THE MAMMOTH
ENCYCLOPEDIA OF THE
UNSOLVED

THE MAMMOTH ENCYCLOPEDIA OF THE
UNSOLVED

Colin Wilson
& Damon Wilson

CARROLL & GRAF PUBLISHERS, INC.
New York

Carroll & Graf Publishers, Inc.
19 West 21st Street
New York
NY 10010–6805

First published in the UK by Robinson,
an imprint of Constable & Robinson Ltd 2000

First Carroll & Graf edition 2000

ISBN 0–7867–0793-3

Printed and bound in the EU

10 9 8 7 6 5 4 3 2

Contents

Author's Note

This book contains most of the chapters from two earlier works: *An Encyclopedia of Unsolved Mysteries* and *Unsolved Mysteries Past and Present*. This explains why some chapters contain nuggets of information that can be found in other chapters: they were originally part of different books. We have not removed such repetitions, because they are always relevant to the chapter in which they occur, and readers who read this book piecemeal will probably not notice them anyway.

CW and DW

Introduction

In 1957 the science writer Jacques Bergier made a broadcast on French television that caused a sensation. He was discussing one of the great unsolved mysteries of prehistory, the sudden disappearance of the dinosaurs about sixty-five million years ago. He suggested that the dinosaurs had been wiped out by the explosion of a star fairly close to our solar system – a "supernova". He then went on to make the even more startling suggestion that the explosion may have been deliberately caused by superbeings who wanted to wipe out the dinosaurs and to give intelligent mammals a chance.

Even the first part of his theory was dismissed by scientists as the fantasy of a crank, and the reaction was no better when in 1970 Bergier repeated it in a book called *Extra-Terrestrials in History*, which began with a chapter called "The Star that Killed the Dinosaurs". But five years later an American geologist named Walter Alvarez was studying a thin layer of clay on a hill side in Italy – the clay that divides the age of the dinosaurs (Mesozoic) from our own age of mammals – and brooding on this question of what had wiped out whole classes of animal. He took a chunk from the hillside back to California, and showed it to his father, the physicist Luis Alvarez, with the comment: "Dad, that half-inch layer of clay represents the period when the dinosaurs went out, and about 75 per cent of the other creatures on the earth".

His father was so intrigued that he subjected the clay to labouratory tests, and found it contained a high proportion of a rare element called iridium, a heavy element that usually sinks to the middle of planets, but which is thrown out by explosions. Alvarez also gave serious consideration to the idea of an exploding star, and only dismissed it when further tests showed an absence of a certain radioactive platinum that would also be present in a supernova explosion. The only other alternative was that the earth had been struck by a giant meteorite, which had filled the atmosphere with steam and produced a "greenhouse effect" that had raised the temperature by several degrees.

Modern crocodiles and alligators can survive a temperature of about 100 degrees C; but two or three degrees higher is too much for them, and they die. This is almost certainly what happened to the dinosaurs, about sixty-five million years ago. And that is why this present book contains no entry headed: "What became of the dinosaurs"? We know the answer. And we also know that Bergier's "lunatic fringe" theory was remarkably close to the truth.

This is the basic justification for a volume like this. It underlines the point that it is always dangerous to draw a sharp, clear line between "lunacy" and orthodox science. In the article on spontaneous human combustion, I have quoted a modern medical textbook which states that spontaneous combustion is impossible, and that there is no point in discussing it. But the evidence is now overwhelming that spontaneous combustion not only occurs, but occurs fairly frequently.

In 1768 the French Academy of Sciences asked the great chemist Lavoisier to investigate a report of a huge stone that had hurtled from the sky and buried itself in the earth not far from where some peasants were working. Lavoisier was absolutely certain that great stones did not fall from the sky, and reported that the witnesses were either mistaken or lying; it was another half century before the existence of meteorites was accepted by science.

The "poltergeist", or noisy ghost, is even more commonplace than spontaneous human combustion; at any given moment there are hundreds of cases going on all over the world. Yet in America scientists have formed a kind of defensive league called CSICOP (Committee for the Scientific Investigation of Claims of the Paranormal) whose basic aim is to argue that the "paranormal" simply does not exist, and is an invention of cranks and "pseudos". Anyone who has taken even the most superficial interest in the paranormal knows that such a view is not merely untenable, but that it represents a kind of wilful blindness.

Let us be quite clear about this. I am not arguing that scepticism is fundamentally harmful. Reason is the highest faculty possessed by human beings, and every moment of our lives demands a continuous assessment of probabilities. Our lives depend upon this assessment every time we cross a busy street. I have to judge the likelihood of that car or bus reaching me before I can step on to the opposite pavement. And when a scientist is confronted by the question of whether, let us say, an Israeli "psychic" can bend keys by merely stroking them, he can only appeal to his general experience of keys and try to assess the probabilities. Yet I think every scientist would agree that it would be wrong to make an *a priori* judgment and decide that the question is not worth investigating because keys cannot be bent by merely stroking them. If he is honest, then he must at least be willing to be prepared to study the matter more closely.

Most scientists would reply that this is precisely how they operate, and in principle this is perfectly true. In fact, they are human beings, and are subject to boredom, impatience and touchiness like the rest of us, which means that they can easily drift over the borderline that separates scientific detachment from emotional commitment.

One of CSICOP's less dogmatic members was the mathematician Martin Gardner, whose book *Fads and Fallacies in the Name of Science* is an amusing and delightful study in "cults of unreason". We can read of the prophet Voliva, who believed that the earth is flat, of Captain Symmes, who believed it is hollow, of Cyrus Teed, who believed it is shaped like an egg and that we are living on its inner surface. Gardner is wickedly amusing on the Jehovah's Witnesses and the cranks who believe that the Great Pyramid contains information about the second coming of Christ. But after half-a-dozen chapters the reader begins to find this attitude of constant superiority rather cloying. Is the author some kind of super-intellect who has discovered the secret of eternal truth? Is he quite sure that dowsing for water is a laughable superstition, that everyone who has seen a UFO is deluded or mistaken, that the continent of Atlantis was a figment of Plato's imagination, that Wilhelm Reich's later ideas were pure lunacy? It is surely a question of where one decides to draw the line. I am inclined to agree that Immanuel Velikovsky was, in the last analysis, a crank – that is, that his theories about the connection between Venus and Biblical catastrophes are the result of inspiration rather than careful scientific reasoning. But many of his inspired guesses were amazingly accurate – for example, his belief that earth is surrounded by powerful magnetic fields. And there are influential philosophers of science like Sir Karl Popper, Michael Polanyi and Abraham Maslow who believed that all scientific thinking is based on "inspiration" rather than on careful scientific reasoning. In short Gardner seems to me to be drawing his line in the wrong place.

I have written a biography of Wilhelm Reich, and I agree that Reich was dogmatic and paranoid, as well as being a thoroughly disagreeable character. But then, the trouble with Reich was that he had, like so many other psychoanalysts, borrowed from Freud a mantle of papal infallibility. All neurosis is sexual in origin, and a neurotic person is incapable of facing up to the sexual nature of his problems. You disagree? It only proves that you have sexual problems that you are afraid to acknowledge. In this respect Reich is like Dr Johnson; if his pistol misfires he will knock you down with the butt. Anyone who disagrees with him must be "mentally sick". But Gardner's own book is full of this same tone of brutal dogmatism. There is an underlying assumption that he is infallible. And while the reader is willing to entertain this as a possibility, he would like to know more of the methods by which Gardner arrives at his unshakeable certainties.

In fact, it would be disastrous if Gardner's attitude became widely accepted and part of the "conventional wisdom". The progress of human knowledge depends on maintaining that touch of scepticism even about the most "unquestionable" truths. A century ago, Darwin's theory of evolution by natural selection was regarded as scientifically unshakeable; today, most biologists have their reservations about it. Fifty years ago, Freud's sexual theory of neurosis was accepted by most psychiatrists; today, it is widely recognized that his methods were highly questionable. At the turn of this century, a scientist who questioned Newton's theory of gravity would have been regarded as insane; twenty years later, it had been supplanted by Einstein's theory although, significantly, few people actually understood it. It seems perfectly conceivable that our descendants of the twenty-second century will wonder how any of us could have been stupid enough to be taken in by Darwin, Freud or Einstein.

Gardner devotes a chapter to attacking the ideas of Charles Fort, the New Yorker who spent his life insisting that scientists are too dogmatic, and ought to be more willing to question their basic assumptions. He objects that, since Fort is merely a destructive critic, with no theories of his own to offer, he is basically barren. There is an element of truth in this. But Gardner fails to grasp that what Fort is really objecting to is the rigid, commissar-like attitude that characterizes his own book. Fort is arguing that scientific discovery has its roots in a sense of wonder, and that a sense of wonder, even with a touch of gullibility, is preferable to a kind of humourless Marxian dogmatism. Newton himself was fascinated by alchemy, and regarded his greatest work as his commentary on the Book of Daniel. Does this qualify Newton as a crank? Obviously not. The inference is surely that it is more fruitful to be intrigued by the possibility of some prehistoric monster in the depths of Loch Ness than to dismiss it as a childish absurdity. It is more fruitful to concede that UFOs may be real than to dismiss them as hallucinations. It may even be more fruitful to admit that the evidence suggests that Shakespeare may not have written his own plays, or that Andrew Crosse created life in his labouratory, or that Orffyreus may have discovered the secret of perpetual motion, than to take the attitude that such extravagances are not even worth discussing.

The career of another "sceptical" friend, Ian Wilson, has also provided me with a great deal of wry amusement. A Roman Catholic convert, he began by writing an important book that argued that the "Holy Shroud of Turin" is genuine. He followed this with a book about reincarnation entitled *Mind Out of Time*, which brilliantly attacked a number of cases of alleged "memories of past lives", like the famous Bridey Murphy case. (The Catholic Church has officially condemned the notion of reincarnation.) He was then asked to participate in a television series based on the files of the Society for Psychical Research, and although he was again able to use his debunking technique to considerable effect in cases like that of the "Croglin vampire", he had to admit that in other cases, particularly those involving ghosts, the evidence simply could not be dismissed. When Wilson turned his attention to "the after-death experience" (in a book of that title), the same thing happened, and even after dismissing much of the evidence as fraudulent, he ended by acknowledging that the overall case for "survival" was very powerful indeed. A more recent book of Wilson's, *Superself* concerns unusual powers of the mind, including dowsing and healing, and ends by acknowledging the reality of what might be called the "superconscious mind". Here we have an example of a man who has the patience and honesty to study many cases of apparently paranormal powers in some detail and who ends with his scepticism deeply eroded – although he finds himself too embarrassed to come out openly and admit that he has, in effect, made a 180 degree turn.

Another interesting example of the "wholesale" attitude toward paranormal phenomena can be found in a book entitled *Secrets of the Supernatural* by Joe Nickell and John Fischer. The authors' aim is to solve a number of mysteries through the investigative approach. The first chapter describes an investigation into a haunting at Mackenzie House, in Toronto. They cite various witnesses, who claim to have seen ghosts over the years and some who have heard spooky noises at night. They then describe how they spoke to the caretaker of the house next door, who demonstrated that various noises made in the basement were "telegraphed" to the "haunted house".

The authors leave us in no doubt that many of the "spooky" noises in Mackenzie House were the result of a rumbling boiler. But this fails to explain the ghost sightings of the witnesses. The tacit assumption is that the demonstration about the noises allows us to dismiss actual sightings. In fact, it may or it may not. If you happen to believe, as I do, that there are such things as ghosts, then you would require a further demonstration that the sightings of a shadowy woman and a man in a frock coat were also the result of the rumbling boiler.

Sceptical investigators all seem to make this same curious logical error. William James pointed out that if you want to disprove that all crows are black, you do not have to try and prove that no crows are black; you only have to produce one single white crow. So a bookful of cases of fraud or excessive gullibility proves nothing except that those particular cases are fraudulent. But one single case of a paranormal event for which the evidence is overwhelming *does* demolish the argument that the paranormal is, by definition, fraudulent.

The truth is that the expansion of human knowledge depends on asking questions. A cow learns nothing because it cannot ask questions; the cow's world is exactly what it looks like, nothing more and nothing less, and there is nothing to ask questions about. But when Thales saw an eclipse he wanted to know what caused it. Newton asked the apparently absurd question: why does an apple fall to the ground instead of staying where it is? And Einstein asked the ultimately absurd question: what would it be like to sit astride a beam of light? All these questions led to fruitful results. If Martin Gardner had been standing behind them with folded arms, they would probably have decided to keep quiet.

Consider a question raised by the zoologist Ivan Sanderson. On a moonlit night, on a dust-covered road in Haiti, he and his wife both experienced a curious hallucination of being back in Paris in the fifteenth century. (The story is told in full in "Time in Disarray" in this volume.) Gardner would declare that this is a question that should simply not be asked unless the answer is that Sanderson was either drunk or lying. But it is obvious that he was neither. Those who knew him (and I have a letter on my desk from one of them at the moment) agree that he was an honest man who was not remotely interested in the "supernatural". It is also worth asking how Sanderson's servants knew he had been involved in an accident – although it occurred in a remote and deserted spot – and that he would be home at dawn.

And so is another question that Sanderson's experience leads him to discuss: whether the mind is identical with the brain. He mentions a case of a man who died in a New York hospital, and who an autopsy revealed to have no brain, only "half a cupful of dirty water". This sounds, admittedly, like another of those absurd stories that are not worth discussing. But in the early 1980s Professor John Lourber of Sheffield University discovered a student with an IQ of 126 whose head was entirely filled with "water". A brain scan showed that the student's brain was merely an outer layer, only one millimetre thick. How can a person function with virtually no brain? Lourber, who specializes in hydrocephalis ("water on the brain") replies that he has come across many cases of perfectly normal people whose heads are filled with 95 per cent of fluid, and that 70 to 90 per cent is actually quite common.

If a person can think without using the brain, the obvious conclusion would seem to be that the being who does the thinking exists apart from his brain.

The real problem posed by experiences such as that of the Sandersons is one concerning the nature of time. All scientific reasoning, even the least dogmatic, tells us that it is totally impossible to slip back into the past or foretell the future. Where the past is concerned, we can admittedly speculate that the "time slip" is some kind of "tape recording". But a vision of the future should be a total impossibility, since the future has not yet happened. In spite of which, there are many well authenticated cases of "glimpses" into the future. (I once presented a television programme about one of these – an Irish peer named Lord Kilbracken who dreamed repeatedly about the winners of horse races, and won money by backing them.) It seems to follow that there is something fundamentally wrong with the vision of the world presented to us by our senses – in fact, we have only to think for a moment to see that there must be something wrong with a logic that tells us that everything has a beginning and an end, and then presents us with the paradox of a universe that apparently has neither.

This is why the views of CSICOP should be treated with suspicion. It is not simply a question of whether ESP or telepathy deserve to be taken seriously, but whether – as Martin Gardner would like to believe – the universe is ultimately as rational and "normal" as a novel by Jane Austen or Anthony Trollope. This is an easy belief to maintain, because the universe that confronts us when we open our eyes in the morning looks perfectly "normal", and it is unlikely that we shall encounter any event during the day that contradicts this assumption. But then the universe looks "unquestionable" to a cow for the same kind of reason. We know that the moment we begin to use our intelligence to ask questions, the universe becomes a far more strange and mysterious place. Most scientists would, in fact, agree wholeheartedly with this sentiment, for science begins with a sense of mystery. But a certain type of scientist – and they are, unfortunately, in the majority – would also like to believe that the mysteries can all be solved by the kind of simple deductive logic employed by Sherlock Holmes. And the problems presented by "time slips" or precognitions or synchronicities, or by poltergeists and out-of-the-body experiences, make it clear that this is wishful thinking. We can only keep science within comfortable logical boundaries by refusing to acknowledge the existence of anything that lies outside those boundaries.

It may seem reasonable to ask: Where is the harm in that? No one blames a policeman for not being interested in mysticism or philosophy – that is not his job. Why blame a physicist for taking no interest in poltergeists and ESP?

The answer is that his preconceptions about the universe also involve preconceptions about the human mind. In the nineteenth century it made no difference whatever whether a scientist was interested in psychical research or regarded it as a delusion. But by the second half of the twentieth century, science was speculating whether the universe might contain eleven dimensions and whether black holes might be an entrance into a dimensionless "hyperspace" – even whether we might be able to use black holes to travel across the universe. Russian and American scientists have been experimenting with ESP as a means of communicating with submarines under the polar ice. Suddenly the question of the limits of the human mind has become a question of major scientific importance. If we are merely chance products of a material universe, then our position is basically that of spectators, and the extent to which we can "intervene" is limited. But if – to take just one example – Sanderson's vision of fifteenth century Paris was not a hallucination, but was some kind of glimpse of a hidden power of his own mind, then it would challenge the whole Darwinian picture of evolution.

Consider the strange case of the calculating twins discussed in the article on identical twins. A prime number is a number that cannot be divided exactly by any other number, like 3, 7 and 13. But there is no easy, quick way to tell whether a number is a prime or not: you just have to patiently divide all the smaller numbers into it and see if any of them "goes" precisely. If a number is very large – say five figures – then the only quick way to find out if it is prime is to look it up in a table of prime numbers. Yet these twins can do it instantaneously, and that is absurd. Quite apart from the mystery of how they can do it, there is the even more baffling mystery of how such a power could have developed during the course of human history. According to Darwin, the basic mechanism of evolution is "survival of the fittest". The cheetah can run faster than a man and the kangaroo jump higher because they had to in order to survive. Most animals cannot count beyond a few figures. Man had to learn to count as his social life became more complex. Even so, most people are "bad at figures". So how could any human being have developed this amazing ability to recognize five figure primes instantaneously, when even a computer would be unable to do it?

There can only be one answer: that we are wrong to think that human intelligence has to operate like a computer. It seems to have some "alternative method". And presumably it was the same alternative method that accidentally allowed Sanderson his curious glimpse of the past. That statement sounds reasonable enough, for we all agree that "intuition" seems to operate in mysterious ways. But then we come upon a case in which someone has clearly foreseen the future, and we know this is not simply a question of intuition. The notion that time has a one-way flow is the very foundation of western science; everything depends on it. If precognition is possible, then our basic assumptions need revising.

For the scientists of the nineteenth century, such an idea was deeply disquieting; that is why so many of them were so hostile to "psychical research". It seemed the opposite of what all science stood for; a return to superstitions and old wives' tales instead of experiment and analysis. In 1848 this reaction of science had swung so far that a novelist named Catherine Crowe decided it was time to protest. So she went to a great deal of trouble to gather together some of the best authenticated cases of the "supernatural" she could find – the kind of cases that would later be carefully examined by the Society for Psychical Research – and published them in a book called *The Night Side of Nature*. It had a considerable impact on thoughtful people.

But Mrs Crowe was unfortunate. The year of its publication also happened to be the year when strange poltergeist disturbances took place in the home of the Fox family in New York State – curious rappings and bangings that occurred in the presence of the two children, Kate and Margaret. In a code of raps, the "entity" claimed to be a murdered peddler who had been buried in the basement. (In fact, a human skeleton was found buried in the basement in 1907.) These manifestations caused a sensation, and soon "Spiritualism" had begun to spread across America and Europe. Scientists were outraged at this fashionable tide of "superstition" – particularly when a number of "mediums" proved to be frauds – and Mrs Crowe's highly reasonable arguments were forgotten. In fact she encountered so much hostility that a little over a decade after the publication of *The Night Side of Nature* she had a nervous breakdown and spent some time in a mental home; during the last sixteen years of her life, she wrote no more.

Now, more than a century and a half later, Spiritualism has ceased to be a challenge to science, and has become little more than a harmless minority religion; nowadays it is perfectly obvious that it never was a challenge to science. We can also see that there was never any question of science being supplanted by superstition and old wives' tales, and that therefore CSICOP was quite wrong to imagine that the success of Uri Geller heralded a return to the Middle Ages.

What it *would* involve is a recognition that the history of life on earth may be a little more complex than Darwin thought. If paranormal powers, such as telepathy and "second sight", actually exist, then it also seems fairly certain that they were possessed in a far greater degree by our primitive ancestors, just as they are now possessed in a greater degree by many "primitive" people. Sanderson makes it clear, for example, that he believes that some of the Haitians he encountered possessed powers of "second sight". One of these remarked to him after his "timeslip" experience, "You saw things, didn't you? You don't believe it, but you could always see things if you wanted to". In short, Sanderson himself could have developed or perhaps simply rediscovered his paranormal faculties.

In my book *The Occult* I have cited many cases that seem to illustrate the same point. For example, the famous tiger-hunter Jim Corbett describes in *Man Eaters of Kumaon* how he came to develop what he calls "jungle sensitiveness", so he knew when a wild animal was lying in wait for him. Obviously, such a faculty would be very useful to a tiger hunter in India, but virtually useless to a stockbroker in New York. So it would seem that civilized man has deliberately got rid of it. Or rather, the development of another faculty – the ability to deal with the complications of civilized life – has suppressed the "paranormal" faculty, because we no longer need it.

But is this actually true? Is it even true that a New York stockbroker does not need "jungle sensitiveness". After all, he lives in other kinds of jungle – not only the commercial jungle, but the concrete jungle where muggers lurk in pedestrian subways and public parks. His real problem is more likely to be the problem that caused Catherine Crowe's nervous breakdown; that he has allowed civilized life to "get on top of him". We have all, to some extent, lost that primitive vital force that can be found in most "savage" peoples. But what has really been lost is a certain sense of wonder, a certain basic optimism. The child thinks that this world of adults is a magical place, full of endless adventures: going into bars, driving motorcars, catching aeroplanes . . . He would find it very hard to believe that as he grows up the world will turn into a hard and ruthless and rather nasty place, where the basic rule is, "Nobody gets anything for nothing".

The adult's problem is that his attitudes have become negative. I have described elsewhere how in 1967 I went to lecture at a university in Los Angeles, then went to meet my family in Disneyland. I had forgotten just how big Disneyland is, and when I walked in through the turnstile and saw the crowds my heart sank. But I was feeling cheerful and optimistic, having just given a good lecture. So I relaxed, placed myself in a mood of confidence and then simply allowed my feet to take me to them. I strolled at random for about fifty yards, turned left, and found them standing at a Mexican food stall.

Forty-eight hours ago I was looking for a book on the Habsburg Empire, and I searched through three book cases without success. The next morning I made another search, and this time found the book on a shelf I had searched several times. Why had I missed it? Because I was in a state of tension as I searched (as if I was in a hurry) and sheer "haste" made me look at it without seeing it. Conversely, I have noticed again and again that when I am in a mood of relaxed confidence I can find things by some kind of "sixth sense".

But I have noticed something even more interesting: that when I am in these moods of relaxed confidence, things just somehow seem to "go right". And this obviously has nothing to do with me or with any "sixth sense". I just happen to "stumble upon" an important piece of information the day before I am due to write about it, or avoid some unpleasant experience by sheer serendipity.

Our basic civilized problem is that our attitudes have become quite unjustifiably negative. Everyone is familiar with the experience of how relief can place us in an optimistic frame of mind. The plumbing goes wrong and you have to flush the lavatory with buckets of water for a couple of days. When the plumber finally arrives you feel immense relief, and for the next twenty-four hours feel how delightful it is to have a lavatory that flushes at the touch of a button. And whenever we experience this relief we also recognize that we are surrounded by reasons for delight: with bath taps and light switches and electric toasters that actually work, and doors that open without squeaking, and televisions that provide us with news as often as we want it. It has taken man about fifty thousand years to move out of caves and achieve this felicity. Yet we have become so accustomed to our civilization that we take it for granted, and spend most of our time worrying about trivialities.

Yet whenever some minor inconvenience is followed by relief, we recognize that we have allowed ourselves to discount our blessings, and fall into a narrow and joyless state of mind. Civilization was designed to give us leisure and freedom; instead, we waste our days concentrating obsessively on minor problems that will appear totally unimportant in a week's time. And this anxiety-ridden shortsightedness is due to certain left-brain qualities that we have developed over the past few thousand years. (The left-brain deals with logic and language, the right with meaning and intuition.) The only way to regain our birthright of leisure and freedom is to recognize that everyday left-brain awareness some-how tells us lies, and that we have to learn to relax into a wider type of awareness.

Consider the following example from a book called *The States of Human Consciousness* by C. Daly King; he is speaking of experiences of what he calls "Awakeness".

> The first of them took place upon the platform of a commuters' railway station in New Jersey as the writer walked along it to take a coming train to New York late one sunny morning. On the platform there were several small housings for freight elevators, news-stands and so on, constructed of dun-coloured bricks. He was emotionally at ease, planning unhurriedly the schedule of his various calls in the city and simultaneously attempting to be aware, actively and impartially, of the movements of his body's walking . . .
>
> Suddenly the entire aspects of his surroundings changed. The whole atmosphere seemed strangely vitalized and abruptly the few other persons on the platform took on an appearance hardly more important or significant than that of the door-knobs at the en-trance of the passengers' waiting room. But the most extraordin-ary alteration was that of the dun-coloured bricks, for there was no concomitant sensory illusion in the experience. But all at once they appeared to be tremendously alive; without manifesting any exterior motion they seemed to be seething almost joyously inside and gave the distinct impression that in their own degree they were living actively and liking it. This impression so struck the writer that he remained staring at them for some minutes, until the train arrived . . .

The first thing to note about this is his comment that "he was emotionally at ease, planning unhurriedly the schedule of his various calls". That is, he was in a "right-brain" state, free of tension. Then some curious effort, some slight movement of the mind, so to speak, propelled him in the right direction, and made him aware that the bricks he would normally have taken for granted were somehow glowing with inner life. It is also significant that the human beings who would normally have occupied the centre of his field of attention now ceased to seem important. Long habit has made us select human beings as the centre of our field of attention, for we are social animals whose peace of mind depends upon "fitting into" society.

There is no need to assume that his perception of the bricks was a "mystical" experience. We can all induce something of the sort by simply staring intently at a perfectly ordinary wall in the sunlight. Our problem is that we do not normally concentrate on anything; we "scan" things automatically, like the girl on a supermarket checkout. But if anything attracts our interest and we focus our full attention on it, we instantly experience this sense of heightened meaning.

I am only trying to point out that the chief reason our experience usually seems to unmemorable is that we have become accustomed to responding "robotically" to our surroundings, leaving the automatic pilot to do the driving for us.

And what difference would non-robotic experience make? Basically this: it would make Daly King aware that the normal assumption he shares with the rest of us, that the world "out there" is a rather ordinary place, is mistaken. His senses are telling him lies. Or rather, his senses are doing their best; it is his attitudes, his assumptions, that reduce their testimony to "ordinariness". His "glimpse" would have told him that he is surrounded by an unutterably strange vicious circle in which most of us are trapped. This consists in the assumption that the world out there is rather ordinary and dull. And when we are bored our energies sink. And when our energies sink it is rather like a cloud coming over the sun, making the world seem dimmer and less interesting. This feeling that the world is uninteresting prevents us from making any kind of effort. The normal human tendency – unaided by external stimulus – is to sink into a state of lethargy, rather like Samuel Beckett characters sitting in dustbins.

Every glimpse of reality – every "moment of vision" – even setting out on holiday – tells us the opposite. This tells us that when a cloud seems to obscure the sun, what has actually happened is that we have allowed our senses to become dimmer, like the device in a cinema that lowers the lights. Perception is "intentional". You see things by a beam of light generated by a dynamo inside your head. When you are bored the dynamo works at half speed, and everything you look at seems dull.

But if you can persuade your subconscious mind that the world out there is fascinating – as holidays persuade it – the dynamo will accelerate, and you will see that this is true.

Wordsworth talked about the time of childhood, when everything seem "apparelled in celestial light". This is because the child knows that there is an infinitely marvellous world out there, and automatically makes that effort that keeps the dynamo working at top speed. Human beings begin to die when they become trapped in the "vicious circle", and become convinced they have "seen it all". And unless circumstances force them to continue to make an effort they sink gently into a kind of swamp of boredom, of "taken-for-grantedness", that finally engulfs them. (This is why so many people die after they retire from a lifetime of work.)

Now, obviously, the human race is on the point of an extremely interesting evolutionary development. The first step towards escape from this vicious circle is to recognize that the apparent "ordinariness" of the world is a delusion. If we could become deeply and permanently convinced that the world "out there" is endlessly exciting, we would never again allow ourselves to become trapped in the swamp of "taken-for-grantedness". And we would become practically unkillable. Shaw says of his "Ancients" in *Back to Methuselah*: "Even in the moment of death, their life does not fail them". "Life failure" is that feeling that there is nothing new under the sun, and that we all have to accept defeat in the end. If we could learn the mental trick of causing the dynamo to accelerate, this illusion would never again be able to exert its power over us.

Let me state my own fundamental belief about human existence. Man consists of a highly complex body, a "computer" that has taken millions of years to evolve, controlled by an entity which we call the soul, spirit or whatever. But to place the "spirit" in charge of such a complicated piece of machinery is like asking a baby to drive a Rolls-Royce. We fail to understand about 90 per cent of its potentialities. Besides, it is simply too "heavy" for us to handle comfortably. As we drag this massively heavy body around, we are in the position of a space-traveller who has been cast away on a planet where gravity is several times greater than on earth, so he cannot even stand upright, and it takes him all his strength just to crawl on his hands and knees. When he is galvanized by some emergency he can summon far more strength, and even stagger briefly on to his feet. Then he can catch a glimpse of the real answer: that he has to develop far more powerful muscles – mental as well as physical muscles.

Whenever I am faced by some exciting challenge or crisis I can see the answer. I can then see that if I could be "galvanized" like this all the time, I could rise up to a far higher level of purpose and vitality. Our trouble is that after a crisis we quickly lose that sense of emergency, and sink back into the old dull, sleepy state in which every molehill becomes a mountain, and the mind falls into a curious apathy in which it loses all sense of purpose. In fact we are so accustomed to this state that we accept it as normal. We only tend to glimpse our true potentialities when we set out on voyages – either physical or mental.

The answer lies in generating (through the use of determination) a far more powerful imagination, a sense of reality, that will make us continually aware of the potential challenges and problems, and keep us in the "galvanized" state. It is a total absurdity that a man sitting on a train should stare dully out of the window, when his mind contains a vast library of past experiences that could keep him entertained for years.

All this explains, of course, why we spend so much of our time seeking out challenges and stimulants – travel, adventure, sport, sex, alcohol; it is a pathetic and misguided attempt to hurl ourselves beyond these stupid limitations. If we could learn to identify and face the basic problem, we would have taken the most decisive step towards solving it. We would become incapable of boredom, and "discouragement" would lose its power over us. We would begin to see the way out of the trap that has been killing off human beings prematurely for thousands of generations.

Now it should be clear why I feel such impatience with those people who want to convince us that the universe is a perfectly rational and logical place, and that any attempt to suggest the opposite is a return to medieval superstition. I am prepared to admit that poltergeists are not particularly important – the scientist's instinct is perfectly sound on that point – and neither are "time slips" or precognitions or out-of-the-body experiences; I myself feel that people who are too obsessed with the paranormal are as boring as people who are too obsessed with football or television soap operas. But these experiences are only a small part of the vast panorama of strangeness that will confront us when we learn that mental trick of slipping out of the bonds of habit, and making a powerful and continuous effort to tear aside the "curtains of everydayness" that surround us.

If this book needs any justification, it is that it is a modest attempt to catch a few glimpses of the strangeness that lies on the other side of the curtain.

1

King Arthur and Merlin

Legend or Reality?

King Arthur and his magician, Merlin, are two of the most popular figures in world mythology. But did either of them really exist? Or are they merely characters in a charming fairy tale?

We can understand, of course, why historians would cast doubt on the existence of Merlin. But some modern scholars have even doubted that King Arthur was a real historical character. This is obviously a question that must be settled before we go any further.

We first hear about Arthur and Merlin in a book entitled *History of the Kings of Britain*, written around 1135 by a Welsh bishop named Geoffrey of Monmouth – whose reliableness may be judged by his opening chapter, in which he explains how Britain was named after the warrior Brutus, who sailed there from the siege of Troy. A hundred or so pages later, Geoffrey describes how a king named Vortigern – who was a real historical character – ordered an impregnable tower to be built on Mount Snowdon, in Wales. The tower kept collapsing, whereupon some soothsayers told him that if he wanted the tower to remain standing, he would have to sprinkle the stones with the blood of a boy who had no father. His messengers traveled throughout the kingdom in search of such a youth, until they overheard two boys quarreling and one of them jeering that the other had no father. The fatherless boy was named Merlin.

King Vortigern sent for Merlin and his mother, who proved to be the daughter of the king of South Wales. She described how she had been seduced by a handsome youth who subsequently vanished into thin air – although she sometimes heard his voice speaking to her when she was alone. Vortigern then explained that since Merlin was literally father-less, he had to sacrifice him and sprinkle his blood on the foundations of the tower. Merlin promptly offered to prove that the soothsayers were liars and asked to have them brought before him. "Do you know why the tower keeps on collapsing"? he asked them. They shook their heads. "Because there is a pool underneath it which makes the earth soggy". Vortigern's men were ordered to dig and found the pool. Merlin then went on to foretell that if they drained it they would find two dragons (or serpents). And when this also proved to be true, Vortigern decided to spare his life. Merlin then went on to make a series of prophecies – including the augury that Vortigern would be burned to death in a tower. This came about just as Merlin foretold, when a king named Aurelius Ambrosius – the rightful heir to the throne – invaded Britain and set fire to Vortigern's tower.

When Aurelius was poisoned his brother, Uther Pendragon, became king. After conquering Scotland, he invited all the nobles of his realm to a feast to witness his coronation. Among these were Duke Gorlois of Cornwall and his beautiful wife, Igerna. Uther fell madly in love with Igerna, and when Gorlois realized this he hurried back to Cornwall. This insulted the King, who pursued Gorlois with an army. Gorlois forestalled the rape of his wife by hiding her away in the castle of Tintagel, which was virtually impregnable, for it stood on an island that was approached only by a narrow neck of land. When he learned about this, Uther Pendragon fell into a deep depression, for he could think about nothing but possessing Igerna.

The problem was solved by Merlin, who used his magic to transform Uther into Duke Gorlois's double. Uther went to the castle of Tintagel and was immediately admitted. That night, in Igerna's arms, he conceived the boy who would become King Arthur.

While Uther was away his men attacked the castle in which Gorlois had taken refuge. Gorlois was killed, and Uther Pendragon married Igerna and made her queen. He reigned for another fifteen years until he was also poisoned, and then Arthur became king.

Readers of Geoffrey of Monmouth (whose book is still in print in a popular edition) will wonder what happened to the sword in the stone, the Knights of the Round Table, and other famous parts of the legend. The answer is that they were added by later (mostly French) chroniclers and given their definitive form in one of the first printed books, Sir Thomas Malory's *Morte D'Arthur*, printed by William Caxton in 1485. Little was known about its author until 1926, when literary research revealed – to the dismay of scholars – that Malory was a robber chief who sacked monasteries and rustled cattle, and who raped a woman named Joan Smyth, the wife of one Hugh Smyth, on at least two occasions. He apparently wrote *Morte D'Arthur* in Newgate Prison, where he is buried.

But if Arthur was a teenager when his father died, why should he have had to prove his right to the throne by pulling a sword out of a stone (or an anvil set in a stone, as Malory tells the story)? Malory overcomes this problem by having Merlin take charge of Arthur from the moment he is born; Merlin then hands the baby over to a knight named Sir Ector, whose wife suckles Arthur.

It all sounds so absurd that it is not surprising that some scholars have dismissed Arthur as a legend. They point out, for example, that one of the main sources of information on Arthur's period is a monk named St. Gildas who wrote a bitter and disgruntled book entitled. *The Downfall and Conquest of Great Britain (De excidio et conquestu Britanniae)* and who does not even mention Arthur – although he speaks of the Battle of Badon, which is Arthur's most famous battle.

But a biography of Gildas by Caradoc of Llancarfan mentions that Arthur killed Gildas's brother, Hueil, who fought against him; that in itself would obviously explain why Gildas could not even bring himself to mention Arthur's name.

So what do we actually know about the legendary hero called King Arthur? Well, to begin with, he was not a king but a general. He did not ride around on a white charger dressed in a suit of medieval armor, because he belonged to a far earlier period – he was probably born about AD 470, during the period when the Romans had just left Britain. He was, in fact, a Roman – or at least a Roman citizen. So his horse would have been a small Roman horse, about the size of a modern pony, and his sword would have been a short Roman sword, not a long broadsword like the legendary Excalibur.

Around AD 410 the Romans decided to pull out of Britain – they needed all their forces to defend Rome from the barbarians. A chieftain named Vortigern set himself up as king of Britain but soon encountered trouble with the wild Picts from north of the Scottish border; around AD 443 he invited Saxon mercenaries from the Continent to come and fight for him. They did, but when Vortigern ran out of money to pay them, they decided to stay and conquer Britain. The original Britons – whom we now call Celts – were slowly driven west into Wales, Cornwall, and Scotland. However, an ex-Roman warrior named Ambrosius Aurelianus rallied the Celts and went to war with Roman thoroughness, inflicting many defeats on the invaders. When he died, his brother, Uther Pendragon, replaced him. And one of his most brilliant generals was a young man named Artorius, the legendary King Arthur – who may or may not have been the son of Uther Pendragon.

It was Arthur who brought the Saxon invasion to a standstill in a series of twelve great battles, the last of which, the Battle of Badon, took place about AD 518. This established him as the Dark Age equivalent of General Montgomery or General Eisenhower. If his allies had remained loyal, it seems probable that the Saxons would have been driven back to the Continent, and it would now be Arthur's Celtic descendants who rule Britain, not the Anglo-Saxons.

Unfortunately, Arthur's former allies now fell to squabbling among themselves, and Arthur spent the remainder of his life trying to avoid being stabbed in the back. When he finally died, in the Battle of Camlann – which, according to Geoffrey, took place near the River Camel in Cornwall – he was fighting his own nephew Mordred, not the Saxon invaders. According to Geoffrey of Monmouth, Arthur's body was carried off to the "Isle of Avalon", which has been identified as Glastonbury, a small town in the west of England with a famous abbey and a tor – a hill surmounted by a tower. (Although Glastonbury is now inland, there was a time when it was surrounded by the waters of the Bristol Channel.) Because the burial was secret, to prevent the Saxons from finding the body, a widespread story soon arose that Arthur was not really dead but would return to help Britain in her hour of need.

In the summer of 1113, about twenty years before Geoffrey of Monmouth wrote his *History*, a group of French priests came to Bodmin, in Cornwall, carrying holy relics. When one of the locals mentioned that Arthur was still alive and was expected to return any day, the servant of one of the clerics was tactless enough to sneer. This caused a violent confrontation, and a group of armed Cornishmen burst into the church with the intention of teaching the skeptical foreigners a lesson; it was only with some difficulty that they were pacified. This seems to demonstrate that Arthur was already a legendary figure before Geoffrey of Monmouth wrote his bestseller.

In fact, Arthur is mentioned many times in various Welsh poems written within a century of his death. But the next major reference to him comes in a confused collection of historical material compiled by a monk named Nennius some time between AD 800 and 820. The earliest material about Arthur that Nennius quotes is a collection of Welsh "Easter Annals", tables of the dates of Easter (which is a movable feast) compiled by monks. These tables have wide margins, and in one of these – for the year AD 518 – there is a jotting (in Latin): "Battle of Badon in which Arthur carried the cross of Our Lord Jesus on his shoulders for three days and three nights and the Britons were victors". And another, for the year AD 539 reads: "The strife of Camlann in which Arthur and

Modred [*sic*] perished". So if we can believe the Easter Annals, Arthur ruled for twenty-one years after the Battle of Badon.

But the most dramatic incident in the story of Arthur occurred about thirty years after the death of Geoffrey of Monmouth (in AD 1154), during the reign of Henry II – the king who is best remembered in connection with the murder of Archbishop Thomas à Becket. Henry was an indefatigable traveler, and on one of his trips to Wales he met a Welsh bard, a "singer of the past", who told him that King Arthur was buried in the grounds of Glastonbury Abbey. To protect the body from the Saxons, said the bard, it had been buried sixteen feet deep. He even mentioned the exact location – between two "pyramids".

The king was naturally delighted, for Geoffrey of Monmouth's *History* had represented Arthur as one of the greatest conquerors since Julius Caesar. (According to Geoffrey, Arthur had conquered Ireland, Scandinavia, and France and was about to march on Rome when news of Mordred's rebellion forced him to return to England.) He was also relieved to hear that Arthur *was* buried in Glastonbury. As the great-grandson of William the Conqueror, he was familiar with the legend that Arthur would return in England's hour of need. If he could prove that Arthur was well and truly dead, the latter would cease to be a rallying cry for rebels like the men of Bodmin.

Besides, Henry had an affection for Glastonbury, because the abbot Henry of Blois had played a part in making him king. So Henry went to call on the abbot to tell him the good news.

Oddly enough, the abbot was not as pleased as he might have been. Glastonbury Abbey was already one of the richest in England; it didn't need any more fame to attract pilgrims. And "between two pyramids" might mean anything.

Then the situation changed dramatically. On 25 May 1184, the abbey caught fire and was left in ruins. The encouraging thing about it was that the image of Our Lady of Glastonbury had survived undamaged, which suggested that God still had great things in store for the abbey. Henry II produced funds to start rebuilding; many nobles contributed. And in 1191 one of the monks died after expressing a wish to be buried on the grounds, between two crosses. These stood on two marble pillars that tapered toward the top and might have been described as tall pyramids. For some reason – perhaps because they remembered the words of the Welsh bard – the monks went on digging below six feet and at seven feet encountered a stone slab. They prized it up. On its underside was a leaden cross, with a Latin inscription that read: *Hic jacet sepultus inclytus Rex Artorius in insula Avalonia* ("Here lies buried the renowned King Arthur in the Isle of Avalon").

They went on digging – it probably took days to make a hole sixteen feet deep and wide enough to allow several diggers to operate. But at sixteen feet, just as the old bard had foretold, the mattocks struck wood. An enormous coffin, hollowed out of oak, was unearthed. Inside, they found the huge skeleton of a man, whose skull had been smashed by heavy blows. A monk saw a lock of yellow hair and leaned over to grab it. It dissolved in his fingers, and the monk fell into the coffin. Later, they identified fragments of a smaller skeleton and realized that the hair was that of Arthur's wife, Guinevere. One chronicler, Giraldus Cambrensis (Gerald of Wales), who actually saw the bones and the cross in the following year, says the inscription on the cross also mentioned "Queen Wenneverla" (Guinevere).

From that moment on, the abbey became the most popular tourist site in England, if not in Europe. The abbey was soon rebuilt on a magnificent scale.

Scholars have accused the monks of Glastonbury of inventing the whole story, yet this seems unlikely. Giraldus Cambrensis seems to have been an honest man – he was one of the few to denounce Geoffrey of Monmouth's *History* as a pack of lies – and he specifically claims to have seen both skeletons and the leaden cross. This cross was still around for many centuries, and in 1607 an antiquarian named William Camden published a picture of it. His text spells Arthur *Arturius*, an ancient form that was in use in the time of King Arthur but had not been used since. (Even the Easter Annals spell his name *Arthur*.)

Moreover, a re-excavation of the site in 1963 by C. A. Radford showed that the monks were telling the truth about digging down sixteen feet. Besides, as the Arthurian scholar Geoffrey Ashe has pointed out, Glastonbury is also supposed to be the burial site of Joseph of Arimathea, the man who gave Jesus a decent burial; if the monks faked the grave of Arthur, why did they not go on and fake Saint Joseph's too?

So, on the whole, there can be no doubt that King Arthur – or rather, General Arturius – really existed and that he deserved his reputation as a great hero. Dozens of questions still remain, but some of these are slowly being answered. For example, many scholars believe that we now know the location of King Arthur's court at Camelot. In 1542 a writer named John Leland wrote that a fortified hill in South Cadbury, Somerset, was, in fact, "Camallate, sometime a famous town or castle . . . Arthur much resorted to Camallate". In 1966 excavations were begun at Cadbury Castle (not a castle in the medieval sense, but a fortified hill). On top of Roman remains were found the foundations of impressive buildings that were clearly occupied, in Arthur's period, by a chieftain of considerable power and authority.

Even Geoffrey of Monmouth's absurd story about Tintagel Castle begins to look as if it has some foundation. The present Tintagel Castle was built around 1140, at the time of Geoffrey's *History*. Historians have pointed out that in the time of King Arthur there was only a Celtic monastery on the site. In 1924 the "visionary" Rudolf Steiner visited Tintagel and devoted a lecture to it, identifying various places as the Hall of the Round Table, the sleeping place of the knights, and so on. It all sounded like pure fantasy.

But in the dry summer of 1983 a fire on the island destroyed the grass, and wind and rain went on to reveal the foundations of more than a hundred small rectangular buildings and of a hall more than eighty feet long. Down below, at the foot of the cliff, is a small natural harbor, and pottery discovered on the island indicated that large quantities of wine and oil were once imported. (There is more imported pottery on the site than on all the other British and Irish sites put together.) A stone "footprint" on the opposite side of the island looks out over old Celtic Christian burial mounds; such a "footprint" was often made by a chieftain who planted his foot and surveyed his kingdom. (In this case, he would have looked across to the graves of his ancestors.) All this sounds as if Tintagel were once the fortress of a considerable chieftain, not simply a monastery. The objection that Tintagel was essentially uninhabited in the time of Arthur cannot be sustained.

So the evidence for the real historical existence of King Arthur is very strong indeed. In a book entitled *Arthur: Roman Britain's Last Champion*, Beram Saklatvala has even argued that there is evidence for the existence of the sword Excalibur and of the Holy Grail. The Latin word for stone is *saxo*, which is close to "Saxon". If some early chronicle mentioned Arthur taking a sword from a Saxon – some warrior he had killed – then it could well have been the origin of the legend of the sword in the stone. Geoffrey of Monmouth calls Arthur's sword *Caliburn*; and *Caliburn* is a combination of two words for "river" – the Celtic *cale* and the Saxon *burn*. Swords need, of course, to be tempered in cold water, and as the Anglo-Saxon word *cale* means "cold", *caliburn* could be translated as "the cold stream". So Arthur's sword could have been named after the stream it was tempered in, the Cale, near Sturminster, in Dorset.

As to the Grail – the cup that Jesus was supposed to have used at the Last Supper and that Joseph of Arimathea is said to have brought to

Glastonbury – this was probably a much larger vessel, too large for a drinking cup, that was used for ritual purposes. In 1959 a large marble urn was found during excavations of a Roman palace in North Africa; the palace dated from the same period as did Arthur. The urn had a cross carved on it, and the lid had rivet holes in the shape of a cross, indicating that it had once had a metal cross on it. The urn probably contained the bones of a saint and was almost certainly used for administering oaths, as we now swear on the Bible. A libation hole suggests that it was used in some special ritual. Arthur would fairly certainly have had a similar urn in his own chapel for the administering of oaths. If this sacred vessel had been captured during one of Arthur's many wars, Saklatvala suggests, then the quest for the Grail could well have been based on fact.

But what of the magician Merlin? Surely *he* was an invention of Geoffrey of Monmouth? In fact, Geoffrey followed up his successful *History* with a *Life of Merlin*, a poem written for a smaller audience. If Geoffrey had invented Merlin, we would expect the poet more or less to repeat the story as told in the *History* – or at least, not to contradict it. Merlin was obviously a great deal older than Arthur, for he was a boy when King Vortigern was alive – and the monk Gildas tells us that Vortigern made the fatal mistake of inviting the Saxons into England in AD 443. Yet in the Merlin poem, Geoffrey has Merlin fighting with a king named Rodarcus against a Scottish king named Guennolous – and these real historical characters lived a century later, *after* the death of Arthur. Geoffrey is aware of this and explains it by saying that Merlin lived to a phenomenally old age – more than a century. But it looks as if Geoffrey has found material about Merlin that obliges him to try to explain why his original dates were wrong.

The explanation that is accepted by most scholars is that Merlin was based on a Welsh bard named Myrddin, who was alive after AD 573. The Welsh language only came into existence after the death of Arthur, so Myrddin could not have been older than Arthur. This identification of Merlin with Myrddin is accepted by Robert Graves in his mythological study *The White Goddess* (1948) and by Nicolai Tolstoy in *The Quest for Merlin* (1985). But it is obviously a somewhat disappointing theory, for if it is correct, Merlin was not even called Merlin. (The usual view is that Geoffrey of Monmouth changed Myrddin to Merlin because *merde* in French means "shit", and a magician named Myrddin would have invited ridicule in an age when England was ruled by the French.) Moreover, Myrddin cannot have known Arthur, for even if their lives overlapped, he would only have been a child at the time of Arthur's death. Geoffrey Ashe agrees that Merlin is Myrddin and that Geoffrey of Monmouth made him Arthur's senior merely for the sake of a good story.

The American professor Norma Lorre Goodrich rejects this notion in her book *Merlin* (1988) and argues convincingly that Merlin *was* a real person who was about thirty years older than Arthur, although she agrees that some of the legends of Myrddin have been incorporated into the Merlin story. She suggests that Arthur's Merlin was born in Wales and buried in Scotland. In fact, she ends by suggesting that "Merlin" was a title rather than a name (a merlin is a type of hawk) and that the original Merlin was a bishop named Dubricius, who crowned Arthur. Myrddin, on the other hand, was a "Wild Man of the Woods", a poet who went mad, lived in the wilderness, and achieved certain magical powers. *This* Merlin is, in fact, the one Geoffrey of Monmouth learned about after writing his *History*. His *Life of Merlin* is, indeed, about a Welsh leader and prophet who went mad after fighting in a battle against a Scottish king and who became a wanderer in the wilderness, delivering a great many prophecies. The Merlin of the *History* is also, we may recall, a prophet: in fact, Geoffrey published a book of Merlin's prophecies first, then incorporated them into the *History*. It sounds as if he learned about the Welsh prophet Myrddin after writing the *History* and decided that Myrddin and Merlin must be the same person. Nicolai Tolstoy agrees with this theory and devotes much of his *Quest for Merlin* to an analysis of various poems and legends that tell of the "Wild Man of the Woods".

It would seem, then, that we have two contesting theories: that there were two Merlins, a view first suggested by Giraldus Cambrensis; and that there was only one Merlin, who was really called Myrddin and who was a Welsh bard and soothsayer. Yet Goodrich and Tolstoy both argue their theories so brilliantly that it seems a pity to have to choose one or the other. Goodrich is most convincing on the subject of the two Merlins and in her argument that the original Merlin *was* the counselor of King Arthur. But Tolstoy has some profoundly important things to say about Merlin the Wizard.

To understand what he is suggesting, we have to forget our modern images of wizards and magicians, derived from Shakespeare's Prospero, Tolkien's Gandalf, and T. H. White's amiable and bumbling Merlin. These are recent inventions. In the age of Arthur a magician would have been a combination of a priest and a witch doctor, a *shaman*.

For an account of a magician in action, it is necessary to turn to *A Pattern of Islands*, Arthur Grimble's account of his years as Land

Commissioner in the Gilbert Islands in the South Pacific. Told that he ought to eat porpoise flesh, Grimble inquired how he could obtain some. He was told that some islanders farther up the coast were the hereditary porpoise-callers of the island and that his informant's cousin could also call them. Grimble was invited to the village, where a feast was laid out. The fat and friendly porpoise-caller retired into his hut, and for several hours there was silence. Then the man rushed out and fell on his face, crying, "They come, they come"! The villagers all rushed into the water and stood breast-deep, and to Grimble's amazement, hundreds of porpoises began to swim in to the shore. It seemed that they were in a trance. The "hypnotized" porpoises were then gently lifted into boats, taken ashore, and slaughtered.

It is not difficult to hypnotize animals, and it has been argued elsewhere in this book (see chapter 25) that hypnosis may involve a kind of telepathy. But "hypnosis" of porpoises from a distance sounds absurd.

Absurd or not, it seems fairly clear that this *is* a power possessed by many primitive witch doctors and shamans. The study of modern primitives leaves no doubt that Stone Age cave drawings of "magicians" dressed in animal skins are not a form of Palaeolithic art but are dipictions of rituals that were designed to attract animals into the vicinity of the hunters, exactly as Grimble's shaman summoned porpoises. A remarkable book, *Wizard of the Upper Amazon* by F. Bruce Lamb, describes the experiences of a Peruvian named Manuel Cordova, who was kidnapped by Amahuaca Indians and spent his life among them. Lamb makes it clear that the primitive hunters of the twentieth century use exactly the same techniques as their Stone Age counterparts. Cordova describes how the hunters kill the sow who leads a herd of pigs, then bury the head with ritual chants, to ensure that the herd will always return that way. And in one remarkable sequence he describes how the Indians drink a "vision extract" called *hini xuma*, and how they then shared visions of snakes, birds, and animals; a black leopard appears among them at the height of the ceremony but does no one any harm.

In another firsthand narrative of years spent among the natives of Papua, New Guinea, *Mitsinari* (1954), Father André Dupreyat gives an account of a sorcerer named Isidoro who can turn himself into a cassowary (a kind of ostrich) and is consequently able to make a five-hour journey over a mountain in two hours. He also describes his own clash with sorcerers who place him under a "snake curse", after which snakes attack him on several occasions. (Snakes will normally do their best to escape from the vicinity of human beings.)*

So it is a mistake to think of a magician as a Walt Disney cartoon character wearing a tall conical hat with stars painted on it. Real sorcerers are closely related to modern "spirit mediums"; they assert that their power comes from spirits. Modern "magicians" – such as the notorious Aleister Crowley – believe that power can be obtained over spirits by the use of certain precise rituals, which must be performed with punctilious accuracy.

The traditional role of tribal witch doctors and shamans is as intermediaries between human beings and the spirit world, and their chief function is to ensure good hunting or good harvests. Celtic druids belonged to this tradition. Druidism was a form of nature worship; it came to Britain around 600 BC with the Celts, but many older forms of nature religion had existed long before that: Stonehenge, for example, was a temple for such worship and is precisely aligned to the stars.

Nicolai Tolstoy is convinced that Merlin was "the last of the druids". Druidism was driven into Wales with the Celts and survived there long after Christianity had stamped it out in the rest of the British Isles. Tolstoy points out that the Myrddin stories – particularly those of bards like Taliesin – are full of clues that link the magician with druidism. He invokes sacred apple trees (the druids worshiped in sacred groves) and has as familiars a pig and a wolf. He takes on many of the characteristics of the horned god of pagan mythology. Tolstoy places the "wood of Calidon", to which Merlin fled after going mad, in Scotland, near Hart Fell, where the rivers Annan and Clyde both have their source. And, according to Tolstoy, Merlin fulfilled his own prophecy that he would meet a "threefold death", clubbed, speared, and drowned. After being beaten for days by shepherds, he slipped into the river Tweed and was impaled on a stake before he drowned.

Professor Goodrich prefers the traditional story, in which Merlin is murdered by a maiden named Ninian or Nimue, the Lady of the Lake (also called Vivian), of whom he becomes enamored and to whom he offers to teach magic. She refuses to become his mistress and finally uses one of his own spells to bind him and entomb him in a cave under an enormous rock. Another commentator has argued that the maiden Nimue is actually the Christian Saint Nimue and that the story of her final triumph over Merlin is really the triumph of Christianity over paganism.

* These and many similar cases are discussed in my 1981 book *Poltergeist*, in the chapter entitled "The Black Magic Connection".

The books by Nicolai Tolstoy and Norma Lorre Goodrich are rich and complex detective stories that will leave most readers in a state of "enlightened confusion". The final picture that emerges is of a real King Arthur, who was one of the greatest generals of the Dark Ages, and of a real Merlin, a shaman and druid, who was Arthur's counselor and adviser. Both were men of such remarkable stature that, even within a few decades of their deaths, they became the subject of endless legends. The legends have blurred the reality to such an extent that it is now virtually impossible to discern the outline of the real men who lived sometime between AD 450 and 550. But the outcome of all the detective work is at least a certainty that they actually existed.

2

Atlantis

The Submerged Continent

Atlantis has been described as the greatest of all historical mysteries. Plato, writing about 350 BC, was the first to speak of the great island in the Atlantic Ocean which had vanished "in a day and a night", and been submerged beneath the waves of the Atlantic.

Plato's account in the two late dialogues of *Timaeus* and *Critias* has the absorbing quality of good science fiction. The story is put into the mouth of the poet and historian Critias, who tells how Solon, the famous Athenian lawgiver, went to Saïs in Egypt about 590 BC, and heard the story of Atlantis from an Egyptian priest. According to the priest, Atlantis was already a great civilization when Athens had been founded about 9600 BC. It was then "a mighty power that was aggressing wantonly against the whole of Europe and Asia, and to which your city [Athens] put an end". Atlantis, said the priest, was "beyond the pillars of Hercules" (the Straits of Gibraltar), and was larger than Libya and Asia put together. It was "a great and wonderful empire" which had conquered Libya and Europe as far as Tyrrhenia (Etruria in central Italy). Deserted by their allies, the Athenians fought alone against Atlantis, and finally conquered them. But at this point violent floods and earthquakes destroyed both the Athenians and the Atlantians, and Atlantis sank beneath the waves in a single day and night.

In the second dialogue, the *Critias*, Plato goes into far more detail about the history and geography of the lost continent. He tells how Poseidon (Neptune), the sea god, founded the Atlantian race by fathering ten children on a mortal maiden, Cleito, whom he kept on a hill surrounded by canals. The Atlantians were great engineers and architects, building palaces, harbours, temples and docks; their capital city was built on the hill, which was surrounded by concentric bands of land and water, joined by immense tunnels, large enough for a ship to sail through. The city was about eleven miles in diameter. A huge canal, 300 feet wide and 100 feet deep, connected the outermost of these rings of water to the sea. Behind the city there was a plain 230 by 340 miles, and on this farmers grew the city's food supply. Behind the plain there were mountains with many wealthy villages and with fertile meadows and all kinds of livestock. Plato goes into great detail about the city, suggesting either that he had been told the story at length or that he had the gifts of a novelist. The long account of magnificent buildings with hot and cold fountains, communal dining halls and stone walls plated with precious metals has fascinated generations of readers for more than two thousand years.

But eventually, says Critias, the Atlantians began to lose the wisdom and virtue they inherited from the god, and became greedy, corrupt and domineering. Then Zeus decided to teach them a lesson. So he called all the gods together . . .

And there, frustratingly, Plato's story breaks off. He never completed the *Critias*, or wrote the third dialogue that would complete the trilogy, the *Hermocrates*. But we may probably assume that the final punishment of the Atlantians was the destruction of their continent.

Many later scholars and commentators assumed that Atlantis was a myth, or that Plato intended it as a political allegory: even Plato's pupil Aristotle is on record as disbelieving it. Yet this seems unlikely. The *Timaeus*, the dialogue in which he first tells the story, is one of his most ambitious works; his translator Jowett called it "the greatest effort of the human mind to conceive the world as a whole which the genius of antiquity has bequeathed to us". So it seems unlikely that Plato decided to insert a fairy tale into the middle of it; it seems more likely that he wanted to preserve the story for future generations.

For more than two thousand years the story of Atlantis remained a mere interesting curiosity. But in the late nineteenth century an American congressman named Ignatius Donnelly became fascinated by it, and the result was a book called *Atlantis, the Antediluvian World* (1882), which became a bestseller and has been in print ever since. Even a century later, the book remains surprisingly readable and up to date. Donnelly asks whether it is possible that Plato was recording a real catastrophe, and concludes that it was. He points out that modern earthquakes and volcanic eruptions have caused tremendous damage, and that there is evidence that the continent of Australia is the only visible part of a continent that stretched from Africa to the Pacific, and which scientists have named Lemuria. (Lemuria was named by the zoologist L.P. Sclater, who noted that lemurs existed from Africa to Madagascar, and suggested that a single land-mass had once connected the two.) He also studied flood legends from Egypt to Mexico, pointing out their similarities, and indicated all kinds of affinities connecting artifacts from both sides of the Atlantic. He notes that there is a mid-Atlantic ridge, and that the Azores seem to be the mountain-tops of some large submerged island. Donnelly's knowledge of geology, geography, cultural history and linguistics appears encyclopedic. The British prime minister Gladstone was so impressed by the book that he tried to persuade the cabinet to allot funds to sending a ship to trace the outlines of Atlantis. (He failed.)

Writing seventy years later in his book *Lost Continents*, the American writer L. Sprague de Camp commented on this impressive theory: "Most of Donnelly's statements of facts, to tell the truth, either were wrong when he made them, or have been disproved by subsequent discoveries". And he goes on to say: "It is not true, as he stated, that the Peruvian Indians had a system of writing, that the cotton plants native to the New and Old Worlds belong to the same species, that Egyptian civilisation sprang suddenly into being, or that Hannibal used gunpowder in his military operations . . ." De Camp demonstrates that Donnelly's scholarship is not as reliable as it looks; but there is still a great deal in the 490-page book that he leaves unchallenged.

Five years before the publication of Donnelly's book, the subject of Atlantis had been raised in an immense two-volume work called *Isis Unveiled* by the Russian "occultist" Helena Blavatsky, who had dashed off its fifteen hundred pages at a speed that suggests automatic writing. But her comments on Atlantis occupy only one single page of Volume One (593), in which she explains that the inhabitants of Atlantis were the fourth race on earth, and that they were all natural "mediums". Having acquired their knowledge without effort, this people was an easy prey for "the great and invisible dragon" King Thevetat, who corrupted them so that they became "a nation of wicked magicians". They started a war which ended in the submersion of Atlantis . . .

Isis Unveiled astonished its publisher by becoming a best-seller; it made its author a celebrity, and she went on to leave New York for India and to found the Theosophical Society. After a shattering expose in which she was declared a fraud, she returned to London and died of Bright's disease at the age of sixty in 1891. But she left behind her the manuscript of a book that was even larger and more confusing than *Isis Unveiled*, a book called *The Secret Doctrine*. This is a commentary on a mystical work called *The Book of Dzyan*, allegedly written in Atlantis in the Senzar language, and it explains that man is not the first intelligent race on earth. The first "root race" consisted of invisible beings made of fire mist, the second lived in northern Asia, the third lived on the lost island continent of Lemuria or Mu in the Indian Ocean, and consisted of ape-like giants who lacked reason. The fourth root race were the Atlantians, who achieved a high degree of civilization, but were destroyed when the island sank after a battle between selfish magicians. The present human species is the fifth root race, and we are the most "solid" so far; the sixth and seventh that succeed us will be more ethereal. According to Madame Blavatsky, all knowledge of the past is imprinted on a kind of psychic ether called Akasa, and this knowledge is called the Akasic records. She also claims that the survivors of Atlantis peopled Egypt and built the pyramids about a hundred thousand years ago. (Modern scholarship dates the earliest about 2500 BC.)

By the time *The Secret Doctrine* appeared, Donnelly's book had popularized the subject of Atlantis. A leading member of the Theosophical Society in London, W. Scott-Elliot, now produced a work called *The Story of Atlantis* (1896), which achieved immense popularity; Scott-Elliot claimed to possess the ability to read the Akasic records. He made the astonishing claim that Atlantian civilization was flourishing a million years ago. There were seven sub-races, one of which, the Toltecs, conquered the whole continent and built a magnificent city, which is described by Plato. When some of the Atlantians practised black magic, a great lodge of initiates moved to Egypt and founded a dynasty; others built Stonehenge in England.

Scott-Elliot later used his insight into the Akasic records to write an equally startling book about Lemuria. Both books are regarded together with *Isis Unveiled* and *The Secret Doctrine* as basic scriptures of the Theosophical Society.

After Madame Blavatsky, the most influential of all Theosophists was the Austrian Rudolf Steiner, who quarrelled with the British Theosophists and developed his own system of "occult philosophy" known as Anthroposophy. In 1904, before the break, Steiner produced a work called *From the Akashic Records* (Akashic being an alternative spelling), which deals with Atlantis and Lemuria. It would be easy to dismiss this as yet another production of the lunatic fringe; yet, like most of Steiner's work, it has a solid core of intellectual understanding that rings true. Steiner thinks in terms of the evolution of worlds, and according to his scheme, higher beings called hierarchies are in charge of the process. The basic aim of evolution is for spirit to conquer the realm of matter. Man began as a completely etherialized being, and has become steadily more solid with each step in his evolution. But the increase in solidity has meant that he has become a slave to matter. When, after evolving through three earlier "worlds", man was reborn on our present earth, his body was little more than a cloud of vapour. By the time he had developed to the "third root race" (the Lemurians) he had learned the secret of telepathy, and of direct use of his will-power. Fear, illness and death entered human history during this period. In the next epoch of Atlantis man was able to control the vegetable life forces and use these as an energy source; he was unable to reason but possessed an abnormally powerful memory. But hostile forces which Steiner called Ahriman pushed man into mere scientific achievement; he became increasingly corrupt and egotistic, and his attempt to use destructive forces finally caused the catastrophe that overwhelmed Atlantis . . . Unlike Madame Blavatsky, Steiner dates this catastrophe around 8000 BC, which places it within the realm of reasonable possibility. (It is true that, according to archaeological research, the first mesolithic farmers had only just made their appearance on earth at this time. However, one American professor of history, Charles Hapgood, has argued seriously that certain "maps of the ancient sea kings" suggest that there was an advanced civilization covering the globe in 8000 BC, see chapter 25.)

Just as it began to look as if Atlantis had fallen into the hands of occultists and the purveyors of science fiction, a new and more serious advocate appeared on the scene. Lewis Spence was a Scottish newspaper editor who also wrote scholarly studies of the mythologies of Babylonia, Egypt, Mexico and Central America. His *Problem of Atlantis* appeared in 1924, and, like Donnelly's book, reached a wide audience. What Spence proposed was that there is geological evidence for the existence of a great continent in the Atlantic region in late Miocene times (25 to 10 million years ago). It disintegrated into smaller island masses, the two largest of which were in the Atlantic close to the Mediterranean. Another large island existed in the region of the West Indies. Further disintegration of the eastern continent began about 25,000 years ago, and it finally vanished about 10,000 years ago, as Plato said. The other continent to the west – Antillia – survived until more recently. Spence argued that man was not a seafarer ten thousand years ago (Hapgood would probably disagree) so there should be evidence of the inhabitants of Atlantis taking refuge in nearby lands. Studying the coast of south-western France, northern Spain and the Bay of Biscay, Spence adduces evidence that three primitive races, the Cro-Magnon, the Caspian and the Azilian, all migrated from the west. He believes that Cro-Magnon man arrived about 25,000 years ago and wiped out Neanderthal man. (Modern students of prehistory would place the date of the disappearance of Neanderthal at least ten thousand years earlier than this.)

The Caspian and Azilian people came 15,000 years later; the Azilians are known to have used boats for deep-sea fishing, and Spence reasons that the land bridge that had joined Atlantis and Europe had now ceased to exist. Spence believed that the Azilians founded the civilizations of Egypt and Crete. Other "Atlantians" fled westward to Antillia, and remained there until it was also partly submerged some time before the Christian era; its inhabitants became the Mayans. (This identification of the Mayans with Atlantians is one of the usual features of Atlantis speculation.) One of Spence's odder theories is that lemmings – the small rodents who often drown themselves in large numbers – are attempting to migrate back to Atlantis. In fact, we now know that lemmings are simply responding to overcrowding, like so many other animals, and that mass suicide is not one of their usual habits – they simply tend to disperse randomly from areas where the birth rate has risen too steeply.

There are other objections to Spence's theory. He argues that the cultures of Egypt, Crete and South America appeared suddenly; archaeology has since established that this is untrue; they evolved slowly from primitive beginnings. Nevertheless, there is a great deal in Spence's first three Atlantis books – *The Problem of Atlantis* was followed by *Atlantis in America* and *The History of Atlantis* – that deserves to be taken seriously. The same cannot be said of the two later books: *Will Europe Follow Atlantis?*, in which he speculates whether the modern world is plunging into the same wicked excesses that destroyed Atlantis (this was in the Hitler period) and *The Occult Sciences in Atlantis*, in which he is inclined to build bricks without straw ("the reader must bear in mind that here we are dealing with the question of Alchemy in Atlantis only . . .") But altogether, Spence is probably the most interesting and reliable writer on Atlantis, and his *Problem of Lemuria* shows the same sober, scholarly approach, even though he is forced to rely too heavily on speculation and guesswork.

Spence advised Conan Doyle on his Atlantis novel *The Maracot Deep*, and also corresponded with the explorer Colonel Percy H. Fawcett, who was convinced that Brazil was part of ancient Atlantis – a theory Doyle utilized in *The Lost World*. The novelist Rider Haggard presented Fawcett with a basalt image inscribed with characters, and when the British Museum was unable to identify it, Fawcett took it to a psychometrist (psychometry is the ability to "read" the history of an object by holding it in the hands).* Although the psychometrist had no clue to

* For the history of psychometry, see my book *The Psychic Detectives*.

Fawcett's identity, he told him: "I see a large irregularly shaped continent stretching from the north coast of Africa across to South America. Numerous mountains are spread over its surface, and here and there a volcano looks as though about to erupt . . . On the African side of the continent the population is sparse. The people are well-formed, but of a varied nondescript class, very dark complexioned though not negroid. Their most striking feature are high cheek bones and eyes of piercing brilliance. I should say their morals leave much to be desired, and their worship borders on demonology . . ."

On the western side, the inhabitants are "far superior to the others. The country is hilly and elabourate temples are partly hewn from the faces of the cliffs, their projecting facades supported by beautifully carved columns . . . Within the temples it is dark, but over the altars is the representation of a large eye. The priests are making invocations to this eye and the whole ritual seems to be of an occult nature, coupled with a sacrificial . . . Placed at various parts of the temple are a few effigies like the one in my hand – and this one was evidently the portrait of a priest of very high rank".

The psychometrist went on to say that this image would eventually come into the possession of a reincarnation of the priest "when numerous forgotten things will through its influence be elucidated". "The teeming population of the western cities seems to consist of three classes; the hierarchy and the ruling party under an hereditary monarch, a middle class, and the poor or slaves. These people are absolute masters of the world, and by a great many of them the black arts are practised to an alarming extent". The psychometrist went on to describe how, as punishment for presumption, the land is destroyed by volcanic eruptions, and sinks beneath the sea. "I can get no definite date of the catastrophe, but it was long prior to the rise of Egypt, and has been forgotten except, perhaps, in myth".

So Fawcett became a firm believer in the reality of Atlantis, and considered that he would find further evidence for it in certain lost jungle cities of Brazil and Bolivia. He had another reason for wishing to go to the Mato Grosso of south-western Brazil. In Rio de Janeiro he had found an old document in Portuguese written by a man called Francisco Raposo, who had gone into the jungle in 1743 in search of the lost mines of Muribeca – Muribeca being the son of a Portuguese adventurer and an Indian woman. According to Raposo's manuscript (which is cited in Fawcett's posthumous book *Exploration Fawcett*), he found a remarkable ruined city that had obviously been destroyed by earthquakes, "tumbled columns and blocks weighing perhaps fifty tons and more".

After spending some time in this ruined city, Raposo and his party made their way back to Bahia, where he wrote his account for the viceroy, who pigeonholed it.

So when Fawcett finally set off in 1924, after endless frustrations and delays, he had a threefold objective: the search for the mines of Muribeca, for the lost city of Raposo, and for Atlantian remains like his basalt idol. With his son Jack and a friend named Raleigh Rimell, he made his way finally to Dead Horse Camp in the Xingu Basin, where he took a final photograph of Jack and Rimell. On 29 May 1924 he wrote a final note to his wife. Then all three men vanished. In 1932 a Swiss trapper named Rattin reported that Fawcett was a prisoner of an Indian tribe. Rattin himself went in search of the "white colonel", but never returned. Various other rumours about Fawcett were carried back by explorers and missionaries, and in 1951 the chief of the Kalapalos tribe, Izarari, made a deathbed confession to killing Fawcett and his companions. He had refused Fawcett carriers and canoes, "on grounds of intertribal strife", and Fawcett slapped his face, whereupon the chief had clubbed him to death, then killed the other two men when they attacked him. He also alleged that Jack Fawcett had been consorting with one of his wives, and the Brazilian who reported this story mentioned that the chief's eldest son seemed to have white blood. However, a team of experts announced that bones found in a jungle grave were not those of Colonel Fawcett; so the mystery of his disappearance remains unsolved. It has even been suggested that Fawcett found his lost city and preferred to stay there rather than return to civilization . . .

Other students of the Atlantis myth preferred to believe that it was to be found on the other side of the Atlantic ocean. A group of German archaeologists named Schulten, Herman, Jessen and Hennig began searching for another lost city, Tartessos, in 1905; it was supposed to be on the Atlantic coast of Spain near the mouth of the Guadalquivir, and had been captured by the Carthaginians in 533 BC. They believed that the lost Tartessos had been Plato's Atlantis – it was certainly on the right side of the Straits of Gibraltar. Another archaeologist, Elena Maria Whishaw, also spent twenty-five years studying the same area – around the ancient fortress of Niebla – and was led by evidence of masonry and skilled hydraulic engineering in the Rio Tinto mines to the conclusion that Andalusia had once been colonized by people from North Africa who had fled from Atlantis. This explains the title of her book, *Atlantis in Andalusia* (1930).

By the 1930s another interesting theory of the destruction of Atlantis had gained millions of followers; it was the work of a Viennese mining engineer named Hans Hoerbiger (1860–1931). As a child Hoerbiger had been an amateur astronomer, and while he was looking at the moon and the planets through a telescope he was suddenly struck by the certainty that the way they reflect the sunlight indicates that they are covered in ice. Later he saw waterlogged soil exploding with puffs of steam, as molten iron ran over it, and thought he saw the answer to the explosive energies of the universe. Space, according to Hoerbiger, is full of hydrogen and oxygen, although in an extremely rarified state. (This is certainly true of hydrogen!) This condenses around small stars as ice, and when these balls of ice fall into a hot star there is a tremendous explosion – the same kind of explosion that formed our solar system. Most of the planets, Hoerbiger insisted, are covered with a layer of ice hundreds of miles thick, while our present moon has an ice-covering 125 miles thick. It is necessary to speak of our *present* moon (Luna) because it is only the latest of a considerable number, perhaps as many as six. The natural movement of all planetary bodies, says Hoerbiger, is a spiral, and the planets are spiralling in towards the sun like the needle on a gramaphone record. Small objects move faster than large ones, so as they spiral past larger planets they are likely to be captured and become "moons". A quarter of a million years ago our earth had another moon – a captured comet. When this approached close to the earth it was moving so fast that it caused the seas to bunch together into a ridge of water that had not time to retreat. The rest of the earth became covered with ice; human beings were forced to move to the tops of mountains, like those of Ethiopia and Peru. (Colonel Fawcett also believed that Tiahuanaco, in the Peruvian Andes, contained evidence of some mysterious lost civilization.) The lighter gravity at these heights turned men into giants – hence the comment in the Bible that there were "giants in the earth" in those days. When the moon finally exploded the result was a great flood, like the one recorded in the Bible and in many other sacred books. When the earth captured our present moon (about twelve thousand years ago) the result was again a tremendous flood, together with earthquakes and volcanic eruptions, and this destroyed Atlantis and Lemuria.

Hoerbiger died in 1931, but his work was continued by one of his foremost disciples, Hans Schindler Bellamy. Bellamy was an Austrian, whose book *Moon, Myths and Man* – published in the year of Hoerbiger's death – made thousands of converts in England and America. Hoerbiger's German converts included Hitler, who proposed to build an observatory dedicated to the three greatest astronomers of all time,

Ptolemy, Copernicus and Hoerbiger. Hitler's belief in Hoerbiger may have cost him the war. A weather bureau based on Hoerbiger's principles forecast a mild winter for 1941–2, and Hitler sent his troops into Russia in light summer uniforms . . . Hoerbiger continued to have hosts of disciples until the 1960s, when space exploration finally made it clear that his belief that the moon and planets were covered in thick ice was erroneous.

The chief problem with "crank" books like Hoerbiger's *Glacial Cosmogony* (1913) is that they often contain more than a grain of truth. This is certainly the case with that astonishing bestseller of the 1950s, *Worlds in Collision*, by Immanuel Velikovsky. Velikovsky, a Russian Jew born in 1895, was startled and impressed by Freud's book *Moses and Monotheism*, which suggested that Moses was not a Jew but an Egyptian, and that he was a follower of the "sun-worshipping" pharaoh Akhnaton. Velikovsky reached the even more startling conclusion that Akhnaton was the Greek king Oedipus. In 1939, the year he moved from Palestine to the United States, Velikovsky was much preoccupied with Hoerbiger's theory, but finally decided against it. But he was impressed by the theory of W. Whiston, Newton's successor at Cambridge, that the comet of 1680 had caused the Biblical deluge on an earlier encounter. He also encountered Donnelly's *Ragnarok, The Age of Fire and Ice* (1883), successor to *Atlantis*, in which Donnelly concludes that the "drift", the vast deposit of sand, gravel and clay which lies in irregular patches over much of the earth's surface, was the result of a tremendous explosion that occurred when a comet struck the earth. Whiston and Donnelly were seminal influences on the book Velikovsky now went on to write, *Worlds in Collision* (see Chapter 40), in which a close brush with a comet is blamed for the destruction of Atlantis, as well as for various Biblical catastrophes.

A rather more credible theory of Atlantis was propounded in the late 1960s by a Greek archaeologist, Professor Angelos Galanopoulos, based on the discoveries of Professor Spyridon Marinatos on the island of Santorini or Thera, in the Mediterranean. Around the year 1500 BC a tremendous volcanic explosion ripped apart Santorini, and probably destroyed most of the civilization of the Greek islands, the coastal regions of eastern Greece, and of northern Crete. This, Galanopoulos suggests, was the catastrophe that destroyed Atlantis. But surely the date is wrong? – the destruction of Santorini took place a mere nine hundred years before Solon, not nine thousand. This is the essence of Galanopoulos's argument – he believes that a scribe accidentally multiplied all the figures by ten. He points out that all Plato's figures seem far too large. The 10,000 stadia (1,150 mile) ditch around the plain would stretch around modern London twenty times. The width and depth of the canal 300 feet wide and 100 feet deep seems absurd; surely 30 feet wide by 10 feet would be more likely? As to the plain behind the city, 23 by 34 miles would be a more reasonable size than 230 by 340 miles. If all Plato's figures are reduced in this way, then Santorini begins to sound altogether more like Atlantis although Galanopoulos suggests that the Atlantian civilization stretched all over the Mediterranean, and that Crete itself was probably the Royal City. And how could such a mistake come about? Galanopoulos suggests that the Greek copyist mistook the Egyptian symbol for 100 – a coiled rope – for the symbol for 1,000 – a lotus flower.

There is only one major objection to all this: Plato states clearly that Atlantis was beyond the Pillars of Hercules. Galanopoulos argues that Hercules performed most of his labours in the Peloponnese, and that the Pillars of Hercules could well refer to the two extreme southern promontories of Greece, Cape Matapan and Cape Maleas. But Plato says clearly: "They [the Atlantians] held sway . . . over the country within the pillars as far as Egypt and Tyrrhenia". And no amount of revisionary geography can place Egypt and Etruria within the promontories of Greece. So another fascinating theory must be reluctantly abandoned. But the notion that Santorini was the legendary Atlantis has brought thousands of tourists to the island and greatly improved its economy . . .

In 1975 a symposium held at the University of Indiana discussed the question: Atlantis, fact or fiction? Various experts stated their views, and reached the predictable conclusion that Atlantis was a myth. And it must be admitted that, apart from the kind of "cultural" evidence adduced by Donnelly, Spence and Whishaw, there is not one grain of solid proof of the existence of the sunken continent. And the kind of "proof" that convinced Colonel Fawcett – the evidence of a psychometrist – is understandably dismissed by geologists, archaeologists and classical scholars alike. Yet anyone who has studied such evidence will agree that, while it is far from convincing, it still leaves a great deal to explain. How did Fawcett's psychometrist come to think of Atlantis? For the evidence to be of any value, we would need to know a great deal more about the psychometrist – whether, for example, he had read Donnelly or Spence. And if he could convince us that his unconscious mind was not playing him tricks, there would still remain the possibility that he was somehow reading Fawcett's mind. Yet anyone who is willing to study the evidence for psychometry with an open mind will end by agreeing that there are many cases that cannot be explained as unconscious self-deception or telepathy.

Similar questions are raised by the detailed descriptions of Atlantian civilization produced by the "psychic healer" Edgar Cayce (pronounced Casey). When Cayce was twenty-two (in 1899) he suffered from psychosomatic paralysis of the vocal cords, which was cured by hypnosis. The hypnotist then asked Cayce some questions about his own medical problems, and Cayce's replies revealed a medical knowledge that consciously he did not possess. Cayce's ability to produce "trance diagnosis" soon made him a minor celebrity. In 1923 Cayce was questioned as to whether there is life after death; when he woke from his trance he was shocked to learn that he had been preaching the doctrine of reincarnation – as an orthodox Christian, he rejected the idea. Eventually he came to accept it. In 1927, giving a "life reading" on a fourteen-year-old boy, Cayce described his previous lives under Louis XIV, Alexander the Great, in ancient Egypt, and in Atlantis. For the remainder of his life Cayce continued to add fragments to his account of Atlantis.

According to Cayce, Atlantis extended from the Sargasso Sea to the Azores, and was about the size of Europe. It had experienced two periods of destruction, in the first of which the mainland had divided into islands. The final break-up occurred, as Plato said, about 10,000 BC, and the last place to sink was near the Bahamas. What he says echoes Steiner to a remarkable extent: ". . . man brought in the destructive forces that combined with the natural resources of the gases, of the electrical forces, that made the first of the eruptions that awoke from the depth of the slow-cooling earth . . ." He claimed that archives dealing with Atlantis now exist in three places in the world, one of these in Egypt. In June 1940 Cayce predicted that the island called Poseidia would rise again, "expect it in '68 or '69". It would happen in the area of the Bahamas.

Early in 1968 a fishing guide called Bonefish Sam took the archaeologist Dr J. Manson Valentine to see a line of rectangular stones under twenty feet of water in North Bimini, in the Bahamas. Valentine was startled to find two parallel lines of stones about 2,000 feet long. They became known as the Bimini Road. But scientists disagreed from the beginning. John Hall, a professor of archaeology from Miami, said they were natural formations; John Gifford, a marine biologist, thought that if the stones were produced by "geological stress", then there would be far more of them over a wider area; he concluded that "none of the evidence conclusively disproves human intervention". One of the investigators, Dr David Zink, wrote a book called *The Stones of Atlantis*, and had no doubt whatsoever that some of the stones were hand-made – in fact, one object was a stone head. But even if the Bimini Road could be shown to be part of a temple, this would still not prove that it was built more than ten thousand years ago; it could be the product of a much more recent culture.

Obviously, Cayce's prediction that Atlantis would "rise again" has not been fulfilled. This in itself does not prove the prediction to have been pure imagination; parapsychologists who have studied precognition have often noted that the time scale is seldom correct. But it *does* mean that for the time being Cayce must be classified with Scott-Elliott, Steiner and Madame Blavatsky as a highly suspect witness.

Of all the theories of the destruction of Atlantis, a recent one by an English geologist, Ralph Franklin Walworth, is in some ways one of the most convincing. Walworth's book *Subdue the Earth* is only incidentally concerned with Atlantis; it is basically an attempt to explain the problem of the ice ages. So far no geologist has produced a convincing theory to account for the tremendous variations in climate that have periodically covered the earth with immense sheets of ice. Robert Ardrey's *African Genesis* contains several fascinating pages in which the various theories are outlined. A "wandering north pole" could not explain why the ice sheets extended down to Africa. A near-brush with a comet could not explain why there have been so many ice ages, and why they are at irregular intervals (the same comet would return regularly). A Jugoslav, M. Milankovitch, produced a marvellously convincing theory based on the known fact that our planet goes through minor cyclical variations in the weather, and argued that when such variations happen to coincide – like lightning striking twice in the same place – the result is an ice age. Ardrey points out that even Milankovitch's simultaneous variations cannot account for twenty million cubic miles of ice. Sir George Simpson produced a highly convincing theory to the effect that ice ages are due to a rise in solar temperature, which causes more rain to fall on highlands in the form of snow. Eventually, there is so much snow that it cannot melt away during the summers, and an ice age begins. But if Simpson's theory is correct, then the seas should become a great deal warmer during ice ages; in fact, studies of sea-bottom deposits during the Pleistocene – the last great ice age – show that there was a variation in temperature of only a few degrees. Ardrey's own theory is that the earth passes periodically through some vast intergalactic gas cloud, and that the earth's magnetic field sucks murky gas into our atmosphere, thus excluding the sunlight. But he admits that his theory fails to explain why, in that case, ice ages do not occur at regular intervals . . .

Walworth sets out to explain some of the problems already noted by Donnelly and Velikovsky: the evidence for great upheavals that buried whole forests. Most geologists, he points out, are now "Uniformitarians"; they propose that the earth has evolved very slowly over vast epochs of time, and that the great catastrophes (floods, earthquakes and so on) that were posited by scientists in the eighteenth century, when the earth was thought to be only a few thousand years old, are unnecessary to explain earth's evolution. Walworth points out that, be that as it may, there is still a great deal of evidence for giant catastrophes. And he asks some simple but very puzzling questions. How, for example, can we account for fossils? The standard explanation is that fossilized fishes, animals, etc, became stuck in mud, which hardened around them and "preserved" them. But if a fish dies in a river it quickly decays, or is eaten by predators; even if it sinks into a few inches of mud, it still decays. Walworth believes that fossils are best formed in the presence of the "activated dust which a volcano ejects".

His theory is that ice ages are caused by tremendous volcanic eruptions, great enough to eject gas, magma and dust far out into space. The air that was hurtled out into space would lose all its heat; when gravity pulled it back to earth it would be "an icy, lethal gas" that would extinguish life in vast areas, and plunge even large creatures like mammoths into an instantaneous deepfreeze. The volcanic dust would cause an ice age. Snow would fall on high ground, until the oceans were hardly more than puddles. "The evidence from the sea floors indicates that sea level has, for long periods of time, been three miles lower than it is now". Human settlements would move to the shores of these seas, since the temperature close to the sea is always slightly higher than inland. The ice sheets would raise soft sediments and magmas to high altitudes, where they would set like concrete, forming mountains and the "drift" that so puzzled Donnelly. Then, as the ice age gradually ended, the settlements would be forced to retreat higher and higher as their former homes were submerged. Some people would even move to mountain-tops like the civilization of Tiahuanaco. And great civilizations would disappear beneath the waves . . .

But if this is true, then why do we not have such tremendous explosions nowadays? Krakatoa, which erupted in 1883, and sent a giant tidal wave across the Pacific, devastating whole islands, only hurled its vapours seventeen miles into the atmosphere. Walworth points to the planet Jupiter, which produces tremendous eruptions of energy every ten years, and he suggests that this is basically an electromagnetic phenomenon: "eddy currents developed by Jupiter's motion through the electrified solar wind cause a buildup of heat under the planet's surface". Because earth is so much smaller, the same mechanism could cause such eruptions at far longer intervals, accounting for the ice ages.

Perhaps the most controversial aspect of Walworth's theory is his suggestion that the earth's core may not be a mass of molten iron, as geologists believe. If volcanic activity is caused by the "electrified solar wind" acting upon the earth's magnetic field and setting up tremendous stresses just below the surface, then presumably the centre of the earth is relatively cool and solid. Presumably science should one day be able to develop "depth sounders" that could prove or disprove this unorthodox notion. As far as the human race is concerned, it would probably be a relief if Walworth proved to be mistaken, since his theory also involves another catastrophic eruption over the next thousand years or so, followed by an ice age that would re-create the conditions that destroyed Atlantis.

3

The Baader-Meinhof Gang

Suicide or Murder?

On the afternoon of Thursday, 13 October 1977, four Palestinians seized control of Lufthansa Flight LH181 as it flew from Majorca to Frankfurt. Two men and two women held the passengers and crew at gunpoint and forced the pilot to change course for Rome's Leonardo da Vinci Airport. After wiring the aircraft with explosive charges, they issued their demands in the name of the Struggle Against World Imperialism Organization.

Few informed sources were surprised when the Palestinian hijackers' main demand turned out to be the release of "all German political prisoners"; it was an open secret that Palestinian paramilitary organizations had close links with the left-wing revolutionary terrorists in West Germany. The demand was later reduced to the release of eleven high-ranking members of the Red Army Faction (RAF; generally referred to by the nickname Baader-Meinhof) then in custody in the GDR.

Over the next three days the hijacked jet was flown on to Cyprus and then Dubai to keep the security forces from launching an attack. Then, on Friday, 16 October only hours before the ransom deadline expired, it was flown to Aden in Yemen.

Shortly after landing, the pilot, Jürgen Schumann, asked permission to inspect the front landing gear, which he thought had been damaged by the last touchdown. He checked the gear, found it to be still serviceable, and started to walk back, but on the way he made the mistake of speaking to a group of airport security men. As he re-entered the aircraft he was made to kneel down and was "executed" in front of the other hostages with a shot through the back of the head. Schumann's body was dumped onto the runway, and the co-pilot was forced to fly them to Mogadishu Airport in Somalia.

As the deadline the terrorists had set for the destruction of the jet approached, the West German government played for time. They offered to release the eleven prisoners and fly them to Mogadishu to join the Palestinians; they would then be given a substantial sum of money and a jet to fly them wherever they chose. The leader of the hijackers, who called himself Martyr Mahmoud, agreed to extend the deadline to facilitate the arrangements but added, "There must be no tricks. This will not be another Entebbe".

By "Entebbe" he was referring to a similar hijacking that had taken place a year earlier. An Air France jet had been seized on a flight from Tel Aviv to Paris and had been flown to Entebbe Airport in Uganda. The hijackers, five Arabs and two Germans, had negotiated with the president of Uganda, Idi Amin, demanding the release of fifty-three pro-Palestinian terrorists held in Israel and around the world; these had included two members of the Baader-Meinhof gang and four from the affiliated Second June Movement, imprisoned in West Germany.

Two days later three army transport planes had landed unannounced at Entebbe; several squads of Israeli commandos had poured out onto the runway and gone on to storm both the hijacked jet and the airport's main building. During the hour's fighting that ensued, twenty Ugandan soldiers, one Israeli commando, three hostages, and all seven hijackers had been killed. The remaining hostages had been rescued.

Martyr Mahmoud's misgivings in the case of the Mogadishu hijacking proved justified. At two o'clock on the morning of Tuesday, 18 October the newly formed West German antiterrorist squad, the GSG-9, stormed the hijacked airliner. Lighting an oil drum under the front of the aircraft to distract the terrorists, they forced the rear emergency exits and tossed in stun grenades. In the resulting confusion they engaged the hijackers in gunfire over the heads of the crouching passengers. Within minutes three of the terrorists were dead, including the leader, and the fourth was badly wounded. This time only one of the ninety hostages was hurt in the cross fire, and the GSG-9 squad suffered no casualties.

The Mogadishu hijack was the third attempt within a year to force the German authorities to free members of the Baader-Meinhof gang. Entebbe had been the first. The second had occurred five weeks before the Mogadishu incident. On 5 September 1977, a sixty-one-year-old German industrialist, Dr Hans-Martin Schleyer, had been kidnapped in Cologne by the RAF; his driver was killed by submachine gun fire; so were three armed guards who were driving immediately behind him. His ransom demand included the same eleven RAF members later demanded by the Mogadishu hijackers. (In fact, both ransom notes proved to have been written on the same typewriter.)

The Mogadishu hijack ended at 2:15 on the morning of Tuesday, 18 October 1977. Shortly after 7:30 the same morning, guards at Stammheim Prison in Stuttgart, West Germany, began to take breakfast around to the prisoners in the seventh-floor cells. Baader-Meinhof terrorist Jan-Carl Raspe, who was serving a life sentence for the murder of four American soldiers in a bombing incident, was found propped up in bed with a bullet wound in his head. He was still alive but died a few hours later. Three cells away, Andreas Baader, the leader of the gang, was found dead with a gun lying beside him. Gudrun Ensslin, Baader's mistress, was found hanging from the barred window of her cell. The fourth RAF terrorist, Irmgard Moller, was found lying in bed with four stab wounds in her chest. She underwent emergency surgery and survived.

That evening the West German minister of justice, Traugott Bender, announced that the three RAF leaders were dead and that a fourth was seriously ill. They had apparently entered into a suicide pact when the news from Mogadishu had made it plain that they had no immediate hope of release. And although Bender insisted that there was no suspicion of foul play, most of the world press took the view that the terrorists had been "executed" to circumvent further hijackings or kidnappings. In fact, Schleyer was murdered by his kidnappers a few hours later – they shot him three times in the head and cut his throat – and his body was found in a car trunk in Mulhouse, France, the next day.

The Baader-Meinhof story, which ended so abruptly that October morning in 1977, began in the late sixties, with the death of a student named Benno Ohnesorg, who was shot by a West Berlin policeman in a protest demonstration against the visit of the shah of Iran. This event soured the whole tone of political debate in Germany. The sixties had been marked by left-wing protest – against the atom bomb, against the Vietnam War, against capitalism in general – but it had remained basically peaceful.

Ohnesorg's killer, Detective Sergeant Kurras, was tried on a manslaughter charge seven months later but was acquitted on a plea that the heat of events at the protest had affected his judgment. The radical Left was incensed by the verdict, which confirmed their view that Germany was still a fascist state. On the day after the shooting, Gudrun Ensslin, a tall, attractive blond dressed in the habitual black sweater and jeans of the revolutionary Left, addressed a meeting of the Socialist German Students Union (SDS) in Berlin. Shrilly emotional to the point of tears, she insisted that the "fascist state" was out to kill them all. It was stupid to aim for a peaceful resolution, she told them; in order to survive they would have to fight violence with violence: "It's the generation of Auschwitz – you can't argue with them"!

Ensslin, born in 1940, was the daughter of an Evangelical pastor who was also a Communist. She had studied philosophy at Tübingen, then moved to Berlin with the left-wing writer Bernward Vesper, with whom she had a son.

In 1967, not long after her impassioned address to the German students, Ensslin met a good-looking, dark-eyed young man named Andreas Baader at a demonstration. At the time Baader was living with – and off – a female action painter named Elly Michell, who bore him a daughter. But this did not prevent him from spending the night with Gudrun Ensslin, who had recently acted in a porno movie called *Das Abonnement* (Subscription).

Baader was entirely without political convictions; he was more interested in fast cars and women. But his own lack of money and success made him an easy convert to the notion that society was rotten and could be improved only by bloody revolution. He deserted his action painter, Ensslin deserted her writer-lover, and together they moved to Frankfurt, where the leftist student movement operated on a more sophisticated level than its Berlin counterpart. Ensslin tended to do the talking at the meetings while Baader, still out of his depth, maintained a tough but silent image. Ensslin was very much the intellectually dominant partner and referred to Baader as her "baby".

It was soon decided, however, that action must replace words. On 2 April 1968, Baader and Ensslin entered the Schneider department store just before closing time. They exited shortly, leaving behind their shopping bags. At midnight fire broke out on three floors but was soon put out by the fire brigade. The following evening Baader and Ensslin were arrested at the apartment of a friend – the police spoke of a "concrete denunciation" – and identified by employees at the department store. Two other militants – Thorwald Proll and Horst Sohnlein – who at the same time had planted a bomb that failed to go off in another department store were also arrested. All four were sentenced to three years' imprisonment for arson. At the trial Ensslin declared, "We don't care about burned mattresses. We are worried about burned children in Vietnam".

Fourteen months later all four were released pending the outcome of an appeal. They now discovered that they had become heroes within extreme-Left circles. When the time came to hear the appeal-court verdict, only Sohnlein turned up; the others – Baader, Ensslin, and Proll

– had fled to Switzerland. They returned secretly in 1970, and in April of that year Baader was arrested as he was on his way to dig up a cache of arms hidden in a cemetery. This time he was sent to Tegel Prison in West Berlin.

There he was visited by a well-known left-wing journalist named Ulrike Meinhof, who had covered the arson trial and interviewed Ensslin and Baader at the time. In a subsequent article she had stated: "It is better to burn a department store than to own one".

At thirty-six – nine years Baader's senior – the divorced Ulrike was something of a celebrity; she had written plays for radio and television, was a popular talk-show guest, and was the mother of twin daughters. In recent years, while lecturing part-time at Berlin's Free University, she had become increasingly involved in extreme-Left student groups. Her apartment was frequently used for their meetings, and these were often attended by associates of Baader and Ensslin. Among these was Horst Mahler, Baader's defense lawyer and the founder of the RAF. (Baader had been in Mahler's car when arrested.) It was Mahler, together with the still-fugitive Ensslin, who convinced Meinhof to help in a plan to free Baader.

The authorities had given Baader permission to write a book on maladjusted juveniles and to conduct his research at the German Institute for Social Questions in the West Berlin suburb of Dahlem – a concession that hardly seems to support Ensslin's assertion that they were confronting a ruthless fascist state.

Another member of the rescue group, Peter Homann, later claimed that no political motive was behind the plan. Gudrun Ensslin desperately wanted her "baby" back, and the others wanted to help her, that was all. It was only later, when they were all on the run, that the idea of becoming full-time revolutionary terrorists seems to have occurred to them, partly through the logic of necessity.

On 14 May 1970, Ulrike Meinhof walked into the German Institute for Social Questions. The librarian who opened the door told her it was closed that morning. Meinhof replied that she already knew this; she had been given permission to work with Andreas Baader on his book. Since she was a well-known journalist, the librarian took her word for it. Baader was brought in and his handcuffs removed. Soon the doorbell rang again, and two young women entered, explaining that they needed to do some research. Moments later a masked man rushed into the room waving a gun; the two women produced guns from their bags, and in the gunfire that followed – mostly aimed at the floor – Baader and Meinhof leapt from a window and into an Alfa Romeo, driven by Thorwald

Proll's sister, Astrid. A librarian had been seriously wounded in the gunfire.

Mahler now arranged for the group – which included Baader, Meinhof, Ensslin, and himself – to escape from Germany to the Middle East, where they were trained in terrorist tactics by the Popular Front for the Liberation of Palestine (PFLP). It was at this point that they decided to call their movement the Red Army Faction, after the Japanese Red Army terrorist group.

Back in Germany, Mahler organized bank raids to finance the movement. Mahler himself was arrested in October 1970. In May 1972 the RAF planted bombs at the headquarters of the U.S. Fifth Army Corps in Frankfurt, killing a colonel and injuring thirteen others. Damage was estimated at more than a million dollars. An anonymous phone call stated that the bombing was in retaliation for Vietnam. The following day suitcases containing time bombs exploded in the police station in Augsburg, Bavaria, injuring five policemen. Three days later the wife of a judge was injured by a car bomb in Karlsruhe. On 19 May, two time bombs exploded in the offices of the right-wing publishing house of Springer in Hamburg. And on 25 May 1972, bomb explosions at the American army base in Heidelberg killed three and injured five.

Soon after the Heidelberg bombing, the Frankfurt police received a tip-off that led them to the garage of an apartment building in the north of the city. Bomb-making equipment was seized and bombs defused. And when Andreas Baader reached the garage in the early hours of 1 June 1972, driving a lilac Porsche, he was met by armed police. In the car with him were Jan-Carl Raspe and another terrorist, Holger Meins. Raspe opened fire and tried to escape but was overpowered. Baader and Meins shut themselves in the garage but were overcome by tear-gas grenades. Baader was shot in the thigh, and Meins emerged in his underpants, with his hands held high.

Six days later Gudrun Ensslin was arrested in a Hamburg boutique – an assistant had noticed a gun in her pocket and called the police.

Ulrike Meinhof was arrested in Hanover a week later, as a result of a tip-off from a left-wing teacher who felt that the terrorists were harming the leftist cause. On 25 June a Briton named Ian MacLeod was shot and killed as police tried to arrest him in Stuttgart; he is believed to have been negotiating an arms deal for the gang.

The gang members were placed in Stuttgart's top-security Stammheim Jail; the trial would be delayed for another three years, until an escape-proof top-security courtroom could be built. Meanwhile, evidence that the terrorist threat was as menacing as ever was provided at the Munich Olympics, when Arab terrorists from the Black September movement took nine Israeli athletes hostage and shot two more; the nine hostages died in a gun battle at the military airport, together with five terrorists. The terrorists' demands had included the release of the Baader-Meinhof gang.

Terrorist outrages continued. In June 1974 an extremist named Ulrich Schmucker was executed by fellow gang members, accused of betraying a plot to blow up the Turkish embassy in Bonn in reprisal for the execution of three Turkish terrorists. And after the death by hunger strike of Holger Meins, on 9 November 1974, a judge named Gunter von Drenckmann was shot down by flower-bearing terrorists when he answered the door on his birthday.

Judges and leading industrialists were now forced to live in a state of siege. On 27 February 1975, terrorists seized Peter Lorenz, leader of the Christian Democratic Party, as he was being driven to his West Berlin office. The release of six terrorists was demanded in exchange for his life; these included Horst Mahler but not, oddly enough, Baader or Meinhof. The West German government caved in: five terrorists were released and flown out of Germany; perhaps sick of being on the run, Horst Mahler declined to accompany them. Lorenz was freed unharmed.

The success of the escapade suggested that the next kidnapping would involve a demand for the release of the Baader-Meinhof gang. In fact, on 24 April 1975, six terrorists who called themselves the "Holger Meins commando" seized the West German embassy in Stockholm and threatened a massacre of hostages unless the Baader-Meinhof gang was released and half a million dollars paid in ransom. To emphasize their seriousness they shot to death the military attaché, Baron von Mirbach. The Bonn government refused to meet the terrorists' demands but offered them safe passage out of the country in exchange for releasing the hostages. Before further negotiations could take place, there was a tremendous explosion on the top floor of the embassy – explosives placed in a refrigerator had been set off accidentally. One terrorist was killed; the hostages made their way out of the building through the smoke. Five terrorists were caught as they tried to escape through a window. One of them died from the after-effects of the explosion; the others were imprisoned in Germany.

Finally, on 21 May 1975, the Baader-Meinhof trial began in a building that was virtually a fortress. Objections and harangues from the four defendants – Baader, Meinhof, Ensslin, and Raspe – threatened to reduce it to a farce. But when, almost a year later, on 4 May 1976,

Gudrun Ensslin claimed responsibility for three of the four bombings, it was all virtually over.

Five days later, on 9 May Ulrike Meinhof was found hanging from her cell window bars, her neck encircled by a noose made from her sheets. An autopsy led to a verdict of suicide. But a second autopsy, carried out at her family's behest, threw doubt on the verdict. Traces of semen were alleged to have been found on her underwear. Bruises on the inside of her thighs also suggested rape. A saliva track ran from her breast to her navel, suggesting that she had been unclothed at the time of her death and had been dressed later. A group of medical experts later agreed that throttling during rape could not be ruled out.

The trial dragged on until April 1977, when the three remaining defendants each were given life plus fifteen years' imprisonment. (Mahler had been sentenced to fourteen years for bank robbery in 1972.)

Six months later, in October 1977, the Lufthansa airliner was hijacked at Palma, Majorca, and the last act of the drama began; it ended with the "suicides" of Baader, Ensslin, and Raspe on 18 October. The German Left was quick to accuse the government of murder, and even the Right had to concede that it was highly likely – in fact, that it was the only logical solution to the problem of further attempts to free the gang.

It looked as if one person now held the solution to the mystery: Irmgard Moller. If the others had been murdered, then clearly the killers had made a serious mistake in leaving her alive. It seemed that she owed her life to the shortness of the knife blade that had stabbed her but that had failed to reach her heart. But when Moller was able to speak, her testimony was disappointing. She brought criminal charges of murder against an "unknown person", and in a hearing in January 1978, denied that she had attempted suicide or that the four had been able to communicate with one another during the Mogadishu hijacking. But she was unable to describe how she came to be found unconscious – she could only recall hearing "two soft popping noises" and a voice saying, "Baader and Ensslin are dead already". Her ninety-minute appearance ended when she was dragged out of court as she tried to confer with her lawyers. In 1979 she was again sentenced to life imprisonment.

Ingrid Schubert, one of the women who had helped free Baader in 1970, and who had been jailed for her part in bank robberies, was found hanging in her cell on 5 November 1977, three weeks after the deaths of Baader, Ensslin, and Raspe.

Was the Baader-Meinhof gang "executed" by its captors? The Bonn government denied it. There had, they insisted, been a suicide pact, whose aim was to fuel the revolutionary fervor of the comrades outside. (Even during the trial there had been another murder – of chief federal prosecutor Siegfried Bruback, on 7 April 1977, and soon after the trial, on 30 July 1977, Jürgen Ponto was murdered by his own goddaughter, Susanne Albrecht.) A portable transistor radio *had* been discovered in the cell of Raspe, and the wires left in the walls of the gang members' cells could have been used as a primitive signaling device. Explosives found in the cells were alleged to have been smuggled in to the gang members at the same time as the pistols that had killed Baader and Raspe. The aim, said the official statement, had been to make suicide look like murder. Baader even wrote a letter to a Stuttgart court insisting that he would never commit suicide – although there was no particular need for this admission. Similarly, Ensslin had sent for two clergymen and indicated that she thought she might be murdered. All this, like Moller's accusation, could certainly be interpreted as evidence of a plot to embarrass the authorities with a final act of desperation and defiance.

The evidence against this view is sparse yet highly disturbing: the semen stains on Ulrike Meinhof's underwear; and the stab wounds – made with a blunt butter knife – in Irmgard Moller's chest. One expert stated that there would be an overwhelming inhibition against the self-infliction of such wounds.

The irony of the Baader-Meinhof story is that nearly all the protagonists came from comfortable middle-class backgrounds and had little firsthand experience of poverty or injustice. If they had been living under Hitler or Stalin, it would be easier to sympathize with the violence of their reactions. But in the democratic regime of West Germany, the argument that they were fighting "the generation of Auschwitz" sounds somehow exaggerated. One student leader commented about Gudrun Ensslin's "Auschwitz" speech: "She was too hysterical". Andreas Baader, who had always been cynically nonpolitical, allowed Ensslin's hysteria to draw him into the fire-bombing. From then on, like some character in Sophocles or Shakespeare, he was drawn into a whirlpool of events over which he had no control and that made him the central figure in a grotesque tragedy that involved the whole country. The verdict of history on the Baader-Meinhof orgy of terrorism will probably be: It was all so unnecessary.

4

The Barbados Vault

Mystery of the Moving Coffins

On 9 August 1812 the coffin of the Hon. Thomas Chase, a slave-owner on the Caribbean island of Barbados, was carried down the steps of the family vault. As the heavy slab was moved aside and the lamplight illuminated the interior, it became clear that something strange had happened. One of the three coffins it already contained was lying on its side. Another, that of a baby, was lying, head-downward, in a corner. It seemed obvious that the tomb had been desecrated. The odd thing was that there was no sign of forced entry. The coffins were replaced in their original positions, and the tomb resealed. The local white population had no doubt that Negro labourers were responsible for the violation; Thomas Chase had been a cruel and ruthless man. In fact, the last coffin to be laid in the vault – only a month before Chase's – was that of his daughter, Dorcas Chase, who was rumoured to have starved herself to death because of her father's brutality.

Four years went by. On 25 September 1816 another small coffin – this time of eleven-month-old Samuel Brewster Ames – was carried into the vault; once again, it was found in wild disorder. Someone had tumbled all four coffins about the floor, including the immensely heavy lead-encased coffin of Thomas Chase, which it had taken eight men to lift. Once more the coffins were arranged neatly, and the vault resealed.

It was opened again seven weeks later, this time to receive the body of Samuel Brewster, a man who had been murdered in a slave uprising the previous April, and who had been temporarily buried elsewhere in the meantime. Yet again the vault was in disorder, the coffins tumbled about in confusion. No one doubted that Negro slaves were responsible, and that this was an act of revenge. The mystery was: *how* had it been done? The great marble slab had been cemented into place each time, and there was no sign that it had been broken open and then recemented.

One of the coffins – that of Mrs Thomasina Goddard, the first occupant of the vault – had disintegrated into planks, apparently as a result of its rough treatment. They were tied together roughly with wire, and the coffin was placed against the wall. Since the vault (which was only 12 feet by 6½ feet) was becoming somewhat crowded, the children's coffins were placed on top of those of adults. Then once more the vault was resealed.

The story had now become something of a sensation in the islands. Christ Church, and its rector, the Rev. Thomas Orderson, became the focus of unwelcome curiosity. He showed understandable impatience with some of the sensation-seekers; but to those whose rank demanded politeness he explained that he and a magistrate had made a careful search of the vault after the last desecration, trying to find how the vandals had got in. There was undoubtedly no secret door; the floor, walls and curved ceiling were solid and uncracked. He was also convinced that the problem had not been caused by flooding. Although the vault was two feet below ground-level, it had been excavated out of solid limestone. And floods would have left some mark. Besides, it was unlikely that heavy leaden coffins would float. Orderson naturally dismissed the theory held by the local black population that the tomb had some kind of curse on it, and that supernatural forces were responsible.

By the time the next and last burial took place, there was universal interest and excitement. On 7 July 1819 (other accounts say the 17th), Mrs Thomazina Clarke was carried into the vault in a cedar coffin. The cement took a long time to remove from the door – it had been used in abundance to reseal the vault – and even when it had been chipped away, the door still refused to yield. Considerable effort revealed that the massive leaden coffin of Thomas Chase was now jammed against it, six feet from where it had been placed. All the other coffins were disturbed, with the exception of the wire-bound coffin of Mrs Goddard. This seemed to prove that flooding was not the answer – would leaden coffins float when wooden planks lay unmoved?

The governor, Lord Combermere, had been one of the first into the vault. He now ordered an exhaustive search. But it only verified what Orderson had said earlier; there was no way that vandals could have forced their way into the vault, no hidden trapdoor, no entrance for floodwater. Before he ordered the tomb resealed, the governor ordered that the floor should be sprinkled with sand, which would show footprints. Then once more the door was cemented shut. Combermere even used his private seal on it so that it could not be opened and then recemented without leaving obvious traces.

Eight months later, on 18 April 1820, a party was gathered at Lord Combermere's residence, and conversation turned as it often did on the vault. Finally, the governor decided that they would go and investigate whether their precautions had been effective. There were nine of them in all, including the governor, the rector, and two masons. They verified that the cement was undisturbed and the seals intact. Then the masons opened the door. Once again the place was in chaos. A child's coffin lay on the steps that led down into the chamber, while Thomas Chase's coffin was upside down. Only Mrs Goddard's bundle of planks remained undisturbed. The sand on the floor was still unmarked. Once again the masons struck the walls with their hammers, looking for a secret entrance. And finally, when it seemed obvious that the mystery was insoluble, Lord Combermere ordered that the coffins should be removed and buried elsewhere. After that the tomb remained empty.

None of the many writers on the case have been able to supply a plausible explanation. The obvious "natural" explanations are flooding and earth tremors. But flooding would have disarranged Mrs Goddard's coffin and moved the sand on the floor; besides, someone would have noticed if rain had been so heavy that it flooded the graveyard. The same applies to earth tremors strong enough to shake coffins around like dice in a wooden cup. Conan Doyle suggested that the explanation was some kind of explosion inside the vault, and to explain this he suggests that the "effluvia" (sweat?) of the Negro slaves somehow combined with unnamed forces inside the vault to produce a gas explosion. Nothing seems less likely.

Yet a "supernatural" explanation is just as implausible. It has often been pointed out that the disturbances began after the burial of a woman believed to have committed suicide; the suggestion is that the other "spirits" refused to rest at ease with a suicide. But the movement of the coffins suggest a poltergeist (*qv*), and all the investigators are agreed that a poltergeist needs some kind of "energy source" – often an emotionally disturbed adolescent living on the premises. And an empty tomb can provide no such energy source.

The Negroes obviously believed there was some kind of voodoo at work – some magical force deliberately conjured by a witch or witch doctor, the motive being revenge on the hated slave-owners. It sounds unlikely, but it is the best that can be offered.

5

The Basa Murder

The Voice from the Grave

There have been many folktales in which the dead have returned to give evidence against their murderers; but there is only one example that has been authenticated beyond all shadow of a doubt. It is the case of a Filippino physical therapist named Teresita Basa, who was stabbed to death in Chicago on February 21, 1977.

Toward 8:30 on the evening of that day, the Chicago fire department was called to put out a blaze in a high-rise apartment building on the North Side. Two fire fighters crawled into Apartment 15B through black smoke and saw that the fire was in the bedroom. A mattress lying at the foot of the bed was blazing. Within minutes the firemen had put the blaze out and opened the windows to let out the smoke. When they lifted the waterlogged mattress, they found the naked body of a woman, with her legs spread apart and a knife sticking out of her chest.

Forty-eight-year-old Teresita Basa had been born in the city of Damaguete, in the Philippines, the daughter of a judge. She had become a physical therapist specializing in respiratory problems – perhaps because her father had died of a respiratory illness – and was working at Edgewater Hospital in Chicago at the time of her death.

Forensic examination postulated that Teresita had answered the door to someone she knew – she had been talking to a friend on the telephone when the doorbell rang. The intruder had encircled her neck from behind with his arm and choked her until she lost consciousness. He then had taken money from her handbag and ransacked the apartment. After that he had stripped off all her clothes, taken a butcher knife from the kitchen drawer, and driven it virtually through her body. Then he had set the mattress on fire with a piece of burning paper, dumped it on top of her, and hurried out of the apartment. The fire alarm had sounded before he had gone more than a few blocks.

Forensic investigation also revealed that there had been no sexual assault. Teresita Basa had died a virgin.

Although Remy (short for Remibias) Chua, another Filippino, had worked with Teresita Basa in the respiratory therapy department of Edgewater Hospital, the two had been only slightly acquainted. Two weeks after the murder, during the course of a conversation, Chua remarked, only half seriously, "If there is no solution to her murder, she can come to me in a dream". She then went for a brief nap in the hospital locker room – it was two o'clock in the morning. As she was dozing on a chair, her feet propped on another, something made her open her eyes. She had to suppress a scream as she saw Teresita Basa – looking as solid as a living person – standing in front of her. She lost no time in running out of the room.

During the course of the next few weeks, two of Mrs Chua's fellow employees jokingly remarked that she looked – and behaved – like Teresita Basa. Her husband, Dr José Chua, also noticed that his wife seemed to have undergone a personality change. Normally sunny and good-natured, she had become oddly peremptory and moody. Teresita Basa had also been prone to moods.

In late July, five months after the murder, Remy Chua was working with a hospital orderly named Allan Showery when she found herself experiencing an inexplicable panic. Showery was a sinewy but powerfully built black man with an open and confident manner. When Showery was standing behind Mrs Chua, she caught a movement out of the corner of her eye – just as Teresita Basa may have when her killer stepped up behind her to lock his forearm round her neck – and, inexplicably, her heart began to pound violently. She decided that she was suffering from nervous problems and asked for time off from work.

That night her husband heard her talking in her sleep – she was repeating, "Al–Al–Al . . ." She told him later that she had dreamed of being in a smoke-filled room. The next day she felt so ill that she asked her parents to come over. After taking a strong sedative, she climbed into bed. But after a few hours' sleep she began to babble in Spanish – a language Remy Chua did not speak. Her husband knelt beside the bed and asked, "How are you"? His wife replied, "I am Teresita Basa". When José Chua asked what she wanted, the voice replied, "I want help . . . Nothing has been done about the man who killed me". A few minutes later "Teresita" disappeared and Remy Chua was herself again.

Two days later Remy Chua felt a pain in her chest, followed by a heavy sensation, "as if someone was stepping into her body". She told her mother (who was still with them), "Terrie is here again".

When her husband returned he found his wife in bed. The voice of Teresita Basa issued from her mouth, asking accusingly, "Did you talk to the police"? José Chua acknowledged that he hadn't, because he needed proof. "Allan killed me" insisted the voice. "I let Al into the apartment and he killed me".

The strain of Remy Chua's "possession" was beginning to adversely affect the whole family (the Chuas had four children). José Chua finally went to his boss at Franklin Park Hospital, Dr Winograd, and told him the whole story; Dr Winograd took the "possession" seriously but believed that the police would dismiss it as an absurdity. He advised Dr Chua to write them an anonymous letter.

The "possessing entity" had other ideas. The next time Remy Chua went into a trancelike state, the voice demanded to know why José Chua had not done as she asked. He explained that he had no proof. "Dr Chua", said the voice, "the man Allan Showery stole my jewelry and gave it to his girlfriend. They live together".

"But how could it be identified"?

"My cousins, Ron Somera and Ken Basa, could identify it. So could my friends, Richard Pessoti and Ray King". She went on to give Dr Chua Ron Somera's telephone number. After that she told him, "Al came to fix my television and he killed me and burned me. Tell the police".

Dr Chua finally decided to do as she asked; he telephoned the Evanston police headquarters. On 8 August 1977, Investigator Joseph Stachula was assigned to interview the Chuas. Their story left him stunned, yet he had an intuitive certainty that they were not cranks. All the same, he could see no obvious way to make use of what they had told him. He could hardly walk up to Allan Showery and arrest him on the grounds that his victim had come back from the dead to accuse him.

A check on Showery revealed that he might well be the killer. He had a long criminal record that included two rapes, each of which had taken place in the victim's apartment. Moreover, he had lived only four blocks from Teresita Basa.

Showery was brought to the police station, and was asked if it were true that he had agreed to repair Teresita Basa's television on the evening of her murder. He acknowledged that it was but insisted that he had gone to a local bar for a drink and simply forgotten. Asked if he had ever been in the Basa apartment, he denied it. Then, when asked for fingerprint samples to compare with some found in the apartment, he changed his mind and acknowledged that he had been there some months earlier. Finally, he admitted that he had been there on the evening of her death but claimed that he had left immediately because he did not have a circuit plan for that particular television.

Now the suspect was obviously nervous, and the interviewers left him alone while they went back to talk to Yanka. She recalled that on the evening of the murder – she remembered it because the fire engine had passed her window – Showery had come home early. Asked by the interviewers if he had recently given her any jewelry, she showed them an antique cocktail ring. She was asked to accompany them back to the police station, together with her jewelry box. Meanwhile, Teresita Basa's two friends, Richard Pessoti and Ray King, were brought to the station. As soon as Pessoti glimpsed the ring on Yanka's finger, he recognized it as one belonging to Teresita Basa. The two were also able to identify other jewelry in Yanka's jewelry box.

Stachula's partner, Detective Lee Epplen, confronted Showery and told him, "It's all over". Showery screamed angrily, "You cops are trying to frame me". When shown the jewelry, he insisted that he had bought it at a pawnshop but had failed to get a receipt. Minutes later he realized that the evidence against him was overwhelming. He asked to speak to Yanka, and in the presence of the detectives said, "Yanka, I have something to tell you. I killed Teresita Basa".

He had believed that Teresita was rich and that robbing her would solve all his financial problems. But after killing her, he found that her purse contained only thirty dollars. In order to make the murder look like a sex crime he had undressed her and spread her legs apart. Then he had stabbed her with the butcher knife and set the mattress on fire, hoping that the fire would destroy any clues he might have left behind.

The "Voice from the Grave" case made national headlines. Showery came to trial on 21 January 1979, before Judge Frank W. Barbero. But the story of the "possession" of Remy Chua was so astounding that the jury was unable to agree on a verdict. The defense also objected that the evidence of a ghost was not admissible in a court of law. Five days later a mistrial was declared. But on 23 February 1979, Allan Showery acknowledged that he was guilty of the murder of Teresita Basa. He was sentenced to fourteen years for murder and to four years each on charges of armed robbery and arson.

6

The Bermuda Triangle

On the afternoon of 5 December 1945 five Avenger torpedo-bombers took off from Fort Lauderdale, Florida, for a routine two-hour patrol over the Atlantic. Flight 19 was commanded by Flight Leader Charles Taylor; the other four pilots were trainees, flying what is known as a "milk run" that is, a flight whose purpose is simply to increase their number of hours in the air without instructors. By 2.15 the planes were well over the Atlantic, and following their usual patrol route. The weather was warm and clear.

At 3.45 the control tower received a message from Taylor: "This is an emergency. We seem to be off course. We cannot see land . . . repeat . . . we cannot see land".

"What is your position"?

"We're not sure of our position. We can't be sure where we are. We seem to be lost".

"Head due west", replied the tower.

"We don't know which way is west. Everything is wrong . . . strange. We can't be sure of any direction. Even the ocean doesn't look as it should".

The tower was perplexed; even if some kind of magnetic interference caused all five compasses to malfunction, the pilot should still be able to see the sun low in the western sky. Radio contact was now getting worse, restricting any messages to short sentences. At one point the tower picked up one pilot speaking to another, saying that all the instruments in his plane were "going crazy". At four o'clock the flight leader decided to hand over to someone else. At 4.25 the new leader told the tower: "We're not certain where we are".

Unless the planes could find their way back over land during the next four hours, they would run out of fuel and be forced to land in the sea. At 6.27 a rescue mission was launched. A giant Martin Mariner flying-boat, with a crew of thirteen, took off towards the last reported position of the flight. Twenty-three minutes later, the sky to the east was lit briefly by a bright orange flash. Neither the Martin Mariner nor the five Avengers ever returned. They vanished completely, as other planes and ships have vanished in the area that has become known as "the Devil's Triangle" and "the Bermuda Triangle".

What finally happened to the missing aircraft is certainly no mystery. The weather became worse during the course of that afternoon; ships reported "high winds and tremendous seas". Flight 19 and its would-be rescuer must have run out of fuel, and landed in the sea. The mystery is *why* they became so completely lost and confused. Even if the navigation instruments had ceased to function, and visibility had become restricted to a few yards, it should have been possible to fly up above the clouds to regain their bearings.

What seems stranger still is that this tragedy should have failed to alert the authorities that there was something frightening and dangerous about the stretch of ocean between Florida and the Bahamas – a chain of islands that begins a mere fifty miles off the coast of Florida. But then the authorities no doubt took the view of many more recent sceptics, that the disappearance was a rather complex accident, due to a number of chance factors: bad weather, electrical interference with the compasses, the inexperience of some of the pilots and the fact that the flight leader, Charles Taylor, had only recently been posted to Fort Lauderdale and was unfamiliar with the area.

Similar explanations were adopted to explain a number of similar tragedies during the next two decades: the disappearance of a Superfortress in 1947, of a four-engined Tudor IV in January 1948, of a DC3 in December 1948, of another Tudor IV in 1949, of a Globemaster in 1950, of a British York transport plane in 1952, of a Navy Super Constellation in 1954, of another Martin seaplane in 1956, of an Air Force tanker in 1962, of two Stratotankers in 1963, of a flying boxcar in 1965, of a civilian cargo plane in 1966, another cargo plane in 1967, and yet another in 1973 . . . The total number of lives lost in all these disappearances was well in excess of two hundred. Oddly enough, the first person to realize that all this amounted to a frightening mystery was a journalist called Vincent Gaddis; it was in February 1964 that his article "The Deadly Bermuda Triangle" appeared in the American *Argosy* magazine, and bestowed the now familiar name on that mysterious stretch of ocean. A year later, in a book about sea mysteries called *Invisible Horizons*, Gaddis included his article in a chapter called "The Triangle of Death". His chapter also contained a long list of ships which had vanished in the area, beginning with the *Rosalie*, which vanished in 1840, and ending with the yacht *Connemara IV* in 1956. In the final chapter Gaddis entered the realm of science fiction, and speculated on "space-time continua [that] may exist around us on the earth, interpenetrating our known world", implying that perhaps some of the missing planes and ships had vanished down a kind of fourth-dimensional plughole.

Soon after the publication of his book Gaddis received a letter from a man called Gerald Hawkes, who told of his own experience in the Bermuda Triangle in April 1952. On a flight from Idlewild Airport (now Kennedy) to Bermuda, Hawkes's plane suddenly dropped about two hundred feet. This was not a nose-dive, but felt if he had suddenly fallen down a lift-shaft in the air; then the plane shot back up again. "It was as if a giant hand was holding the plane and jerking it up and down", and the wings seemed to flap like the wings of a bird. The captain then told them that he was unable to find Bermuda, and that the operator was unable to make radio contact with either the US or Bermuda. An hour or so later the plane made contact with a radio ship, and was able to get its bearings and fly to Bermuda. As they climbed out of the plane they observed that it was a clear and starry night, with no wind. The writer concluded that he was still wondering whether he was caught in an area "where time and space seem to disappear".

Now, all pilots know about air pockets, where a sudden change in pressure causes the plane to lurch and fall, and about air turbulence which causes the wings of a plane to "flap". What seems odd about this case is the total radio blackout.

This was an anomaly that had also struck students of UFOS (see Chapter 39), or flying saucers, who had been creating extraordinary theories ever since that day in June 1947 when a pilot named Kenneth Arnold saw nine shining discs moving against the background of Mount Rainier in Washington State. The flying-saucer enthusiasts now produced the interesting notion that the surface of our earth has a number of strange "vortices", whirlpools where gravity and terrestrial magnetism are inexplicably weaker than usual. And if extra-terrestrial intelligences happened to know about these whirlpools, they might well find them ideal for collecting human specimens to be studied at leisure upon their distant planet . . .

Ivan Sanderson, a friend of Gaddis's and a student of earth mysteries, felt that this was going too far. His training had been scientific, so he began by taking a map of the world, and marking on it a number of areas where strange disappearances had occurred. There was, for example, another "Devil's Triangle" south of the Japanese island of Honshu where ships and planes had vanished. A correspondent told Sanderson about a strange experience on a flight to Guam, in the western Pacific, when his ancient propeller-driven plane covered 340 miles in one hour, although there was no wind – about 200 miles more than it should have covered; checks showed that many planes had vanished in this area.

Marking these areas on the map, Sanderson observed that they were shaped like lozenges, and that these lozenges seemed to ring the globe in a neat symmetry, running in two rings, each between 30°C and 40°C north and south of the equator. There were ten of these "funny places", about 72°C apart. An earthquake specialist named George Rouse had argued that earthquakes originated in a certain layer below the earth's surface, and had speculated that there was a kind of trough running round the central core of the earth, which determined the direction of seismic activities. Rouse's map of these seismic disturbance areas corresponded closely with Sanderson's "lozenges". So Sanderson was inclined to believe that if "whirlpools" really caused the disappearance of ships and planes, then they were perfectly normal physical whirlpools, caused, so to speak, by the earth's tendency to "burp".

Sanderson's theory appeared in a book entitled *Invisible Residents* in 1970. Three years later a female journalist, Adi-Kent Thomas Jeffrey, tried to put together all the evidence about the Bermuda Triangle in a book of that name, printed by a small publishing company in Pennsylvania. It was undoubtedly her bad luck that her book failed to reach the general public. For one year later Charles Berlitz, grandson of the man who founded the famous language schools, once again rehashed all the information about the Bermuda Triangle, persuaded a commercial publisher, Doubleday, to issue it, and promptly rocketed to the top of the American best-seller lists. It had been twenty years since the disappearance of Flight 19, and ten years since Vincent Gaddis invented the phrase "Bermuda Triangle". But Berlitz was the first man to turn the mystery into a worldwide sensation, and to become rich on the proceeds.

Berlitz's *Bermuda Triangle*, while highly readable, is low on scholarly precision – it does not even have an index. One reason for its popularity was that he launched himself intrepidly into bizarre regions of speculation about UFOs, space-time warps, alien intelligences, chariots of the gods (à la Von Däniken) and other such matters. And among the weirdest of his speculations were those concerning the pioneer "Ufologist" Morris K. Jessup, who had died in mysterious circumstances after stumbling upon information about a certain mysterious "Philadelphia experiment". This experiment was supposed to have taken place in Philadelphia in 1943, when the Navy was testing some new device whose purpose was to surround a ship with a powerful magnetic field. According to Jessup's informant, a hazy green light began to surround the vessel, so that its outlines became blurred; then it vanished – to reappear in the harbour of Norfolk, Virginia, some three hundred miles away. Several members of the crew died; others went insane. According to Jessup, when he began to investigate this story, the Navy asked him whether he would be willing to work on a similar secret project; he declined. In 1959 he was found dead in his car, suffocated by exhaust gas; Berlitz speculates that he was "silenced" before he could publicize his discoveries about the experiment.

And what has all this to do with the Bermuda Triangle? Simply that the Philadelphia experiment was supposed to be an attempt to create a magnetic vortex, like those suggested by Sanderson, and that (according to Jessup) it had the effect of involving the ship in a space-time warp that transported it hundreds of miles.

Understandably, this kind of thing roused sceptics to a fury, and there were suddenly a large number of articles, books and television programmes all devoted to debunking the Bermuda Triangle. These all adopted the common-sense approach that had characterized the Naval authorities in 1945: that is to say, they assumed that the disappearances were all due to natural causes, particularly to freak storms. In many cases it is difficult not to agree that this is indeed the most plausible explanation. But when we look at the long list of disappearances in the area, most of them never even yielding a body or a trace of wreckage, the explanation begins to sound thin.

Is there, then, an alternative which combines common sense with the boldness necessary to recognize that all the disappearances cannot be conveniently explained away? There is, and it rests on the evidence of some of those who have escaped the Bermuda Triangle. In November 1964 a charter pilot named Chuck Wakely was returning from Nassau to Miami, Florida, and had climbed up to 8,000 feet. He noticed a faint glow round the wings of his plane, which he put down to some optical illusion caused by cockpit lights. But the glow increased steadily, and all his electronic equipment began to go wrong. He was forced to operate the craft manually. The glow became so blinding that he was dazzled; then slowly it faded, and his instruments began to function normally again.

In 1966 Captain Don Henry was steering his tug from Puerto Rico to

Fort Lauderdale on a clear afternoon. He heard shouting, and hurried to the bridge. There he saw that the compass was spinning clockwise. A strange darkness came down, and the horizon disappeared. "The water seemed to be coming from all directions". And although the electric generators were still running, all electric power faded away. An auxiliary generator refused to start. The boat seemed to be surrounded by a kind of fog. Fortunately the engines were still working, and suddenly the boat emerged from the fog. To Henry's amazement, the fog seemed to be concentrated into a single solid bank, and within this area the sea was turbulent; outside it was calm. Henry remarked that the compass behaved as it did on the St Lawrence River at Kingson, where some large deposit of iron – or a meteorite – affects the needle.

Our earth is, of course, a gigantic magnet (no one quite knows why), and the magnetic lines of force run around its surface in strange patterns. Birds and animals use these lines of force for "homing", and water-diviners seem able to respond to them with their "dowsing rods". But there are areas of the earth's surface where birds lose their way because the lines somehow cancel one another out, forming a magnetic anomaly or vortex. The *Marine Observer* for 1930 warns sailors about a magnetic disturbance in the neighbourhood of the Tambora volcano, near Sumbawa, which deflected a ship's compass by six points, leading it off course. In 1932 Captain Scutt of the *Australia* observed a magnetic disturbance near Freemantle that deflected the compass 12° either side of the ship's course. Dozens of similar anomalies have been collected and documented by an American investigator, William Corliss, in books with titles like *Unknown Earth* and *Strange Planet*. It was Corliss who pointed out to me the investigations of Dr John de Laurier of Ottawa, who in 1974 went to camp on the ice-floes of northern Canada in search of an enormous magnetic anomaly forty-three miles long, which he believes to originate about eighteen miles below the surface of the earth. De Laurier's theory is that such anomalies are due to the earth's tectonic plates rubbing together – an occurrence that also causes earthquakes.

The central point to emerge from all this is that our earth is not like an ordinary bar magnet, whose field is symmetrical and precise; it is full of magnetic "pitfalls" and anomalies. Scientists are not sure why the earth has a magnetic field, but one theory suggests that it is due to movements in its molten iron core. Such movements would in fact produce shifting patterns in the earth's field, and bursts of magnetic activity, which might be compared to the bursts of solar energy known as sunspots. If they *are* related to earth-tensions and therefore to earthquakes then we would expect them to occur in certain definite zones, just as earthquakes do. What effects would a sudden "earthquake" of magnetic activity produce? One would be to cause compasses to spin, for it would be rather as if a huge magnetic meteor was roaring up from the centre of the earth. On the sea it would produce an effect of violent turbulence, for it would affect the water in the same way the moon affects the tides, but in an irregular pattern, so that the water would appear to be coming "from all directions". Clouds and mist would be sucked into the vortex, forming a "bank" in its immediate area. And electronic gadgetry would probably be put out of action . . .

All this makes us aware why the "simplistic" explanations of the problem – all those books explaining that the mystery of the Bermuda Triangle is a journalistic invention – are not only superficial but dangerous. They discourage the investigation of what could be one of the most interesting scientific enigmas of our time. With satellites circling the earth at a height of 150 miles, it should be possible to observe bursts of magnetic activity with the same accuracy that earth tremors are recorded on seismographs. We should be able to observe their frequency and intensity precisely enough to plot them in advance. The result could not only be the solution of the mystery, but the prevention of future tragedies like that of Flight 19.

7

Bigfoot

Like the gun-fight in OK Corral, the siege of Ape Canyon has become part of American folklore.

It begins in 1924, when a group of miners were working in the Mount St Helen's range in Washington State, seventy-five miles north of Portland, Oregon. One day they saw a big ape-like creature peering out from behind a tree. One of the miners fired at it, and thought the bullet hit its head. The creature ran off into the forest. Then another miner, Fred Beck – who was to tell the story thirty-four years later – met another of the "apes" at the canyon rim, and shot it in the back three times. It toppled over into the canyon; but when the miners went to look there was no body.

That night the miners found themselves under siege. From dusk until dawn the next day the creatures pounded on the doors, walls and the roof, and rocks were hurled. The miners braced the heavy door from inside, and fired shots through the walls and roof. But the creatures were obviously angry and determined, and the assault ceased only at sunrise. That day the miners decided to abandon the site.

Beck's description of the "Bigfoot" is of a creature about eight feet tall, and very muscular. It looked not unlike a gorilla, but if it could use rocks as a weapon of assault, then it was clearly humanoid.

Fred Beck's account of the siege, together with other sightings on the West Coast, made Bigfoot something of a national celebrity in the late 1950s. But stories about the creature had been in circulation for centuries. The Salish Indians of British Columbia called the creature "Sasquatch", meaning "wild man of the woods". In northern California the Huppa tribe call them "Oh-mah-ah"; in the Cascades they are known as "Seeahtiks".

The notion of colonies of monsters living quietly in the modern US and Canada admittedly sounds absurd; but this is partly because few people grasp the sheer size of the North American coniferous forests – thousands of square miles of totally uninhabited woodland, some still unexplored, where it would be possible to hide a herd of dinosaurs.

The first recorded story of a Sasquatch footprint dates back to 1811. The well-known explorer and trader David Thompson was crossing the Rockies towards the mouth of the Columbia river when, at the site of modern Jasper, Alberta, he and his companion came upon a footprint fourteen inches by eight inches, with four toes and claw marks. Thompson thought it was probably a grizzly bear, but his companion insisted that it could not have been a bear because bears have five toes. In any case, few bears leave behind fourteen-inch footprints.

The *Daily Colonist* of Victoria, British Columbia, for Friday, 4 July 1884, published an account of the capture of a Bigfoot. Jacko (as his captors called him) seems to have been a fairly small specimen, only 4 ft 7 in high, and weighing 127 pounds. He was spotted from a train which was winding its way along the Fraser river from Lytton to Yale, in the shadow of the Cascade mountains, and apparently captured without too much difficulty. He was described as having long black, coarse hair and short glossy hairs all over his body. The forearms were much longer than a man's, and were powerful enough to be able to tear a branch in two. Regrettably, Jacko's subsequent fate is unknown, although the naturalist John Napier reports that he may have been exhibited in Barnum and Bailey's Circus.

In 1910 Bigfoot was blamed for a gruesome event that took place in the Nahanni Valley, near Great Slave Lake in the Northwest Territories. Two brothers named MacLeod were found headless in the Valley, which subsequently became known as Headless Valley. It seems far more likely that the prospectors were murdered by Indians or desperados; nevertheless, Bigfoot was blamed, and the legend acquired a touch of horror.

In 1910 the *Seattle Times* contained a report about "mountain devils" who attacked the shack of a prospector at Mount St Lawrence, near Kelso. The attackers were described as half human and half monster, and between seven and eight feet tall. To the Clallam and Quinault Indians the creatures are known as Seeahtiks. Their legends declare that man was created from animals, and that Seeahtiks were left in a half-finished state.

One of the most remarkable Bigfoot stories dates from 1924, although it was not written down until 1957, when it was uncovered by John Green, author of *On the Track of the Sasquatch*. Albert Ostman, a logger and construction worker, was looking for gold at the head of the Toba

Inlet in British Columbia, and was unalarmed when an Indian boatman told him tales of "big people" living in the mountains. After a week's hiking he settled down in a campsite opposite Vancouver Island. But when he woke up in the morning he found that his supplies had been disturbed. He decided to stay awake that night, so when he climbed into his sleeping-bag he removed only his boots; he also took his rifle into the sleeping-bag with him. Hours later, he reported, "I was awakened by something picking me up. I was asleep and at first I did not remember where I was. As I began to get my wits together, I remembered I was on this prospecting trip, and in my sleeping-bag".

Hours later, his captor dumped him down on the ground, and he was able to crawl out of the sleeping-bag. He found himself in the presence of a family of four Sasquatches – a father eight feet tall, a mother and teenage son and immature daughter. Ostman described them in considerable detail – the woman was over seven feet tall, between forty and seventy years of age, and weighed between 500 and 600 pounds. They apparently made no attempt to hurt him, but seemed determined not to let him go. Possibly they regarded him as a future husband for the girl, who was small and flat-chested. He spent six days in their company until, choosing his moment, he fired off his rifle. While his captors dived for cover, Ostman escaped. Asked by John Green why he had kept silent for so long, Ostman explained that he thought nobody would believe him.

In 1928 an Indian of the Nootka tribe called Muchalat Harry arrived at Nootka, on Vancouver Island, clad only in torn underwear, and still badly shaken. He explained that he had been making his way to the Conuma river to do some hunting and fishing when, like Ostman, he was picked up – complete with sleeping bag – and carried several miles by a Bigfoot. At daybreak he found himself in the midst of a group of about twenty of the creatures, and was at first convinced they intended to eat him. When one of them tugged at his underwear it was obviously astonished that it was loose – assuming it to be his skin. He sat motionless for hours, and by afternoon they had lost interest and went off looking for food. Harry took the opportunity to escape, and ran a dozen or so miles to where he'd hidden his canoe, then paddled another forty-five miles back to Vancouver Island, where he told this story to Father Anthony Terhaar, of the Benedictine Mission. Terhaar says that Harry was in such a state of nervous collapse that he needed to be nursed carefully back to health, and that his hair became white. The experience shook him so much that he never again left the village.

In 1967 a logger called Glenn Thomas from Estacada, Oregon, was walking down a path at Tarzan Springs near the Round Mountain when he saw three big hairy figures pulling rocks out of the ground, then digging down six or seven feet. The male figure took out a nest of rodents and ate them. Investigators looking into his story found thirty or forty holes, from which rocks weighing as much as two hundred-weight had been shifted. Chucks and marmots often hibernate under such rocks, and there were many of these animals in the area.

By that time one of the most convincing pieces of evidence for the existence of Bigfoot had emerged. In October 1967 two young men called Roger Patterson and Bob Gimlin were in Bluff Creek in Del Norte country, northern California, when they were thrown from their horses as they rounded the bend in the Creek. About a hundred feet ahead, on the other side of the Creek bed, there was a huge, hairy creature that walked like a man. Roger Patterson grabbed his ciné-camera, and started filming. The creature – which they had by now decided was a female – stopped dead, then looked around at them. "She wasn't scared a bit. The fact is, I don't think she was scared of *me*, and the only thing I can think of is that the clicking of my camera was new to her". As Patterson tried to follow her the creature suddenly began to run, and after three and a half miles they lost her tracks on pine needles.

The film – which has become famous – shows a creature about seven feet high, weighing around 350 to 450 pounds, with reddish-brown hair and prominent furry breasts and buttocks. As it strides past it turns its head and looks straight into the camera, revealing a fur-covered face. The top of the head is conical in shape. Both mountain gorillas and Bigfoot's cousin the Yeti or Abominable Snowman (of which more in a moment) display this feature. According to zoologists, its purpose is to give more anchorage to the jaw muscles to aid in breaking tough plants.

Inevitably, there were many scientists who dismissed the film as a hoax, claiming that the creature was a man dressed in a monkey suit. But in his book *More "Things"* the zoologist Ivan Sanderson quotes three scientists, Dr Osman Hill, Dr John Napier and Dr Joseph Raight, all of whom seem to agree that there is nothing in the film that leads them, on scientific grounds, to suspect a hoax. Casts taken of the footprints in the mud of the Creek indicate a creature roughly seven feet high.

The Asian version of Bigfoot is a Yeti, better known as the Abomin-able Snowman. When Eric Shipton, the Everest explorer, was crossing the Menlung Glacier on Everest in 1951 he observed a line of huge footprints; Shipton photographed one of them, with an ice axe beside it to provide scale. It was eighteen inches long and thirteen inches wide, and its shape was curious – three small toes and a huge big toe that seemed to be almost circular. The footsteps were those of a two-legged creature, not a wolf or a bear. The only animal with a vaguely similar foot is an orang-utan. But they have a far longer big toe.

Ever since European travellers began to explore Tibet they had reported legends of a huge ape-like creature called the Metoh-kangmi, which translates roughly as the filthy or abominable snowman. The stories cover a huge area, from the Caucasus to the Himalayas, from the Pamirs, through Mongolia, to the far eastern tip of Russia. In central Asia they are called Mehteh, or Yetis, while tribes of eastern Asia refer to them as Almas. The earliest reference to them in the West seems to be a report in 1832 by B.H. Hodgson, the British Resident at the Court of Nepal, who mentioned that his native hunters were frightened by a "wild man" covered in long dark hair. More than half a century later, in 1889, Major L.A. Waddell was exploring the Himalayas when he came across huge footprints in the snow at 17,000 feet; his bearers told him that these were the tracks of a Yeti. And the Yeti, according to the bearers, was a ferocious creature which was quite likely to attack human beings and carry them off for food. The best way to escape it was to run downhill, for the Yeti had such long hair that it would fall over its eyes and blind it when it was going downhill.

In 1921 an expedition led by Colonel Howard-Bury, making a first attempt on the north face of Everest, saw in the distance a number of large dark creatures moving against the snow of the Lhapta-la Pass; the Tibetan porters said these were Yetis. And in 1925 N.A. Tombazi, a Fellow of the Royal Geographical Society, almost managed to get a photograph of a naked, upright creature on the Zemu Glacier; but it had vanished by the time he sighted the camera. And so the legends and the sightings continued to leak back to civilization, always with that slight element of doubt which made it possible for scientists to dismiss them as lies or mistakes. Shipton's photograph of 1951 caused such a sensation because it was taken by a member of a scientific expedition who could have no possible motive for stretching the facts. Besides, the photograph spoke for him.

At least, so one might assume. The Natural History Department of the British Museum did not agree, and one of its leading authorities, Dr T.C.S.Morrison-Scott, was soon committing himself to the view that the footprint was made by a creature called the Himalayan langur. His assessment was based on a description of the Yeti by Sherpa Tensing, who said it was about five feet high, walked upright, had a conical skull and reddish-brown fur. This, said Dr Morrison-Scott, sounded quite like a langur. The objection to this was that the langur, like most apes, walks on all fours most of the time; besides, its feet have five very long toes, quite unlike the four rounded toes of the photograph. Morrison-Scott's theory was greeted with hoots of disdain, as it undoubtedly deserved to be. But that brought the identification of the strange creature no closer.

A more imaginative view was taken by the Dutch zoologist Bernard Huevelmans in a series of articles published in Paris in 1952. He pointed out that in 1934 Dr Ralph von Koenigwald had discovered some ancient teeth in the shop of a Chinese apothecary in Hong Kong – the Chinese regard powdered teeth as a medicine. One of these was a human-type molar which was twice as large as the molar of an adult gorilla, suggesting that its owner had stood about twelve feet tall. Evidence suggested that this giant – he became known as Gigantopithecus – lived around half a million years ago. Huevelmans suggested that Shipton's footprints were made by a huge biped related to Gigantopithecus. But few scientists considered his theory seriously.

In 1954 the *Daily Mail* sent out an expedition to try to capture (or at least photograph) a Yeti. It spent fifteen weeks plodding through the Himalayan snows without so much as a glimpse of the filthy snowman. But the expedition gathered one exciting piece of information. Several monasteries, they learned, possessed "Yeti scalps", which were revered as holy relics. Several of these scalps were tracked down, and proved to be fascinating. They were all long and conical, rather like a bishop's mitre, and covered with hair, including a "crest" in the middle, made of erect hair. One of these scalps proved to be a fake, sewn together from fragments of animal skin. But others were undoubtedly made of one piece of skin. Hairs from them were sent to experts for analysis, and the experts declared that they came from no known animal. It looked as if the existence of the Yeti had finally been proved. Alas, it was not to be.

Sir Edmund Hillary was allowed to borrow one of the scalps – he was held in very high regard in Tibet – and Bernard Huevelmans had the opportunity to examine it. It reminded him of a creature called the southern serow, a kind of goat, which he had seen in a zoo before the war. And serows exist in Nepal, "abominable snowman" country. Huevelmans tracked down a serow in the Royal Institute in Brussels. And comparison with the Yeti scalp revealed that it came from the same animal. The skin had been stretched and moulded with steam. It was not, of course, a deliberate fake. It was made to be worn in certain religious rituals in Tibet; over the years its origin had been forgotten, and it had been designated a Yeti scalp.

All this was enough to convince the sceptics that the Yeti was merely a legend. But that conclusion was premature. Europeans who went out searching for the snowman might or might not catch a glimpse of some dark creature moving against the snow. But their tracks were observed, and photographed, in abundance. A Frenchman, the Abbè Bordet, followed three separate lots of tracks in 1955. Squadron Leader Lester Davies filmed huge footprints in the same year. Climber Don Whillans saw an ape-like creature on Annapurna in June 1970, and Lord Hunt photographed more Yeti tracks in 1978.

In Russia more solid evidence began to emerge. In 1958 Lt Col Vargen Karapetyan saw an article on the Yeti – or, as it is known in Russia, Alma – in a Moscow newspaper, and sought out the leading Soviet expert, Professor Boris Porshnev, to tell him his own story. In December 1941 his unit had been fighting the Germans in the Caucasus near Buinakst, and he was approached by a unit of partisans and asked to go and look at a man they had taken prisoner. The partisans explained that Karapetyan would have to go along to a barn to look at the "man", because as soon as he was taken into a heated room, he stank and dripped sweat; besides, he was covered in lice. The "man" proved to be more like an ape: naked, filthy and unkempt, he looked dull and vacant, and often blinked. He made no attempt to defend himself when Karapetyan pulled out hairs from his body, but his eyes looked as if he was begging for mercy. It was obvious that he did not understand speech. Finally, Karapetyan left, telling the partisans to make up their own minds about what to do with the creature. He heard a few days later that the "wild man" had escaped. Obviously this story could have been an invention. But a report from the Ministry of the Interior in Daghestan confirmed its truth. The "wild man" had been court-martialled and executed as a deserter.

It was in January 1958 that Dr Alexander Pronin, of Leningrad University, reported seeing an Alma. He was in the Pamirs, and saw the creature outlined against a cliff-top. It was man-like, covered with reddish-grey hair, and he watched it for more than five minutes; three days later he saw it again at the same spot. For some reason good Marxists poured scorn on the notion of a "wild man"; but the evidence went on accumulating, until Boris Porshnev began to make an attempt to co-ordinate the sightings. The considerable body of evidence he has accumulated is described in some detail in Odette Tchernine's impressive book *The Yeti*.

To summarize: the evidence for the existence of the Yeti, or Alma, or Bigfoot, or Sasquatch, is very strong indeed; hundreds of sightings make it unlikely that it is an invention. If, then, we assume for a moment that it really exists, what is it?

Dr Myra Shackley, lecturer in archaeology at Leicester University, believes she knows the answer. She is convinced that the Yeti is a Neanderthal man. And this is also the conclusion reached by Odette Tchernine on the basis of the Soviet evidence.

Neanderthal man was the predecessor of modern man. He first seems to have appeared on earth about a hundred thousand years ago. He was smaller and more ape-like than modern man, with the well-known receding forehead and simian jaw. He lived in caves, and the piles of animal bones discovered in such caves suggest that Neanderthal woman was a sluttish housewife, and that his habitation must have stunk of rotting flesh. He was also a cannibal. But he was by no means a mere animal. Colouring pigments in Neanderthal caves suggest that he loved colour; he certainly wove screens of coloured flowers. And since he buried these with his dead, it seems certain that he believed in an after-life. Mysterious round stones found in his habitations suggest that he was a sun-worshipper.

Our ancestor, Cro-Magnon man, came on earth about fifty thousand years ago; it was he who made all the famous cave paintings. Neanderthal man vanished completely over the next twenty thousand years, and the mystery of his disappearance has never been solved. The general view is that he was exterminated by Cro-Magnon man (William Golding's novel *The Inheritors* is a story of the encounter between the two; so is H.G. Wells's earlier *The Grisly Men*).

The psychologist Stan Gooch advanced a startling thesis in his book *The Neanderthal Question*: that Neanderthals were not entirely exterminated, but that their women occasionally bore children to Cro-Magnon males. The descendants of these products of cross-breeding became the Jews. (It should be noted that Gooch is himself Jewish.) Gooch believes that Neanderthal man was more "psychic" than Cro-Magnon, and that such psychic faculties as present-day man now possesses are inherited from these Neanderthal ancestors.

Whether or not we can accept Gooch's theory, it seems reasonable to suppose that Neanderthal man may have survived, driven into the wilder and less hospitable places of the earth by his conqueror. Myra Shackley has travelled to the Altai mountains of Mongolia and collected evidence for the existence of Almas. "They live in caves, hunt for food, use stone tools, and wear animal skins and fur". And she mentions that in 1972 a Russian doctor met a family of Almas. In fact, Odette Tchernine cites a number of such stories. Professor Porshnev discovered again and again evidence among mountain people that they knew of the existence of "wild men"; the Abkhazians still have stories of how they drove the wild men out of the district they colonized. Tchernine refers to these wild men as "pre-hominids".

Porshnev himself investigated a case of a female Alma who had been caught in the Ochamchir region in the mid-nineteenth century. Hunters captured a "wild woman" who had ape-like features and was covered in hair; for several years in captivity she was so violent that she could not be approached, and food had to be thrown to her. They called her Zana. Porshnev interviewed many old people – one was a hundred and five – who remembered Zana. They told him how she had become domesticated, and would perform simple tasks like grinding corn. She had a massive bosom, thick muscular arms and legs, and thick fingers; she could not endure warm rooms but preferred the cold. She loved to gorge herself on grapes in the vineyard, and also enjoyed wine – she would drink heavily, then sleep for hours. This may explain how she became a mother on several occasions, to different fathers. Her children usually died because she washed them in the freezing river. (Presumably, having half-human characteristics, they lacked her tremendous inherited endurance of cold.) Finally, her newborn children were taken away from her, and they grew up among the people of the village. Unlike their mother, they could talk and were reasonable human beings. The youngest of these died as recently as 1954 (Zana died about 1890). Porshnev interviewed two of her grandchildren, and noted their dark skin and Negroid looks. Shalikula, the grandson, had such powerful jaws that he could pick up a chair with a man sitting on it. Here, it would seem, is solid, undeniable evidence of the existence of "wild men".

8

Christie, Agatha

The disappearance of the novelist

In 1926 Agatha Christie was involved in a mystery that sounds like the plot of one of her own novels. But unlike the fictional crimes unravelled by Hercule Poirot, this puzzle has never been satisfactorily solved.

At the age of thirty-six, Agatha Christie seemed an enviable figure. She was an attractive redhead, with a touch of grey, and lived with her husband, Colonel Archibald Christie, in a magnificent country house which she once described as "a sort of millionaire-style Savoy suite transferred to the country".

She was also the author of seven volumes of detective fiction, of which the latest, *The Murder of Roger Ackroyd*, had caused some controversy because of its "unfair" ending. Yet the authoress was hardly a celebrity; few of her books achieved sales of more than a few thousand.

Then on the freezing cold night of 3 December 1926 she left her home at Sunningdale, in Berkshire, and disappeared.

At eleven the next morning, a Superintendent in Surrey Police was handed a report on a "road accident" at Newlands Corner, just outside Guildford. Agatha Christie's Morris two-seater had been found halfway down a grassy bank with its bonnet buried in a clump of bushes. There was no sign of the driver, but she had clearly not intended to go far, because she had left her fur coat in the car.

By mid-afternoon the Press had heard of the disappearance, and were besieging the Christie household. From the start the police hinted that they suspected suicide. Her husband dismissed this theory, sensibly pointing out that most people commit suicide at home, and do not drive off in the middle of the night. But an extensive search of the area around Newlands Corner was organized and the Silent Pool, an allegedly bottomless lake in the vicinity, was investigated by deep-sea divers.

What nobody knew was that Agatha Christie's life was not as enviable as it looked. Her husband had recently fallen in love with a girl who was ten years his junior – Nancy Neele – and had only recently told her that he wanted a divorce. The death of her mother had been another psychological shock. She was sleeping badly, eating erratic meals, and moving furniture around the house in a haphazard manner. She was obviously distraught, possibly on the verge of a nervous breakdown.

The next two or three days produced no clues to her whereabouts. When it was reported that some female clothes had been found in a lonely hut near Newlands Corner, together with a bottle labelled "opium", there was a stampede of journalists. But it proved to be a false alarm, and the opium turned out to be a harmless stomach remedy. Some newspapers hinted that Archibald Christie stood to gain much from the death of his wife, but he had a perfect alibi: he was at a weekend party in Surrey. Other journalists began to wonder whether the disappearance was a publicity stunt. Ritchie-Calder suspected that she had disappeared to spite her husband, and bring his affair with Nancy Neele out into the open. He even read through her novels to see whether she had ever used a similar scenario. When the *Daily News* offered a reward reports of sightings poured in. They all proved to be false alarms.

Another interesting touch of mystery was added when her brother-in-law Campbell revealed that he had received a letter from her whose postmark indicated that it had been posted in London at 9.45 on the day after her disappearance, when she was presumably wandering around in the woods of Surrey.

In the *Mail* the following Sunday there was an interview with her husband in which he admitted "that my wife had discussed the possibility of disappearing at will. Some time ago she told her sister, 'I could disappear if I wished and set about it carefully . . .'" It began to look as if the disappearance, after all, might not be a matter of suicide or amnesia.

On 14 December, eleven days after her disappearance, the head waiter in the Hydropathic Hotel in Harrogate, North Yorkshire, looked more closely at a female guest and recognized her from newspaper photographs as the missing novelist. He rang the Yorkshire police, who contacted her home. Colonel Christie took an afternoon train from London to Harrogate, and learned that his wife had been staying in the hotel for a week and a half. She had taken a good room on the first floor at seven guineas a week, and had apparently seemed "normal and happy", and "sang, danced, played billiards, read the newspaper reports of the disappearance, chatted with her fellow guests, and went for walks".

Agatha made her way to the dinner table, picked up an evening paper which contained the story of the search for herself, together with a photograph, and was reading it when her husband made his way over to her. "She only seemed to regard him as an acquaintance whose identity she could not quite fix", said the hotel's manager. And Archibald Christie told the Press: "She has suffered from the most complete loss of memory and I do not think she knows who she is". A doctor later confirmed that she was suffering from loss of memory. But Lord Ritchie-Calder later remembered how little she seemed to correspond with the usual condition of amnesia. When she vanished, she had been wearing a green knitted skirt, a grey cardigan and a velour hat, and carried a few pounds in her purse. When she was found she was stylishly dressed, and had three hundred pounds on her. She had told other guests in the hotel that she was a visitor from South Africa.

There were unpleasant repercussions. A public outcry, orchestrated by the Press, wanted to know who was to pay the £3,000 which the search was estimated to have cost, and Surrey ratepayers blamed the next big increase on her. Her next novel, *The Big Four*, received unfriendly reviews, but nevertheless sold nine thousand copies – more than twice as many as *The Murder of Roger Ackroyd*. And from then on (as Elizabeth Walter has described in an essay called "The Case of the Escalating Sales") her books sold in increasing quantities. By 1950 all her books were enjoying a regular sale of more than fifty thousand copies, and the final Miss Marple story, *Sleeping Murder*, had a first printing of sixty thousand.

Agatha Christie divorced her husband (who wed Miss Neele) and in 1930 married Professor Sir Max Mallowan. But for the rest of her life she refused to discuss her disappearance, and would only grant interviews on condition that it was not mentioned. Her biographer, Janet Morgan, accepts that it was a case of nervous breakdown, followed by amnesia. Yet this is difficult to accept. Where did she obtain the clothes and the money to go to Harrogate? Why did she register under the surname of her husband's mistress? And is it possible to believe that her amnesia was so complete that, while behaving perfectly normally, she was able to read accounts of her own disappearance, look at photographs of herself, and still not even suspect her identity?

Lord Ritchie-Calder, who got to know her very well in later life, remains convinced that "her disappearance was calculated in the classic style of her detective stories". A television play produced after her death even speculated that the disappearance was part of a plot to murder Nancy Neele. The only thing that is certain about "the case of the disappearing authoress" is that it turned Agatha Christie into a best-seller, and eventually into a millionairess.

Postscript to "The Disappearance of Agatha Christie"

The mystery of Agatha Christie's disappearance was finally solved after her death on 12 January 1976. Then it was clear why it had been kept secret – the truth would have been highly embarrassing to the writer and her family.

Ritchie Calder had been right all along; the disappearance had been staged with the connivance of her sister-in-law Nan, and the motive was simply to spite her husband and to spoil the weekend he had meant to spend with his mistress. What Agatha Christie had not reckoned with was the immense public interest that her disappearance would generate. The subsequent publicity appalled her – even though it also had the effect of turning her into a celebrity and a bestselling author – and she had no wish to confess that the reason for the disappearance was that her husband had a mistress.

The root of Agatha Christie's problems almost certainly lay in her childhood. She was a highly imaginative and very private person. When a toddler she was horrified to overhear her nanny tell a housemaid that Miss Agatha had been playing again with her imaginary friends, the Kittens. Her lifelong dislike of invasions of her privacy seems to have begun there.

Agatha Christie was born on 15 September 1890, in a white villa called Ashfield, on the outskirts of Torquay, the seaside resort on the south coast of Devon. Her father, Frederick Miller, was a wealthy American and he and his wife Clarissa had three children, of whom Agatha was the third. Her elder sister Madge was regarded as the clever one of the family. It was her father's devotion to Madge that was to cause tragedy. He spent so much money on her coming-out in New York that the family's finances became straitened. For the first time in his life he began to think of taking some kind of a job in the City. But he had no qualifications, and a combination of depression and a chill that turned into double pneumonia killed him when Agatha was eleven.

For a while, it looked as if Clarissa Miller would have to sell Ashfield, but by means of extreme economies she managed to hang on to it, to Agatha's enormous relief. But the change from affluence to poverty was traumatic for the child and was – at least partly – responsible for that determination to hang on to her money that led to the eventual break-up of her marriage.

In the year following her father's death, Madge married James Watts, the son of a wealthy Manchester manufacturer, and the bridegroom's younger sister Nan was to become Agatha's lifelong friend and co-conspirator.

It was Agatha's regular visits to the magnificent Victorian Gothic home of James Watt Senior, Abney Hall in Cheshire, that provided her with the kind of experience of high living that she was to use so effectively in her detective novels.

As a teenager, with her long red-blonde hair and shy manner, Agatha was highly attractive and she quickly became involved with a young man she met at amateur theatricals in Torquay. But they drifted apart when she went to a finishing school in Paris where she took singing and piano lessons. Her sister-in-law Nan was at this time at a finishing school in Florence, and Agatha frequently visited her there. She also made her first acquaintance with Egypt when she had her coming-out season in Cairo. And in 1912, when she was twenty-two, she met her future husband, Archibald Christie, at a dance given by Lord and Lady Clifford at their home in Devon. He was tall, handsome, and had learned soldiering at the Royal Woolwich Military Academy, after which he became a lieutenant, stationed at Exeter.

The hero-worshipping Agatha was swept off her feet. Archie wanted to marry her immediately, but Agatha's mother objected – there was something about Archie, perhaps a touch of selfishness or irresponsibility, that made her suspicious. But eighteen months later, the First World War broke out, and Archie and Agatha married when he was home on leave.

Archie went to serve his country in France, and his wife returned home to live with her mother. But Agatha also decided to join in the war effort and became a voluntary nurse at the Red Cross hospital in Torquay. To take her mind off the war, she began to devour detective stories.

Her elder sister Madge had become a published writer, whose stories often appeared in *Vanity Fair* and other magazines. Agatha had also been writing for years, but her stories had invariably been rejected. But it was a bet with her sister that she could write a good detective novel that led Agatha to write *The Mysterious Affair at Styles*, whose hero was a Belgian because at that time Torquay happened to be full of Belgian refugees. As might have been expected, the murder in the novel was committed by poison – a subject upon which Agatha was to become increasingly knowledgable.

The war came to an end, Archie returned home, and husband and wife moved to London where Archie was working for the Air Ministry. Their finances were straitened, so much so that it took Agatha many weeks to decide to call on her old friend Nan, who had acquired herself a wealthy husband. The two found they enjoyed being together just as much as they had in childhood. In 1919, Agatha gave birth to a daughter, Clanssa.

Meanwhile, Agatha had decided that it would improve their finances if she could find a publisher for *The Mysterious Affair at Styles*. In 1920, it was accepted by John Lane of the Bodley Head, who was so confident of her ability to write that he gave her a contract for five books. The book was published in England and America and sold two thousand copies. All Agatha made from it was £25.

As it became clear to Agatha that her publishers were taking advantage of her, she determined to break with them as soon as possible.

Archie had joined the staff of the Imperial and Foreign Corporation, and in 1922, when he became Financial Advisor on the British Empire Mission, they went on a world tour which included South Africa, Australia and the United States. But when they got back from the tour, Archie suddenly found that he had been made redundant. Agatha's detective stories now became doubly important to their finances. Archie hated being redundant, and the marriage began to show signs of strain. Things did not improve when a series of Poirot stories appeared in *The Sketch*, and Agatha was described as the "writer of the most brilliant detective novel of the day". And although Archie soon found himself a job, his feeling that his wife was the family's main provider continued to rankle.

When the five book contract with The Bodley Head came to an end, Agatha turned down an offer to renew it on better terms, and moved to Collins, who offered her an advance of £200 on each novel – an impressive sum for those days.

When Agatha refused to share her literary earnings with her husband, Archie became even more resentful. Busy with her career, his wife failed to notice the warning signs. She was probably rather relieved when Archie became a golf enthusiast, for it kept him occupied. But it was on the golf course that Archie met a typist named Nancy Neele, and fell in love with her.

On holiday with her husband in France, Agatha noticed that he seemed moody and irritable but had no idea that this was because he had transferred his affections elsewhere. In fact, she knew Nancy Neele well, and the girl often spent weekends with them. She had no suspicion that Nancy was her husband's mistress.

So far, the name Agatha Christie had become known only to readers of detective stories, and she seldom made more than a few hundred pounds from each book. But in 1925, the serialisation of *Who Killed Roger Ackroyd*? brought her a new level of celebrity, as critics squabbled about whether it was not cheating to make the killer the harmless Watson who tells the story. It became her most successful book to-date.

The Christies had moved by now into a large house not far from Sunningdale, in Berkshire, and had decided to call it Styles, after Agatha's first book. That was hardly auspicious, since the fictional Styles had been the scene of a murder. In fact, the real Styles had a bad reputation as the last three owners had all encountered disasters. But Agatha felt no misgivings. She was cheerful and full of confidence, her marriage seemed happy, and she even tried to persuade Archie that it was time to have another baby.

In April 1926, Agatha was shattered when her mother died after a bout of bronchitis. She was on her way to see her when she suddenly had a strong conviction that her mother was already dead.

Her intuition was to manifest itself again a few months later when Archie came back from a trip abroad and Agatha had a strong feeling that there was something wrong. She pressed him to tell her – and then was horrified when he admitted that he was in love with Nancy Neele and that she had been his mistress for the past eighteen months. Agatha felt totally betrayed. For a while, Archie moved to London, living at his club, and Agatha sank into a depression. Finally, when Archie confessed that he was not quite sure whether they should divorce, she pressed him to keep their marriage going on a trial basis for another year. Archie would only agree to three months. Agatha got a little of her own back by writing a story in which the "other woman" commits suicide by jumping off a cliff. But Nancy was disinclined to do anything so convenient.

And so came that evening on 3 December 1926, when she walked out of Styles and disappeared – and became known to every newspaper-reader in England.

In fact, she and Archie had quarrelled violently that morning because Archie intended to go and stay the weekend with friends, and Nancy Neele would also be a guest. When Archie left for London, Agatha wrote him a long letter full of recriminations. After that, she left the house at about 10 p.m, drove to Newlands Corner and put her pre-arranged plan into operation. She parked on the edge of the road and then pushed the car down the slope, with its headlights full on. She left her fur coat and a case of her clothes – as well as her driving license – in the car. It had stopped in a clump of bushes on the edge of a chalk pit. After that, Agatha walked to West Clandon Station and took a train to London. There she went along to the home of her sister-in-law Nan, at 78 Chelsea Park Gardens, and stayed there the night. She had been to see Nan a few days before to tell her about her husband's betrayal, so the visit was not wholly unexpected.

The next morning, Agatha posted a letter she had written to Archie's brother Campbell, telling him that she was on her way to a Yorkshire spa. She sent this to his office in Woolwich so that he would not receive it until after the weekend. But in fact, on opening the letter Campbell Christie only glanced at it and then somehow managed to mislay it. This explains why it took so long for Archie and the police to find her – eleven days after her disappearance. Meanwhile, Archie got a little of his own back by telling a newspaper reporter that his wife had discussed the possibility of "disappearing" – implying that it might be a kind of practical joke or publicity stunt.

And so Agatha sat in the Harrogate Hydro Hotel, reading the newspaper accounts of herself and doing the kind of things that overseas visitors – she claimed to be from South Africa – did when they stay at a hotel during the Christmas holiday period.

On Sunday, 12 December, hundreds of members of the public set out to comb the Surrey hills for the missing novelist when in fact two members of a band who played in the Harrogate Hydro Hotel already thought they had recognized Agatha Christie on the dance floor, and went to inform the local police. A chambermaid called Rosie Asher had confirmed the bandsmens' suspicions. She had noticed that the woman's handbag had a zip, which was the first time she had ever seen this newly fashionable item but she was afraid to mention it to the management in case she lost her job. During the following Monday, plain-clothed police mingled with the hotel guests and quickly arrived at the conclusion that they had found Agatha Christie. The following day, the Yorkshire police rang Archie at work and asked him if he would travel to Harrogate to identify his wife. It must have been a relief to Archie to know that he was no longer suspected of his wife's murder.

Early that evening, Archie sat in the hotel lounge hidden behind a newspaper as Agatha walked in and paused to look at her own photograph on the front of a newspaper lying on a table. Then she saw her husband looking across at her. With typical English coolness, the couple said hello, and then, a few minutes later, went in to dinner. There, apparently, Agatha admitted that she had staged her disappearance to spite her husband and that the prank had expanded beyond her expectations.

Now Archie learned that her sister-in-law Nan had known where she was all the time and had even lent her the money to travel to Harrogate and stay in the hotel. Agatha had posted the letter to Campbell – which was supposed to have guaranteed that she would be found quickly – and then had lunch with Nan in London. She then caught a train at 1.40 from King's Cross to Harrogate, where she arrived six hours later.

The following morning, decoys who looked like the Christies left the hotel to be pursued by a crowd of reporters, while the *Daily Mail* cameraman, who was the only one who was left behind, took a photograph of the real Mr and Mrs Christie as they hurried out of the hotel at 9.15. At Harrogate station, they entered – by prior arrangement – by the goods entrance, but nevertheless found the London platform jammed with dozens of reporters and photographers. Agatha's sister Madge had arrived, together with her husband Jimmy, but the attempt by the party to deceive the reporters by splitting into two pairs, male and female, failed in its purpose and flashbulbs popped as the sisters scrambled on to the train, with Agatha close to tears. At Leeds, they managed to mislead the reporters by changing trains, but the press caught up with them again in London where a photographer snapped Agatha as she walked up the platform. She then had to run the gauntlet of another crowd of reporters and managed to scramble on to the Manchester train. But one of the photographs of her that appeared that evening showed her grinning broadly, and strengthened the general impression that this was some kind of publicity stunt or hoax.

Seeking refuge at Abney Hall, in Cheadle, they were again besieged by newsmen, and Archie finally gave a single interview to a journalist who happened to be wearing his old school tie, explaining that his wife had lost her memory. No one, of course believed him. When Archie finally returned home to Styles, he received a bill from the Surrey Constabulary for cost of the search – £25. He refused to pay. But it was clear that the Surrey Police also felt that the Christies had been wasting their time.

Agatha herself escaped further publicity by leaving the country, together with her secretary and her daughter, for the Canaries. While she was abroad Members of Parliament raised questions in the House about the cost of the search, and one MP denounced the whole episode as a "cruel hoax".

In fact, although the disappearance did her reputation no harm in the long run, Agatha was to discover on her return to England, that many old friends no longer wanted to know her.

Her disappearance had also failed in its immediate purpose – to persuade her husband to stay with her. Archie Christie was the kind of person who disliked publicity even more than his wife did, and he resented the spotlight that had been thrown on his affair with Nancy Neele. Less than two years later, in April 1928, his wife divorced him, and shortly after that, he married Nancy Neele, with whom he continued to live happily until her death in the summer of 1958. Archie himself died in December 1962.

Agatha Christie herself also found happiness of a kind. In 1930, she visited the archaeological site at Ur, in Mesopotamia, where Leonard Woolley had found evidence of what he believed to be the biblical Flood. There, Agatha met Woolley's 25-year-old assistant, Max Mallowan, who was asked to take her on a sight-seeing tour. She was fourteen years his senior but the two found they had so much in common that when he asked her to marry him, she took very little time to accept. She also insisted that they should pool their finances – Mallowan was relatively poor – and divide them equally. She had evidently learned from her mistake with her first husband. She also made Max promise never to play golf, to which he immediately agreed.

In 1947, after the war, Max was appointed to the archaeological chair at London University. Here he was immensely popular with his students and since he was in his early forties, he could not resist the temptation to have the occasional affair. Agatha found out about this from Nan, but she now reacted less violently than with Archie, and so the two remained married until her death.

In 1948 Agatha's financial fortunes reached a new peak when Penguin Books published a million of her paperbacks in one day. She was now the most successful detective writer of all time.

As she approached her eighties her health began to deteriorate and on 12 January 1976, she died quietly while Max pushed her in her wheelchair.

In 1997 the BBC made a documentary on the disappearance of Agatha Christie, and a young writer named Jared Kade was appointed as research assistant. The final result of that assignment was his book *Agatha Christie and the Eleven Missing Days* (1998), to which this present account is greatly indebted.

9

The Cleveland Torso Murders

Who Was "the Mad Butcher"?

The American equivalent of the Jack the Ripper murders (described in chapter 27) was the Cleveland Torso case. The Cleveland murders were more numerous, and in some ways – as will be seen – more horrific, than their Victorian counterparts.

On a warm September afternoon in 1935, two boys on their way home from school walked along a dusty, sooty gully known as Kingsbury Run, in the heart of Cleveland, Ohio. On a weed-covered slope known as Jackass Hill, one challenged the other to a race, and they hurtled sixty feet down the slope to the bottom. Sixteen-year-old James Wagner was the winner, and as he halted, panting, he noticed something white in the bushes a few yards away. A closer look revealed that it was a naked body and that it was headless.

The police who arrived soon after found the body of a young white male clad only in black socks; the genitals had been removed. It lay on its back, with the legs stretched out and the arms by the sides, as if laid out for a funeral. Thirty feet away the policemen found another body, that of an older man, lying in the same position; it had also been decapitated and emasculated.

Hair sticking out of the ground revealed one of the missing heads buried a few yards away; the second proved to be buried nearby. Both sets of genitals were also found lying nearby, as if thrown away by the killer.

One curious feature of the crimes was that there was no blood on the ground or on the bodies, which were quite clean. It looked as if the victims had been killed and beheaded elsewhere, then carefully washed when they had ceased to bleed.

Forensic examination revealed even more baffling evidence. The older corpse was badly decomposed and the skin discoloured; the pathologists discovered that this was due to some unidentifiable chemical substance, perhaps used by the killer in an attempt to preserve the body. The man had been dead about two weeks. The younger man had only been dead three days. His fingerprints enabled the police to identify him as twenty-eight-year-old Edward Andrassy, who had a minor police record for carrying concealed weapons. He lived near Kingsbury Run and had a reputation as a drunken brawler.

But the most chilling discovery was that Andrassy had actually died as a result of decapitation. Rope marks on his wrists revealed that he had been tied and had struggled violently. The killer had apparently cut off his head with a knife. The skill with which the operation had been performed suggested a butcher – or possibly a surgeon.

It proved impossible to identify the older man. But the identification of Andrassy led the police to hope that it would not be too difficult to trace his killer. Andrassy had spent his nights gambling and drinking in a slummy part of town – the third precinct – and was known as a pimp. Further investigation also revealed that he had had male lovers. Lead after lead looked extremely promising. The husband of a married woman with whom he had had an affair had sworn to kill him. But the man was able to prove his innocence. So were various shady characters who might have borne a grudge. Lengthy police investigation led to a dead end – as it did in another ten cases involving the killer who became known as "the Mad Butcher of Kingsbury Run".

Four months later, on a raw January Sunday, the howling of a dog finally led a woman who lived on East Twentieth Street – not far from Kingsbury Run – to go and investigate. She found the chained animal trying to get at a basket standing near a factory wall. Minutes later she told a passing neighbour that the basket contained hams. But the neighbour soon recognized the "hams" as being parts of a human arm. A burlap bag proved to contain the female torso. The head was missing, as were the left arm and the lower parts of both legs. But fingerprints again enabled the police to trace the victim, who had a record as a prostitute. She proved to be forty-one-year-old Florence ("Flo") Polillo, a squat, double-chinned woman who was well known in the neighbourhood bars.

Again, there were plenty of leads, and again, all of them petered out. Two weeks later the victim's left arm and lower legs were found in a vacant lot. The head was never recovered.

The murder of Flo Polillo raised an unwelcome question. The first two murders had convinced the police that they were looking for a homosexual sadist, which at least simplified the investigation; this latest crime made it look as if the killer was quite simply a sadist – like Peter

Kürten, the Düsseldorf killer executed in 1931; he had killed men, women, and children indiscriminately, and he was not remotely homosexual. The pathologist also recalled that a year before that first double murder, the torso of an unknown woman had been found on the edge of Lake Erie. It began to look as if the Mad Butcher was a psychopath who was simply obsessed with the dissection of human corpses, as some boys enjoy pulling the wings off flies.

Cleveland residents felt they had one thing in their favour, however. Since the double killing, the famous Eliot Ness had been appointed Cleveland's director of public safety. Ness and his "Untouchables" had cleared up Chicago's Prohibition rackets, and in 1934 Ness had moved to Cleveland to fight its gangsters. With Ness in charge, the newspapers were confident that the Head Hunter of Kingsbury Run – another press sobriquet – would find himself becoming the hunted.

But it was soon clear to Ness that hunting a sadistic pervert was totally unlike hunting professional gangsters. The killer struck at random, and unless he was careless enough to leave behind a clue – like a fingerprint – then the only hope was to catch him in the act. And Ness soon became convinced that the Mad Butcher took great pleasure in feeling that he was several steps ahead of the police.

The Head Hunter waited until the summer before killing again, then lived up to his name by leaving the head of a young man, wrapped in a pair of trousers, under a bridge in Kingsbury Run; again, two boys found it – on 22 June 1936. The body was found a quarter of a mile away, and it was obvious from the blood that the man had been killed where he lay. Again, medical examination revealed that the victim had died as a result of decapitation – though it was not clear how the killer had prevented the victim from struggling while he removed his head. The victim was about twenty-five and heavily tattooed. There was no record of his fingerprints in police files. Three weeks later a young female hiker discovered another decapitated male body in a gully, with the head lying nearby. The decomposition made it clear that this man had been killed before the previously discovered victim.

The last "butchery" of 1936 was that of a man of about thirty, who was also found in Kingsbury Run; the body had been cut in two and emasculated. A hat found nearby led to a partial identification: a housewife recalled giving it to a young tramp. Not far away was a "hobo camp" where down-and-outs slept; this was obviously where the Butcher had found his latest victim.

The fact that Cleveland had been the scene of a Republican convention and was now the site of a Great Exposition led to even more frantic police activity and much press criticism. The murders were reported all over the world, and in Nazi Germany and Fascist Italy they were cited as proof of the decadence of the New World.

As month after month went by with no further grisly discoveries, Clevelanders began to believe they had heard the last of the Mad Butcher. But in February 1937 that hope proved unfounded when the killer left the body of a young woman in a chopped-up pile on the shores of Lake Erie. She was never identified. The eighth victim *was* identified from her teeth as Mrs Rose Wallace, age forty; only the skeleton remained, and it looked as if she might have been killed in the previous year.

Victim number nine was male and had been dismembered; when his body was fished out of the river, the head was missing, and it was never found. This time the killer had gone even further in his mutilations, disemboweling the corpse in the manner of Jack the Ripper. It was impossible to identify the victim. It was believed that two men seen in a boat might be the Butcher and an accomplice, but this suggestion led nowhere.

The killer now seemed to take a rest for nine months. Then the lower part of a leg was pulled out of the river. Three weeks later two burlap bags found in the river proved to contain more body fragments, which enabled the pathologist to announce that the victim was a brunette female of about twenty-five. She was never identified.

The killer was to strike twice more. More than a year after the last discovery, in August 1938, the dismembered torso of a woman was found at a dump on the lakefront, and a search of the area revealed the bones of a second victim, a male. A quilt in which the remains of this twelfth victim were wrapped was identified as one that had been given to a junkman. Neither body could be identified.

One thing was now obvious: the Butcher was selecting his victims from vagrants and down-and-outs. Ness decided to take the only kind of action that seemed left to him: two days after the last find police raided the shantytown near Kingsbury Run, arrested hundreds of vagrants, and burned it down. Whether by coincidence or not, the murders ceased.

Two of the most efficient of the man hunters, Detectives Merylo and Zalewski, had spent a great deal of time searching for the killer's "labouratory". At one point they thought they had found it, when a negative left behind by one of the earliest victims, Edward Andrassy, was developed and showed Andrassy lounging on a bed in an unknown room. The photograph was published in newspapers and the room was finally identified by a petty crook as being the bedroom of a middle-aged homosexual who lived with his two sisters. Upon investigation, blood was found on the floor of the room, and a large butcher knife was discovered in a trunk. But the blood proved to be the suspect's own – he was subject to nosebleeds – and the butcher knife showed no trace of blood. And when another body turned up while the suspect was in jail for sodomy, it became clear that he was not the Torso killer.

Next the investigators discovered that Flo Polillo and Rose Wallace had frequented the same saloon and that Andrassy had been a regular there too. They also learned of a middle-aged man named Frank Dolezal who carried knives and threatened people with them when drunk. When they learned that this man had also been living with Flo Polillo, they believed they had finally identified the killer. Dolezal was arrested, and police discovered a brown substance resembling dried blood in the cracks of his bathroom floor. Knives with dried bloodstains on them provided further incriminating evidence. Under intensive questioning, Dolezal, a bleary-eyed, unkempt man, confessed to the murder of Flo Polillo, and the newspapers triumphantly announced the capture of the Butcher. Then things began to go wrong. Forensic tests showed that the "dried blood" in the bathroom was not blood after all. Dolezal's "confession" proved to be full of errors about the corpse and the method of disposal. And when, in August 1939, Dolezal hanged himself in jail, the autopsy revealed that he had two cracked ribs, which suggested that his confession had been obtained by force.

The two victims of August 1938 proved to be the Butcher's last – at least in Cleveland. In Pittsburgh in 1940 three decapitated bodies were found in old boxcars. Members of Ness's team went to investigate, but no clue to the treble murder was ever discovered. The Mad Butcher was also blamed for the Black Dahlia killing in Hollywood in 1947, when an aspiring film actress named Elizabeth Short was dissected, like victim number seven. It seems highly unlikely, however, that the Mad Butcher survived that long; a large percentage of sadistic killers commit suicide.

Steven Nickel's book on the case, *Torso* (1989), makes it clear that there were many suspects in Cleveland who might have been capable of committing the murders. One man, nicknamed the "Chicken Freak", was known to the prostitutes of the third precinct because he could achieve orgasm only when watching a chicken being decapitated; he would go to a brothel with two live chickens and a large butcher knife. Naked prostitutes would be asked to behead the chickens while he looked on and masturbated; if he failed to reach a climax, the bloody knife had to be rubbed against his throat. Finally arrested, the "Chicken

Freak" proved to be a truck driver who admitted that he made a habit of intercourse with chickens. But he was so obviously nauseated when shown photographs of the Torso victims that he was allowed to go.

Why have the Torso murders never achieved the same grim celebrity as the crimes of Jack the Ripper? The reason is that Cleveland in the mid-1930s was a far more violent city than London in the 1880s and the crimes made far less impact on the public imagination than the Ripper's sadistic murder of prostitutes in Victorian London. Ten years before the Cleveland murders began, six decapitated male bodies were found in a swamp near New Castle, a small town ninety miles southeast of Cleveland. The victims were never identified; the local police concluded that they had been killed by gangsters in the course of bootleg wars and that the swamp was a convenient dumping ground.

Sadly, the last decade of Eliot Ness's life – he died in 1957, at the age of fifty-four – was full of poverty and disappointment. He resigned as Cleveland's Safety Director in April 1941, after a scandal involving a hit-and-run accident. In 1947 he was heavily defeated when he ran for the post of mayor of Cleveland. A year later he was even turned down for a sixty-dollar-a-week job. "He simply ran out of gas" said one friend. In 1953, after five years of obscurity and poverty, he became involved with a paper-making company tottering on the verge of bankruptcy. But it was through a friend in the company that Ness met a journalist named Oscar Fraley and began telling him the story of his anti-bootlegging days. In the course of their conversations, Ness told Fraley that he was reasonably certain that he knew the identity of the Torso killer and that he had driven him out of Cleveland.

Ness told Fraley the following: He had reasoned that the killer was a man who had a house of his own in which he could dismember the bodies and a car in which he could transport them. So he was *not*, after all, a down-and-out. The skill of the mutilations suggested medical training, or at least a certain degree of medical knowledge. The fact that some of the victims had been strong men suggested that the Butcher had to be big and powerful – a conclusion supported by a size-12 footprint near one of the bodies.

Ness had three of his top agents, Virginia Allen, Barney Davis, and Jim Manski, make inquiries among the upper levels of Cleveland society. Virginia was a sophisticated woman with contacts among Cleveland socialites, and it was she who learned about a man who sounded like the ideal suspect. The suspect, whom Ness was to call "Gaylord Sundheim", was a big man from a well-to-do family who had a history of psychiatric problems. He had also studied medicine. When the three "Untouchables" called on him, he leered sarcastically at Virginia and closed the door in their faces. Ness invited him – pressingly – to lunch, and he came under protest. He refused either to admit or deny having performed the murders. Ness persuaded him to take a lie detector test, and "Sundheim's" answers to questions about the murders were registered by the stylus as lies. When Ness finally told him he believed he was the Torso killer – hoping that shock tactics might trigger a confession – "Sundheim" sneered, "Prove it".

Soon after this, "Sundheim" had himself committed to a mental institution. Ness knew *he* was now "untouchable", for even if Ness could prove his guilt, he could plead insanity.

Ness went on to collabourate with Fraley on a book entitled *The Untouchables*. It came out in 1957 and was an immense success, becoming a bestseller and leading to a famous TV series. But Ness never knew about its success; he had died of a heart attack on 16 May 1957, six months before *The Untouchables* was published.

10

Crop Circles

UFOs, Whirlwinds, or Hoaxers?

On 15 August 1980, the *Wiltshire Times* carried an odd report concerning the apparently wanton vandalism of a field of oats near Westbury in Wiltshire, England. The owner of the field, John Scull, had found his oats crushed to the ground in three separate areas, all within sight of the famous White Horse of Westbury, a hillside figure cut into the chalk. It seemed obvious to Scull that the crops had been damaged by people rather than natural phenomena since the areas were identical in shape and size: almost perfect circles, each sixty feet in diameter.

It was also noted that the circles had apparently been produced manually rather than mechanically, since there was no sign that any kind of machinery had been moved through the field. In fact, there seemed to be no evidence of *anything* crossing the field; the circles were surrounded by undamaged oats, with no paths that would indicate intruders. One speculation was that the vandals had used stilts.

Close examination of the flattened cereal revealed that the circles had not been made at the same time – that in fact, the damage had been spread over a period of two or three months, probably between May and the end of July. The edges of the circles were sharply defined, and all the grain within the circles was flattened in the same direction, creating a clockwise swirling effect around the centres. None of the oats had been cut – merely flattened. The effect might have been produced by a very tall, strong man standing in the centre of each circle and swinging a heavy weight around on a long piece of rope.

Dr Terence Meaden, an atmospheric physicist from nearby Bradford-on-Avon and a senior member of the Tornado and Storm Research Organization (TORRO), suggested that the circles had been produced by a summer whirlwind. Such wind effects are not uncommon on open farmland. But Dr Meaden had to admit that he had never seen or heard of a whirlwind creating circles. Whirlwinds tend to scud about randomly, pausing for only a few seconds in any one place, so one might expect a random pathway through the crop.

Another interesting fact was noted by Ian Mrzyglod, editor of the "anomaly" magazine *The PROBE Report*. The "centre point" on all three circles was actually off centre by as much as four feet. The swirling patterns around these points were therefore oval, not circular. This seemed to contradict the vandal theory – vandals would hardly go to the trouble of creating precise ellipses. It also made Meaden's whirlwind explanation seem less plausible.

Almost exactly a year later, on 19 August 1981, another three-circle formation appeared in a wheatfield below Cheesefoot Head, near Winchester in Hampshire. These circles had been created simultaneously and, unlike the widely dispersed circles in Wiltshire, were in close formation – one circle sixty feet across with two twenty-five-foot circles on either side. But the sides of these circles had the same precise edges as the Wiltshire circles, and again, the swirl of the flattened plants was slightly off-centre, creating ellipses. And again there were no paths through the grain to indicate intruders.

The new evidence seemed to undermine the natural-causes theory. Instead of a neat, stationary whirlwind creating only one circle, Meaden now had to argue the existence of an atmospheric disturbance that hopscotched across the landscape and produced circles of different sizes. Meaden suggested that perhaps peculiarities of terrain created this effect – the field in question was on a concave, "punchbowl" slope, and this might indeed have caused the vortex to "jump".

There were a few isolated reports of similar incidents in 1982, but they were unspectacular and excited little attention. As if to make up for it, a series of five-circle phenomena began in 1983, one of them at Bratton, again close to the White Horse of Westbury. These were clearly not caused by whirlwinds, for they consisted of one large circle with four smaller ones spaced around it like the number five on a die. A "quintuplet" appeared in Cley Hill, near Warminster – a town that, in earlier years, had had more than its share of "flying saucer" sightings. Another appeared in a field below Ridgeway near Wantage in Oxfordshire. Quintuplets were no longer freaks but were virtually the norm.

Now the national press began to cover the phenomena. The British press often refer to the summer as the "silly season" because, for some odd reason, there is often a shortage of good news stories in the hot months of the year, and newspapers tend to make up for the deficiency by blowing up trivia into major news stories. Crop circles answered the need perfectly, with the result that the British public soon became familiar with the strange circle formations. UFO enthusiasts appeared on television explaining their view that the phenomena could be explained only by flying saucers. Skeptics preferred the notion of fraud.

This latter view seemed to be confirmed when a second quintuplet found at Bratton turned out to be a hoax sponsored by the *Daily Mirror*; a family named Shepherd had been paid to duplicate the other Bratton circles. They did this by entering the field on stilts and trampling the crops underfoot. But, significantly, the hoax was quickly detected by Bob Rickard, the editor of an anomaly magazine, the *Fortean Times*, who noted the telltale signs of human intruders, which had not been present in earlier circles, and the fact that the edges of the circles were quite rough and imprecise. The aim of the hoax was to embarrass the competing tabloid, the *Daily Express*, which had originally scooped the cropcircle story.

Over the next two years the number of circles increased, as did their complexity. There were crop circles with "rings" around them – flattened pathways several feet wide that ran around the outer edge in a neat circle. Some were even found with two or three such rings. At the same time the quintuplet formations and "singletons" also continued to appear.

It began to look as if whoever – or whatever – was creating the circles took pleasure in taunting the investigators. When believers in the whirlwind theory pointed out that the swirling had so far been clockwise, a counterclockwise circle promptly appeared. When it was suggested that a hoaxer might be making the circles with the aid of a helicopter, a crop circle was found directly beneath a power line. When an aerial photographer named Busty Taylor was flying home after photographing crop circles and mentioned that he would like to see a formation in the shape of a Celtic cross, a Celtic cross appeared the next day in the field over which he had been flying. And, as if to rule out all possibility that natural causes could be responsible, one "sextuplet" in Hampshire in 1990 had keylike objects sticking out of the sides of three circles, producing the impression of an ancient pictogram. Another crop "pattern" of 1990 (at Chilcomb) seemed to represent a kind of chemical retort with a long neck, with four rectangles neatly spaced on either side of it, making nonsense of Meaden's insistence that the circles were caused by "natural atmospheric forces".

Rickard brought together a number of eyewitness descriptions of the actual appearance of circles:

Suddenly the grass began to sway before our eyes and laid itself flat in a clockwise spiral . . . A perfect circle was completed in less than half a minute, all the time accompanied by a high-pitched humming sound . . . My attention was drawn to a "wave" coming through the heads of the cereal crop in a straight line . . . The agency, though invisible, behaved like a solid object . . . When we reached the spot where the circles had been, we were suddenly caught up in a terrific whirlwind . . . [The dog] went wild . . . There was a rushing sound and a rumble . . . then suddenly everything was still . . . It was uncanny . . . The dawn chorus stopped; the sky darkened . . .

The high-pitched humming sound may be significant. It was noted on another occasion, on 16 June 1991, when a seventy-five-foot circle (with a "bull's-eye" in the centre) appeared on Bolberry Down, near Salcombe in Devon. A local ham-radio operator named Lew Dilling was tuned into a regular frequency when strange high-pitched blips and clicks emerged. He recognized the sounds as being the same as others that had been heard in connection with crop-circle incidents. "The signals were so powerful", said Dilling, "that you could hear them in the background of Radio Moscow and Voice of America – and they would normally swamp everything".

The landlord of the local pub, Sean Hassall, learned of the crop circle indirectly when his spaniel went berserk and began tearing up the carpet, doing considerable damage.

The owner of the field, Dudley Stidson, was alerted to the circle by two walkers. He went to the six-acre hayfield and found a giant circle in the centre. But this one differed from many such circles in that the hay was burned, as if someone had put a huge hot-plate on it. Stidson emphasized that there was no sign of intrusion in the field, such as trampled wheat.

Another local farmer, Peter Goodall, found a sixty-foot circle in his winter wheat (at Matford Barton) at the same time.

A few days before these incidents occurred, a Japanese professor announced that he had solved the crop-circle mystery. Professor Yoshihiko Ohtsuki, of Tokyo's Waseda University, had created an "elastic plasma" fireball – a very strong form of ionized air – in the labouratory. When the fireball touched a plate covered with aluminum powder, it created beautiful circles and rings in the powder. Ohtsuki suggested that plasma fireballs were created by atmospheric conditions and that they would flatten crops as they descended toward the ground.

This certainly sounded as if it could be the solution of the mystery – until it was recalled that some of the crop circles had rectangles or keylike objects sticking out of their sides. Another objection was that fireballs are usually about the size of footballs and are clearly visible. Surely a fireball with a seventy-five-foot diameter would be visible for many miles? And why were no fireballs seen by the eyewitnesses cited by Rickard, who simply saw the corn being flattened in a clockwise circle?

Another recent suggestion is that an excess of fertilizer will cause the corn on which it is used to shoot up much faster than that which surrounds it, after which it will collapse and lie flat. There are two objections to this theory: Why would a farmer spray an excess of fertilizer in a circle – or some even more complicated design? And why would the corn collapse in a clockwise direction?

In a symposium entitled "The Crop Circle Enigma" (1990), John Michell made the important suggestion that the crop circles have a meaning and that "the meaning . . . is to be found in the way people are affected by them". In conjunction with this idea, Michell noted that "Jung discerned the meaning of UFOs as agents and portents of changes in human thought patterns, and that function has been clearly inherited by crop circles".

In order to understand this fully, we have to bear in mind Jung's concept of "synchronicity" or "meaningful coincidence", His view is basically that "meaningful coincidences" are somehow *created* by the unconscious mind – probably with the intention of jarring the conscious mind into a keener state of perception. Preposterous synchronicities imbue us with a powerful sense that there is a hidden meaning behind everyday reality. Certain pessimistically inclined writers – such as Shakespeare and Thomas Hardy – have taken the view that accidents and disasters indicate a kind of malevolent intelligence behind life. Jung's view is that synchronicities produce a sense of a *benevolent* intelligence behind life. He once suggested that the UFO phenomenon was an example of what he called "projection" – that is, of a physical effect somehow produced by the unconscious mind, in fact, by the "collective unconscious".

Michell was, in effect, suggesting that the crop-circle phenomenon serves the same purpose. Yet to say, as he did, that the crop circles have a "meaning" could also imply that some "other intelligence" is trying to influence human thought patterns. This is an idea that has been current since the earliest UFO sightings in the late 1940s and was popularized by Arthur C. Clarke in the screenplay of the film *2001: A Space*

Odyssey: specifically, the notion that "higher intelligences" have been involved in the evolution of the human brain.

The logical objection to this theory is that to "make" man evolve is a contradiction in terms; evolution is the result of an *inner* drive. Presumably, a higher intelligence would recognize this better than we do. Yet it is also true that intelligence evolves through a sense of curiosity, of mystery, and that such apparent absurdities as flying saucers and crop circles certainly qualify as mysteries.

Michell concluded by quoting Jung's words that UFOs are "signs of great changes to come which are compatible with the end of an era". And whether or not Jung was correct, there can be no doubt that the UFO phenomenon has played an enormous part in the transformation of human consciousness from the narrow scientific materialism of the first half of the twentieth century to the much more open-minded attitude of its second half. Whether or not the crop circles prove to have a "natural" explanation, this may be their ultimate significance in the history of the late twentieth century.

Postscript: In early September 1991, a number of self-proclaimed hoaxers made simultaneous confessions to fabricating crop circles. Two of them, Dave Chorley and Doug Bower, claimed to have been making crop circles for thirteen years. Fred Day declared that he had been making them "all his life". Chorley and Bower demonstrated their technique by flattening corn in a field with a plank in front of TV cameras and crop-circle investigators. As in the case of the earlier *Daily Mirror* hoax, the investigators pointed out that the Chorley-Bower circle was visibly amateurish.

At the time of writing, the position taken by "cereologists" is that while some of the circles may be hoaxes, the majority show signs of being genuine, such as geometric perfection and an obvious lack of trampling of surrounding crops by human feet. The ultimate test, of course, will be whether crop circles now simply cease to appear – the silliest hoaxer gets tired of repetition – or whether, like "flying saucer" sightings, they continue to be as numerous as ever. Readers who pick up this book in the year 2025 will be in a better position to assess the possibilities than the authors are in 2000.

11

The Curse of the Pharaohs

On 26 November 1922 the archaeologist Howard Carter peered through a small opening above the door of the tomb of Tutankhamon's tomb, holding a candle in front of him. What he saw dazzled him: "everywhere the glint of gold". He and his colleague Lord Carnarvon had made the greatest find in the history of archaeology. But a few days later they found a clay tablet with the hieroglyphic inscription: "Death will slay with his wings whoever disturbs the peace of the pharaoh". The following April Lord Carnarvon died of some unknown disease. By 1929 – a mere six years later – twenty-two people who had been involved in opening the tomb had died prematurely. Other archaeologists dismissed talk about "the curse of the pharaohs" as journalistic sensationalism. Yet it is difficult to imagine that this long series of deaths was merely a frightening coincidence.

Tutankhamon was the heir of the "great heretic" Akhnaton (about 1375 BC to 1360), the first monotheist king in history. He abandoned the capital Thebes, with all its temples, and built himself a new capital, called Akhetaton (Horizon of Aton), at a place now called Tell el Amarna. He worshipped only one god, the sun god Aton. His people, who were more comfortable with the host of old animal gods, disliked this new religion, and were relieved when Akhnaton died young, or perhaps possibly murdered. (So were the priests!) His successor was his son-in-law – possibly his son – Tutankhamon, who was a mere child when he came to the throne, and who died of a blow on the head at the age of eighteen. Historically speaking, therefore, Tutankhamon is a nonentity, whose name hardly deserves to be remembered. His only achievement – if it can be called that – was to restore the old religion, and move his capital back to Thebes. No one knows how he died, whether from a fall, or possibly from the blow of an assassin.

The strangest part of this story is still to come. The high priest (and court chamberlain) was a man called Ay. He seized power, and married Tutankhamon's fifteen-year-old widow, Enhosnamon. He reigned less than four years, and once again the throne was seized by a usurper, a general called Horemheb, who had been a little too slow off the mark when Tutankhamon died. The wait for the throne had apparently filled him with resentment; as soon as he became pharaoh, he behaved like a dictator, and set out to erase the names of Akhnaton and Tutankhamon from history; he had their names chiselled off all hieroglyphic inscriptions, and used the stones of the great temple of the sun at Tell el Amarna to build three pyramids in Thebes. He even destroyed many tombs of the courtiers of Ay and Tutankhamon.

Yet he omitted to do the most obvious thing of all: to destroy the tomb of Tutankhamon, and to seize its treasures for his own treasury. Why? One possible explanation is that the location of the tomb was kept secret. But that is unlikely; after all, Horemheb came to the throne a mere four years after the death of Tutankhamon; even if the tomb's location was a secret, there must have been dozens of priests or workmen who could have been "persuaded" to reveal it. It is natural to suspect that Horemheb had some other reason for deciding to leave the tomb inviolate . . .

Howard Carter, the man who finally discovered the tomb, had come out to Egypt as a teenager – he was born in 1873 – and while still in his twenties became Chief Inspector of Monuments for Upper Egypt and Nubia. Acting on his advice, a wealthy American, Theodore Davis, began excavating the Valley of the Kings in 1902. In the previous year grave-robbers had mounted an armed attack on the men guarding the newly discovered tomb of Amonhotep II – a bloodthirsty character who was the great-grandfather of Akhnaton – and made off with all its gold and jewels. Carter had rounded them up and prosecuted them, an action that made him so unpopular with the Egyptians that he found himself without a job. Theodore Davis took him on as a draughtsman, and with Carter's help made some astonishing discoveries, including the tomb of Horemheb, of the great Queen Hatshepsut, and of Akhnaton's grandfather Thutmose IV.

It was during this period that there was a curious curtain-raiser to the story of the curse of the pharaohs. Joe Linden Smith was another skilled draughtsman who worked closely with the excavators; he was married to an attractive 28-year-old American named Corinna. Among their closest friends were Arthur and Hortense Weigel; Weigel was an English archaeologist, while Hortense, like Corinna, was a young American. One day when they were descending the slope into the Valley of the

Queens, Smith and Weigel came upon a natural amphitheatre that struck them as the ideal site for the presentation of a play. They decided to present their own "mystery play", and to invite most of the archaeological community from Luxor. But the purpose was not mere entertainment. Both men had immense admiration for Akhnaton and for the artistic productions of his reign, which were far more lifelike than the stylized works of other periods. Their aim was nothing less than to intercede with the ancient gods to lift the curse that consigned Akhnaton's spirit to wander for all eternity.

According to tradition, Akhnaton died on 26 January 1363 BC. Smith and Weigel decided to present their play on 26 January 1909, and the invitations were sent. On 23 January they held their dress rehearsal. The god Horus appeared and conversed with the wandering spirit of Akhnaton – played by Hortense – offering to grant him a wish; Akhnaton asked to see his mother, Queen Tiy. The Queen was summoned by a magical ceremony; she spoke of her sadness to see her son condemned to eternal misery. Akhnaton replied that even in his misery he still drew comfort from the thought of the god Aton; he asked his mother to recite his hymn to Aton . . .

As Corinna Smith began to recite the hymn her words were drowned by the rising wind. Suddenly a violent storm was upon them; the gale blew sand and small stones, so the cowering workmen thought the gods were stoning them. The rehearsal had to be abandoned, and the actors hurried back to their headquarters, the nearby tomb of Amet-Hu, once governor of Thebes. Later that evening Corinna complained of a pain in her eyes, and Hortense of cramps in her stomach. That night both had similar dreams; they were in the nearby temple of Amon, standing before the statue of the god; he came to life and struck them with his flail – Corinna in the eyes, Hortense in the stomach. The next day Corinna was in agony with inflamed eyes, and had to be rushed to a specialist in Cairo, who diagnosed one of the worst cases of trachoma – Egyptian ophthalmia – he had ever seen. Twenty-four hours later, Hortense joined Corinna in the same nursing-home; during the stomach operation that followed she came close to losing her life. The play had to be abandoned.

Howard Carter and Lord Carnarvon had both been invited to the play; at this period Carter was working for Theodore Davis. By 1914 Davis had decided that he had now found all there was to be found in the Valley of the Kings, and decided to abandon his labours. Carnarvon snapped up the concession. He knew that Davis was convinced that he had found the grave of Tutankhamon, a pit grave containing gold plates and other items; but neither Carnarvon nor Carter believed that a pharaoh would be buried so modestly.

The war made it impossible to begin digging until 1917. Then Carter began to dig, slowly and systematically, moving hundreds of tons of rubble left from earlier digs. He found nothing. By 1922 Carnarvon felt he had poured enough money into the Valley of the Kings. Carter begged for one more chance.

On 1 November 1922 he began new excavations, digging a ditch southward from the tomb of Rameses IV. On 4 November the workmen uncovered a step below the foundations of some huts Carter had discovered in an earlier dig. By evening twelve steps had been revealed, then a sealed stone gate. Carter hastened to send a telegram to Carnarvon in England; Carnarvon arrived just over two weeks later. Together Carnarvon and Carter broke their way through the sealed gate, now in a state of increasing excitement as they realized that this tomb was virtually unplundered. Thirty feet below the gate, they came upon a second. With trembling hands, Carter scraped a hole in the debris in its upper corner, and peered through; the candlelight showed him strange animals, statues and gold. There were overturned chariots, lifesize figures, gilded couches, a gold-inlaid throne. But there was no mummy, for this was only the antechamber. However, it was in this antechamber that they found the tablet with the inscription: "Death will slay with his wings whoever disturbs the peace of the pharaoh". It was recorded by Carter, then disappeared – they were afraid rumours of the inscription might terrify the workmen. A statue of Horus also carried an inscription stating that it was the protector of the grave. On 17 February 1923 a group of distinguished people was invited to witness the opening of the tomb itself. It took two hours to chisel a hole through into the burial chamber. Then only two sets of folding doors separated them from the magnificent gold sarcophagus that was to become world-famous; they decided to leave that for another day. The wealth that surrounded them made them all feel dazed.

Carnarvon was never to see it. That April he fell ill. At breakfast one morning he had a temperature of 104, and it continued for twelve days; his doctors suspected that he had opened an old wound with his razor while shaving, but the fever suggested a mosquito-bite. Howard Carter was sent for. Carnarvon died just before two in the morning. As the family came to his bedside, summoned by a nurse, all the lights suddenly went out, and they were forced to light candles. Later they went on again. It was a power failure that affected all Cairo. Some accounts of Lord Carnarvon's death state that the failure has never been explained, but none of them mention whether any inquiry was actually addressed to the Cairo Electricity Board.

According to Lord Carnarvon's son, another peculiar event took place that night; back in England, Carnarvon's favourite fox terrier began to howl, then died.

The newspapers quickly began printing stories about the "curse of the pharaohs". This was partly Carnarvon's own fault; he had sold exclusive rights in the Tutankhamon story to the London *Times*, and other newspapers had to print any stories they could unearth or concoct. But the curse story hardly needed any journalistic retouching. Arthur Mace, the American archaeologist who had helped unseal the tomb, began to complain of exhaustion soon after Carnarvon's death; he fell into a coma and died in the same hotel – the Continental – not long after Carnarvon. George Jay Gould, son of the famous American financier, came to Egypt when he heard of Carnarvon's death, and Carter took him to see the tomb. The next day he had fever; by evening he was dead. Joel Wool, a British industrialist who visited the grave site, died of fever on his way back to England. Archibald Douglas Reid, a radiologist who X-rayed Tutankhamon's mummy, suffered attacks of feebleness and died on his return to England in 1924. Over the next few years thirteen people who had helped open the grave also died, and by 1929 the figure had risen to twenty-two. In 1929 Lady Carnarvon died of an "insect bite", and Carter's secretary Richard Bethell was found dead in bed of a circulatory collapse. Professor Douglas Derry, one of two scientists who performed the autopsy on Tutankhamon's mummy, had died of circulatory collapse in 1925; the other scientist, Alfred Lucas, died of a heart attack at about the same time.

In his book *The Curse of the Pharaohs*, Philip Vandenburg not only lists the deaths associated with Tutankhamon, but goes on to mention many other archaeologists associated with Egypt who have died prematurely. He points out how frequently these deaths seem to involve a curious exhaustion – Carter himself suffered from this, as well as from fits of depression – and speculates whether the ancient priests of Egypt knew of poisons or fungoid growths that would retain their power down the centuries. Among the premature deaths he mentions François Champollion, who decoded the Rosetta Stone, the great Egyptologist Belzoni, the Swabian doctor Theodore Bilharz (after whom the disease bilharzia was named), the archaeologist Georg Möller, and Carter's close associate Professor James Henry Breasted. It was James Breasted who reported that Carter became sick and feeble after excavating the tomb, that he seemed at times "not all there", and that he had difficulty making decisions. Carter died at sixty-six.

Vandenberg begins his book by citing a conversation he had with Dr Gamal Mehrez, director-general of the Antiquities Department of the Cairo Museum. Mehrez, who was fifty-two, expressed disbelief in the idea of a curse. "Look at me. I've been involved with tombs and mummies of pharaohs all my life. I'm living proof that it was all coincidence". Four weeks later Mehrez had died of circulatory collapse . . .

Yet although Vandenberg himself seems to discount the coincidence theory, his attempts to explain the "curse" scientifically are unconvincing – he even considers the possibility that the shape of the pyramid can cause it to absorb certain cosmic energies capable of affecting human health, and that the Egyptians "knew how to influence radioactive decay".

The ancients themselves would have dismissed such theories as absurd. For them a curse was the result of a ritual to evoke a guardian "demon" or spirit. Such beliefs have survived down to modern times. The psychical researcher Guy Lyon Playfair has described the years he spent in Brazil, and how he investigated "poltergeist" hauntings which appeared to be the result of a curse – that is to say, of "black magic". Most investigators of the paranormal are inclined to believe that the poltergeist – "noisy ghost" – is some kind of unconscious manifestation of the mind of a "disturbed" teenager, and that when objects suddenly fly around the room, this is due to "spontaneous psychokinesis". Playfair, while accepting this explanation in some cases, nevertheless came to believe that most poltergeists are in fact disembodied "spirits". Such spirits can be persuaded, by means of rituals, to "haunt" certain individuals, or to cause disturbances in houses. When this happens another *candomblé* specialist (*candomblé* is an African-influenced cult) is called in to dispel the malign influence. In fact, traditional magic through the ages has been based upon this belief in the use of spirits for magical purposes.

Another modern investigator, Max Freedom Long, studied the Huna religion in Hawaii, and became convinced that the Huna priests – known as kahunas – were able to cause death by means of the "death prayer". He writes:

> The truth was that over a period of several years during which time I checked the data through doctors frequenting the Queen's Hospital in Honolulu, not a year passed but one or more victims of the potent magic died, despite all the hospital doctors could offer by way of aid.

The kahunas, Long says, believe that man has three "selves" or souls, known as the low self, the middle self and the high self. The low self corresponds roughly to what Freud called the unconscious; it controls man's vital forces, and seems to be predominantly emotional. The middle self is man's "ordinary consciousness", his everyday self. The "high self" might be called the superconscious mind; it has powers that are unknown to the everyday self. These three selves inhabit the body, and are separated from it after death. But sometimes a "low self" may become detached from the other two. It becomes an "earthbound spirit" of the sort that causes poltergeist disturbances. The low self, according to the kahunas, possesses memory, while the middle self does not. So a disembodied "middle self", separated from the other two, is a wandering wraith without memory – what we would regard as a ghost.

According to Long, the "death prayer" involves disembodied "low spirits", who are highly susceptible to suggestion, and can easily be persuaded to obey. The victim of the death prayer experiences an increasing numbness as the spirits drain his vital energies.

Long obtained much of his information about the kahunas (recorded in his book *The Secret Science Behind Miracles*) from a doctor, William Tufts Brigham, who had studied them for many years. Brigham told him a typical story of the death prayer. He had hired a party of Hawaians to climb a mountain, and a fifteen-year-old boy became ill, experiencing a numbness that rose from his feet. He told Brigham that he was a victim of the death prayer. The kahuna in his local village hated the influence of the white men, and declared that any Hawaian who worked for the whites would become a victim of the death prayer. When the boy accepted the job with Brigham the kahuna knew it by clairvoyance, and had invoked the death prayer.

The Hawaians, who also believed that Brigham was a magician, asked him to try to save the boy. Brigham decided to try. Acting upon the assumption that the lad was being attacked by highly suggestible "lower spirits", he stood over him and addressed the attackers, flattering them and arguing that the boy was an innocent victim, and telling them that it was the witch doctor who sent them who ought to be destroyed. He kept his mind concentrated on this idea for another hour, when suddenly the tension seemed to vanish and he experienced a sense of relief. The boy declared that he could now feel his legs again. When Brigham visited the boy's village he learned that the kahuna had died, after telling the villagers that the "white magician" had redirected the spirits to attack him. Within hours of this he was dead. Brigham thought he had gone to sleep early, and awoke to find himself under attack, by which time it was too late.

Long believes that the kahunas originated in Africa, possibly in Egypt. "Their journey commenced at the 'Red Sea of Kane', which fits neatly into the idea that they came from Egypt by way of the Red Sea".

The Egyptians also believed that man is a multiple being, a body animated by several spirits, the main ones being the *ka* or double (corresponding roughly to what is sometimes called the "astral body"), the *ba*, or heart-soul, and the *khu*, or spiritual soul. There was also the *ab* (heart-soul), *khaibit* (shadow), *sekhem* (or vital force) and the *ren*, the man's name.

Long writes: 'In Egypt, as we might expect . . . there are definite traces of the kahuna system to be found", and he goes on to describe the Egyptian beliefs in some detail. He believes that the kahunas came to Hawaii by way of Egypt, and also left traces of their system in the Hindu religion.

The strange debilitating effects experienced by some of the archae-ologists including Carter sound in many ways like the effects of the death prayer as described by Brigham and Long. But it is unnecessary to establish some direct connection between the kahunas of Hawaii and the religion of ancient Egypt. *If* Long and Playfair are correct, and pol-tergeists or "low spirits" can be used for magical purposes, then it is logical to believe that they were used by the priests of ancient Egypt as the "guardians of the tomb".

In *A Search in Secret Egypt* the English occultist Paul Brunton describes a night spent in the King's Chamber in the Great Pyramid. He speaks of "a strange feeling that I was not alone", which developed into a feeling of being surrounded by "antagonistic beings". "Mon-strous elemental creations, evil horrors of the underworld, forms of grotesque, insane, uncouth and fiendish aspect gathered around me . . . The end came with startling suddenness. The malevolent ghostly invaders disappeared . . ." After this Brunton experienced a feeling that a benevolent being was present in the chamber, then thought that he saw two high priests.

Vandenberg, who quotes this, admits that it may all have been Brunton's imagination. But he goes on to describe how when he was visiting the pyramid in 1972 a woman screamed, then collapsed and was unable to move. She said to Vandenberg later: "It was as if something had suddenly hit me". The guide told Vandenberg that such attacks were not unusual.

If these odd effects are merely the result of imagination, then it is also arguable that the same applies to the curse of the pharaohs. After all, Carnarvon died of something that resembled a mosquito bite, others of heart attacks, others of circulatory failure – nothing that sounds like the creeping numbness of the death curse. In a BBC programme on the curse of the pharaohs, Henry Lincoln, investigator of the mystery of Rennes-le-Château (*q.v.*), stated emphatically: "There never was a curse of the pharaohs". It is certainly more comfortable to think so.

12

The Devil's Footprints

The winter of 1855 was an exceptionally severe one, even in the south-west of England, where winters are usually mild. On the morning of 8 February Albert Brailsford, the principal of the village school in Topsham, Devon, walked out of his front door to find that it had snowed in the night. And he was intrigued to notice a line of footprints – or rather hoofprints – that ran down the village street. At first glance they looked like the ordinary hoofprints of a shod horse; but a closer look showed that this was impossible, for the prints ran in a continuous line, one in front of the other. If it was a horse, then it must have had only one leg, and hopped along the street. And if the unknown creature had two legs, then it must have placed one carefully in front of the other, as if walking along a tightrope. What was odder still was that the prints – each about four inches long – were only about eight inches apart. And each print was very clear, as if it had been branded into the frozen snow with a hot iron.

The villagers of Topsham were soon following the track southward through the snow. And they halted in astonishment when the hoofprints came to a halt at a brick wall. They were more baffled than ever when someone discovered that they continued on the other side of the wall, and that the snow on top of the wall was undisturbed. The tracks approached a haystack, and continued on the other side of it, although the hay showed no sign that a heavy creature had clambered over it. The prints passed under gooseberry bushes, and were even seen on rooftops. It began to look as if some insane practical joker had decided to set the village an insoluble puzzle.

But it was soon clear that this explanation was also out of the question. Excited investigators tracked the prints for mile after mile over the Devon countryside. They seemed to wander erratically through a number of small towns and villages – Lympstone, Exmouth, Teignmouth, Dawlish, as far as Totnes, about halfway to Plymouth. If it was a practical joker, he would have had to cover forty miles, much of it through deep snow. Moreover, such a joker would surely have hurried forward to cover the greatest distance possible; in fact, the steps often approached front doors, then changed their mind and went away again. At some point the creature had crossed the estuary of the river Exe – it looked as if the crossing was between Lympstone and Powderham. Yet there were also footprints in Exmouth, farther south, as if it had turned back on its tracks. There was no logic in its meandering course.

In places it looked as if the "horseshoe" had a split in it, suggesting a cloven hoof. It was the middle of the Victorian era, and few country people doubted the existence of the Devil. Men armed with guns and pitchforks followed the trail; when night came people locked their doors and kept loaded shotguns at hand.

It was another week before the story reached the newspapers; on 16 February 1855 the London *Times* told the story, adding that most gardens in Lympstone showed some trace of the strange visitor. The following day the *Plymouth Gazette* carried a report, and mentioned the theory of a clergyman that the creature could have been a kangaroo – apparently unaware that a kangaroo has claws. A report in the Exeter *Flying Post* made the slightly more plausible suggestion that it was a bird. But a correspondent in the *Illustrated London News* dismissed this idea, pointing out that no bird leaves a horse-shoe-shaped print. He added that he had passed a five-month winter in the backwoods of Canada, and had never seen a more clearly defined track.

In the *Illustrated London News* for 3 March the great naturalist and anatomist Richard Owen announced dogmatically that the footmarks were those of hind foot of a badger, and suggested that many badgers had come out of hibernation that night to seek food. He did not explain why all these badgers hopped along on one hind foot. (Five years later, he was to be equally dogmatic – and equally wrong – on the subject of Charles Darwin and the origin of species.) Another correspondent, a doctor, described how he and another doctor "bestowed considerable time in endeavouring to discover the peculiarities of this most singular impression" (the Victorians loved this kind of pompous language). He claimed that "on more minute examination of the tracks, we could distinctly see the impressions of the toes and pad of the foot of an animal". His own candidate was an otter. Another correspondent, who signed himself "Ornither", was quite certain that they were the prints of a Great Bustard, whose outer toes, he claimed, were rounded. Another gentleman, from Sudbury, said he had recently seen impressions of rats surrounding a potato patch, and that they looked exactly like the drawings of "the devil's footprints". He thought that the rats had been leaping through the snow, landing with their full body weight and producing a roughly horseshoe-shaped impression. A Scottish correspondent thought that the culprit could be a hare or polecat bounding through the snow. These suggestions are less absurd than they sound. They would certainly explain the most baffling feature of the footprints – that they followed one upon another, as if made by a one-legged animal. But they still fail to explain why they continued for forty miles or so.

Perhaps the likeliest hypothesis is one put forward by Geoffrey Household, who edited a small book containing all the major correspondence on the matter.* He comments as follows, in a letter to the author:

> I think that Devonport dockyard released, by accident, some sort of experimental balloon. It broke free from its moorings, and trailed two shackles on the end of ropes. The impression left in the snow by these shackles went up the sides of houses, over haystacks, etc. . . . A Major Carter, a local man, tells me that his grandfather worked at Devonport at the time, and that the whole thing was hushed up because the balloon destroyed a number of conservatories, greenhouses, windows, etc. He says that the balloon finally came down at Honiton.

This information is fascinating, and could well represent the solution of the mystery. But if so there is still one major anomaly to be explained. A glance at the map of the "footprints" will show that they meandered in a kind of circle between Topsham and Exmouth. Would an escaped balloon drift around so erratically? Surely its route would tend to be a more or less straight line, in the direction of the prevailing wind which, moreover, was blowing from the east.

The fact that it took a week for the first report of the mystery to appear in print means that certain vital clues have been lost for ever. It would be interesting to know, for example, whether the snow that fell that night was the first snow of February 1855. It had been a hard winter that year, and many small animals, including rats, rabbits and badgers, must have been half starved by February, and have been out looking for food. The letter to the *Plymouth Gazette* (dated 17 February) begins:

* *The Devil's Footprints*, edited by G.A. Household, Devon Books 1985.

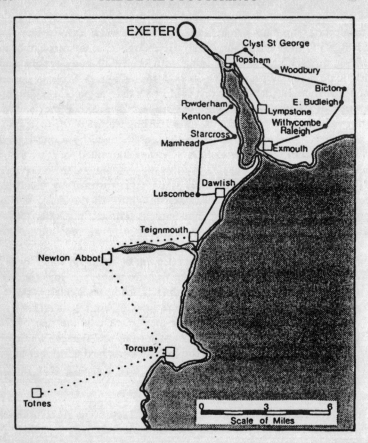

"Thursday night, the 8th of February, was marked by a heavy fall of snow, followed by rain and boisterous wind from the east, and in the morning frost". Small animals had probably been out every night, but it was not until that Friday morning, with its fresh carpet of snow, that their tracks were noticed for the first time. Such tracks would have sunk deep into the soft snow, and would have been further deepened by the rain before they were frozen solid. This would explain why they seemed to be "branded" into the snow.

But if the ground was already covered with snow before the night of 8 February, then one more plausible theory would have to be abandoned. And in any case it fails to explain how the tracks managed to wander over rooftops and haystacks ... At this distance in time, the only certainty seems to be that the mystery is now insoluble.

13

Was Philip K. Dick Possessed by an Angel?

By the time of his death in March 1982, Philip K. Dick had become perhaps the most respected of modern science-fiction writers. The reason for this was expressed in an essay on Dick by Brian Stableford. "He has done more than anyone else to open up metaphysical questions to science fictional analysis".*

He was also, with the possible exception of H. P. Lovecraft, the most neurotic of major science-fiction writers, obsessed by the notion that human beings are trapped in a web of unreality. His persecution mania developed to a point where he could undoubtedly have been described as a paranoid schizophrenic. Yet, toward the end of his life, Dick became convinced that he had been "taken over" by a kind of super-alien, who went on to reorganize his life. And although Lawrence Sutin, in his full-length biography of Dick, *Divine Invasions* (1991), casts doubts on some of Dick's claims, the case is too complex to be dismissed as simple self-delusion.

Philip Kindred Dick was an oversensitive little boy whose childhood was not designed to make him buoyant and optimistic. His twin sister died soon after his birth – as a result, he was later convinced, of his mother's neglect. He was a lonely child; his mother was cold and, in Sutin's words, "emotionally constrained". She was often in pain and spent long periods bedridden – she suffered from Bright's disease. Dick himself suffered from asthma and had eating and swallowing phobias. He was an introverted child who liked to retreat into daydreams of cowboys; he resisted all of his father's attempts to interest him in sports. His parents divorced when he was five. When he was nine, he and his

* In E. F. Bleiler, ed., *Science Fiction Writers* (New York: Scribner), 1982.

mother moved to Berkeley, California, and Dick attended high school there. His relationship with his mother, who was slim and pretty, had classic Freudian overtones; when he was a teenager he even had a dream that he was sleeping with her. He finally left home at nineteen – he claimed his mother threatened to call the police to stop him – and moved into a bohemian rooming house populated by gay artists. From the age of fifteen he had worked in a local TV and record store and so was able to support himself.

At nineteen Dick was still a virgin who had never even kissed a girl. Then one of his customers – a short, overweight woman named Jeanette, who was ten years his senior – remedied the situation in a storeroom in the basement, and Dick decided to marry her; she was the first of five wives. When they had been married two months, Jeanette told him that she had a right to see other men; he dumped her possessions outside their apartment and changed the locks. His love life became sporadic and not particularly satisfying; one woman he fell in love with preferred his partner in the store; another went off with a lesbian. Another beautiful woman with whom he had an affair dropped him because he was so socially inept. A nervous breakdown – accompanied by agoraphobia – led him to leave the University of California a year later. "I managed to become universally despised wherever I went", he later told an interviewer. This led him, he said, to identify with the weak and to make the heroes in his stories weak.

From an early age Dick was obsessed by pain and misery. He records that when he was four his father, who had fought on the Marne in World War I, told him about gas attacks and men with their guts blown out. And during World War II, when he was still a child, he saw a newsreel showing a Japanese soldier who had been hit by a flamethrower and was "burning and running, and burning and running", while the audience cheered and laughed. Dick wrote of the incident: "I was dazed with horror . . . and I thought *something is terribly wrong*". And in an autobiographical essay he wrote: "Human and animal suffering makes me mad; whenever one of my cats dies I curse God and I mean it; I feel fury at him. I'd like to get him where I could interrogate him, tell him I think the world is screwed up, that man didn't sin and fall but was pushed". Forced to kill a rat that had been caught in a trap in his children's bedroom, he was haunted for the rest of his life by its screams. As a youngster, Dick had had an urge to cruelty, but after an incident in his childhood that involved tormenting a beetle, the urge suddenly vanished and was replaced by a sense of the oneness of life – what he called satori: "I was never the same again".

Dick's obsession with the problem of cruelty resembled that of the Russian writer Dostoyevsky, whose Ivan Karamazov confesses that the cruelty and brutality of the world makes him want to "give God back his entrance ticket". It is unsurprising, therefore, that Dick's first science-fiction story, "Beyond Lies the Wub", concerned space explorers on an alien planet who buy a piglike creature called a wub, which is delighted to discuss philosophy with them – while their only desire is to eat it. A later wub story describes how wub fur is used to bind books because it is self-repairing, though the fur causes the texts to alter. Thomas Paine's *Age of Reason* vanishes completely – an expression of Dick's feeling that it is an absurd form of hubris for human beings to believe they are rational creatures.

From then on most of Dick's work had a morbid, not to say paranoid, streak. In "Second Variety", machines get out of hand and create duplicate humans to trap real people. "The Imposter" is about a man who finds himself subjected to the nightmarish experience of being suspected of being a robot bomb; the final twist of the story is that it turns out to be true. (Dick's early stories were heavily influenced by the work of the older science-fiction writer, A. E. Van Vogt, who often chooses such themes – e.g., a hero caught in a nightmare world of apparently insane misunderstandings – although his basic outlook is optimistic.)

There is a Kafkaesque quality to Dick's work, which often features individuals beset by endless complications that frustrate all attempts at purposeful action. Like so many modern writers – notably Arthur C. Clarke – Dick likes to play with the idea of computers developing their own intelligence and taking over from human beings. He is also inclined to experiment with the idea that the word "reality" is meaningless – that, instead, there are as many "realities" as there are living creatures and that the notion of "reality" is therefore purely subjective. This view, of course, leads easily to solipsism, the belief that you are the only person in the universe. After all, if the reality around us is "relative" and self-created, then perhaps other people are illusions we create to defend us from the recognition of our loneliness.

One of Dick's early novels, *Eye in the Sky* (1957), encapsulates his views about "reality"; a group of people find themselves in an "alternative reality" where other people's beliefs can become "reality"; a religious cult imposes its own views on everyone's mind. They then realize that they are trapped in the insane reality of one of their own number. When they escape this illusion, they immediately find themselves entrapped in yet another. Their return to "reality" is a painful process in which they have to escape the "individual reality" of every member of the group. But in this early work Dick at least believes that a "return to reality" is possible. His later work becomes more darkly pessimistic, infused with the underlying conviction that there is no overall "reality", only our individual illusions. This could be regarded as a dramatized version of the pessimistic philosophy of Schopenhauer and possibly that of Buddha.

In 1963 Dick finally achieved relatively wide recognition with a novel entitled *Man in the High Castle*, which won the Hugo Award for best science-fiction novel of the year. It is another "alternative reality" novel, about a world in which the Allies lost the Second World War, with the result that America is divided into a German zone and a Japanese zone. A character named Tagomi has flashes of an alternative reality in which the Allies won the war, but they seem absurd. Dick apparently plotted this novel with the aid of the *I Ching*, the Chinese book of oracles; the result is a certain arbitrary quality. A later novel, *Do Androids Dream of Electric Sheep?*, concerns an attempt by "real people" to root out the robots that are trying to take over the earth and that are virtually indistinguishable from humans. (It was made into a successful film, *Blade Runner*.) All of Dick's work seems to express his own sense of having an extremely insecure foundation in reality and his inability to cope with life. He wrote, "For us . . . there can be no system. Maybe *all* systems . . . are manifestations of paranoia. We should be content with the meaningless, the contradictory, the hostile".

Meanwhile, Dick's life lurched from crisis to crisis: nervous breakdowns, suicide attempts, divorces, novels written at top speed to stave off debt, paranoid delusions – at one point he saw a great metal face, with slots for eyes, looking down at him from the sky. His sexual relationships were reminiscent of those of the Swedish playwright Strindberg; again and again it looked as if the lonely, fear-ridden writer had found peace when some attractive woman thought that she could give him the security he needed. But his fundamental instability wrecked every relationship. And his loneliness and paranoia brought about writer's blocks. His biographer remarks, "If there is a dominant mood to his novels of the late sixties, it is that of a dark night of the soul". The novels themselves usually have a stifling, airless atmosphere that contrasts strongly with the wind of reality that seems to blow through the best of Tolstoy or Hemingway.

A quarrel he had with the science-fiction writer Harlan Ellison seems to embody everything that was wrong with Dick. At a science-fiction conference in Metz, France, Dick bewildered and bored his audience with a typically rambling speech entitled "If You Find This World Bad, You Should See Some of the Others", Audience members suspected he was drunk or on drugs. (He was, in fact, addicted to numerous prescription drugs.) Dick and Ellison had parted company before because Ellison felt Dick was unreliable and "possibly loony". When they met in the bar they engaged in a bitter philosophical debate that was basically a quarrel. Dick's girlfriend at the time gives a memorable word-portrait of the encounter:

> Phil was very antithetical to Harlan. Harlan is very cocky, glib, cool, and here is Phil going clunk clunk clunk. Phil was not a very debonair or self-assured man. Snuff falling out of his nose, ninety-two spots on his tie – you know. And Harlan thought Phil treated people very badly because he wandered away, got lost, had people support him rather than be master of his own ship.
>
> Anyway, they got into this huge debate. Phil does very well in these kinds of situations. Here is Harlan banging his chest, and Phil was more a philosopher. Phil was just great – more dynamic and sexy than I'd ever seen him.

Clearly, Dick *could* pull himself together and organize his ideas. Yet, as Ellison realized, he preferred to "have people support him rather than be master of his own ship".

But on 2 March 1974, Dick experienced a "vision" that transformed his life. He later told an interviewer, Charles Platt, "My mental anguish was simply removed from me as if by a divine fiat . . . Some transcendent divine power, which was not evil, but benign, intervened to restore my mind and heal my body and give me a sense of the beauty, the joy, the sanity of the world".

In February 1974 Dick was convinced that he was being persecuted by both American and Soviet authorities; he was also convinced that he was destined to die the following month.

One night, lying awake and wrestling with "dread and melancholy", he began to see whirling lights. A week later he again had visions but this time of "perfectly formed modern abstract paintings" – hundreds of thousands of them replacing each other at dazzling speed. Then he experienced the "Bardo Thodol journey" (an after-death journey, as described in the *Tibetan Book of the Dead*) and found himself face to face with the goddess Aphrodite. After this he began hearing female voices as he hovered in hypnagogic states on the edge of sleep. On March 16 "it appeared – in vivid fire, with shining colours and balanced patterns –

and released me from every thrall, inner and outer". Two days later "it, from inside me, looked out". In other words, Dick now felt another being inside himself; he was "possessed". But the entity seemed benevolent: "It denied the reality, the power, the authenticity, of the world, saying, 'This cannot exist; it cannot exist.'" Two days later: "It seized me entirely, lifting me from the limitations of the space-time matrix; it mastered me as, at the same instant, I knew that the world around me was cardboard, a fake. Through its power I suddenly saw the universe as it was; through its perception I saw what really existed, and through its power of no-thought decision, I acted to *free myself*".

All this sounds like the typical rambling of a psychotic. Yet what actually took place was by no means entirely in the realm of fantasy. Dick had a conviction that he would receive a letter that would kill him. His wife, Tessa, confirms that one morning he selected a letter from a large batch of mail, handed it to her unopened, and told her that this was what he had been expecting. In fact, it was a photocopy of a book review about the decline of American capitalism, and every negative word, such as *die, decline, decay*, and *decomposition*, had been underlined. Paranoid or not, Dick seemed to have a sixth sense that enabled him to detect the strange letter unopened.

Now, says Dick, he was taken over by the "intelligence". "On Thursdays and Saturdays I would think it was God, on Tuesdays and Wednesdays I would think it was extraterrestrial . . . It set about healing me physically, [as well as] my four-year-old boy, who had an undiagnosed life-threatening birth defect that no one had been aware of".

The "intelligence", which Dick called Valis (*Vast Active Living Intelligence System*), fired information into his brain by means of pink light beams. It told him that his son, Christopher, suffered from a potentially fatal inguinal hernia. The Dicks checked with the doctor and found that the information was correct; the hernia was remedied by an operation. Dick told Charles Platt:

> This mind was equipped with tremendous technical knowledge – engineering, medical, cosmological, philosophical knowledge. It had memories dating back over two thousand years, it spoke Greek, Hebrew, Sanskrit, there wasn't anything that it didn't seem to know.
>
> It immediately set about putting my affairs in order. It fired my agent and my publisher. It remargined my typewriter. It was very practical; it decided that the apartment had not been vacuumed recently enough; it decided that I should stop drinking wine

because of the sediment – it turned out I had an abundance of uric acid in my system – and it switched me to beer. It made elementary mistakes, such as calling the dog "he" and the cat "she" – which annoyed my wife; and it kept calling her "ma'am".

His wife, Tessa, told Dick's biographer, Lawrence Sutin, that she had no doubt of the genuineness of these "mystical" experiences. But she herself also had reason to believe that there was some basis for her husband's paranoia. Dick thought that the radio was transmitting programs in which a popular singer called him names, told him he was worthless, and advised him to die. This sounds like a typical schizophrenic delusion. But Tessa herself verified that the radio would go on at two in the morning and play music (she did not hear the voice); the odd thing was that the radio was unplugged.

Dick goes on:

My wife was impressed by the fact that, because of the tremendous pressure this mind put on people in my business, I made quite a lot of money very rapidly. We began to get checks for thousands of dollars – money that was owed me, which the mind was conscious existed in New York but had never been coughed up. And it got me to the doctor who confirmed its diagnoses of the various ailments I had . . . it did everything but paper the walls of the apartment. It also said it would stay on as my tutelary spirit. I had to look up "tutelary" to see what it meant.

Sutin verifies that Dick galvanized his agent – the one he had fired for a time – into pursuing back royalties from Ace Books and that the agent was able to send him a check for $3,000.

Tessa also confirmed that Dick normally refused to go to the doctor but that the "spirit" insisted and that the doctor immediately had Dick check into a hospital for treatment of high blood pressure. He came out physically much improved. His wife wrote, "It made Phil more fun to be with. Every day brought an adventure". And his experiences culminated in this insight: "This is not an evil world . . . There is a good world under the evil. The evil is somehow superimposed over it . . . and when stripped away, pristine, glowing creation is visible".

Dick's life began to improve. He had always been poor. In 1974 he made $19,000, and in the following year, $35,000. As his reputation increased, so did demands for interviews, and an increasing number of his novels were translated into foreign languages. Several books were optioned by Hollywood, and one of them, as mentioned earlier, became a classic movie, *Blade Runner*. When Dick died – of a stroke and heart failure – in 1982, he had achieved cult status among thousands of science-fiction fans and had become something of a legend.

How far can we accept Dick's own estimate of his "possession" experience? His biographer, Lawrence Sutin, is obviously ambivalent about the subject. Yet the title of his book, *Divine Invasions*, indicates that he feels the experience to be the most important in Dick's life. His ambivalence is understandable. Dick sounds like a paranoid schizo-phrenic, and paranoid schizophrenics have "visions". Yet there is enough factual evidence to suggest that Dick may not have been suffering from delusions after all.

The problem, of course, is that a rational human being finds it practically impossible to believe in "possession" – except as a psychia-tric label. Chapter 42 in this book argues that such an attitude may not be as reasonable as it sounds. It depends upon the assumption that disembodied "spirits" cannot exist, and while no one will disagree that this is a perfectly sensible *assumption* for a rational and practical human being, we cannot assume that it is *true* for that reason. And if we are willing even to admit the logical possibility of spirits, then we have also admitted the logical possibility of "possession".

An American psychiatrist, Wilson Van Dusen, found himself in this position, simply as a result of his work with mental patients at Mendo-cino State Hospital in California. In a book entitled *The Natural Depth in Man* (1972), Van Dusen defined madness as "a turning in on one's self that makes one a constricted uselessness that misses one's highest potentials". In other words, madness is a *limitation* of our natural potential – which inevitably raises the question: What is our natural potential? Van Dusen's conclusion was that all human beings have the potential to undergo "mystical" experiences, in which consciousness seems to expand far beyond its normal limitations, and that therefore, in a certain sense, we are all "mad".

He went on to describe how he managed to establish contact with one of his patient's hallucinations. The girl had a phantom lover, and "just for the heck of it", Van Dusen asked her to "report faithfully what [the lover] said and did". Van Dusen was thus able to hold "conversations" with the hallucination, using the patient as a go-between. He then found, to his surprise, that he was able to give psychological tests to his patients *and* to their hallucinations, separately. He next made a startling and disturbing discovery: the hallucinations were sicker than the patients. That should have been quite impossible, since the hallucinations *were* the patients. Yet "what was revealed of the hallucinations looked remarkably like ancient accounts of spirit possession". There could be no doubt in Van Dusen's mind that the hallucinations behaved like real people, and really replied to his remarks; for example, the patient's eyes would sometimes flash sideways as Van Dusen was talking and the hallucination interposed some remark.

Patients often told stories of how they had come to "meet" their hallucinations: "One woman was just working in her garden and a kindly man started talking to her when no one else was around. One alcoholic heard voices coming up a hotel light well. Another man saw a spaceship land and green men getting out". (This experience is worth bearing in mind, when one considers so-called contactees of flying saucers; if Van Dusen is correct, these may not always be hallucinations.) "It takes a while for the patient to figure out that he is having private experiences that are consequently not shared by others".

There was evidence that the "hallucinations" were not entirely subjective and unreal. One of the patients was a woman who had "murdered a rather useless husband". The Virgin Mary had come to her in the hospital and advised her to drive to the southern part of the state and stand trial for murder. The Virgin told her there would be an earthquake on the day she left for the south and another on the day she arrived. In fact, both earthquakes took place on cue.

Van Dusen soon noted that there seemed to be two types of hallucinations, which he termed "higher order" and "lower order". The lower order were stupider than the patient. They would lie, cheat, deceive, and threaten. They might repeat the same word over and over again for days on end; they might tell the patient he was useless and stupid and that they were going to kill him. They behaved, says Van Dusen, like "drunken bums in a bar".

The "higher order", on the other hand, were more intelligent and talented than the patient, and far from attacking him, they respected his freedom. They were "helpers". In one case, Van Dusen was introduced by his patient – a "not very gifted gas fitter" – to a "beautiful lady" who referred to herself as the Emanation of the Feminine Aspect of the Divine and who seemed to have an incredible knowledge of religious symbols: "When I or the patient said something very right, she would come over to us and hand us her panties". One day Van Dusen went home and spent the evening studying Greek myths. The next day he asked the "hallucination" about some of the obscurer parts. "She not only understood the myth, she saw into its human implications better than I did. When asked, she playfully wrote the Greek alphabet all over the place. The patient couldn't even recognize the letters, but he could copy hers for me". As the gas fitter was leaving the room, he turned to Van Dusen and asked him to give him a clue as to what the conversation had been about.

The detail of handing over the panties makes it sound as if, whatever Van Dusen thought, this hallucination was conjured up by the gas fitter – who admitted that he had made "immoral" proposals to the woman and had been rejected. Yet her description of herself as the "Emanation of the Feminine Aspect of the Divine" offers an important clue. She was describing herself as the archetypal symbolic woman, Goethe's "eternal womanly". For a male, the incredible essence of the female is that she is willing to give herself; the handing over of her panties may be regarded as a singularly apt symbol for this essence.

Van Dusen was fascinated to discover that the Swedish mystic Emanuel Swedenborg (1688–1772) had described the lower and higher orders with considerable accuracy. They were, according to Swedenborg, "spirits", and the lower order were earthbound spirits who were driven by malice or boredom. These tended to outnumber the higher spirits by about four to one. Like Kardec (see chapter 26), Swedenborg commented that spirits could only "invade" people with whom they had some affinity – which probably explained why the low spirits outnumbered the high ones. Swedenborg referred to "high spirits" as angels and said that their purpose was to help; low spirits might be regarded as devils, yet their function was often – in spite of themselves – a helpful one, for they pointed out the patient's sins and shortcomings.

Could Swedenborg have been mad? asks Van Dusen, and replies that there is no evidence for it whatever. What is odd is that his high and low spirits are not confined to Christian mental homes; they transcend cultural barriers and can be found just as frequently among Muslim or Hindu lunatics.

Van Dusen reaches the interesting conclusion that "the spiritual world is much as Swedenborg described it, and is the unconscious".

If he is correct, and the "spirit world" lies *inside* us – as another remarkable mystic, Rudolf Steiner, asserted – then we can begin to see why mental patients might experience hallucinations. They might have "opened" themselves to their own depths, to the curious denizens of those regions.

When Philip K. Dick's strange experiences are considered in the light of these comments, it becomes clear that it is impossible to dismiss him as a paranoid schizophrenic. We must at least be willing to leave open the possibility that he was aware – as expressed in the title of Wilson Van Dusen's second book – of "the presence of other worlds".

14

The Dogon and the Ancient Astronauts

Evidence of Visitors from Space?

The theory that the earth has been visited, perhaps even colonized, by beings from outer space has been a part of popular mythology since Stanley Kubrick's cult movie *2001: A Space Odyssey* (written by Arthur C. Clarke), came out in 1968. But it had already been "in the air" for many years – in fact, since 1947, when a businessman named Kenneth Arnold, who was flying his private plane near Mount Rainier, in Washington, reported seeing nine shining disks traveling at an estimated speed of one thousand miles an hour. Soon "UFO" sightings were being reported from all over the world – far too many and too precise to be dismissed as pure fantasy.

In 1958, in a book entitled *The Secret Places of the Lion*, a "contactee" named George Hunt Williamson advanced the theory that visitors from space had arrived on earth 18 million years ago and had since been devoting themselves to helping mankind evolve. It was they who built the Great Pyramid. Perhaps because it is so full of references to the Bible, Williamson's book made little impact.

In 1960 there appeared in France a book entitled *The Morning of the Magicians (Le Matin des Magiciens)* by Louis Pauwels and Jacques Bergier, which became an instant bestseller and which may claim the dubious credit of having initiated the "occult boom" of the 1960s. (Before that the fashion was for political rebellion with a strong Marxist flavor.) Its success was largely due to its suggestion that Hitler may have been involved in black magic, but it also included speculations about the Great Pyramid, the statues of Easter Island, Hans Hoerbiger's theory that the moon is covered with ice (soon to be disproved by the moon landings), and the reality of alchemical transformation. Fiction writers like Arthur Machen, H. P. Lovecraft, and John Buchan are discussed alongside Einstein and Jung. And there is, inevitably, a section on the famous Piri Re'is map (see chapter 49), in which the authors succeed in mixing up the sixteenth-century pirate Piri Re'is with a Turkish naval officer who presented a copy of the map to the Library of Congress in 1959. They conclude the discussion: "Were these copies of still earlier maps? Had they been traced from observations made on board a flying machine or space vessel of some kind? Notes taken by visitors from Beyond"?

These speculations caused excitement because the world was in the grip of flying-saucer mania. Books by people who claimed to be "contactees" – like George Adamski – became best-sellers. And while many "sightings" could be dismissed as hysteria – or as what Jung called "projections" (meaning religious delusions) – a few were too well authenticated to fit that simplistic theory.

In 1967 a Swiss writer named Erich von Däniken eclipsed *The Morning of the Magicians* with a book entitled *Memories of the Future*. Translated into English as *Chariots of the Gods?*, it soon sold more than a million copies. This work was also devoted to the thesis that visitors from space had landed on earth when men were still living in caves and had been responsible for many ancient monuments, such as the Great Pyramid, the Easter Island statues, the Nazca lines drawn in the sand of southern Peru (he suggested they were runways for spaceships), and the step pyramids of South America.

But von Däniken's almost wilful carelessness quickly led to his being soon discredited. Perhaps the most obvious example of this carelessness was his treatment of Easter Island. Von Däniken alleged that the island's gigantic stone statues – some of them twenty feet high – could only have been carved and erected with the aid of sophisticated technology, which would have been far beyond the resources of primitive savages. In fact, the Norwegian explorer Thor Heyerdahl persuaded modern Easter Islanders to carve and erect statues with their own "primitive technology". Von Däniken had also pointed out that Easter Island has no wood for rollers – unaware that only a few centuries ago, the island was covered with woodland and that the Easter Islanders had been responsible for the destruction of their own environment.

Most of von Däniken's other arguments proved equally vulnerable. He had insisted that a stone tablet – known as the Palenque tablet – from Chiapas, Mexico, depicted a "spaceman" about to blast off. Archaeologists who had studied the religion of ancient Mexico demonstrated that what von Däniken mistook for instruments of space technology were traditional Mexican religious symbols. Von Däniken's assertions about the pyramids proved equally fanciful and uninformed. He asked how such monuments could have been constructed without the aid of ropes and managed to overstate the weight of the Great Pyramid by a multiple of five. Experts on the pyramids pointed out that ancient paintings show the Egyptians using ropes and were able to prove that ancient Egyptian engineers were more knowledgeable than von Däniken realized. As to the famous Nazca lines, it required no expert to see that lines drawn in the sand – even if made of small pebbles – would soon be blasted away by any kind of spacecraft coming in to land. In fact, the purpose of the Nazca lines – like that of all ancient fertility ceremonies – seems to have been to control the weather.

Much of von Däniken's literary evidence is equally dubious. He discusses the Assyrian *Epic of Gilgamesh* (getting the date of its discovery wrong) and describes how the sun-god Enkidu bore the hero Gilgamesh upward in his claws "so that his body felt as heavy as lead" – which to von Däniken suggests an ascent in a space rocket. The tower of the goddess Ishtar – visited by the hero – is also, according to von Däniken, a space rocket. A door "that spoke like a living person" is obviously a loudspeaker. And so on. Anyone who takes the trouble to check the *Epic of Gilgamesh* – readily available in a paperback translation – will discover that none of these episodes actually occurs.

But the von Däniken bubble finally burst in 1972 when, in *Gold of the Gods*, the author claimed to have visited a vast underground cave system in Ecuador, with elabourately engineered walls, and examined an ancient library engraved on metal sheets. When his fellow explorer, Juan Moricz, denied that von Däniken had even ventured into the caves, von Däniken admitted that his account was fictional, but argued that his book was not intended to be a scientific treatise; since it was designed for popular consumption, he had allowed himself a certain degree of poetic license. Yet in a biography of von Däniken, Peter Krassa ignores this admission, insisting that the case is still open and that von Däniken may have been telling the truth after all. But Krassa has a skillful technique of making an admission and then quickly taking it back again. He concludes: "Of course his report was mad, and untrue; this story about underground caverns; his description of the golden treasure to be found there was a lie. This was the judgment of many scientists and journalists".

In fact, a British expedition to the caves found them to be natural, with evidence of habitation by primitive man but no signs of von Däniken's ancient library or perfectly engineered walls. A two-hour TV exposé of von Däniken subsequently punctured every one of his major claims.

Having said which, it must be admitted that von Däniken and other "ancient astronaut" theorists have at least one extremely powerful piece of evidence on their side. Members of an African tribe called the Dogon, who live in the Republic of Mali, some 300 miles south of Timbuktu, insist that they possess knowledge that was transmitted to them by "spacemen" from the star Sirius, which is 8.7 light-years away. Dogon mythology insists that the "Dog Star" Sirius (so called because it is in the constellation Canis) has a dark companion that is invisible to the naked eye and that is dense and very heavy. This is correct; Sirius does indeed have a dark companion known as Sirius B.

The existence of Sirius B had been suspected by astronomers since the mid-nineteenth century, and it was first observed in 1862 – although it was not described in detail until the 1920s. Is it possible that some white traveler took the knowledge of Sirius B to Africa sometime since the 1850s? It is possible but unlikely. Two French anthropologists, Marcel Griaule and Germaine Dieterlen, first revealed the "secret of the Dogon" in an obscure paper in 1950; it was entitled "A Sudanese Sirius System" and was published in the *Journal de la Société des Africainistes*.

The two anthropologists had lived among the Dogon since 1931, and in 1946 Griaule was initiated into the religious secrets of the tribe. He was told that fishlike creatures called the Nommo had come to Earth from Sirius to civilize its people. Sirius B, which the Dogon call *po tolo* (naming it after the seed that forms the staple part of their diet, and whose botanical name is *Digitaria*), is made of matter heavier than any on earth and moves in an elliptical orbit, taking fifty years to do so. It was not until 1928 that Sir Arthur Eddington postulated the theory of "white dwarfs" – stars whose atoms have collapsed inward, so that a piece the size of a pea could weigh half a ton. (Sirius B is the size of the earth yet weighs as much as the sun.) Griaule and Dieterlen went to live among the Dogon three years later. Is it likely that some traveler carried a new and complex scientific theory to a remote African tribe in the three years between 1928 and 1931?

An oriental scholar named Robert Temple went to Paris to study the Dogon with Germaine Dieterlen. He soon concluded that the knowledge shown by the Dogon could not be explained away as coincidence or "diffusion" (knowledge passed on through contact with other peoples). The Dogon appeared to have an extraordinarily detailed knowledge of our solar system. They said that the moon was "dry and dead", and they drew Saturn with a ring around it (which, of course, is only visible through a telescope). They knew that the planets revolved around the sun. They knew about the moons of Jupiter (first seen through a telescope by Galileo). They had recorded the movements of Venus in their temples. They knew that the earth rotates and that the number of stars is infinite. And when they drew the elliptical orbit of Sirius, they showed the star off-centre, not in the middle of the orbit – as someone without knowledge of astronomy would naturally conclude.

The Dogon insist that their knowledge was brought to them by the amphibious Nommo from a "star" (presumably they mean a planet) which, like Sirius B, rotates around Sirius and whose weight is only a quarter of Sirius B's. They worshiped the Nommo as gods. They drew diagrams to portray the spinning of the craft in which these creatures landed and were precise about the landing location – the place to the northwest of present Dogon country, where the Dogon originated. They mention that the "ark" in which the Nommo arrived caused a whirling dust storm and that it "skidded". They speak of "a flame that went out as they touched the earth", which implies that they landed in a small space capsule. Dogon mythology also mentions a glowing object in the sky like a star, presumably the mother ship.

Our telescopes have not yet revealed the "planet" of the Nommo, but that is hardly surprising. Sirius B was only discovered because its weight caused perturbations in the orbit of Sirius. The Dog Star is 35.5 times as bright (and hot) as our sun, so any planet capable of supporting life would have to be in the far reaches of its solar system and would almost certainly be invisible to telescopes. Temple surmises that the planet of the Nommo would be hot and steamy and that this probably explains why intelligent life evolved in its seas, which would be cooler. These fish-people would spend much of their time on land but close to the water; they would need a layer of water on their skins to be comfortable, and if their skins dried, it would be as agonizing as severe sunburn. Temple sees them as a kind of dolphin.

But what were such creatures doing in the middle of the desert, near Timbuktu? In fact, the idea is obviously absurd. Temple points out that to the northwest of Mali lies Egypt, and for many reasons, he is inclined to believe that the landing of the Nommo took place there.

Temple also points out that a Babylonian historian named Berossus – a contemporary and apparently an acquaintance of Aristotle (fourth century BC) – claims in his history, of which only fragments survive, that Babylonian civilization was founded by alien amphibians, the chief of whom is called Oannes – the Philistines knew him as Dagon (and the science-fiction writer H. P. Lovecraft borrowed him for his own mythology). The Greek grammarian Apollodorus (about 140 BC) had apparently read more of Berossus, for he criticizes another Greek writer, Abydenus, for failing to mention that Oannes was only one of the "fish people"; he calls these aliens "Annedoti" ("repulsive ones") and says they are "semi-demons" from the sea.

But why should the Dogon pay any particular attention to Sirius, even though it was one of the brightest stars in the sky? After all, it was merely one among thousands of stars. There, at least, the skeptics can produce a convincing answer. Presumably, the Dogon learned from the Egyptians, and for the ancient Egyptians, Sothis (as they called Sirius) was the most important star in the heavens – at least, after 3200 BC, when it began to rise just before the dawn, at the beginning of the Egyptian New Year, and signaled that the Nile was about to rise.

So the Dog Star became the god of rising waters. The goddess Sothis was identified with Isis; and Temple points out that in Egyptian tomb paintings, Isis is usually to be found in a boat with two fellow goddesses, Anukis and Satis. Temple argues convincingly that this indicates that the Egyptians knew Sirius to be a three-star system – the unknown "Sirius C" being the home of the Nommo. An ancient Arabic name for one of the stars in the Sirius constellation (not Sirius itself) is Al Wazn, meaning "weight", and one text says that it is almost too heavy to rise over the horizon.

Temple suggests that the ancients may have looked toward the Canis constellation for Sirius B and mistaken it for Al Wazn. He also suggests that Homer's Sirens – mermaidlike creatures who are all-knowing and who try to lure men away from their everyday responsibilities – are actually "Sirians", amphibious goddesses. He also points out that Jason's boat, the Argo, is associated with the goddess Isis and that it has fifty rowers – fifty being the number of years it takes Sirius B to circle Sirius A. There are many other fish-bodied aliens in Greek mythology, including the Telchines of Rhodes, who were supposed to have come from the sea and to have introduced men to various arts, including metalwork. Significantly, they had dogs' heads.

But if the Egyptians knew about Sirius B and the Nommo, then why do we not have Egyptian texts that tell us about aliens from the Dog Star system? Here the answer is obvious: Marcel Griaule had to be "initiated" by Dogon priests before he was permitted to learn about the visitors from Sirius. If the Egyptians knew about Sirius B, the knowledge was revealed only to initiates. But it would have left its mark in Egyptian mythology – for example, in the boat of Isis.

Temple's book *The Sirius Mystery* (1976) is full of such mythological "evidence", and much of it has been attacked for stretching interpretation too far. Yet what remains when all the arguments have been considered is the curious fact that a remote African tribe has some precise knowledge of an entire star system not visible to the human eye alone and that they attribute this knowledge to aliens from that star system. That single fact suggests that in spite of von Däniken's absurdities, we should remain open-minded about the possibility that alien visitors once landed on our planet.

15

The Mystery of Eilean More

The Island of Disappearing Men

In the empty Atlantic, seventeen miles to the west of the Hebrides, lie the Flannan Islands, known to seafarers as the Seven Hunters. The largest and most northerly of these is called Eilean More – which means in fact "big island". Like the *Mary Celeste*, its name has become synonymous with an apparently insoluble mystery of the sea.

These bleak islands received their name from a seventh-century bishop, St Flannan, who built a small chapel on Eilean More. Hebridean shepherds often ferried their sheep over to the islands to graze on the rich turf; but they themselves would never spend a night there, for the islands are supposed to be haunted by spirits and by "little folk". In the last decades of the nineteenth century, as Britain's sea trade increased, many ships sailing north or south from Clydebank were wrecked on the Flannans, and in 1895 the Northern Lighthouse Board announced that a lighthouse would be built on Eilean More. They expected construction to take two years; but rough seas, and the problems of hoisting stones and girders up a 200-foot cliff, made it impossible to stick to the schedule; Eilean More lighthouse was finally opened in December 1899. For the next year its beam could be seen reflected on the rough seas between Lewis and the Flannans. Then, eleven days before Christmas 1900, the light went out.

The weather was too stormy for the Northern Lighthouse Board steamer to go and investigate, even though the lighthouse had been built with two landing-stages, one to the west and one to the east, so one of them would always be sheltered from the prevailing wind. Joseph Moore, waiting on the seafront at Loch Roag, had a sense of helplessness as he stared westward towards the Flannans. It was inconceivable that all three men on Eilean More – James Ducat, Donald McArthur and Thomas Marshall – could have fallen ill simultaneously, and virtually impossible that the lighthouse itself could have been destroyed by the storms.

On Boxing Day, 1900, the dawn was clear and the sea less rough. The *Hesperus* left harbour soon after daylight; Moore was so anxious that he refused to eat breakfast, pacing the deck and staring out towards the islands; the mystery had tormented him, and now he was too excited to take food.

The swell was still heavy, and the *Hesperus* had to make three approaches before she was able to moor by the eastern jetty. No flags had answered their signals, and there was no sign of life.

Moore was the first to reach the entrance gate. It was closed. He cupped his hands and shouted, then hurried up the steep path. The main door was closed, and no one answered his shouts. Like the *Mary Celeste*, the lighthouse was empty. In the main room the clock had stopped, and the ashes in the fireplace were cold. In the sleeping quarters upstairs – Moore waited until he was joined by two seamen before he ventured upstairs, afraid of what he might find there – the beds were neatly made, and the place was tidy.

James Ducat, the chief keeper, had kept records on a slate. The last entry was for 15 December at 9 a.m., the day the light went out. But this had not been for lack of oil; the wicks were trimmed and the lights all ready to be lit. Everything was in order. So it was clear that the men had completed their basic duties for the day before tragedy struck them; when evening came there had been no one on the island to light the lamp. But the 15th of December had been a calm day . . .

The *Hesperus* returned to Lewis with the men's Christmas presents still on board. Two days later investigators landed on Eilean More, and tried to reconstruct what had happened. At first it looked as if the solution was quite straightforward. On the westward jetty there was evidence of gale damage; a number of ropes were entangled round a crane which was sixty-five feet above sea-level. A tool chest kept in a crevice forty-five feet above this was missing. It looked as if a hundred-foot wave had crashed in from the Atlantic and swept it away, as well as the three men. The fact that the oilskins belonging to Ducat and Marshall were missing seemed to support this theory; they only wore them to visit the jetties. So the investigators had a plausible theory. The two men had feared that the crane was damaged in the storm; they had struggled to the jetty in their oilskins, then been caught by a sudden huge wave . . . But in that case, what had happened to the third man, Donald McArthur, whose oilskins were still in the lighthouse? Had he perhaps rushed out to try to save them and been swept away himself?

All these theories came crashing when someone pointed out that the 15th had been a calm day; the storms had not started until the following day. Then perhaps Ducat had simply entered the wrong date by mistake? That theory also had to be abandoned when, back at Loch Roag, Captain Holman of the *Archer* told them he had passed close to the islands on the night of the 15th, and that the light was already out . . .

Then what if the three men had been on the jetty on a calm morning – which would explain why McArthur was not wearing his oilskins – and one of them had slipped into the water? Perhaps the other two had jumped in after him and been drowned. But then there were ropes and lifebelts on the jetty – why should men leap into the water when they only had to throw in a lifebelt?

Suppose the drowning man was unconscious, and could not grab a lifebelt? In that case only one of his companions would have jumped in after him, leaving the other on the jetty with a rope . . .

Another theory was that one of the three men had gone insane and pushed the others to their deaths, then thrown himself into the sea. It is just possible; but there is not the slightest shred of evidence for it.

The broadcaster Valentine Dyall – the "Man in Black" – suggested the most plausible explanation in his book *Unsolved Mysteries*. In 1947 a Scottish journalist named Iain Campbell visited Eilean More on a calm day, and was standing near the west landing when the sea suddenly gave a heave, and rose seventy feet over the jetty. Then, after about a minute, it subsided back to normal. It could have been some freak of the tides, or possibly an underwater earthquake. Campbell was convinced that anyone on the jetty at that time would have been sucked into the sea. The lighthouse keeper told him that this curious "upheaval" occurs periodically, and that several men had almost been dragged into the sea.

But it is still hard to understand how *three* men could be involved in such an accident. Since McArthur was not wearing his oilskins, we can presume he was in the tower when it happened – *if* it happened. Even if his companions were swept away, would he be stupid enough to rush down to the jetty and fling himself into the sea?

Only one thing is clear: that on that calm December day at the turn of the century, some accident snatched three men off Eilean More, and left not even a shred of a clue to the mystery.

16

Fairies

Are the "Little People" Just a Fairy Tale?

In the summer of 1897 the poet W. B. Yeats went to stay at Coole Park, in Galway, with Lady Augusta Gregory, who was to become his close friend and patroness, and the two of them began collecting fairy stories from the local peasantry. Yeats had already compiled two collections of Irish myths and fairy tales by interviewing peasants in his home county of Sligo. But he now came to recognize that the majority of Irish country folk accepted the existence of fairies, not as some kind of half-believed superstition – like touching wood – but as a concrete fact of life.

Yeats's father was a total skeptic, and Yeats himself had been inclined to toy with a belief in fairies as a kind of reaction to the materialism of the modern world – in short, as a kind of wishful thinking. His collabouration with Lady Gregory made him aware that belief in fairies could hardly be dismissed as wishful thinking. G. K. Chesterton, who met him several years later, was impressed by his insistence on the factual reality of fairies and wrote of Yeats in his autobiography.

He was the real original rationalist who said that the fairies stand to reason. He staggered the materialists by attacking their abstract materialism with a completely concrete mysticism; "Imagination"! he would say with withering contempt; "There wasn't much imagination when Farmer Hogan was dragged out of bed and thrashed like a sack of potatoes – that they did, they had 'um out"; the Irish accent warming with scorn; "they had 'um out and thumped 'um; and that's not the sort of thing that a man wants to imagine".

Chesterton goes on to make a very important point:

It is the fact that it is not abnormal men like artists, but normal men like peasants, who have borne witness a thousand times to such things; it is the farmers who see the fairies. It is the agricultural labourer who calls a spade a spade who also calls a spirit a spirit; it is the woodcutter with no axe to grind . . . who will say he saw a man hang on the gallows, and afterwards hang round it as a ghost.

A few years later Yeats was to encourage the orientalist W. Y. Evans Wentz – best known for his translation of the *Tibetan Book of the Dead* – to study the folklore of the fairies; the result was Wentz's first book, *The Fairy Faith in Celtic Countries* (1911), a bulky and scholarly volume based upon his own extensive field-work. Yeats's friend, the poet AE (George Russell), contributed an anonymous piece to the book (under the title "An Irish Mystic's Testimony") in which he described his own fairy sightings with the factual accuracy and precision of an anthropologist describing primitive tribes: shining beings, opalescent beings, water beings, wood beings, lower elementals:

The first of [the fairies] I saw I remember very clearly . . .: there was first a dazzle of light, and then I saw that this came from the heart of a tall figure with a body apparently shaped out of half-transparent or opalescent air, and throughout the body ran a radiant electrical fire, to which the heart seemed the centre. Around the head of this being and through its waving luminous hair, which was blown all about the body like living strands of gold, there appeared flaming wing-like auras. From the being itself light seemed to stream outwards in every direction; and the effect left on me after the vision was one of extraordinary lightness, joyousness or ecstasy.

Wentz concludes that the factual and scientific evidence for the existence of fairies is overwhelming, that in fact, "there are hundreds of proven cases of phenomena".

But AE's fairies were essentially "visions" and could therefore be classified with unicorns or centaurs. In 1920, nine years after Wentz's book appeared, the British public was intrigued to learn of new scientific evidence that seemed to place belief in "the little people" on an altogether more solid foundation. The front cover of the Christmas issue of the *Strand* magazine announced: "An Epoch-Making Event . . . Described by Conan Doyle". Facing the opening page of the article was a photograph of a teenage girl in a white cotton dress, sitting in a grassy field and holding out her hand to a dancing gnome. Another photograph showed a younger girl gazing mildly into the camera over a group of four cavorting fairies, complete with gossamer wings. The caption under the first photograph stated: "This picture and the even more extraordinary one of fairies on page 465 are the two most astounding photographs ever published. How they were taken is fully described in Sir A. Conan Doyle's article".

It was not a seasonal joke. Doyle and his fellow investigators were convinced that the two photographs virtually proved the existence of "the little people". The resulting controversy was to remain unsettled for the next sixty years.

The girls in the photograph were Elsie Wright and Frances Griffiths, and they lived in the village of Cottingley, in Yorkshire. They had taken the photographs three and a half years earlier, in the summer of 1917, and had consistently claimed, often in the face of extremely skeptical cross-examination, that the photographs were of real fairies.

The village of Cottingley is situated near Bradford, although it has today been swallowed up by suburbs. In 1917 it was surrounded by green English countryside. It was in April of that year that ten-year-old Frances Griffiths had moved to the village with her mother, Annie, from South Africa; her father was fighting in France. She later claimed that she soon realized there were fairies in the fields around her home, especially near the local beck (stream), which ran down a steep-sided dell at the bottom of her garden. She later described the first time she said she had seen a fairy down by the stream.

One evening after school I went down to the beck to a favourite place – the willow overhanging the stream . . . then a willow leaf started shaking violently – just one. I'd seen it happen before – there was no wind, and it was odd that one leaf should shake . . . as I watched, a small man, all dressed in green, stood on the branch with the stem of the leaf in his hand, which he seemed to be shaking at something he was looking at. I daren't move for fear of frightening him. He looked straight at me and disappeared.

But she had decided not to tell anyone for fear of being laughed at.

She explained how, as the summer wore on, she had become increasingly fascinated by the stream and how she would spend hours "fairy-watching" in the dell. She occasionally missed her footing on the slippery bank and landed up to her waist in the water. When she returned home her mother would slap her and make her promise not to go near the stream, but Frances never kept her promise – she could not resist the urge to see the fairies.

One day, when she arrived home soaked yet again, her mother and her Aunt Polly pressed hard for an explanation. What they heard left them both slightly breathless: "I go to see the fairies! That's why – to see the fairies"!

At this point, to the surprise of the two women, Frances's cousin, seventeen-year-old Elsie Wright, came to her defense and insisted that she, too, had seen fairies. No amount of questioning could shake the girls' story. According to Doyle's article, it was this confrontation that convinced the two cousins that they must produce some indisputable evidence to make the grown-ups eat their words.

That is why, on a Saturday afternoon in July 1917, Elsie asked her father, Arthur Wright, if she could borrow his plate camera. He was understandably reluctant, since the camera was new and the plates expensive, but he eventually gave way. The girls hurried off to the stream and were back in half an hour. After tea Arthur was coaxed into developing the plate.

As the plate started to develop, he realized that it was a picture of Frances leaning on a bank that seemed to be scattered with sandwich papers. Then, to his amazement, he saw that the "papers" were tiny human forms with wings growing from their backs; they were apparently four dancing fairies.

The girls' mothers didn't know what to think. Both had recently become interested in Theosophy – the movement founded by Madame Blavatsky, who taught that behind the solid world of everyday reality there was an invisible world peopled with spiritual beings, including nature spirits or fairies. In theory, at any rate, they agreed.

Arthur Wright, on the other hand, was skeptical:

"You've been up to summat".

"No we haven't", Elsie insisted.

He knew that Elsie was a gifted artist and was convinced that the fairies were paper cutouts – although a search of the girls' room and the wastebaskets failed to turn up any snippets of paper left over from manufactured fairies. And in spite of all their protestations, he remained unconvinced. Eventually, the matter was dropped. But in August the girls borrowed the camera again; this time they returned with a picture of Elsie sitting in a field watching a dancing gnome. They explained that they often saw gnomes in the field just above the stream. After this, in the interest of peace and quiet, Arthur Wright refused further loans of his camera. But several prints were made of each plate.

The whole affair might have been forgotten if it had not been for the Theosophical Society. After the war, with its appalling casualties, Spiritualism and Theosophy had made thousands of new converts, and the Bradford Unity Hall, where the Society held its meetings, was always packed.

After a meeting in which fairies had been mentioned, Polly Wright approached the speaker and told him about the photographs. He asked to see them, and copies were soon circulating among the Bradford Theosophists.

Shortly afterward Polly Wright received a letter from Edward L. Gardner, head of the Theosophist Lodge in London; he was excited about the photographs and asked to see the original prints and negatives. Upon receiving the negatives, Gardner had them copied and the copies then retouched. He was quite open about this; in a letter to Doyle he wrote:

> I begged the loan of the actual negatives – and two quarter plates came by post a few days after. One was a fairly clear one, the other much under exposed . . . the immediate upshot was that a positive was taken from each negative, that the originals might be preserved untouched, and then new negatives were prepared and intensified to service as better printing mediums.

He then took the original prints and negatives to a professional photographer, Harold Snelling. Snelling's previous employer had assured Gardner that "what Snelling doesn't know about faked photography isn't worth knowing".

It was Snelling who examined the four-dancing-fairies negative (the better-exposed plate). He reported to Gardner:

> This plate is a single exposure . . . These dancing fairies are not made of paper nor of any fabric; they are not painted on a photographed background – but what gets me most is that all these figures have *moved* during exposure.

Gardner, delighted with this verdict, began showing lantern slides of the photographs at Theosophy meetings around the country. And in the summer of 1920 he was flattered to receive a letter from the creator of Sherlock Holmes.

The sixty-year-old Doyle was not a Theosophist, but in recent years he had become convinced of the truth of Spiritualism. He had already been commissioned by the *Strand* to write an article on fairies, and the news of the Cottingley photographs must have sounded like a gift from the beyond. When he saw the photographs, Doyle was at first skeptical about them. But a meeting with Gardner convinced him that they could be genuine. The next step, obviously, was to try to obtain more of them.

Toward the end of July 1920 Edward Gardner went to visit the Wrights for the first time – Frances was then in Scarborough with her father and so was not present. Elsie's father made no attempt to conceal the fact that he was unhappy about the whole situation. He still felt that the photographs were fakes, and the high esteem in which he held Doyle had declined sharply when he heard that Doyle was now convinced "by our Elsie, and her at the bottom of her class"!

But his wife had a long and thoughtful talk with Gardner, and Elsie later showed him the field, and the spot by the stream where the photographs had been taken. Some people had felt that the stream photograph looked a little too "magical" to be true, with its little toadstools and waterfall; Gardner was delighted to find that it looked exactly as in the photograph. He reported to Doyle that he was convinced that the girls were genuine. Doyle still felt that more photographs were needed to prove the case. So, as Doyle embarked on a steamship south to Australia to lecture on Spiritualism, Gardner went north again; this time armed with new cameras and two dozen carefully numbered plates. (Oddly enough, nobody bothered to note how many plates were eventually used by the girls, so the numbering was wasted.)

On this occasion Gardner also met Frances, then fourteen, who had returned from Scarborough for the summer holidays. He soon formed the conviction that both girls were psychic. Since the weather was rainy and dull – bad visibility for fairly-spotting, according to the girls – he left the cameras behind and returned to London. The rain continued for the next two weeks.

The morning of August 19 was dull and misty, but when it brightened up later, the girls decided to try out the cameras. They returned with two more photographs, which were promptly developed by the unbelieving Arthur Wright. One was of a winged fairy, with stylish-looking bobbed hair, standing placidly on a branch, offering Elsie a tiny bunch of harebells. The other was of a slightly blurred Frances jerking her head back as another winged fairy leapt toward her. It was clear that it was leaping rather than flying because the wings were unblurred by movement. Gardner later had these photographs examined by an expert, who again reported that they showed no signs of fraud.

The last photograph was taken on a drizzly day, 21 August 1920. Later referred to by Frances as a "fairy sunbath", it seems to show two fairies hanging a gossamerlike material over a tuft of grass, to make a shelter or suntrap. Frances said she often saw the little people doing this on dull days, as if to keep themselves warm. Oddly enough, this phenomenon has been reported in various unconnected fairy sightings before and after the Cottingley photographs. The fairies in this last photograph have a semi-transparent quality, which detractors claimed was a sign of double exposure but which believers ascribed to the effect of cold on the fairy constitution.

Since Doyle had written the *Strand* article before he left for Australia, it made no reference to these last three photographs. Even so, when the magazine was published that Christmas – with retouched, much sharper prints – it caused a sensation. The Cottingley fairies became the talk of every London dinner table. But skeptics were outraged at what they regarded as the public's infantile gullibility. Their basic argument was summed up in the January 5 issue of *Truth*: "For the true explanation of these fairy photographs what is wanted is not a knowledge of occult phenomena but a knowledge of children".

One detractor, a doctor by the name of Major Hall-Edwards, even went so far as to say:

I criticize the attitude of those who declared there is something supernatural in the circumstances attending to the taking of these pictures because, as a medical man, I believe that the inculcation of such absurd ideas into the minds of children will result in later life in manifestations of nervous disorder and mental disturbances.

(One wonders how he felt about parents telling their children that Santa Claus was a real person.)

On the other hand, the Cottingley fairies had their supporters in the media. The *South Wales Argus* commented: "The day we kill our Santa Claus with our statistics we shall have plunged a glorious world into deepest darkness". The *City News* said more pragmatically: "It seems at this point that we must either believe in the almost incredible mystery of the fairy or in the almost incredible wonders of faked photographs".

Doyle himself, still in Australia, was delighted by the new pictures. He wrote to Gardner:

> My heart gladdened when out here in far Australia I had your note and the photographs, which are confirmatory of our published results. When our fairies are admitted other psychic phenomena will find a more ready acceptance . . . we have had continued messages at séances for some time that a visible sign was coming through.

In March 1921, three months after the first article, the *Strand* published Doyle's second, illustrated with the new photographs. The reaction was much as before – one major criticism being that the dresses and hair-styles looked too contemporary. Other critics objected that the fairies looked *too* much like typical "storybook" fairies. Defenders suggested that the physical appearance of the fairies might be an ectoplasmic projection based on what the spirits thought was expected of them. And since Elsie and Frances were interested in contemporary fashions, their fairies might well look like a strange hybrid of the two elements.

As the photographs were reproduced in foreign publications, and the debate spread overseas, it became more heated. But the second set of photographs failed to tip the balance. Few people felt that they made any real difference.

One basic problem was that both girls were minors, and as such their testimony was legally inadmissible; their parents were also unable to offer proof since they had never claimed to have seen any "little people". A photograph taken by an adult who could swear under oath that no trickery had been used might have been enough to swing the debate.

A friend of Doyle's the psychic Geoffrey Hodson – who also claimed to have seen fairies – went to Cottingley to see what he could find out. Hodson arrived in Cottingley with his wife and Edward Gardner in August 1921. Gardner stayed for just over a week, during which the weather was generally poor and no fairies were seen. On the day before he left both Hodson and the girls claimed to have sighted many "nature spirits" (as Hodson called them in his notebook) but failed to get any pictures. Hodson and his wife stayed on, and the fairy sightings became more frequent; but he still failed to capture any of them with a camera. In the end he admitted defeat and left.

At this point the debate ran out of steam; there seemed to be too little evidence to prove the case either way. In 1922 Doyle published a book entitled *The Coming of the Fairies*, but although it contained many photographs and reported fairy sightings, it failed to convince the skeptics. For the next forty years or so Elsie and Frances were forgotten.

In 1965 Elsie, then in her sixties, was tracked down in the Midlands by a *Daily Express* reporter, Peter Chambers. He believed that the pictures were faked, and Elsie's comment that people should be left to make up their own minds on the subject only deepened his skepticism. Elsie made the curious remark: "As for the photographs, let's say they are pictures of figments of our imagination, Frances's and mine, and leave it at that".

This might be taken in one of two ways; either she was making an oblique reference to the ectoplasm theory; or she was admitting that the fairies never existed outside her imagination. Now that the subject had been revived, there were many more interviews with both Frances and Elsie. Much was made of a new admission that they had seen *no* fairies during the visit of Geoffrey Hodson; they explained that they were thoroughly bored by the whole subject and felt him to be a fraud, so they amused themselves by pretending to see fairies and were maliciously amused when he said he could see them too. (In his own book on fairies Hodson insists that he *did* see "little people" at Cottingley.)

In 1971 Elsie was asked by the BBC's "Nationwide" program if her father had had a hand in the taking of the photographs. She replied, "I would swear on the Bible that father didn't know what was going on". But when asked if she would swear on the Bible that the photographs were not tricks, she replied after a pause, "I'd rather leave that open if you don't mind . . . but my father had nothing to do with it, I can promise you that". Again she seemed to be close to admitting that there was some kind of fraud.

On the other hand, when Frances was asked by Yorkshire Television if the photographs were fabricated, she replied, "Of course not. You tell us how she could do it – remember she was sixteen and I was ten. Now then, as a child of ten, can you go through life and keep a secret"?

This, it seemed, was the chief argument in favour of the fairy photographs – that it seemed unlikely that Frances and Elsie would and could keep such a secret for so long.

Frances made this comment in 1976; the occasion was a television program about Frances and Elsie, which had been suggested by the Yorkshire psychical investigator Joe Cooper. That is why, on 10 September 1976, the two women turned up at a house on Main Street, Cottingley, opposite the house where the Wright family had lived half a century earlier. In the intervening years, Elsie had lived in India with her husband, Frank Hill, a Scottish engineer; Frances had married a soldier, Frank Way, and had spent much time with him abroad.

Cooper describes Frances as "a bespectacled woman of middle class and height wearing fashionable denim clothes but with a dash of red and black about the scarf and blouse". Elsie, when she arrived, looked a good ten years younger than her seventy-five summers, dressed in fashionable slacks and "mod" gear, including a black derby hat. During the day Cooper became friendly with the two women, even carrying Elsie over a stile. The camera team interviewed locals – who all expressed extreme skepticism about the photographs – and filmed the women down by the stream. Interviewer Austin Mitchell made no secret of believing that the case of the Cottingley fairies had started as a joke, but had gotten out of hand. Cooper was inclined to believe Frances and Elsie. On camera, Elsie and Frances identified the place where they had seen a gnome and flatly denied that they had fabricated the photographs. When interviewed by Mitchell, Cooper stated his view that the girls had seen an "elemental form of fairy life" – that is to say, nature spirits. After all, he noted, W. B. Yeats and thousands of his fellow countrymen were quite certain about the existence of fairies.

In 1977 there was an interesting development. A researcher named Fred Gettings, working on nineteenth-century fairy illustrations, came upon *Princess Mary's Gift Book*, published during the First World War to make money for the Work for Women fund. It contained a poem entitled "A Spell for a Fairy" by Alfred Noyes, illustrated by Claude Shepperson. Two of the fairies in the illustration were virtually identical to the fairies in the first Cottingley photograph, which showed Frances gazing over the heads of five prancing sprites. Their positions had merely been reversed.

In August 1978 *The New Scientist* reported that the magician James Randi ("the Amazing Randi") and the Committee for the Scientific Investigation of Claims of the Paranormal (CSICOP) had put the photographs through an image-enhancement process and found that this revealed strings holding up the fairies. When Cooper told Elsie about the article she merely laughed and pointed out that there was nowhere in the region of the stream where string could have been tied. After a TV play about the fairies had been broadcast in October 1978, Randi expressed indignation that the BBC had failed to state clearly that the photographs had been proved to be fakes.

In 1981 Cooper was writing a book on telepathy and had some correspondence with Frances – who now lived in Ramsgate – about the subject. In September 1981 she asked him to come see her, telling him that there were "some things he should know". When he arrived she was still not ready to specify what these were. But the following day she asked him to drive her to Canterbury; once there, she asked him to wait for her while she went into the cathedral. When she returned they sat in a coffee shop, and she asked him what he thought of the first fairy photograph. He commented that it had been greatly touched up. Then Frances dropped her bombshell:

"From where I was, I could see the hatpins holding up the figures. I've always marveled that anybody ever took it seriously".

"Why are you telling me"? asked the flabbergasted investigator.

"Because Elsie has already told Glenn" [Elsie's son].

"What about the other four? Are they fakes"?

Her answer was, in its way, as astonishing as the original admission: "Three of them. The last one's genuine".

Cooper and Frances now discussed writing a book together and giving Elsie a share of the proceeds; Frances was adamant that Elsie should play no part in writing the book. Cooper went to London to talk to his publisher. Unfortunately, the publisher was not particularly interested in a sixty-year-old story about fairies, especially since it ended so anticlimactically.

By this time, the present writer (CW) had also become involved. I had met Joe Cooper at a weekend conference on parapsychology (at the Swanwick Conference Centre in Derbyshire) in 1980, and he had told me he had written a book on the Cottingley fairies – this, of course, was a year before Frances told him the true story. He sent me the manuscript, and I found it fascinating. I had also come across people – one of them a hardheaded Scottish TV interviewer – who claimed to have seen fairies, and I was simply not willing to rule out the possibility that "nature spirits" might exist. Joe's own research into the paranormal had convinced him that "elementals" could not merely be ruled out as an absurdity.

In fact, I was on my way to Yorkshire to research a poltergeist haunting in Pontefract, and that weekend was something of a turning point in my life, for just before I left the conference centre I met Guy Lyon Playfair, a psychical researcher with whom I had been in correspondence for some time. At this time I accepted the view of most people involved in psychical research – that poltergeists were a strange manifestation of the unconscious mind of a psychologically disturbed teenager. What Playfair suggested left me rather bewildered. He felt that while some poltergeists may be "spontaneous psychokinesis", mind over matter, the majority are genuine spirits who draw their energy from human beings, particularly children on the verge of puberty.

I have described in my book *Poltergeist* how my visit to the Pritchard household in Pontefract soon convinced me that Guy Playfair knew what he was talking about. When Diane Pritchard, who had been the focus of the disturbances (i.e., the person whose energy was "stolen" by the poltergeist), described how she was dragged up the stairs by some unknown force, I suddenly knew beyond all doubt that the poltergeist was not some manifestation of her own unconscious mind. It was a spirit. This meant that as a writer on the paranormal, I had to get off the fence and stop keeping an "open mind" about whether such things as spirits can exist.

It seemed clear to me that the spirits involved in most poltergeist cases are those of the dead – in the Pontefract case, possibly that of a Cluniac monk who had been hanged for rape in the time of Henry VIII. (The gallows had been on the site of the Pritchard house.) But that did not necessarily mean that no other kinds of spirits can exist. The travel writer Laurens Van der Post, for example, had no doubt whatsoever that the nature spirits or gods of the Kalahari bushmen are real and can cause all kinds of problems. In *The Lost World of the Kalahari* he describes how "the spirits of the Slippery Hills" became offended when one of his team killed a warthog on their territory and caused endless mishaps until they received a proper apology. In *Poltergeist* I cited many similar stories. So it was hardly logical for me to deny the existence of nature spirits on the grounds that only a child could believe in them.

But the problem with Joe Cooper's book, even in its original version, was that the story was too slight – it could be told in fifty pages, which seemed to mean that the rest had to be some kind of "padding". And since, at that point, both Frances and Elsie were still insisting that the photographs were genuine, the story had no real conclusion. I tried to find a publisher for the book but was unsuccessful. And at this point Joe said he wanted to rewrite it anyway; and there the matter rested.

It was in the following year that Frances finally "came clean". Oddly enough, Joe was excited that the case had finally reached a definite conclusion. When he told me about Frances's confession, I was less optimistic. If the book ended with an admission of fraud, it would be an anticlimax.

Joe Cooper came to the same conclusion. Late in 1982 an anthology called *The Unexplained*, of which I was a consulting editor, published his article "Cottingley: At Last the Truth", in which he revealed that the fairies in the first four photographs were cutouts stuck to the branches with hatpins. Understandably, this upset both Frances and Elsie. When Frances called Joe's wife on New Year's Day, 1983, and Joe answered the phone, she called him a traitor and hung up. She died in

1986. Elsie died in 1988, maintaining to the end that she did not believe in fairies.

Which seems to be the end of the story . . .

Or is it? Certainly the skeptics are justified in regarding the case as closed. Possibly they are correct. Yet before we make up our minds, there are a few interesting points to be made.

What Frances is asking us to believe is this: She came to England from South Africa in 1917, when she was ten, and went to stay with her sixteen-year-old cousin, Elsie, in Cottingley. Elsie claimed to have had some odd ghostly experiences. For example, she insisted that when she was four she was regularly visited in bed by a woman who wore a tight dress buttoned up to her neck. And when she was six she woke up one night and called for a drink; when no one replied, she went downstairs and found a strange man and woman in the house. She asked where her parents were and was told they had gone out to play cards with the neighbours. Elsie said she wanted to go and find them, and the man opened the front door and let her out. Her parents – who were, in fact, playing cards with the neighbours – were startled to see her and even more startled to hear about the man and woman, for they had left the house empty. But when they went to investigate, the house *was* empty.

Frances had had no "psychic" experiences. But in the spring of 1918 she saw her first gnome. She had gone down to the stream after school and observed a phenomenon she had often observed before: a single willow leaf began to shake on the tree by the stream. Then a small man, all dressed in green, was standing on the branch. Frances watched, breathless, terrified of disturbing him. The little man looked straight at her, then disappeared. After that, she claimed, she often saw little men wearing coats of grayish green and matching caps by the stream. She gradually reached the conclusion that the little men were engaged in some kind of purposeful activity, perhaps associated with helping plants to grow. Later, she began to see fairies, with and without wings. These were smaller than the elves; they had white faces and arms and often seemed to be holding some kind of meeting. Elsie, she insists, never saw the fairies or little men.

It was after falling into the stream yet again that Frances admitted that she went there to see fairies. And it was the total skepticism of the adults that led Elsie to decide to take some fairy photographs. This was not simply a desire to deceive. Elsie believed Frances when she said she saw fairies; her own psychic experiences made it seem quite plausible. She wanted to shake the credulity of the grown-ups. So the photographs were taken with cutouts propped up by hatpins.

When the world suddenly became interested in the fairies, the girls were in a difficult position. The photographs were fakes. Yet – according to the girls – the fairies really existed. If the whole thing had been a hoax, it would have been easier to confess. But it was not a hoax – not totally, anyway. They were in an embarrassing and anomalous position. If they admitted that the photographs were fakes, they would be implying that the whole affair was a deception. And that would be as untrue as continuing to maintain that the photographs were genuine. So they decided to keep silent.

When the whole affair blew up again in 1965, the situation was unchanged. It is true that Elsie, now a hardheaded woman in her sixties, was no longer convinced that Frances had seen fairies; yet she was absolutely certain that *she* had had "psychic" experiences and was therefore prepared to be open-minded. As to Frances, she *had* seen fairies and had nothing to retract. In a letter to Leslie Gardner, the son of Edward Gardner, Elsie remarked that after her interview with Peter Chambers (in 1965), in which she had declared that people must judge for themselves and that the pictures were "figments of our imaginations", Frances had said indignantly, "What did you say that for? You know very well that they were real".

In fact, Frances had always maintained that the fairies were real. In November 1918 she sent the first fairy photograph to a friend in South Africa and scrawled on the back: "Elsie and I are very friendly with the beck Fairies. It's funny I never used to see them in Africa. It must be too hot for them there".

In his original manuscript of the Cottingley book, Joe Cooper had included a chapter entitled "Other Sightings", consisting of accounts of fairies related to him by various witnesses, and it makes clear why he believed Frances. One man, a healer, told how he was sitting with a girl in Gibraltar, eating a sandwich, when it was snatched from him by "a little man about eighteen inches high". An eighty-year-old official of the Theosophical Society insisted that when he was a small boy he was often visited in bed by a green-clad gnome. Another old man described seeing a green-clad gnome, about two feet high, walking along a path in a cornfield. Some young male students told how, when walking in a wood near Bradford, they saw fairies who were "circling and dancing" but who were invisible to the direct gaze; they could only be seen "out of the corner of the eye". An elderly woman showed Cooper a photograph of a gnome seen through a frosty window; she claimed that she had come down one morning, seen the gnome, and rushed upstairs to get her camera. The photograph also shows diminutive white rabbits.

Joe Cooper finally published most of these accounts in his book *Modern Psychic Experiences*, together with many more. A New Zealand medium named Dorothy described how she used to play with a "spirit" girl named Mabel as a child and how she had first seen fairies, who came from under plants. One day she came home to find her father unconscious on the floor – a gastric ulcer had perforated – and the fairies took charge and escorted her to the doctor's house. Joe Cooper's own niece, Jo, who was in her thirties, described how, at the age of sixteen, she had seen three little men crouching on top of a wall.

When I wrote about the Cottingley fairies in *Poltergeist* (before Frances had "confessed"), I also went to some trouble to find accounts of "real" fairies. I described being interviewed on television at the 1978 Edinburgh Festival by a man named Bobbie (whose surname I forgot to note in my journal); in the pub next door he told me casually that he had once seen a gnome standing on the pavement outside a convent gate and that it had "scared the hell out of him".

My friend Marc Alexander, author of many books on the paranormal, told me a story of a friend in New Zealand named Pat Andrew, who claimed to have seen a pixie when he was six. Years later, after seeing a stage hypnotist, Marc and Andrew began experimenting with hypnosis on each other. Marc had no doubt that Andrew was genuinely hypnotized, and one day he decided to try and "regress" him to the age at which he saw the pixie. The result was an amazing one-sided conversation that left Marc in no doubt whatever that, whether Andrew had really seen a pixie or not, he undoubtedly *believed* he had.

One of the most convincing accounts I know of is an encounter with a pixie as recounted by another friend, Lois Bourne, in her book *Witch Among Us*. Lois is a "witch" in the sense that she possesses odd psychic powers, of whose reality I have not the slightest doubt. She is an extremely sensible and down-to-earth woman. And in her book, among many stories that psychical researchers will find credible enough, she tells a story that will obviously cause most readers to doubt her truthfulness or her sanity. While on holiday at a cottage at Crantock, in Cornwall, she met a member of a "wicca" coven and spent an evening at her home. The woman's husband, Rob, asked her if she would like to see a goblin, explaining that one appeared among the rushes of the millstream at Treago Mill, Cuberts Heath, every morning at sunrise; if she wanted to see him, she had to be up early. The next morning Lois and her husband, Wilfred, joined Rob at the mill gate, and they crept up to the stream. Bourne writes:

I have never been able to decide, and still cannot decide, whether I really saw that goblin, or if Rob made me see it . . . Whatever it was, there, sitting on a stone calmly washing his socks, was an elfin creature with a red hat, green coat and trews, one yellow sock on, and one in his tiny hands in the process of being washed. I remember thinking at the time, in my sleepy, befuddled, but practical way, "What an atrocious colour combination". Suddenly he saw us and he disappeared . . . "Now do you believe me"? asked Rob.

I have known Lois for years. I may be gullible and she may be a liar, but I believe her. She is not the type to invent such a silly story. And her husband, Wilfred – who also saw it – is not the type to support a downright lie.

As already mentioned, the poet W.B. Yeats had been convinced of the existence of fairies ever since he and Lady Gregory went door to door collecting information from the local peasants. They recorded these interviews in a 1920 book entitled *Visions and Beliefs*. Evans Wentz concludes his *Fairy Faith in Celtic Countries* by acknowledging: "We seem to have arrived at a point . . . where we can postulate scientifically . . . the existence of such invisible intelligences as gods, genii, daemons, all kinds of true fairies, and disembodied men". (By the latter he means ghosts.) And he goes on to cite the very sound evidence for the existence of the poltergeist. George Russell (AE) and Evans Wentz emphasize that these entities are seen only by "psychics", and Russell believes that such beings are not "individuals" in the human sense: "Theirs is a collective life, so unindividualised and so calm that I might have more varied thoughts in five hours than they would have in five years".

When all of this is taken into account, we may feel that the notion that Frances really saw fairies by the stream in Cottingley no longer seems quite so absurd.

17

Fulcanelli and
the Mysteries of Alchemy

In the autumn of 1926 there appeared in Paris a limited edition of a book called *The Mystery of the Cathedrals – La Mystère des Cathédrales* – whose author was named on the title page simply as "Fulcanelli". It was a book written by a man who claimed to be an alchemist, and was addressed to his fellow-alchemists. Its thesis is that the great Gothic cathedrals are not simply temples of the Christian religion but are also "stone books" whose pages contain the encoded secrets of alchemy. According to Fulcanelli, the word "Gothic" is not derived from the Germanic people known as the Goths but from the word *argot*, meaning slang. *Arts gothiques* – Gothic art – should be spelt *argotiques*: for argot is a language used by those who do not wish their meaning to be understood by outsiders. The rest of the book is an elegant exposition of some of the "stone secrets" of the cathedrals of Notre Dame, Amiens and Bourges.

The preface to the first edition was written by one "Eugene Canseliet", who declares that the author of the book, his "Master", has now disappeared. "Having achieved the pinnacle of knowledge, could he refuse to obey the commands of Destiny"? "Fulcanelli is no more", says Canseliet, and then goes on to thank the artist, Julien Champagne, "to whom my master has entrusted the illustration of his work".

Although printed only in an edition of three hundred copies – or possibly because of this – the reputation of *Mystery of the Cathedrals* continued to grow, so that another edition was called for in 1957. In his new preface Canseliet admits that "Fulcanelli" is a pseudonym under which his master has chosen to conceal his identity, and he quotes a long letter from Fulcanelli to *his* master, congratulating him on finally achieving the "Gift of God" or the "Great Work", the Philosopher's Stone of the alchemists.

When the book was translated into English in 1971 it contained an additional introduction by the translator's husband, Walter Lang – the pseudonym of Edward Campbell – in which he reveals that he has met Canseliet, and learned that Canseliet *had* seen Fulcanelli after his "disappearance" in 1922. That meeting occurred thirty years later, yet according to Canseliet, his master appeared to be thirty years younger than when he had last seen him. Fulcanelli had been eighty in 1924; now he looked a mere fifty. What was stranger still was that Fulcanelli was now dressed as a woman. Canseliet's story was that he had received a summons from Fulcanelli, and journeyed to a château in the mountains. There he was greeted by Fulcanelli in his normal male guise, and assigned an alchemical labouratory to work in. A few days later he strolled downstairs early in the morning and stood in his braces. Across the courtyard he saw a group of three women dressed in the style of the sixteenth century. As they passed him one of them turned, and he recognized Fulcanelli. But later Canseliet recollected that one of the basic symbols of alchemy is the androgyne or hermaphrodite, and that this is sometimes used as a symbol of the "completed work" – the achievement of the philosopher's stone. Was Fulcanelli telling him that he had now achieved the aim of a lifetime?

By the time *Mystery of the Cathedrals* appeared in English, Fulcanelli had achieved a legendary status, rather like that of the Comte de Saint-Germain (see chapter 47). This was largely due to the role he plays in a best-selling work by Louis Pauwels and Jacques Bergier, *The Morning of the Magicians* (1960), which was largely responsible for the "occult revival" of the 1960s. According to Pauwels, his friend Bergier was studying chemistry in 1933 when he confided to his professor his desire to study alchemy – and was instantly and predictably rebuffed. The student protested that one form of alchemy – nuclear energy – should be possible, but the professor assured him that this was also an impossibility. All the same, Bergier continued to study alchemy. From 1934 to 1940 he worked with André Helbronner, the distinguished physicist who died in Buchenwald. And among Helbronner's acquaintance there were many pseudo-alchemists, and at least one genuine alchemist, whose name Bergier never learned. "The man of whom we are speaking disappeared some time ago without leaving any visible traces, to lead a clandestine existence, having severed all connection between himself and the century in which he lived". Bergier can only guess that he may have been the man who, under the pseudonym of Fulcanelli, wrote "two strange and admirable books, *Les Demeures Philosophales* and *La Mystère des Cathédrales* . . ."

Pauwels goes on to tell how, one afternoon in June 1937, Bergier thought he was in the presence of Fulcanelli. At Helbronner's request Bergier met the "alchemist" at the labouratory of the Gas Board in Paris. What the man had to tell him was that Helbronner's researches into nuclear energy were very close to success, and that "the research in which you and your colleagues are engaged is fraught with terrible dangers . . . for the whole human race". Radioactivity, said the alchemist, could poison the atmosphere of the planet, and a few grams of metal could produce enough energy to destroy a whole city. "Alchemists have known it for a very long time". Picking up Soddy's book *The Interpretation of Radium*, he read aloud a paragraph suggesting that earlier civilizations (Atlantis?) had been destroyed by atomic radiation.

But the most interesting part of the account lies in the alchemist's reply to Bergier's question about the nature of his researches.

> I can tell you this much: you are aware that in the official science of today the role of the observer becomes more and more important . . . The secret of alchemy is this: there is a way of manipulating matter and energy so as to produce what modern scientists call a "field of force". This field acts on the observer and puts him in a privileged position *vis-à-vis* the Universe. From this position he has access to the realities which are ordinarily hidden from us by time and space, matter and energy. This is what we call "The Great Work".
>
> "But what about the philosopher's stone? The fabrication of gold"?
>
> "These are only applications, particular cases. The essential thing is not the transmutation of metals, but that of the experimenter himself. It's an ancient secret that a few men rediscover once in a century".

Jacques Sadoul, another modern student of alchemy, makes the same point in his book *Alchemists and Gold*.

> Actually the transmutatory powder was simply *an experiment* carried out at the end of the Master Work, to make certain that the substance manufactured was indeed the Philosopher's Stone . . . Their aim, after having transmuted a metal, was to transmute themselves by swallowing a homoeopathic dose of the Stone twice a year.

When he swallows this dose, the alchemist loses all his hair, nails and teeth; but they grow again, stronger and healthier than before. The adept becomes younger, and no longer needs food although he may still eat for enjoyment.

Most modern readers will be understandably sceptical about all this, and the only full-length book on Canseliet's mysterious Master, *The Fulcanelli Phenomenon* by Kenneth Raynor Johnson (1980), will do little to undermine his scepticism. He tells how in the 1930s a student of the occult named Robert Ambelain became so intrigued by Fulcanelli's books (the second, *The Dwelling Places of Philosophy*, is an expansion of the ideas of the first) that he set out to try to track him down. He called on the publisher, Jean Schemit, to ask permission to quote Fulcanelli's books in a work of his own, *In the Shadow of the Cathedrals*. Schemit told him how, in the early part of 1926, he was visited by a shortish man with a long Gallic moustache. The stranger began talking to Schemit about Gothic architecture, and claimed that it was a kind of code ("argot"), known as the "green language". He went on to argue that slang contained many plays on words and puns that actually indicated a profound philosophical depth: in fact, it was the ancient hermetic language, the "Language of the Birds" – that is to say, of the initiates. He then left. A few weeks later Canseliet appeared in Schemit's office, and left with him the manuscript of *The Mystery of the Cathedrals*. Schemit read it, and recognized the speech patterns of his previous visitor. He decided to publish it. Soon after, Canseliet called again, bringing with him the artist who would illustrate the book, Jean-Julien Champagne. And in Champagne Schemit recognized his previous visitor. Canseliet showed him "extraordinary respect and admiration, addressing him one minute as "Master", the next as "my Master". Canseliet also referred to Champagne as "my Master" in his absence. Schemit consequently reached the conclusion that Fulcanelli was Champagne.

Canseliet always insisted that his friend Champagne was simply an illustrator, but this was flatly contradicted by an article in a popular occult magazine containing a description of an illustration by Champagne; the illustration was full of alchemical symbols, and the author of the article admitted that the description was by Champagne himself. The same author, a man called Jules Boucher, told Ambelain that Champagne possessed a biscuit tin containing gum resin, and that Champagne would often inhale its odours deeply, telling Boucher that it possessed some magical quality that enabled him to gain "intuitive insights into the knowledge he sought". Boucher also said that Champagne could induce "OBE's" – "out-of-the-body experiences" – at will.

Champagne had died in 1932, in his mid-sixties. His former landlady told Ambelain that Canseliet and Champagne had occupied rooms at 59 bis rue de Rochechouart – the attic – and that Canseliet treated Champagne with great respect, addressing him as Master. So it would seem to be a logical conclusion that Champagne *was* Canseliet's "master" – i.e., Fulcanelli.

Boucher – who was also a "pupil" of Champagne – had no doubt that Champagne and Fulcanelli were the same person. When Champagne was correcting the proofs of *The Mystery of the Cathedrals* he became extremely indignant at printing errors, and the proofs of the two books "were redrafted eight times under the watchful eyes of their author". Moreover, said Jules Boucher, Champagne wrote the introductions to the books, which he asked Canseliet to sign.

Canseliet, predictably, denies all this. He claims that Schemit never met Champagne, and insists that he himself wrote the introductions. He tends to be dismissive of Boucher's claims to have known Champagne intimately. But then if Champagne and Canseliet invented Fulcanelli between them, this would be perfectly understandable. Having gone to the trouble of creating a modern myth – not unlike that of Saint-Germain – why should he admit that the whole thing is a straightforward piece of mystification?

Kenneth Raynor Johnson's arguments against the Champagne-Fulcanelli identification are also unconvincing. He points out that Champagne was a well-known practical joker, as well as an alcoholic. As an example of Champagne's sense of humour, he tells how Champagne advised a gullible student that the first step in alchemy was to fill his room with bags of coal. When the student had heaved sack after sack up several flights of stairs, and had scarcely enough room left to lie down on his bed, Champagne told him that the search for the philosopher's stone was a waste of time, and that he had better forget it. This suggests that Champagne's sense of humour was both puerile and cruel. This, Johnson argues, hardly sounds like the author of *The Mystery of the Cathedrals*, to which the obvious answer is: why not? Immersion in magic and "occultism" seems to demand a peculiar temperament; it can be seen in a dozen cases, from Paracelsus and Cornelius Agrippa to Macgregor Mathers and Aleister Crowley, all of whom combined the temperament of a genuine "seeker after truth" with that of a confidence trickster. Contemporary accounts reveal that the "great adept" Saint-Germain was vain, talkative and boastful, and among "adepts" this seems to be the rule rather than the exception.

Does this mean then that alchemy should be regarded as a fantasy or a waste of time? The commonsense answer should obviously be yes. But common sense can easily lead us into error, as when it tells us that the sun revolves round the earth or that matter is solid. Jung's studies of alchemy led him to conclude – like Bergier's mysterious alchemist – that the real purpose of alchemy is to transform the alchemist: in other words, that it is, like yoga or mysticism, a spiritual discipline. The main difference between Jung and Freud was that for Freud the world is divided into sick people and "normal" people, while Jung had always been fascinated by "supernormal" people – saints and men of genius. Jung wanted to find a connection between "depth psychology" and supernormal people, and thought that he might have found it in alchemy, which like certain earlier researchers he was inclined to see as a "mystery religion". But after studying obscure alchemical texts for many years, and attempting to "interpret" them as if they were full of dream symbolism, he reached the somewhat disappointing conclusion that the alchemist "projected" his own basic obsessions into his experiments, much as we might "see" faces in the clouds, so that alchemy became a kind of mirror in which he saw his own hidden depths. In other words, it was a kind of unconscious self-deception.

Yet in his later work on synchronicity (see Chapter 54) Jung had stumbled on some vital clues to this problem. By synchronicity Jung meant "meaningful coincidence as, for example, when we hear a name for the first time, then hear it half a dozen times more over the next twenty-four hours, almost as if "fate" is trying to make sure we learn it by heart. Jung tried hard to find "scientific" explanations for such coincidences, talking about an "acausal connecting principle" and about Heisenberg's uncertainty principle. Critics like Arthur Koestler have suggested that Jung was merely trying to dress up "occult" ideas in acceptable scientific terminology.

But it is generally agreed that the basis of "occultism" is the statement attributed to Hermes Trismegistos (after whom the "hermetic art" is named) "As above, so below", which means the pattern of the greater universe is repeated in the smaller universe of the human soul (microcosm). In *Alchemists and Gold* Jacques Sadoul begins by quoting a translation of the so-called Emerald Tablet of Hermes by Fulcanelli: "As below, so above; and as above, so below. With this knowledge alone you may work miracles".

What we might call the Jungian interpretation of this is as follows. It is self-evident that external events influence our states of mind (or soul). But perhaps the most fundamental tenet of occultism is that the human soul can influence external events, possibly by some process of induction not unlike that employed in an induction coil. The principle of the latter is as follows. When an electric current is passed through a coil of wire it creates a "field" around the wire. And if another coil of wire, with more "circles" of wire, is wound around the first, a far more powerful current is somehow induced in the second coil. A piece of American electrical equipment runs off a current of 120 volts; in England the voltage is twice as high; so if I wish to use an American electric razor in England, or vice versa, I merely have to buy a small transformer which will either "step up" 120 to 240 volts, or "step down" 240 volts to 120. The electrical vibrations in one coil communicate themselves to the other, and induce a stronger – or weaker – current.

The law "As above, so below" may be thus interpreted: the human soul can, under the right circumstances, induce its own "vibrations" in the material world; one result of this process is coincidence – or rather, synchronicity.

It is also true, of course, that the "mind-transformer" can be used for the opposite purpose: to "step down" the vital current to a lower level. This is in fact the problem with most human beings: we use our mind-transformer the wrong way round. More often than not, a vague general sense of "discouragement" or pessimism causes "negative induction" in the environment. We are all familiar with the feeling that this is just "one of those days", and how on such days everything seems to go wrong. Moreover, we all recognize instinctively that this is due to our own negative attitudes; they seem to attract bad luck.

The reverse is the feeling that things are somehow destined to go right, and that in some odd way the optimism induced by this intuition will *induce* "serendipity". In such moments we also have a glimpse of an exciting insight: that if we could learn to create this mood of optimism *at will* we could somehow *make* things go right. Everyone recognizes the other side of the same coin: that pessimistic people who "expect the worst" somehow attract bad luck. Yet the feeling that the right mental attitudes can induce good luck is oddly worrying; it seems to be tempting fate . . .

All this, I would argue, is implied in the Jungian theory of synchro-nicity, and in the "hermetic law", As above, so below. And if this law is also the starting-point of alchemy, then it is obviously a mistake to think of alchemy as a misguided form of chemistry whose aim is the trans-mutation of lead into gold. Sadoul is obviously right; the transmutation is merely a symbol of something else. But if the transmutation is merely another name for mystical insight, a synonym for satori or enlight-enment, then why waste time with retorts and crucibles?

What seems to be implied is that alchemy is *a method*, like yoga or the disciplines of Zen. Ancient alchemists may well have believed that lead can be transmuted into gold by some straightforward chemical process, but their modern counterparts know better. They recognize that, in a basic sense, alchemy is a symbol for the actual process of living. The traditional alchemist begins with the so-called *prima materia* (which some believe to be salt, some mercury, others earth, even water), which must be mixed with "secret fire" and heated in a sealed vessel; this should first of all become black (the "nigredo") then white (the "albedo"). This is mixed with "mercury" (but not necessarily the mercury of the chemist), and then dissolved in acid; after a process known as "the green lion" it finally turns red – the philosopher's stone. For all human beings, the *prima materia* is the world of their everyday experience. Pleasant surprises, enjoyable physical stimuli, flashes of "holiday consciousness" can transmute everyday experience into what J.B. Priestley calls "delight", and that strange feeling that "all is well". When we experience such moments we always find ourselves confronting the same insight: that, as absurd as it sounds, the pleasant experience that triggered the insight *was unnecessary*; we should be able to achieve it *by an act of will*.

The whole chemical process of alchemy may be seen as a parallel to this experience. Canseliet remarks that Fulcanelli would never have attempted "the great work" unless he started with a conviction that it was possible. And this seems to be the initial step in the process we are discussing: the creation of a state of optimism, a pragmatic state of "intentionality". The implication of the classic texts of alchemy is that the alchemist must somehow "support" the chemical process by a psychological process. It is only when he has achieved the right state of mind, of "positive induction", that the transformation can be achieved. And the ultimate aim of the process is not the philosopher's stone but the state of mind in which the philosopher's stone can be manufactured. The aim of the alchemical process is to make the "operator" recognize that he can control his own mental states. The use of sexual symbolism in alchemy may be a hint that the nearest most human beings come to this control is in the mental component of sexual experience.

In a sense, therefore, it is irrelevant whether Fulcanelli really existed or whether he was Jean-Julien Champagne, or even whether Canseliet invented him. The "adepts" themselves recognize this basic principle when they insist upon anonymity. All the classic texts seem to agree that physical transmutation *is* a genuine possibility; yet even this may be regarded as an irrelevant by-product. Sadoul states that this is why no successful alchemist has ever bothered to make large quantities of gold.

In a *Books and Bookmen* review of Timothy Leary's *Flashbacks* (November 1983) John Walsh remarked: "Expanded consciousness, Leary maintains, leads to a radically different, wider and more libertarian system of 'imprinting' by which the human brain gives itself, in a single blinding moment, an image of the whole world within which it moves, and thereafter draws strength and mental sustenance from such a paradigm". This could also be taken as a convenient summary of the fundamental purpose of "alchemy".

18

The Glozel Mystery

Archaeological Riddle or Fraud?

One day in 1869 a band of hunters from the castle of Santillana del Mar, at the foot of the Cantabrian Hills of northern Spain, realized that they had lost a dog. They whistled and searched and eventually heard the animal yelping from a crack in the ground. Cold air blew up from the crack. They made their way down the crack, and their torches revealed a large cave. They rescued the dog and returned to tell their master, Don Marcelino de Sautuola, of their discovery. The Don made his way down the crack, determined that the cave was just a hole in the ground of no particular interest, and decided to seal it up to prevent village boys from playing in it. For the next nine years he forgot about it.

But in 1878 he visited the Paris Exhibition and was fascinated by glass cabinets full of Ice Age tools and engravings. (The last Ice Age ended about 12,000 years ago.) On his return home, Don Marcelino consulted an expert on the correct procedure for searching for Ice Age artifacts, then set out for the cave armed with a spade and a torch.

His early excavations were disappointing; he found nothing. Finally, nearly a year later, he was rewarded by the discovery of a hand axe and some stone arrowheads. He began to dig with renewed vigor. And one day, when his five-year-old daughter, Maria, was in the cave with him, he heard her call out with astonishment. She was in a recess that the Don had ignored because it was too low for him. But the child had seen pictures of charging bulls on the walls. At first the Don was unable to see anything; then, as he moved his candle closer to the wall, he recognized the eye of a bison. A closer examination revealed that the wall was covered with pictures of bison – bulls, cows, and calves – in all sorts of postures. The one he had first seen was lying on its side, in the process of dying. The ceiling and the other walls were covered with even more extraordinary paintings. When he touched them he realized that the pigment was still wet.

Together with his friend Professor Vilanova, Marcelino announced his discovery to the world; visitors – including the king of Spain – flocked to the cave (today known as Altamira). But when he went to a congress of prehistorians in Lisbon, Marcelino was stunned to discover that they regarded his cave paintings as a fraud. Indeed, all the learned men of Europe denounced them. Marcelino had them reproduced in a book; it was ignored. Ancient cavemen could not possibly paint like that, said the experts; it had to be a confidence trick. His chief enemy, a prehistorian named Cartailhac, even refused him admission to a congress in Algiers.

Years later Cartailhac went to look at newly discovered caves at Les Eyzies, in the Vézère Valley, and found them full of paintings like those at Altamira. Too late, he returned to Altamira to apologize for his mistake; the child Maria, now a grown woman, could only take him to see her father's grave.

This story, not untypical of the behavior of "experts", may serve as a prelude to another tale of discovery that began in 1924, when a cow stumbled into a hole in southern France. This happened on a farm owned by the Fradin family, near Glozel, not far from Vichy. The family had turned up a few pottery fragments during the First World War; now, investigating the hole into which the cow had stumbled, they found "a kind of tomb", containing various pots and inscribed tablets. There was an oval paving of bricks, some of which had melted glass on them, and other lumps of glass lay around. A local schoolmistress told the Fradins that they had found a cremation grave and that this explained the melted glass. But another visitor to the site thought it more likely that they had stumbled upon a Roman or medieval glass kiln.

In the following year a Vichy doctor named Morlet, who was also an amateur archaeologist, came to the farm. He had recently found a skeleton in his own garden. When the Fradins told him that they had been trying to persuade the local historical society to defray the cost of their digging, Morlet made the mistake of offering to buy their finds – and any more they might stumble upon – and told them to fence off the site. It was a mistake because it later led to the accusation that the Fradins had devised a hoax for the sake of money. Yet it seems clear that they had made no attempt to profit from their discovery before Morlet came on the scene.

The Fradins and Morlet now began to excavate the site – which became known as "the Field of the Dead" – together. They soon uncovered an astonishing variety of objects. These included bone carvings of animals and pictures of reindeer on stones, as well as marks that seemed to be writing. In fact, they unearthed many inscribed tablets. They also found carved faces – each about an inch high – and a figure of a human being standing on an animal. One French writer, Robert Charroux, whose books on ancient mysteries have been credited with inspiring Erich von Däniken (see chapter 8), declared confidently in 1969: "Little is known about the Glozel civilization, except that it must have existed before the Flood, the great cataclysm which blocked the caves at Lascaux and swallowed up the necropolis or religious centre at Glozel, all the inhabitants having died in the disaster". He estimated that Glozel flourished about 15,000 years ago, toward the end of the last great ice age.

This was the period of the Magdalenian culture, to which the paintings of Altamira and Lascaux (discovered in 1940) belong. Because the hunters and fishers of this period were surrounded by an abundance of food, a population explosion occurred, and large numbers of people began to live in lakeside dwellings. If, as Charroux believes, Glozel belongs to this period, then the tablets with writing on them certainly support his thesis that civilization is far older than we believe – which in turn provides an argument for the "ancient astronaut" theory discussed in chapter 8.

The Glozel pottery makes this thesis unlikely, however, for the earliest known pottery dates from many thousands of years later – 9,000 years ago in Japan and much later in Europe. Some of the Glozel pottery has owl-like faces on it, like French Bronze Age pottery (from around 2000 BC). On the other hand, Morlet dated certain polished axe heads to the Neolithic (New Stone Age) period, after 9000 BC. If he was correct, then writing was not invented in the Middle East (Sumer) around 3500 BC but in France five thousand years earlier.

One noted French authority on the subject was Professor Salomon Reinach, the author of a best-selling book on the history of religion entitled *Orpheus*. His first reaction to the Glozel finds was that they might be forgeries. But when he went to Glozel he became convinced that they were in fact genuine. The skeptics were later to point out that Glozel seemed to support some of Reinach's pet theories, such as that reindeer lived on in France much later than archaeologists believed, and that France was the cradle of civilization. In any event, he announced his conviction that the finds were genuine, and the result was a great deal of publicity, which made Glozel a tourist attraction.

Other archaeologists reacted by declaring their conviction that Glozel was a fraud and that the Fradins were busily manufacturing "ancient" artifacts and burying them. When roughly built tombs were discovered, the anti-Glozelians pointed out that no earth had found its way between the cracks in thousands of years and that this seemed unlikely. The curator of the museum at Villeneuve-sur-Lot announced that he had taken shelter in a barn in Glozel in September 1927 and had seen some half-finished artifacts and some unbaked clay tablets. If true, this evidence was damning. On the other hand, as the Glozelians pointed out, the curator of a rival museum might have his own reasons for raising doubts about Glozel.

A commission sent to Glozel by the International Anthropological Congress of 1927 came up with an unfavourable report, declaring that the finds were "of no great age". Police now descended on Glozel and seized various artifacts, which were sent off to the police labouratory in Paris. Reinach countered by getting a Swedish policeman named Soderman to have the bone objects tested in a Stockholm labouratory. The lab reported that the bone had a lower organic content than modern bone. The Paris police report, on the other hand, declared that the artifacts seemed to be modern and that one Neolithic axe head looked as if it had been worked with a file. But the Glozelians declined to be convinced. When accused of fraud, Emile Fradin sued and won his case – although he was awarded only one franc.

The controversy dragged on, but – as in the case of Altamira – skepticism prevailed, and it became generally accepted that the Glozel finds were fraudulent. And when, in 1953, the famous "Piltdown skull" was shown to be a hoax (see chapter 35), it became the fashion to classify Glozel and Piltdown together. Glozel had also been hailed as a kind of missing link – in this case, the missing link between Old Stone Age hunters and Neolithic farmers – a gap archaeologists referred to as "the ancient hiatus". Old Stone Age hunters were supposed to have followed the retreating reindeer north and the New Stone Age farmers to have come in from elsewhere, possibly Asia. Reinach was convinced – rightly, as it turned out – that this never happened and that the New Stone Age farmers were the descendants of the Old Stone Age hunters. So Glozel filled the hiatus. Eventually, the hiatus dissolved, like the missing link. And Glozel became not merely suspect but irrelevant.

Then, in 1974, Emile Fradin – who had been seventeen at the time of the first finds – announced that scientific examination of Glozel artifacts in Denmark had proved their authenticity. The technique used was called *thermoluminescence*. When pottery is fired, it gives off trapped electrons that originate in radioactive traces in the clay. Then the pot gradually reaccumulates trapped electrons from radioactivity. If the pot is heated to between 300 and 500°C, it gives off a glow, which results from the release of trapped electrons. The greater the glow, the older the pot. Samples of Glozel pottery had been given to Dr. Hugh McKerrel of the National Museum of Antiquities of Scotland, and Dr Vagn Mejdahl of the Danish Atomic Energy Commission. They measured the thermoluminescence of the Glozel pottery and concluded that it had been fired about the time of Christ, some of it possibly eight hundred years earlier.

This, of course, contradicted Reinach's thesis that the pottery was Neolithic. But it also contradicted the notion that the pottery finds at Glozel had been fired in a kiln on the farm. Some of the tablets with writing were also dated to the same period.

Archaeologists were outraged and accused the physicists of bungling. The BBC "Chronicle" program promptly invited a team of experts to go and have another look at Glozel. Their conclusion was that the new evidence was still at variance with the facts. If the Glozel pottery dated from between 2,000 and 2,800 years ago, then the later examples should have been like other pottery of the period when France (Gaul) was occupied by the Romans. It wasn't. It was *sui generis* – of its own unique type.

And so the mystery remains. Is Glozel another Piltdown hoax? That is a tempting conclusion, but if we accept it, we have to ignore some facts to the contrary. Charles Dawson, the man who found the Piltdown skull, was an amateur archaeologist, so he may have had a motive for the forgery (although it is still not clear what this was). But when Emile Fradin and his grandfather found the first "tomb" (or glass kiln), they had no reason for deception. And if it is true that earlier finds had turned up during the First World War, then this point is underlined. They made no attempt to cash in on the find, and it was not until a year later that Dr. Morlet arrived on the scene and the Fradins finally began to make a profit from their finds.

Did this tempt them to begin faking artifacts? That is certainly possible. But would an uneducated French farmer have the kind of knowledge to fake pottery, axe heads, bone figurines, and engraved clay tablets? Besides, one of the earliest finds was a brick with "writing" on it. If this was genuine, then the later finds may have been genuine too. And the conclusion would have to be that, at the time of Socrates, Glozel housed a small and flourishing community with its own special culture.

Reinach was undoubtedly wrong. Glozel does not prove that writing originated in France in the New Stone Age. But the (admittedly confusing) evidence seems to indicate that the experts may also be wrong and that – like Don Marcelino – the Fradins may one day be due for a belated apology.

19

The Grey Man of Ben MacDhui

At the 27th Annual General Meeting of the Cairngorm Club in Aberdeen, in December 1925, the eminent mountaineer Professor Norman Collie made a startling disclosure. He told how in 1890 he was climbing alone on Ben MacDhui, 4,000 feet above sea-level, when he had a terrifying experience. As he was returning from the cairn on the plateau there was a heavy mist, and Collie heard crunching noises behind him, "as if someone was walking after me, but taking steps three or four times the length of my own". He told himself it was nonsense, but as he walked on, and the footsteps continued to sound behind him, "I was seized with terror and took to my heels, staggering blindly among the boulders for four or five miles down to Rothie-murchus Forest".

In fact Collie had told the story twenty-three years earlier, to friends in New Zealand, and the result was a report in a New Zealand news-paper headlined: "A Professor's Panic". As a result of this story, another Scottish mountaineer, Dr A.M. Kellas – who was to die during the Mount Everest Reconnaissance expedition of 1921–2 – wrote to Collie telling him of his own curious experience on Ben MacDhui. Kellas and his brother Henry had been chipping the rock for crystals late one afternoon when they saw a giant figure coming down towards them from the cairn. It passed out of sight briefly in a dip, and as the two men fled down the mountainside again in mist both of them were convinced that they were being followed by the "giant".

This account makes it sound as if some form of "Yeti", or Abomin-able Snowman, lives on the slopes of Ben MacDhui. But accounts by other climbers make it clear that the explanation may not be as simple as this. Peter Densham, who was in charge of aeroplane rescue work in the Cairngorms during the Second World War, described in an interview with a journalist how in May 1945 he had left the village of Aviemore and climbed to the cairn on the summit. Suddenly, as he was looking across at Ben Nevis, the mist closed in. He sat there eating chocolate, conscious of strange noises which he attributed to the expansion and contraction of the rocks, when he had a strong feeling that there was someone near him. Then he felt something cold on the back of his neck, and a sense of pressure. He stood up, and heard crunching noises from the direction of the cairn. He went towards the cairn to investigate, "not in the least frightened". Then suddenly he experienced a feeling of apprehension, and found himself running towards Lurcher's Crag, with its sheer drop. "I tried to stop myself and found this was extremely difficult to do. It was as if someone was pushing me. I managed to deflect my course, but with a great deal of difficulty . . ." He ran most of the way back down the mountain.

On another occasion Densham was on the mountain with his friend Richard Frere, searching for an aeroplane that was reported to have crashed. They were sitting close to the cairn when Densham was surprised to hear Frere apparently talking to himself on the other side of the cairn. Then he realized that Frere was talking to someone else. "I went round and found myself joining in the conversation. It was a strange experience which seemed to have a psychic aspect. We talked to someone invisible for some time, and it seemed we had carried on this conversation for some little time when we suddenly realized that there was no one there but ourselves. Afterwards, neither of us, strangely, could recall the purport of this extraordinary conversation". What seems even stranger is that when Frere himself was tracked down by Affleck Gray, the author of a book called *The Big Grey Man of Ben MacDhui*, he had no recollection of the episode described by Densham. But he had had his own strange experiences on the mountain, and described it to Gray as "the most mysterious mountain I have ever been on". He told Gray of a day when he had climbed to the high pass of Lairig Ghru, above Ben MacDhui, and sat gazing down on the cliffs of Lurcher's Crag with its cascade of water. Then he found himself slipping into a "weird and disagreeable" train of thought, so he stood up and walked. But the gloom turned to a sense of deep depression and apathy. Then suddenly he became certain that he was not alone. "Very close to me, permeating the air which moved so softly in the summer's wind, there was a Presence, utterly abstract but intensely real".

Then Frere noticed something else. "The silence of the mountain was violated by an intensely high singing note, a sound which was just within the aural capacity, which never rose or fell . . . The sound, it seemed, was coming from the very soil of the mountains". This sound continued until he was below Lurcher's Crag, when the music became so faint that he was not sure whether it was there at all. But the "abstract Presence" seemed to cling to him "with some sort of desperate eagerness as if it passionately desired to leave the mountain which it haunted . . ." Then there was a momentary flash of terror, and it was gone.

The experience of the strange, sustained note is not as unusual as Frere apparently thought. In her autobiography *The Infinite Hive* the eminent psychical investigator Rosalind Heywood calls it "the Singing". She describes it as "a kind of continuous vibrant inner *quasi*-sound, to which the nearest analogy is the noise induced by pressing a seashell against the ear, or perhaps the hum of a distant dynamo". Rosalind Heywood could hear "the Singing" fairly constantly – although very faintly – if she switched her full attention to it. She says that "it is far more evident in some places than in others; particularly so in a quiet wood, for instance, or on a moor or a mountain . . ." She notes that she also hears it in churches and college libraries, "places where thought or devotion have been intense for years". She finds that "mountain Singing conveys a different "atmosphere" from church Singing, as an oboe conveys a different "atmosphere" from a trumpet". And she says that she has met four other people who have heard it; in one case, she mentioned it to a young engineer, convinced that he was a thorough pragmatist; to her surprise, he replied, "Oh yes, I hear that too, in places where there have just been strong emotions". So to some extent the "Singing" seems to be a kind of "recording": Rosalind Heywood says that she can also "feel" it when she goes into a room where intense thought has been going on. Yet it cannot be wholly due to human "vibrations", since she mentions that the Hampstead tube station – the deepest in London – is the only place where she has not heard it. "The silence was dead".

If "the Singing" can be heard in places where intense thought or worship has taken place, this verifies that it could be regarded as some kind of "recording". In the 1840s an American professor of anatomy named Joseph Rodes Buchanan came to the interesting conclusion that every object has its own history somehow "imprinted" on it, and that "psychics" can sense this history by holding it in their hands; he called this faculty "psychometry". He observed that handwritten letters seem to be particularly good "recorders" of the writer's state of mind, particularly if the writer was feeling some powerful emotion at the time. In the early twentieth century the scientist and psychical researcher Sir Oliver Lodge advanced the theory that "ghosts" may be "recordings" – that the powerful emotions associated with some tragedy may be imprinted on the walls of the room in which it has taken place, so that a "sensitive" person who walked into the room would have a strange feeling of misery and oppression, or perhaps even see the tragedy re-enacted. A Cambridge don named Tom Lethbridge suggested a very similar "tape recording" theory half a century later. Lethbridge suggested that these "recordings" are imprinted on some kind of electrical field, and he believed that mountains, deserts and woodlands each have their own special type of "field". (He seemed to feel that the field of water is the best "recorder", so that ghosts are often associated with damp places).

It seems conceivable, then, that when Rosalind Heywood heard "the Singing" she was simply picking up some kind of electrical field – a field which, on account of its properties, we might christen "the psychic field". Why Richard Frere should suddenly have become aware of this field on the slopes of Ben MacDhui must remain an open question. But at least it seems to offer some kind of confirmation that his feeling of menace and depression was not merely imagination.

The episode in which Frere and Densham held a conversation with some invisible entity seems even stranger; presumably they were responding to some "presence" on a subconscious level, almost as if dreaming. This could also explain why Frere could not even remember the episode later.

Frere also told Affleck Gray a curious story about a friend – whose identity he was not at liberty to disclose – who decided to spend the night on Ben MacDhui to win a bet. He set up his tent by the summit cairn on a January night. (This is not a man-made cairn, but a natural formation eroded by the weather.) He also began to experience the familiar sense of unreality, and "the morbidly analytical directioning of thought". Frere explained: "He did not feel in any way mad: the terror which possessed him concerned the imminent impact of knowledge which he knew would always set him aside from his fellows. It was as if he was the unwilling recipient of a vast range of new revolutionary thought impulses built up in some all-powerful mind. And the mind was neither human nor anti-human; it just had nothing to do with him at all".

He fell asleep and woke up "to a fear of a more terrifying nature". Moonlight fell through the crack of the flysheet of his tent, and as he stared at it he saw a brown blur, and "knew that something lay between himself and the moon". He lay there in frozen immobility until the shadow went away. He now pulled aside the flysheet of the tent. "The night was brilliant. About twenty yards away a great brown creature was swaggering down the hill. He used the word "swaggering" because the creature had an air of insolent strength about it". His impression was that the creature was about twenty feet high, and was covered with shortish brown hair. It was too erect to be a huge ape; it had a tapering waist and very broad shoulders. Affleck Gray's book contains a photograph of footprints in the snow taken on Ben MacDhui, and they look oddly like the famous photograph of the footprints of the "Abominable Snowman" discovered on the Menlung glacier on Everest by Eric Shipton in 1951.

Frere was inclined to wonder whether the brown-haired creature was real, or whether perhaps it was somehow created by his friend's imagination in that oddly "unreal" state of mind.

In her book *The Secret of Spey* the writer Wendy Wood describes her own experience on Ben MacDhui. She had reached the entrance to the pass of Lairig Ghru on a snowy day, and was preparing to return when she heard a voice "of gigantic resonance" close behind her. "It seemed to speak with the harsh consonants and full vowels of the Gaelic". She wondered if someone was lying injured in the snow, and tramped around in circles until she was convinced that she was alone. Now feeling afraid, she began to hurry back, and as she descended the mountain, thought she could hear footsteps following her. "She had a strange feeling that something walked immediately behind her". At first she thought it might be echoes of her own footsteps, until she realized that the crunching noises did not exactly correspond with her steps. She asks in her book whether perhaps the strange happenings on Ben MacDhui might be "the concretion of the imaginings of the race, clinging to a particular place, discernible only to those whose racial sensitiveness is open to receive the primal impressions and fears of a bygone day". In other words, she is suggesting that the "ghost" of Ben MacDhui is a "recording".

This seems to be confirmed, to some extent, by an experience recounted by the novelist Joan Grant in her autobiography *Time Out of Mind*. Her book reveals her to be highly psychic. She and her husband were not even on Ben MacDhui but down below near Aviemore; Gray suggests they were on the Lairig Ghru path near Coylum Bridge. For no apparent reason, she was suddenly overwhelmed with fear. "Something – utterly malign, four legged, and yet obscenely human, invisible and yet solid enough for me to hear the pounding of its hooves, was trying to reach me. If it did I should die for I was far too frightened to know how to defend myself". She fled in terror. "I had run about half a mile when I burst through an invisible barrier behind which I knew I was safe. I knew I was safe now, though a second before I had been in mortal danger; knew it as certainly as though I were a torero who has jumped the barrier in front of a charging bull".

What seems to be emerging from most of these stories about Ben MacDhui is that the chief manifestation is a sudden feeling of depression followed by panic. Joan Grant's account underlines another important point. Tom Lethbridge, who has already been quoted, had observed repeatedly that these sudden unpleasant sensations of fear or "nastiness" seem to have a precisely defined area, so that it is possible to step in or out of them in one single stride. He describes for example how one day he and his wife Mina went to Ladram beach in Devon to gather seaweed for the garden. At a point on the beach where a small stream flowed from the cliff both experienced an odd feeling of gloom. "I passed into a kind of blanket, or fog, of depression, and, I think, of fear". Mina Lethbridge went off to gather seaweed at the other end of the beach but soon hurried back. "I can't stand this place any longer. There's something frightful here". The following week they returned, on another dull, grey day, and were again greeted by the same feeling of depression – Tom compared it to a bad smell. It was at its worst around the stream, making him feel almost giddy. Mina went to the cliff-top to make a sketch, and had a sudden feeling that she was being urged to jump. Later they verified that someone had committed suicide from this precise spot.

Tom noted that it was possible to step in and out of the "depression" – and he noticed it once again when the old lady next door died under strange circumstances after an attempt to practise black magic. An "unpleasant" feeling hung around her house, but it was possible to step in and out of it, as if it was some kind of invisible barrier, like Joan Grant's bullring barrier.

Gray recounts many stories that seem to support Lethbridge's "tape recording" theory. The Scots poet James Hogg, known as the Ettrick Shepherd (because he was a shepherd by profession), once saw a herd of Highland cattle on the far side of the stream, and since they had no right to be there he sent a shepherd to drive them off the land, together with two more farmhands armed with cudgels. But they found no sign of a herd, or even of hoofmarks. No one had seen a herd of cattle in the district that day. It had been some kind of "mirage", or perhaps a "recording" of something long past.

Gray also quotes *The Mountain Vision* by the mountaineer Frank S. Smythe. Smythe describes how, crossing the hills from Morvich to Loch Duich, on a bright sunny day, with a wonderful panorama of cloud-dappled hills and the distant sea, he entered a grassy, sun-warmed defile and "became instantly aware of an aura of evil" in the place. "It was as if something terrible had once happened there, and time had failed to dissipate the atmosphere created by it".

On impulse, Smythe decided to eat lunch there. As he smoked his pipe the atmosphere seemed to become increasingly unpleasant. Then, as he strove to be receptive to the strange influence, he seemed to witness a massacre: a score or so of ragged people were straggling wearily through the defile when concealed men rushed down on them with spears and axes, and killed them all. As Smythe hurried on, he seemed to hear screams behind him. He was later able to confirm that a massacre of Highlanders by British troops *had* taken place on the road, but he remained convinced that this is not what he had seen. "The weapons I saw, or seemed to see, were those of an earlier date".

Yet the many strange accounts of invisible presences on Ben MacDhui seems to throw doubt on the notion that the "big grey man" is nothing more than a "recording". George Duncan, an Aberdeen lawyer and a mountaineer, was totally convinced he had seen the devil on the slopes of the mountain. He and a fellow-climber, James A. Parker, had descended from Devil's Point, and were driving in a dog cart along the Derry Road. Duncan said: "All at once, I got the shock of my life by seeing before me a tall figure in a black robe – the conventional figure of the Devil himself, waving his arms, clad in long depending sleeves, coming towards me". He seemed to see the figure surrounded by smoke. In a few moments it passed from view as the cart went round a corner. James A. Parker verified the story. "It was only at dinner that evening he told me that when we were about a mile below Derry Lodge he had looked up to the hillside on his right and seen the Devil about a quarter of a mile away waving his arms to him".

Perhaps the oddest and in some ways the most interesting explanation that Gray encountered was given by Captan Sir Hugh Rankin, Bart, and his wife. Rankin was a Mahayana Buddhist, and his wife was a Zen Buddhist. He and Lady Rankin were cycling from Rothiemurchus to Mar via the Lairig Ghru pass, and although it was July it was bitterly cold in the pass. At the Pools o' Dee they suddenly felt "the Presence" behind them; they turned and saw a big, olive-complexioned man dressed in a long robe and sandals, with long flowing hair. "We were not in the least afraid. Being Buddhists we at once knew who it was. We at once knelt and made obeisance". They had instantly recognized the stranger as a Bodhisattva, "one of the five 'Perfected Men' who control the destinies of this world, and meet once a year in a cave in the

Himalayas". According to Sir Hugh, the Presence addressed them in a language he thought was Sanskrit, and he replied respectfully in Urdu. "All the time the Bodhisattva was with us [he gave the time as about ten minutes] a heavenly host of musicians was playing high up in the sky . . . Immediately the Bodhisattva left us the music ceased and we never heard it again". It sounds as if they had heard some version of "the Singing". But his comment that the Presence spoke in Sanskrit raises the question of whether Wendy Wood had not mistaken Sanskrit for Gaelic when she heard it on the mountain.

Shortly before his death, F.W. Holiday, author of a classic book on the Loch Ness monster (see Chapter 18), advanced the startling theory that the Grey Man, like the Loch Ness monster and the Surrey puma, and possibly the Abominable Snowman of the Himalayas, is a member of "the phantom menagerie", creatures who belong to some other world or dimension. In *The Goblin Universe* (chapter 6) he cites various stories about the *Fear Liath More* (the Celtic name for the Grey Man), and goes on:

> Pan, the goat-footed god, is not so funny when you encounter him . . . The chief symptom of being in the presence of Pan is panic, which the Oxford dictionary defines as "unreasoning and excessive terror, from Greek *panicos*, of god Pan, reputed to cause panic . . ." The phenomenon is certainly not localised to the Cairngorms. Hamish Corrie, when he was nearing the summit of Sgurr Dearg on Skye, turned back when he was overcome by "an unaccountable panic".

The late John Buchan reported the same effect in the Bavarian Alps. He describes how in 1910 he was returning through a pinewood on a sunny morning with a local forester when panic struck them out of the blue. Both of them fled without speaking until they collapsed from exhaustion on the valley highway below. Buchan comments that a friend of his "ran for dear life" when climbing in Jotunheimen in Norway. The Pan effect may be worldwide.

Holiday connects "the phantom menagerie" with Unidentified Flying Objects, and cites the authority on UFOs, John Keel, who began by assuming that UFOs are some kind of unknown aircraft, perhaps from other planets, and ended by accepting that they come from "another dimension", and that they seem to have a distinctly supernatural element. In one of his books, *The Mothman Prophecies*, Keel speaks of a gigantic winged figure sighted again and again in West Virginia, and describes his own feeling of "panic" on a road close to one of the sightings. Like Lethbridge, Keel found that the area of "panic" seemed to be sharply defined, so that he could walk in and out of it with one stride. And the area of sightings of "Mothman" also has many sightings of UFO phenomena.

Oddly enough, Affleck Gray is willing to consider the "space visitors" theory as an explanation of the Ben MacDhui phenomena. He points out that in 1954 an ex-taxi driver named George King inaugurated the Aetherius Society in Caxton Hall, London. King claimed that he had met the Master Jesus on Holdstone Down, North Devon, and been made aware that he had been chosen as the primary mental channel of certain Space Intelligences. He was told to travel the world, his task being to serve as the channel for "charging" eighteen mountains with cosmic energy. One of these mountains was Creag an Leth-Choin, three miles north-west of Ben MacDhui, and King asserts that there is a huge dome-shaped auditorium, a retreat of the Great White Brotherhood, in the bowels of Ben MacDhui. Another group of "seekers", the Active Truth Academy in Edinburgh, also believe that Ben MacDhui "has become the earth-fall for space beings". But it is clear from Gray's chapter on Space Beings that he regards this explanation with skepticism.

If we wish for a "scientific" explanation of the Ben MacDhui phenomena, then the likeliest seems to be that the answer lies in Ben MacDhui itself: that the "panic" is caused by some natural phenomenon, a kind of "earth force" which may be connected with the earth's magnetic field. There are areas of the earth's surface where birds lose their way because the lines of earth magnetism somehow cancel one another out, forming a magnetic vortex. "Ley-hunters" also believe that so-called "ley lines" – which connect sacred sites such as churches, barrows and standing stones – are basically lines of magnetic force. Many are also convinced that places in which this force is exceptionally powerful are likely to be connected with "supernatural" occurrences – in fact, that such places "record" human emotions, producing the effects that are described as "hauntings". This explanation would account for Frank Smythe's experience of the "haunted" valley where the massacre had occurred.

The non-scientific explanation may be sought in the belief of most primitive peoples that the earth is alive, that certain places are holy, and that such places are inhabited by spirits. The Western mind is inclined to dismiss such beliefs as superstition; but many travellers who have been in close contact with them are inclined to be more open-minded. In

The Lost World of the Kalahari Laurens Van der Post tells how, when he was seeking the vanished Bushmen of South Africa, his guide Samutchoso took him to a place called the Slippery Hills. The guide insisted that there must be no hunting as they approached the hills, or the gods would be angry. Van de Post forgot to tell his advance party, and they shot a warthog. From then on they ran into an endless stream of bad luck. When Samutchoso tried to pray Van der Post saw that he was pulled over backward by some unknown force. All their technical equipment began to malfunction. Then Samutchoso "consulted" the spirits and began to speak to invisible presences. He told Van der Post that they *were* angry, and would have killed him if he had tried to pray again. Van der Post suggested that they should all write a message of apology, and that this should be buried in a bottle at the foot of a sacred rock. Apparently this worked; the spirits were propitiated, and suddenly the equipment ceased to malfunction. Through the guide, the "spirits" told Van der Post that he would find bad news waiting for him when he reached the next place on his route. In fact his assistant found a message saying that his father had died and he had to return home immediately. After all this, Van der Post had no doubt of the real existence of the "earth spirits" worshipped by primitive people.

F.W.Holiday's view was that the explanation of such phenomena as the "Grey Man" lay somewhere between these two sets of explanations: the scientific and the "supernatural". But he believed that the Western mind will be capable of grasping the answer only when it has broadened its conception of science.

20

Kaspar Hauser

The Boy from Nowhere

The case of Kaspar Hauser is perhaps the greatest of nineteenth-century historical mysteries. But it is rather more than that. The unfortunate youth was the subject of a cruel experiment in what would now be called "sensory deprivation", and the results of this experiment were in some ways more interesting than the admittedly fascinating enigma of Kaspar's identity.

On Whit Monday, 26 May 1828, the Unschlitt Square in Nuremberg was almost deserted, most people being in the surrounding countryside enjoying the *Ausflug* (or holiday excursion). At about five in the afternoon a weary-looking youth dragged himself into the square, and almost fell into the arms of the local cobbler, George Weichmann. He was well built, but poorly dressed, and walked in a curious, stiff-limbed manner. Weichmann took the letter that the youth held out to him, and saw that it was addressed to the captain of the 4th Squadron, 6th Cavalry Regiment. The lad seemed to be unable to answer questions, replying in a curious mumble – Weichmann suspected he was drunk. He led the youth to the nearest guardroom, and the sergeant in charge took him to the captain's home. When Captain Wessenig came home a few hours later he found the place in a state of excitement. The youth seemed to be an idiot. He had tried to touch a candle flame with his fingers, and screamed when he was burned. Offered beer and meat, he had stared at them as if he had no idea what to do with them; yet he had fallen ravenously on a meal of black bread and water. The grandfather clock seemed to terrify him. The only words the boy seemed to know were "*Weiss nicht*" – I don't know.

The envelope proved to contain two letters. The first began: "Honoured Captain. I send you a lad who wishes to serve his king in the army. He was brought to me on October 7, 1812. I am but a poor labourer with children of my own to rear. His mother asked me to bring up the boy . . .

Since then I have never let him go outside the house". The letter had no signature. The other note stated: "This child has been baptised. His name is Kaspar; you must give him a second name yourself. His father was a cavalry soldier. When he is seventeen take him to Nuremberg to the Sixth Cavalry regiment: his father belonged to it. He was born on April 30, 1812. I am a poor girl; I can't take care of him. His father is dead". This was presumably the letter that had accompanied Kaspar when he had been handed over to the "poor labourer".

Taken to the police station, the boy accepted a pencil and wrote "Kaspar Hauser". But to other questions he answered "Don't know".

It all seemed straightforward enough – an illegitimate child left on someone's doorstep and brought up by a kind stranger. But in that case why keep him indoors for seventeen years? The boy's feet were so tender – he was bleeding through his shoes – because he was unaccustomed to walking on them. His skin was pale, as if he had been confined in darkness. Moreover, on close examination it became clear that the two letters had been written by the same hand at about the same time, not sixteen years apart. The clothes he was wearing looked as if they had been taken from a scarecrow, and they were obviously not his own. Someone was trying to draw a red herring across the trail.

The boy was locked in a cell, and his gaoler observed that he seemed perfectly contented to sit there for hours without moving. He had no sense of time, and seemed to know nothing about hours and minutes. It soon became clear that he had a small vocabulary. He could say that he wanted to become a Reiter (cavalryman) like his father – a phrase he had obviously been taught like a parrot. To every animal he applied the word "horse", and he seemed to be fascinated by horses. When a visitor – one of the crowd who flocked to stare at him every day – gave him a toy one he adorned it with ribbons, played with it for hours, and pretended to feed it at every meal. The audience caused him no concern, and he caused amusement by performing his natural functions quite openly, with no sense of shame. He did not even seem to know the difference between men and women – he referred to both as "boys" (*Junge*).

One of the most curious things about him was his incredible physical acuteness. He began to vomit if coffee or beer was in the same room; the sight and smell of meat produced nausea. The smell of wine literally made him drunk, and a single drop of brandy in his water made him sick. His hearing and eyesight were abnormally acute – in fact, he could see in the dark, and would later demonstrate his ability by reading from a Bible in a completely black room. He was so sensitive to magnets that he could tell whether the north or south pole was turned towards him.

He could distinguish between different metals by passing his hand over them, even when they were covered with a cloth. (A few years later, the American doctor Joseph Rodes Buchanan would stumble upon the faculty he called psychometry (see Chapter 43) when he learned that many of his students could do the same thing.)

At first Kaspar seemed to be an imbecile; he lived in a daze. Like an animal, he was terrified of thunderstorms. But the notion that he was mentally retarded soon had to be abandoned. The attention of his visitors obviously gave him pleasure, and he became visibly more alert day by day – exactly like a baby learning from experience. His vocabulary increased from day to day, and his physical clumsiness vanished – he learned to use scissors, quill pens and matches. And as his intelligence increased, his features altered. He had struck most people as a typical idiot, coarse, lumpish, clumsy and oddly repulsive; now his facial characteristics seemed to change and become more refined. But he continued to walk rather clumsily: in the place at the back of the knees where most of us have a hollow he had protrusions, so that when he sat with outstretched legs, the whole leg was in contact with the ground.

As he learned to speak he was gradually able to tell something of his own story. But it seemed to make the mystery even more baffling. A bulletin issued by Burgomeister Binder and the town council of Nuremberg stated that for as long as Kaspar could remember he had lived in a small room, about seven feet long by four feet wide, and its windows were boarded up. There was no bed, only a bundle of straw on the bare earth. The ceiling was so low that he could not stand upright. He saw no one. When he woke up he would find bread and water in his cell. Sometimes his water had a bitter taste, and he would go into a deep sleep; when he woke his straw would have been changed and his hair and nails cut. The only toys were three wooden horses. One day a man had entered his room and taught him to write his name, Kaspar Hauser, and to repeat phrases like "I want to be a soldier" and "Don't know". One day he woke up to find himself wearing the baggy garments in which he had been found, and the man came and led him into the open air. As they trudged along the man promised him a big, live horse when he was a soldier. Then he was abandoned somewhere near the gates of Nuremberg.

Suddenly Kaspar was famous; his case was discussed all over Germany. This must doubtless have worried whoever was responsible for turning him loose; his captor, or captors, had hoped that he would vanish quietly into the army and be forgotten; now he was a national celebrity, and everyone was asking questions.

The Burgomaster and town council decided to take Kaspar under their protection; he would be fed and clothed at the municipal expense. In the rather dull town of Nuremberg he was an object of endless interest, and everyone wanted to solve the mystery. The town paid for thousands of handbills appealing for clues to his identity, and even offering a reward. The police made a careful search of the local countryside for his place of imprisonment, which was obviously within walking distance; but they found nothing.

The town council also appointed a guardian for its celebrity, a lecturer and scientist named Georg Friedrich Daumer. He was interested in "animal magnetism", and it was he who conducted the tests that revealed that Kaspar could distinguish the poles of a magnet and read in the dark. Under Daumer's tutelage Kaspar finally developed into a young man of normal intelligence. Like any teenager, he enjoyed being the centre of attention. His appearance became almost foppish, and in the last months of his life he looked not unlike Roman busts of Nero, with his plump face and little curls.

One of the many learned men who examined him was the lawyer and criminologist Anselm Ritter von Feuerbach, distinguished author of the Bavarian penal code; and he reached the interesting conclusion that Kaspar must be of royal blood. There could be no other explanation for the boy's long imprisonment; he must be *somebody*'s heir. Kaspar was obviously not displeased at this notion.

Then, a mere seventeen months after he had been "found", someone tried to kill him. It happened on the afternoon of 7 October 1829, when Kaspar was found lying on the floor of the cellar of Daumer's house, bleeding from a head-wound, with his shirt torn to the waist. Later he described being attacked by a man wearing a silken mask, who had struck him either with a club or a knife. The police immediately made a search of Nuremberg, but had no success in finding anyone who fitted Kaspar's description of his assailant. There were those in Nuremberg who muttered that there had never been an assailant, and that Kaspar had invented the whole episode to attract attention. Not everyone believed, as Daumer did, that Kaspar was some sort of angel. But most people took the view that his life was in danger. He was moved to a new address, and two policemen were appointed to look after him; Ritter von Feuerbach was appointed his guardian. And for the next two years Kaspar vanished from the public eye. But not from the public mind. Now the novelty had worn off, there were many in Nuremberg who objected to supporting Kaspar on the rates.

Then a solution was proposed that satisfied everyone. A wealthy and eccentric Englishman, Lord Stanhope – nephew of the former prime minister Pitt – became interested in Kaspar and came to interview him. The two seemed to take an instant liking to one another; they began to dine out in restaurants, and Kaspar was often to be seen in Lord Stanhope's carriage. Stanhope was convinced that Kaspar was of royal blood, and was evidently fascinated by the mystery. When he offered to take Kaspar off on a tour of Europe the town council was delighted. And from 1831 until 1833 Kaspar was exhibited at many minor courts of Europe, where he never failed to arouse interest. But various members of the Bavarian royal houses, particularly that of Baden, threatened lawsuits if their names were publicly linked with Kaspar's . . .

It seems that all this attention and good living was not good for Kaspar's character; predictably, he became vain, difficult and conceited. Stanhope became disillusioned with him. In 1833, back in Nuremberg, Stanhope asked permission to lodge him in the town of Ansbach, twenty-five miles away, where he would be tutored by Stanhope's friend Dr Meyer, and guarded by a certain Captain Hickel, a security officer. Then, feeling that he had done his duty, Stanhope disappeared back to England.

Kaspar was not happy in Ansbach. It was even more of a backwater than Nuremberg – in fact, Nuremberg was a glittering metropolis by comparison. Kaspar resented being made to do lessons, particularly Latin, and longed for the old life of courts and dinner parties. His homesickness became stronger after a brief visit to Nuremberg. He seems to have felt that Ansbach was hardly better than the cell in which he had spent his early years.

Then, only a few days before Christmas, he died. On 14 December 1833, on a snowy afternoon, he staggered into Mayer's house gasping: "Man stabbed . . . knife . . . Hofgarten . . . gave purse . . . Go look quickly". A hastily summoned doctor discovered that Kaspar had been stabbed in the side, just below the ribs. The blow had damaged his lung and liver. Hickel rushed to the park where Kaspar had been walking, and found a silk purse containing a note, written in mirror-writing. It said: "Hauser will be able to tell you how I look, whence I came and who I am. To spare him from that task I will tell you myself. I am from . . . on the Bavarian border . . . On the River . . . My name is M.L.O".

But Kaspar could not tell them anything about the man's identity. He could only explain that he had received a message through a labourer, asking him to go to the Hofgarten. A tall, bewhiskered man wearing a black cloak had asked him, "Are you Kaspar Hauser"? and when he nodded handed him the purse. As Kaspar took it the man stabbed him, then ran off.

Hickel revealed a fact that threw doubt on this story; there had only been one set of footprints – Kaspar's – in the snow. But when two days later, on 17 December, Kaspar slipped into a coma his last words were: "I didn't do it myself".

His death was a signal for a flood of books and pamphlets, each with its own theory about the mystery. Feuerbach published a book called *Example of a Crime Against the Soul of a Man*, arguing that Kaspar must be of royal blood. To avoid libel, he avoided naming any suspects, but his readers had no difficulty supplying their own names. The favourite candidates were the Grand Dukes of Baden. The old Duke Karl Frederick had contracted a morganatic marriage with a pretty eighteen-year-old, Caroline Geyer, who was rumoured to have poisoned his sons by an earlier marriage to make sure her own children became the future Grand Dukes. Kaspar Hauser was supposed to have been one of these children. The story was obviously absurd, for it would have meant stealing him away as a baby and handing him over to a "minder". One suggestion was that this "minder" was a man named Franz Richter, and that Kaspar's childhood home was Castle Pilsach, near Nuremberg. (The castle is in fact merely a large farmhouse.) It was suggested that Richter had decided to send Kaspar Hauser to Nuremberg when his wife died. But there is no conclusive evidence for this view, or for any other theory of Kaspar's origin.

There is of course no evidence whatsoever that Kaspar was of royal blood. If he was the legitimate heir to some throne, or even to some rich estate, it is difficult to understand why he should be kept in a small room all his life; it would have been enough to hand him over to a "minder" in some distant place. Kaspar's strange and inhuman treatment sounds more typical of ignorant peasants than of guilt-stricken aristocrats. In a Cornish case of the twentieth century, an army deserter of the First World War, William Garfield Rowe, was kept concealed in his family's farmhouse for thirty years. It does not seem to have struck anyone that this was a kind of insanity – far worse than the few months' imprisonment he might have suffered if he had given himself up.* The theory that Kaspar was the step-child of some wicked Grand Duke seems on the whole less likely than that he was the illegitimate child of some respectable farmer's daughter who was engaged to a local landowner, and was terrified that her secret would become local gossip.

---

* Rowe achieved a different kind of notoriety in 1963 when he was murdered by two out-of-work labourers, who were later hanged.

In that case, who was behind the attacks? It is just possible that they never happened. After the first attack, in Daumer's cellar, Nuremberg gossip suggested that his wound was self-inflicted, and that Kaspar was trying to draw attention to himself after the failure of his recently published Autobiography. By the time the second attack occurred his fame was in decline, and he was desperately unhappy about his situation.

It is important to try to gain some insight into the psychology of a boy who has spent the first seventeen years of his life in a kind of prison cell. Most boys love being the centre of attention and will go to great lengths to achieve it. (Mark Twain shows how deeply he understands the mentality in the episode where Tom Sawyer pretends to be drowned, and attends his own funeral.) Most boys crave the approval of adults, and will tell lies to get it. In his book about Kaspar, Jacob Wassermann describes how disappointed Daumer felt when he discovered that Kaspar was not as truthful as he seemed. Kaspar emerged quite literally from obscurity, to find himself the centre of sympathetic attention – in fact a European celebrity. But although his chronological age was seventeen, he was in the most basic sense a two-year-old boy. Intellectually speaking, he grew with astonishing rapidity; emotionally speaking, he remained a child. So it *is* perfectly conceivable that he was prepared to go to desperate lengths to retain public sympathy.

In the light of this suspicion, Kaspar's story of both attacks begins to seem implausible. Would a masked man somehow find his way into the basement of Daumer's house, then merely hit Kaspar on the head with a club (or a knife; there seems to be some conflict about the weapon) and rush away without making sure he was dead? As to the second attack, could Hickel have been mistaken when he asserted that there were only one set of footprints in the snow? And why was the mysterious letter written in mirror writing? Was it because Kaspar wrote it with his left hand, looking in a mirror, in order to disguise his writing? (It is a well-known fact that it is easy to train the left hand to write backward, using a mirror.) Why was the message so nonsensical: "Hauser will be able to tell you how I look, whence I came and who I am . . ." etc. Why should a paid assassin write a letter at all? Is it not more likely that Kaspar, in a desperate state of unhappiness, decided to inflict a harmless wound, and stabbed himself too deeply?

If so, Kaspar at least achieved what he wanted – universal sympathy and a place in the history books.

21

Rudolf Hess

Was It Hitler's Deputy
Who Died in Spandau Prison?

On 17 August 1987, the man referred to as Prisoner Number 7 committed suicide by hanging in Berlin's Spandau Prison. The prison records gave his real name as Rudolf Walter Richard Hess, aged ninety-three years – the last member of the Nazi high command to be held in that prison.

Hess had been Hitler's deputy and personal secretary and was third in line to the Führership. Then, in 1941, only a few weeks before the launch of the German attack on the Soviet Union, he vanished from Berlin and flew to Scotland as a self-appointed peace ambassador. The result of that well-meant mission was a lifetime of imprisonment. At the time of his death he had been incarcerated for almost forty-six years, had been convicted of preparing and waging aggressive war, and had attempted suicide several times. Ignoring complaints by human-rights groups, the Soviet Union insisted that Hess be held in prison until he died – the real motive being to maintain that nation's access to West Berlin, where Spandau Prison was situated.

For more than ten years before his suicide, there had been odd rumors that Prisoner Number 7 was not Hess at all but a double, planted on the British for reasons unknown. The findings of a prison doctor in 1973, in fact, seem to prove that the prisoner was not Hess. But why, if that were true, would he have kept the secret so long and at such cost? Why would the authorities have imprisoned an innocent man for nearly half a century? Close scrutiny of the facts throws up a number of bizarre anomalies that suggest that, as absurd as it sounds, Number 7 may not, after all, have been Hitler's deputy.

Shortly before eleven o'clock on the night of Saturday, May 10, 1941, David MaClean, the head plowman at Floor's Farm, outside Eaglesham near Glasgow, was startled by a tremendous roar that shook the whole cottage. Rushing outside, he saw that an aircraft had crashed in a nearby field; he also saw a lone parachute descending in the moonlight. Unarmed, MaClean ran across the field and found the parachutist disentangling himself from his harness – hampered somewhat by a twisted ankle. MaClean, keeping his distance, called, "Who are you? Are you German"? The pilot, a big man, pulled himself upright with some difficulty and replied, "Yes, I am German. My name is Hauptmann Alfred Horn. I want to go to Dungavel House. I have an important message for the Duke of Hamilton".

The "Hauptmann" gave no trouble and waited quietly until a constable arrived and took him into custody. He was held at the local home guard headquarters for a few hours, then was transferred to the Mayhill Barracks in Glasgow. When questioned, he simply repeated his name and insisted that he must see the Duke of Hamilton on a matter of urgency.

The next morning this information was passed on to the Duke, who was then a wing-commander with the city of Glasgow (bomber) squadron. Together with an RAF intelligence officer, he hurried immediately to interview the captured pilot – who was by then laid up in bed with a painfully swollen ankle. After the introductions the prisoner insisted on speaking to the Duke alone. The intelligence officer obligingly went outside; as soon as they were alone, the prisoner greeted the Duke of Hamilton as an acquaintance. He explained that they had met in Germany during the 1936 Olympics and that the Duke had even attended a luncheon party at his house. When Hamilton continued to look puzzled, the "Hauptmann" said, "I do not know if you recognize me, but I am Rudolf Hess".

Hamilton was staggered. If the man before him was indeed Hess – and the resemblance was striking – it meant that they had captured the deputy Führer of the Nazi Party – one of the top men in the Nazi high command and third in line to Hitler himself. Yet why would one of the most powerful men in Europe risk his life by flying into an enemy country at night and then hand himself over as if he were a common criminal hoping for amnesty?

Hess went on to explain that he was on a "mission of humanity"; a diplomatic errand of the highest importance, carrying a message that could save thousands, perhaps millions of lives. He was here, he told the astonished duke, to try to negotiate peace between Britain and Germany.

Rudolf Hess had the reputation of being the most intellectual member of Hitler's inner circle. Born in 1894 in Egypt, he had been schooled in Germany and had immediately volunteered for active service at the outbreak of war in 1914. Shot through the left lung on the Rumanian front in 1917, he was given a medical discharge from the army, but after a six-month recovery period he joined the Imperial Flying Corps. He successfully completed pilot training in time to serve only ten days before the armistice.

The National Socialist Workers Party, led by a spellbinding orator named Adolf Hitler, consisted mainly of ex-servicemen who felt that the peace had betrayed them. Hess joined in 1920, the year Hitler took over the leadership. He quickly achieved prominence and in 1923 helped Hitler plan the attempted overthrow of the Bavarian government – later known as the "Beerhall Putsch". When this failed, and Hitler was arrested, Hess fled the country. After a spectacular self-defense that was virtually a condemnation of his judges, Hitler was sentenced by a sympathetic court to five years' imprisonment but was offered a considerably reduced sentence if he remained on good behavior. When he heard the news, Hess returned of his own free will and gave himself up. He was sentenced to an eighteen-month term and sent to serve his time with Hitler in the Landsberg fortress.

During their imprisonment Hitler and Hess kept busy, Hitler writing a book and Hess acting as his secretary. It is certain that Hess had an important influence on the development of ideas in *Mein Kampf*; he had a better intellectual and academic training than Hitler and had already developed his own strong views on German racial purity and the need for territorial expansion. The two worked well together, and the foundations of Hess's future influence in the Nazi Party were laid.

When Hitler won an election and became Reichschancellor in 1933, Hess was appointed his deputy, and during the establishment of the totalitarian dictatorship he was never far from Hitler's side. But when Hess announced plans to make the first east-west trans-Atlantic flight, Hitler turned down the scheme, insisting that Hess was too valuable to the Reich to risk his life.

In February 1938 Hess was appointed head of a department whose purpose was to make secret plans for the war of German expansion, which broke out a year later. Hess is known to have advocated expansion eastward, into Poland and then into the Soviet Union, but he was strongly against war on two fronts. And when France capitulated in 1940, he seems to have decided that Germany's new western frontier was reasonably secure and that therefore the war with Great Britain was dangerous and unnecessary. The question was, would Hess have felt strongly enough about the subject to risk his own life to make peace, and would such a madcap scheme have had Hitler's backing?

Although stating that he was acting on his own initiative, the man who claimed to be Hess insisted to Hamilton that he was speaking for Hitler in all but name. The Führer had never wanted to go to war with the British Empire, he said. Britain's impending total defeat – and in 1941 many people thought this increasingly likely – was something Hitler truly wished to avoid. There was a chance now for the nations to come to peace and perhaps even to join forces to smash the threat from Communist Russia. He was there to try to put an immediate stop to the war.

Hamilton asked him why he had specifically asked to see him, and the prisoner replied that a mutual friend, Dr Albrecht Haushofer, had recommended the duke as a man who would support his peace initiative. To back this he pointed out that among his confiscated belongings were the visiting cards of Haushofer and his father, Professor Karl Haushofer. He also mentioned a letter that Albrecht Haushofer had sent to the Duke, inviting him to a secret diplomatic meeting in neutral Portugal.

The Duke had indeed received this letter, after it had been intercepted and investigated by M15, but he was still dubious about the identity of the prisoner. For one thing, he was carrying no identification other than the visiting cards and some photographs of Rudolf Hess as a small child – a very odd choice of material to back such an incredible story.

It all seemed beyond belief. Capturing Rudolf Hess – under any circumstances – was almost too good to be true, and it occurred to Hamilton that it might be a trick using a look-alike, in order to sound out the British government's willingness to continue fighting. Even so, he found himself more than half believing that the prisoner was indeed Hess, but he was careful not to give this away during the interview.

The Duke, wary of using the telephone system, flew to inform Churchill in person. Ushered in to see the Prime Minister a few hours later, he told his strange story. Churchill exclaimed, "Do you mean to tell me that the Deputy Führer of Germany is in our hands? . . . Well, Hess or no Hess, I'm going to see the Marx Brothers"! Which in fact he did – *The Marx Brothers Go West* – at a local cinema.

On his return he interrogated Hamilton more thoroughly. The Duke said that the more he thought about the secret letter from Dr Haushofer, the more certain he was that only the real Hess could have known about it. Hess was known to be a close associate of Haushofer, and it was quite possible that the letter had been sent on his orders. If this was the case, or even if Hess had simply condoned the letter, it was highly unlikely that he would broadcast the fact to his colleagues, many of whom would have argued that it was treason. After a three-hour session, Churchill sat deep in thought and was heard to mutter, "The worm is in the bud".

The next day Hamilton, who admitted that his memory of meeting Hess in 1936 was a dim one, was sent back to Glasgow with Ivone Kirkpatrick, a man who had served as First Secretary to the embassy in Berlin from 1933 to 1938 and had met Hess on many occasions. When they landed they were greeted by a call from the Foreign Secretary, Anthony Eden. The following broadcast had just been sent out on German public radio:

> On Saturday 10th May Rudolf Hess set out at 18:00 hours on a flight from Augsburg from which he has so far not returned. A letter that he left behind unfortunately shows by its distraction traces of a mental disorder, and it is feared that he was a victim of hallucinations . . . In the circumstances it must be considered that party member Hess either crashed or met with an accident.

Hamilton and Kirkpatrick were told that the Ministry of Information was shortly going to release a statement headed "Rudolf Hess in England". The British government was committing itself.

If this was indeed some cunning Nazi trick, then Hitler was playing for high stakes. The real Hess might have dropped out of sight for a while to give an impostor a chance to convince the British, but Hess's public credibility would be destroyed in Germany if the "mission" came to nothing. And if this were to happen, the Nazi high command would have to admit that they had been attempting a confidence trick on the highest diplomatic level; the loss of face to the party as a whole would be enormous. Since nobody could imagine what such a plot might achieve that would be worth such a risk, it seemed logical that the simple explanation – that Hess had flown to England without Hitler's knowledge – was the only possible one.

The prisoner did not recognize Kirkpatrick when they were first introduced, but as they talked he seemed to remember him and mentioned several incidents they had witnessed together in Germany. This convinced Kirkpatrick and Hamilton that they were talking to Hess. Then, just as the interview was becoming more relaxed, the prisoner drew out a large packet of manuscript notes and launched into a four-hour diatribe on the subject of Anglo-German historical relations and the unfairness of Britain's declaration of war on Germany.

The exhausted Kirkpatrick later telephoned the Foreign Office, to be told that Churchill had definitely ruled out any possibility of negotiating with the Deputy Führer. To do so might be interpreted, by friend and foe alike, as unwillingness to fight – perhaps just the result the Nazis were hoping for. Hess, said Churchill, was to be treated as a prisoner of war and nothing else. He was to be told that if, after the war, he was found guilty of war crimes, his repentance would stand in his favour; other than that the British government had no interest in him.

After eighteen months of imprisonment, Hess began to show signs of mental illness; he complained that his food was being poisoned and made a number of suicide attempts. He was moved to a mental hospital and held there for the rest of the war.

It was now generally accepted that the prisoner was Rudolf Hess – even his mental illness seemed to support the Nazi statement that he had been suffering from a breakdown at the time of his flight. Yet an observant doctor might have noted reasons for doubt. To begin with, Hess insisted that he was suffering from periodic bouts of amnesia, which made it impossible for him to answer questions about himself. But he also seemed to have undergone a personality change. The Deputy Führer had been known to be obsessed with his health. Like Hitler, he had been a strict vegetarian, who refused even to eat eggs, fried foods, or any products grown with artificial fertilizer, considering them "impure". He was known to have eaten with fastidious care and to have been punctiliously neat and tidy. In confinement in England, he ate anything set before him voraciously and messily and seemed to have lost all interest in his appearance.

While held in Britain he was allowed to write to his wife, Ilsa Hess, via neutral Switzerland. She later said that the handwriting seemed to be that of her husband and that she never had any doubts that that was who he was. What did bother her occasionally was that her husband seemed to be desperately trying to prove to her that he *was* Rudolf Hess.

The war ended; in October 1945 the prisoner was transferred to Nuremberg, Germany, to face the War Crimes Tribunal. On his arrival he seemed to suffer a total memory breakdown and was judged incapable of standing trial. The doctors tried to jog his memory by introducing him to old colleagues; but although he showed some sign of recognition when confronted by his two secretaries, he failed to recognize Hermann Göring or Karl Haushofer, the father of the man who had recommended that he seek out the Duke of Hamilton.

Perhaps understandably, the prisoner was also in poor physical shape. Hess had once been a large, well-built man in excellent health. He was now gaunt and sickly; although in defense of his jailers it should be noted that he had already been in poor physical condition when captured.

As the authorities wrangled over his mental competence, the prisoner suddenly issued the following statement;

> Henceforth my memory will again respond to the outside world. The reasons why I simulated loss of memory were tactical. The fact is that it is only my ability to concentrate that is somewhat reduced. However, my capacity to follow the trial, to defend myself, to put questions to witnesses, or even to answer questions is not being affected thereby.

He subsequently stood trial, and though clearly tired and less than fully alert, gave a reasonable account of himself. On September 2, 1946, he was found guilty of conspiracy and crimes against peace. Since it could not be proved that he had known about the death camps, he was acquitted of the charge of war crimes. Together with Walter Funk, Admiral Donitz, Admiral Raeder, Baldur von Schirach, Constantin von Naurath, and Albert Speer, Rudolf Hess was sentenced to life imprisonment in Spandau Prison in West Berlin. There he was simply referred to as Prisoner Number 7.

Throughout the trial and for the next twenty-three years, the prisoner declined to see his wife or his only son. When he finally agreed to allow Ilsa Hess to visit him, she expressed surprise that his voice had deepened – it might have been expected to become higher with increasing age.

Spandau Prison was an oddly anomalous product of the cold war. Situated in the British-occupied section of West Berlin, it was administered by the four major victorious powers: the United States, Britain, France, and the Soviet Union. Under a special convention drawn up for the prison, control of the prison alternated between these four nations every month; this included a total change of guard.

In the course of time the other six prisoners were released, the last two being von Schirach and Speer in 1966. But Prisoner Number 7 was offered no hope of release. The Soviets made it clear that they would block any such move and that Hess was to remain imprisoned until he died.

There were two reasons for this. First, the Soviet people felt particularly bitter toward Hess, who had collaborated with Hitler on the plan to conquer and enslave them. But the main reason was undoubtedly that Hess's release would involve the Soviets losing their foothold in West Berlin, and with it, presumably, all kinds of opportunities for spying.

And so, on 17 August 1987, the last Spandau prisoner committed suicide by hanging at the age of ninety-three. But for at least fourteen years before that, there were very real doubts about his identity. In 1972 Dr Hugh Thomas was appointed consultant in general surgery at the British Military Hospital in Berlin. Three years earlier, in 1969, Hess had almost died when a duodenal ulcer perforated, and his Russian captors allowed several days to pass before sending for a doctor; now Thomas insisted on giving him a complete medical checkup – although it was not until the following year, 1973, that he was finally allowed to examine Hess in the presence of representatives of all four powers. Thomas was revolted by the inhumanity toward Hess shown by Voitov, the Soviet commandant; any attempt to show sympathy was immediately met by a command of "Stop that! It is contrary to the Nuremberg convention".

What Thomas now discovered puzzled him deeply. Hess had been wounded in the chest in the First World War, and the resultant lung injury had caused him much bronchial trouble in the days when he was Hitler's deputy. Now there was no sign of a war wound and no bronchial trouble. Examination of Hess's medical records made it clear that there should have been many scars from war wounds, none of which was visible on the body of the Spandau prisoner. When, at a second examination, Thomas asked him, "What happened to your war wounds"?, Hess blanched, began to tremble, then muttered, "Too late, too late". What did that mean? That there would now be no point in admitting that he was not Rudolf Hess?

Thomas concluded that it was impossible that this prisoner – who had been code-named "Jonathan" when in England – could be Hess. X-rays should at least have shown signs of tissue scarring, but there were none.

Thomas went on to study the documents concerning Hess's flight to Scotland and concluded that it should have been impossible for a Messerschmitt 110D to carry enough fuel to make the 850-mile journey if it had included as many detours as Hess claimed. The range of the aircraft – on full tanks – was only a little more than 850 miles. It could possibly have been carrying spare tanks under the wings, but Hess's adjutant, Pintsch, had taken a photograph of the plane as it took off, and it showed no spare fuel tanks.

In his book *The Murder of Rudolf Hess*, Dr Thomas suggests that Hess never left Germany; rather, he died there and was replaced by a double. The commander of fighter squadrons along the Dutch coast, Adolf Galland, tells in his book *The First and Last* how, on the night of Hess's flight, Hermann Göring – who loathed Hess – rang him and ordered him to intercept an aircraft flying out of Germany, claiming, "The Deputy Führer has gone mad and is flying to England . . . He must be brought down". But Galland's planes were unable to locate Hess's Messerschmitt.

What do we know to support the notion that Hess flew to Britain on a peace mission? To begin with, it is clear that Hitler wanted peace. He was known to admire the British and would have preferred them as allies rather than enemies; Russia was his real target. On 25 June 1940, Hitler made a speech in which he appealed to England from a position of strength ("since I am not the vanquished") for peace "in the name of reason". Churchill rejected this offer.

But Hess is known to have favoured a direct appeal to the British. One of his closest friends was the aforementioned Albrecht Haushofer, whose father, Karl, had been Hess's personal adviser in the mid-1930s and was sent on a number of diplomatic missions. It seems certain that he knew about Hess's plans to appeal directly to the British. On the day after Hess's adjutant Pintsch delivered Hess's "farewell" letter to Hitler at Berchtesgaden, describing his peace mission, Albrecht Haushofer was summoned to write an account of his own attempts to make contact with the British to make peace. Unfortunately, Albrecht was murdered by the S.S. in the last days of the war, so the one witness who might have been able to tell the truth about the prisoner in Spandau was silenced.

But if we know that Hess wanted to make peace, and even that he went to talk to the Duke of Windsor in Lisbon in July 1940, why should we doubt that it was Hess who landed in Scotland on 10 May 1941? Because, as we have seen, the medical evidence suggests that the prisoner code-named "Jonathan" was not the man who received so many wounds in World War I. If "Hauptmann" Horn was Hess, why was he carrying so little documentation, so few papers to establish his identity? Why did he refuse to see his wife and son for twenty-three years after being incarcerated in Spandau?

Thomas's theory, briefly, is this: Göring detested Hess and would have been glad to see him dead. And Heinrich Himmler, head of the S.S., is known to have nurtured plans to replace Hitler. For either of them, Hess's death would have been a bonus. But if Hess was murdered on his peace flight – or intercepted and shot down – Hitler would have been unforgiving. It was important that "Hess" should arrive. So when

Hess's planned flight became known to Göring, a double was found and carefully schooled. And when Hess had been eliminated – sometime on that night of 9–10 May 1941 – the double was hastily sent off, probably from a Danish airfield. This is why the Duke of Hamilton did not recognize him. This is why he began feigning loss of memory at the earliest opportunity.

But British intelligence must have found out very soon that he was not Rudolf Hess. This could explain why the British made no attempts to use their prisoner for propaganda purposes.

Then, why did Hess's double not reveal his secret after the war? Thomas speaks of Himmler's known habit of eliminating whole families of "traitors" to the Reich. This would have explained the double's silence before Himmler's death – before the Nuremberg trials began. And after that, he may either have continued to believe his family to be in danger from ex-Nazis or simply have assumed that he stood no chance of being believed. If, in fact, he had been virtually brainwashed during a series of breakdowns and suicide attempts, and mental exhaustion, he may simply have settled into the state of blank indifference that is sometimes seen in the very old.

Whatever the reason, it seems clear that Prisoner Number 7 recognized that it was "too late, too late" when Dr Thomas finally began asking the right questions.

22

The Holy Shroud of Turin

The notion that a fourteen-foot oblong of cloth preserved in the Cathedral of Turin could be the shroud in which the founder of Christianity was laid in the tomb seems on the face of it an obvious absurdity, particularly since the Turin shroud had forty-odd rivals in other parts of Europe. Yet if the "Holy Shroud" is a fake, then the mystery is in a sense greater than ever; for we are then left with the problem of trying to explain away a great many pieces of remarkably convincing evidence.

The known history of the shroud begins in 1353, when Geoffroy de Charny, Lord of Savoisie and Lirey, built a church at Lirey and put on show "the true burial sheet of Christ". This was a strip of linen, just over fourteen feet long and three and a half feet wide. On this linen there was the dim brown image of a man – or rather, two images, one of his front and one of his back. Apparently the body had been laid out on the bottom half of the sheet, which had then been folded down over the top of the head. And, in some strange way the image of the man had been imprinted on the shroud like a very poor photographic image.

A "relic" like this was worth far more than its weight in gold, as pilgrims poured into the church to see it and dropped their coins into the collection box. In 1389 the bishop of Troyes, Peter D'Arcis, declared the shroud to be a fake, painted by an artist, and tried to seize it; but he was unsuccessful. In 1532 the shroud was almost destroyed in a fire in the Sainte Chapelle at Chambéry, France, and when it was recovered it had been badly damaged – many holes had been burnt in it by molten silver. Fortunately, these completely missed the central part which contained the image, and when the nearby nuns of St Clair had patched it it looked almost as good as new.

As far as the modern reader is concerned, the real history of the shroud begins on 28 May 1898. The shroud had been in Turin cathedral since 1578 – it was now the property of the Duke of Savoy – and on 25 May 1898 it was again put on public display. A Turin photographer, Secondo Pia, was commissioned to photograph it. And it was in his apartment, towards midnight, that the photographer removed the first of two large plates from the developing fluid. What he saw almost made him drop the plate. Instead of the dim, blurred image he was looking at a real face, quite plainly recognizable. Yet he was looking at a photographic negative, not the final product. This could only mean one thing: that the image on the shroud was itself a photographic negative, so by "reversing" it Pia had turned it into a positive – a real photograph. If the relic was genuine, Pia was looking at a photograph of Christ.

The Duke of Savoy – now King Umberto I (he would be assassinated two years later) – was told the news; a procession of distinguished visitors began to arrive at the photographer's house. Most of them, understandably, were convinced that this must be the true Holy Shroud, since no painter would have thought of forging a photographic negative. The only other possibility was that the effect had been achieved accidentally by a forger, but this seemed unlikely. Two weeks later a journalist broke the story, and it spread round the world.

But the shroud's fame was not to last for long. Two years later a detailed report on it by a medieval scholar, Fr. Ulysse Chevalier, defused the excitement. Chevalier studied all the documents he could find, including Peter D'Arcis's assertion that it was a fake (D'Arcis claimed that the artist had confessed), and declared firmly that the image on the shroud was a painting; he quoted a well-known photographer to the effect that the "negative" aspect of the picture was merely a technical accident. Scholars were convinced; the Holy Shroud was just another false relic, like the thousands of pieces of the "true cross" in churches all over the world.

But a new defender had already appeared on the scene. Paul Vignon, a painter with an interest in biology, had become the assistant of Professor Yves Delage of the Sorbonne. Vignon was a Catholic, Delage an agnostic. But it was Delage who in 1900 showed Vignon photographs of the shroud, and aroused his interest in the problem. Surely, Vignon reasoned, close examination should prove once and for all if the shroud had been painted by hand? He went to Turin and obtained copies of Secondo Pia's photographs, as well as two snapshots of the shroud taken at the same time by other men.

The first question Vignon asked himself was how the brown stains could have been made. If it *had* been painted by an artist, could he have produced such an impressive negative? It would mean painting without really seeing what he was doing, and as an artist, Vignon knew this was virtually impossible. And since photography did not exist in 1353, the artist would have had no means of checking his work. And why should he have wanted to produce a negative if the intention was to deceive pilgrims? They would prefer a recognizable face . . .

Vignon tried coating his face in red chalk-dust, then lying down and covering his face with a cloth, which was then pressed gently against his face. The result was not a negative; it was just blotches.

So if the image had been produced by "contact", it could not have been this kind of crude, direct contact. But in that case, what kind of contact? One mystery was that even the hollows of the face had been "imprinted"; the image showed the bridge of the nose, yet a cloth laid over someone's face would not touch the bridge of the nose.

Suppose the image had been produced by sweat? The commonest burial ointments were myrrh and aloes at the time of the Crucifixion. Vignon and Delage tried impregnating a cloth with myrrh and aloes, then seeing what effect sweat had on it. Sweat contains a substance called urea, which turns into ammonia (hence the disagreeable smell of people with BO). They found that sweat would produce brown stains on their impregnated cloth.

Oddly enough, the agnostic Delage finally became convinced that the shroud was genuine – although he stopped short of becoming converted to Christianity. This man's "photograph" showed signs of scourging, and of being pierced in one side with a spear; the forehead had marks that would correspond to a crown of thorns. There were nail-marks in the wrists and the feet. Most paintings of the Crucifixion show nails driven through the hands, but Vignon established that the hands would not support a man on the cross – they would tear. In fact, historical research has shown that crucifixion involved nailing the wrists, not the hands.

The report by Vignon and Delage was read on 21 April 1902 at the Academy of Sciences, and caused a sensation, Vignon and Delage were praised and denounced. Yet, oddly enough, some influential Catholics still regarded the shroud as an imposture; the Jesuit Father Herbert Thurston, of London's Farm Street, contributed a piece to the *Catholic Encyclopedia* in which he stated his view that the shroud was a mere "devotional aid", painted by some fourteenth-century monk.

The controversy died down; almost thirty years passed. In May 1931 it was decided to exhibit the shroud again in belated celebration of the marriage of Crown Prince Umberto. More photographs were taken, by Giuseppe Enrie. They were far better in quality than Pia's earlier photographs, and the sense of reality was even stronger. Moreover, close examination of the cloth showed that the paint theory was unlikely; paint would have soaked in, and the brown stain seemed to be on the surface. Even under a microscope, no fragments of paint were visible.

The photographs were shown to an eminent French anatomist, Pierre Barbet, who proceeded to study them in minute detail. The photograph showed that the nail that had penetrated the wrist had emerged in the back of the hand. Could this be a forger's mistake? Barbet tried nailing a severed wrist; when the nail struck the bone it slipped upward, and emerged at exactly the spot shown in the photograph. The wrists showed two streaks of blood, as if the wrist had been in two different positions. Barbet showed that a man hanging by the wrists would soon suffocate; in order to breathe he would have to force himself upright, literally standing on the nails that held his feet; but he would soon become exhausted, and slump again. The bloodstains corresponded precisely to the two positions. Brooding on the apostle John's description of the lance-thrust into the side of the dead Christ, "and immediately there came out blood and water", Barbet tried to experiment of thrusting a knife into the side of a corpse above the heart; the result was "blood and water" – a mixture of blood and pericardial fluid.

All these investigations gave Barbet an appalling insight into the sufferings of a man dying on the cross – to such an extent that he admitted he no longer dared to think about them and his book *The Corporal Passion of Jesus Christ* became the subject of endless Easter sermons. Barbet was himself overcome with emotion when he succeeded in catching a close-up glimpse of the shroud in October 1933, and realized that some of the brown stains were bloodstains – the blood of Christ . . . He sank to his knees and bowed his head.

One thing was by now obvious: that the information contained in the shroud was so complex that the chances of it being a fake were a thousand to one against. The study of the shroud became something of a science in its own right. It was christened sindonology (the Italian for the shroud being *sindone*), and Paul Vignon became its acknowledged leader. It was Vignon who made the interesting suggestion that the shroud might be responsible for a sudden change in the representations of Jesus in the time of the emperor Constantine (AD 274–337); in the first three centuries after the Crucifixion, Jesus is represented as a beardless youth, but after that as a bearded man with a moustache. Could it have been the discovery of the shroud that caused the change? Vignon studied hundreds of paintings, and concluded that a large number of them seemed to have been influenced by the shroud. For example, there was a small square above the nose, due to an imperfection in the weave of the cloth, and he found this in many of the portraits of Jesus. In the so-called "holy face of Edessa" a portrait dating from a century after Constantine there is a distinct resemblance to the face on the shroud.

A later scholar, Ian Wilson, has argued convincingly that the shroud is identical with a relic known as the Mandylion, the handkerchief with which St Veronica wiped the face of Jesus when he was on his way to Calvary, and on which Jesus miraculously imprinted his image. The Mandylion (or a relic claiming to be the original handkerchief of St Veronica) was preserved in Byzantium until it was sacked by the Crusaders in 1204; it had come there from Edessa (Urfa, in modern Turkey) in August AD 994. Wilson argues that the shroud was folded so that only the face was visible, and that this was the Mandylion. In his book *The Turin Shroud*, Wilson devotes more than a hundred pages to studying documentary sources and attempting to trace the history of the shroud-Mandylion before it appeared in Lirey in the mid-fourteenth century. His arguments are too long to detail here, but his tentative reconstruction is as follows.

After the Crucifixion (about AD 30), the shroud was folded and disguised as a portrait, to hide its "unclean" nature as a burial cloth. It was taken to Edessa, then a thriving Christian community; but when Ma'nu VI reverted to paganism in AD 57 and persecuted the Christians it was hidden in a niche in the wall above Edessa's west gate. Although Christians were once again tolerated about 120 years later, the shroud's existence remained unknown. In 525 severe floods in Edessa cost 30,000 lives and destroyed many public buildings; the shroud was rediscovered when the walls were being rebuilt. (This version, of course, contradicts Vignon's hypothesis that it was rediscovered in the reign of Constantine three centuries earlier.) In the spring of 943 the Byzantine army besieged Edessa and offered to spare the city in exchange for the Mandylion; so the Mandylion was transferred to Constantinople. It was discovered to be a burial shroud in about AD 1045, probably when someone unpinned the Mandylion from its frame to remount it. In 1204, when the Crusaders took Constantinople from the Greek Christians, the shroud vanished again. What happened next is unknown, but one conjecture is that it fell into the hands of the Knights Templars, who were accused of worshipping a man's head with a red beard. In 1291, after the fall of Acre (where the Templars had their treasury), the cloth was brought to Sidon, then to Cyprus.

In 1306 the Treasury of the Templars came to France, brought by Jacques Molay. On 13 October 1307 the Templars were arrested on the orders of King Philip the Fair, who was anxious to lay his hands on their money, and in March 1314 Jacques Molay was burnt at the stake, together with Geoffrey de Charnay, the order's Normandy master. It is not known if this Geoffrey de Charnay was related to the Geoffroy de Charny who built the Lirey church in 1353, and who seems to have exhibited the shroud there about 1355. When Geoffroy was killed at Poitiers in September 1356 the shroud became the property of his infant son, also called Geoffroy; the shroud was exhibited (perhaps to raise money) in 1357, but Bishop Henry of Poitiers ordered the exhibition (or "exposition") to be stopped. In 1389 another exposition aroused the anger of Peter D'Arcis, Bishop of Troyes, who appealed to the king, then to the pope, to gain possession of the relic; he insisted that the shroud had been forged by an artist around 1355. The pope supported the de Charny family, and the Bishop's attempt was a failure. In 1400, after the death of the younger Geoffroy de Charny, his daughter Margaret married Humbert of Villersexel, and the shroud was handed over to him for safe-keeping. It was kept in the chapel at St Hippolyte-sur-Doubs, and was exhibited yearly in a meadow on the banks of the Doubs (Known as the Saviour's Meadow, Pré du Seigneur). The Lirey canons tried hard to recover it from about 1443, and even succeeded in having Margaret excommunicated; but they failed to regain it. When Margaret died in 1460 the shroud already seems to have been in the possession of the Duke of Savoy, who gave Margaret two French castles. In 1502 the shroud was deposited in Chambery castle, where thirty years later it was almost destroyed in a fire. And in 1578 the shroud was taken to Turin, where it has remained ever since, except for the Second World War, when it was taken to the Abbey of Monte Vergine at Avellino for safety.

In 1955 Group Captain Leonard Cheshire took a crippled Scottish girl to Turin, and she was allowed to hold the shroud in her lap; however, no cure took place. Possibly this failure decided Cardinal Pellegrino of Turin to make a determined attempt to establish the shroud's authenticity or otherwise by scientific means. In June 1969 a scientific commission was allowed to examine the shroud, and more photographs (some in colour) were taken by Giovanni-Battista Judica-Cordiglia. For two days the commission examined the shroud, and recommended a series of tests that would involve the "removal of minimum samples". In Portugal exiled King Umberto II gave his permission for the tests. On 23 November 1973 the shroud was shown for the first time on television. The next day it was removed to a small room at the rear of Turin cathedral, and a total of seventeen samples were carefully removed. Part of the backing-cloth sewn on by the nuns after the fire was also removed, and this revealed the interesting fact that the image on the cloth had not "soaked through" to the other side. In fact, closer examination of a thread showed that the brown stain was restricted to the very surface of the cloth. This also seemed to rule out the possibility that there was actual blood on the shroud – we may recall the fact that Pierre Barbet had fallen on his knees when it had struck him that he was looking at a real bloodstain. In fact tests showed that there was no blood on the shroud.

Another scientist, Dr Max Frei of Zurich, had noticed that there was dust on the shroud, and he took samples by pressing adhesive tape to the surface of the linen. Back in his labouratory, a microscope revealed that there were many pollen grains among the dust and mineral particles. Frei, a criminologist, was an expert on pollens. One of his first discoveries was of pollen from a cedar of Lebanon. That looked promising – except that such trees have spread far from Lebanon, especially in public parks. Then he came upon something more revealing: pollens from plants unique to the Jordan valley, adapted to live in a soil with a high salt content. He went on to identify forty-nine varieties of pollen, many from Jerusalem, others from Istanbul (Constantinople), others from Urfa (Edessa), others from France or Italy. This constituted powerful evidence that the shroud had originated in the Holy Land, had travelled to Turkey, then to France and Italy. This was undoubtedly the most exciting discovery to emerge from the 1973 examination.

By the time of this examination, important research was also being carried on in America by a physicist, John Jackson, and his friend Dr Eric Jumper, a USAF captain. They made a "dummy" shroud by using a transparency and marking all the shroud's main features on a similar piece of cloth. Placing the dummy over a man who was lying down, they then plotted the relative darkness of the brown markings. This revealed the curious fact that the markings were strongest where the cloth would have touched the body, and that they seemed to be in exact proportion to the distance the cloth would have been from the flesh – for example, being faintest below the chin, where the cloth would have been stretched between the chin and the chest.

But it was in 1976 that the two stumbled on their most fascinating piece of information – and perhaps the most exciting discovery since Secondo Pia's original photograph. They decided to subject the shroud to "image-enhancement". This is a modern technique whose purpose is to analyze the relative brightness of areas of a photograph – for example, one taken by a space-probe – and to intensify them selectively to "bring out" underlying images. (It has been used on photographs of the Loch Ness monster.) Since the image-enhancer can also interpret information about distance, it can also turn a flat photograph into a three-dimensional image, the equivalent of turning it into a statue. The "statue" can then be turned from side to side. From a small transparency of the shroud Jackson and Jumper obtained an amazingly perfect image of the face. It proved that the brown marks on the shroud actually provided enough information for the computer to reconstruct the original and, in doing so virtually ruled out the possibility that the shroud was a painted forgery. In fact, as Jackson and Jumper pointed out, the shroud was in many respects superior to a modern photograph. A photograph may not contain enough "distance information" to produce an accurate "statue" – so an attempt to translate a photograph of Pope Pius XI into a three-dimensional image flattened the nose, distorted the mouth and made the eyes too deeply set. The image on the shroud was more accurate than that. It even revealed something never before recognized – that coins had been placed on both eyes, according to the Jewish burial custom of the time. Other researchers, Donald Lynn and Jean Lorre, were even able tentatively to identify the coins – as "leptons", the "widow's mite" of the New Testament.

In 1977 Dr Walter McCrone, a Chicago microanalyst, submitted a request to take samples from the shroud. McCrone had disproved the authenticity of the "Vinland map", which was supposed to prove that Vikings discovered America, by showing that although the parchment was medieval, the ink contained a component only used after 1920. McCrone stated that with the use of the ion microscope he could identify the nature of the shroud's image. But in 1977 his chances of laying his hands on material from the shroud seemed minimal; Turin had demanded the return of the small samples. Then a new Cardinal of Turin was appointed, Anastasio Ballestrero, former archbishop of Bari. In August 1978 Ballestrero mounted another exposition of the shroud, and it was clear that he was not averse to more scientific tests. Jackson and Jumper, Lynn and Lorre, were able to take more material; Max Frei took more dust and pollen samples. And McCrone got his test samples.

For the believers, McCrone's results were disappointing. He announced that his microscopic examination had revealed traces of iron oxide and of paint fragments on the shroud, and concluded that this proved that it was a forgery. Other scientists pointed out that flax is soaked in water before it is made into linen, and that this could easily be the source of the minute traces of iron oxide. Moreover, the shroud has often come into contact with artists – many copies around Europe bear an inscription certifying that they have been in actual contact with the Holy Shroud of Turin (and have thus, presumably, absorbed some of its virtue). Nothing is more likely than that it has some traces of the pigments used to make such copies.

At the time of writing these questions remain unresolved. The sceptical school has returned to the old assertion, first made by Fr. Ulysse Chevalier, that the shroud is a forgery whose peculiar properties – when subjected to photography and image-enhancement – are due somehow to the "decay" of the original pigment. This belief seems as absurd now as it seemed at the turn of the twentieth century. Carbon 14 dating could perhaps resolve the question once and for all, if it proved that the linen of the shroud dates from long after the Crucifixion. This had still not been carried out when this book was written, partly because carbon dating techniques would still involve the destruction of a small amount of the cloth of the shroud, but permission for this has apparently now been granted.

But if, as seems likely on the basis of Max Frei's pollen results, the shroud proves to be of the right date, we are still faced with the mystery of *how* the image was "imprinted" on it. American investigators have pointed out the similarity of the markings to "radiation burns" produced by atomic explosions, and suggested that the image may have been impressed on the shroud by a very brief and intense burst of radiation – perhaps when the body of Jesus was brought back to life in the tomb. The sceptics counter this by asking why a "miracle" should involve atomic radiation. Their question seems unanswerable. But then, so does the evidence of the extraordinary amount of "information" encoded in the shroud. If the shroud proves to be a fourteenth-century forgery, the miracle will be almost as great as if it is proved genuine.

Postscript to "The Holy Shroud"

The developments in the Turin Shroud case since this article was written are extremely interesting.

In 1977, an American organization called the Shroud of Turin Research Project (STURP) was formed. The Catholic Church continued to reject all proposals to have the shroud subjected to carbon dating, but finally gave way, and agreed to a test on 21 April 1988. Three labouratories were involved: from Arizona, Oxford and Zurich. The results were published on 13 October 1988, and showed with ninety-nine per cent certainty that the material of the shroud dated from between AD 1260 and 1390.

So it seemed that the shroud was a fake. Then who faked it, and why?

In 1994, Lynn Picknett and her fellow researcher Clive Prince came up with a rather interesting answer to this question. Their book, *The Turin Shroud – In Whose Image?* was subtitled "The Shocking Truth Unveiled".

According to Picknett and Prince, the "fake" was the work of Leonardo da Vinci, and he was probably commissioned to do it by the pope.

But how about the fact that Leonardo was born in 1452, 99 years after the shroud had first been put on display? Their theory is that Leonardo was commissioned by the pope to make a copy of the shroud that would be exhibited to draw the tourists – because, we presume, the other was becoming worn.

This story, apparently, was told by a Neapolitan named Giovanni Battista della Porta, who is usually credited with the invention of photography, since he described the process in 1552, 33 years after Leonardo's death. Then Leonardo's notebooks were translated, (he had written them in a kind of code) and they showed that Leonardo had invented what he called "the artificial eye" (*oculus artificalis*). Leonardo explained that if the façade of a building is illuminated by the sun, and a small hole is made in the face of the building facing it, the light passing through this hole will throw an upside-down image of the façade on a wall. It would be about another 150 years, in the 1640s, until the Jesuit scientist Athanasius Kircher used the principle in the first "magic lantern".

What Picknett and Prince then have to prove is that silver nitrate or chloride, the chemicals that "photograph" the image, were known at the time of Leonardo. They are able to show that these had been known since the beginning of that century.

The theory is original, but most people will feel, rightly, that it is simply too speculative, without solid evidential proof. For example, if carbon dating has shown that the linen of the shroud was woven between 1200 and 1390, then Leonardo's lifetime is simply a century too late. Of course, the linen he used may have been lying around for a century – but it seems unlikely.

This objection does not apply to another recent theory about the nature of the shroud, explained in *The Second Messiah* (1997) by Christopher Knight and Robert Lomas. These researchers argue that the image on the shroud is that of Jacques de Molay, Grand Master of the Knights Templar.

The Templars (who are also discussed in the article on Rennes-le-Chateau) were a group of knights who were formed in the Holy Land after the fall of Jerusalem and the success of the First Crusade in AD 1099. Their purpose was to make the roads of the Holy Land safe for pilgrims, but the original band of nine knights clearly seems inadequate for this purpose, suggesting that it was a "blind".

Lomas and Knight argue that the Templars had another purpose when they moved in to the remains of Solomon's Temple in Jerusalem, which had been destroyed by the Romans when they crushed the Jewish revolt of AD 70. The Templars, they suggest, were actually searching for old scrolls or documents.

The most famous scrolls of the Holy Land are, of course, the Dead Sea Scrolls, discovered in a cave by an Arab shepherd in 1947. He took them home with him, and fortunately decided against using them as fire-lighters.

Lomas and Knight believe that the scrolls in the Temple came from the same source as the Dead Sea Scrolls, but were of far greater significance. There is evidence that the Templar who took some of the scrolls back to France was Geoffrey de St Omer, the second in command after Hugh de Payen. The scrolls were taken to an old priest called Lambert of St Omer, who is mainly known to historians because of a copy of a drawing that depicts the Heavenly Jerusalem. It was made about AD 1120, and – Lomas and Knight point out – shows the basic symbols of Freemasonry five centuries before Freemasonry is said to have been founded. Lomas and Knight argue convincingly that the drawing originated in Solomon's Temple.

But what were these scrolls?

The Dead Sea Scrolls were the property of a Jewish sect called the Essenes, also known as the Nazoreans. These were what we might describe as Jewish Puritans, strict vegetarians who rejected animal sacrifice, and therefore refused to recognize the divine inspiration of Moses.

The Essenes were founded because of a fundamental split among the Jews. When the Jews were dragged off into their Babylonian exile by the armies of King Nebuchadnezzar in 587 BC, they dreamed of a Messiah who would lead them to freedom. And when they returned to Jerusalem fifty years later, and a priest named Zerubbabel rebuilt the Temple, Zerubbabel was regarded by many as the Messiah – although he himself preferred to avoid that responsibility.

Two centuries later, Alexander the Great conquered Palestine, and it was his generals, known as Seleucids, who then ruled. But when the Greek conquerors were rash enough to place a statue of Zeus on the altar of the Temple, the Jews under Judas Maccabeus, began a highly successful guerrilla campaign, and finally rededicated the Temple to Jehovah in 164 BC. The Maccabees became kings, as well as high priests, of Jerusalem.

This caused outrage among the descendants of Zerubbabel, who regarded the Maccabees as upstarts, and around 187 BC, many withdrew to the wilderness near the Dead Sea, and became the Qumran community. They lived in tents, and used the caves as store houses. They were also known as the Essenes, and were led by a man who was referred to simply as the Teacher of Righteousness. Lomas and Knight argue that the rituals of the Essenes bore many resemblances to those of the Freemasons.

In the Jewish revolt of AD 66, the Essenes hid their scrolls and manuscripts in the Dead Sea caves, and – Lomas and Knight believe – in Solomon's Temple, which was reserved for the most valuable.

These, Lomas and Knight argue, is what the Templars were actually seeking. This was the "treasure" that they found. They went on during the course of the next two centuries, to achieve an enormous amount of wealth and influence. The documents they had found in the Temple were, according to Lomas and Knight, the title deeds that authorized them to become the founders of a new religious order.

The most controversial part of the argument of Lomas and Knight is that the leader of the Essenes in the first century AD were Jesus, who became known as Jesus Christ, and his brother James. Jesus, they claim, was actually known as Jesus the Nazorean, not the Nazarene. Nazareth, they say, did not even exist in Jesus' time.

According to Lomas and Knight, it was Jesus' younger brother James, also known as Ya'cov, who was the leader of the Essenes and the "Teacher of Righteousness".

The Roman Catholic Church has denied that Jesus had brothers or sisters, although this is actually contradicted by the Gospel of Matthew (13: 55): "Is this not the carpenter's son? Is not his mother called Mary, and his brothers James, Simon and Jude? And his sisters, are they not all with us"?

Lomas and Knight argue that Jesus was not simply a preacher of universal love; he wanted to get rid of the Romans, and was prepared to lead a revolt to do it. A large number of the Essenes preferred Jesus' less radical brother James.

Both Jesus and his cousin John the Baptist were regarded as "messiahs".

After the death of John the Baptist, Jesus took up his ministry (which only lasted one year) gathering followers and preaching in remote places. Then he made what, historically speaking, was his great mistake – he rode into Jerusalem on an ass, to fulfill the prediction of the prophet Zachariah that the king would arrive on a donkey. Then he caused a riot in the temple and attacked the money changers.

The Romans issued a wanted poster for Jesus which still survives, describing him as short, (about 4ft 6ins), bald-headed and humpbacked. His brother James was arrested first, then Jesus was arrested in Gethsemane.

It seems highly probable that Jesus was hoping that his act of rebellion would cause an uprising that would bring people flocking to his banner. He had announced that the end of the world would occur within the lifetime of people who were then listening to him. He was mistaken on both counts. Instead, he was arrested, tried and sentenced to death. Lomas and Knight argue that Barrabas, the "thief" who was acquitted was Jesus' brother James – Barrabas is a title meaning "son of the Father". An early manuscript of Matthew gives Barrabas' surname as Jesus.

So Jesus was crucified, while James returned to being the leader of the Qumran community. Thirty years later he would be murdered by priests, who threw him from the top of the temple then stoned him to death.

Jesus' body disappeared from the rock tomb, and so began rumours that he had not died on the cross, but had been seen alive.

It was St Paul–Saul – who plays the central part in the early story of Christianity.

When Saul became a Roman citizen, he changed his name to Paul and was given the job of stamping out the remains of the Jewish freedom movement. This was ten years after the death of Jesus, in AD 43. And it was seventeen years later that Paul had his experience on the road to Damascus, and was suddenly converted to Christianity. Lomas and Knight state that this would not have been the Damascus in Syria, where he would have had no authority, but probably Kumran, which was also referred to as Damascus. And it was probably on the way to Kumran to persecute the Essenes that Paul received his revelation. He became temporarily blind, and when he recovered, became romantically enthralled by the doctrine that would be later labeled Christianity. This doctrine, of Paul's own invention, declared that Jesus had died on the cross to redeem humankind from the sin of Adam, and that all who believed in Jesus would become free of Original Sin.

James and the other Nazoreans must have been astonished and delighted to discover that their persecutor had suddenly become Jesus' chief admirer. But when, in due course, they learned the details of the Christianity that had been invented by Paul, they were enraged, and habitually referred to him as "the spouter of lies".

Now in fact, these two versions of Christianity – the militant version of James, and the "gentle Redeemer" version of Paul – might well have continued to be rivals for centuries to come. But the Jewish revolt put an end to that, James was murdered, and most of the rebels were slaughtered or driven into exile.

Paul, who was abroad preaching to the Gentiles, survived, and so did his version of Christianity.

The immense popularity of Christianity was due to the fact that it preached the end of the world within a decade or so – say, by the end of the first century – and by the time that that came and went without any sign of Armageddon St Paul's version of Christianity was so well established that no one noticed.

For the next two centuries, the fortunes of the Christians varied, but more often than not they were persecuted. Then, they suddenly achieved power. This happened in the year AD 312, when the emperor Constantine made Christianity the official religion of his empire. It is usually assumed that Constantine was converted when he saw the sign of a cross in the sky, before the battle of the Milvian Bridge, and the words "In this sign shall ye conquer". But the truth is that Constantine never became a Christian – he remained a follower of the sun god Sol Invictus. There can be little doubt that his "conversion" was entirely political. It was basically an attempt to prevent the shaky Roman Empire from falling apart. What the Empire needed, he suddenly recognized, was not a vast army, but a new religion. His mother Helena, a British princess, had been converted to Christianity. And although the Christians were a long way from being a majority, there were probably a few of them in every town and village in his empire. If he handed them power, then he had a supporter in every town and village. If the Roman Empire could be compared to a British public school, then the headmaster had decided to hand over part of his authority to the prefects, who now had good reason to want to keep order.

It was true that, as soon as they gained power, these gentle, peace-loving Christians immediately began to quarrel and murder one another. But at least they held the empire together.

Lomas and Knight quote Pope Leo X as saying: "It has served us well, this myth of Christ".

The Roman Catholic Church had every reason for supporting this new, authoritarian version of Christianity, based on St Paul's inspired invention, but the older version – of the Nazoreans and Messianists – had not entirely died out. For example, Paul – in the days when he was still a persecutor of Christians – drove a group of Messianists known as Mandaeans – who regarded John the Baptist as the Messiah – to Iraq, where they still continue to flourish.

Lomas and Knight believed that it was this older version of Christianity, with its roots in the Kumran community, that one day became Freemasonry. And it is here that the story touches on the strange history of Rennes-le-Chateau. Henry Lincoln has argued that the order of the Priory of Sion, which was founded at the end of the first Crusade by Hugh de Payen and his knights, actually dates back many centuries, through the dynasty known as the Merovingians. (See Postscript to the article on Rennes-le-Chateau.)

During the twelfth century, the Crusaders lost what ground they had gained in the Holy Land; a second crusade ended in failure, and the Muslims under the leadership of Saladin recaptured Jerusalem in 1187. During the next century, seven more crusades failed to restore power to the Christians. The fall of Acre in 1291 completed their defeat, and the Knights Templar had lost their *raison d'etre*.

Their wealth – based on exemption from taxes – remained. But the French king Philip the Fair (1265–1314) was eyeing them like a cat watching a mouse. He had reason for feeling hostile, since the Templars were dedicated to the service of the pope, and Philip the Fair was in conflict with Pope Boniface VIII. Philip simply wanted an excuse to pounce on the Templars, and seize their wealth.

After being ejected from the Holy Land, the Templars had moved to Cyprus, but the island was insecure. The ideal solution would have been for the Templars to return to France. None of them was aware how deeply the king – who had once been turned down for membership – detested them.

Boniface VIII died; his successor, Boniface IX, soon followed him – probably poisoned by Philip. At that point – 1305 – Philip succeeded in having his own candidate appointed pope – Archbishop Bertrand de Gotte of Bordeaux. Bertrand and Philip disliked one another, but the prizes were too great to allow this to stand in their way. So Bertrand became Pope Clement V, and the king – now he had the pope in his pocket – decided to move the papal seat from Rome to Avignon, and to seized the wealth of the Templars.

It was an immense undertaking, since the number of Templars was now enormous, and they were among the most influential men in France. In spite of which, sealed orders went out in mid-September, 1307, ordering a swoop on the Templars on Friday, 13 October 1307. What is so amazing is that the coup actually worked, and most of the Templars fell into the trap. The exception were the Templars of Bezu, near Rennes-le-Chateau, who were almost certainly tipped off by the pope himself – it can hardly be coincidence that the chief Templar of Bezu was called de Gotte.

Philip's excuse for having the Templars arrested was that they were actually a kind of satanist organization – they were accused of homosexuality, worshipping a demon called Baphomet, and spitting upon the cross. Most of this was almost certainly nonsense – except that the Templars probably did *not* believe in orthodox Christianity. If, as Lomas and Knight believe, they were descendants of the Essenes and the Priory of Sion, then they would certainly have regarded St Paul as a "spouter of lies", and Pauline Christianity as a gross distortion of the truth.

Most of the Templars were subjected to appalling tortures, so that many confessed to these absurd charges. The Grand Master himself, Jacques de Molay, was among those who confessed, and so was his second-in-command, Geoffrey de Charney. But at their sentencing seven years later – on 18 March 1314 – Molay withdrew his confession, declaring it had been forced on him by torture. The king was so enraged at having his plans thwarted that he immediately ordered Molay and Charney to be roasted alive, over a slow fire. This happened the following day, on an island in the Seine called the Ile de Palais, and it is said that Molay, dying in horrible agony, summoned the king and the pope to meet him before the throne of God within a year. Whether this is true or not, both the king and the pope were dead within the year.

In fact, Philip's main purpose in destroying the Templars was thwarted. The knights of Bezu and other Templars sailed out of La Rochelle in eighteen ships on the day before the arrest of the Templars, and they vanished from history. So Philip's coffers were not replenished after all.

At least one of the Templar ships escaped to Scotland, and it was there that a knight named William St Clair built a chapel called Rosslyn, not far from Edinburgh, which is full of evidence that St Clair was a Templar.

The chapel of Rosslyn is certainly amazing enough. To begin with, it seems to be built on the plan of Solomon's Temple. Second, some of its decorations show cobs of sweet corn, which at that time was only found in the New World, which would not be discovered for another half century – St Clair began to build Rosslyn in 1440. The decorations also include aloes, another American plant. It is difficult not to agree with Lomas and Knight that some of the eighteen missing Templar ships sailed to America. But would they take a voyage as dangerous as that if they had no idea of what lay across the Atlantic? The highly plausible suggestion made by Lomas and Knight is that the "treasure" found by the first Templars in Solomon's Temple included maps which showed America. And this presupposes that the Templars had access to some ancient maps like the "maps of the ancient sea kings" discussed elsewhere in this book (p 91).

Now Lomas and Knight discovered a four-inch tableau hidden away at the top of a pillar in Rosslyn chapel showing a headless figure holding up a piece of cloth, on which there is the face of a bearded man. The head has obviously been cut off to prevent recognition. But none of the other figures has a missing head. Moreover, the faces are highly distinctive, as if they were portraits of living people. So it seems likely that the figure with the missing head may have had the face of William St Clair himself, or possibly of a member of the de Charney family, who now owned the Holy Shroud. Lomas and Knight are convinced that the cloth being held by the figure *is* the Holy Shroud.

They also argue strongly that the image on the Holy Shroud is Jacques de Molay, the Master of the Templars.

The argument they put forward in their book *The Second Messiah* – the sequel to *The Hiram Key* – is that it was, in fact, Jacques de Molay whose outline is still preserved on the Holy Shroud.

Now de Molay had not been tortured in the chamber of the Inquisition, but in the Paris headquarters of the Templars. The rack and suspension chains would not have been available in the headquarters. Lomas and Knight argue that de Molay was, in fact, tortured by being crucified, and that this was carried out by nailing him to a door in a chamber at the Paris headquarters. The inquisitor William Imbert a devout Catholic, would certainly have been horrified to learn that the Templars denied that Christ was the Son of God, and would have felt that it was highly appropriate to torture de Molay by nailing him to a door.

After Molay had confessed to whatever the inquisitors accused him of, he was taken down and wrapped in a piece of cloth which was probably there in the Paris Temple. He was laid on his bed in this "shroud", his body streaming with perspiration, and with blood (with a high lactic acid content) and the authors introduce some interesting evidence to the effect that this mixture would have "photographed" de Molay's image on the cloth of the shroud. (In an appendix to *The Second Messiah*, they introduce the evidence of Dr Alan Mills, a photographic expert, on the chemistry of this process.)

This cloth, they think, was returned to the home of Geoffrey de Charney, either before or after the two men were roasted to death. Less than forty years later, the shroud was put on display in a church at Lirey, near the home of Geoffrey de Charney's grandson, who had the same name.

Thousands of people regarded Jacques de Molay as a martyr – hence the title of the book *The Second Messiah*. Four and a half centuries later, when Louis XVI was guillotined during the French Revolution, someone in the crowd shouted: "Jacques Molay is avenged"!

Lomas and Knight's theory of the origin of the Holy Shroud is certainly one of the most controversial so far. It is, of course, supported by the carbon-dating of the Shroud. And the notion that the Shroud is a fake, propounded by Picknett and Prince, seems to have been disproved by the fact that chemical tests have shown that the Shroud was genuinely soaked with blood and perspiration.

It is true that the one weak point of the theory of Lomas and Knight is that there is no positive evidence that Jacques de Molay was tortured by being crucified. But if the man on the Shroud was not de Molay, then who was he?

23

Homer and the Fall of Troy

Are They Both a Myth?

Although Shakespeare is acknowledged to be England's greatest poet, serious doubts have been expressed about whether he wrote any of the works attributed to him. In the case of Homer – the first great poet of Western civilization – many schoolars have gone even further and raised doubts as to whether he actually existed. A children's book entitled *How Much Do You Know*? carries the following entry under the question: "Who Was Homer"?:

> The traditional author of the *Iliad* and the *Odyssey*. No evidence exists that such a person ever lived, though every known test has been applied to the poems, and every possible source of information scrutinized. All the *Lives* of Homer are apocryphal. The best one can say is that an authoritative text of the two poems existed at Athens between 550 and 500 BC. According to tradition, Homer was blind, and conventional busts and pictures show him as sightless.

How could a famous poet be nonexistent? One widely held opinion is that various Greek bards (or *rhapsodes*) invented poems about the Trojan War and its aftermath and that these various accounts were later stitched together into the poems we know as the *Iliad* and the *Odyssey*. We can add to this question about the existence of Homer the question of whether the Trojan War really took place or whether – as many scholars have suggested – it was a purely mythical event, like the wars of the gods. However, no one who has actually read straight through these two poems can believe that they were written by a committee.

There is one very sound reason for believing that Homer really existed. By studying the language of the *Iliad* and the *Odyssey*, scholars have dated the poems to some time between 750 and 650 BC. Now this is a mere two or three centuries before the Golden Age of Athens, the age of Plato and Aristotle and Euripides. In other words, it was closer to the age of Plato than Shakespeare is to our own period at the time of this writing. Moreover, the Greek bards learned their poetry by heart and could recite many thousands of lines from memory – as their modern descendants still can today. So there was no question of Homer being lost in the dim mists of antiquity, in the days before there were any historical records. The memories of the bards themselves were the historical records. And it is impossible to believe that they simply invented a poet named Homer and attributed various poems to him – as unlikely as believing that Sir Isaac Newton was the invention of a group of seventeenth-century scientists, who also wrote his *Principia*.

What seems to emerge from the available evidence is that Homer was a blind poet who was born some time around 750 BC in Asia Minor (now Turkey) and who spent much of his life in poverty, wandering from place to place, until he found a measure of fame on the island of Chios. Many fragmentary biographies of him exist among the works of the classical writers, the longest and best of which is attributed to the historian Herodotus (known as the Father of History), who was also born in Asia Minor about two and a half centuries later.

Herodotus's story is as follows. Homer's mother was a poor orphan girl named Critheis who became pregnant out of wedlock, as a result of which she moved from Asia Minor to a place near the river Meles in Greece (Boeotia) and gave birth to a son, whom she named Melesigenes (pronounced Mellis-igenees), after the river. He was to acquire the nickname Homer (which means "blind man"*) many years later. She then returned to Smyrna (now called Izmir) and became housekeeper to a teacher of literature and music named Phemius, who fell in love with her and married her. So Homer acquired a stepfather who knew all about poetry and music.

The young Homer distinguished himself at school. When his step-father died – followed shortly by his mother – he took over the school with brilliant success and became something of a celebrity among his fellow citizens. He became friendly with a traveler named Mentes, from the island of Leucadia (now called Leukas) in western Greece, who persuaded Homer to accompany him on his travels and offered to pay all Homer's expenses. Unable to resist this offer to see the world, Homer

---

* Other meanings suggested by scholars are "hostage", "comrade", and "orderer", in the sense of one who gives order to thoughts.

set off with Mentes and traveled by land to what is now called Italy. Full of curiosity, he asked questions everywhere he went. But in the course of his travels, he picked up an eye infection, and by the time he reached Ithaca – just south of Leucadia – it had become so serious that Mentes left him behind with a doctor named Mentor. It was Mentor who taught Homer about the legends of Odysseus (whom the Romans would call Ulysses★) and the story of his epic voyage home from the Trojan War. When he came to compose the *Odyssey*, Homer gave the name Mentor to the teacher of Ulysses's son Telemachus, and the name has become synonymous with "teacher". But Mentor was unable to cure Homer's eye problems. Homer decided to try to get back home, but in Colophon, in Asia Minor, he finally became blind.

Back in Smyrna, he continued to devote himself to poetry. But now he had no school to support him, and he set out on the wanderings that would last the rest of his life. In a place called Neon Teichos (New Wall) he was befriended by an armorer named Tychias and earned his bread by reciting verse. And although poverty drove the blind poet to move on, the inhabitants of Neon Teichos remembered him with affection and would point out the spot where he used to recite. In Cumae, his mother's birthplace (from which she had fled to conceal her pregnancy), he once again found such a sympathetic audience for his verses that he decided he would like to settle there and asked the town council if they would support him with public funds in exchange for entertainment – promising them that he would make their city famous. But one grumpy councillor declared that if they fed every Homer ("blind man") who came to Cumae, they would soon be overrun with vagabonds. Thereupon the council decided not to grant the poet's request. The name "Homer" stuck, however.

Homer moved to nearby Phocoae, on the island of Chios, where a would be poet named Thestorides persuaded him to enter into an odd bargain. Homer would write poetry for Thestorides, in exchange for food and lodging. But his host finally broke his bargain and threw the blind man out. Homer continued as a homeless wanderer, singing for his supper. Sometime later, back on the mainland, he met some merchants from Chios who told him that their local poet, Thestorides, was singing verses that were virtually identical with Homer's. Enraged that Thestorides was passing off his (Homer's) verses as his own, Homer hastened back to Chios, where he met a kindly goatherd named Glaucus

---

★ And I shall follow their example, as well as changing the names of other Greek gods to their more familiar Latin equivalents.

who put him up for the night in his hut. Homer's story of his travels so moved Glaucus that he went to his master and asked him to help the poet. The master was scornful, feeling that Glaucus had been taken in by a vagabond. But when he actually met Homer, he was so impressed by his learning and by his poetry that he engaged him as a tutor for his children.

Now, at last, Homer's misfortunes were over. In the town of Chios he became a celebrity, and when the truth became known about Thestorides, the imposter was driven from the island. Homer became highly successful, both as a poet and a teacher of youth, and he married and had two daughters. Chios became so proud of Homer that it claimed to be his birthplace. As his reputation spread to Greece, he decided to travel there again. On the island of Samos he was recognized and played a part in a religious festival, then was a guest in many rich houses. After this he set sail for Athens but had only reached the island of Ios when he fell ill and died, probably of a stroke. (The legend claims that his death was brought on by frustration at being unable to answer a riddle propounded by the children of fishermen.) But as his fame spread throughout Greece, and bards recited his poems, Chian bards formed a school known as the children of Homer – or Homeridae – which was still flourishing when Herodotus wrote his life of Homer.

So while scholars insist on preserving caution, it seems a commonsense assumption that a blind poet named Homer was born in Asia Minor, traveled in Greece and Italy – perhaps even as far as Spain – settled in Chios, and died on his way to Athens. The school he founded learned his words by heart; why not the events of his life? The dates of these events are altogether more doubtful. Herodotus thinks Homer lived some four hundred years before himself – around 900 BC. A later scholar, Crates, placed him around eighty years after the Trojan War (which has generally been dated about 1180 BC but which modern scholars place as early as 1250 – a question to which we shall return in a moment). We now know that to be virtually impossible; for example, a reference in the *Odyssey* to the Phoenicians as traders dates it later than 900 BC.

But anyone who has read the two epics will have noticed basic differences between them. Although a great deal longer than the *Odyssey*, the *Iliad* covers only a small part of the Trojan War – a few weeks in its tenth year – and is full of slaughter and violence. (The story is a simple one: The Greek hero, Achilles, quarrels with King Agamemnon about a pretty slave girl and refuses to take any part in the battle – until his closest friend, Patroclus, is killed by the Trojan Hector;

then Achilles goes out to meet Hector, chases him three times around the walls of Troy, and kills him.) The *Odyssey* is altogether softer and more lyrical in tone, describing the adventures of Ulysses as he tries to make his way back home from Troy to Ithaca. The Greek scholar Longinus, author of *On the Sublime*, takes the view that this difference is attributable to the fact that Homer wrote the *Iliad* when he was young and at the height of his powers, and the *Odyssey* in old age. But most modern scholars explain the difference by suggesting that two different poets wrote the two works. The author of the *Iliad*, they claim, was the blind poet described by Herodotus. The *Odyssey* was written by a later poet, whose identity is unknown. A widely held view is that the *Iliad* was composed about 750 BC and the *Odyssey* about 700.

There is one very obvious difference between the two poems. In the *Iliad*, the gods play as prominent a part as the men; they are always interfering in the battle, and the goddess of love, Aphrodite, even swoops down and carries off Paris when he is about to be defeated by Menelaus. In the *Odyssey*, the gods still interfere in the narrative, but they could be eliminated without making much difference to the story of Ulysses. One example will suffice: when Ulysses is slaying his wife's suitors, the goddess Minerva (Athena) puts in an appearance, disguised as the estate manager; but after the suitors have threatened her with violent reprisals, she turns herself into a swallow and flies up to the rafters. Such an event, one would expect, would clearly convince the suitors that something supernatural was going on and would lower their morale; in fact, they seem not to notice and proceed to attack Ulysses as if nothing had happened. The appearance of the goddess is not only pointless, it makes the scene absurd. It is almost as if the *Iliad* belongs to an earlier period of belief, while the *Odyssey* was written by someone for whom the gods were little more than a convenient plot mechanism.

But if the author of the *Odyssey* was not the blind Homer, then who was he?

The English writer Samuel Butler became aware of the puzzle in 1891. Butler is best known for his amusing satirical novel *Erewhon*, but it would be a mistake to think of him as a satirist. He was a serious thinker who devoted an important part of his life's work to attacking Darwin's theory of evolution. He objected to Darwin's view that mutations cause species to change *at random* and that evolution is due simply to the survival of the fittest. Butler objected that Darwin had "banished God from the universe" and turned the universe into a gigantic machine. He preferred the views of the earlier zoologist Lamarck, who believed that species change because they make determined *efforts* to change. (For a more detailed account of the problem, see chapter 35.)

At the age of fifty-six Butler decided to compose a cantata entitled *Ulysses*. (He was also an amateur composer who wrote in the style of Handel.) His librettist, Henry Festing Jones, was relying on Charles Lamb's *Adventures of Ulysses*, but Butler felt he should reread the *Odyssey*, of which he retained only vague memories from his schooldays. Butler found Homer's Greek simple and straightforward and decided to make his own prose translation. As he worked, he became aware of a feeling of unease, of "a riddle that I could not read". The *Iliad* is full of larger-than-life heroes. The *Odyssey*, by comparison, struck Butler as far more lifelike, in fact, as a kind of novel rather than an epic, full of real people and real observations. The latter begins by telling how Ulysses's son Telemachus, sick of the horde of suitors who surround his mother, Penelope, goes off to see if he can find news of his father; he calls on King Menelaus, who is now living happily with his errant wife, Helen of Troy, and the domestic scene has an almost tongue-in-cheek atmosphere. Here he learns that his father is a prisoner of the nymph Calypso.

The scene shifts to Calypso's island, where Ulysses has been allowed to leave (owing to the intervention of Jupiter). But the god Neptune, who disliked Ulysses, caused a storm, which wrecked the hero on the coast of a country called Scheria. Here he was found lying asleep by Nausicaa, the king's daughter, who took him back to the palace. And here, in due course, Ulysses tells the story of what happened to him after he left Troy (which was captured by means of a wooden horse). At this point, we have a long story-within-a-story, which forms the main part of the *Odyssey*.

Butler was struck by the realism of the Nausicaa episode and its many homely touches. It confirmed his feeling that the *Odyssey* was a kind of novel, based on real people. A few books later, after Ulysses has encountered the Cyclops, the god of wind (Aeolus), and the man-eating Laestrigonians, he lands on the island of the enchantress Circe, who changes his men into swine. And it was as he was reading about Circe that Butler was suddenly struck by a dazzling intuition: that Circe was not created by a man but by a woman – and, moreover, by a young one. Closer reading convinced him of this. The males of the *Odyssey* are wooden creatures compared to the women, who have that touch of life. Butler also concluded that while the author of the *Odyssey* shows intimate knowledge of the affairs of women, he is often oddly uncomfortable when describing things that are the province of males, especially seamen or farmers. What male would place the rudder in front of the ship? What seaman would believe that seasoned timber can be cut from a growing tree? Or make the wind "whistle" over the waters? (It whistles on land, because of obstacles, but there are no obstacles at sea.) What man with any knowledge of farming would make a herdsman milk the sheep, then give them their lambs to feed (presumably with empty udders)? What countryman would make a hawk tear its prey *on the wing*? The author of the *Odyssey* makes these curious errors, and many more. Butler goes on to argue with great skill and conviction that the author of the *Odyssey* had to be a woman, and a young one at that.

Now if, for the sake of argument, we are willing to admit the possibility that the *Odyssey* was written by a young woman, a kind of Greek Jane Austen or Elizabeth Barrett Browning, then certain things become obvious. The first is that she had a great deal of leisure. In Jane Austen's day the daughter of a country vicar would have had sufficient leisure to write novels; but in ancient Greece, life was far harder. (What moderns find so hard to grasp is that life in ancient Greece was a poverty-stricken affair, with most people living on a diet of olive oil and vegetables, with some boiled mutton every week or so.) For a woman to have had leisure enough to write, she would have had to have been a member of the aristocracy, one who had servants to look after her. (And we note that even Princess Nausicaa goes to the beach to do her own washing.)

Second, a Greek Jane Austen, like the English one, would have had a fairly restricted knowledge of life (in those days, girls stayed at home), and you would expect her to use her own background in her poem. Butler felt that all the older women in the poem – Helen, Penelope, Queen Arete (Nausicaa's mother) – are basically the same person and that the same applies to the younger women – Nausicaa, Circe, and Calypso – and to the men – Ulysses, Nestor, Menelaus, and King Alcinous (Nausicaa's father). And if, like any young lady novelist, the authoress of the *Odyssey* put a portrait of herself into her book, then we have to choose between Nausicaa, Circe, and Calypso. Nausicaa is the obvious choice. And presumably, Queen Arete and King Alcinous are portraits of the authoress's parents.

But if the young authoress knew only her own home, then how did she manage to describe the travels of Ulysses so convincingly? Presumably, by using places she actually knew and transforming them into the lands of Polyphemus, Circe, the Laestrigonians, and so on. In other words, if one could find out where "Nausicaa" lived, one might recognize various features of the poem in its geography.

Now Nausicaa, as we have said, lived in a land called Scheria – which means "jut-land" – a peninsula jutting into the sea, which, according to Homer, was the land of a people called the Phaecians. When the naked Ulysses approaches her on the beach – covering himself with a bough for decency – she gives him food and clothing and instructs him precisely how to get back to her father's house: "You will find the town lying between two harbors, approached by a narrow neck of land". Later in the *Odyssey*, after the Phaecians have taken Ulysses back to his own land of Ithaca, the angry sea-god, Neptune, turns their ship into a rock in the mouth of the harbor. So Butler felt he had a number of clues about Scheria: it had to have a neck of land jutting into the sea between two harbors and a large rock that resembled a ship in the mouth of one of the harbors. It also seems clear from the *Odyssey* that Ulysses approaches Scheria from the east, so that the harbor must be on the western coast. Butler went to the British Museum and studied a map of Greece and Italy, looking for any west coast that had two harbors on either side of a promontory. He could find only one – the site of the town of Trapani, on the west coast of Sicily. Butler looked at Trapani more closely and became convinced that this had to be the home of Nausicaa. It was the only western coast in the whole area – including Italy and Greece – that fit the description. There was also a mountain – Mount Eryx – above Trapani, and Neptune is also reported in the *Odyssey* as threatening to bury the city of the Phaecians under a high mountain.

Two earlier Greek history scholars, Stolberg and Mure, had also been convinced that Mount Eryx fit the geography of the Cyclops episode. And the Greek historian Thucydides, writing around 403 BC, had mentioned that Sicily was probably the home of the Cyclops and the Laestrigonians. In the *Odyssey*, of course, these episodes take place far from the home of Nausicaa. But what would be more natural than for a young authoress writing a kind of novel about Ulysses to use local scenery as its background?

The next step was to visit Trapani; this Butler did in 1892. Now he had the satisfaction of finding that everything confirmed his views. Admittedly, one of the two harbors was now silted up and contained a saltworks; but it was obvious that it had once been just such a harbor as "Homer" had described. A few miles away, on the lower slopes of Mount Eryx, was a cave that the locals still called the "grotto of Polyphemus". Near the entrance to the northern harbor was a rock that looked not unlike a ship. Local legend said it was a Turkish pirate ship turned to stone by the Blessed Virgin – obviously a Christianized form of the ancient legend.

Now Butler no longer had any doubt that he was on the right track. He noted that the description of Ithaca in the *Odyssey* is quite unlike the real Ithaca: it is described as "highest up in the sea" with a clear view to the west, whereas the real Ithaca is completely masked by the much bigger island of Samos (now Cephalonia) to the west. But if the authoress of the *Odyssey* modeled her Ithaca on the little island of Marettimo, facing the harbors of Trapani, it would correspond to the description in the *Odyssey*.

A voyage around Sicily convinced Butler that his authoress had simply taken the island she knew and used its scenery as the geographical background for the voyage of Ulysses. Ulysses himself describes how he sailed down to the island of Cythera, just south of Greece, and then was prevented from turning northward (for Ithaca) by strong winds that drove him west to the land of the lotus-eaters, which must have been on the coast of north Africa. But after this, according to Butler, he made for Sicily, to the north, hunted goats on the island of Favagnana (known to the ancients as Goat Island – Aegusa), then landed on Sicily and had his adventure with the one-eyed giant, Polyphemus, whose eye he burned out with a stake. Then he sailed north to the island of Aeolus, the god of winds, which Butler identifies as the little island of Ustica. The town of Cafalu, on the north coast, he thinks is the site of the adventure of the man-eating Laestrigonians. The site of Scylla and Charybdis is off the east coast, near present-day Messina. Finally, on his way back, he encountered Calypso's island, which Butler identifies as the island of Pantelleria. And so back to Trapani – or rather, to Marettimo, which is Homer's Ithaca.

If Butler had lived a century later, he would have taken a good photographer with him to Sicily and published a series of colour photographs of the various sites of the adventures of Ulysses in a coffee-table book, together with Homer's descriptions. In fact, in his book *The Authoress of the Odyssey* (finally published in 1897), Butler includes half a dozen or so photographs, but none are as convincing as they might be. Probably the best way for a modern reader to make up his own mind would be to go to Sicily with a copy of Butler's book. It has to be admitted that Butler's own sheer excitement and enthusiasm convey a great deal of conviction. But the section of the book that describes the various places is less thorough than it could be. My own suspicion is that Butler was disheartened by the general skepticism he encountered and by the total lack of response from the various scholars to whom he sent pamphlets about his theory. The famous Professor Jowett, an Oxford scholar and translator of Plato, admitted frankly that he had not even glanced at the two pamphlets Butler sent him. A dozen publishers turned down Butler's excellent prose translation of the *Odyssey*. So on the whole, it is not surprising that he failed to summon the necessary energy to argue the topographical part of the book as thoroughly as the rest.

The achievement is nevertheless considerable. At the time Butler was writing his book, most scholars took it for granted that Homer was the author of both the *Iliad* and the *Odyssey*. Nowadays, very few take that position. Butler was admittedly wrong about the dates – he thought that at least a hundred years separated the two epics and that the *Odyssey* was composed around 1050 BC But then, Butler lacked the tools – and the archaeological information – that have enabled later scholars to be far more precise. As to his essential thesis – that the *Odyssey* was written by a woman – few people who follow his arguments with the *Odyssey* in the other hand will fail to admit that he could be right. George Bernard Shaw attended a Fabian Society meeting at which Butler lectured on the female authorship of the *Odyssey* and admitted that, while initially skeptical about the idea, he took up the *Odyssey* and soon found himself saying, "Of course it was written by a woman".

Robert Graves was another classical scholar who allowed himself to be convinced, and whose novel *Homer's Daughter* is inspired by the theory. The story is told by Princess Nausicaa, who describes how her brother disappeared after a quarrel with his wife and was assumed to have gone off to foreign parts. In fact, he has been murdered by a treacherous friend. Her father, King Alpheides, sails off to look for him, leaving Uncle Mentor in charge. Nausicaa's suitors then behave exactly like Penelope's suitors in the *Odyssey* and move into the palace. But when Nausicaa and her attendants are doing the laundry near the sea, they are approached by a naked man who has been shipwrecked; he is a Cretan nobleman named Aethon, and it is he who eventually slays the suitors and marries Nausicaa. Nausicaa then goes on to write the *Odyssey*, in which biography and legend freely intermingle. The merit of the book is that it enables us to grasp the sheer plausibility of Butler's theory. *Homer's Daughter* is one of Graves's most underrated books – a careful re-creation of Sicily around 800 BC that deserves to be as widely read as *I, Claudius*.

Another interesting footnote to the Butler theory is that James Joyce used his prose translation of the *Odyssey* as the basis of *Ulysses*.

To summarize this part of the argument: it is probably fair to say that *if* the *Odyssey* was indeed the work of one single person – and was not the collective work of many bards – then the contention that it was written by a woman is highly plausible.

But what of our second question: did the siege of Troy really take place, or was it simply a myth? After all, it is obvious that the *Odyssey*, with its one-eyed giants, wandering rocks, and enchantresses who turn men into pigs, is basically a fairy tale. And the action of the *Iliad* is even more mythical, with the gods playing as important a part in the action as the heroes.

Let us review the story again. According to Greek legend, mostly based on the works of Homer, a prince named Paris (or Alexandros), son of King Priam of Troy, was a guest of King Menelaus of Sparta when he fell in love with Menelaus's wife, Helen, who was a famous beauty. She was the daughter of the god Jove (or Zeus) and a princess named Leda, whom Jove seduced by turning himself into a swan. Many princes had sought her hand before she accepted Menelaus. So when Paris carried her off – with or without her consent – the indignant Menelaus went to ask for help from his brother, King Agamemnon, in Mycenae (he would have had to travel by sea, for roads were almost nonexistent), and an armada of ninety ships sailed for Troy. These included contingents led by many of Helen's rejected suitors.

Troy – or Ilion – was a town whose wealth was founded on trade (like Mycenae, which was so rich that it was known as "golden Mycenae"). Its main industry seems to have been horse breeding. It is important for us to realize that in those days, the Mediterranean was swarming with pirates, so that no town could afford to be on the sea unless it had mighty defenses. Troy was a mile inland, but it had mighty defenses anyway, including immense walls with defensive towers. It is also important to realize that in the ancient world, peace was a rare commodity. The first thing man seems to have done when he began to live in settlements was to wage war on his neighbours, so that in the ancient world, the words "peaceable nation" were virtually a contradiction in terms. It was not until relatively modern times – about 1700 or so – that the rules of history changed and it became such a costly and highly destructive business to go to war that long periods of peace became the norm.*

So the Greeks attacking Troy found themselves in the position of a hawk trying to attack a tortoise. This was no ordinary siege – no town could hold out for ten years, as Troy did, if it was surrounded. The plain of Troy was notoriously windy – it still is – so the Greeks camped in a sheltered spot between two headlands and built a rampart to protect themselves. The Trojans had allies in other parts of Asia Minor, who sallied out to help them periodically. So it was less a siege than a spasmodic series of engagements.

---

* For a longer account of all this, see my *Criminal History of Mankind* (1984).

But in the tenth year of the war something happened, and Troy fell and was destroyed; all its men were massacred, and its women and children were carried off into slavery. According to Ulysses in the *Odyssey*, it was he who suggested the stratagem of building a wooden horse and filling it with armed men, then pretending to sail away. But of course, this could well have been an invention of the author (or authoress) of the *Odyssey*.

The story of the search for Troy is one of the most fascinating in the history of archaeology, and its conclusions are more satisfyingly positive than those in the case of the search for Homer's identity.

One story concerning the search for Troy begins in 1829, when a seven-year-old boy named Heinrich Schliemann received a copy of Jerrer's *Universal History* for Christmas. When he saw the picture of Troy in flames, he was struck by the thought that nothing could possibly destroy such mighty walls. The young Schliemann resolved that he would one day go and investigate the matter for himself. His father was a country parson in Neu-Buckow, Germany, who was dismissed after being falsely accused of misappropriating church funds. Heinrich had to become a grocer's assistant at the age of fourteen. Tuberculosis led him to give up his job and embark for South America as a cabin boy. After a shipwreck he drifted to Amsterdam, where he became a clerk and learned English. At the age of thirty-two he learned that his brother had died in California and sailed for America to claim his estate. It was a good time to go; the gold rush made him rich, and in 1863 he was finally able to realize his ambition to search for Troy. Together with a sixteen-year-old Greek schoolgirl, whom he married, he sailed for the northern coast of Turkey to begin his search.

Most scholars accepted the notion that the remains of Troy would be found on a mountain near Bunarbashi, about three hours from the sea. Schliemann, using the *Iliad* as a guide, disagreed – Homer's heroes rode between Troy and the coast several times a day. Schliemann concluded that a more likely site was a mound called Hissarlik in present-day Turkey, about an hour from the sea. (And in ancient times, the sea came much farther inland.)

It was an inspired guess, typical of Schliemann's incredible luck. When he had obtained permission to dig there, Schliemann began excavations – in 1871 – with a large gang of workmen. They soon encountered the remains of a town, but it dated from the Roman period, and it was a mere hundred yards in diameter. Below this was another ruined town. And then another. And then another. Eager to find Homer's Troy, Schliemann ordered his men to slice a great trench through the middle of the mound and keep going until they reached bedrock. All told, there proved to be the ruins of nine cities, one on top of the other.

Twelve years later, Schliemann announced that he had found the treasures of King Priam – treasures that, for some odd reason, he had always been convinced would still be there. (He never explained why the conquerors had not simply stolen them when they destroyed Troy and massacred its inhabitants.) In his autobiography he tells a remarkable story of how he had glimpsed a copper vessel through a hole in the wall and waited until his workmen had gone to lunch – he was afraid they might be tempted to steal – before he and his wife removed a treasure of drinking vessels and jewelry. The finds were to make him world famous.

There is, in fact, a disappointing postscript to this story. When, in 1972, Professor William Calder, of the University of Colorado, decided to start checking on Schliemann's biographical information, he soon discovered that the great archaeologist was a mythomaniac of the first order. His story about being received by the president of the United States on his first visit to America was pure invention; so was his tale of being present in San Francisco on the night of the great fire in May 1851. It became clear that his fortune was founded on cheating the bankers to whom he sold gold dust and that the story of the finding of the Trojan treasure was also an invention – it had actually been found over a considerable period and concealed from the eyes of his partners in the enterprise, a Turkish pasha and an American named Frank Calvert. Calder's research proved that Schliemann was a crook. Yet there can be no doubt that, in spite of this, he was an inspired archaeologist.

In fact, Schliemann's next major venture was to excavate Mycenae, in southern Greece, the home of Agamemnon, the Bronze Age king who led the expedition to Troy; here he uncovered still more treasure and revealed again that, where archaeology was concerned, his intuition was awesome. A dig at Tiryns, the home of King Diomedes (another Homeric hero), in 1884 uncovered some of the finest remains of Bronze Age civilization to date.

In 1889 Schliemann returned to Hissarlik and renewed his search for evidence of Homer's Troy. What he found, in 1890, was at once exciting and depressing. Outside the mound, and well beyond the limits of what he had believed to be Homer's Troy, he came upon the remains of a large building that in turn contained the remains of pottery that was unmistakably Mycenaean. The conclusion was obvious: he had sliced straight through the Troy he was looking for. In the following year,

Schliemann died of a stroke, collapsing in the street; his death frustrated his plans for still more ambitious excavations.

Schliemann had indeed proved that Troy existed – ancient records make it clear that there was simply no other great city in the area. But of the nine cities that had been uncovered, which one was it? Schliemann had been convinced that it was the second from the bottom – because it showed signs of having been destroyed by fire – and in order to reach it, he had ordered his workmen to slice a huge trench through the seven layers of ruins that lay above. He was to learn too late that *his* Troy was a thousand years too old and that his brutal methods had destroyed a large part of the city he was looking for. But again, which of the other eight *was* Homer's Troy?

Schliemann's collabourator, Wilhelm Dörpfeld, continued and completed Schliemann's work. The discovery of the large building containing Mycenaean pottery – probably a royal hall – had furnished him with the clue he needed. It indicated that the walls of Homer's Troy extended well beyond the boundaries of the mound of Hissarlik. And when Dörpfeld excavated at the southern edge of the mound, he soon uncovered walls greater than any Schliemann had found. This – the sixth city from the bottom – was the city they had all been looking for. These walls had a slight inward slope, just as Homer had indicated in the *Iliad* (Patroclus had made a determined attempt to scale them), and there was a mighty tower that must have been about sixty feet high before it had been reduced by more than half. There was a gate in the east wall and the remains of another tower, built of limestone blocks. Inside the walls he uncovered the ruins of five large houses and deduced that the citadel had risen in concentric circles. And although "Troy 6" measured only two hundred yards by a hundred and fifty yards, it must have been as impressive as a medieval castle. It was obvious now why the Greeks had failed to take it by storm. It must have towered over the plain of Scamander as Mont Saint Michael still towers over the flat Britanny marshes.

The next great step forward in Mediterranean archaeology was taken by the Englishman Arthur Evans, who began to excavate near the city of Heraklion, on the island of Crete, in 1900 and uncovered the remarkable royal palace at Knossos. He announced this as the palace of the legendary King Minos. According to Greek legend, the king's wife, Pasiphae, had a taste for bestiality and became pregnant by a bull, giving birth to a monster called the Minotaur, which was half man and half bull. The legend also tells how Minos demanded a yearly tribute of seven youths and seven maidens from Athens and how these were thrown to the Minotaur, which was kept in a specially built labyrinth. The Greek hero Theseus went to Crete as part of the yearly tribute, killed the Minotaur, and escaped from the labyrinth with the help of a thread, given to him by Minos's daughter Ariadne. Evans's excavations revealed pictures of youths and maidens turning somersaults over the back of a bull, suggesting that there had been a bull cult at Knossos. And the mazelike palace was full of symbols of a double-headed axe, known as *labrys*. It began to look as if the legend of Theseus and the Minotaur was based on fact after all. If so, the same could apply to the story of the Trojan War.

One of Evans's most important discoveries at Knossos was a quantity of clay tablets written in a form of hieroglyphics – actually, two forms, which became known as Linear A and Linear B. Evans was convinced that they were written in the unknown language of the ancient Cretans, which would mean that the Minoan civilization of Crete was not Greek. However, Linear B was deciphered by the scholar Michael Ventris in 1952, eleven years after Evans's death, and proved to be an early form of Greek. (Linear A remains undeciphered.) And names found in the Linear B tablets included many place-names that had been mentioned in Homer.

Evans's view dominated British archaeology for many years. An American named Carl Blegen disagreed. His excavations on mainland Greece in the 1920s convinced him that the Greeks had dominated Mediterranean civilization for a very long time indeed – as far back as 1900 BC. In 1932 he began a new series of excavations at Hissarlik, whose aim was to use the latest dating techniques (which relied heavily on pottery) to try to establish the age of *all* the levels and to learn as much as possible about each.

Blegen was able to establish that the bottom layer dated back as far as the fourth millennium BC (Modern dating is 3600.) But when he came to study the sixth Troy, which Dörpfeld had believed to be Homer's, he reached a conclusion that seemed to contradict Dörpfeld: that it had been destroyed by an earthquake. The walls had crumbled, and in one place the foundations had even shifted. That seemed to rule it out as the Troy burned down by Agamemnon. And Dörpfeld, who visited the site in 1935, had to agree. Blegen dated Troy 6 about 1260 BC, possibly ten years earlier.

But at the next layer, which he called 7a (because he found many subordinate layers in the course of his digging – a total of no less than fifty), he found something that looked much more promising. The streets of 7a were a kind of shantytown, where there had formerly been houses of the nobility, now there were cramped "bungalows". It looked as if all the people who normally lived outside Troy had been crowded into its confines – which is what you would expect in a siege. Inside the gate was a building that Blegen called the "snack bar" – a combination of bakery and wine shop. (Blegen imagined the Homeric heroes rushing in there after battle to refresh themselves.) Moreover, this Troy *had* been burned. He found smashed skulls, charred skeletons, and an arrowhead. It was this that led Blegen to announce triumphantly, "The sack of Troy is a historical fact".

There was one obvious objection to this shantytown being Homer's Troy: if the walls had been badly damaged by earthquake at some earlier stage, then surely the Greeks would have had no trouble in conquering the unprotected citadel? But closer examination disposed of this objection. Although the walls had been damaged, the circuit still remained complete; they would still have been a formidable obstacle. Many scholars were convinced that Blegen had found the Troy of the *Iliad*.

But other objections began to appear. There *was* evidence of burning in Troy 6 – Dörpfeld had noted it at the turn of the century. What is more, the "bungalows" and the "snack bar" had been built on the sites of the noble houses. But the *Iliad* is full of noblemen and women. Surely, the obvious scenario is that Troy 6 – "earthquake Troy" – was the Troy besieged by the Greeks, and that when it fell, its noblemen were slaughtered; that is why their houses gave way to lesser structures.

It is possible, however, that an earthquake caused the downfall of Homer's Troy. It has even been suggested that the story of the wooden horse may be a "folk memory" of this event. The sea-god Neptune (Poseidon) was often worshiped in the form of a horse and was supposed to be the master of horses. He was also the god of earthquakes. Suppose a great earthquake occurred in the tenth year of the war, which shook the walls and destroyed some of the noble houses in the citadel. And suppose the Greeks seized this opportunity to scale the walls – perhaps even using a siege engine that looked not unlike a horse?

What we *do* know is that the palaces of these Greek heroes – Agamemnon and Nestor and Diomedes – were themselves destroyed half a century later (about 1200 BC), probably by mysterious raiders known as the "sea peoples". So the mighty Achaean civilization was brought to its knees not long after it had destroyed Troy. Writing still did not exist, except on clay tablets (and they were used only for making lists or writing letters, not for preserving poetry); but the stories of Troy and its heroes lived on in the memories of the bards. Centuries passed; the Mediterranean was plunged into a dark age. Finally, writing in its modern form – with paper and ink – was invented and at last the great epics were written down. Apart from the *Iliad* and the *Odyssey*, there were other epic poems – the *Thebais*, about the siege of Thebes and the *Cypria*, about how Paris stole Helen – and comic epics like the *Margites* (whose hero is a fool) and the unpronounceable *Batrachomyomachia*, or Battle of the Frogs and Mice. All these are attributed to Homer. Yet since scholars are inclined to date writing in Greece as late as 650 BC, this means that Homer may have been alive six centuries after the fall of Troy.

So far, we have been obliged to admit that there is not the slightest scrap of real evidence for the siege of Troy, as described by Homer. Schliemann claimed to have found the jewels of Helen and the mask of Agamemnon, and Blegen claimed to have found the palace of King Nestor at Pylos. This may all have been wishful thinking – in fact, it undoubtedly *was* in the case of Schliemann. But confirmation of the Trojan War and its heroes was to come from a completely unexpected source.

In 1834 a young Frenchman named Charles Texier was riding through central Turkey when he heard of some ruins near the village of Bogazköy. They proved to be the gigantic remains of an earlier civilization, with tremendous walls and magnificent ruined buildings ornamented with winged demons and unknown hieroglyphs. It took half a century before it was recognized that these were the remains of a mighty empire that had once extended from Asia Minor down to Syria – the empire of the people known as the Hittites, who had once attacked Babylon. Their empire, like that of the Greeks, collapsed about 1200 BC; but two centuries earlier it had been one of the greatest nations of the Middle East. The period of the fall of Troy had been the period of the slow disintegration of the Hittite empire. Moreover, most of Asia Minor had been a part of that empire. So Troy was, in a sense, a Hittite town.

The ruins discovered by Texier were those of the Hittite capital, Hattusas, and in excavations undertaken between 1906 and 1908, the archaeologist Hugo Winkler found a mighty library of clay tablets, some in Hittite and some in Akkadian, the language in which diplomacy was conducted. Deciphered during the First World War, the tablets, from the Hittite equivalent of the foreign office, gave a detailed impression of the working of Hittite foreign policy.

These documents provided some fascinating glimpses into Near Eastern history. They revealed, for example, that after the death (around 1360 BC) of the Egyptian pharaoh Tutankhamen (he died of a blow to the head at the age of eighteen), his widow, Enhosnamon, wrote to the emperor of the Hittites, Suppiluliumas, requesting a husband. An ambassador was sent to Egypt and was there shown tablets containing details of an old treaty between Egypt and the kingdom of Hatti (the land of the Hittites); this convinced him of their good faith, and a prince named Zannanza was sent to Egypt. However, the high priest Ay wanted to marry the widow, and Zannanza was murdered – which caused a diplomatic crisis. All this was told in a document by the son of Suppiluliumas, King Mursilis II.

Was there anything about Troy or the Mycenaean civilization in these amazing records? In 1924 the Swiss historian Emile Forrer announced that he had found references to a country named *Ahhiyawa*, somewhere to the west, and he identified this as meaning "Achaia-land" – Homer always referred to the Greeks as Achaeans, or Achaiwoi. And although a philologist named Ferdinand Sommer criticized Forrer's findings in a 1932 book entitled *The Ahhiyawa Documents*, Forrer's case remains remarkably convincing.

Moreover, in 1963 an archaeological dig at Thebes (northwest of Athens) revealed more Hittite documents dating from the right period. Oddly enough, some of these were from the Hittite "foreign office" to the king of Ugarit, the great trading centre in northern Syria. There were also seals from Babylon, which research has shown to have been plundered from the temple of Marduk, sacked by the Assyrians around 1225 BC. It seems that the Assyrians, who were gaining power in the area and were therefore enemies of the Hittites, regarded the Greeks as allies. So it appears certain that the Hittites were aware of the Greeks (a fact that has been denied by some of Forrer's critics). In some Linear B tablets, Greece is called Achaiwia, which sounds very like the Hittite Ahhiyawa.

What also emerges from the Hittite records is that the Ahhiyawans controlled some territory of the coast of Asia Minor, including a city called Millawanda or Milawata. Now on the coast of Asia Minor, some two hundred miles south of Troy, there was a Greek-controlled city called Miletus, earlier known as Milatos. Geographical accounts make it clear that Miletus is Milawata. And since the Hittite records refer to the land of the Ahhiyawa as "overseas" from Miletus, this seems to suggest that it *is* "Achaiwia" or Achaea – that is, mainland Greece. Relations between the Miletan Greeks and the Hittites were basically friendly, although Miletus was sacked by the Hittites in 1315 BC in the course of a quarrel.

The records also show that a Greek king was in dispute with the Hittites around 1260 BC over a northern city called Wilusa. We know that the early Greeks called Ilios (Troy) "Wilios". And 1260 was, of course, the approximate date of the Greek expedition against the Trojans. At about this date the Hittite king Hattusilis mentions in a letter his troubles with the Greeks as well as the sack of the city of Carchemish – far to the east – by his new enemy, the Assyrians.

Some ten years later the Hittite emperor wrote to the king of the Greeks, whom he addressed as *brother*. It seems that this king's brother had been causing trouble for the Hittites. What seems to have been happening was this: the brother of the Greek king, a man named Tawagala, had joined with a rebel from Arzawa – a region northeast of Miletus – in harassing the Hittite garrison. The emperor of the Hittites marched with an army to Miletus, found that his enemies had fled, and wrote an aggrieved letter to the Greek "king" that made it clear that the Greeks were then a major power in the Mediterranean. The king to whom the Hittite emperor was writing could well have been Agamemnon. His rebellious brother Tawagala has been identified as a Greek named Eteocles, and if we knew that Agamemnon had a brother of that name, it would clinch that argument. Unfortunately, we only know of his other brother, Menelaus.

In the television series, "In Search of the Trojan War", the historian Michael Wood argues strongly that Wilusa was Troy (not just the city, but the whole area around it), using a great deal of geographical evidence from the Hittite records. Moreover, the king of Wilusa is called Alaxandus. Homer often refers to Paris – who abducted Helen – as Alexandros of Troia. Wood cites other Hittite records that show the king of the Greeks was in Asia Minor in the reign of Hattusilis III (1265–35 BC – which would include the date of the Trojan War). If that king was Agamemnon – as seems likely from the dates – then we have powerful evidence for Homer's story.

There is another piece of evidence for the existence of the Trojan War, unearthed by Blegen in his excavations at Pylos, the home of Homer's King Nestor. Among the Linear B tablets found at Pylos were many referring to a large number of "Asian" women who were apparently slaves, and whose main tasks were grinding corn and preparing flax. Asia is short for Asia Minor and actually refers to the kingdom of Lydia, south of Troy. But references to the places from which these captives were taken make it clear that they came from many places on the coast of Asia Minor, including Chios and Miletus. We know, of course, that the Greeks were pirates, so these women may have been captured on raids. But the sheer number – seven hundred women, four hundred girls, and three hundred boys – suggests that they were captives of war. Some of these women are referred to as *To-ro-ja*, which sounds like "people from Troy". Again, the date is right – the period of the Trojan War. No men are mentioned – and Homer tells us that the men of Troy were killed, and their women and children enslaved and taken back to Greece.

So what seems to emerge from the historical record is this: The period of the Trojan War was, in fact, a period of many wars in Asia Minor. The empire of the Hittites was weakening, and the Greeks took advantage of this to raid "Asian" settlements and to encourage rebellion. Troy (or Wilios) had always been a faithful ally of the Hittites, and records show that the Trojan prince Alaksandus had fought on the side of the Assyrian king Muwatallis (1296–1272 BC), the elder brother of Hattusilis. Another independent tradition from southwest Asia Minor declares that the lover of Helen is an ally of Muwatallis. So *if* this Alaksandus is indeed Prince Alexandros – Homer's Paris – then he was not a young man when he seduced Helen but a grizzled veteran.

Some ten years after fighting on the side of Muwatallis at the battle of Kadesh (in Syria) in 1274 BC, Alexandros went to call on Menelaus, brother of Agamemnon, in Sparta. We may surmise that Menelaus was not a particularly strong character – legend represents him as unlucky in love and war – and that Helen found the battle-scarred veteran Paris much more attractive, and eloped with him.

When Menelaus went to his brother, the mighty "King of the Achaeans", to complain, Agamemnon may or may not have been indignant at the abduction of his sister-in-law. But he knew perfectly well that the west coast of Anatolia ("Asia") was highly vulnerable since the Hittites had been forced to go to war with various neighbours, including the Assyrians. It was just the kind of opportunity for plunder that the piratical Greeks loved. So off they sailed with a vast fleet. Achilles, we learn from Homer, landed by mistake in Mysia, south of Troy, but was driven back to his ships by Telephus, the king of Mysia – though not before ravaging the country.

The Greeks attacked Troy, and the Hittites were too weak to send aid. But Troy was virtually impregnable, and it was not until the tenth year of the war that an earthquake caused a certain amount of chaos and finally permitted the Greeks to take the city. The men were killed, and the women and children were taken back to Greece as slaves. Troy itself was burned and its noble houses destroyed. In its place there sprang up a city of "bungalows". The Greeks continued to make nuisances of themselves with impunity, aiding rebels against the Hittites – who had to do their best to make peace with them – and carrying off more captives from other cities of "Asia".

What happened during the next half century is still not clear to historians. All we know is that raiders who are known only as the "sea peoples" wreaked havoc throughout the Mediterranean area; some ancient records credit them with causing the downfall of the Hittite empire. They certainly fought against Egypt and caused the downfall of Agamemnon's Mycenae, Nestor's Pylos, and the new "bungalow" Troy. (Agamemnon, of course, had long been dead, murdered by his wife, Clytemnestra, and her lover, Aegisthus, who were in turn killed by Agamemnon's children, Orestes and Electra.)

The identity of the "sea peoples" used to be one of the great mysteries of ancient history: Who were they? Where did they come from? How did they succeed in overthrowing great empires? But the answer that is beginning to emerge shows that the question itself is too simple. The sea peoples were not a single racial group: they came from many countries.

We must remember that Mediterranean civilizations were not as stable as those of, say, northern Europe. To begin with, the Mediterranean is a poor region, where even today, a large proportion of farmers only scratch out a subsistence living. In the midst of this widespread poverty, a few powerful rulers became rich, usually by plundering their neighbours. Piracy was regarded as a respectable way of living. But such a situation was rather like Al Capone's Chicago; you might become very rich, but you were likely to die violently.

In this crime-ridden Mediterranean slum, empires rose and fell fairly quickly. While you were at your peak, you had plenty of allies; but as soon as you were past your peak, or your attention was distracted elsewhere, your former allies lost no time in attacking you. What happened around 1200 BC was that the two mighty empires – the Egyptian and the Hittite – were buckling, like the earth's tectonic plates under stress, and around 1190 BC there was an earthquake that caused a great collapse and released hordes of "criminal rats" all over the Mediterranean.

The ancient world virtually came to an end. The twelfth century BC was a period of collapse, a dark age, in which Greece was full of wandering tribes; the age of great kings and great palaces was over. Recovery came slowly. Around 800 BC Greeks began trading again with overseas partners; some may have settled on the west coast of Italy and founded the city of Rome. Meanwhile, the Assyrians became the new empire builders – the most blood-thirsty and cruel so far. But they did not reach Greece, which became a conglomeration of city-states and invented democracy. Out of the chaos came law giving and a sense of order. And one of the major voices of this new order was the poet we call Homer, a traveler with an immense appetite for old tales of gods and heroes. We do not know whether Homer memorized these stories or whether he was the first to write them down, in the days before his blindness. All we know is that he became a legend and that he founded a school of bards who continued his work.

If Samuel Butler is correct, Homer's greatest disciple was a young girl from Sicily, a girl of noble family who shared his passion for ancient tales, and who one day decided that she would write a sequel to the *Iliad*, a sequel that would not be a tale of bloodshed and treachery but a gentler story of the aftermath of the war, and of noble women as well as heroic men. The result was the *Odyssey*, the first novel, whose translation into rough-and-ready prose by Samuel Butler would inspire a twentieth-century novelist, James Joyce, to create his own peculiar version of the Ulysses legend.

Much of this story is speculation. All that we can say for certain is that Homer – whether one person or two – created a concept that is now almost synonymous with the human imagination: the concept of literature.

24

The Hope Diamond

The Famous Cursed Jewel

Like the "skull of doom" (described in chapter 52), the story of the Hope diamond seems to suggest that crystals have some power to absorb human emotions.

The diamond was purchased by Louis XIV in 1668 from a French trader named Jean-Baptiste Tavernier, who is believed to have stolen it (like Milton Hayes's "Green Eye of the Little Yellow God") from the eye socket of an idol in an Indian temple. (One writer mentions the temple of Rama-sitra, near Mandalay.) Tavernier subsequently went bankrupt, sailed for India to try to recoup his fortune, and died en route.

The King had the diamond cut into the shape of a heart, and it was worn by Mme. de Montespan, the King's mistress, who was also involved in the notorious "affair of the poisons", in which a number of old crones who told fortunes provided poisons for killing off unwanted husbands. Black magic was involved, and an abbé named Guiborg took part in black masses in which babies were sacrificed; the naked body of Mme. de Montespan was used in these ceremonies as an altar. The scandal was suppressed, but Mme. de Montespan fell from favour, and the old crones were secretly tried in the *chambre ardente* ("candlelit chamber") and later burned. So after Tavernier, it would seem that Mme. de Montespan was the next person on whom the "French blue" (as it was then known) brought misfortune.

A century later the stone was given by Louis XVI to his Queen, Marie Antoinette; her involvement in the scandal of the diamond necklace caused her to lose credit with the populace and was an indirect cause of the French Revolution in which she lost her head. The Princesse de Lamballe, to whom Marie Antoinette lent the diamond, was murdered by a mob.

The diamond reappeared in London, but now greatly reduced from its original 112.5 carats (22.5 grams) to 44.5 carats – less than half its original size. It was purchased in 1830 by the London banker Henry Thomas Hope for £18,000 and from then on was known as the Hope diamond. As far as we know, Hope suffered no ill effects from the diamond. Neither did any other member of his family until the diamond passed into the hands of singer, May Yohe, who married Lord Francis Hope; they were plagued by marital problems, and the wife prophesied that the diamond would bring ill luck to all who owned it. She herself died in poverty, blaming the diamond.

Lord Francis, in severe financial trouble, sold it in the early 1900s to a French broker, Jacques Colot, who went insane and committed suicide – but not before he had sold it to a Russian, Prince Kanitovsi, who lent it to a French actress at the Folies Bergère, then shot her from his box the first night she wore it. He was stabbed by revolutionaries.

A Greek jeweler, Simon Mantharides, bought it and later fell over a precipice (or, according to another account, was thrown). The Turkish sultan Abdul Hamid, known as "Abdul the Damned", bought it in 1908 and was deposed in the following year; he went insane. Habib Bey, its next owner, drowned.

The diamond then passed, via the French jeweler Pierre Cartier, to America, to Edward Beale Maclean, proprietor of the *Washington Post*. Soon after he purchased it, his mother died, and so did two servants in the household. His son, ten-year-old Vinson, who was always heavily protected and watched over, evaded his minder one day and ran out of the front of the house, where he was knocked down and killed by a car. Maclean himself parted from his wife, Evalyn, was involved in the famous Teapot Dome scandal, and ended as an insane alcoholic. Evalyn kept the diamond and frequently wore it, dismissing stories about its malign properties. But when her daughter committed suicide in 1946 – with an overdose of sleeping pills – it was recalled that she had worn the diamond at her wedding.

After Evalyn Maclean's death in 1947, all her jewels were purchased by the New York jeweler Harry Winston for a sum rumored to be a million dollars. He displayed the diamond in New York but eventually decided to present it to the Smithsonian Institution; the fact that he sent it by ordinary parcel post seems to indicate that he had no misgivings about the "curse". The packet is now exhibited together with the diamond.

When it was tested under ultraviolet light at the De Beers Laboratory in Johannesburg in 1965, it continued to glow like a red-hot coal for several minutes afterwards – a unique phenomenon among diamonds.

Skeptics regard the curse of the Hope diamond, like "the curse of

Tutankhamen" as mythical, pointing out that many of its owners suffered no misfortune. Yet while skepticism may be the correct attitude in this case, it would undoubtedly be premature to dismiss the whole notion of curses as superstition. The late T. C. Lethbridge (see chapter 60) was convinced that tragedies and unpleasant events can leave behind their "imprints" on the places where they occurred – a theory first put forward in the early twentieth century by Sir Oliver Lodge, who felt that certain so-called hauntings could be explained as a kind of "recording". Lethbridge called such recordings "ghouls" – meaning the unpleasant sensations that may be experienced in certain places. When he was eighteen he and his mother had been on a walk in the Great Wood near Wokingham when they both felt suddenly depressed. Later they learned that the body of a man who had committed suicide had been lying close to the spot where they were standing; Lethbridge believed that the man's depression had been somehow "recorded" by his surroundings. Four decades later Lethbridge and his wife, Mina, set out one afternoon to collect seaweed from a nearby beach – Ladram, in Devon. As they walked to the beach, Lethbridge again experienced a "blanket" of depression, as if he had walked into a fog. A few minutes later Mina said, "I can't stand this place any longer", and they left.

The following weekend they repeated the trip. Again, he experienced the same "blanket of depression". This time Mina went to the top of a cliff to make a sketch and suddenly experienced an unpleasant sensation, as if someone was urging her to jump.

Later, Lethbridge discovered that a man *had* recently committed suicide by jumping from the spot where Mina had been standing. He concluded that this was again the reason for the depression; the man's misery had somehow been "recorded" on the electrical field of water. (Both days had been warm and damp, and he had also noted that a small stream ran on to the beach at the point where the "depression" was strongest.) It was not the suicide's ghost that was urging Mina to jump; rather, she was responding to his own suggestion of jumping. This notion of "tape recording" lies behind the theory of *psychometry*, the ability of certain people to "read" the history of an object by holding it in their hands (see chapter 43).

Clairvoyants believe that crystals possess this power of absorption to a high degree – hence the popularity of crystal balls, which are kept wrapped in black velvet to protect them from light and heat (on the same principle that recorded tapes should not be left in hot sunlight or on radiators).

There is also a great deal of documentation on "curses", which seems to indicate that certain objects can carry "bad luck". For example, a whole book has been devoted to the career of the ship called *The Great*

Eastern, built by the great nineteenth-century engineer Isambard Brunel. During its construction, a riveter and his boy apprentice vanished; no one realized that they had been sealed into the hull. The ship (the largest ever built at that time) got stuck during its launching and took three months to free. Brunel then collapsed on its deck and died a week later. From then on the career of *The Great Eastern* was a long series of disasters. Five firemen died when a funnel exploded. While in port for repairs, the ship was damaged in a storm. The captain was drowned in a boat with a cabin boy. A sailor was crushed by the wheel; a man was lost overboard. The disasters and the damage continued until the ship was abandoned, a mere fifteen years after its launching. When it was broken up for scrap, the skeletons of the riveter and his apprentice were found sealed in the hull.

Many similar stories could be told of "jinxed" ships, houses, airplanes, and cars.* The car in which the Archduke Ferdinand was assassinated at Sarajevo (thus precipitating the First World War) went on to bring death or disaster to its next seven owners.

Now if Lethbridge is correct, and a curse is merely a kind of negative tape recording, it also suggests a reason why some people may be affected and others escape unscathed. Lethbridge believed that "sensitives" like himself – for example, good dowsers – would be unusually receptive to these "recordings", while other people would not even notice them.

If physical objects – like crystals – *are* sensitive to the vibrations of the human mind, it would also seem to follow that under certain circumstances, a "curse" might be deliberately imprinted on them – rather like marking one's possessions with an invisible marking pen. The ancient Egyptians certainly believed that their tombs could be "cursed" against robbers. The priests of the temple of Rama-sitra may have taken the same precaution with the Hope diamond.

* See my book *Mysteries* (1978), part 2, chapter 10.

25

The Mystery of Hypnosis

Real-Life Svengalis
and the Telepathy Theory

In May 1991 a hypnotist named Nelson Nelson (his real name was Nelson Lintott) was tried in Bristol Crown Court on the charge of raping and/or otherwise sexually assaulting 113 girls under hypnosis. Nelson, fifty-seven, had apparently learned hypnosis in South Africa at a party. After a varied career as a driving instructor, swimming pool superintendent, barkeep, and restaurateur, he established the Britannia Lodge Health Centre in Appledore, Devon, where, among other things, he undertook to cure people of all kinds of complaints, from nail biting to smoking.

While the girls were in a trance, Nelson would remove their clothes and commit sexual assaults that were described in court as "perverted". Nelson also videotaped many of these assaults. His downfall came when one of his employees borrowed a videotape from his bedroom without permission and found that it contained footage of Nelson undressing girls who appeared to be in a trance and committing sexual acts with them. The employee went to the police, who raided Nelson's premises and found a video camera behind a two-way mirror in his bathroom. They also found forty-five videotapes, loaded guns, and numerous photographs that Nelson had taken over the years; the latter featured 113 different girls and women, ranging in age from ten to thirty-four.

One girl who had worked for Nelson as a barmaid from the age of sixteen described how he had hypnotized her twice a week over a long period to cure her of nail biting. While she was under hypnosis, Nelson had induced her to commit various sex acts; the girl was "distraught and horrified" when she viewed the videotapes and realized what had been happening. Other girls – the police succeeded in identifying 112 out of the 113 – were equally astonished to learn what had happened to them.

Nelson was sentenced to eleven years' imprisonment.

The case appears to contradict one of the most basic assertions of psychiatric medicine – that no one can be made to perform acts under hypnosis that he or she would not perform when awake. A mischievous student of the great nineteenth-century French doctor – and hypnotist – Jean-Martin Charcot tried to make a hypnotized girl remove her clothes in a medical class; she immediately woke up. As to criminal acts, the general view is stated by Bernard Hollander in his book *Hypnosis and Self-Hypnosis* (1928): "Criminal suggestions would be accepted only by criminal minds".

The general public became fascinated by hypnosis in the last years of the nineteenth century, when George Du Maurier's novel *Trilby* (1894) achieved tremendous success. It tells the story of an attractive artist's model (Trilby) in the Latin Quarter of Paris, who is one day hypnotized by a Hungarian musician named Svengali in order to cure her headache. Three young English artists firmly refuse to allow him to hypnotize her again. But when the English men leave Paris, Svengali again approaches Trilby and hypnotizes her into becoming a great singer. (In her normal state, she cannot even sing in tune.) When her English friends see Trilby again, she fails to recognize them and merely looks vague and confused – until Svengali murmurs something in her ear, whereupon she becomes cold and hostile. Later, when Svengali is stabbed by a fellow musician, she becomes virtually an imbecile. And when he dies, she loses all memory of her years as Svengali's "slave". Without her sinister master, her vitality seems to drain away, and she also dies.

Svengali became one of the most famous villains of the century, and his name became a synonym for an evil manipulator, someone who takes over another's will. (The book implied, of course, that Trilby was also Svengali's "sex slave".) But since hypnosis was by that time beginning to achieve a certain medical respectability, psychiatrists lost no time in assuring the public that a real-life Svengali was an impossibility. If a person under hypnosis was ordered to do something that he would normally find repugnant, he would instantly wake up. Charcot's mischievous student might have induced the girl to undress if he had told her that she was in her own bedroom, about to go to bed; otherwise, her natural modesty would have caused her to wake up.

The hypnosis of human beings dates from the last years of the eighteenth century. Hypnosis of animals has been known in Europe since 1636, when the mathematician Daniel Schwenter observed that if a small piece of bent wood was fixed on a hen's beak, the hen would stare at it and go into a trance. The same thing would happen if a hen's head was held on the ground and a chalk line drawn in front of its beak. Ten years later a German Jesuit priest, Athanasius Kircher, described how, if a hen's head was tucked under its wing, a few gentle swings through the air would send it into a trance. French peasants still use this method at market when buying a live hen. Africans probably knew about animal hypnosis long before that; in his book *Hypnosis of Men and Animals* (1966), Ferenc Volgyesi describes how wild elephants can be tamed by tying them to a tree and waving leafy boughs in front of their eyes until they blink and become docile.

The man with whose name hypnosis is usually associated – Franz Mesmer – was, in fact, the discoverer of a completely different technique. Convinced that our health depends upon the flow of "vital currents" around the body, Mesmer came to believe that the flow could be increased by stroking with magnets. When, later, he observed that bleeding increased or decreased when he moved his hand above the bleeding, he concluded that human beings exercise "animal magnetism". He "magnetized" trees and got his patients to embrace them; he magnetized tubs of water and made his patients sit with their feet in them. All of this was supposed to increase the flow of vital energy around their bodies.

One of Mesmer's disciples, Armand Marie Jacques de Chastenet, the Marquis de Puységur, practiced "mesmerism" on his estate at Buzancy. One day he tied a young peasant named Victor Race – whom he was treating for asthma – to a tree, and was making "mesmeric" passes over him when Race's eyes closed. Yet he continued to reply to Puységur's remarks. And on Puységur's orders, he untied himself and walked off across the park. Puységur had discovered hypnosis. He also made another important discovery that has since been forgotten. He could give Race *mental* orders – for example, to repeat the words of a song that he was singing mentally – and Race would obey them. With another excellent hypnotic subject named Madeleine, Puységur would give public demonstrations of mind reading; one total skeptic was converted when he himself was able to order Madeleine – mentally – to put her hand in his pocket and take out an object he had placed there. This ability to influence hypnotized subjects *telepathically* was demonstrated again and again during the nineteenth century; but medicine has continued to dismiss it as a myth.

Mesmer's enemies drove him out of Paris and Vienna; he died, discredited and embittered, in 1815. And the medical profession made sure that hypnosis was treated as a fraud throughout the nineteenth century; any doctor who practiced it was likely to be struck off the register. It was only toward the end of the century that Charcot rediscovered it. Charcot had noticed that patients suffering from hysteria behaved as if they were hypnotized. For example, a man who was convinced that his arm was paralyzed would behave exactly as if it *was* paralyzed, although there was nothing physically wrong with his arm. But he could be cured by being told under hypnosis that his arm was not paralyzed – and the paralysis could also be reinduced by hypnosis. When Charcot announced to the medical profession that hypnosis was simply a form of hysteria, his colleagues believed that he had solved the mystery and ceased to regard hypnosis as a fraud. It took some time before it was recognized that Charcot had inverted the truth and that hysteria is, in fact, a kind of hypnosis. A hysterical patient becomes convinced that he is suffering from some disability and "suggests" himself into it. Freud was one of the many who were impressed by Charcot's theory of hypnosis; he later made it the basis of his own theory of the unconscious.

But what precisely is hypnosis? This is a question that no one at that time could answer – and that remains (officially, at all events) unanswered today. Bernard Hollander's book includes a chapter entitled "Explanation of Hypnosis" that has some useful suggestions. He points out that a subject under hypnosis *forgets his body*; if his attention is drawn to his body, it feels heavy and immobile. Yet the patient is not asleep. Hollander compares a hypnotized patient to someone absorbed in a play – the mind is wide-awake but totally abstracted. We have all seen a child staring at the television with his thumb in his mouth, so absorbed that he has to be prodded to gain his attention. This seems to imply that we have *two minds*, one of which deals with the world that surrounds us and copes with immediate experience, while the other can go off "inside itself", into a subjective world, a kind of cinema inside the head.

At about the time Freud was studying under Charcot in Paris, an American newspaper editor named Thomson Jay Hudson was also puzzling over the mystery of hypnosis. Hudson had attended a hypnotic performance by the eminent physiologist William B. Carpenter in Washington, D.C., and what he saw amazed him. Carpenter placed a young college graduate under hypnosis and asked him if he would like to meet Socrates. The young man objected that Socrates was dead, and Carpenter told him that he had the power to evoke the spirit of Socrates. Then he pointed to a corner of the room and exclaimed, "There he is". The young man – whom Hudson called C. – looked awestruck. Carpenter then urged C. to enter into conversation with Socrates and ask him any question he liked – mentioning that, since the audience could not hear Socrates, C. would have to repeat his replies aloud. For the next two hours the audience witnessed an incredible conversation, in which the replies of Socrates seemed so brilliant and plausible that some of the audience – who were interested in Spiritualism – were inclined to believe that Socrates was actually there.

After this Carpenter introduced C. to the spirits of various modern philosophers, and more brilliant and plausible conversations followed. These were quite different from one another and from the conversation with Socrates – although they usually had nothing whatever in common with the ideas of the philosophers under interrogation. Finally, to convince the audience that they were not listening to the words of spirits, Carpenter summoned a philosophic pig, which discoursed learnedly on Hinduism.

What impressed Hudson was that C. was obviously of fairly average intelligence, whereas the answers of the philosophers were close to genius level. Obviously, C.'s "unconscious mind" – or whatever it was – was far cleverer than *he* was. And as Hudson studied similar cases he came to the conclusion that we possess two minds – what he called the "objective mind", which copes with everyday reality, and the "subjective mind", which can become totally absorbed in an *inner* world. C. only became a man of genius under hypnosis, when the operations of his objective mind, like those of his body, were suspended. Then the subjective mind could operate freely. In other words, the objective mind serves as a kind of anchor, or ball-and-chain, on the subjective mind. But men of great genius, Hudson concluded, have an odd faculty for allowing the two to work in harmony – like children. He cited the case of an American orator, Henry Clay, who was once called upon to answer an opponent in the Senate when he was ill. He asked the friend sitting next to him to tug on his coattails when he had been speaking for ten minutes. Two hours later he sank down exhausted – then looked at the clock and asked his friend why he had failed to interrupt. The friend explained that he had not only tugged at Clay's coattails, he had pinched him repeatedly and even jabbed a pin into his leg. Clay had remained totally oblivious to all this. It would seem that Clay was in the same trancelike state as the child watching television with his thumb in his mouth, and that it was, in fact, a kind of hypnosis.

The theory that Hudson developed in his book *The Law of Psychic Phenomena* (1893) is that the "subjective mind" has virtually miraculous powers. All men of genius – particularly those whose talent seems to burst forth like a wellspring, such as Shakespeare and Mozart – are able to tune in at will to the enormous powers of the subjective mind. The miracles of Jesus, and of various saints, were simply manifestations of the same mysterious power.

Hudson himself became convinced that he could also perform miracles of healing with the aid of the subjective mind and decided to try to cure a relative of severe rheumatism that had almost killed him. The man lived a thousand miles away. Hudson decided that the best time to send "healing suggestions" was on the edge of sleep, when the "objective mind" is passive – exactly as in hypnosis. On 15 May 1890, he told a number of friends that he meant to start the experiment. A few months later one of the friends met the invalid and found that he was well again; the attacks had ceased and he was working normally. Asked when the attacks ceased, he said, "About mid-May" – exactly when Hudson had started his "experiments".

Hudson claimed that he went on to cure about five hundred people in the same way. He failed in only two cases and these – oddly enough – were patients who had been told that he intended to try to cure them.

This, Hudson believed, underlined another peculiarity of the subjective mind: its powers have to work *spontaneously*, without self-consciousness. As soon as it becomes self-conscious, it freezes up, like the hand of a schoolboy when the teacher looks over his shoulder as he is writing. This also explains why so many "psychics" fail when they are tested by skeptics. It is like trying to make love in a crowded public square.

Because we have two minds, our powers tend to interfere with one another. In the 1870s a stage hypnotist named Carl Hansen loved to demonstrate a spectacular trick; he would tell the hypnotized subject that he (the subject) was about to become as rigid as a board. The subject was then placed across two chairs, with his head on one and his heels on the other, and several people would sit or stand on his stomach; he never bent in the middle. What happened was that the objective mind had been put to sleep, and the hypnotist then *took over the role of the objective mind*. Normally, "you" tell your body to stand up or sit down. But "you" are often negative or tired or unsure of yourself, so your "orders" are given in a hesitant voice. We are undermined by self-doubt. The hypnotist delivers his orders like a sergeant major, and this has the effect of unlocking the powers of the subjective mind. It obviously follows that if *you* could learn to give orders with the same assurance, you would also be capable of "miraculous" feats.

But in that case, why aren't self-confident people capable of miraculous feats? Because they have developed the objective mind, the conscious "self" that copes with reality, rather than the subjective mind. Genius – and miracles – is about *contact* between the two minds.

Hudson was also certain that all so-called psychic phenomena are due to the powers of the subjective mind. He attended a séance at which a pencil wrote of its own accord on a slate, delivering messages that were relevant to Hudson and to the other "sitter", a general. Yet when thinking it over later, Hudson concluded that nothing was written that could not have emanated from the mind of the medium, if the medium had telepathic powers. He decided that the medium had – unconsciously – read the mind of his sitters and then used the miraculous powers of his own subjective mind to make the pencil write on the slate. And if *that* was possible, Hudson argued, then all psychical phenomena, including ghosts and poltergeists, could be explained in the same way. In fact, Hudson was ahead of his time. It would be several years before psychical researchers came to the conclusion that poltergeists are due to the unconscious minds of disturbed adolescents.

Here it could be argued that Hudson was carried away by his own brilliant insights into the powers of the subjective mind. I have argued elsewhere that the evidence for "spirits" cannot be so easily dismissed. In fact, he was quite definitely wrong when he came to deal with the curious power known as *psychometry*, the ability of certain people to "read" the history of an object they hold in their hands. Some of the most remarkable tests in the history of psychical research were carried out by a professor of geology named William Denton. He would wrap geological and archaeological specimens in thick brown paper packages, shuffle them until he no longer knew which was which, then get his "psychometrists" – his wife and sister-in-law – to describe the contents and history of packages chosen at random. Their accuracy was amazing – for example, a fragment of volcanic lava from Pompeii produced an accurate description of the eruption, while a fragment of tile from a Roman villa produced a description of Roman legions and a man who looked like a retired soldier. However, this latter experiment worried Denton, because the tile came from the villa of the orator Cicero, who was tall and thin, and the "soldier" was described as heavily built. It was only some years later, after publishing his first account, that Denton learned that the villa had also belonged to the Roman dictator Sulla, who *did* correspond accurately to the description.

But all this leaves Hudson's central insight untouched: that man has two minds and it is because of these two minds impede each other instead of supporting each other that our powers are so limited. His basic proposition is that if we could learn to tap the powers of the subjective mind, we would develop into supermen.

Hudson's book became a bestseller and went into edition after edition between 1893 and Hudson's death in 1903. Why, then, did its remarkable new theory not make a far greater impact? The reason can be summarized in a single word: Freud. The objective and subjective minds obviously correspond roughly to Freud's ego and id – or conscious and unconscious. But there is a major difference. Freud was a pessimist who saw the unconscious mind as a *passive* force, a kind of basement full of decaying rubbish that causes disease – or neurosis. The conscious mind is the victim of these unconscious forces, which are basically sexual in nature. Hudson would have been horrified at such a gloomy and negative view of the subjective mind. But because Freud was a "scientist" and Hudson was merely a retired newspaper editor, the latter's achievement was ignored by psychologists.

Yet the "two minds" theory was to receive powerful scientific backing a few decades later. Even in the nineteenth century it had been recognized that the two halves of our brains have different functions. The speech function resides in the left half of the brain; doctors observed that people with left-brain damage became inarticulate. The right side of the brain controls recognition of shapes and patterns, so that an artist who had right-brain damage would lose all artistic talent. One man could not even draw a clover leaf; he put the three leaves of the clover side by side, on the same level.

Yet an artist with left-brain damage only became inarticulate; he was still as good an artist as ever. And an orator with right- brain damage could sound as eloquent as ever, even though he could not draw a clover leaf.

The left brain also governs logic and reason, which are involved in such tasks as adding up a laundry list or doing a crossword puzzle. The right is involved in such activities as musical appreciation or facial recognition. In short, you could say that the left is a scientist and the right is an artist.

One of the odd facts of human physiology is that the left side of the body is controlled by the right side of the brain, and vice versa. No one quite knows why this is, except that it probably makes for greater integration. If the left brain controlled the left side and the right brain the right side, there might be "frontier disputes"; as it is, each has a foot firmly in the other's territory.

If you removed the top of your head, the upper part of your brain – the cerebral hemispheres – would look like a walnut with a kind of bridge connecting the two halves. This bridge is a knot of nerves called the *corpus callosum*, or commissure. But doctors learned that there are some freaks who possess no commissure yet seem to function perfectly well. This led them to wonder if they could prevent epileptic attacks by severing the commissure. They tried it on epileptics and it seemed to work. The fits were greatly reduced, and the patients seemed to be unchanged. It led the doctors to wonder what the function of the commissure was. Someone suggested it might be to transmit epileptic seizures; another suggested it might be to keep the brain from sagging in the middle.

In the 1950s experiments in America began to shed a good deal of light on the problem. Someone noticed that if a "split-brain" patient knocked against a table with his left side, he didn't seem to notice. It began to emerge that the split-brain operation had the effect of preventing one half of the brain from learning what the other half knew. If a cat was taught a trick with one eye covered, then asked to do it with the other eye covered, it was baffled. It became clear that we literally have two brains.*

Moreover, if a split-brain patient was shown an apple with the left eye and an orange with the right, then asked what he had just seen, he would reply, "Orange". Asked to write what he had just seen with his left hand, he would write *Apple*. A split-brain patient who was shown a dirty picture with her right brain blushed; asked why she was blushing, she replied truthfully, "I don't know". The person who was doing the blushing was the one who lived in the right half of her brain. *She* lived in the left half.

This is true of all of us (except left-handed individuals, whose brain hemispheres are reversed). The person you call "you" lives in the left half – the half that "copes" with the real world. The person who lives in the right is a stranger.

You might object that you and I are not split-brain patients. That makes no difference. Mozart once remarked that tunes were always walking into his head fully fledged, and all he had to do was write them down. Where did they come *from*? Obviously, from the right half of his brain, the "artist". Where did they *go to*? To the left half of his brain,

---

* For the sake of simplicity I speak here of the left eye and the right eye; in fact, both eyes are connected to both sides of the brain, so it would be more accurate to speak of the right and left *visual fields*. In visual experiments with split-brain patients, the patient is asked to keep his eyes fixed either to the left or the right. This piece of information is unimportant for understanding what follows.

where Mozart lived. In other words, Mozart was a split-brain patient. And if Mozart was, then so are the rest of us. The person we call "I" is the scientist. The "artist" lives in the shadows, and we are scarcely aware of his existence, except in moods of deep relaxation or of "inspiration". We all become more "right brain", for example, after an alcoholic drink; it makes us more aware of our "other half". It does this, to some extent, by anesthetizing the left brain (which explains why you find it harder to do a mathematical problem when you have had a few glasses of wine). This is why alcohol is so popular. The same – unfortunately – applies to other drugs.

We can see that the left and right halves of the brain correspond roughly to Hudson's objective and subjective minds. And how does this help us to understand hypnosis? Well, it would seem that the hypnotist "anesthetizes" the left brain – makes it fall asleep – while the right remains wide awake. If Hudson is correct – and there seems every reason to believe that he is – the right brain is then able to operate with the full powers of the subjective mind. There seem to be obvious clues here to how we could all make better use of our powers.

According to modern medicine, hypnosis merely enables you to relax and become less self-conscious. It has no power to make you "superhuman". Yet once again, this is contradicted by the facts. We have already seen that the Marquis de Puységur was able to communicate telepathically with Victor Race when Victor was in a trance. And anyone who takes the trouble to look into the four volumes of Eric J. Dingwall's *Abnormal Hypnotic Phenomena* – which is devoted mainly to the nineteenth century – will find dozens of cases that leave no doubt whatever that "telepathy under hypnosis" has been demonstrated over and over again. One of Dingwall's most astonishing accounts concerns the brothers Alexis and Adolphe Didier, who could both perform remarkable paranormal feats under hypnosis. For example, the two would play a game of cards with cards that were turned facedown. Nevertheless, one brother would be able to tell his partner which cards the other held, as if he were looking over his shoulder.

The father of the Didiers was himself a remarkable hypnotic subject who would sometimes go into a trance at the breakfast table while reading the newspaper – and continue reading the newspaper although he had dropped it onto the table and was not looking at it. Alexis, the more talented of the two brothers, was particularly expert at "traveling clairvoyance". The person he was talking to could ask him to describe what he (the "client") had been doing that day, or to "travel" to his home and describe it. This sounds as if it could be explained by telepathy – except that Didier could tell the client things he did not know himself. On one occasion Didier described a magistrate's study with great accuracy and mentioned that there was a bell on the table; the magistrate denied this. But when he got home he found that Didier was correct; his wife had placed the bell there since he had left home.

Alfred Russel Wallace, codeveloper (with Darwin) of the theory of evolution in the mid-nineteenth century, became interested in hypnosis when he was a young schoolteacher, and he discovered that some of his pupils were excellent hypnotic subjects. One boy would actually share Wallace's perceptions when in a trance; if Wallace pinched his own arm, the boy started and rubbed his arm; if Wallace tasted sugar, the boy smiled and licked his lips; if Wallace tasted salt, the boy grimaced.

In the 1880s, the French psychologist Pierre Janet was able to place one of his patients, a woman named Leonie, in a hypnotic trance *from the other side of Le Havre* and summon her to come to him. The experiments were performed under test conditions under the auspices of the Society for Psychical Research.

Almost a century later Dr Gustav Pagenstecher discovered that one of his patients, Maria Reyes de Zierold, was able to share his own sensations, tasting substances he put on his tongue and wincing if he held his hand over a lighted match. The first time he hypnotized her, she told him that her daughter was listening at the door; Pagenstecher opened the door and found that this was true. This sounds as if she may simply have heard the girl outside; but she was also able to describe what Pagenstecher was doing when he was in the next room. Under hypnosis, Maria also became an excellent psychometrist and could describe with great accuracy the history of objects placed in her hands.*

All of this obviously raises a fascinating possibility – that hypnosis may not merely involve placing someone in a trance through suggestion but that it might be *the direct influence of one mind upon another*. In *Over the Long High Wall*, writer J. B. Priestley tells how, at a boring literary dinner in New York, he told the person sitting next to him that he intended to try to make one of the poets wink at him. He chose a serious-looking woman, "no winker", and concentrated on her. After a while she turned and winked at him. Priestley's neighbour was inclined to doubt whether it had been a wink, but after the dinner, the woman came up to him to apologize for winking at him, remarking, "I don't know what made me do it".

* For a longer account of Pagenstecher and Maria Reyes de Zierold, see my book *The Psychic Detectives* (1985).

This brings us back to the question raised at the beginning of this article: whether a hypnotist can influence someone to commit a criminal act against his will. The evidence suggests that it is possible. In 1865, in France, a vagabond named Thimotheus Castellan was tried for abducting and raping a young peasant girl named Josephine. He had knocked on the door of her father's cottage, begging shelter for the night. The next morning, when the father and brothers had gone off to work, neighbours noticed him making passes in the air behind Josephine's back. Over the midday meal, Castellan made a movement with his fingers, and she felt her senses leaving her; he then carried her into the next room and raped her. She said she wanted to resist but was paralyzed. Later, he left and took her with him, demonstrating his power over her at various farms where they stayed by making her walk on all fours like an animal. He was finally arrested and sentenced to twelve years in prison.

In 1934 a Heidelberg hypnotist named Franz Walter met a woman on a train and caused her to pass into a trance simply by taking her hand. After raping her, he ordered her to work for him as a prostitute. He subsequently ordered her to make several attempts on her husband's life; when these failed, he ordered her to commit suicide. She was saved by passersby on two occasions. Finally, a police surgeon guessed that she had been hypnotized and ordered to keep silent about it; he succeeded in "unlocking" her memory, and Franz Walter was sentenced to ten years in prison.

In 1985 two Portuguese criminals, both named Manuel, succeeded in parting a number of victims from their life savings through hypnosis. One woman described how she had simply been talking to one of the men when he took her hand and she felt "cold all over", then went into a stupor in which she obeyed orders to go home and withdraw her savings; she handed over more than £1,000. The two men were caught by accident when a hairdresser heard one of her clients agreeing (over the telephone) to meet them and give them money; she had heard of the earlier case and notified the police. The men were deported.*

All of this seems to suggest that there is a telepathic element in hypnosis – of one mind directly influencing another – and that legends about real-life Svengalis may have some basis in fact. Ferenc Volgyesi, whose book *Hypnosis in Men and Animals* has already been mentioned, was convinced that legends about the "hypnotic gaze" of the snake were

---

* For a longer account of all these cases, see my *Mammoth Book of the Supernatural* (1991).

not without foundation; he cites examples of toads, frogs, and rabbits being "transfixed by a snake's gaze", which involved the expansion of its pupils; but he has photographs of other creatures engaged in "battles of will" in which they simply stare at each other. In one case, a toad won a "battle of will" against a snake.

This is not, of course, to deny the validity of the generally accepted theory of hypnosis – that it is basically a matter of suggestion. Hypnosis, as we have seen, is based on a state of abstraction, and hypnotists undoubtedly create this state by suggestion – usually by suggesting that the subject is becoming sleepy, that his limbs are becoming heavy, and so on. But it is the right brain – the "other you" – that accepts these suggestions and puts "you" to sleep, while *it* remains wide awake. Its powers are then at the disposal of the hypnotist (which suggests, in turn, that a good hypnotic subject ought to be able to cure people at a distance, as Hudson did).

What seems to have happened, in the case of Nelson Nelson, the rapist described at the beginning of this chapter, is that his suggestions made his patients totally unaware of their bodies and that he committed the sexual assaults while the patients were virtually asleep, as if under anesthesia.

But it would be a mistake to assume that this supports the view that a hypnotist could not persuade an unwilling subject to submit to sexual intercourse. In his book *Open to Suggestion* (1989), a study of the abuse of hypnosis, Robert Temple devotes a whole chapter to rape under hypnosis. One assault victim describes how the hypnotist raised her bra and caressed her breasts, yet she still made a further appointment. The next time, after placing her in a light trance,

> he caressed my breast again and after a while pulled down my pants and panties, and he even put his hand in my vagina . . . He wanted me to take his genitals in my hand. I said no . . . After a while I held his penis . . . I would have liked to have knocked him away, but in one way or another I couldn't do it. [When] he started to get closer with his genitals, I started to panic and cried.

Here it seems clear that she had no more desire to be raped than the victim of the two Portuguese criminals had to hand over her life savings. This is clearly a case in which – as with Thimotheus Castellan and Franz Walter – the will of the hypnotist prevailed over the will of the victim. Temple also cites a case of a homosexual assault on a soldier by a hypnotist – his colonel – in which the soldier felt immobilized and unable to get up from the bed, although he objected to the colonel's advances.

Temple himself describes a personal episode that throws an interesting light on hypnosis. He was undergoing a course of hypnotic treatment and one day failed to "wake up". But because he was aware that his doctor was in a hurry to get away, he pretended to be fully conscious. Outside, he told his wife – who was waiting in the car – that he was still hypnotized and asked her to blow on his face; she thought it funny and screamed with laughter. On the way home, he saw a tree and ordered her to stop. Then he went and embraced the tree and burst into tears, telling it how beautiful it was. After that he lay on his back, staring at the night sky and uttering maudlin remarks. In fact, he behaved exactly as if drunk. Back at home, he drank down half a glass of neat gin – a drink he disliked – and finally "came to". It is clear that he knew that a part of his mind was still under hypnosis but was unable to awaken it.

This raises another important point. William James has pointed out that there are certain days on which we feel that our vital powers are simply not at their best; "our fires are damped; our draughts are checked". We feel curiously dull, like a car whose engine is still cold and that keeps "cutting out". In fact, the remarkable teacher Gurdjieff asserted that our ordinary consciousness is literally a state of sleep and that we have to make superhuman efforts if we are to wake up. (*Hypnosis* comes from the Greek *hypnos* – "sleep".)

Clearly, then, hypnosis is not some abnormal, freak condition that we can ignore. It offers clues to what is wrong with human beings and to why it is the easiest thing in the world to waste one's life. Our basic problem is to "shake the mind awake".

Notice that when we are dull and bored, we feel "alienated" from reality. We feel trapped in the physical world and in the present moment; "reality" is a prison. This is the opposite of what happens when we are happy and excited – for example, when looking forward to some eagerly anticipated event – or when we are deeply relaxed. In these states, the world seems infinitely fascinating; reality seems to stretch around us in endless vistas, like a view from a mountaintop.

It is obvious that in such states, the right and left brains are in close communication. When you are bored, you are trapped – not only in the physical world, but in your left brain. You are, in essence, a split-brain patient. The same thing happens if you are absorbed in a daydream, except that in this case you are trapped in your inner world – your right brain. If you spend too much time in such states – what is sometimes called "escapism" – you begin to find the real world unbearable, and you alternate between being trapped inside yourself and feeling trapped in the physical world.

On the other hand, in moods of happiness or relaxation, you become, for a short time, a "whole-brain" patient. Your right brain – your intuitive self – now feels awake, and you realize that this "whole" state is far closer to what human consciousness was intended to be. One of the oddest things about these states is that, when we look back on our miseries and misfortunes, most of them seem laughably trivial, the result of the lopsided half-consciousness that we regard as "normal".

The French philosopher Sartre had a word for these states in which we feel trapped in the present moment: "nausea". And, oddly enough, he regarded "nausea" as the fundamental reality of human existence – what you might call the basic state of human consciousness – rather like seeing an attractive woman with her hair in curlers and cold cream smeared all over her face. It follows, of course, that Sartre felt that human life is meaningless and that – as he put it in a famous phrase – "man is a useless passion". His close associate Simone de Beauvoir captured the spirit of "nausea" when she wrote: "I look at myself in vain in a mirror, tell myself my own story. I can never grasp myself as an entire object. I experience in myself the emptiness that is myself. I feel that I am not". But obviously, she was simply talking about the experience of being trapped in left-brain consciousness. Yet it is quite clear that she was mistaken when she said that she could never grasp herself as an entire object and that she felt "she is not". In "whole-brain" states, we have a curious sense of our own reality *and* that of the world. We suddenly *know* that "we are".

What is so interesting here is that Sartre's whole philosophy of human existence – he is known as one of the founding figures of existentialism – is based on his mistaken notion that "nausea" is some fundamental truth about human reality – the beautiful woman in hair curlers. Moreover, it is a philosophy that is echoed by some of the most respectable figures in modern literature, from Ernest Hemingway and Albert Camus to Graham Greene and Samuel Beckett. It could be said to dominate modern philosophy and modern literature. Yet we can see that it is simply a misunderstanding. "Nausea" is not some glimpse of reality; it is as unimportant as a headache, and in some ways curiously similar. If Sartre had known about the right and left hemispheres, he would have recognized that he was greatly exaggerating the importance of "nausea". And if we could grasp, once and for all, that "alienation" in left-brain consciousness is not a glimpse of the reality of the human condition, we would experience an enormous and immediate rise in our level of optimism and vitality.

There is another important inference to be drawn from all this. Hypnosis, as we have seen, is basically suggestion. The hypnotist's suggestion ("your eyelids are feeling heavy . . .") has the effect of trapping us in left-brain consciousness. Boredom and pessimism have the same effect. But if you believe – like Sartre – that life is meaningless and "man is a useless passion", then you are in a permanent condition of negative self-suggestion, and entrapment in left-brain consciousness becomes your normal mode of awareness. So "nausea" becomes a kind of self-fulfilling prophecy. Entrapment in left-brain consciousness is bad enough, but it becomes ten times worse if you accept it as a norm. On the other hand, if you are aware that whole-brain consciousness is the norm, then states of "trapped" left-brain consciousness would be accepted as casually as a headache.

This, then, is the real importance of Puységur's discovery of hypnosis. It was the recognition of a curious anomaly that raised enormous questions about the human mind. The total eclipse of hypnosis during the nineteenth century reveals that these questions were too uncomfortable to be faced; it was easier to dismiss them and to stick to the old commonsense view of human awareness. Now we find ourselves at an interesting crossroads when we accept the reality of hypnosis (although there are still a few academics who dismiss it as a delusion) yet fail to grasp its implications. When these are finally grasped and taken for granted by every high school student – as we now take for granted the notion of the unconscious mind or of childhood eroticism – man will be prepared to begin a voyage of discovery into his own unexplored potentialities.

26

The Enigma of Identical Twins

One Mind in Two Bodies

When Jim Lewis was six years old, he learned that he had an identical twin brother. Their unmarried mother had put them up for adoption soon after they were born in August 1939. Jim had been adopted by a couple named Lewis in Lima, Ohio; his brother was adopted by a family named Springer in Dayton, Ohio. Oddly enough, both boys were christened "Jim" by their new parents.

In 1979, when he was thirty-nine, Jim Lewis decided to try to find his twin brother. The court that had arranged the adoption was exceptionally helpful. Six weeks later, Jim Lewis knocked on the door of Jim Springer in Dayton. The moment they shook hands they felt close, as if they had been together all their lives. But when they began to compare notes they became aware of a staggering series of coincidences. To begin with, they had the same health problems. Both were compulsive nail-biters and suffered from insomnia. Both had started to experience migraines at the age of eighteen, and stopped having them at the same age. Both had heart problems. Both had developed haemorrhoids. They were exactly the same weight, but had both put on ten pounds at exactly the same period of their lives, and then lost it again at the same time.

All this might seem to indicate that genetic programming is far more precise and complex than anyone had suspected. But their coincidences went much further than genetics. Both had married girls named Linda, divorced, then married girls called Betty. Both had named their sons James Allan. Both had owned a dog named Toy. Both had worked as deputy sheriff, petrol-station attendant, and at McDonald's Hamburger restaurants. Both spent their holidays on the same Florida beach. Both chain-smoked the same make of cigarette. Both had basement work-shops in which they made furniture . . .

The twins were fascinated, not only by these similarities in experience but by their mental similarities – one would start to say something and the other would finish it.

Their reunion received wide press coverage, and they appeared on the Johnny Carson chat show. And in Minnesota a psychologist named Tom Bouchard was so intrigued that he persuaded the University to give him a grant to study the "Jim twins" scientifically. Then he went on to look for other similar pairs: that is, twins who were separated at a very early age, and who had not seen each other since. In their first few years of research they discovered thirty-four sets of such twins. And again and again they discovered the same extraordinary coincidences – coincidences that cannot be scientifically explained. Two British twins, Margaret Richardson and Terry Connolly, who did not even know they were twins until they were in their mid-thirties, had married on the same day within an hour of each other. Two others, Dorothy Lowe and Bridget Harrison, had decided to keep a diary for just one year, 1962, and had both filled in exactly the same days. The diaries looked identical because they were of the same make and colour. Both played the piano as children but gave it up in the same year. Both like eye-catching jewellery.

Since then work on twins has continued to show that in many cases – particularly of identical twins – there are incredible coincidences. Identical twins are those who are formed by a splitting of the same ovum. They have identical genes, which means they have identical eyes, ears, limbs, even fingerprints. The scientific term for such twins is *monozygotic*, or MZ for short. *Dizygotic* twins (DZ) are formed from two different eggs. The astonishing level of "coincidence" applies mainly to MZ twins. In fact, the similarities in many cases become almost monotonous. For example, the twins last mentioned, Bridget Harrison and Dorothy Lowe, had sons called respectively Richard Andrew and Andrew Richard. Their daughters were called Katherine Louise and Karen Louise, but Dorothy Lowe had originally intended to call her daughter Katherine, and changed it to Karen to please a relative. Both wear the same perfume. Both leave their bedroom doors ajar. Both had had meningitis. Both collect soft toys and had cats called Tiger. Bouchard's intelligence tests showed they had identical IQs.

Barbara Herbert and Daphne Goodship were the twins of an un-married Finnish student, and were adopted by different families at birth. Both their adoptive mothers died when they were children. Both had fallen downstairs when they were fifteen and broken an ankle. Both met their future husbands at town-hall dances when they were sixteen, and married in their early twenties. Both had early miscarriages, then each had two boys followed by a girl. Both have a heart murmur and a slightly enlarged thyroid. Both read the same popular novelists and take the same women's magazine. And when they met for the first time both had tinted their hair the same shade of auburn, and were wearing beige dresses, brown velvet jackets and identical white petticoats.

In 1979 Jeanette Hamilton and Irene Read each discovered they had twin sisters, and hastened to get together. They discovered that both suffered from claustrophobia and dislike of water, both sit with their backs to the sea on beaches, both hated heights, both got a pain in the same spot in the right leg in wet weather, and both are compulsive calculators. As children they had led scout packs, and they had both worked at one time for the same cosmetics firm.

Two male twins studied by Bouchard had been brought up in backgrounds that could scarcely have been more different. Oscar Stohr and Jack Yufe were born in Trinidad in 1933, then their parents went off in opposite directions, each taking a twin. Oscar went to Germany and became a member of the Nazi youth movement, while Jack was brought up as an orthodox Jew. They met for the first time at the airport in 1979, and found they were both wearing square, wire-rimmed glasses and blue shirts with epaulettes; they had identical moustaches. Closer study showed remarkable similarities in their habits. Both flushed the lavatory before and after using it, stored rubber bands on their wrists, and liked to eat alone in restaurants so they can read. Their speech rhythms were identical, although one spoke only German and the other only English. Both had the same gait and the same way of sitting. Both had the same sense of humour – for example, a tendency to sneeze loudly in lifts to startle the other passengers.

It is obviously very difficult, if not impossible, to explain such a series of "coincidences" without positing some form of telepathy – that is, some form of hidden connection between the twins – that persisted even when they were separated by long distances. In fact Jung, who invented the word "synchronicity" (see Chapter 54) for "meaningful coincidences", would have accepted the telepathic explanation: there are many anecdotes in his work that are designed to illustrate the reality of telepathy. But even telepathy cannot explain how two sisters met their husbands under similar circumstances or worked for the same cosmetic firm; it must be either dismissed as coincidence or explained in terms of some peculiar theory about "individual destinies", or even what Professor Joad once called "the undoubted strangeness of time". If people can have glimpses of the future, or dream of events before they happen, it suggests that, in some odd way these events are already "programmed", like a film that has already been made. If individual lives are to some extent "pre-programmed", then perhaps the lives of MZ twins have the same basic programming . . .

Other cases certainly seem to demonstrate the reality of telepathy. In 1980 two female twins appeared in court in York, and attracted the attention of reporters because they made the same gestures at the same time, smiling simultaneously, raising their hands to their mouths at the same moment, and so on. The Chaplin twins, Freda and Greta, were in court for a peculiar reason: they had both apparently developed a powerful "crush" on a lorry-driver, Mr Ken Iveson, who used to live next door, and had been pursuing him for fifteen years. They seem to have had rather a curious way of showing affection, shouting abuse and hitting him with their handbags. When this had been going on for fifteen years Mr Iveson decided to ask the court for protection.

The publicity surrounding the court case led to various medical studies of the twins. Their obsession with Mr Iveson was defined medically as erotomania, a condition in which a patient sinks into melancholy or mental disturbance due to romantic love. The twins proved to be mentally subnormal, although this seems to have been a later development. At school they had been slow, but not backward, and teachers described them as neat, clean and quiet. The deputy head-master placed the blame on their mother. "It was quite clear that they had a doting mother who never allowed them a seperate identity". They were apparently dressed identically and allowed no friends.

The twins showed a tendency to the "mirror imaging" which is often typical of MZ twins. (That is to say, if one is left-handed, the other is right-handed; if the whorls of the hair grow clockwise in one, they grow anti-clockwise in the other, and so on.) One twin wears a bracelet on the left wrist, the other on the right. When one broke a shoelace the other removed her own shoelace on the opposite side.

At some point the twins had been forced to leave home – neither they nor their mother would disclose why. At thirty-seven they were un-married and jobless; they lived in a local service hostel. They cooked breakfast in their room together, both holding the frying-pan, then went out in identical clothes. When they both had identical grey coats with different-coloured buttons they simply swapped half the buttons so each had both colours. When given different pairs of gloves, they took one of each pair. When given two different bars of soap, they cut both in half and shared them. They told a woman journalist that they had one brain, and were really one person, claiming to know exactly what the other is thinking. Their "simultaneous behaviour" suggests that some form of telepathy exists between them. They occasionally quarrel, hitting one another lightly with identical handbags, then sulking for hours. But in spite of these disagreements, it seems clear that their common aim is to exclude the external world and to live in their own small private universe.

Two Californian twins, Grace and Virginia Kennedy, even developed a private language in which they conversed; this started when they were seventeen months old. By 1977, when they were seven, a speech therapist in the San Diego children's hospital began to study their private language, and discovered that it seemed to be a mixture of invented words, like "nunukid" and "pulana", and a mixture of English and German words mispronounced (their parents were respectively American and German). They called one another Poto and Cabenga, and spoke their unknown language swiftly and fluently. Eventually they were coaxed into speaking English; but they declined to explain their former language – or perhaps they were simply unable to.

One of the strangest cases involving twins was recorded in the *New York Review of Books* (28 Feb 1985) by the psychiatrist Oliver Sacks. Michael and John, known simply as The Twins, have been in state institutions since they were seven (in 1947). They have been diagnosed as autistic, psychotic and severely retarded. Yet they possess one extraordinary ability: the ability to say on what day of the week any date in the past or future will fall; asked, say, about 11 June 55 BC, they would instantly snap "Wednesday" – and prove correct. They are, says Sacks, a grotesque Tweedledum and Tweedledee, mirror-image twins who are identical in face, personality and body movements, as well as in their brain and tissue damage. They wear glasses so thick that their eyes seem distorted.

They can repeat any number of digits after one hearing – as many as three hundred. Yet they are not "calculating prodigies", able to multiply huge numbers within seconds or extract tenth roots from twenty digit numbers, as many such prodigies have been able to. But when a box of matches fell on the floor, both murmured "111" before the matches hit the floor – and again, proved to be correct.

One day Sacks found them sitting in a corner, wearing an odd, contented smile and swopping six-digit numbers. He noted down several of these, and when he got home, checked through a book of mathematical tables, and discovered that all the numbers were primes – numbers that cannot be divided by any other number without a "left-over". Now, the odd thing is that there is no mathematical method of determining whether some large number is a prime or not – except painstakingly to try dividing all the smaller numbers into it; if it gives a "remainder" with every smaller number up to half its own size, then it is a prime. Yet the twins were apparently pulling primes out of the air without the slightest effort.

The next day Sacks again sat in on their game, and suddenly interupted it with an eight-figure prime (taken from his book of tables). They looked at him in astonishment; then, after a half-minute pause their faces broke into broad smiles. Then the twins began swopping nine-figure primes. Sacks offered a ten-figure prime; once again there was wonderment. After a long silence John brought out a twelve-figure number. Sacks had no way of checking this, because his book only went up to ten-figure primes; but he had no doubt it *was* a prime. An hour later the twins were swopping twenty-figure numbers.

What were the twins *doing* during their half-minute silence when Sacks introduced the eight-figure prime? The answer can only be that they were making the effort to *see* the number – to see it in some symmetrical way so they could see if there was any "remainder". Most of us can visualize, say, nine or sixteen by imagining a group of dots laid out in three rows of three or four rows of four; the twins must have been doing the same thing on a far vaster scale.

This offers us an important clue. We know that the two hemispheres of the brain have different functions: in effect, the left is a scientist, the right an artist. The left is concerned with language and logic; the right with intuitions and insights. The left sees the world from a "worm's-eye view", the right from a "bird's-eye view". In civilized human beings the left is the "dominant hemisphere", and my *sense of identity* resides there, so that when I use the word "I" it is the left brain speaking. (See also article on synchronicity.) In most of us the powers of the right brain – to visualize patterns, for example – are fairly limited compared to the reasoning powers of the left. It seems clear that in the Twins the powers of the left are extremely limited, but the powers of the right are apparently hundreds of times greater than in the rest of us.

It would seem that the general lesson to be learned from twins is that the non-stop left-brain activity demanded by civilization has suppressed all kinds of "natural" powers in the right, such as telepathic communication, physical empathy, and the ability to grasp reality with a "bird's-eye vision" – with a "telescope" instead of the microscope we habitually use. And cases like those of the Jim twins – in which the same kind of things have happened to twins who have been separated since birth – seem to hint there are laws and patterns of events scientists and philosophers have not even begun to suspect.

27

Jack the Ripper

Shedding New Light on the World's Most Infamous Serial Killer

In spite of the epidemic of twentieth-century serial killers with sobriquets like the Boston Strangler, the Buffalo Slasher, and the Sunset Slayer, Jack the Ripper still remains far and away the world's most famous – or infamous – serial killer. This is not due simply to the grisly picturesqueness of the nickname but to the fact that the murders took place in the fog-shrouded London of Sherlock Holmes and that – unlike the three killers mentioned above – the identity of Jack the Ripper is still a total mystery.

One other interesting fact deserves to be taken into account: Jack the Ripper was the first sex killer in the modern sense of the term. The notion that sex crimes made their first appearance as late as 1888 sounds rather strange. What about Roman emperors like Tiberius, who enjoyed deflowering altar boys? What about Gilles de Rais and Vlad the Impaler and Ivan the Terrible? The first thing we notice about these men is that they were all rulers or members of the aristocracy. They had leisure – which can also lead to boredom – and sufficient authority to be able to impose their will on their victims. But the majority of criminals throughout history have killed or robbed for purely economic reasons. *The Newgate Calendar*, a compilation of crimes published in London in the late eighteenth century, contains only half a dozen "sex crimes", and these were not violent rapes but what we would call seductions. The lower classes were too hungry to bother about "forbidden" sex, and the upper classes could obtain it so easily that rape would have been pointless.

In the early nineteenth century a significant development occurred; the rise of pornography. The man most responsible for this was the Marquis de Sade – again an aristocrat – who died in an asylum in 1816.

He was very highly sexed, and since he spent most of his life in prison, he had little to do but fantasize about sex. His books, with their monstrous daydreams of rape and torture, inspired many imitators in the 1820s, not all of whom shared his taste for flogging and being flogged, but every one of whom was excited by the notion of the forbidden.

In the two decades preceding Jack the Ripper, there *were* a few crimes that we would nowadays describe as sex murders, but these were usually perpetrated by people who would today be committed to an asylum – like the Italian youth Vincent Verzeni, who graduated from killing chickens to disemboweling women and "sucking their blood", or the Boston teenager Jesse Pomeroy, who enjoyed inflicting pain on younger children and ended by killing two of them.

Compared to these, there was something utterly calculated about the Jack the Ripper murders, which took place in the Whitechapel area of East London, in the autumn of 1888, and which produced a morbid sense of shock and panic.

It was still dark on the morning of September 1 when a cart driver named George Cross walked along Bucks Row on his way to work. It was a narrow, cobbled street with the blank wall of a warehouse on one side and a row of terraced houses on the other. In the dim light Cross saw what he thought was a bundle of tarpaulin and went to investigate. It proved to be a woman lying on her back, her skirt above her waist. Cross decided she was drunk, and when another man approached, he said, "Give me a hand getting this woman on her feet". The other man, a market porter, looked down dubiously; his first impression was that she had been raped and left for dead. He bent down and touched her cheek, which was cold, and her hand. "She's dead", he said. "We'd better find a policeman". He pulled down her skirt to make her decent.

In fact, the beat of Police Constable John Neil took him through Bucks Row, and a few minutes after the men had left, the light of his bull's-eye lantern showed him the woman's body, which lay close to a stable door. It also showed him something the men had been unable to see: that the woman's throat had been cut so deeply that the vertebrae were exposed.

An hour later the body, which was that of a middle-aged woman, lay in the yard of the local mortuary, and two paupers from the workhouse next door were given the job of stripping it, while a police inspector took notes. It was when they pulled off the two petticoats that the inspector saw that the woman's abdomen had been slashed open with a jagged incision that ran from the bottom of the ribs to the pelvis.

The woman was identified through a Lambeth Workhouse mark stenciled on her petticoat. She was Mary Ann Nicholls, a prostitute who had been living at a common lodging house in Thrawl Street – one of the worst slums even in that poverty-stricken area. A few hours before her death she had staggered back to the lodging house, her speech slurred with drink, and admitted that she lacked the fourpence necessary for a bed. The keeper had turned her away. "I'll soon get the money", she had shouted as she went off down the street. "See what a jolly bonnet I've got". She went looking for a man who would give her the price of a bed in exchange for an uncomfortable act of intercourse on the pavement in a back alley. What had happened, the police surgeon inferred, was that her customer had placed his hands around her throat as she lay on the ground and strangled her into unconsciousness – there were bruises on her throat. Then he had cut her throat with two powerful slashes that had almost severed the head, raised her skirt, and stabbed and slashed at her stomach in a kind of frenzy.

Oddly enough, the murder caused little sensation. Prostitutes were often killed in the slums of London, sometimes by gangs who demanded protection money. The previous April a prostitute named Emma Smith had dragged herself into London Hospital, reporting that she had been attacked by four men in Osborn Street. They had rammed some object, possibly an iron bar, into her vagina with such force that it had penetrated the uterus; she had died of peritonitis. In July dismembered portions of a woman's body had been recovered from the Thames. And on 7 August 1888, a prostitute named Martha Tabram had been found dead on a landing in George Yards Buildings, Whitechapel; she had been stabbed thirty-nine times with a knife or bayonet. Two soldiers were questioned about her murder but proved to have an excellent alibi. Evidently some sadistic brute had a grudge against prostitutes, it was hardly the kind of story to appeal to respectable newspaper readers.

That attitude was to change dramatically eight days after the murder of Mary Ann Nicholls, when another disemboweled body was found in the backyard of a barber's shop in Hanbury Street, Whitechapel. It was a place where prostitutes often took their customers, and this is evidently what Annie Chapman had done at about 5:30 on the morning of Saturday, 8 September 1888; a neighbour had seen her talking to a dark-looking man "of foreign appearance", dressed in shabby genteel clothes and wearing a deerstalker hat. Half an hour later a lodger named John Davis went downstairs and into the yard, where the lavatory was situated. He saw the body of a woman lying against the fence, her skirt drawn up above her waist and her legs bent at the knees. The stomach had been cut open and some of the intestines pulled out. As in the case of Mary Ann Nicholls, the cause of death was a deep gash in the throat. The murderer had placed the woman's rings and some pennies at her feet and a torn envelope near her head. Medical examination revealed that the killer had also removed the uterus and upper part of the vagina.

Now, suddenly, the press awoke to the fact that the unknown killer was a sadistic maniac. The *Star* that afternoon carried the headline: "Latest Horrible Murder in Whitechapel". When Mrs Mary Burridge, of Blackfriars Road, South London, read the story, she collapsed and died "of a fit". Sir Melville Macnaghten, later head of the Criminal Investigation Department (CID), would eventually write in his memoirs: "No one who was living in London that autumn will forget the terror created by these murders. Even now I can recall the foggy evenings, and hear again the raucous cries of the newspaper boys: 'Another horrible murder, murder, mutilation, Whitechapel.'"

In our own age of mass violence, we find it impossible to imagine the shock created by the murders. A journalist who reported the crimes later began his account of them in a popular booklet: "In the long catalogue of crimes which has been compiled in our modern days there is nothing to be found, perhaps, which has so darkened the horizon of humanity and shadowed the vista of man's better nature as the series of mysterious murders committed in Whitechapel during the latter part of 1888". "Shadowed the vista of man's better nature" – this is what so frightened Londoners. It was as if an inhuman monster, a kind of demon, had started to hunt the streets. Hysteria swept over the whole country. There had been nothing like it since the Ratcliffe Highway murders of 1811, when two families were slaughtered in East London, and householders all over England barricaded their doors at night.

On 29 September 1888, the Central News Agency received a letter that began: "Dear Boss, I keep on hearing the police have caught me but they won't fix me just yet". It included the sentence; "I am down on whores and I shan't quit ripping them till I do get buckled" and promised: "You will soon hear of me with my funny little games". It was signed "Jack the Ripper" – the first time the name had been used. The writer requested: "Keep this letter back till I do a bit more work, then give it out straight". The Central News Agency decided to follow his advice.

That night, a Saturday, the "ripper" killed again – this time not one, but two prostitutes. At 1:00 A.M. on Sunday morning a hawker named Louis Diemschutz drove his pony and cart into the backyard of a workingman's club in Berner Street. The pony shied and Diemschutz saw something lying in front of its feet; a closer look showed him that it was a woman's body. The Ripper was either in the yard at that moment or had only just left it when he heard the approach of the horse and cart. When Diemschutz returned a few moments later with a lighted candle, he was able to see that the woman's throat had been cut. There had also been an attempt to cut off her ear. She was later identified as Elizabeth Stride, an alcoholic Swedish prostitute.

The killer had been interrupted but his nerve was unshaken. He hastened up Berner Street and along Commercial Road – this murder had been farther afield than the others – and reached the Houndsditch area just in time to meet a prostitute who had been released from Bishopsgate police station ten minutes earlier. Her name was Catherine Eddowes, and she had been held for being drunk and disorderly. He seems to have had no difficulty persuading the woman to accompany him into Mitre Square, a small square surrounded by warehouses, only a few hundred yards away. A policeman patrolled the square every fifteen minutes or so, and when he passed through at 1:30, he saw nothing unusual. At 1:45 he found the body of a woman lying in the corner of the square. She was lying on her back, with her dress pushed up around her waist, and her face had been slashed. Her body had been gashed open from the base of the ribs to the pubic region, and the throat had been cut. Later examination revealed that a kidney was missing and that half of one ear had been cut off.

The murderer had evidently heard the approach of the policeman and hurriedly left the square by a small passage that runs from its northern side. In this passage there was a communal sink, and he had paused long enough to wash the blood from his hands and probably from his knife. In Goulston Street, a ten-minute walk away, he discarded a blood-stained piece of his victim's apron. The policeman who found it also found a chalked message scrawled on a nearby wall: "The Juwes are not the men that will be blamed for nothing". The police commissioner, Sir Charles Warren, ordered the words to be rubbed out, in spite of a plea from a local CID man that they should be photographed first; he thought they might cause a riot against the Jews, thousands of whom lived in Whitechapel.

Macnaghten admitted later: "When the double murder of 30th September took place, the exasperation of the public at the non-discovery of the perpetrator knew no bounds". The "Jack the Ripper" letter was released, and the murderer immediately acquired a nickname. And early on Monday morning the Central News Agency received another missive – this time a postcard – from Jack the Ripper. It read: "I was not codding [joking] dear old boss when I gave you the tip. You'll hear about Saucy Jack's work tomorrow. Double event this time. Number one squealed a bit. Couldn't finish straight off. Had not time to get ears for police. Thanks for keeping last letter back till I got to work again".

The public exploded in fury. Meetings were held in the streets, criticizing the police. Sir Charles Warren's resignation was demanded. Because the murderer was suspected of being a doctor, men carrying black bags found it dangerous to walk through the streets. The police decided to try bloodhounds, but the dogs promptly lost themselves on Tooting Common.

Yet as October passed with no further murders, the panic began to die down. Then, in the early hours of 9 November the Ripper staged his most spectacular crime of all. Mary Jeanette Kelly was a young Irish-woman, only twenty-four years old, who lived in a cheap room in Miller's Court, off Dorset Street. At about two o'clock that morning she was seen talking to a swarthy man with a heavy moustache; he seemed well dressed and had a gold watch chain. They entered the narrow alleyway that led to her lodging: room 13.

At 10:45 the next morning a rent collector knocked on her door but received no reply. He put his hand through a broken pane of glass in the window and pulled aside the curtain. What he saw sent him rushing for a policeman.

Jack the Ripper had surpassed himself. The body lay on the bed, and the mutilations must have taken a long time – an hour or more. One of the hands lay in the open stomach. The head had been virtually removed and was hanging on only by a piece of skin, as was the left arm. The breasts and nose had been removed and the skin from the legs stripped off. The heart lay on the pillow, and some of the intestines were draped around a picture. The remains of a fire burned in the grate, as if the Ripper had used it to provide himself with light. But this time, medical examination revealed that the Ripper had taken away none of the internal organs; his lengthy exercise in mutilation had apparently satisfied his peculiar sadistic fever.

This murder caused the greatest sensation of all. The police chief finally resigned. Public clamour became louder than ever; even Queen Victoria made suggestions on how to catch the murderer. Yet the slaughter of Mary Kelly proved to be the last of the crimes of Jack the Ripper. The police, hardly able to believe their luck as weeks and months went by without further atrocities, reached the conclusion that the Ripper had either committed suicide or been confined in a mental home. A body taken from the river early the following January was identified as that of a doctor who had committed suicide, and Scotland Yard detectives told themselves that this was almost certainly Jack the Ripper. But their claims have never been confirmed.

There have, of course, been many fascinating theories. Forty years after the murders, an Australian journalist named Leonard Matters wrote the first full-length book on Jack the Ripper. He ended by telling an extraordinary story: how a surgeon in Buenos Aires was called to the bedside of a dying Englishman, whom he recognized as the brilliant surgeon Dr Stanley, under whom he had studied. Stanley told him a horrifying story. In 1888 his son Herbert had died of syphilis contracted from a prostitute two years before; her name had been Mary Jeanette Kelly. Dr Stanley swore to avenge Herbert's death and prowled the East End of London looking for the woman. He would pick up prostitutes, question them about Mary Kelly, then kill them to make sure they made no attempt to warn her. Finally, he found the woman he was seeking and took his revenge. Then he left for Argentina.

Matters admitted that his own search of the records of the British Medical Association had revealed no Dr Stanley nor anyone who even resembled him. But there are other reasons for regarding the Stanley story as fiction. If Dr Stanley was only trying to silence his first four or five victims, why did he disembowel them? In any case, syphilis is unlikely to kill a man in two years – ten is a more likely period. But the most conclusive piece of evidence against the Dr Stanley theory is that Mary Kelly was not suffering from syphilis.

Ten years later an artist named William Stewart published *Jack the Ripper: A New Theory*. Stewart had studied the inquest report on Mary Kelly and discovered that she was pregnant at the time of her death. He produced the remarkable theory that Jack the Ripper was a woman – a midwife who had gone to the room in Miller's Court to perform an abortion. After killing Mary Kelly in a sadistic frenzy, she had dressed up in her spare clothes and left, after burning her own bloody garments in the grate. The immediate objection to this theory is that Mary Kelly had no spare clothes – she was too poor. But the major objection is that there has never yet been a case of sadistic mutilation murder in which the killer was a woman. Stewart's "Jill the Ripper" is a psychological improbability.

In 1959 the journalist Donald McCormick revived a theory that dated to the 1920s. A journalist named William LeQueux described in a book called *Things I Know* how, after the Russian revolution, the Kerensky government had allowed him to see a manuscript written in French by the "mad monk" Rasputin and found in a safe in the basement of Rasputin's house. It was called *Great Russian Criminals*, and it declared that Jack the Ripper was a sadistic maniac named Alexander Pedachenko, who was sent to England by the Russian secret police to embarrass the British police force. Pedachenko, said LeQueux, was later arrested after he tried to kill a woman in Tver (Kalinin). In fact, LeQueux wrote three books about Rasputin, all full of cynical invention. And although they were written before *Things I Know*, they all fail to mention this extraordinary theory. But the strongest objection to the Rasputin-Pedachenko theory is that Rasputin did not speak a word of French and that he lived in a flat on the third floor, in a house with no cellar.

In the same year that McCormick's book was published, Daniel Farson investigated the Ripper murders for a television program and succeeded in securing an extraordinary scoop. Sir Melville Macnaghten had hinted strongly in his memoirs that he knew the identity of Jack the Ripper and spoke of three suspects, although he finally dismissed two of these. Farson succeeded in getting hold of Macnaghten's original notes and learned the name of this chief suspect: an unsuccessful barrister named Montague John Druitt – the man whose body was found in the Thames in early January 1889. Farson did some remarkable detective work and learned a great deal about Druitt's life and death.

Alas, when Macnaghten's comments are examined closely, it becomes very clear that he knew little or nothing about Druitt. He calls him a doctor when he was a barrister. He says he believes Druitt lived with his family, when in fact he lived in chambers, like most lawyers. He says he believes Druitt's mind snapped after his "glut" in Miller's Court and that he committed suicide the following day. We know that Druitt killed himself three weeks later and that he did so because he was depressed after going to see his mother, who had become insane – he was afraid that the same thing was happening to him. In fact, Macnaghten joined the police force six months after the Ripper murders came to an end, and it is obvious that his Druitt theory was pure wishful thinking, without a shred of supporting evidence.

When, in 1960, I published a series of articles entitled "My Search for Jack the Ripper" in the London *Evening Standard*, I was asked to lunch by an old surgeon named Thomas Stowell, who told me his own astonishing theory about the Ripper's identity: that it was Queen Victoria's grandson – the heir to the throne – the Duke of Clarence, who died during the flu epidemic in 1892. Sowell told me that he had seen the private papers of Sir William Gull, Queen Victoria's physician, and that Gull had dropped mysterious hints about Clarence and Jack the Ripper, as well as mentioning that Clarence had syphilis, from which he died. When, subsequently, I asked Stowell if I could write about his theory, he said no. "It might upset Her Majesty". But in 1970 he decided to publish it himself in a magazine called *The Criminologist*. Admittedly, he did not name his suspect – he called him *S* – but he dropped dozens of hints that it was Clarence. Journalists took up the story and it caused a worldwide sensation. Stowell was so shaken by all the publicity that he died a week later, trying to repair the damage by claiming that his suspect was *not* the Duke of Clarence.

A writer named Michael Harrison, working on a biography of Clarence, carefully reread Stowell's article and realized that there were many discrepancies between the career of *S* and that of the Duke of Clarence. He concluded that Sir William Gull had indeed referred to a suspect as *S* but that it was not the Duke of Clarence, but someone who was closely acquainted with him. Studying Clarence's acquaintances, he discovered the ideal suspect: James Kenneth Stephen, a poet, lawyer, and man-about-town who had become distinctly odd after being struck on the head by the vane of a windmill and who, like Clarence, had died – in a mental home – in 1892. Harrison had no trouble in disposing of Clarence as a suspect, pointing out that at the time of the Miller's Court murder, Clarence was celebrating his father's birthday at Sandringham. But he was far less successful in finding even a grain of evidence to connect Stephen with the crimes. It is almost impossible to imagine the intellectual young aesthete, author of a great deal of published verse, stalking prostitutes with a knife.

The next major book on Jack the Ripper was optimistically entitled *Jack the Ripper: The Final Solution* (1976) and was written by a young journalist named Stephen Knight; he was following up a story propounded in a BBC television series called "The Ripper File", which in turn was based on an astounding story told by Joseph "Hobo" Sickert, son of the famous Victorian painter Walter Sickert. This story also involved the Duke of Clarence – although not, this time, as the murderer.

According to Hobo Sickert, his father and the heir to the throne were close friends, and the Duke often went slumming with the bohemian painter. In Sickert's studio in Cleveland Street, Soho, Clarence met an attractive young artist's model named Annie Crook. She became his mistress and in 1885 gave birth to a baby girl they named Alice Margaret. Then, according to Sickert, Clarence and his mistress got married in a private ceremony.

The story becomes more preposterous. When the secret marriage reached the ear of Queen Victoria, she was horrified. Annie was not only a commoner but a Catholic. The Prime Minister, Lord Salisbury, gave orders that Annie and the baby were to be kidnapped. A carriage drove up to the house at 6 Cleveland Street, and Annie and her baby daughter were hustled into a carriage and taken off to a mental home; there Sir William Gull performed a sinister brain operation on Annie to make her lose her memory. (This, incidentally, is virtually impossible; even nowadays scientists are uncertain where the source of memory lies, and in 1888 ignorance was total.)

The child, Alice, was handed over to a nanny in the East End of London – one Mary Kelly. Eventually, Alice found her way back to Walter Sickert and became his mistress. Joseph "Hobo" Sickert was the outcome of this union.

But Mary Kelly made the mistake of deciding to blackmail the royal family. She had taken a number of fellow prostitutes into her confidence, and the Prime Minister decided they all had to be killed. The task was given to Sir William Gull, who had sadistic tendencies anyway. His method was complicated but original; he would drive around the streets of Whitechapel in a coach until he saw his prospective victim, who would then be lured inside and disemboweled. His coachman, a man named Netley, was an accomplice. (A more recent theory suggests that Netley himself was Jack the Ripper.) And since Gull was also a Freemason, he left various clues in the form of hints of masonic ritual, such as the objects arranged so carefully around Annie Chapman and the misspelling of Jews as *Juwes*. Mary Kelly, of course, was the final victim.

It is not clear whether Knight believed this incredible farrago of nonsense. He probably did not. He knew that Gull had suffered a stroke in 1887 and would have been incapable of the murders. And a fellow investigator named Simon Wood had uncovered Annie Crook's rent book and discovered that she left the Cleveland Street address in 1886, a year before she is supposed to have been kidnapped. Moreover, the records show that she was living a perfectly normal life until 1920, when she died in a workhouse. Her religion was Church of England, not Roman Catholic. Simon Wood told Knight all of this soon after publication of *The Final Solution*, but Knight made no attempt to correct his "facts" in the paperback edition. Since his book had become something of a bestseller, it was not in his interests to admit that he had been deceived by Hobo Sickert.

It was, in fact, Hobo Sickert himself who pulled the rug out from under Knight by publicly admitting that the Jack the Ripper part of his story was pure invention. He insisted, however, that the story of Annie Crook giving birth to the Duke of Clarence's daughter – and the daughter becoming his own mother – was true. And in this he was probably being truthful. The most convincing part of Knight's book is his description of the various "clues" to the affair that Sickert slipped into his paintings.

In fact, this part of the story was confirmed – or at least strongly supported – in a book entitled *Sickert and the Ripper Crimes* (1990) by Jean Overton Fuller. It also demonstrates that Hobo Sickert did not invent his Jack the Ripper story out of whole cloth; it looks as if a remarkable coincidence led him to believe that there *was* some connection between the Duke of Clarence and the Ripper murders.

Jean Overton Fuller's mother had a friend named Florence Pash, an artist who was also an intimate of Walter Sickert. Florence had told Mrs Fuller that Sickert knew the identity of Jack the Ripper and that he had carried some sinister secret around with him for the rest of his days – a secret that, at times, made him fear for his life. Florence Pash also confirmed that Mary Kelly *had* worked for Sickert as a nursemaid before the murders. We know that Sickert was obsessed by the Ripper murders and that he painted several pictures based on them.

All this, according to Jean Fuller, proves that Sickert was himself Jack the Ripper and that his motive was to kill the blackmailing prostitutes who knew the secret of Annie Crook.

This is obviously absurd. Why should Sickert go around murdering prostitutes because they knew that the Duke of Clarence had fathered an illegitimate child? Protecting his royal friend's good name is obviously an insufficient motive. Besides, Jack the Ripper was a sadist who enjoyed disemboweling women. Walter Sickert seems to have been one of the nastiest and most spoiled men who ever lived, but as far as we know, he was not a sadist.

What the Florence Pash evidence *does* seem to prove is that the Duke really fathered an illegitimate daughter, who became the mother of Joseph Sickert. It also confirms the unlikeliest part of Hobo Sickert's story: that Mary Kelly acted as a nursemaid to the baby. She may even have tried to blackmail Sickert. But even without the blackmail motif, we can understand why Sickert thought he was the custodian of a frightening secret. When Mary Kelly became – almost certainly by pure chance – the Ripper's final victim, he must have felt certain that the long arm of Buckingham Palace was involved. And when Hobo Sickert, the child of Walter Sickert and Annie Crook, came to hear of this tale of a royal love affair followed by murder, he understandably came to believe that the Palace was somehow involved in the murders. At least Fuller's book enables us to understand how the whole silly story came to be invented.

But that leaves us with the question: Who *was* the Ripper? In 1988, the centenary of the murders, half a dozen books propounded new theories – or old theories with a new twist.

Martin Fido's *Crimes, Detection and Death of Jack the Ripper* returned to Macnaghten's original notes, which listed three men as the chief Ripper suspects: Druitt (whom we have already dismissed), an insane Russian doctor named Ostrog (the origin of "Pedachenko"), and an insane Polish Jew named Kosminski, who was committed to an asylum in 1889. Sir Robert Anderson, the Assistant Commissioner of Police, is on record as remarking that the Ripper was a Polish Jew. Fido looked through the records of insane asylums and found a man named Aaron Kozminski, who died in 1891; but he was suffering from paranoid delusions and obviously lacked the cunning and intelligence to be the Ripper. A further search, however, uncovered a Nathan Kaminsky, treated for syphilis in March 1888, but about whom nothing more is known. Fido identifies him with David Cohen, another Polish Jew, who was committed to an asylum in December 1888 and died in the following year; Cohen was too violent to associate with his fellow patients. Fido speculates that a man who mumbled his name as "Nathan Kamin" might have been misheard as saying "David Cohen". This is true; it is also true that Cohen *might* have been Jack the Ripper. But there is not a shred of real evidence that he was.

Paul Begg, another "Ripperologist", points out in *Jack the Ripper: Uncensored Facts* that a close associate of Anderson, D. S. Swanson, wrote in the margin of Anderson's autobiography the comment that the Polish Jew died in "the Seaside Home". This would seem to rule out Kaminsky-Cohen as the Ripper.

In *The Ripper Legacy*, Martin Howells and Keith Skinner describe their fruitless investigation into an "Australian connection" mentioned by Daniel Farson: the notion that Druitt's cousin Lionel moved to Australia and wrote a pamphlet entitled "Jack the Ripper – I Knew Him". This trail led nowhere. Nevertheless, Howells and Skinner endorse Farson's conclusion that Druitt was Jack the Ripper and suggest that his "suicide" in the Thames was actually murder – that former associates from his Cambridge days, a society called The Apostles, learned that he was the Ripper and killed him in order to prevent a scandal. The book reveals their remarkable tenacity as researchers, but their theory contains as many "ifs" as Martin Fido's.

The "black magician" Aleister Crowley was convinced that the Ripper was another "magician" by the name of Roslyn D'Onston Stevenson (who preferred to be called "D'Onston"), who committed the murders as part of a ritual to gain supreme magical powers. Crowley tells a preposterous story about how D'Onston ate parts of the bodies at the scene of the crime and in so doing stained his ties with blood. The bloodstained ties were then found in a tin box under D'Onston's bed by his lesbian landlady.

In fact, D'Onston wrote a letter to Scotland Yard claiming to know the identity of Jack the Ripper: a doctor named Morgan Davies. His grounds for this belief were that he had heard Davies describing the murders to some fellow doctors and enacting the crimes with a gruesome realism that convinced D'Onston that Davies had actually committed them. The police seem to have treated it as yet another crank letter. In *A Casebook on Jack the Ripper* (1976), criminologist Richard Whittington-Egan went into the D'Onston theory at length but concluded that D'Onston was a fantasist and something of a con man.

Whittington-Egan's friend Melvin Harris decided to investigate D'Onston and discovered that Whittington-Egan had been less than just. Many of D'Onston's "fantasies" about his service in India and fighting under Garibaldi turned out to be true. Harris's *Jack the Ripper: The Bloody Truth* is an impressive piece of research. But it utterly fails to explain why a man who went to the police alleging that someone else was Jack the Ripper (on grounds that cannot be taken seriously) should himself have been the Whitechapel murderer.

Another brilliant piece of investigation was carried out by a Norwich accountant named Steward Hicks, who searched through the lunacy records for 1888 and came upon the name of a doctor named John Hewitt, who had been a patient in Coton Hill, an asylum in Staffordshire. Walter Sickert once described how he had taken a room near Camden Town and how his landlady was convinced that one of her previous lodgers, a student vet named John Hewitt, was Jack the Ripper – Hewitt had burned all his clothes in the grate (presumably to destroy bloodstains) and often stayed out all night. Hewitt's mother had finally removed him to Bournemouth, where he died of tuberculosis.

Could it be, wondered Hicks, that Hewitt's mother had actually realized he was Jack the Ripper and had had him committed to an asylum in Staffordshire? His research revealed that Hewitt had died of "general paralysis of the insane" in 1892, so he *could* be the Ripper. Hicks approached me with his theory, and I was able to help him gain access to the records of Coton Hill asylum, which had now been removed to the

Staffordshire asylum. Alas, they revealed that Hewitt had committed himself to the asylum before the murders began. There was, however, still a slim hope for Mr Hicks's theory. Since Hewitt had committed himself voluntarily to the asylum, he was allowed to go in and out as he pleased. If he had been away on the dates of the Whitechapel murders, that would constitute almost overwhelming circumstantial evidence that he was the Ripper. Regrettably, when Hicks finally gained full access to the papers in the Public Records Office, they made it clear that the dates when Hewitt was absent from the asylum were not the dates of the murders. Hicks tells me that, in spite of this, he still believes he may find evidence to show that Hewitt could have been Jack the Ripper. I wish him luck but cannot share his optimism.

Other theories that surfaced around the time of the Ripper centenary are that the killer was Frank Miles, a homosexual artist who was a friend of Oscar Wilde's (and who died insane), and that he was Joseph Barnett, the man who had lived with Mary Kelly until shortly before her murder. The Frank Miles theory – advocated by Mr Thomas Toughill – is open to the same objection as Harrison's Stephen theory: that highly educated, "aesthetic" young poets (or artists) are not likely to turn to disemboweling. Bruce Paley, author of the Joseph Barnett theory, has a stronger case, in that whoever killed Mary Kelly locked the door behind him – yet the key is known to have been missing for some time. Barnett *could* easily have had the key. On the other hand, it may simply have turned up again before Mary Kelly was killed. And since Barnett is known to have been a mild little man, the theory that he killed five women because he was madly in love with Mary and disapproved of her habit of selling her favours is, to say the least, unlikely.

Jack the Ripper: Summing Up and Verdict, by myself and Robin Odell, also appeared during the centenary. In *Jack the Ripper in Fact and Fiction* (1965), Robin Odell had suggested that Jack the Ripper was a Jewish *shochet*, or ritual slaughterer, whose sadistic tendencies were stimulated by his profession until he began killing women. This is conceivable – except that it is hard to see why a sadist whose job involved slaughtering cattle by cutting their throats should have felt the need to kill women. And since all the records that might have enabled Odell to identify his slaughterer were destroyed during the Second World War, it seems that we must regard his theory as one more interesting might-have-been.

Since the early 1980s the phenomenon of serial murder has seized the public imagination, and careful psychological studies – particularly by the FBI's Behavioral Science Unit at Quantico, Virginia – have thrown some important new light on the phenomenon.* What can they tell us about Jack the Ripper? To begin with, the great majority of serial killers have emerged from working-class backgrounds. The middle- or upper-class serial killer is virtually unknown – presumably because the kind of frustrations that lead to multiple murder tend to spring from childhood poverty and ill treatment. This means that we can fairly confidently dismiss all the theories that involve an upper-class Ripper (or even a middle-class doctor like Matters's Dr Stanley or D'Onston's Morgan Davies).

We must also recognize that part of the fascination of the Ripper murders lies in the mistaken notion that the murderer must have been a master criminal, a kind of Dracula who preferred to mutilate his victims rather than drink their blood. In fact, the surprising thing about most serial killers is that they tend to be ordinary, nondescript individuals. In many cases, they seem so gentle and polite that their acquaintances find it impossible to believe they were capable of murder. The Boston Strangler, Albert DeSalvo, falls into this category; so does Peter Kürten, the Düsseldorf sadist, and Earl Nelson, the Gorilla Murderer – a charming young man who liked to discuss the Bible.

In many cases, the killer himself is totally unable to understand the urges that drive him to kill, and criminologists admit to being equally baffled. In September 1980 four black men were shot with a .22 rifle in Buffalo and Niagara Falls; in October two black cab drivers were stabbed to death and their hearts cut out. The killer had opened the ribcages and seemed to possess some medical skill. In December 1980 four black men were stabbed to death in New York by a man who simply approached them in the street.

The following January an eighteen-year-old army private named Joseph C. Christopher – a white – attacked a black soldier with a potato knife and then tried to emasculate himself. In custody, Christopher confessed to being the "Buffalo Slasher" as well as the .22 killer and the knife-wielding maniac of New York. People who had known Christopher in Buffalo were astounded; he was a quiet, ordinary teenager who was not known as a racist or a homosexual. (All the victims were male.) He had been raised in an Italian neighbourhood by a dominant father and a passive mother – in that respect he resembled the Boston Strangler – and had adored his father, who had taught him to shoot. Christopher had been much affected by his father's death, which had occurred in 1976, when he was fourteen. He himself seemed to have no idea of why

---

* See Colin Wilson and Donald Seaman, *The Serial Killers* (1990).

he had killed. As a "monster", Joe Christopher is a total disappointment. Yet he provides us with a more realistic image of the serial killer than the notion of a raving maniac.

The probability is that Jack the Ripper was as "ordinary" and as nondescript as Christopher. He was probably not even insane, like "Pedachenko", or violent, like Kaminsky-Cohen. So there is almost certainly no hope of establishing his identity more than a century after the murders. He was a "nobody".

Yet, oddly enough, there is a suspect who fits this description of a "murderous nobody". After Daniel Farson had presented his television program on Jack the Ripper in 1959, he received a letter from a man who signed himself *G.W.B.* and who explained that he was a seventy-seven-year-old who lived in Melbourne, Australia. He wrote:

When I was a nipper, about 1889, I was playing in the streets about 9.00 P.M. when my mother called, "Come in Georgie or JTR [Jack the Ripper] will get you". That night a man patted me on the head and said, "Don't worry, Georgie. You would be the last person JTR would touch". [This man was apparently Georgie's own father, who was born in 1850 and so would have been thirty-eight at the time of the murders.] My father was a terrible drunkard and night after night he would come home and kick my mother and us kids about something cruelly. About the year 1902 I was taught boxing, and after feeling proficient to hold my own, I threatened my father that if he laid a hand on my mother or brothers I would thrash him. He never did after that, but we lived in the same house and never spoke to each other. Later, I emigrated to Australia. I was booked to depart with three days' notice, and my mother asked me to say goodbye to my father. It was then he told his foul history and why he did those terrible murders, and advised me to change my name because he would confess before he died. Once settled in Melbourne I assumed another name. However, my father died in 1912 and I was watching the papers carefully, expecting a sensational announcement.

This, of course, never came. Georgie's explanation for his father's heavy drinking is that he had always wanted a daughter but that his first child – a female – was an imbecile; later children were all boys. "During the confession of those awful murders, he explained that he did not know what he was doing but his ambition was to get drunk and an urge to kill every prostitute that accosted him".

His father, Georgie explained, was a dung collector, and on one occasion, after killing a woman, he had removed his outer pair of trousers, which were saturated with blood, and hidden them in the manure. Later, while his partner went to have a meal of sausage and mash, Jack (this was the father's name) buried himself in the manure to keep warm and upon hearing a policeman asking questions about Jack the Ripper felt "scared to death".

Many sadistic killers commit their crimes only after they have been drinking heavily, and "Georgie's" account of his father rings psychologically true. A highly dominant individual, a bully who beat his wife and probably felt a contempt for all women, might well have experienced a kind of homicidal rage when accosted by prostitutes. It is also hard to imagine why a seventy-seven-year-old man should bother to write an anonymous letter from Melbourne with a completely false story. And, assuming his story to be true, it is equally hard to see why his father should have invented the story about being Jack the Ripper.

It is possible that, even at this distance in time, a check of the records of ships bound for Australia in 1902 could reveal the identity of "G.W.B". and that this in turn might lead to uncovering the identity of a man called Jack (surname probably beginning with a *B*) who was born in 1850, died in 1912, and was a manure collector in Whitechapel in 1888. We would have no means of being certain that this man was Jack the Ripper; but he would seem to me far and away the likeliest candidate.

Postscript to Jack the Ripper

In 1993, a new – and highly plausible – candidate was added to the list when a book called *The Diary of Jack the Ripper* was published. The author of the *Diary* (found scrawled in an old notebook) was James Maybrick, a Liverpool cotton merchant, whose young wife Florence was accused of poisoning him. Florence was found guilty and sentenced to death, but later reprieved. The *Diary* revealed that Maybrick was an 'arsenic eater' (in small quantities arsenic is a powerful stimulant), and that he was driven to a frenzy of jealousy by his young wife's infidelities. Maybrick spent a great deal of time in Whitechapel on business and, according to the *Diary*, vented his fury against Florence by murdering prostitutes.

Although the authenticity of the *Diary* has been widely questioned, powerful internal evidence suggests that it *was* written by James Maybrick, and that Maybrick was Jack the Ripper.

28

Did Joan of Arc
Return from the Dead?

On 30 May 1431 Joan of Arc was burnt as a heretic by the English; she was only nineteen years old. She regarded herself as a messenger from Heaven, sent to save the French from their enemies the English (who were in league with the Burgundians who captured her). At the age of thirteen Joan began to hear voices, which she later identified as those of St Gabriel, St Michael, St Marguerite and St Catherine. When the news of the encirclement of Orleans reached her little village in Lorraine, Domremy, her voices told her to go to lift the siege. Her military career was brief but spectacular: in a year she won many remarkable victories, and saw Charles VII crowned at Rheims. Then she was captured by the Burgundians, sold to the English for ten thousand francs, tried as a witch, and burnt alive.

But that, oddly enough, was not quite the end of "the Maid". "Now one month after Paris had returned to her allegiance to King Charles", writes Anatole France, "there appeared in Lorraine a certain damsel. She was about twenty-five years old. Hitherto she had been called Claude; but now she made herself known to divers lord of the town of Metz as being Jeanne the Maid". This was in May 1436, five years after Joan had died at the stake.

It sounds very obviously as if some imposter had decided to pose as Joan the Maid. But there is some astonishing evidence that suggests that this is not so. Joan's two younger brothers, Petit-Jean and Pierre, were still serving in the army, and they had no doubt whatever that their sister had been burnt at Rouen. So when they heard that a woman claiming to be Joan was at Metz, and that she had expressed a wish to meet them, the brothers hastened to Metz – Petit-Jean was not far away, being the provost of Vaucouleurs. One chronicler describes how the brothers went to the village of La-Grange-aux-Ormes, two and a half miles south of Metz, where a tournament was being held. A knight in armour was galloping around an obstacle course and pulling stakes expertly out of the ground; this was the person who claimed to be their sister. The brothers rode out on to the field, prepared to challenge the impostor. But when Petit-Jean demanded, "Who are you"?, the "impostor" raised her visor, and both brothers gaped in astonishment as they recognized their sister Joan.

In fact Joan was surrounded by various people who had known her during her spectacular year fighting the English, including Nicole Lowe, the king's chamberlain. If she was in fact an impostor, it seems absurd that she should go to a place where she would be sure to be recognized. (John of Metz was one of her first and most loyal supporters.) And the next day her brothers took her to Vaucouleurs, where she spent a week, apparently accepted by many people who had seen her there seven years earlier, when she had gone to see the local squire Robert de Baudricourt, to ask him to send her to see the Dauphin, the heir to the throne. After this she spent three weeks at a small town called Marville, then went on a pilgrimage to see the Black Virgin called Notre Dame de Liance, between Laon and Rheims. Then she went to stay with Elizabeth, Duchess of Luxembourg, at Arlon. Meanwhile her brother Petit-Jean went to see the king and announced that his sister Joan was still alive. We do not know the king's reaction, but he ordered his treasurer to give Petit-Jean a hundred francs. An entry in the treasury accounts of Orléans for 9 August 1436 states that the council authorized payment of a courier who had brought letters from "Jeanne la Pucelle" (Joan the Maid).

The records of these events are to be found in the basic standard work on Joan of Arc, Jules Quicherat's five-volume *Trial and Rehabilitation of Joan of Arc* (1841), which contains all the original documents. One of these documents states that on 24 June 1437 Joan's miraculous powers returned to her. By then she had become something of a protégée of Count Ulrich of Württemberg, who took her to Cologne. There she became involved in a clash between two churchmen who were rivals for the diocese; one had been appointed by the chapter, the other by the pope. Count Ulrich favoured one called Udalric, and Joan apparently also pronounced in his favour. But her intervention did no good; the Council of Basle considered Udalric a usurper, and the pope's nominee was appointed. The Inquisitor general of Cologne became curious about the count's guest (remember that this was at the height of the "witchcraft craze"), and was apparently shocked to learn that she practised magic, and that she danced with men and ate and drank more than she ought. (The magic sounds more like conjuring: she tore a tablecloth and restored it to its original state, and did the same with a glass which she broke against a wall.) He summoned her before him, but she refused to appear; when men were sent to fetch her the count hid her in his house, then smuggled her out of the town. The inquisitor excommunicated her. Back at Arlon, staying with the Duchess of Luxembourg, she met a nobleman named Robert des Armoires and – no doubt to the astonishment of her followers – married him. (The original Joan had sworn a vow of perpetual chastity under a "fairy tree" at Domremy.) Then they moved to Metz, where Robert had a house, and during the next three years she gave birth to two children.

Two years later, in the summer of 1439, the "Dame des Armoires" went to Orléans, whose magistrates gave her a banquet and presented her with 210 livres by way of thanking her for her services to the town during the siege. Oddly enough, these same burgesses had paid for Masses in memory of the Maid's death three months earlier; presumably they must have changed their minds in the meantime. After 1439 the Masses ceased.

After two weeks she left Orléans in rather a hurry, according to one chronicler, and went to Tours, where she sent a letter to the king via the Baillie of Touraine, Guillaume Bellier, who had been the Maid's host ten years earlier. Moreover, she soon afterwards went to Poitou, where she seems to have been given the nominal command of a place called Mans – presumably by the king she had enthroned. Then the king transferred this command to Joan's ex-comrade in arms, Gilles de Rais. Since the days when he had fought beside Joan before the walls of Paris, Gilles had begun to practise black magic – in an attempt to repair his fortunes, drained by his excesses – and had become a sadistic killer of children. In the following year, 1440, Gilles would be tried and condemned to be hanged and burned. Meanwhile – assuming he met the Dame des Armoises (which seems practically certain, since she had to hand over her command to him) – he seems to have accepted her as his former comrade-in-arms. He also placed her in authority over the men-at-arms.

In 1440 Joan finally went to Paris and met the king. And for the first time she received a setback; after the meeting the king declared her an impostor. It may be significant that he did so after the interview. Surely if he could see she was a fraud he would have said so at the time? He even attempted to practise on her the same trick he had tried at their first meeting eleven years earlier, concealing himself and asking one of his men to impersonate him. But as on the previous occasion Joan was not to be deceived; she walked straight up to the king and knelt at his feet, whereupon the king said: "Pucelle, my dear, you are welcome back in the name of God". It seems, to say the least of it, strange that he should then have decided she was an impostor.

And now, according to the journal "of a Bourgeois of Paris", Joan was arrested, tried and publicly exhibited as a malefactor. A sermon was preached against her, and she was forced to confess publicly that she was an imposter. Her story, according to the "Bourgeois of Paris", was that she had gone to Rome about 1433 to seek absolution for striking her mother. She had, she said, engaged as a soldier in war in the service of the Holy Father Eugenius, and worn man's apparel. This, presumably, gave her the idea of pretending to be the Maid . . .

But the whole of this story is doubtful in the extreme. To begin with, Joan then returned to Metz, and continued to be accepted as "la Pucelle". In 1443 her brother Pierre refers to her in a petition as "Jeanne la Pucelle, my sister", and her cousin Henry de Voulton mentions that Petit-Jean, Pierre and their sister la Pucelle used to visit the village of Sermaise and feast with relations, all of whom accepted her. Fourteen years later she makes an appearance in the town of Saumur, and is again accepted by the officials of the town as the Maid. And after that she vanishes from history, presumably living out the rest of her life quietly with her husband in Metz.

What then are we to make of the story that the king declared her an impostor, and that she admitted it publicly? First of all, its only source is the "journal of a Bourgeois of Paris". This in itself is odd, if she was involved in such a public scandal. Moreover, the "bourgeois" was hostile to the earlier Joan, in the days before her execution. Anatole France mentions that the common people of Paris were in a fever of excitement at the news that the Maid was still alive and was returning to Paris. The University of Paris was still thoroughly hostile to the Maid, who had been condemned as a witch.

Her sentence could only be reversed by the pope, and he showed no sign of doing this, in spite of a movement to rehabilitate Joan. So as far as the clerks and magistrates of Paris were concerned, the return of Joan would have been nothing but an embarrassment. As to those authorities of the Church who were trying to have the Maid declared innocent (they succeeded in 1456, and Joan was finally canonized in 1922), they would have found the return of their heroine – alive, healthy and married – an obstacle to their patriotic campaign. The king must have found himself under intolerable pressure to declare Joan an impostor. After all, if *he* declared her genuine, then it was "official", and no one in France had a right to doubt her identity. Moreover, there would be some question of public recognition . . . On the other hand, if he expressed doubts about her, the whole scandal was defused. She could return home and drop out of sight. And everyone would be much happier. And that, it seemed, is precisely what happened.

Anatole France takes it for granted that the Dame des Armoises was an impostor. But then his biography of Joan of Arc is permeated with his famous irony, and takes the view that she was a deluded peasant girl; France was basically a disciple of Voltaire. The notion that she was an impostor is indeed the simplest explanation. But it leaves us facing the problem: why, in that case, did so many people who knew "the Maid" accept the Dame des Armoises as genuine? It is conceivable that her brothers may have decided that it would be to their advantage to have their famous sister alive, and so condoned the imposture. But why should so many old comrades have agreed to support the story?

The Dame des Armoises never as far as we know explained how she came to escape the flames. But then presumably she would not know the answer to this question. She would only know that she had been rescued, and that someone else had died in her place – perhaps another "witch". It is easy to see how this could have come about. We know that Joan was an extraordinarily persuasive young lady, and that dozens of people, from Robert de Baudricourt to the Dauphin, who began by assuming she was mad, ended by believing that she was being guided by divine voices. We know that even in court Joan declared that she could hear St Catherine telling her what to say. Even at her trial she had certain friends; a priest called Loyseleur was her adviser. When Joan complained about the conduct of her two guards the Earl of Warwick was furious, and had them replaced by two other guards – which suggests that the earl held her in high regard. So it would not be at all surprising if there was a successful plot to rescue her. And it is possible that the English themselves may have been involved in such a plot; when Joan was apparently burnt at the stake in Rouen the crowd was kept at a distance by eight hundred English soldiers, which would obviously prevent anyone coming close enough to recognize her. At the trial for her rehabilitation in 1456 the executioner's evidence was entirely second-hand, although three of Joan's comrades who were with her at the "end" – Ladvenu, Massieu and Isambard – were actually present. *If* Joan was rescued, presumably they also were involved in the plot.

The rehabilitation itself has its farcical aspects. It began in 1450, and Joan's mother was the person who set it in motion, supported by Joan's brother Pierre. We do not know whether Joan's mother accepted the Dame des Armoires as her daughter, but there can be no doubt that she lent credence to the claim by not denouncing her as an impostor. Yet now she and Pierre joined in the claim that was based on the assertion that Joan was executed by the English in 1431. But then the aim of the rehabilitation was financial; Joan had been a rich woman, thanks to the generosity of the king, and the wealth remained frozen while Joan was excommunicated. So, whether or not Joan's family believed that the Dame des Armoires was the Maid, they now had good reason to try to have her rehabilitated – even if it meant swearing that she was dead.

If the Dame des Armoires was genuine, she must have felt there was a certain irony in the situation. She had been an embarrassment to everyone during her first career as the saintly virgin warrior; now she was just as much an embarrassment as the heroine returned from the dead. It is thankless work being a saint.

29

Junius

Who Was the Eighteenth Century's Most Feared Satirist?

In these days of investigative journalism, it is almost impossible to imagine a man who succeeds in maintaining a secret identity when everyone in the country is agog with curiosity to know who he is. It happens only in children's comics. Yet that is precisely what happened in England in the final years of the eighteenth century. The mystery man was a writer who called himself Junius and whose murderously satirical letters set the whole country laughing at the government, and even at the King himself. As a satirist and literary stylist, Junius compares favourably with Daniel Defoe, Jonathan Swift, and Samuel Butler – all of whom published their early works anonymously. But in these famous cases, the sheer brilliance of the satire made it inevitable that the identity of the authors of *Robinson Crusoe, Gulliver's Travels*, and *Erewhon* should be discovered. Junius's secret went with him to the grave.

The story begins in the reign of George III, the King whose "tea tax" was to cause the American Revolution and whose general Wellington later defeated Napoléon.

George III came to the throne in 1760, and his reign was troubled almost from the beginning. Under its greatest war leader, Prime Minister William Pitt, Britain had been fighting France for four years and was winning the war. The new King was anxious to end it, to the disgust of his subjects, who wanted to see the French well and truly thrashed. And Pitt – who not only wanted to thrash the French but to go to war with the Spaniards as well – resigned in 1761. The war came to an end two years later, and the "surrender" made the King still more unpopular.

But the real trouble – which brought England close to revolution –

was caused by a radical politician named John Wilkes. He was the kind of man who made every old-fashioned English gentleman foam at the mouth. He was blasphemous, ugly, cross-eyed, and a tireless seducer – but such a natural charmer that he liked to boast that he needed only half an hour's start on the handsomest man in England. He had been a member of Sir Francis Dashwood's Hell-Fire Club, a group that liked to dress as monks and invoke the Devil; Wilkes had terrified them when he introduced a sooty baboon into one of their orgies and they mistook it for Satan.

When Wilkes was elected to Parliament in 1757, he became a supporter of William Pitt. And when the King appointed his old tutor, a Scot named Lord Bute, as Secretary of State, and Bute began making peace with the French, Pitt resigned in disgust. Wilkes naturally regarded Bute as an enemy. Besides, most of the English detested the Scots – it was less than twenty years since Bonnie Prince Charlie had marched on London. So Wilkes founded a violently anti-Scottish newspaper called *The North Briton*. (A north Briton was, of course, a Scot – it was rather as if someone had founded an anti-Semitic newspaper called *The Israelite*.) Among other things it hinted that Lord Bute had gained his position by sleeping with the Queen Mother, an accusation that made the King apoplectic. The smear campaign was so successful that Bute resigned.

But now Wilkes went too far and put into the King's mouth a satirical speech – supposedly written by Bute – that amounted to an accusation of base betrayal of Britain's allies in the war. Wilkes was seized and thrown into the Tower of London, which – inevitably – boosted his popularity with the disgruntled populace. Wilkes claimed "Parliamentary privilege" – whereby a Member of Parliament has a right to speak his mind freely on political issues – and was released after a week. He now proceeded to make the King and his government still more embarrassed by suing Lord Halifax, the Secretary of State, for trespass. (He was backed financially by Lord Temple, Pitt's brother-in-law, who had also financed *The North Briton*.) Wilkes won his case; he was awarded vast damages – $5,000 – and the Secretary of State lost his job.

The King was now out for Wilkes's blood. To anybody with any sense, it should have been obvious that his administration was accident-prone and had better keep its head down. Instead, the new Secretary of State, Lord Sandwich,* decided to make Wilkes pay for his victory. The

---

* This was the man who invented the sandwich; rather than interrupt his gambling, he would eat a piece of meat between two slices of bread.

House of Commons voted that Wilkes's attack on the King had been a "seditious libel". They also bribed a printer to hand over a pornographic poem – entitled "An Essay on Woman" – that Wilkes was having printed, and some of its juicier passages were read aloud in the House of Lords. The Lords thought it a joke, for everyone knew that Lord Sandwich had looser morals than Wilkes. (When Sandwich told Wilkes that he would either die of the pox or on the gallows, Wilkes retorted, "That depends on whether I embrace your mistress or your principles".) But Parliament was shocked and voted that Wilkes had no right to Parliamentary privilege after all. Wilkes was force to flee abroad to avoid prison, but this only increased his popularity with the mob. The printer who had handed over the "Essay on Woman" could find no one to employ him and committed suicide.

The King's next choice as Prime Minister was George Grenville, a former ally of Pitt. He was capable enough but proved to be a bore who was inclined to deliver long lectures; the King got rid of him in 1765. But it was under Grenville that the government first stirred up revolution in the American colonies by imposing a Stamp Act – a tax on newspapers, advertisements, and legal documents. This met with such violent resistance in America that the next administration was forced to repeal it. It was a "dry run" for the Boston Tea Party seven years later.

Grenville had been one of the chief persecutors of John Wilkes. Now the King turned to a defender of Wilkes, the Marquis of Rockingham, who had friends on both sides, Whig and Tory. Wilkes decided to return to England, and the King's troubles began all over again. Wilkes stood for a London Parliamentary seat and was soundly beaten. Since he was an outlaw, the government did its best to have him arrested. He evaded them and got himself elected MP for Middlesex. Then he gave himself up. If the King had had any sense, he would have pardoned him. Instead, Wilkes received two years in prison and a fine of a thousand pounds. Wilkes instantly became the most popular man in England. An angry crowd rescued him from the officers of the law. He gave himself up again and was put in jail. A mob gathered and looked as if it would storm the jail; troops fired and killed five, wounding fifteen.

Wilkes wrote a violent article attacking the use of force against the rioters; Parliament voted it libelous and expelled him again. He got himself reelected by rebellious voters; Parliament threw him out again. He became the most popular cause of his time; there had been nothing like it since Daniel Defoe had got himself stuck in the pillory – for the same kind of offense – in 1703 and was pelted with flowers instead of rotten eggs. The well-meaning King, with his pathetic desire for popularity and his determination to be a "true Briton" (like all the Hanovers, he was a German by parentage), was stumbling from disaster to disaster.

Rockingham resigned; party quarrels were too much for him. Now the King had an idea that he must have regarded as brilliant and foolproof: to persuade Pitt to take over again. That ought to undo all the squabbling and bitterness of the past six years. Unfortunately, Pitt's manic depression was turning into madness. When the King made him Earl of Chatham, Pitt virtually retired to the House of Lords, and the administration was left in the hands of a much younger man, Lord Grafton. The country was in a state of chaos.

And it was at this point that Junius stepped into the picture.

Now whoever Junius was, he was a man who, for some reason, detested the King and his political allies and was a supporter of Pitt and Wilkes. He had a particular antipathy toward Lord Grafton, who had by now quarreled with Pitt. In 1768 Pitt and Grenville – who had also quarreled – received letters signed Junius, urging them to make up and unite against Grafton. In fact, Pitt resigned shortly afterward. Now Junius decided to take his case to the public.

His first letter was sent to a newspaper called *The Public Advertiser*, owned by Henry Sampson Woodfall. Newspapers were still something of a novelty in England. They had begun about fifty years earlier; by Junius's time there were eleven of them in London alone. Most of their profit came from advertisements, but readers' letters were also immensely popular – in fact, Junius's first letter, dated 21 January 1769, was held up for several days while a backlog of letters was printed.

The style of Junius's letters is not immediately appealing to a modern audience; it seems rather ponderous and pedantic. As far as his contemporaries were concerned, however, that was an advantage; they could see that he was a serious minded man who knew how to turn a good phrase. And the very first sentence of his first letter makes it clear that what concerns him is the freedom of the British people and the feeling that designing politicians like Prime Minister Grafton were trying to steal it. Junius starts with a contentious but rather dull statement: "The submission of a free people to the executive authority of government is no more than a compliance with laws which they themselves have enacted". The English, he goes on to say, are a generous and good-natured people, who naturally respect the law and love their King. So it fills him with indignation to see these good qualities abused by schemers: "The situation of this country is alarming enough to rouse the attention of every man . . ." So far, his readers must have stifled a yawn. But a few sentences later they were startled into attention: "The finances of a nation, sinking under its debts and expenses, are committed to a young nobleman already ruined by play". To accuse the King's Prime Minister of being a dissolute gambler was strong stuff.

Next, Junius turned his attention to Britain's most popular soldier, the Marquis of Granby, whose victories in the seven-year war with France had fired British patriotism and led hundreds of pubs and inns to call themselves the Marquis of Granby. At the battle of Minden, Granby wanted to charge the French, but his superior, Lord Sackville, ordered him not to. It later became obvious that if Granby had been allowed to charge, the French would have been utterly routed. Sackville was dismissed and Granby took his place.

But like many fine soldiers, he was out of his depth in politics, and when he was made peacetime commander-in-chief, he was less than brilliant. Even so, when Junius remarked with suave malice: "Nature has been sparing of her gifts to this noble lord", it was as shocking as if someone had dismissed Winston Churchill or General Eisenhower as a dithering idiot after the Second World War. And when Junius went on to accuse Granby of using his position to "heap promotion on his favourites and dependants" and ignore merit in the rest of the army, he was virtually accusing Britain's war hero of being a crook.

It is not clear whether Junius made these accusations to produce shock and outrage. But he could hardly have chosen a better way to make himself famous – or infamous. For one of Granby's most distinguished fellow soldiers, Sir William Draper, quickly leapt to his defense and wrote an indignant letter to *The Public Advertiser*, whose owner must have been rubbing his hands with glee. Draper began by furiously accusing Junius of being a "felonious robber of private character", a "cowardly base assassin" who did not have the courage to sign his real name. Then Draper went on to defend his commander-in-chief, saying, in essence, that he was a "decent chap" whom everybody liked and who was too generous for his own good.

This kind of thing must have made readers groan with boredom. As to not keeping his promises – another of Junius's slanders – there were some cases, said Draper, where it was better not to keep promises. He was obviously thinking of some scheming friend of Granby's who had persuaded the general to make rash promises when he had had too much to drink – a person, says Draper indignantly, "who would pervert the open, unsuspecting moments of convivial mirth into sly, insidious applications for preferment . . . and who would endeavour to surprise a good man who cannot bear to see anyone leave him dissatisfied".

Junius, of course, had achieved his goal. He was being treated seriously by a famous soldier, and the delighted public was being allowed to witness their squabble. Junius's next letter began with deceptive benevolence and generosity: "Your defense of Lord Granby does honour to the goodness of your heart". He went on to praise Draper's "honest unreflecting indignation" – although the word *unreflecting* gave warning of what was to come. Then he took the gloves off and went straight for the chin: "It is you, Sir William, who makes your friend appear awkward and ridiculous, by giving him a laced suit of tawdry qualifications which nature never intended him to wear". And he became positively murderous when he answered Draper's ill-advised remarks about promises made in "convivial mirth". "It is you, Sir William Draper, who have taken pains to represent your friend in the character of a drunken landlord, who deals out his promises as liberally as his liquor, and will suffer no man to leave his table sorrowful or sober. None but an intimate friend, who must have seen him frequently in these unhappy, disgraceful moments, could have described him so well".

Draper must have winced. But he lacked the common sense to see that he was giving Junius exactly the kind of publicity he wanted. Besides, he had been an academic and felt he could exchange urbane insults with the best of them. So back he came for more, this time accusing Junius (probably correctly) of being a bitter and disappointed man who "delights to mangle carcasses with a hatchet". Then he took up the impossible task of defending his friend Granby against the hatchet, failing to realize that he was only succeeding in making him look like a helpless dummy. He went on to answer Junius's charges that he had feathered his own nest and entered into precise details about his income that only revealed how much Junius had him on the defensive.

Junius came back in his smoothest and deadliest form: "I should justly be suspected of acting upon motives of more than common enmity to Lord Granby, if I continued to give you fresh materials or occasion for writing in his defense". But then he proceeded to indulge in another of his favourite tricks: an appearance of omniscience. He went on to talk about Draper's income and career as if he knew more about them than Draper did. Then he accused Draper of being a money-grubbing liar who had turned his back on the army in exchange for a pension – which Junius called a "sordid provision for himself and his family".

Now we can begin to see Junius's technique. There can be no doubt that he *was* bitter and twisted. He was a man with a grievance, and his specialty was libelous accusations that would cause maximum suffering to the accused, as well as maximum glee to the general public. One gets the impression that he was a kind of sadist who didn't care what he said so long as it hurt; but he was clever enough to make his accusations sound plausible – as if he was an insider with a secret source of knowledge.

The general public, of course, loves to see authority attacked and ridiculed. Things have not changed in the slightest in the two centuries or so that have passed since the days of Junius; any kind of scandal about a politician can still sell newspapers. In present-day America, politicians have no legal redress against libel – provided malice cannot be established – so that journalists can invent virtually what they like. After the Kennedy assassination, a play called *Macbird* accused Lyndon Johnson of being the murderer; it was pure invention, but its author, a dissident academic, must have been bewildered when it became the hit of the season on Broadway. In England, a magazine called *Private Eye* has specialized since the sixties in libelous and insulting stories that might have been concocted by Junius; but although the magazine has been sued to the verge of bankruptcy, it continues to flourish as the public appetite for malicious "dirt" remains insatiable. Junius was simply the first to discover that there is a permanent demand for "dirt".

The naïve Draper went on to increase Junius's fame by writing more pained and explanatory letters; Junius continued to treat him with ferocious contempt. In his third letter he dismissed him partronizingly: "And now, Sir William, I shall take my leave of you for ever . . . In truth, you have some reason to hold yourself indebted to me. From the lessons I have given you, you may collect a profitable instruction for your future life".

Junius ignored Draper's third reply and turned his attention to the Prime Minister, the Duke of Grafton. True to form, Junius accused him of being a scheming politician who preferred his own interests to the public good. Then he turned his attention to a recent scandal concerning the Middlesex by-election, which the government had fervently hoped that Wilkes would lose – and which, in fact, Wilkes had won with the aid of a drunken rabble. (Wilkes was now, of course, in jail.)

A man named Clarke had been killed in a brawl, and an Irishman named MacQuirk, a local chairman of the anti-Wilkes party, was accused of his murder, together with another man named Balf. Both were sentenced to death, but this was obviously unfair; the evidence against Balf was weak, and MacQuirk had obviously not intended to commit murder. Both were pardoned by Grafton. Junius pretended to think that this was an outrageous interference in the course of justice, a deliberate tampering with the evidence; a murderer went free because he was against Wilkes. He ended by asking: "Has it never occurred to you that, while you were withdrawing this desperate wretch from justice . . . that there is another man, who is the favourite of the country, whose pardon would have been accepted with gratitude"?

He meant, of course, John Wilkes, and he went on to use his favourite technique of invention: "Have you quite forgotten that this man was once your Grace's friend"? Grafton was to protest again and again that Wilkes was only a casual acquaintance; Junius ignored him and went on repeating his charge; that Grafton had stabbed his friend in the back. Subsequent investigation by historians indicates that Grafton was telling the truth. But Junius never let the truth spoil a good accusation.

What so alarmed the government – and the King – was that Wilkes's imprisonment had made him potentially the most dangerous man in England. Junius went on to accuse Grafton of fleeing London for two nights during the Wilkes riots and leaving the city to be defended by two of his incompetent underlings. Grafton had apparently spent those two nights with his mistress, Nancy Parsons, and Junius jeered at her "faded beauty" – although he later pretended to be shocked when Grafton broke with her and married someone else, declaring: "His baseness to this woman is beyond description or belief". When Grafton married, Junius sneered at him as a reformed rake who had tired of debauchery.

Junius's next letter to Grafton reached new heights of malice: "Let me be permitted to consider your character and conduct", he wrote ominously, "merely as a subject of curious speculation". And after calling him lazy, dishonest, and inconsistent, he added generously: "For the sake of your mistress, the lover shall be spared. I will not lead her into public, as you have done, nor will I insult the memory of her departed beauty. Her sex, which alone made her amiable in your eyes" – he is implying that Grafton will mount anything that wears a skirt – "makes her respectable in mine".

He went on to give what he claimed to be a sympathetic account of Grafton's ancestors – "those of your Grace . . . left no distressing examples of virtue" – and of his own career – "grave and plausible enough to be thought fit for business; too young for treachery". But, he claimed, Grafton lost no time in stabbing his patron William Pitt in the back, then grabbing power under Rockingham and betraying his friend Wilkes. Like Dr Goebbels, Junius felt that the best way to make people believe a lie was to repeat it.

After more than two centuries these insults make us smile. But if we try to put ourselves in the place of his victims, we can see that they must have felt choked with hopeless rage. Junius was not a man so much as a scorpion. When one angry victim challenged Junius to a duel, Junius declined politely: "You would fight, but others would assassinate". He was probably right. The sheer malice and unfairness of his attacks would have led some of his victims to make sure he was stabbed in the dark.

In December 1769 Junius shocked everyone, including his own supporters, by launching an attack on the King himself. His success in evading exposure had obviously given him the confidence to risk imprisonment. In earlier letters he had been careful to speak of the King with the deepest respect, referring to him in a letter to Grafton as "an amiable, accomplished prince". Now he addressed the King directly, reminding him of one of his earliest utterances when he came to the throne: "I glory in the name of Briton". The King undoubtedly meant that he regarded himself as a Briton rather than a German; Junius pretended to think that he was deliberately making a distinction be-tween Britons and Englishmen, to emphasize his affection for the Scots: "While the natives of Scotland are not in actual rebellion, they are undoubtedly entitled to protection; nor do I mean to condemn the policy of giving some encouragement to the novelty of their affections".

He patronizingly told the King that he attributed his blunders to inexperience. He went on to defend Wilkes and to describe the King's campaign against him as mean and ridiculous. After taking swipes at the King for oppressing the Irish and the Americans, he warned him against the "fawning treachery" of the Scots. Finally, he told him condescend-ingly that "the affections of your subjects may still be recovered" but that this would mean ceasing to be driven by petty resentments. The King, wrote Junius, should face his subjects like a gentleman and "tell them you have been fatally deceived" by crooked ministers. He ended on a note of warning that sounded dangerously like sedition. The people were loyal to the House of Hanover, he wrote, because they expected justice. The House of Stuart – to which Bonnie Prince Charlie belonged – was "only contemptible", but armed with royal power it would become formidable. "The prince who imitates their conduct should be warned by their example" (i.e., by King Charles losing his head), "and while he plumes himself upon the security of his title to the crown, should remember that, as it was acquired by one revolution, it may be lost by another".

That made everyone gasp. The novelist Horace Walpole – son of a former Prime Minister – described it as "the most daring insult ever offered to a prince but in times of open rebellion". The printer, Woodfall, was arrested on a charge of seditious libel. The jury refused to convict, and he was released on payment of costs. Recognizing his own danger, Junius warned Woodfall to take every possible precaution, as "I would not survive a discovery three days".

How *had* he survived discovery for so long? By an elabourate system of concealment. It was easy to get his letters to the *Public Advertiser* – he could send them by messenger or by post. But communications from the newspaper were altogether more dangerous. Many people wrote to Junius and sent him "sensitive" information. Junius had letters addressed to him, via the printer, under various pseudonyms at various coffeehouses (there were literally hundreds), and the printer would signal that a letter was waiting by inserting a coded advertisement in the newspaper. Junius frequently changed his poste restante address at short notice, informing Woodfall with messages like: "Change to the Somerset Coffee House, and let no mortal know the alteration". And he obviously spent some time worrying about what would happen if Woodfall became careless: "I am persuaded that you are too honest a man to contribute to my destruction".

Junius also corresponded with Wilkes, who was released from jail in 1770 and promptly returned to Parliament; Wilkes made a few tactful attempts to persuade Junius to reveal his identity but respected his determination to have no confidantes.

In fact, Junius was beginning to feel tired; the sheer strain of taking on opponent after opponent, like a masked swordsman, was obviously beginning to tell. Besides, when Grafton resigned in 1770 – undoubtedly rattled by Junius's insults – and Wilkes was released in the same year, Junius had achieved his basic purpose. The King refused to be stampeded into making more concessions to the Libertarian Party and appointed the efficient and good-natured Lord North as his First Minister Junius had earlier attacked Lord North: "It may be candid to suppose that he has hitherto voluntarily concealed his talents; intending, perhaps, to astonish the world when we least expect it". But he proved wrong, and Lord North developed into an excellent administrator.

Junius wrote his last public letter in January 1772. When, a year later, Henry Woodfall did his best to induce Junius to return to the fray with hints in the *Public Advertiser*, Junius replied: "If I were to write again I must be as silly as any of the horned cattle that run mad through the City . . . The cause and the public – both are given up". In fact, the world had heard its last of Junius – although his collected letters, in book form, achieved considerable popularity. In this collection Junius wrote: "I am the sole depository of my own secret, and it shall perish with me". And as far as we know, he kept his word.

So who was Junius? In the days of Rockingham's Prime Ministership, the chief suspect was the brilliant Irishman Edmund Burke, who was passionately liberal – although by no means radical, like Wilkes. He was a friend of Dr Johnson, Oliver Goldsmith, Sir Joshua Reynolds, and David Garrick (the most famous actor of his time). Like Wilkes, he wanted to curb the corrupt practices in the royal court and so was detested by the King. He argued strongly against the King's policies in America, suggesting – correctly – that they would lead to revolution, and after the Boston tea party he argued for the repeal of the tea tax. If Burke had been listened to, America might well still be a British colony. He was later horrified by the French Revolution and became one of its most passionate opponents, thus endearing himself to all his former enemies.

Burke was brilliant enough to have written the Junius letters. But he was also a man of immense integrity. So when he wrote to a friend, Charles Townshend, "I now give you my word and honour that I am not the author of Junius", we may take it to be the truth.

In the nineteenth century book after book about Junius appeared; speculations about his identity became as popular as speculations about the identity of Jack the Ripper did a century later. (In his edition of the Junius letters, Professor John Cannon offers a "short list" of sixty-one names.) An obvious possibility is Wilkes himself; but the exchange of letters between Wilkes and Junius that later came to light makes it clear that this is out of the question.

One writer announced confidently that Junius was George III himself, averting revolution by giving his subjects a chance to let off steam. Another writer identified Junius as the historian Edward Gibbon, resting his case upon the sheer absence of evidence, which, the writer claimed, only went to prove how far the historian had gone to conceal his guilty secret. Another staked the claim of Lord George Sackville, the military commander who had been dismissed after the battle of Minden in favour of the Marquis of Granby; certainly, Junius's attacks on Granby make this plausible, if unlikely. (Sackville was a warm supporter of the King.) Lord Chesterfield, the author of the famous *Letters to His Son*, is another candidate; but his health at the time was so poor – he was half-blind and bedridden – that it is virtually impossible that he was Junius. Perhaps the unlikeliest nominee was Thomas Paine, the author of *The Rights of Man* (1791), a polemic directed at Burke. At the time of the Junius letters, Paine was still struggling to make a start in life – as a grocer, a tobacconist, a schoolmaster, and an exciseman – and still had a number of years to go before he learned to write; it was not until 1774 that Benjamin Franklin persuaded him to emigrate to America.

All this seems to suggest that Junius was one of the lesserknown names of the period. Charles Everett, the editor of the 1927 edition of the letters, devotes a long introduction to proving that Junius was Lord Shelburne, a member of the opposition and later Prime Minister; the historian Sir Lewis Namier destroyed that case in a brief review in which he pointed out that Shelburne was on the Continent in the summer of 1771 when Woodfall received two private letters from Junius that had to have been written in London. Shelburne's private secretary, Laughlin Macleane, has been strongly suggested by two recent academics, one of whom has claimed to have a statement, signed by Shelburne, identifying Macleane as Junius. The chief problem here is that Macleane was attacked by Junius, who made fun of his stammer. This could have been a deliberate attempt to mislead; but Junius did not use his own name in this attack but another of his pseudonyms, Vindex. And since no one but Woodfall knew that Vindex was Junius, this seems to dispose of Macleane – whether or not Shelburne believed his secretary to be Junius. Besides, Macleane was an ardent Scottish patriot, and Junius clearly loathed the Scots, losing no opportunity to jeer about their corruption, stupidity, and cowardice.

This brings us to the chief suspect: Sir Philip Francis, who was at the time a twenty-eight-year-old senior civil servant in the War Office. Francis came under suspicion in 1812, when the private letters of Junius to Woodfall were published in a new edition. They revealed that Junius used various other pseudonyms, including Vindex and Veteran. These letters pay close attention to the affairs of the War Office and indicate that Junius knew far more about it than any outsider could learn.

In 1772, the year the Junius letters ceased, Francis went to India, where he clashed with Warren Hastings – the chief servant of the East India Company, which virtually governed India. On his return to England, he entered Parliament as a Liberal, was knighted, and pursued Hastings with considerable vindictiveness, being largely instrumental in having him impeached for corruption and exceeding his powers.

In 1813, when he was seventy-three, Francis was identified as Junius in a book by a man named John Taylor. He flatly denied it, calling the accusation "silly and malignant". Yet when he married again in the following year, he gave his wife the Junius letters as a wedding present. He also gave her Taylor's book on the mystery of Junius. His wife took the hint; she had no doubt that he was Junius. And Francis was aware of this. He had only, she remarked, to deny it, and she would have given up the idea; but he never did.

Professor Cannon has no doubt whatever that Francis was Junius. He points out that in 1772 – before Francis was posted to India at the huge salary of £10,000 a year – Junius changed his pseudonym to *Veteran*. In 1771 Christopher D'Oyly, a friend of Francis, told him he intended to resign as Deputy Secretary of War; it is obvious from their correspondence that both disliked their chief, Lord Barrington. Francis hoped to succeed D'Oyly but was passed over in favour of a man named Chamier. "Veteran" was soon writing to his printer: "Having nothing better to do, I propose to entertain myself and the public with torturing that bloody wretch Barrington. He has just appointed a French broker his deputy. I hear from all sides it is looked upon as a most impudent insult to the army. Be careful not to have it known to come from me. Such an insignificant creature is not worth the generous rage of Junius". In which case, why bother with such small fry?

In March 1772 Francis resigned his post. Junius wrote to the printer: "The enclosed is fact, and I wish it could be printed tomorrow. The proceedings of this wretch are unaccountable. There must be some mystery in it, which I hope will soon be discovered to his confusion. Next to the Duke of Grafton, I verily believe that the blackest heart in the kingdom belongs to Lord Barrington". The "enclosed" declared: "I desire you will inform the public that the worthy Lord Barrington, not contented with having driven Mr D'Oyly out of the War Office, has at last contrived to expel Mr Francis".

Handwriting evidence also links Francis and Junius. In 1771 a Miss Giles in Bath was the recipient of some polite verses, and the handwriting on the cover was that of Junius. In 1870 a handwriting expert, Charles Chabot, identified the verses as being written by Francis's cousin, Richard Tilman. Francis's second wife later produced copies of the verses in her husband's handwriting, saying that he had given them to her as examples of his own early verses. In letters discovered in the late nineteenth century, Francis's authorship was confirmed by his cousin.

This raises an obvious question: Surely we have only to compare the handwriting of Junius with that of Francis to have our solution? But it is not as simple as that. Junius must have known that unless he went to considerable lengths to disguise his handwriting, it could be his downfall. It was only after careful study that Charles Chabot concluded that the handwriting of Junius was a disguised version of Francis's.

Another piece of evidence emerged in 1969, when French research revealed that a French ambassadorial report sent to Louis XVI in the 1770s attributed the letters to one Thaddeus Fitzpatrick, a man-about-town. Now in fact, we know this is impossible because Fitzpatrick died in 1771, while Junius was still writing. But the report declares that Fitzpatrick obtained his information from his friend Philip Francis, a clerk in the War Office.

Fitzpatrick had quarreled with the actor David Garrick and with Lord Chief Justice Mansfield, two men who were savaged by Junius. So there is a strong case to be made for Fitzpatrick being a collabourator of Junius. This does not contradict Junius's assertion that he was "the sole depository of his own secret", since this was made in the year after Fitzpatrick's death.

Wherever the French ambassador obtained his information – information that seems to have been denied to his British colleagues – it certainly has the ring of plausibility. One of the reasons that posterity has found the Junius problem so fascinating is that he seems to be a solitary outsider figure, a man with a truly awesome gift for savage invective and the cut and thrust of polemic, who succeeded, like the Scarlet Pimpernel, in keeping his light hidden under a bushel. It is a fascinating and romantic conception, but the major objection to it is that it is too romantic. Scarlet Pimpernels exist only in the imagination of novelists.

What seems far more plausible is that a middle-aged man-about-town, who nurses powerful grudges against people he actually knows, should decide to deliver some sharp rebukes under the cloak of anonymity and should take into his confidence a sarcastic and disaffected young clerk from the War Office who can provide inside information. (One of Francis's jobs was to report speeches in the House of Lords, so he had the opportunity to overhear much political gossip.) The picture of two men chuckling and egging one another on is somehow more believable than the picture of a solitary misanthrope nursing his own secret. Moreover, if Thaddeus Fitzpatrick was the initiator of the project, this would also explain why the later Junius letters – those that followed his death in 1771 – show a falling off in quality. The rear end of the pantomime horse found himself sadly missing his partner.

This could also explain Francis's curious attitude toward the book that accused him of being Junius. More than forty years after the smoke of battle had cleared and most of his victims were dead – including

Grafton himself – surely there could have been no harm in acknowledging that he was Junius? But if this meant acknowledging that he was merely a *half* of Junius – and the lesser half at that – then it would obviously be far better to keep silent and allow his contemporaries – and posterity – to give him the full credit, while continuing to deny it in a manner that convinced nobody. It was a way of having his cake and eating it.

Certainly, everything we know of Francis indicates that he could have been Junius (or half-Junius). Cannon describes him as "a man of fierce animosities, harsh and sarcastic". He quarreled with most of his friends and benefactors, says his biographer Herman Merivale, with all "those who wished well to him, defended him, showered benefits on him". All "appear . . . in his written records, branded with some unfriendly or contemptuous notice, some insinuated or pronounced aspersion". Francis broke with two of his former patrons, Henry Fox and John Calcraft, and when they quarreled, made his typically stinging and ungenerous assessment of them: "There was not virtue enough in either of them to justify their quarreling. If either of them had common honesty he could never have been the friend of the other". The phrase has the typical Junian ring. Dining with Francis in the last year of his life, Cannon reports, the philosopher Sir James Mackintosh was led to comment, "The vigorous hatreds which seemed to keep Francis alive were very amusing".

In other words, Francis had a streak of paranoia. And this is how Cannon summarizes Junius: "Junius believed . . . that it was necessary to save the constitution from violation, but the desperate plot to destroy the liberties of the subject existed only in his own mind".

There is not enough space here to describe the affair of the impeachment of Warren Hastings and Francis's part in it; but it confirms that Francis was a man who, like Junius, was a good hater with little generosity.

Finally, in the 1950s, a Swedish philologist, Alvar-Ellegard, undertook a computer analysis of the writing of Junius and of forty of his contemporaries, looking for recurrent words, tricks of style, and so on. Ellegard began by being a skeptic about Francis; he ended by being totally convinced that he was Junius: "The statement that Sir Philip Francis was Junius may henceforth be allowed to stand without a question mark".

But does the identity of Junius *matter*? The answer must be yes, for he appeared at a vital moment in history. When George III came to the throne, British politics was notoriously corrupt; it was taken for granted that a man went into the House of Commons to make his fortune. He expected to take money in exchange for favours. It was not even regarded as reprehensible – merely as normal and natural. The King himself spent his vast "privy purse" – more than a million pounds – in bribing Members of Parliament. (At least he was not, like some of his European counterparts, an absolute monarch who could merely order them to vote as he pleased.) Junius lost no opportunity to jeer at this corruption.

Newspapers had begun in the reign of Queen Anne (1702–14), but they were little more than entertainment. Junius changed all that. His outrageous letters revealed that you did not have to be a King or a Member of Parliament to exert pressure on the government. Under Queen Elizabeth or Charles I, such attacks would have been regarded as high treason; there would have been torture and executions by the dozen. Woodfall's trial and acquittal (1770) revealed that even Parliament lacked the power to silence criticism.

Newspapers began to report Parliamentary debates and laid themselves open to prosecution. In 1771 a newspaper referred to a Member of Parliament, Colonel George Onslow, as "the little scoundrel" and "that paltry, insignificant insect". When he complained, the House ordered the arrest of the printers. The printers fought back, arrested the men sent to arrest them, and hauled them in front of the Lord Mayor and two aldermen (one of whom was Wilkes, recently out of jail). When the Lord Mayor countermanded the arrest order, Parliament ordered that he be committed to the Tower of London. His supporters rose up and rioted; they hissed the King, invaded Parliament, and attacked the carriages of MPs. The Lord Mayor was hastily released. And the newspapers took advantage of this triumph to resume their reports of Parliamentary debates.

Parliament itself was forced to order publication of its debates in full – the first "Hansard" (named for Luke Hansard, the publisher) appeared in 1774. From then on, a free press was taken for granted, and the opinions of the people became as important as the opinions of the King and his ministers. Bribery and corruption became the exception rather than the rule.

Junius, of course, cannot take all the credit for this revolution; Wilkes had started it with his *North Briton* article, which in turn was inspired by Pitt and his brother-in-law. But Junius added yeast to the mixture; he stirred up the issues and raised a spirit of rebellion that looked, at one point, as if it would lead to a revolution like the one that swept France two decades later.

It is difficult to feel much sympathy for Junius as a man; he was obviously a thoroughly unpleasant character: mean, envious, and paranoid. His rage was not generous but vindictive. But his formidable literary talent, comparable to that of Swift, changed the course of British history, creating a spirit of freedom that went on to change the course of world history. It is impossible to think of any historical figure of comparable influence whose identity has remained unknown. But then, as Junius himself remarked smugly: "The mystery of Junius increases his importance".

30

Fedor Kuzmich

Did the Tsar Die an Unknown Monk?

In 1836 a sixty-year-old beggar named Fedor Kuzmich was arrested as a vagrant near the town of Krasnophinsk, in the province of Perm, Russia, and was sentenced to twenty blows of the knout (whip). Then he was sent to Siberia – Russia's penal colony. There, at Nerchinsk, near Tomsk, he became a hermit and acquired a reputation for saintliness.

Fedor Kuzmich impressed all who saw him. He was tall and broad-shouldered, and of majestic appearance, producing in everyone a sense of awe and veneration. His voice, too, seems to have been that of an educated man, and his speech was gentle and deliberate. In spite of his gentleness, however, there were times when he became impatient and imperious, and the peasants who approached him felt the urge to fall to their knees.

Kuzmich always turned aside inquiries about his early life. But occasionally, he made some remark that suggested he had fought in the Russian Army against Napoléon; he spoke of the campaign of 1812 and of the victorious entry into Paris of the Russians and their allies on 31 March 1814. The meticulous tidiness of his cell suggested army training.

Kuzmich had remarkable powers as a healer, and people came to see him from all over Siberia. And according to his biographer, Schilder (author of a pamphlet that became immensely popular in the 1890s), two former servants from the Tsar's palace were among these visitors – they had been exiled to Siberia, and when one of them fell ill, his companion decided to go and see the healer, to ask if he could help his sick comrade. According to Schilder, the man entered the cell alone, leaving a guide – probably a monk – outside; and when he saw the hermit, he felt obliged, like so many others, to fall to his knees. The old man raised him to his feet and began to speak; with astonishment, the man recognized the voice of Tsar Alexander I. And as he stared at the white-bearded features, he recognized the face of his former master. He fell down in a swoon. The guide outside heard his cry and came in; Fedor Kuzmich told him gently, "Take him back home. And when he regains his senses, warn him not to tell anybody what he saw. Tell him that his friend will recover". Kuzmich proved to be right.

The story that Alexander had been recognized by one of his former servants soon spread all over Russia and was the subject of some official correspondence. Alexander's biographer, Maurice Paleologue, described (in *The Enigmatic Tsar*, 1938) how an old soldier who had been sent to the prison of Nerchinsk saw the hermit and instantly stiffened to attention, saying, "It's our beloved Tsar Alexander Pavlovich"!

Fedor Kuzmich died in 1864 at the age of eighty-seven – precisely the age Alexander I would have been if he had lived.

Is it conceivable that a modern Tsar of Russia, the man who defeated Napoléon, should have quietly vanished and become a hermit? It is true that Ivan the Terrible abdicated in his mid-thirties and retired to a monastery; his subjects had to go and beg him to return. But that was in 1564, in a Russia that was still virtually medieval, not in the enlightened nineteenth century. To understand how it might be possible, we need to know a little of Russia's appallingly bloody and violent history.

The first absolute Tsar was Ivan the Terrible, who came to the throne in 1547 and who was a paranoid maniac. He began his reign by having his chief adviser torn apart by his hunting dogs – Ivan was in his teens at the time. He then embarked on a career of rape, murder, and torture – he regarded every woman in Moscow as a member of his private harem. Marriage seemed to reform him, but when his wife died, he became more paranoid than ever and went on to perpetrate some of the most appalling cruelties in history. While besieging the city of Novgorod, he had a timber wall built around it so that no one could escape. When the city fell, he directed a massacre that went on for five days; husbands and wives were forced to watch one another being tortured; mothers saw their babies ill treated before they themselves were roasted alive. Sixty thousand people were executed. When he besieged Weden, in Livonia, hundreds of citizens preferred to blow themselves up in a castle rather than fall into his hands; he had all the remaining townsfolk tortured to death.

Ivan was the worst of the Tsars, but only just. Even rulers we like to think of as "enlightened" – Peter the Great, Catherine the Great – were capable of ordering mass executions and torture. Peter the Great's niece earned herself the title of Anna the Bloody, while Catherine's son Paul – the child of her first lover, Saltykov – was a madman who oppressed the peasantry in a way that made them feel Ivan the Terrible was back. (Since 1649 – the year Charles I was executed in England – Russian peasants were not allowed to leave their owners' estates and were merely "property".)

By 1801 the paranoid Tsar Paul was living in seclusion in a newly built palace that was surrounded by canals and had imposed a nine o'clock curfew on St Petersburg – whose reaction to it was much as it would have been in London or Paris. On March 23 the regiment of his son Alexander was guarding the palace. Alexander had suffered greatly from his father's arbitrary despotism and had imbibed liberal ideas from Europe; he agreed with his father's chief adviser, Count Pahlen, that Paul had to be deposed. He is supposed to have insisted that Paul's life should be spared, but few historians believe that he meant it. A group of conspirators was admitted to the palace after dark and entered the Tsar's bedroom; he was ordered to abdicate, then strangled with a scarf. The people of Russia went mad with joy when Alexander became their Tsar; they felt that a nightmare was over.

It certainly looked as if it was. The handsome, charming young Tsar met every day with a group of liberal friends to discuss over coffee the way to regenerate his country through freedom of the individual. He quickly made peace with the English – to the disgust of Napoléon. He had no doubt that the first major step was the abolition of serfdom; but that was easier said than done. His minister Speransky, the son of a village priest, was asked to draft a constitution for a democratic Russia; but even he advised against freeing the serfs at one blow. Alexander had to be contented with a decree that allowed anyone to own land, a right that had previously been restricted to the nobility. He also made a determined effort to increase the number of schools and universities. He allowed students to travel abroad, lifted the ban on the import of foreign books, and closed down the secret police department.

A first step toward the liberation of the serfs was left in suspension while Russia went to war with Persia over Russia's annexation of Georgia – a war Russia eventually won. But Alexander's chief problem, of course, was Napoléon, with whom his father, Paul, had been on friendly terms. In 1805 Alexander joined England, Austria, and Sweden in an alliance against Napoléon. Britain defeated Napoléon's fleet at Trafalgar, but the Russians and Austrians were defeated by Napoléon at Austerlitz. A series of treaties with Napoléon followed, and Alexander became Napoléon's ally under the Treaty of Tilsit (1807). Alexander went on to fight successful wars against Turkey and Sweden, acquiring Bessarabia and Finland. The starry-eyed liberal was becoming a conquering hero.

By 1812 it was obvious that Napoléon and Alexander disliked each other too much to remain allies; in June Napoléon's Grand Army, strengthened by Italians, Poles, Swiss, Dutch, and Germans, invaded Russia. It looked like the end for Alexander. Smolensk fell; the Russians were defeated at Borodino; in mid-September the French entered Moscow. The next day the city burst into flames. Alexander declined to make terms, and a month later, Napoléon began his disastrous retreat. Besieged by the Russians and by the Russian winter, the French troops died in droves; Napoléon fled to Paris, leaving behind half a million corpses. The Prussians now deserted Napoléon and joined the Russians. And although Napoléon raised another army and had some remarkable victories, he could not prevent the allies from entering Paris in March 1814. In April, Napoléon abdicated and was exiled to Elba.

Alexander had defeated the "Corsican monster"; he was adored by all his subjects. If history were predictable, he would have completed his reforms and become the most popular monarch in Europe. Unfortunately, Alexander's ten years of war had turned him into a realist and made him repent of the liberal delusions of his youth. Under the influence of a dubious visionary named Julie de Krüdener, he dreamed up an idea called the Holy Alliance, in which the heads of Europe would unite under Christian principles of faith and justice; British statesman Castlereagh called it "sublime mysticism and nonsense". Yet it was deeply typical of Alexander. He had always struck those who knew him well as a self-divided man, and it is said – although it is not clear with how much truth – that he never ceased to reproach himself for the murder of his father. Alexander was a famous charmer, as well as a man of sentiment; but the continual exercise of his charm must have made him wonder sometimes whether he was a man or a mouse. To begin with, he continued to live up to his liberal pledges, conferring a constitution on Poland and emancipating the serfs in the Baltic provinces. But in Russia itself, he took care to maintain the status quo. He began to tighten the screws on education, placing conservatives in charge of universities. Censorship was introduced and liberal professors were purged.

One of Alexander's chief problems was the army. Understandably, he felt that a huge standing army was necessary. But this was enormously expensive. He devised what he considered a brilliant solution to the problem: military colonies. Local peasants had to maintain the army units, and the soldiers had to work the land like peasants. These units were a combination of barracks, collective farms, and concentration camps. They were the most hated feature of Alexander's reign.

Yet, oddly enough, he encouraged the flowering of literature that was taking place, becoming the personal patron – and in some ways the jailer – of the great romantic poet Alexander Pushkin. (One reason for this may have been his desire to get Pushkin's lovely wife into bed – Alexander, like most of the Russian Tsars, lost no opportunity to seduce a pretty girl.) Under Alexander, Russian literature began to develop into one of the great literatures of the world.

It was this combination of freedom and repression that nurtured the Decembrist revolution that would break out three weeks after his death.* Young officers who had imbibed liberal ideas in Europe joined together in 1816 to form a literary discussion group called the Faithful Sons of the Fatherland. It struck them as outrageous that Russia should be drifting back into despotism, and they began to talk revolution. In 1820 Alexander's own Semyonovsky regiment mutinied against a harsh commander; Alexander proceeded to post its officers to other parts of Russia. Alexander soon became aware that his officers were conspiring against him, yet he seemed oddly indifferent and disillusioned. In his mid-forties, he felt the irony of the situation: a liberal Tsar who had conquered Napoléon, he had become a symbol of oppression to the very officers who had once regarded him as Russia's brightest hope. For many years, his marriage to the beautiful Empress Elizabeth had been a marriage in name only; they were childless, and he took a succession of mistresses. Life seemed curiously empty. When told of the proliferation of secret societies he said wearily, "I myself have shared and encouraged these errors and delusions . . . I have no right to punish them". A stronger and more ruthless man would have had all the conspirators arrested and tried; Alexander had no stomach for a bloodbath. He began to speak longingly of abdicating, of becoming a private citizen in Switzerland, or a botanist on the Rhine.

When informed of the death of his child by his Polish mistress, Marie Naryshkin, he burst into tears in front of his officers. A few days later, he began to travel feverishly all over Russia and covered three thousand miles in four months – an achievement that arouses no astonishment nearly two centuries later but which, in those days of bumpy carriages and roads full of potholes, was a considerable feat. Back in St Petersburg in November 1824, he witnessed a major disaster: the river Neva flooded half the city. When he heard a man crying desperately, "It's a punishment for our sins", he replied, "No, it's a punishment for my sins".

* The Decembrist conspiracy was easily suppressed; most of the conspirators were executed.

Revolt was everywhere. Pushkin said, "Holy Russia is becoming un-inhabitable". The Tsar's favourite aide-de-camp died, and the Empress fell ill; Alexander felt that his life was falling apart. And when the Empress decided to try to recuperate in Taganrog, on the Sea of Azov, the Emperor announced that he would go with her. People were puzzled about the choice of Taganrog, which was not a health resort but a small fortress town in wild and swampy country. Why did she not choose Italy?

Before the Emperor set out from the capital, he attended a service at a monastery, then spent some time with an old hermit who was greatly revered. They had a long talk, and when Alexander left he remarked, "I have heard many sermons, but none has moved me as much as that old monk. How sorry I am not to have known him sooner".

He went to Taganrog, and the Empress – whose illness prevented her from hurrying – arrived ten days later. For a month they lived simply and peacefully together, and it seemed that their love had achieved an Indian summer. Then Alexander was again seized by his wanderlust and set out on a tour of the Crimea. When he returned to Taganrog on 16 November, he was feverish.

And, according to the history books, he died there on 1 December 1825. Four eyewitnesses vouch for it: the Empress herself, his aide-de-camp, Prince Volkonsky, his personal physician, the Englishman Sir James Wylie, and the court physician, Tarassov. So why should we not accept this as the truth?

To begin with, because the diaries and letters of the witnesses contradict one another; for example, one says he is getting steadily worse, while another states that he is feeling much better and is gay and smiling. One thing that is certain is that the Tsar consistently refused all medicines during his last illness.

23 November 1825, seems to have been the crucial day. In the morning, after sleeping well, the Tsar sent for his wife and remained in conversation with her for about six hours. They were evidently discussing something of considerable import. She wrote to her mother: "When you think you have arranged everything for the best, there comes an unexpected trial which makes it impossible for you to enjoy the happiness surrounding you". Happiness, when her husband was seriously ill? Does it not sound, rather, as if she is now certain that he is recovering and that after their reconciliation, she is now looking forward to a new and intimate relation with her husband – and then, suddenly, some new obstacle has arisen that has dashed her hopes? Could it be that her husband has confided to her that he sees this illness as an oppor-tunity to put into practice his scheme of "disappearing"?

Moreover, after writing this letter, there is a sudden gap in her diary. Paleologue suggests that the diary entries were destroyed by Tsar Nicholas I – Alexander's younger brother – when he came to the throne. This is plausible, since Nicholas I is known to have destroyed many papers belonging to his older brother, as well as the Empress's diary. But if the Empress had just been told by her husband that he intended to disappear, this would have been a still better explanation; it is surely unlikely that she would have continued to keep her diary, with the incriminating evidence.

Another curious incident occurred. Prince Volkonsky recorded in his diary that Alexander had suggested that his illness should be made known to his younger brother, the Grand Duke Constantine, who was heir to the throne. (In fact, he declined it and allowed Nicholas to take over.) Volkonsky gave the date for this request as 21 November – then amended it to 23 November, the day of the Tsar's long talk with his wife. It may have been a genuine error. Or it may have reflected a desire to support the story that the Tsar began to deteriorate on 23 November. That he was not in an enfeebled state is proved by the fact that after his six-hour talk with his wife, he then wrote a long letter to his mother, the Dowager Empress Marie – a highly dominant woman – *which has since disappeared*. Nicholas I later destroyed the diary of the Tsar's mother, as well as all papers relating to Alexander's last years. The evidence is purely circumstantial, but it certainly fits the hypothesis that 23 November was the day on which Alexander told his wife that he intended to abdicate; the day on which he relayed this news to his mother and to his aide-de-camp and physicians – with instructions to falsify their diaries.

Four days later the parish priest of Taganrog, Father Fedotov, arrived to give Alexander Communion. Four days after that, Alexander died. Is it credible that he failed to ask the priest to come again? We would expect the opposite from a man of his religious and mystical tendencies – that is, that when he believed he was dying, he would have kept the priest by him most of the time. Neither were there any last rites, such as all the previous Tsars had received. Instead, Alexander apparently died without any of the comforts of religion – which sounds as absurd as a pope dying without the final sacrament.

Ten doctors signed the autopsy report on the day after the Tsar's death. This report provides the most positive evidence that the corpse was not that of the Tsar and that another corpse had been found during the thirty-two hours that had elapsed since his death. Alexander is reported to have died of malaria, which causes the spleen to hyper-trophy. But the spleen of the corpse was quite normal. Examination of the brain revealed that the man had suffered from syphilis. But Alexander, says Paleologue, was known to be immune to syphilis. He had had many mistresses, and his favourite mistress, Marie Naryshkin, had many lovers. His promiscuity must have led him to consult his physicians about the possibility of venereal disease on several occasions; medical reports show that he had always remained immune.

The back and loins of the corpse were brownish-purple and red; this might be expected of a peasant who took no care of his skin – or who had been recently flogged – but hardly of a Tsar.

But where could the corpse have been obtained? There is no difficulty in answering this question if we recall that Taganrog was a garrison town full of soldiers. Maurice Paleologue (who was the French ambassador at the court of Nicholas II, the last of the Tsars) reports that there is some evidence (he agrees that it is "faint", because such matters were kept secret) that the head physician of the military hospital, Dr Alexandrovitch, happened to have in his hands the body of a soldier who was roughly the same height and size as the Tsar. If the body was that of a soldier – possibly a Tatar – it could explain why the skin of the loins and back was purple; soldiers were often beaten.

Oddly enough, Dr Tarassov, the royal surgeon, later declared that he had not signed the autopsy report. Yet the report is signed by Tarassov. Why did Tarassov think he had not signed it? Was it because he did not wish to put his name to a document he knew to be false? On the other hand, an unsigned autopsy report would confirm suspicions if any question of the Tsar's "survival" arose, and it would therefore be logical for someone to forge Tarassov's signature.

It is also known that when the Tsar's remains were exposed to public view – as they had to be by custom – in the church at Taganrog, everyone who looked at the face said the same thing: "Is that the Tsar? How he has changed".

Another curious event occurred when the coffin was on its way back to St Petersburg – or rather, to the summer palace in Tsarskoe Selo – in the following March. (In the freezing Russian winter, the body was perfectly preserved, as if it had been kept in a deep freeze.) When the coffin reached Babino, fifty miles from its destination, the Dowager Empress Marie Feodorovna came – alone – to see it. She ordered the coffin to be opened, took a long look at the body, and then left. It seems odd that she should have made the journey to Babino when she could just as easily have seen the body in St Petersburg. It is recorded that she had recently received "a very grave confidence" from Princess Volkonsky, wife of the Tsar's aide-de-camp. If that confidence was that the corpse was not that of the Tsar, it would certainly explain her visit in midwinter. If we assume that the letter of 23 November had simply told her that Alexander had decided to abdicate, and the next news she received was of his death, then it becomes understandable that she was anxious to find out as quickly as possible whether it was true that her son was still alive. She did not want to see the body in the presence of other people.

Alexander was taken to the summer palace in Tsarskoe Selo, although it might have been expected that he would lie in state in St Petersburg so that his subjects could see him for the last time. Instead, only the royal family filed past the coffin in the chapel. As the Dowager Empress did so, she made the curious remark, "Yes, that is my dear son Alexander" and kissed the brow of the corpse. The body was then taken to the Peter and Paul Fortress and placed in a tomb.

Forty years later the new Tsar, Alexander II, heard the rumors that the hermit Fedor Kuzmich, who had died in the previous year, was actually Tsar Alexander I. He ordered the tomb to be opened. This was done at night, under the direction of the minister of the imperial court, Count Adlersberg. The coffin proved to be empty. The tomb was then resealed without the coffin. Paleologue records that the tomb was opened again in the reign of Tsar Alexander III and that the coffin was missing. In contradiction to this, the historian R. D. Charques records, in a footnote in his *Short History of Russia* (1956), that the coffin was opened again by the Bolsheviks in the 1920s and found to be empty.

But in his introduction to Tolstoy's *Death of Ivan Ilyich* (which contains his story "Fedor Kuzmich"), Tolstoy's translator, Aylmer Maude, states that in 1927 the Soviet government had the imperial tombs opened and that that of Alexander I contained only a bar of lead. This sounds altogether more likely. It suggests that Paleologue's account is the correct one and that Charques wrote *coffin* when he meant *tomb*. In fact, a completely empty coffin would not be placed in the tomb, since it would be evident to those who lifted it that it was empty; something would almost certainly be placed inside to give it weight, and that something might well be a bar of lead. When the coffin was found to be empty by Count Adlersberg, this might well have been left behind in the tomb.

Tolstoy was intrigued by the story of Fedor Kuzmich and, as already noted, sketched out a story – unfinished at the time of his death – about it. Tolstoy's "Fedor Kuzmich" purports to be the diary of Alexander I. The protagonist describes himself as "the greatest of criminals", the murderer of hundreds of thousands of people as well as of his own father. In Taganrog, he says, he received a letter from his minister, Arakcheyev, describing the assassination of Arakcheyev's voluptuous mistress; this, he says, filled him with lustful thoughts. Early the next morning he walked out alone, heard the sound of drums and flutes, and realized that a soldier was being made to run the gauntlet – that is, to run halfnaked between lines of colleagues who would beat him with rods. The thought of the murdered girl and of a soldier being beaten with rods "merged into one stimulating sensation". He then realized that the soldier who was being beaten bore a striking resemblance to himself; it was a man named Strumenski, who was sometimes jokingly called Alexander II. He had been in the Tsar's old regiment and was now being punished for attempted desertion. Two days later the Tsar made inquiries and learned that Strumenski was dying. It was when his chief of staff was telling him about various conspiracies that the desire to abdicate again came upon him with tremendous force, and he realized that the death of Strumenski would provide him with the opportunity he needed. And when, the following day, he cut himself badly while shaving, and collapsed on the floor, he decided that the time had come to put his plan into operation.

Tolstoy's version assumes that Alexander decided to vanish on impulse in Taganrog; Paleologue suspects that he chose Taganrog because he had already planned his disappearance.

Oddly enough, Paleologue doubts whether Fedor Kuzmich *was* Alexander I – he cites a story to the effect that an English lord picked up the Tsar in his yacht and that Alexander died as a monk in Palestine. This is, in a sense, more logical than the notion that he became a wanderer in Russia, where he would have been easily recognized.

Many historians, including Charques, dismiss the notion that Alexander I survived his "death" in Taganrog. In *The Court of Russia in the Nineteenth Century* (1908), E. A. Brayley Hodgetts cites the report of Sir James Wylie, the Tsar's English doctor, who examined the body and diagnosed that the death was due to "bilious remittent fever". But if Alexander "disappeared", then Wylie was undoubtedly part of the conspiracy. And the doubts about the disappearance theory must be balanced against the evidence of the empty tomb and against the whole strange story of Alexander's final illness and death. It now seems unlikely that anyone will ever prove that Alexander I arranged his own disappearance. But the reason that it is unlikely – that all the relevant diaries and letters have mysteriously vanished – suggests that it is true.

31

The Loch Ness Monster

Loch Ness, the largest of British lakes, is twenty-two miles long and about a mile wide; at its greatest depth, it is 950 feet deep. It is part of the Great Glen, which runs like a deep crack right across Scotland, from one coast to the other; it opened up between 300 and 400 million years ago as a result of earthquakes, then was deepened by glaciers. At the southern end of the loch there is the small town of Fort Augustus; at the northern end, Inverness. Until the eighteenth century, the loch was practically inaccessible, except by winding trackways; it was not until 1731 that General Wade began work on the road that runs from Fort Augustus up the south side of the loch (although Fort Augustus was not so christened until 1742). But this steep road, which makes a long detour inland, was obviously not the shortest distance between Fort Augustus and Inverness; the most direct route would run along the northern shore. In the early 1930s a road was finally hacked and blasted out of this northern shore, and vast quantities of rock were dumped down the steep sides of Loch Ness.

The road had only just been completed in April 1933, and it was on the 14th of that month that Mr and Mrs John Mackay, proprietors of the Drumnadrochit Hotel, were returning home from a trip to Inverness. It was about three in the afternoon when Mrs Mackay pointed and said, "What's that, John"? The water in the middle of the loch was in a state of commotion; at first she thought it was two ducks fighting, then realized that the area of disturbance was too wide. As her husband pulled up they saw some large animal in the middle of the surging water; then as they watched the creature swam towards Aldourie pier on the other side of the loch. For a moment they glimpsed two black humps, which rose and fell in an undulating manner; then the creature made a half-turn and sank from sight.

The Mackays made no attempt to publicize their story, but gossip about the sighting reached a young water bailiff, Alex Campbell, who also happened to be local correspondent for the *Inverness Courier*; he called on the Mackays, and his report went into the *Courier* on 2 May, more than two weeks after the sighting occurred. The editor is said to have remarked: "If it's as big as they say, it's not a creature it's a monster". And so the "Loch Ness Monster" acquired its name.

This was not, strictly speaking, the first account of the monster to appear in print. This distinction belongs to a *Life of St Columba* dating from about AD 565. This tells (in vol. 6, book 11, chap. 27) how the saint arrived at a ferry on the banks of the loch and found some men preparing to bury a comrade who had been bitten to death by a water monster while he was swimming. The saint ordered one of his own followers to swim across the loch. The monster heard the splashing and swam towards him, at which the saint made the sign of the cross and commanded the creature to go away; the terrified monster obeyed . . .

Other reportings down the centuries are more difficult to pin down; in his book on the monster, Nicholas Witchell mentions a number of references to the "beast" or "water kelpie" (fairy) of Loch Ness in old books between 1600 and 1800. And after Commander Rupert Gould published a book on the monster in 1934, a Dr D. Mackenzie of Balnain wrote to Gould claiming to have seen it in 1871 or 1872, looking rather like an upturned boat but moving at great speed, "wriggling and churning up the water". Alex Campbell, the water bailiff, reported that a crofter named Alexander MacDonald had seen the monster in 1802 and reported it to one of Campbell's ancestors. But hearsay reports like this inevitably led sceptics to suspect that local people, particularly hoteliers, had a financial interest in promoting the monster, so that by the mid-1930s "Nessie" (as she was soon christened in the area) had become something of a joke. In fact the first "modern" report of the monster had occurred in 1930; the *Northern Chronicle* reported that three young men who were out in a boat fishing on 22 July of that year, close to Dores, on the southern shore, saw a loud commotion in the water about 600 yards away, and some large creature swimming towards them just below the surface; it turned away when it was about 300 yards away. The young men commented that it was "certainly not a basking shark or a seal".

That summer of 1933 was one of the hottest on record, and by the end of the summer the Loch Ness monster was known to readers all over the British Isles; it was still to become a world-wide sensation.

By now the monster had also been sighted on land. On a peaceful summer afternoon, 22 July 1933, Mr and Mrs George Spicer were on their way back to London after a holiday in the Highlands. At about four o'clock they were driving along the southern road from Inverness to Fort William (the original General Wade road) and were on the mid-portion between Dores and Foyers. About two hundred yards ahead of them they saw a trunk-like object apparently stretching across the road. Then they saw that it was in motion, and that they were looking at a long neck. This was soon followed by a grey body, about five feet high (Mr Spicer said later "It was horrible – an abomination") which moved across the road in jerks. Because they were on a slope, they could not see whether it had legs or not, and by the time their car had reached the top of the slope it had vanished into the undergrowth opposite. It seemed to be carrying something on its back. They saw no tail, and the drawing that Commander Gould made later under their direction justifies Mr Spicer's description of a "huge snail with a long neck". When Gould heard of this sighting he thought it was a hoax; but after he had interviewed the Spicers in London he had no doubt that they were telling the truth. The Spicers still seemed shaken and upset. It was later suggested the object over the monster's shoulder could have been a dead sheep. In 1971 Nicholas Witchell interviewed Mrs Margaret Cameron, who claimed to have seen the monster on land when she was a teenager, during the First World War; she said, "It had a huge body and its movement as it came out of the trees was like a caterpillar". She also described it as being about twenty feet long, and said that it had two short, round feet at the front, and that it lurched from side to side as it entered the water. She and her friends felt so sick and upset that they were unable to eat their tea afterwards. Witchell also interviewed a man called Jock Forbes, who claimed to have seen the monster in 1919, when he was twelve; it was a stormy night, and he and his father were in a pony and trap when the pony shied, and they saw something large crossing the road ahead of them, then heard a splash as it plunged into the loch.

In November 1933 "Nessie" was photographed for the first time. Hugh Gray, an employee of the British Aluminium Company, was walking on a wooded bluff, fifty feet above the loch, near Foyers. He had seen the monster on a previous occasion, and was now carrying a camera. It was Sunday 12 November 1933, a sunny morning, and Gray sat down for a moment to look out over the loch. As he did so he saw the monster rising up out of the water, about two hundred yards away. He raised his camera and snapped it while it was two or three feet above the surface of the water. It is not the clearest of all photographs – it is easy to focus attention on the dark shadow and to overlook the vague, greyish bulk of the creature rising from the water above it. This was only one of five shots; the others seem to have been even less satisfactory. Gray was so ambivalent about the sighting – afraid of being subjected to derision – that he left the film in his camera for two weeks, when his brother took it to be developed. It appeared in the Scottish *Daily Record* and the London *Daily Sketch* on 6 December 1933, together with a statement from the Kodak film company that the negative had not been retouched. But Professor Graham Kerr, a zoologist at Glasgow University, declared that he found it utterly unconvincing as a photograph of any living thing. It was the beginning of the "debunking" of the monster, in which major zoologists were to be prominent for many decades to come.

And the sightings continued. The day after Hugh Gray had snapped the monster, Dr J. Kirton and his wife were walking down the hill behind the Invermoriston Hotel when they saw the monster swimming away from them. They saw a rounded back with a protuberance in the middle, "like the rear view of a duck in a pond". Gould lists this as the twenty-sixth sighting of 1933. A week later, on the 20th of November, the monster was seen lying motionless in the water for some ten minutes by a Miss N. Simpson, near Altsigh; she judged its length to be about 30 feet. Then she saw it swim underwater to the centre of the loch "at about the speed of an outboard motor boat".

On 12 December 1933 a firm of Scottish film producers, Irvine, Clayton and Hay, managed to film the monster in motion for a few seconds; unfortunately, the film shows little but a long dark shadow moving through the water.

The most famous photograph of the monster was taken in the following April, 1934 – the celebrated "surgeon's photograph". On 1 April 1934 Robert Kenneth Wilson, Fellow of the Royal College of Surgeons, was driving northward with a friend; they had leased a wild-fowl shoot near Inverness, and meant to go to it and take some photographs of the birds. Wilson had borrowed a camera with a telephoto lens. It was early in the morning about seven and they stopped the car on a small promontory two miles north of Invermoriston. As they stood watching the surface they noticed the signs of "considerable commotion" that seem to herald the arrival of the monster, and the friend, Maurice Chambers, shouted, "My God, it's the monster". Wilson rushed to the car, came back with the camera, and managed to expose four plates in two minutes in such a hurry that he did not even look at what he was photographing. The serpentine head, not unlike an elephant's trunk, then withdrew gently into the water. Unsure as to whether he had captured anything, Wilson hurried to Inverness and took the plates to a chemist to be developed. They were ready later that day. Two proved to be blank; one showed the head about to vanish into the water. But the fourth was excellent, showing the dinosaur-like neck and tiny head.

Wilson sold the copyright of the photograph to the *Daily Mail* and it appeared on 21 April 1934, creating a sensation. It also aroused the usual roars of derision from the scientific establishment, who branded the photograph a fake, and pointed out that the "surgeon" (who had withheld his identity) could be an invention of the perpetrator of the fraud. In fact, Wilson soon allowed himself to be identified, and his name appeared in Commander Gould's book *The Loch Ness Monster and Others*, which came out later the same year, with the "surgeon's photograph" as a frontispiece. (The fact that the photograph was taken on 1 April may have increased the general scepticism.) Many years later another monster-investigator, Tim Dinsdale, held the photograph at arm's length and noticed something that convinced him of its authenticity. When viewed from a distance, a faint concentric circle of rings is visible around the monster, while there is another circle in the background, as if some other part of the body is just below the surface. No one, Dinsdale pointed out, would take the trouble to fake a detail that is almost invisible to the eye. Another piece of evidence in favour of its authenticity emerged in 1972, when the photograph was subjected to the computer-enhancement process at NASA; the improved picture showed signs of whiskers hanging down from the lower jaw.

In July 1934 a team of fourteen men was hired by Sir Edward Mountain, at a wage of £2 per week per man, to spend five weeks standing on the shores of the loch, armed with cameras. Five promising photographs were taken; four of them only showed a dark wake, which could have been caused by a boat; the fifth showed a head disappearing in a splash of spray. After the watchers had been paid off, Captain James Frazer, who had been in charge of the expedition, succeeded in shooting several feet of film from a position just above Castle Urquart. It showed an object like an upturned, flat-bottomed boat, about fifteen feet long; it disappeared in a spume of spray. Zoologists who viewed the film said that the creature was a seal. Captain Frazer later admitted that he had to endure a great deal of ridicule.

Sightings continued, and more photographs were taken; but the general public had ceased to be deeply interested in the monster. After the initial excitement, most people were willing to accept the view of sceptics that the monster had been a cynical invention of people involved in the Highland tourist business; if so, it had certainly succeeded, for Loch Ness hotels were crowded throughout the summer. One of the most interesting sightings of 1934 went virtually unnoticed. On 26 May Brother Richard Horan, of St Benedict's Abbey, was working in the abbey boathouse when he heard a noise in the water, and saw the monster looking at him from a distance of about thirty yards. It had a graceful neck with a broad white stripe down its front, and a muzzle like a seal's. Three other people corroborated his sighting. In the December of the following year, a Miss Rena Mackenzie also saw the monster fairly close, and noted that its head seemed tiny, and that the underside of its throat was white. A man named John Maclean, who saw the monster in July 1938, saw the head and neck only twenty yards away, and said that it was obviously in the act of swallowing food, opening and closing its mouth, and tossing back its head "in exactly the same manner that a cormorant does after it has swallowed a fish". When the creature dived Maclean and his wife saw two humps. They described it as being about eighteen feet long, and said that at close quarters its skin was dark brown and "like that of a horse when wet and glistening". Each of these sightings enables us to form a clearer picture of the monster. And in July 1958 the water bailiff Alex Campbell had a sighting which confirmed something he had believed for many years – that there must be more than one of the creatures; he saw one lying quietly near St Benedict's Abbey while another (visible as a large black hump) headed across the loch, churning the surface of the water. (Many accounts indicate that the animals can move at high speed.)

During the Second World War interest in the monster (or monsters) waned, although sightings continued to be reported. In 1943 Commander Russell Flint, in charge of a motor launch passing through Loch Ness on its way to Swansea, reported a tremendous jolt that convinced the crew that they had struck some floating debris. In fact, they saw the monster disappearing in a flurry of water. His signal to the Admiralty, reporting that he had sustained damage to the starboard bow after a collision with the Loch Ness monster, earned him in response "a bit of a blast".

In November 1950 the *Daily Herald* ran a story headed "The Secret of Loch Ness", alleging that dozens of eight-foot-diameter mines had been anchored on the floor of the loch since 1918, some at a depth of a mile. (The *Herald* stated that at its greatest depth, the loch is seven miles deep.) The story apparently had some slight basis in fact; mines *had* been laid in 1918 by HMS *Welbeck* – Hugh Gray, who later took the first monster photograph, was on board – but when a vessel went to collect them in 1922, only the anchors remained. The mines, which were designed to have a life of only a few years, were probably at the bottom. Certainly none of the photographs looks in the least like an eight-foot mine, even one with horns.

In the following year another monster photograph was taken by a woodsman named Lachlan Stuart. He was about to milk a cow early on 14 July 1951 when he saw something moving fast down the loch, so fast that he at first thought it was a speedboat. He grabbed his camera, rushed down the hill, and snapped the monster when it was only fifty yards offshore. The result was a photograph showing three distinct humps.

Four years later a bank manager named Peter Macnab was on his way back from a holiday in the north of Scotland, and pulled up his car just above Urquhart Castle. It was a calm, warm afternoon – 29 July 1955 – and he saw a movement in the still water near the castle; he hastily raised his camera, and took a photograph which has joined the "surgeon's photograph" and the Lachlan Stuart photograph as one of the classic views of the monster. But he was so anxious to avoid ridicule that he released the picture only three years later, in 1958.

Before that happened, interest in the case had been revived by the best book on it so far – *More Than a Legend*, published in 1957. The author was Constance Whyte, wife of the manager of the Caledonian canal, who became interested in the monster after she was asked to write an article about it for a small local magazine. Mrs Whyte interviewed every witness she could find, and produced the first overall survey of the evidence since Rupert Gould's book of 1934. *More Than a Legend* aroused widespread interest, the author was deluged with correspondence, and once again the Loch Ness monster was news. What Mrs Whyte had done, with her careful research, was to refute the idea that the monster was a joke, or the invention of the Scottish Tourist Board. No one who reads her book can end with the slightest doubt that the monster really exists, and that it shows itself with a fair degree of frequency.

The immediate result was a new generation of "monster-hunters". One of these, Frank Searle, was a manager for a firm of fruiterers in London; he bought Constance Whyte's book, and in 1958 decided to camp by Loch Ness. From then on he returned again and again. In June 1965 he was parked in a lay-by near Invermoriston and chatting to some hitch-hikers when he saw a dark object break the surface, and realized he had at last seen the monster. His excitement was so great that in 1969 he gave up his job and pitched his tent by Loch Ness, where he was to remain for the next four years. In August 1971 he saw the tail at close quarters as the monster dived; his impression was of an alligator's tail, "seven feet long, dark and nobbly on top, smooth dirty white underneath". In November 1971 he got his first photograph of the monster – a dark hump in a swirl of water; he admitted that it was "inconclusive". But in the following five years he obtained at least ten of the best pictures of the monster taken so far, including one showing the swanlike neck rising out of the water, and another showing both the neck and one of the humps; these were published in his *Nessie: Seven Years in Search of the Monster* in 1976. During that time his tent had become a "Mecca for visitors" – mostly directed to him by the Scottish Tourist Board – and in 1975 he estimated that he had seen twenty-five thousand in eight months. On 7 June 1974, together with a girl visitor from Quebec, he had a memorable sighting. As they approached a barbedwire fence near Foyers, they noticed a splashing sound. They crept up and peered over the fence, "and saw two of the strangest little creatures I've ever seen. They were about two feet in length, dark grey in colour, something like the skin of a baby elephant, small heads with black protruding eyes, long necks and plump bodies. They had snake like tails which were wrapped along their sides, and on each side of the body, two stump-like appendages". When he tried to get through the fence the small creatures "scuttled away with a kind of crab-like motion" and were submerged in the loch within seconds.

But in his book *The Loch Ness Story* – perhaps the best comprehensive account of the hunt for the monster – Nicholas Witchell comments: "It is a regrettable fact which can easily be proved that these 1972 photographs have been tampered with. Mr Searle has also produced another series identical with the original shots in all respects except that an extra hump has been added to them by some process of superimposition or by rephotography". And he adds: "Because of the highly suspicious content of some of Mr Searle's photographs and the inconsistencies of the facts surrounding the taking of them, it is not possible to accept them as being authentic photographs of animate objects in Loch Ness".

In 1959 an aeronautical engineer named Tim Dinsdale read an article about the monster in a magazine called *Everybody's*, and was intrigued. He spent most of that winter reading everything he could find; it was in the following February that (as already described) he looked at the surgeon's photograph, and noticed the circle of ripples that convinced him that it was genuine. In April that year Dinsdale went off to Loch Ness to hunt the monster. But after five days he had still seen nothing. On the day before he was due to return home he was approaching his hotel in Foyers when he saw something out in the loch; his binoculars showed a hump. He snatched his 16-mm ciné-camera and began to film as the creature swam away. Then, almost out of film, he drove down to the water's edge; by the time he got there the creature had vanished. But Dinsdale had fifty feet of film showing the monster in motion. When shown on television it aroused widespread interest and – as Witchell says – heralded a new phase in the saga of the monster.

That June the first scientific expedition to Loch Ness embarked on a month-long investigation, with thirty student volunteers and a Marconi echo-sounder, as well as a large collection of cameras. A ten-foot hump was sighted in July, and the echo-sounder tracked some large object as it dived from the surface to a depth of sixty feet and back up again. The expedition also discovered large shoals of char at a depth of a hundred feet – an answer to sceptics who said that the loch did not contain enough fish to support a monster; the team's finding was that there was enough fish to support several.

But Dr Denys Tucker, of the British Museum of Natural History, who had organized this expedition, did not lead it as he had intended to; in June he was dismissed from his job – as he believed, because he had publicly expressed his belief in the existence of the monster.

Dinsdale became a close friend of Torquil MacLeod, who had seen the monster almost out of the water in February 1960. MacLeod had watched it for nine minutes, and admitted being "appalled by its size", which he estimated at between 40 and 60 feet. It had a long neck, like an elephant's trunk, which kept moving from side to side and up and down, and "paddles" at the rear and front. In August 1960 MacLeod had another sighting from the shore, while a family in a motor yacht belonging to a company director, R.H. Lowrie, saw the monster at close quarters for about a quarter of an hour, taking a few photographs. At one point they thought the monster was heading straight for them and about to collide; but it veered away and disappeared.

It was also in August 1960 that Sir Peter Scott, founder of the Wildfowl Trust, and Richard Fitter of the Fauna Preservation Society approached the Member of Parliament David James and asked for his help in trying to get government assistance for a "flat-out attempt to find what exactly is in Loch Ness". In April 1961 a panel decided that there was a prima facie case for investigating the loch. The result was the formation of the Bureau for Investigating the Loch Ness Phenomena, a registered charity. In October 1961 two powerful searchlights scanned the loch every night for two weeks, and on one occasion caught an eight-foot "finger like object" standing out of the water. In 1962 another team used sonar, and picked up several "large objects"; one of these sonar recordings preceded an appearance of the monster on the surface.

In 1966 Tim Dinsdale's film was subjected to analysis by Air Force Intelligence, which reported that the object filmed was certainly not a boat or a submarine, and by NASA's computer-enhancement experts, who discovered that two other parts of the body also broke the surface besides the main hump.

In August 1962 another "monster-hunter", F.W. ("Ted") Holiday, parked his van by Loch Ness, on the southern shore opposite Urquhart Castle. As darkness fell he had a feeling that "Loch Ness is not a water by which to linger". Two nights later, on a perfectly still night, he heard the crash of waves breaking on the stony beach, although there was no sound of a boat engine. Two days later he had his first sighting of the monster. On a hill close to the spot where Dinsdale had taken his 1961 film, he suddenly saw a black and glistening object rise three feet out of the water; then it dived like "a diving hippopotamus". He could still see the shape of the animal just below the surface. He judged it to be about 45 feet long. Then a man on a nearby pier started hammering, and the creature vanished.

Every year from then on Holiday returned to the loch; but in 1963 and 1964 he was unlucky. Then in 1965 he saw it on two occasions; on the first he saw it (looking like an upturned boat) from three different positions as he raced his car along the loch to get a better view. But he had already reached a conclusion about the nature of the monster, that it was simply a giant version of the common garden slug, an ancestor of the squid and octopus. In his book *The Great Orm of Loch Ness* he argued that the monster is a type of *Tullimonstrum gregarium*, a creature looking a little like a submarine with a broad tail. He also came to believe that these monsters were once far more plentiful in the British Isles, that they used to be known as "worms" (or "orms"), and that they gave rise to the legend of dragons. A photograph in the book shows the Worm's Head peninsula in South Wales, and argues that it is so called because it resembles the "orm" of legend and of Loch Ness.

In 1963 Holiday interviewed two fishermen who had seen the monster at close range, only 20 or 30 yards away. One said that the head reminded him of a bulldog, that it was wide and very ugly. The neck was fringed by what looked like coarse black hair. In a letter to Dinsdale, Holiday remarked: "When people are confronted by this fantastic animal at close quarters they seemed to be stunned. There is something strange about Nessie that has nothing to do with size or appearance. Odd, isn't it"? He was intrigued by the number of people who had a feeling of horror when they saw the monster. Why were dragons and "orms" always linked with powers of evil in medieval mythology? He also began to feel increasingly that it was more than coincidence that the monsters were so hard to photograph: he once had his finger on the button when the head submerged. Either the monsters had some telepathic awareness of human observation or they were associated with some kind of Jungian "synchronicity", or meaningful coincidence.

Holiday, who was a fishing correspondent, had also had a number of sightings of UFOs (or Flying Saucers), and one or two close brushes with "poltergeists" (or "banging ghosts"). And he was intrigued to learn that Boleskine House, near Foyers, had been tenanted by the notorious "magician" Aleister Crowley in the early years of the twentieth century, and that Crowley had started to perform there a lengthy magical ritual by a certain Abramelin the Mage. Crowley himself claimed that the house was filled with shadowy spirits while he was performing the ritual (which takes many months), and that they drove a coachman to drink and a clairvoyant to become a prostitute. Crowley failed to complete the ritual, and, according to Holiday "misfortune stalked him" from then on. Although he never says so in so many words, Holiday seemed to entertain the suspicion that the monster may have been conjured up by Crowley: certainly he thought it a coincidence that a creature associated with evil should be seen so often from Foyers, near Boleskine House. He also thought it odd when American students exploring the cemetery near Boleskine found a tapestry and a conch shell beneath a grave slab. The tapestry – probably Turkish in origin – had "worm like creatures" embroidered on it, and its freedom from mildew suggested that it had been hidden recently. Holiday suspected that it had been used in some magical ceremony, and that the ceremony had been hastily abandoned when someone walked into the churchyard. It looked as if black magic is still practised near Boleskine House.

Soon after this Holiday went to have dinner with a friend near Loch Ness, and met an American called Dr Dee, who was in England looking up his family tree. Dr Dee said that he had discovered that he had a celebrated Elizabethan ancestor of the same name. It was another coincidence: John Dee, the Elizabethan "magician", had published the ritual of Abramelin the Mage.

In a letter to me in 1971 Ted Holiday described a further coincidence. Looking across the loch, he found himself looking at the word DEE in large yellow letters. Bulldozers engaged in road-widening had scraped away the soil running down to the loch, and the top half of the "letters" was formed by the yellow subsoil. The bottom half of the letters was formed by the reflection of the top half in the perfectly still water.

In fact Holiday was coming to a very strange conclusion about lake monsters; it arose from some investigations he had undertaken in Ireland in 1968, where more monsters had been sighted in lochs (or "loughs") in Galway. The sightings sounded very much like those of "Nessie", and the witnesses were of unimpeachable reputation – on one occasion, two priests. Yet after weeks of careful observation, and even an attempt to "net" a monster in Lough Nahooin, Holiday had failed to obtain the slightest bit of evidence for the monsters. What puzzled him was that these Irish lakes were too small to support a fifteen-foot monster, still less a colony of them. He began to wonder whether the *peiste* (as the Irish called the creature) was a thing of flesh and blood. Jung had suggested that UFOs are a "projection" from the human unconscious, modern man's attempt to recreate lost religious symbols. Could it be, Holiday wondered, that the lake monsters are also some kind of "projection"?

By 1971 Holiday had abandoned the notion that the lake monsters are simply "prehistoric survivals". He was coming round to the admittedly eccentric view that there is some influence at work that actively prevents the final solution of the mystery, just as in the case of Unidentified Flying Objects. And some time in 1972 this view seemed to be confirmed when he read a newspaper controversy between an "exorcist", the Rev. Donald Omand, and some opponent who thought the Loch Ness monster was simply an unidentified animal. Omand had inherited "second sight" from Highland ancestors, and had no doubt of the real existence of powers of evil – or at least of mischief; he often performed exorcisms to get rid of them. He had caught his first glimpse of a lake monster in Loch Long in Ross-shire in 1967. In June 1968, in a boat in Norway's Fjord of the Trolls, he saw another, which came straight towards them; the Norwegian captain who was with him told him not to be afraid: "It will not hurt us – they never do". And in fact the monster dived before it reached their boat. But the Captain, Jan Andersen, was convinced that the monsters were basically evil, that in some way they could do harm to men's characters (or, as Omand would have said, their souls). In 1972 Omand attended a psychiatric conference at which an eminent Swedish psychiatrist read a paper on the monster of Lake Storsjön, and said that he was convinced that the monsters had a malevolent effect on human beings, especially those who hunted them or saw them regularly. He thought their influence could cause domestic

tragedies and moral degeneration. So Omand began to consider the
theory that perhaps lake monsters are not real creatures, but "projections" of something from the prehistoric past.

Holiday wrote to Omand, and the odd result was that in June 1973
Holiday and Donald Omand rowed out into the middle of Loch Ness,
and Omand performed an exorcism of the loch. Holiday said they both
felt oddly exhausted when it was over. And his suspicion that he was
stirring up dangerous forces seemed to be confirmed two days later
when he went to stay the night with a retired Wing Commander named
Carey. Holiday was telling Mrs Carey about a Swedish journalist called
Jan-Ove Sundberg who had been wandering through the woods behind
Foyers when he had seen a strange craft in a clearing, and some odd-
looking men; the craft had taken off at a great speed, and after his return
to Sweden, Sundberg had been plagued by "men in black" – people
claiming to be officials who often seem to harass UFO "contactees".

Holiday said he intended to go and look at the place where the
"UFO" had landed, and Mrs Carey warned him against it. At this
moment there was a rushing sound like a tornado outside the window
and a series of violent thuds; a beam of light came in through the
window, and focused on Holiday's forehead. A moment later, all was
still. The odd thing was that Wing Commander Carey, who had been
pouring a drink only a few feet away from his wife, saw and heard
nothing. The next morning, as Holiday was walking towards the loch he
saw a man dressed entirely in black – including helmet and goggles –
standing nearby; he walked past him, turned his head, and was astonished to find that the man had vanished. He rushed to the road and
looked in both directions; there was nowhere the man could have gone.
One year later, close to the same spot, Holiday had a heart attack; as he
was being carried away he looked over the side of the stretcher and saw
that they were just passing the exact spot where he had seen the "man in
black". Five years later, Holiday died of a heart attack.

Perhaps a year before his death, Ted Holiday sent me the typescript
of his book *The Goblin Universe*, in which he attempted to justify the
rather strange views he had gradually developed since starting his hunt
for the Loch Ness monster. He had already discussed them in his second
book *The Dragon and the Disc*, in which he linked UFOs ("discs") and
"worms" as symbols of good and evil. Then, to my surprise, he changed
his mind about publishing the book.

There were, I suspect, two reasons. The team of investigators from
the Academy of Applied Science at the Massachusetts Institute of
Technology, led by Dr Robert H. Rines, had taken some remarkable

underwater photographs in 1972 and 1975; one of the 1972 photographs showed very clearly an object like a large flipper, perhaps eight feet long, while a 1975 photograph showed very clearly a long-necked creature and its front flipper; this was particularly impressive because the sonar evidence – waves of sound reflected back from the creature – made it clear that this was not some freak of the light or piece of floating wreckage or lake-weed. By the time he was thinking about publishing *The Goblin Universe*, Holiday was probably wondering whether the book would be contradicted by some new evidence that would establish the physical reality of the monster beyond all doubt. Apart from this, the argument of *The Goblin Universe* was not quite as rigorous as it might be – he was attempting to explain why his views had changed so startlingly since 1962, and spent a great deal of time dwelling on "the paranormal". At all events, he decided not to publish the book, and instead wrote another typescript confined to lake monsters. (*The Goblin Universe* was recently published in America.)

This account of Holiday's activities may seem to be something of a digression; yet it illustrates the immense frustration experienced by monster-hunters in the 1970s and 1980s. When Gould wrote his book in 1934 the solution of the problem seemed close; then it receded. Constance Whyte's book revived interest in the mystery, and when the Loch Ness Phenomena Investigation Bureau began to co-operate with the team from the Academy of Applied Science, and to use all the latest scientific equipment, it began to look as if the mystery was about to be solved once and for all. Yet at the time of this writing – eleven years after that remarkable underwater picture of the monster – there has still been no major advance. Nicholas Witchell triumphantly concludes his book *The Loch Ness Story* (1975) with a chapter entitled "The Solution", in which he describes his excitement when Rines telephoned him from America to describe the colour photograph of the monster; it contains the sentence: "With the official ratification of the discovery of the animals in Loch Ness, the world will lose one of its most popular mysteries". And he declares that it would be ignoble now to gloat about the short-sightedness of the scientific establishment for its sceptical attitude towards Loch Ness.

It is now clear that Witchell was premature. Most people still regard the question of the monster's existence as an open one, and the majority of scientists still regard the whole thing as something of a joke. In 1976 Roy Mackal, a director of the Loch Ness Investigation Bureau and Professor of Biochemistry at the University of Chicago, published the most balanced and thoroughgoing scientific assessment so far, *The*

Monsters of Loch Ness. He turns a highly critical eye on the evidence, yet nevertheless concludes that it is now proven that "a population of moderate-sized, piscivorous aquatic animals is inhabiting Loch Ness". If the scientific establishment was willing to change its mind, this book should have changed it; yet it seems to have made no real impact.

One thing seems clear: that Holiday's pessimism about the monster was unjustified; even at the time he was writing *The Dragon and the Disc*, Rines was taking the best underwater photographs of the monster so far. So there seems reason to believe that science will finally solve the problem of establishing its existence beyond all doubt. The problems of capturing the monster either on film or in nets are epitomized in the following description by Dennis Stacy, of San Antonio, Texas, of his own encounter with "Nessie".

In 1972 I went to the Loch with the express purpose of looking for Nessie. The idea was to camp along the shoreline for about two weeks and see what was to be seen. I had a very distinct feeling of confidence that if I went to the Loch I would see Nessie. I met some students on vacation from Oxford and stayed with them just above Drumnadrochit. Every day I would take my camera down to the shoreline and have a good look around. Except for the day it was cold and drizzly and all of us went for a walk in the pinewoods there. A girl student and myself soon wandered off on our own from the others and made it down to the lochside. While we had been under the pines, the sky cleared remarkably and the wind died down. By the time we reached the loch, it was completely still and mirror-like. About three quarters of a mile across the loch, nearly under Crowley/Page's Boleskine, was Nessie, showing about six feet of neck and head above the water. We had jumped up on the little low rock wall skirting the road. We both saw it at the same time and nearly caused each other to tumble over the side by grabbing the other's shoulders and pointing and saying, Look! Do you see what I see?

And my camera, a 35mm, was miles away. My companion, however, had a little small, cheap camera, and the presence of mind to take a shot. All that was visible in the picture was a white wake, about a hundred feet in length, left by Nessie (or whatever), and which showed up clearly against the dark reflection of the trees on the other side in the water.

Nessie herself? The head was definitely angular, as described. Some say like a horse, with the very pronounced wedge-shape. In my own experience, I liken it to the shape of a rattlesnake's head, a square snout running back in a flare to the jaws. The length of neck out of the water, including the head, was five or six feet. The *impression* it gave, in the sense that spiders and snakes seem to exude their own peculiar aura, was one not so much of danger as power. I mean it was really cutting a wake through the water, raising a little wavelet on either side of the neck. At times the head was lowered down and forward, and would sweep a small angle from side to side, as if feeding, by lowering the bottom part of the jaw just into the water. But it was really too far away to be absolutely certain of this last manoeuver; the head, however, could be very plainly seen swinging from side to side.

It was swimming thusly when we first saw it and after no more than a minute, simply sank lower and lower in the water, much in the same way a person comes down from a round of water-skiing, or a submarine submerges. (Letter to the author, 20 Sept 1980.)

Holiday might point out that some points in this narrative seem to support his own quasi-Jungian views. Dennis Stacy expected to see the monster. But he did not see it while he was patrolling the lake with his camera; it happened accidentally on a day he had decided to take off from his vigil. It certainly sounds as if the monster is playing some Jungian game of hide-and-seek. Yet all of us have experienced that same feeling that certain days are lucky or unlucky – everything seems to go right or everything seems to go wrong – and common sense tells us that this is purely subjective; an attitude of pessimism makes us careless and therefore accident-prone; an attitude of optimism awakens a new level of vigilance that anticipates problems.

What seems perfectly clear from Stacy's narrative (and many others quoted in the foregoing pages) is that the creatures of Loch Ness appear above the surface fairly frequently, particularly on calm days. If science can devise methods of detecting the presence of aeroplanes or jet-propelled missiles in the skies, and of submarines under the sea, it should surely be a simple matter to design a system that would detect all objects that move on the surface of Loch Ness on a calm day, and to film them? In these days of laser beams and electronic surveillance, it seems absurd that we should have to wait for chance sightings of the monster, like the one described above. It should also be obvious that attempts to "hunt" it with motor launches, submarines, helicopters and search-lights are self-defeating, since they create exactly the kind of distur-bance that drives the creature(s) to hide in the depths of the loch.

When the "monster" is finally identified and classified it will undoubtedly be something of an anticlimax, and Loch Ness will probably lose most of its tourist industry at a blow. Half the fascination of the monster lies in the notion that it is terrifying and dangerous. In fact all the evidence suggests that like that other legendary marauder the "killer" whale, it will turn out to be shy, amiable and quite harmless to man.

Postscript to "The Loch Ness Monster"

In March 1994 it was revealed that one of the most famous photographs of the Loch Ness Monster, the so-called "surgeon's photograph", was a hoax. As described in the above article, the photograph was taken in April 1934 (the 19th – not, as stated above, the 1st) by a eminent Harley Street gynaecologist Colonel Robert Wilson, who claimed he was driving towards Inverness when a friend who was in the car shouted: "My God, it's the monster" and Wilson took four photographs with a plate camera.

The true story, apparently, begins several months earlier, and concerns a self-styled big game hunter and self-publicist called Marmaduke Arundel Wetherell. He had been hired to track down the monster by *The Daily Mail*. On 18 December 1933, Wetherell went to Scotland with a *Daily Mail* photographer, and forty-eight hours after arriving, claimed that he had found two footprints of the monster on the south shore near Fort Augustus. The "spoor" was, he declared, "less than a few hours old". It was "a four fingered beast, and it has feet or pads about eight inches across, a very powerful soft-footed animal about twenty feet long".

Plaster casts were taken of the footprints and sent to the Natural History Museum, but on 4 January it was announced that the footprints were those of a young hippo. It was probable, said the expert, that the foot was in use somewhere as an umbrella stand. Understandably, Wetherell was upset by the gale of derision that greeted this announcement. The Loch Ness story ceased to be front-page news.

And then, three months later, came the "surgeon's photograph", and the laughter died away.

What no one knew is that the photograph was also the work of Duke Wetherell.

Colonel Robert Wilson was the friend of a man called Maurice Chambers, in association with whom he leased a wildfowl shoot on the Beauly Firth, near Inverness. And Chambers was also a friend of Duke Wetherell.

Another important clue was never revealed to the public – that Colonel Wilson was extremely fond of a practical joke.

The true story of the "surgeon's photograph" began to emerge in December, 1975, when a diary story in *The Sunday Telegraph* reported that Wetherell's son Ian claimed he and his father had fabricated a photograph of the Loch Ness Monster. The article did not specify which photograph, but it named Maurice Chambers as a co-conspirator.

David Martin, a zoologist with the Loch Ness and Morar Scientific Project, and Alistair Boyd, a fellow researcher, recalled reading that Chambers was a friend of Duke Wetherell.

At the time of the diary piece, Ian Wetherell was sixty-three and running a Chelsea pub. But when Martin and Boyd arrived at the pub eighteen years later, he was dead.

The trail then led to Duke Wetherell's stepson, living on the south coast and in poor health. Christian Spurling was then close to ninety, and he was willing to tell the whole story.

When Duke Wetherell returned from Scotland to his home in Twickenham in January 1934, he was furious with *The Daily Mail*, which had made it clear what it thought of his hippopotamus footprints. "All right", he told his son Ian, "We'll give them their monster".

Ian, twenty-one, was sent out to buy the raw materials – a toy submarine and some tins of plastic wood. His step-brother Christian, the son of a marine painter, was a keen model maker. He received a message from Wetherell saying "can you make me a monster"?

Spurling made a small monster of plastic wood with a long neck and a head like a dinosaur. The neck was built over the conning tower of the toy submarine, leaving a space for the clockwork key. A piece of lead was soldered underneath to prevent it from capsizing. The model was tested out on the local pond, and then Duke Wetherell and his son returned to Loch Ness, found a quiet day, and floated the "monster" out into the shallows. It was Ian who took the photographs.

What Wetherell now needed was someone "respectable" who would be willing to claim he had taken the photographs.

Chambers' friend Colonel Robert Wilson entered into the spirit of the thing, took the four photographic plates to a chemist shop in Inverness, and announced that he had photographed the Loch Ness Monster.

In the storm of publicity that followed, the British Medical Association told Colonel Wilson that the story was likely to bring his profession into disrepute, whereupon Wilson began to drop hints that he could not talk to anyone else about his sighting because the companion who had shouted: "My God, it's the monster" was a married woman with whom he was having an affair.

Wilson died in Australia in 1969, and Duke Wetherell and Chambers died in the mid-1950s. Christian Spurling died in November 1993, after recording the story.

As to the toy submarine, it is presumably still somewhere in Loch Ness – when they had photographed "the monster" they heard a water bailiff approaching, and Duke Wetherell put his foot out and sank it.

An equally interesting development in the Loch Ness story came to light in April 1999, through another "hunter" of strange anomalies called Erik Beckjord.

As mentioned in the article above, one of the most eminent investigators of the Loch Ness Monster was the aeronautical engineer Tim Dinsdale, who became fascinated after reading an article about the monster in a magazine called *Everybody's Weekly*. Dinsdale filmed some of the best-known footage of the monster, and became widely known for his theory that it was some kind of dinosaur – a plesiosaurus. This was in 1959.

But twenty-four years later, Erik Beckjord learned from Dinsdale himself that he no longer believed his own theory.

Beckjord describes how he was on his way to a canal-barge holiday with his girlfriend Kathy Quint when he stopped in Reading, where Tim Dinsdale lived. They went for a drink in a nearby pub, and Dinsale confided to Beckjord that his wife had her reservations about his fame as a monster hunter.

The problem, it seemed, was that Dinsdale had become totally convinced that the Loch Ness Monster was a ghost. Ted Holiday, he admitted, had been right all along.

He told Beckjord how, through many long nights watching the Loch, he had experienced a number of paranormal (or abnormal) happenings and became increasingly certain that he was dealing with some aspect of the supernatural. Apparently what convinced him beyond doubt was a night when he anchored his small cruiser off Boleskine House, where the magician Aleister Crowley had performed the occult ritual of Abrahamelin the Mage seventy years earlier, and that, according to Dinsdale's account, "he endured a series of ghosts, ghoulies, 'demons,' crawling into his boat and coming at him. They never harmed him physically, but they finally killed off the plesiosaur idea for him". He was absolutely certain that these were not fatigue-hallucinations, but real events.

He now realized he was faced with a dilemma. A large part of his income came from his books and lectures on the monster. His audiences would simply not want to hear his theory that the monster was somehow "supernatural". Financially, this would be a disaster. He would also be labelled a "nut". Altogether, it would be better to keep silent.

So, according to Beckjord, Dinsdale hid his knowledge from his publishers and his audiences, but at least he confided in a number of researchers.

When, in the mid-1980s, Beckjord pressed him to make plans for his estate, Dinsdale said it was all taken care of. Beckjord himself became totally convinced that the Loch Ness Monster was somehow paranormal, and found that he was shunned by traditional researchers at Loch Ness. In 1987, Beckjord attended the International Society of Cryptozoology in Edinburgh, and was not even allowed to speak at the main conference. However, he showed a 16mm film after the sessions were over and many people agreed that it showed a white, shape-shifting thing that was not a reptile. Tim Dinsdale was there and saw the film, but said nothing to Beckjord. But Dr Jack Gibson, co-sponsor of the meeting, told Beckjord in a voice that could be overheard by Dinsdale that the film was "the most important he had ever seen of Nessie".

Six months later, Dinsdale died at the age of sixty-seven.

32

The Man in the Iron Mask

On 19 November 1703 a masked prisoner died in the Bastille after a brief illness. He had been imprisoned for thirty-four years, and even the king's Lieutenant in the Bastille, Etienne du Jonca, did not know his identity. He made a note in his journal: "I have since learnt that they called him M. de Marchiel". The unknown prisoner was buried the day after his death, under the name of Marchioly, and was quickly forgotten.

He became famous nearly half a century later, as a result of a book by Voltaire, *The Century of Louis XIV*, in which Voltaire finally exposed the mystery of the "man in the iron mask". According to Voltaire, a few months after the death of Cardinal Mazarin (which occurred in 1661), a young prisoner wearing an iron mask – or rather, a mask whose chin was composed of steel springs, so he could eat without removing it – was taken to the prison on the Ile Sainte Marguerite. Orders were given to kill him if he removed the mask. This prisoner, "of majestic height . . . of a graceful and noble figure", was allowed to have anything he desired. His greatest pleasure was fine linen and laces. He was obviously a man of high rank, for the governor seldom sat down in his presence. Even the doctor who attended him was never allowed to see his face. The stranger died in 1704, said Voltaire (getting the date wrong by a year), and the strange thing is that when first he was incarcerated on the Isle of St Marguerite no person of any rank disappeared in Europe. According to Voltaire, the mysterious prisoner once scratched something on a plate, which he threw out of a window of his prison. It was picked up by a fisherman, who took it to the prison governor. "Have you read what is written on it"? asked the governor. The fisherman confessed that he was unable to read. "You are lucky", said the governor . . .

Voltaire's story created a sensation. There had been rumours about a masked prisoner, but no one had ever dared to speak about them openly. In fact a rather absurd novel called *The Iron Mask*, by the Chevalier de

Mouhy, had been banned five years earlier, although its story took place in Spain and it bore no resemblance to the true story of the masked prisoner.

But who was the masked prisoner, and what had he done? Twenty years later, in *Questions on the Encyclopedia*, Voltaire revealed the answer or what he believed to be the answer. To understand his story, we must know a little of French history. King Louis XIII was rumoured to be impotent, and was in any case on bad terms with his wife, Anne of Austria. Anne was far closer to the king's great minister Cardinal Mazarin; politically they were hand in glove, and it is fairly certain that he was her lover; she may even have secretly married him after the death of the king. This then was Voltaire's theory: that Anne of Austria bore Mazarin a son, and that this happened before the birth of Louis XIV; the child, naturally, was kept secret from the king. So Louis XIV had an elder brother, who might have challenged his right to the throne. Which is why Louis kept his brother in prison, his face concealed by a mask, in case the family resemblance gave him away . . .

Nearly a century after Voltaire's "revelation", in 1847, Alexandre Dumas published his famous novel *The Man in the Iron Mask*, one of the many sequels to *The Three Musketeers*. This became by far the most famous account of the mystery, and was the basis of the popular Hollywood film. According to Dumas, the unknown prisoner was the twin brother of Louis XIV. This was not Dumas's own theory; it was first put forward in a work called *Memoires of the Duc de Richelieu*, published in London in 1790. This work claimed that Louis XIV was born at noon, and that his twin brother arrived at 8.30 in the evening, while his father was at supper. The younger twin was hidden away, so as not to cause problems with the succession. But these *Memoirs* are in fact a forgery by the Duc's secretary, the Abbé Soulavie, so this story is probably an invention.

In his introduction to an English translation of Dumas's novel the literary critic Sidney Dark writes:

Other wilder theories have identified the prisoner with the Duke of Monmouth, the illegitimate son of Charles II, with a certain Armenian Patriarch, with Fouquet, the ambitious minister of Louis XIV in his youth, who is one of the central figures in Dumas's novel, and, wildest guess of all, with Molière. It is said that after the successful production of Molière's famous comedy *Tartuffe* the Jesuits persuaded Louis XIV to order his disappearance. All these guesses are romantic and fantastic. Serious historians now hold that the Man in the Iron Mask was an Italian called Matthiolo, a minister of the Duke of Mantua, who aroused the enmity of Louis XIV through some obscure intrigues.

Sidney Dark was not quite correct. The man that many scholars thought was the masked prisoner was Ercole Mattioli, who was born in 1640, and was Secretary of State to the Duke of Mantua. The "obscure intrigue" that aroused the wrath of Louis XIV was a piece of double-dealing. In 1632 France had bought a stronghold in Italy called Pinerolo, or Pignerol. Thirty years or so later, Louis thought he saw a chance to acquire another useful piece of Italian territory by the same means: the town and citadel of Casale, near Turin, which belonged to the Duke of Mantua. Apparently the Duke was financially embarrassed and might be willing to sell. But negotiations had to be carried out with great caution, for Louis was quarrelling with Spain, and the Duke of Mantua was surrounded by friends of Spain. In fact Mattioli allowed news of the proposed deal to leak out to Louis's enemies, with the result that it fell through. Louis was furious, but there was not much he could do about it while Mattioli was on Italian territory. First of all, Mattioli had to be kept in the dark about the king's anger. Next he had to be lured to Pignerol, apparently to conclude the deal. The moment he was on French territory he was arrested, and thrown into goal in the fortress of Pignerol, which was in the charge of a governor named Saint-Mars. The whole thing was kept secret; Mattioli simply "disappeared", and remained in prison until his death; no one knows quite when this was, but the likeliest guess is that it was about fifteen years later, in 1694.

Mattioli is certainly a likely candidate – we may recall that Etienne du Jonca, the King's Lieutenant in the Bastille, said that the masked prisoner was known as "M. Marchiel"; and we know he was buried as "Marchiolly". But *if* Mattioli was the man in the mask, then why did the king go to such lengths to keep his identity secret, especially after he was transferred to the Island of St Marguerite, then to the Bastille? It is true that Mattioli was kidnapped in Italy, which might cause diplomatic problems. But in that pragmatic age, no one would have bothered much about Mattioli after he was imprisoned. And why hide Mattioli's face? Not many people would recognize it.

Then what about the twin brother theory, which is still by far the most popular solution to the mystery? In fact this was exploded half a century before Dumas wrote his novel. After the fall of the Bastille during the French Revolution, its archives were published under the title *The Bastille Unveiled*. The chairman of the commission that investigated the archives, a certain M. Charpentier, studied every document he could lay his hands on relating to the man in the iron mask. Other royal archives were also at his disposal, and he found there was not a scrap of evidence that Anne of Austria had given birth either to an illegitimate son or to twins.

But Charpentier *did* uncover a few interesting facts about the "ancient prisoner", as well as one curious legend. The legend was that the man in the mask was the illegitimate son of Anne of Austria by the Duke of Buckingham, the handsome, daredevil minister of James I and Charles I. Buckingham had risen to power as the favourite of the homosexual James I, but also acquired a strong influence over Charles I. It is known that he did his best to seduce Anne of Austria when he was in France in 1626, but a matter of some doubt whether he succeeded – it would not be easy for two people as well known as they were to find an opportunity for adultery. But according to the legend recorded by M. Charpentier, Anne bore the Duke a son in 1626 who bore a remarkable family resemblance to her later child Louis XIV, born twelve years later – hence the need to keep him masked . . .

This legend had one strong point in its favour. It originated with a certain Madame de Saint-Quentin, who was the mistress of the Marquis de Louvois, Louis XIV's war minister. And if (as is practically certain) she heard it from the Marquis, then surely there must be a certain amount of truth in it? That is true; but the opposite may also be true. Perhaps the Marquis told her the story that Louis wanted people to believe – a story that was close enough to the truth to seem probable, but that would mislead the curious. In any case, this story also has one major drawback. If the man in the iron mask was born in 1626, then he would have been about seventy-three at the time of his death. But other clues about the prisoner suggest that he was at least ten years younger than that. Voltaire says he was young and graceful. But by 1669 – the date at which the Bastille archives revealed that the former prisoner had first been incarcerated – a man born in 1626 would have been forty-three – almost an old man in the Europe of that period.

At least Charpentier was able to find a few useful clues from the archives. The prisoner had been in Pignerol, like Mattioli, as well as on the island of St Marguerite – also like Mattioli. But it was not Mattioli. For other archive material revealed that when Saint-Mars, the prison governor of Pignerol, was given another appointment at nearby Exiles in 1681 the "ancient prisoner" went with him, while Mattioli stayed behind. And as more archive material came to light, it was discovered that various letters between the minister of war and Saint-Mars were in the file. And, more important, there were letters from the king. These proved beyond all doubt that the name of the man in the iron mask was Eustache Dauger. In July 1669 the Marquis de Louvois (the father of the one who told his mistress the fairy tale about the Duke of Buckingham) wrote to Saint-Mars:

> The King has commanded that I am to have the man named Eustache Dauger sent to Pignerol. It is of the utmost importance . . . that he should be securely guarded and that he should in no way give information about himself nor send any letters . . . You must on no account listen to what he may want to say to you, always threatening to kill him if he opens his mouth . . .

And the archive contained two letters from the king himself that underlined the same point. They make one thing very plain: that Eustache Dauger knew some astonishing secret, and that the king was quite determined that no one else should know it. Then why not execute Dauger? Possibly because Louis XIV was not as ruthless and cruel as that; possibly because he had a certain affection for Dauger. Possibly even because the king was hoping that Dauger might one day reveal some great secret . . .

It was a historian called Jules Lair who first advanced the theory that the man in the mask was Eustache Dauger; he did this in a life of the finance minister Nicholas Fouquet, who was also condemned to life imprisonment by the king. Fouquet, born in 1615, had been a protégé of Cardinal Richelieu, and when Mazarin – Richelieu's ally and successor – died in 1661 everyone expected Fouquet to become the king's chief minister. But the young king – he was only twenty-three – was sick of Fouquet, who had become immensely wealthy as a result of his office. He may also have been jealous of Fouquet, who had tried to seduce Louise de la Vallière, the officer's daughter who became the king's mistress. The king appointed Jean-Baptiste Colbert, a shopkeeper's son, assistant to Fouquet, and Colbert soon reported that Fouquet was handing the king falsified accounts every afternoon. Fouquet made the mistake of inviting the king to his château and entertaining him with extravagant magnificence, a magnificence the king knew was bought with public money. Fouquet was arrested, tried, and sentenced to life imprisonment in the fortress of Pignerol. And in 1675 the "ancient prisoner", Eustache Dauger, was allowed to become Fouquet's valet. There can have been only two possible reasons. Either Fouquet already knew Dauger's secret of the "ancient prisoner", or it did not matter if he found out, since he himself would never be released.

But who was Eustache Dauger, and what had he done? The first question proved slightly easier to answer than the second. In the late 1920s the historian Maurice Duvivier set out to track him down. The doctor who had attended him in the Bastille had mentioned his age as about sixty. That meant he must have been born in the late 1630s. Duvivier searched the records tirelessly for a Dauger – or D'Auger, or Danger, or Oger, or Daugé – who might fit the bill. Eventually he found one in the records of the Bibliothèque Nationale, a man called Oger de Cavoye, a member of the minor gentry of Picardy. Eustache Oger (also spelt Dauger) de Cavoye was the son of François de Cavoye, the captain of Cardinal Richelieu's musketeers, and he was born on 30 August 1637. He was one of six brothers, four of whom died in battle. The fifth, Louis Dauger de Cavoye, had become one of Louis XIV's most trusted officials. But Eustache seems to have been the ne'er-do-well of the family. And the more Duvivier studied him, the more certain he became that he was the man in the iron mask.

Eustache's father, François de Cavoye, went to court to seek his fortune about 1620. Like Dumas's D'Artagnan, he soon achieved celebrity for his courage. (D'Artagnan was in fact a real person, and he escorted Fouquet to Pignerol prison.) He married a young widow, Marie de Sérignan, and became the captain of the cardinal's guard in 1630. Marie was extremely popular in her own right, and became a friend of Richelieu and of the king, and a maid of honour to the queen. So her sons were brought up at court, and the young Eustache was a playmate of the young Louis XIV – which seems to explain why Louis was unwilling to have him executed. François de Cavoye was killed at the siege of Bapaume in 1641, but his widow's position ensured that the children continued to be favoured at court. But four of the brothers were to die in the army. Eustache, who was also a soldier, had served in seven campaigns by the time he was twenty-one.

In 1659, when he was twenty-two, Eustache Dauger seems to have been involved in an extremely strange incident. He was present on the Good Friday of that year at a black mass in the Castle of Roissy, in which a pig was christened and eaten. The scandal was tremendous, and a number of careers were ruined, but Eustache seems to have escaped punishment, probably because of the respect in which his mother was held at Court. But six years later he was involved in another scandal which forced him to resign his commission. There was some sort of quarrel with a page-boy outside the old castle of St Germain; one account (by the Duc d'Enghien) says that the page was drunk, and that he managed to strike the Duc de Foix with his pike as he staggered past him. A quarrel flared, and "a man called Cavoye" killed the page. This was regarded as an act of sacrilege, since the place was sanctified by the king's presence. The Duc de Foix escaped unpunished, but Cavoye was forced to sell his commission. That the Cavoye referred to was Eustache Dauger is proved by the fact that he also ceased to be a guards officer in 1665, while his two surviving brothers Louis and Armand continued to serve the king.

Soon after the murder of the page, Eustache's mother died, and in her will declared that Louis Dauger, not his elder brother Eustache, should be the head of the family. She had apparently made this will fourteen months before the murder of the page, so we can only conclude that she already regarded Eustache as a scapegrace. She left him a pension for life of a thousand livres a year. Eustache seems to have been financially secure, and he and his brother Louis shared rooms in the Rue de Bourbon, not far from the Charity Hospital. But in 1668 Louis Dauger found himself in serious trouble. He had been trying to seduce a lady named Sidonia de Courcelles, whose husband objected. Louis fought a duel with him, and was arrested. The war minister Louvois was also interested in Sidonia, and he tried hard to get Louis sentenced to death. The finance minister Colbert saved him; but Louis spent the next four years in the Bastille. When he emerged he continued to rise in the world. But by then his brother Eustache was in Pignerol.

Why? What had Eustache done? Duvivier's theory is that he had played some part in the infamous "affair of the poisons", or rather, in a curtain-raiser to it that occurred in 1668. The "affair of the poisons" began in 1673, when the police chief, Nicolas de la Reynie, heard rumours of wealthy ladies who were admitting in the confessional that they had poisoned their husbands. It took La Reynie four years to uncover an incredible "poisons ring" run by fortune-tellers and priests who practised the black mass. Many ladies of the court were involved, and so (this came as a deep shock to the king) was Madame de Montespan, the king's mistress. Her aim was to secure the king's love and to weaken the influence of her rival Louise de la Vallière, and she took part in a black mass, allowing her naked belly to be used as the altar, while a priest named Guibourg slit the throat of a baby. In another ceremony to concoct a love potion for the king, drops of a woman's menstrual blood were mixed with a man's sperm – the latter obtained by getting a man to masturbate into a holy chalice. All this so horrified the king that he ordered it to be investigated in the utmost secrecy in a room lit only by candles, known as the Chambre Ardente (lighted room) – and that no hint of it should be allowed to reach the public. Most of the leading figures in the affair of the poisons were burned alive. Mme de Montespan was disgraced.

In 1668, five years before La Reynie heard the first hints about the poison ring, there had been another "poison scare" in Paris, and a "sorcerer" named Le Sage and his assistant, the Abbé Mariette, were charged with witchcraft. There was much talk about love potions, black masses, and ladies of the court. The name of Madame de Montespan was mentioned for the first time, but hastily suppressed. Le Sage was sentenced to the galleys for life, while the Abbé Mariette, who had influential relatives, escaped with nine years' banishment.

Now in the later affair of the poisons, the Abbé Guibourg admitted that he had been paid to say a black mass at the home of the Duchesse d'Orléans by a surgeon who lived in the St-Germain quarter, near the Charity Hospital, with his brother. This is where Eustache Dauger and *his* brother lived in 1668. And another piece of evidence from the Chambre Ardente trial referred to a surgeon called d'Auger, who supplied "drugs". Duvivier speculates that this "surgeon" d'Auger was Eustache, and that it was his involvement in the Le Sage-Mariette affair that led to his banishment. Evidence showed that Eustache Dauger had been arrested at Dunkirk by special order of the king; he was apparently about to flee to England. So Duvivier could be right. Eustache Dauger could be the surgeon d'Auger involved in the sorcery case. But that still fails to explain why the king should conduct the whole affair with such secrecy. After all, the Abbé Mariette was banished, and so had plenty of opportunity to open his mouth about any sinister secrets he knew about the king and Dauger. Somehow Duvivier's theory that Dauger's crime was sorcery or selling poisons fails to carry conviction.

There is another and rather more interesting possibility that links Dauger with the mystery of Rennes-le-Château (see Chapter 44). In his book *The Holy Blood and the Holy Grail*, Henry Lincoln states that Fouquet, the disgraced finance minister, may have been the man in the iron mask. This as we know is impossible; Fouquet died in 1680, twenty-three years before the "ancient prisoner". But Lincoln also points out that in 1656 Fouquet's brother Louis was sent to Rome to see the painter Poussin, and that he wrote Fouquet a curious letter about some secret which would give him "through M. Poussin, advantages which even kings would have great pains to draw from him". This secret is assumed to be something to do with the hidden treasure of Rennes-le-

Château. Poussin's painting *The Shepherds of Arcady*, which contains important keys to the mystery, was acquired by Louis XIV and kept in his private rooms where no one could see it. Is it possible that Fouquet knew the secret of Rennes-le-Château, and that the king had him imprisoned in Pignerol – where he was not allowed to speak to anyone – to try to force him to disclose the secret? There is yet another possibility linked with Rennes-le-Château. Lincoln reveals that an important part of the mystery concerns a secret order called the Priory of Sion, whose aim is to restore the Merovingian dynasty to the throne of France. In the seventeenth century the Merovingians – descendants of King Merovech – were the house of Lorraine. The younger brother of Louis XIII, Gaston d'Orléans, was married to the Duke of Lorraine's sister, and there was an attempt to depose Louis and put Gaston in his place – which would have meant that Gaston's Merovingian descendants would have been once more on the throne of France. The attempt failed, but it was still possible that Gaston's heirs would succeed to the throne, since Louis XIII was childless. Then, as we know, Anne of Austria astonished everyone by conceiving the child who became Louis XIV . . .

Lincoln writes: "According to both contemporary and later writers, the child's true father was Cardinal Richelieu, or perhaps a 'stud' employed by Richelieu . . ."

And who could such a "stud" have been? The obvious candidate is Richelieu's handsome young captain of musketeers, François Dauger de Cavoye. There are many stories about the conception of Louis XIV – how, for example, Richelieu plotted to bring the king and his queen together, and how Louis took refuge with Anne of Austria during a thunderstorm, as a result of which the child was conceived. It is of course possible that Louis XIV was conceived as a result of one single encounter between the king and queen, but far more likely that Richelieu arranged the encounter so that Louis would have reason to believe the child was his own . . .

Several writers mention the resemblance between Louis Dauger de Cavoye, Eustache's younger brother, and Louis XIV. This would be understandable if the two were, in fact, half-brothers.

And so at last we have a theory that seems to explain the mystery of the man in the mask. François de Cavoye was the "stud" who made sure that an heir to the throne was born, thus frustrating the aspirations of the Merovingians (and the Priory of Sion). Eustache and Louis Dauger both knew that the king was really their half-brother; this is why Louis became a royal favourite after his release from the Bastille. He could be relied upon to keep a secret. But the ne'er-do-well Eustache was a different story. After his downfall, his resignation from the guards, and the arrest and imprisonment of his brother, he began to talk too much. Perhaps he tried some form of blackmail on the king: release my brother or else . . . That would certainly explain why Louis had him whisked away to Pignerol and kept incommunicado, and why he later made sure that the "ancient prisoner" always accompanied the governor Saint-Mars when he moved to another prison. It is also conceivable that Eustache became involved with the Priory of Sion and the plot to place a Merovingian on the throne of France – after all, what better reason could there be for replacing the king than revealing that he was not the true son of Louis XIII? Fouquet probably knew the secret already, since he also seems to have had connection with the Priory. (Lincoln speculates that this is why Fouquet was arrested and tried; Louis tried hard to have Fouquet sentenced to death, but the court refused.) That is why Eustache was allowed to become Fouquet's valet. But when another old acquaintance of Dauger's, the Duc de Lauzun, was imprisoned in Pignerol after an escapade, he and Dauger were carefully kept apart.

This theory could explain many things. It could explain, for example, why the war minister Louvois (who undoubtedly knew the secret) told his mistress that the masked prisoner was the son of the Duke of Buckingham and Anne of Austria. It was not too far from the truth; it explained why the king should want to keep the prisoner's existence a secret; but it made the prisoner the illegitimate child rather than the king. It would also explain why Dauger was obliged to wear a mask when other people were around: like his brother, he probably resembled the king. It is almost impossible to imagine why a man should be obliged to wear a mask unless his face itself is an important key to his secret.

It must be admitted that there is also one strong objection to this theory. When King Louis XV was finally told the secret of the man in the mask by his regent, the Duc d'Orléans, he is reported to have exclaimed, "If he were still alive I would give him his freedom". Would the king really have thought it unimportant that his grandfather was the son of Richelieu's captain of musketeers? Perhaps; after all, his own throne was now secure. But there is another story of Louis XV that casts rather more doubt on the theory. When the Duc de Choiseul asked him about the mysterious prisoner he refused to say anything except: "All conjectures which have been made hitherto are false". Then he added a baffling afterthought: "If you knew all about it, you would see that it has very little interest". If this comment is true – and not simply an attempt to allay the duke's curiosity – then it suggests that all the thousands of pages that have been written about the man in the iron mask are "much ado about nothing".

33

The Mystery of the *Mary Celeste*

On a calm afternoon of 5 December 1872 the English ship *Dei Gratia* sighted a two-masted brig pursuing an erratic course in the North Atlantic, midway between the Azores and the coast of Portugal. As they came closer they could see that she was sailing with only her jib and foretop mast staysail set; moreover, the jib was set to port, while the vessel was on a starboard tack – a sure sign to any sailor that the ship was out of control. Captain Morehouse of the *Dei Gratia* signalled the mysterious vessel, but received no answer. The sea was running high after recent squalls, and it took a full two hours before Morehouse could get close enough to read the name of the vessel. It was the *Mary Celeste*. Morehouse knew this American ship and its master, Captain Benjamin Spooner Briggs. Less than a month ago both vessels had been loading cargo on neighbouring piers on New York's East River. The *Mary Celeste* had set sail for Genoa with a cargo of crude alcohol on 5 November, ten days before the *Dei Gratia* had sailed for Gibraltar; yet now, a month later, she was drifting in mid-Atlantic with no sign of life.

Morehouse sent three men to investigate, led by his first mate Oliver Deveau, a man of great physical strength and courage. As they clambered aboard they saw that the ship's decks were deserted; a search below revealed that there was not a living soul on board. But the lifeboat was missing, indicating that Captain Briggs had decided to abandon ship.

There was a great deal of water below decks; two sails had been blown away, and the lower foretop sails were hanging by their corners. Yet the ship seemed seaworthy, and was certainly in no danger of sinking. Then why had the crew abandoned her? Further research revealed that the binnacle, the box containing the ship's compass, had been smashed, and the compass itself was broken. Two cargo hatches had been ripped off, and one of the casks of crude alcohol had been stoved in. Both forward and aft storage lockers contained a plentiful supply of food and water.

The seamen's chests were still in the crew's quarters, an indication of the haste in which the ship had been deserted. But a search of the captain's cabin revealed that the navigation instruments and navigation log were missing. The last entry in the general log was dated 25 November; it meant that the *Mary Celeste* had sailed without crew for at least nine days, and that she was now some 700 miles north-east of her last recorded position.

Apart from Captain Briggs and a crew of seven, the *Mary Celeste* had also sailed with Brigg's wife Sarah and his two-year old daughter Sophia Matilda. Faced with the mystery of why they had abandoned ship for no obvious reason, Morehouse experienced a certain superstitious alarm when Deveau suggested that two of the *Dei Gratia's* crew should sail the *Mary Celeste* to Gibraltar; it was the prospect of £5,000 salvage money that finally made him agree to Deveau's scheme.

Both ships arrived in Gibraltar harbour six days later. And instead of the welcome he expected, Deveau was greeted by an English bureaucrat who nailed an order of immediate arrest to the *Mary Celeste's* mainmast. The date significantly was Friday the 13th.

From the beginning the *Mary Celeste* had been an unlucky ship. She was registered originally as the *Amazon*, and her first captain had died within forty-eight hours. On her maiden voyage she had hit a fishing weir off the coast of Maine, and damaged her hull. While this was being repaired a fire had broken out amidships. Later, while sailing through the Straits of Dover, she hit another brig, which sank. This had occurred under her third captain; her fourth accidentally ran the ship aground on Cape Brenton Island and wrecked her.

The *Amazon* was salvaged, and passed through the hands of three more owners before she was bought by J.H. Winchester, the founder of a successful shipping line which still operates in New York. Winchester discovered that the brig – which had now been renamed *Mary Celeste* – had dry rot in her timbers, and he had the bottom rebuilt with copper lining and the deck cabin lengthened. These repairs had ensured that the ship was in excellent condition before she had sailed for Genoa under the experienced Captain Briggs – this helped to explain why she had survived so long in the wintry Atlantic after the crew had taken to the lifeboat.

British officials at Gibraltar seemed to suspect either mutiny or some Yankee plot – the latter theory based on the fact that Captain Morehouse and Captain Briggs had been friends, and had apparently dined together the day before the *Mary Celeste* had sailed from New York. But at the inquiry that followed, the idea of mutiny seemed to have gained favour. To back this theory the Court of Inquiry was shown an axe-mark on one of the ship's rails, scoring on her hull that was described as a crude attempt to make the ship look as if she had hit rocks, and a stained sword that was found beneath the captain's bunk. All this, it was claimed, pointed to the crew getting drunk, killing the master and his family, and escaping in the ship's boat.

The Americans were insulted by what they felt was a slur on the honour of the US Merchant Navy, and indignantly denied this story. They pointed out that Briggs was not only known to be a fair man who was not likely to provoke his crew to mutiny, but also that he ran a dry ship; the only alcohol on the *Mary Celeste* was the cargo. And even a thirsty sailor would not be likely to drink more than a mouthful of crude alcohol – it would cause severe stomach pains and eventual blindness. Besides, if the crew had mutinied, why should they leave behind their sea-chests together with such items as family photographs, razors and sea-boots?

The British Admiralty remained unconvinced, but had to admit that if the alternative theory was correct, and Briggs and Morehouse had decided to make a false claim for salvage, Briggs would actually have lost by the deal – he was part-owner of the ship, and his share of any salvage would have come to a fraction of what he could have made by selling his share in the normal way.

In March 1873 the court was finally forced to admit that it was unable to decide why the *Mary Celeste* had been abandoned, the first time in its history that it had failed to come to a definite conclusion. The *Dei Gratia's* owners were awarded one-fifth of the value of the *Mary Celeste* and her cargo. The brig herself was returned to her owner, who lost no time in selling her the moment she got back to New York.

During the next eleven years the *Mary Celeste* had many owners, but brought little profit to any of them. Sailors were convinced she was unlucky. Her last owner, Captain Gilman C. Parker, ran her aground on a reef in the West Indies and made a claim for insurance. The insurers became suspicious, and Parker and his associates were brought to trial. At that time the penalty for deliberately scuttling a ship on the high seas was death by hanging; but the judge, mindful of the *Mary Celeste's* previous record of bad luck, allowed the men to be released on a technicality. Within eight months Captain Parker was dead, one of the associates had gone mad, and another had committed suicide. The *Mary Celeste* herself had been left to break up on the reef.

Over the next decade or so, as no new evidence came to light, interest in the story waned. During the trial, when fraud was still suspected, a careful watch had been kept on the major ports of England and America. But there was no sign of any of the missing crew.

In the year 1882 a 23-year-old newly qualified doctor named Arthur Doyle moved to Southsea, a suburb of Portsmouth, and screwed up his nameplate. And during the long weeks of waiting for patients he whiled away the time writing short stories. It was in the autumn of 1882 that he began a story: "In the month of December 1873, the British ship *Dei Gratia* steered into Gibraltar, having in tow a derelict brigantine *Marie Celeste*, which had been picked up in the latitude 38°40', longitude 70°15' west".

For such a short sentence, this contains a remarkable number of inaccuracies. The year was actually 1872; the *Dei Gratia* did not tow the *Marie Celeste*, the latter came under its own sail; the latitude and longitude are wrong; and the ship was called plain English Mary, not Marie. All the same, when "J. Habakuk Jephson's Statement" was published in the *Cornhill* magazine in 1884 it caused a sensation, launching Arthur Doyle's career as a writer – he was soon using the name A. Conan Doyle. Most people took it for the truth, and from then on it was widely accepted that the *Mary Celeste* had been taken over by a kind of Black Power leader with a hatred of Whites. Mr Solly Flood, the chief investigator in the *Mary Celeste* case, was so indignant that he sent a telegram to the Central News Agency denouncing J. Habakuk Jephson as a fraud and a liar. From then on the *Cornhill* was willing to publish most of Conan Doyle's stories at thirty guineas a time instead of the three guineas he had been paid so far.

Doyle's story was the signal for a new interest in the mystery, and over the next few years there were a number of hoax accounts of the last days of the *Mary Celeste*. They told all kinds of stories from straight-forward mutinies to mass accidents – such as everyone falling into the sea when a platform made to watch a swimming race gave way, or the finding of another derelict carrying gold bullion, which tempted Captain Briggs to leave his own ship drifting while he escaped in the other one. One author argued that all the crew had been dragged through the ship's portholes at night by a ravenous giant squid, while Charles Fort, the eminent paranormal researcher, suggested the crew had been snatched away by the same strange force that causes rains of frogs and live fish. Fort added, "I have a collection of yarns, by highly individualized liars, or artists who scorned, in any particular, to imitate one another; who told, thirty, forty, or fifty years later, of having been members of this crew". Even today the *Mary Celeste* often sails un-suspectingly into TV serials and Sci-Fi movies to become involved in time warps or attacked by aliens in UFOs.

In fact, a careful study of the facts reveals that the solution of this particular mystery is obvious.

The man most responsible for the perpetuation of the myth about the *Mary Celeste* was Conan Doyle: it was he who insisted that the ship's boats were still intact. This small inaccuracy made an otherwise simple problem virtually insoluble.

In fact, once we know that the boat was missing, we at least know one thing for certain: that the crew abandoned ship, apparently in great haste – the wheel was not lashed, an indication that the ship was abandoned in a hurry. The question then presents itself: what could have caused everyone on board to abandon the ship in such a hurry?

Captain James Briggs, the brother of the *Mary Celeste*'s skipper, was convinced that the clue lay in the last entry in the log, for the morning of 25 November 1872: it stated that the wind had dropped after a night of heavy squalls. James Briggs believed the ship may have become be-calmed in the Azores, and started to drift towards the dangerous rocks of Santa Maria Island. The gash-marks found along the side of the *Mary Celeste* – which the British investigators had claimed were deliberately made by the ship's mutinous crew – may have been made when she actually rubbed against a submerged rock, convincing the crew that she was about to sink.

Oliver Deveau proposed that during the storms some water had found its way from between decks into the hold, giving the impression that the ship was leaking.

Another popular explanation is that a waterspout hit the *Mary Celeste*. The atmospheric pressure inside a waterspout is low; this could have caused the hatch-covers to blow open and forced bilge water into the pump well; this would have made it look as if the ship had taken on six to eight feet of water and was sinking fast.

There are basic objections to all these three answers. If the ship scraped dangerous rocks off Santa Maria Island, then the lifeboat would have been close enough to land on the Island. Since no survivors were found and no wreckage from the lifeboat, this seems unlikely.

Oliver Deveau's theory has a great deal more in its favour. There have often been panics at sea. When Captain Cook's *Endeavour* was in difficulties off the coast of eastern Australia the ship's carpenter was sent to take a reading of the water in the hold. He made a mistake, and the resulting hysteria might have ended with the crew leaving the ship if

Cook had not been able to control the panic. On another occasion a ship which was carrying a hold full of timber dumped the whole lot into the sea off Newfoundland, before anyone realized that it would be next to impossible to sink a ship full of wood. But it seems unlikely that a captain of Briggs's known efficiency would allow some simple misreading to cause a panic.

The objection to the waterspout theory is that, apart from the open hatches, the ship was completely undamaged. If a waterspout was big enough to cause such a panic, it would surely have caused far more havoc.

In any case, the real mystery is why, if the crew left the *Mary Celeste* in the lifeboat, they made no attempt to get back on board when they saw that the ship was in no danger of sinking.

Only one explanation covers all the facts. Briggs had never shipped crude alcohol before, and being a typical New England puritan, undoubtedly mistrusted it. The change in temperature between New York and the Azores would have caused casks of alcohol to sweat and leak. The night of storms, in which the barrels would have been shaken violently, would have caused vapour to form inside the casks, slowly building up pressure until the lids of two or three blew off. The explosion, though basically harmless, might have blown the hatches off the cargo hold on to the deck in the positions in which Deveau later found them. Convinced that the whole ship was about to explode, Briggs ordered everyone into the lifeboat. In his haste, he failed to take the one simple precaution that would have saved their lives – to secure the lifeboat to the *Mary Celeste* by a few hundred yards of cable. The sea was fairly calm when the boat was lowered, as we know from the last entry in the log, but the evidence of the torn sails indicates that the ship then encountered severe gales. We may conjecture that the rising wind blew the *Mary Celeste* into the distance, while the crew in the lifeboat rowed frantically in a futile effort to catch up. The remainder of the story is tragically obvious.

34

Glenn Miller

The Strange Disappearance
of a Bandleader

On 24 December 1944, an official press release stated that "Major Alton Glenn Miller, Director of the famous United States Army Air Force Band, which has been playing in Paris, is reported missing while on a flight from London to Paris. The plane in which he was a passenger left England on 15 December and no trace of it has been found since its take-off".

Glenn Miller's rise to fame and wealth had not been an easy one. Born in Clarinda, Iowa, in March 1904, he learned to play the trombone at thirteen and helped to pay his way at the University of Colorado by playing with local dance bands. He joined Ben Pollack's band at the age of twenty and over the next ten years became known in New York as an arranger as well as a trombonist, playing with Red Nichols, Smith Ballew, and the Dorsey brothers. A dance orchestra he organized for Ray Noble in 1934 became popular through its broadcasts, but Miller's own orchestra, organized in 1937, was a failure. A second orchestra, organized in the following year, did little better.

The breakthrough came in March 1939, when the band played at the Glen Island Casino in a suburb of New York and the audience was overwhelmed with enthusiasm at this new, distinctive, Glenn Miller sound, with its smooth, almost syrupy, brass. Radio broadcasts spread the fever across the country, and Miller was soon a rich man. Although he lacked the sheer inventive genius of other jazzmen of the period – Benny Goodman, Duke Ellington, and Count Basie, for example – the "seamless and rich" perfection of numbers like "Moonlight Serenade" made him the favourite of the American middle classes, while "hot" numbers like "In the Mood" and "Tuxedo Junction" made him popular with a younger generation that was learning to jive. He went to Hollywood and made two classic films, *Orchestra Wives* (1941) and *Sun Valley Serenade* (1942). During this period he became a friend of actor David Niven – a friendship that, as we shall see, plays an odd part in the mystery of Glenn Miller's disappearance.

In 1942, as a patriotic gesture, Miller joined the air force. He soon assembled another band and was assigned to entertaining the troops abroad. He was sent to London. David Niven had also joined up – but in the British Army. Since he was a famous show-business personality, he was also given an important post in armed-forces entertainment, and one of his jobs was to organize Glenn Miller's tours. He was, in effect, Miller's boss. The man actually in charge of organizing the details of Miller's tours – hotel and travel arrangements – was Lieutenant Don Haynes, Miller's former booking agent, now also in the U.S. Air Force.

In November 1944 Niven organized a six-week tour for Miller's band, starting on Saturday, 16 December. The band was due to fly to Paris on that day. But on 12 December, as Don Haynes and Miller were walking back to their London hotel, Miller told Haynes – according to Haynes's later story – that he wanted to go a day early because he had a social engagement. Haynes said he would book Miller on a flight from RAF Bovingdon, northwest of London, the usual takeoff point for Continental flights.

The following day, Wednesday, 13 December, Haynes claims he left Miller in London and drove back to Bedford, where the band was housed in billets, to arrange their flight. The following morning, he claims, he ran into Lieutenant-Colonel Norman Baessell, who was special assistant to the station commander at RAF Milton Ernest, near Bedford. Baessell mentioned that he would be flying to Paris the next day – Thursday – and offered Haynes a lift. Haynes declined, saying he would be flying with the band on Saturday, but mentioned that Glenn Miller would like a lift. Haynes telephoned Miller, who accepted the offer; Haynes went to London to collect him and took him back to RAF Milton Ernest.

The next morning Haynes collected Miller and Baessell and took them to the nearby airfield, Twinwood Farm. At about 1:40, their plane arrived – a small American prop-driven plane called a Norseman, piloted by Flight Officer John R. S. Morgan. In spite of appalling weather conditions, they took off five minutes later – and vanished.

We now know what happened to the plane. It flew across the channel toward Dieppe but began to experience engine trouble; the pilot was forced to ditch in the sea only six miles west of Le Touquet, which is some distance north of Dieppe. The plane was located in 1973 and examined by an independent diver seven years later. Its propeller was missing. This suggested a leak in the hydraulic system, which failed to adjust the blades to the required speed; the propeller "oversped" and probably fell off.

Now as strange as it sounds, no one at the time seems to have realized what had happened. On Monday (the flight was delayed by bad weather) the band arrived at Orly Airport, near Paris, and Haynes was puzzled when Miller failed to turn up to meet them. Haynes spent the rest of Monday, and the whole of the following day, searching Paris – which had recently been liberated – for the bandleader. He finally contacted General Ray Barker, who was in charge of all U.S. military personnel in Paris. Two days later, when the band played its first Paris engagement, the audience was simply told that "Major Miller could not be with the band". Miller's death was announced three days later.

That was the story. But Miller's wife, Helen – the childhood sweetheart whom he had married – didn't want to believe it. To begin with, she hoped that he had been taken prisoner. And when, after the end of the war, it became clear that this was a forlorn hope, she began instituting inquiries that involved searching war cemeteries, hoping that at least she could find a grave that she could visit. In February 1946 a certain Colonel Donnell wrote in answer to her inquiry to tell her that her husband had not been flying in one of the passenger planes but in a combat aircraft not designed for passengers. This aircraft, he said, was cleared to fly from Abbotts Ripton Field, near Huntington, *to Bordeaux*. Now Bordeaux is long way short of Paris, and Helen Miller must have found herself wondering whether her husband was supposed to walk the extra distance. Of course, the Norseman could have been intended to land at Paris and then go on to Bordeaux; but if so, the clearance would have said as much. The letter concluded by telling her firmly that no further information was available.

The rumor that there had been some sort of cover-up in the case led various researchers to try to track down the official documents. One of these, an ex-RAF officer named John Edwards, dismissed the cover-up theory and set out to prove that Glenn Miller *had* been on board the Norseman when it crashed. It was simply, he thought, a matter of getting the official form – called a 201 – about Miller's death from the Washington file where it must be kept. But he found it to be a less simple task than he expected. The Records Office in Washington denied all knowledge of the file. The National Personnel Records Center in St Louis said they thought the records had been lost in a fire. It began to dawn on Edwards that *somebody* had a reason for sitting on the evidence.

Another RAF man, Squadron Leader Jack Taylor, decided to have a try. He succeeded in obtaining the MACR (Missing Air Crew Report) but found that the signature was illegible and the typed details so blurred as to be almost unreadable. Two other documents he succeeded in obtaining showed only that no kind of search for Glenn Miller had been instituted at the time. This in itself seemed odd, for the Allies were by then in control of most of France, and there would have been nothing to prevent a thorough search for the famous bandleader.

It was Taylor who approached another ex-RAF pilot named Wilbur Wright, who had become a highly successful novelist and therefore had time to spare. It was true that, by 1986, most of the witnesses were dead; but Wright reasoned that it ought to be straightforward enough to obtain whatever records existed. If there was any difficulty, he could invoke the Freedom of Information Act. And so Wilbur Wright took a deep breath and wrote to the United States Air Force Inspection and Safety Center in Norton, California, for the accident report on the missing plane. The reply stated that they had no record of an accident involving a Norseman on that date. A second letter drew from them the reply that no Norseman airplanes had been reported missing in December 1944. But Wright had a way of checking this – a document called the Cumulative Loss Listing. And this told him that there had been no fewer than *eight* Norseman airplanes lost in December 1944.

Wright began to smell a rat. And when letters to the Washington Records Office, the Army Casualty Division, and the Air Force History department met with similar blanks, one thing at least became obvious. This was not vagueness or incompetence; he was being deliberately stonewalled. Another letter to the Casualty Division in Alexandria, Virginia, brought a fascinating revelation. They admitted plaintively that they had been trying for years to obtain the Glenn Miller file from Washington and had been totally ignored.

Over the next month or so Wright kept up a furious barrage of letters to various agencies. He even wrote directly to President Reagan, asking him to intervene. He secured one grudging admission from Military Reference, admitting that there were several documents in the Miller file and listing them. But the Washington Records Office continued to insist that all documents had been lost or mislaid. In January 1987 Wright telephoned the records office and demanded to talk to the "top man". He was put through to a Mr George Chalou, and he explained that he was a professional author and wanted to see the Glenn Miller burial file. He added that he had written repeatedly and got nowhere and that the Casualty Division people in Alexandria complained that

Washington would not give them the file. "Right"!, said Mr Chalou, "and there's no way they'll get them back either. Those files have been under lock and key for years, and that's how they'll stay". Wilbur Wright, who was recording the conversation, stared at the phone in dumbstruck astonishment. At last he had an admission that the file was being kept under wraps.

He went on to mention that he had written to Ronald Reagan – but did not mention that so far he had received no reply. That drew a gasp of *"You didn't!"* followed by a demand for Wright's telephone number. But there was no return telephone call – only more letters assuring Wright that he had now received all the information that was available. But further pressure elicited the reply that the missing file had now been found and that when Wright came to visit the office, he would see the "original MACR". That confirmed what Wright had already deduced: that the MACR obtained by Squadron Leader Jack Taylor was a fake.

The Washington Records Office then decided to send the file to the Casualty Division in Virginia, assuring them that it had only just been located. Virginia wrote to Wright telling him that they had now mailed him a copy of the missing file. And eventually, weeks later, the file finally arrived.

This – as might be expected – included no astounding revelations; if it had, presumably it would not have been sent. But it confirmed one thing: the Missing Air Crew Report obtained by Taylor was not the original; close study revealed that it had been altered. Moreover, only page 1 had been included; page 2, which should have contained the signature, was missing. And when, with his usual incredible persistence, Wright obtained the missing page – which turned up in the pilot's Burial File – it had no signature. The later "signed" version *was* a fabrication. So why had the original unsigned version not been given to Taylor – or released soon after the accident? Obviously, because it had *not* been signed, and this would have caused suspicion. Because Captain Ralph S. Cramer, who should have signed it, must have known that he would have been putting his signature to something that was untrue, he preferred not to.

All this, Wright realized, sounded inconclusive; perhaps Cramer was in a hurry and forgot to sign it; perhaps the Washington Records Office genuinely mislaid the file. But there was one other piece of evidence that Wilbur Wright felt was far more striking: the actor David Niven had been a friend of Miller's since they had met in Hollywood in the early 1940s. As mentioned earlier, he was Miller's "boss" when Miller came to London as a member of the U.S. Air Force, and he arranged that final tour, which was never made. Yet in his bestselling autobiography, *The Moon's a Balloon*, Niven did not even mention Glenn Miller. And he also failed to say anything about him to his biographer, Sheridan Morley.

There is an equally odd omission in Niven's autobiography. He was in Paris at the time of Miller's disappearance, arranging a tour for Marlene Dietrich, another old friend – in fact, she, Niven, and Miller met for dinner whenever they could. The Battle of the Bulge – in which the Germans tried to relaunch the offensive against the Allies – began on the day after Miller "disappeared", and Marlene Dietrich (who was, of course, German, and could have been shot as a traitor if captured) had to be hastily evacuated to Paris. Niven made a frantic phone call to a colleague in England, Colonel Hignett, to try to borrow a squad of "rough-necks" (commandos) to go and rescue Miss Dietrich. Hignett had to refuse, since all his men were on red alert. Then why did Niven fail to mention this important episode in his autobiography? He mentions the period but says he was elsewhere, at a place called Spa, two hundred miles from Paris. And a biography of Marlene Dietrich confirms that she and Niven were together on the day before Miller "disappeared" and that she was "rescued" from the German advance and returned to Paris.

Wright's conclusion was that Niven knew exactly what had happened to Glenn Miller and that whatever it was, it was not a drowning accident off Le Touquet. But if Miller was not on the Norseman when it crashed, where was he? Presumably in Paris, where he was supposed to be – and with Niven and Marlene Dietrich.

Assuming that that was correct, and that Miller flew to Paris – either on Thursday (the 14th) from Bovingdon, or on the following day – then what happened to him in Paris that led to a coverup?

Wright's lengthy investigation – far too lengthy to describe in detail – led him to study many possible scenarios. He lists these in his book *Millergate* (1990). Miller's brother Herb was convinced that Glenn never left England but that he died of cancer. This obviously raises the question of why a cover-up would have been necessary. There is nothing disgraceful about dying of cancer.

Another theory studied by Wright was that Miller's plane was shot down by German fighters. But the weather over the Continent on 15 December was so bad that all planes were grounded. Moreover, the Luftwaffe records make no mention of a plane being shot down over the Channel. Oddly enough, Wright's investigations revealed that the weather over Twinwood Airfield was still good and not, as Haynes claimed, appalling. The inference was that Haynes had invented the appalling weather to make his story more convincing.

Another rumor alleged that Miller had been taken prisoner and died in a prisoner-of-war camp. Wright dismisses this theory, pointing out that the Germans would have announced the capture of Glenn Miller to undermine Allied morale.

A more promising lead was connected with Lieutenant-Colonel Normal Baessell, who proved to have an extremely dubious reputation as a drug smuggler. Wright investigated a rumor that Baessell had been smuggling drugs to an airstrip in northern France on that fatal flight, that Glenn Miller had objected, and that Baessell had shot him and concealed the body; on their way back, the plane crashed. Wright's research revealed that Baessell was certainly a swashbuckling character, macho and aggressive, who would have been perfectly capable of drug smuggling. But there is not the slightest piece of confirmatory evidence that this is what happened.

One of the most interesting stories was told by a man named Dennis Cottam, who had gone to Paris in 1954 to pick up a car. In a place called Fred's Bar, not far from the Hotel Olympiades in Montmartre, where the Miller band had stayed, Cottam was told by the bartender, "You English think Glenn Miller died in the Channel on 15 December 1944, yet he was drinking in here that same evening". He told Cottam that if he wanted confirmation of this story, he should go to a blue-painted door on the other side of the street and ask the lady there about Glenn Miller. The door turned out to be that of a brothel, and the Madame there told Cottam that in 1944 her boyfriend had been a Provost Marshall Captain and that he had told her that he saw and identified the body of Glenn Miller. But why was he killed? Cottam wanted to know. "Because he knew too much about the Black Market".

That was certainly interesting. But would Black Marketeers really kill a famous bandleader who had only been in Paris for twenty-four hours or so – scarcely enough time to learn much about the Black Market?

Interviews with researcher John Edwards also brought some interesting insights. He obtained a tape made by a BBC engineer named Teddy Gower, who claimed that he had flown to Paris (Orly) with Glenn Miller from Bovingdon on Thursday, 14 December, the day Miller had actually *wanted* to fly. Don Haynes had admitted that Miller wanted to fly to Orly on the 14th, and that he (Haynes) had promised to arrange a flight from Bovingdon, the usual airfield for Continental flights. Yet, according to Haynes, he had changed his mind and accepted Baessell's offer to give Miller a lift to Paris on the following day, Friday.

But why *should* Miller prefer a "lift" in a small plane (Miller hated small planes) on Friday to a comfortable trip in a larger Dakota on Thursday? Wright had already found many inconsistencies in Haynes's story that led him to believe that he was lying. For example, Haynes claimed that he had driven back to Bedford on the Wednesday afternoon in thick fog, when Wright was able to uncover evidence that he and Glenn Miller had spent that evening at the Milroy Club with a group of officers and a girl singer. This, and much other evidence, convinced Wright that Haynes was closely involved in the cover-up. Miller *had* flown to Paris on the Thursday in a Dakota and had probably been met by David Niven, who was certainly in Paris that day.

John Edwards had another rather odd story to tell Wilbur Wright. Because of the publicity given to his search for Glenn Miller, he had received many letters. One of these was from a World War II veteran who claimed that he had not only known Major Glenn Miller but had been with Miller in a military hospital in Columbus, Ohio, when the bandleader died of head injuries. That sounded so absurd that Edwards had not even followed up the story but had thrown the letter into the wastebasket.

Edwards also told Wright about an American doctor named David Pecora who claimed to have been present at the time Glenn Miller died. With his usual incredible persistence, Wright finally succeeded in tracing Pecora. The result was disappointing – Pecora agreed that he had been in France at the time but said he had no knowledge of Glenn Miller.

Nevertheless, this false lead was to prove productive. Tracking down Pecora had involved much letter writing to New Jersey, the state where Miller had lived before he joined the U.S. Air Force, Wright decided to write to the State Registrar in New Jersey, asking if they had any record of the death of a Major Alton Glenn Miller; he gave all the necessary family details, including place and date of birth. But by accident he gave Miller's state of birth as Ohio instead of Iowa. He was astonished to receive a letter confirming that Alton Glenn Miller had died in Ohio in December 1944. A telephone call to the registrar in New Jersey confirmed that Alton Glenn Miller, later a resident of New Jersey, had died in Ohio. At this point, Wilbur Wright made a mistake. Instead of asking for further details of where Miller died, he told the woman on the other end of the telephone, "You realize we are talking about *the* Glenn Miller who vanished in Europe in 1944"? After a long silence, the woman said, "We'll call you back". In fact, she called back two days later to say that the typist had made an error. They had sent him Glenn Miller's place of birth instead of his place of death.

Wright was baffled. How could they confuse a place of birth in 1904 with a place of death in 1944? What's more, Wright said to the woman, Miller was born in Iowa, *not* Ohio. "It was a typing error", the woman insisted. "And anyway, Ohio, Iowa – it's the same state". Samuel Goldwyn is known to have confused the two, but it sounded strange coming from an employee of a State Registrar.

There was, Wright discovered, another oddity that needed explaining. In 1949 Helen Miller, who had moved to Pasadena, California, had purchased a six-grave burial plot in nearby Altadena. But the family consisted of only herself and the son and daughter she and Glenn had adopted; there were also her parents, who were, in due course, buried in the plot. Who was the extra grave for? The cemetery authorities were asked to deny that Glenn Miller was buried in the plot; it took them fifteen months to do so. They also sent Wilbur Wright's "confidential" inquiry to Glenn Miller's adopted son, Steve, whose response was to write an angry letter to Glenn's brother, Herb – who had replied to Wright's inquiries – saying: "Get this guy off our backs".

Then what *did* happen to Glenn Miller? By far the most persistent rumor Wright encountered was that Miller had received a fatal blow on the head in a brawl in a brothel in Pigalle, Paris. (Pigalle is known as the prostitute's area.) In a 1976 newspaper article, John Edwards speculated that Miller was murdered in Paris on the Monday that the band finally arrived. The article summarized, "Mr Edwards believes that Miller, who was a bit of a lad with the ladies, died of a fractured skull".

Wright was originally skeptical about this story, because he was able to disprove some of the other details given by Edwards – for example, his assertion that a Lieutenant-Colonel Corrigan was able to confirm the "murder". Wright traced Corrigan, who denied it. Edwards also claimed that an American doctor in Paris had signed the death certificate; this was presumably Dr Pecora, who denied all knowledge of Miller's death. Yet the sheer persistence of the story – which surfaced in Paris as early as 1948 – suggested that it could be true. And it certainly fits in with the rest of the information that Wilbur Wright accumulated.

This, then, is the outline of Wright's scenario of what happened to Glenn Miller:

Miller decided to go to Paris two days before the band in order to do some "socializing" – which included buying female companionship. He had arranged to meet his old friend David Niven, who would be there on 14 December to arrange Marlene Dietrich's tour. Niven's autobiography makes it clear that he was not averse to female companionship either, having been a flatmate of Errol Flynn. Niven probably met Miller off the Dakota that brought him from Bovingdon on Thursday, 15 December. Two days later Niven had to rush off to rescue Marlene Dietrich from becoming a victim of the Battle of the Bulge, but the two of them returned to Paris two days later and may well have joined Miller for a meal.

Miller went to a brothel in Pigalle, became involved in some kind of brawl, and was struck on the head. When Don Haynes arrived at Orly, he was puzzled that Miller wasn't there to meet him. He claims that he spent two days searching for Miller in Paris, but (as Wright points out) that would not have been necessary. He must have known where Miller was staying and checked there – probably discovering that Miller had been missing all night.

The badly injured Miller was located; it seemed clear that he might die. How could his death by violence be explained without a scandal? The cover-up began. Miller was flown to a military hospital in Columbus, Ohio. Meanwhile, the disappearance of the Norseman provided the perfect opportunity for explaining his nonappearance at the Paris concerts. When the disappearance of the Norseman was announced nine days after it had happened, Glenn Miller was already dead in Ohio. He was probably buried there. His wife, Helen, was informed that he had died in the Norseman, but she did not believe it. And eventually, the military authorities decided to tell her what had happened – presumably before she purchased the six-grave plot in Altadena.

Some time thereafter, Glenn Miller was transferred from his unmarked grave in Ohio to his resting place in Altadena. Helen joined him there in 1966. His friend Niven, one of the few who knew the secret, maintained an entirely uncharacteristic silence about Miller for the rest of his life, not even mentioning him to his second wife. Don Haynes later published his diaries, which appeared to confirm his story that Miller had flown to Paris from Twinwood on the morning of Friday, 15 December, in exceptionally bad weather. Wright's investigations revealed that the weather was reasonable on that date *but that the airfield was closed*.

Glenn Miller's records are as popular as ever, and their smooth, seamless sound is still one of the delights of the swing era. Perhaps, after all, Niven and Haynes were right when they decided that, as far as posterity was concerned, Miller had died in a mysterious airplane accident rather than in an undignified brawl in a Paris brothel.

35

The Missing Link

The Unsolved Mystery
of Human Evolution

One day in 1908, an amateur archaeologist named Charles Dawson, who made his living as a solicitor, was walking along a farm road near Piltdown Common in East Sussex, England, when he noted some peculiar brown flints that had been used to mend the road. When he learned that they had been found in a gravel bed on the farm, he went along to take a look at it. Two workmen were digging, and Dawson asked them if they had found any fossils; they said no. But when Dawson returned later, one of them handed him a piece of a human skull. Three years later, in the same place, Dawson found another piece.

In the following year, 1912, Dawson decided to show the pieces to his friend, Dr Arthur Smith Woodward, the keeper of the Department of Geology at the British Museum, and during that summer, Smith Woodward came to look at the site, bringing another geologist, the French priest Pierre Teilhard de Chardin (who was to become famous four years after his death, in 1955, for his book *The Phenomenon of Man*). They quickly discovered what Dawson described as a "human mandible" (lower jaw) with two molar teeth. Prehistoric animal bones and primitive human tools in the same gravel pit seemed to date the jaw as being about half a million years old. Part of a human skull also turned up in the pit.

This was a matter of great excitement, for man himself is only about half a million years old. At any rate, the sudden expansion of the brain that has become known as "the brain explosion" began – for reasons no one understands – half a million years ago. (The "first man", *Homo erectus*, dates back about one and a quarter million years but had a brain the size of an ape's.) What was so startling about this find was that the jaw was definitely apelike, yet it fit the cranium. They had apparently discovered something that science had been seeking for almost half a century – what Charles Darwin had called "the Missing Link", the definitive proof that man is descended from the ape.

It's hard for us to understand the scandal that had been caused by the publication of Darwin's *Origin of Species* in November 1859. Most of us take the notion of evolution for granted and regard biblical fundamentalism as an absurd joke. In 1859 Darwin's conclusions seemed to shake the foundations of Christianity, and therefore the foundations of British society. The first edition of the book actually sold out on its first day. And in spite of the caution with which he had phrased his conclusions – that all species emerge through natural selection due to the survival of the fittest – Darwin was soon being accused of atheism and downright wickedness. In 1859 most British people accepted that the account of creation in Genesis was entirely factual, and most accepted Archbishop Usher's estimate of the date of creation (worked out from the Bible) as 4004 BC.

Admittedly, Sir Charles Lyell had disproved this almost thirty years before in his *Principles of Geology*, in which he showed that the earth must be millions of years old. But somehow, this did not bother the Church too much – after all, if God created the rocks, he may well have created them with million-year-old fossils, in much the same way that you might stock a new library with old books. But Darwin was saying that man was not the "Lord of Creation", merely a latecomer descended from the ape. In a speech in Parliament, Disraeli made the famous comment that in the controversy about whether man was an ape or an angel, he was on the side of the angels.

The historic battle – evolutionism's equivalent of the Battle of Hastings – took place in Oxford on 30 June 1860, and the two leading debaters were Bishop Samuel Wilberforce – known as "Soapy Sam" because of his unctuous manner – and "Darwin's bulldog", biologist Thomas Henry Huxley. After Soapy Sam had given a humorous and satirical account of the theory of evolution, he turned politely to Huxley and "begged to know, was it through his grandfather or his grandmother that he claimed his descent from a monkey"? He sat down to roars of laughter and applause.

It is reported that Huxley slapped his knee and whispered to his neighbour, "The Lord hath delivered him into my hands". Huxley rose to his feet and spoke quietly and gravely, explaining Darwin's theory in plain and simple language. He concluded by saying, "I would not be ashamed to have a monkey for my ancestor, but I *would* be ashamed to be connected with a man who used his great gifts to obscure the truth".

The applause that followed was as thunderous as the applause that had followed Wilberforce's attack. One woman fainted. And Wilberforce was so stunned that he declined the opportunity to have a final say.

Eleven years later, in 1871, Darwin declared his belief that archaeology would turn up the proof of his theory in "the Missing Link". Darwinians were eager to have the honour of fulfilling that prophecy. And in 1912 it looked as if Charles Dawson had succeeded triumphantly.

Other finds followed. Teilhard de Chardin found a human canine in the debris that had been thrown out of the pit; it fit the skull. An elephant bone shaped into a club – the earliest known weapon – was also found. And when, in 1915, another "Piltdown cranium" was found two miles away, even the doubters were convinced. This "proved" beyond all doubt that man was the descendant of an ape.

Dawson had only a year longer to live; he died in 1916, at the age of fifty-two, in a glow of celebrity. Woodward had christened his discovery *Eoanthropus dawsoni* – Dawsonian dawn man. And in due course a statue of Dawson was erected near the gravel pit.

The problem was that Dawson's dawn man did not seem to fit into the emerging picture of human evolution. For example, Neanderthal man, which had been discovered in 1857, had a receding jaw; so did the much older Heidelberg man, discovered in 1907 (and also dated at about half a million years old). So did Java man, discovered in 1891. But these all looked much more humanoid, less apelike, than dawn man. In short, Piltdown dawn man was far too late to be the Missing Link.

The bubble finally burst in 1953, when the Piltdown skull was subjected to the latest scientific tests at the British Museum by Dr Kenneth Oakley. These included fluorine analysis. (Fluorine accumulates in buried bones, so the older a bone, the more fluorine it contains.) The Piltdown skull proved to be a mere 50,000 years old, while the jawbone proved to be that of a chimpanzee; both had been stained with iron sulphate and pigment. The Piltdown skull, which had figured in so many books on the evolution of man, was a hoax. But who was responsible for it?

The obvious suspect was Dawson himself. Evidence began to accumulate that he was not as honest as everyone had supposed. Dr J. S. Weiner, the author of a book entitled *The Piltdown Problem* (1955), went down to Sussex, and in a cabinet of fossils belonging to a contemporary of Dawson's, Harry Morris, found a flint described on its accompanying card as "stained by C. Dawson with intent to defraud". In fact, Dawson is known to have stained the bones with bichromate to preserve them –

or at least that is the reason he gave Woodward. Local historians had criticized Dawson for basing his *History of Hastings Castle*, without acknowledgment, on an earlier history. And there was a story that he had bought a house that was being considered for the site of the headquarters of the Sussex Archaeological Society by using his membership to snatch it from under the society members' noses. Whoever "salted" the gravel pit with primitive tools, and bones of hippopotamus, rhinoceros, and deer, had access to this kind of material. And the same person placed the second "Piltdown skull" two miles away to silence the skeptics. Dawson was certainly in a position to do these things.

On the other hand, Francis Vere, author of *The Piltdown Fantasy*, is convinced that Dawson did *not* have sufficient knowledge to carry out the fraud – for example, enough knowledge of dentistry to grind down the teeth. He believes that the hoaxer was one of the many local amateur geologists – like Harry Morris (who is known to have been an embittered man).

But *why* was it done? If Dawson did it, then the reason may have been either the desire for personal aggrandizement or the desire to prove Darwin right once and for all. Fifty years after the publication of *The Origin of Species*, the world was still full of fundamentalists who could not accept Darwinism. In 1925 a schoolteacher named John Scopes was put on trial in Dayton, Tennessee, for teaching his pupils the theory of evolution. Scopes was found guilty and fined $100.

In a pamphlet entitled *Lessons of Piltdown* (published by the Evolution Protest Movement in 1959), Francis Vere even suggests that Teilhard de Chardin could have been responsible for the Piltdown hoax. Vere's protest is also directed at the notion that man is descended from the ape, and he suggests that what the scientists ought to be trying to explain is the "gift to Man from God – the mind". Vere's protest is in the spirit of the complaint of Samuel Butler – another anti-Darwinian – who claimed that the theory of natural selection had "banished God from the universe". Bernard Shaw took up his protest in the preface to *Back to Methuselah*, in which he argued that the failure of Darwinism lies in its rigid determinism, its failure to recognize the part played in evolution by the *will* of the individual.

What, in fact, has happened since the 1950s is that the objections of historians like Vere – and even of the townsfolk of Dayton – have been justified by new discoveries that prove, once and for all, that there is no connection between human beings and apes. Some ninety million years ago, in the age that succeeded the dinosaurs (who lived from about 250 to 150 million years ago), the ancestor of both the apes and man was a tiny insect-eating creature that resembled a mouse or shrew and that lived in the steaming forests that covered the earth. At about this time, these creatures felt confident enough to emerge from the undergrowth and take to the trees, where they ate seeds and tender leaves and a new development called fruit, rather than insects. It was probably as a consequence of living in trees that the "mouse" developed a "hand" with a thumb and four fingers, rather than a paw with all the digits side by side. Many of these creatures were exterminated by their cousins the rodents, who had one major advantage – their teeth never stopped growing and so never wore down. But they survived in Africa – or rather, in the vast continent that included Africa and South America, before they drifted apart forty million years ago. By this time, the tree shrew had turned into a monkey – so in that sense, man is descended from a monkey.

For some reason, monkeys had their eyes in front of their heads, rather than on either side, as rodents have. This enabled them to develop depth perception, which in time would mean that they could handle tools. (If you try driving a car with one eye closed, you will find it far more difficult to judge your distance from the hedge.) As the earth became dryer, and the lush African forests became savannahs, the primates split into two lines, the apes and the monkeys. The earliest ape seems to have been a creature we call *Aegyptopithecus*, which lived about twenty-eight million years ago. Then came *Dryopithecus*, a baboonlike creature, which spread out of Africa and across Europe. About fifteen million years ago, one line of *Dryopithecus* took to the trees and became the ancestor of the modern ape – the kind we encounter in the Tarzan stories.

Next came the ape we call *Ramapithecus*, found in 1934 in northern India. This was so humanlike that paleontologist G. E. Lewis classified it as a hominid. *Ramapithecus* seems to date back between eight and fourteen million years and has a claim to be the "first man".

In 1924, in the part of Africa now called Botswana, miners who were blasting rock discovered fossil bones near a railway station known as Taungs; further investigation revealed the skull of a child; it still had milk teeth and thus was reckoned to be about six years old. The brain case was much smaller than that of a human child, yet the teeth were definitely human. Professor Raymond Dart concluded that this was one of the earliest "true men" yet discovered and called it. *Australopithecus africanus*, or southern ape man. This creature was a meat eater and is nowadays referred to as a "Dartian". Another type of *Australopithecus* was discovered some time later, a vegetarian with a more robust build; he was labeled *Australopithecus robustus*.

Dart's fellow scientists were unwilling to accept that his meat-eating ape-man was an important link in the evolutionary chain, but discoveries made by the paleontologist Robert Broom in the second half of the 1930s left no doubt that the "Dartians" were a truly human species that had originated in Africa. Some dated as far back as three million years ago, others a mere three-quarters of a million years. The "Dartians" seem to have given way to the creature we call *Homo erectus*, the immediate predecessor of *Homo sapiens*, while *robustus* seems to have died out.

At some of the australopithecine sites, Dart found baboon skulls with a kind of double depression in the back. And the discovery of antelope front-leg bones (*humeri*) at these sites suggested to Dart that these early ape-men had used the bones as clubs. It led him to publish, in 1949, a highly controversial paper entitled. "The Predatory Transition from Ape to Man", which argued that human intelligence had developed through the use of weapons. Wielding a club, Dart maintained, requires a certain degree of coordination between the hand and the eye. In short, Dart was suggesting that man evolved because he was the descendant of some primitive killer ape, while his more peaceful brothers stayed in the trees and developed into modern gorillas, orangutans, and so on. Dartian man went on to develop tools – stones with their edges chipped off to make primitive axes, which could be used to extract marrow from bones – about two million years ago.

Dart's version of human evolution was popularized in 1961 by the playwright-turned-anthropologist Robert Ardrey, in a book entitled *African Genesis*. This, briefly, is how Ardrey sees human development: About fifteen million years ago, in the Miocene era, Africa was still covered with lush forests. Twelve million years ago the rains stopped, and the Miocene gave way to the long droughts of the Pliocene era. At some point in the Pliocene era, our human ancestors descended from the trees to take their chance on the savannahs. These became the two types of *Australopithecus* – the meat-eating "Dartians" and the vegetarian *robustus*. During this period, Ardrey believes, the "Dartians" learned to use weapons like bone clubs.

Then, about a million years ago, the rains came, and the Pleistocene era began. It was the bad weather, Ardrey thinks, that led man to develop his intelligence. Pebble tools made their appearance. So did hand axes. The gentle *robustus* vanished as rains gave way to periodic droughts, but "Dartian" man, the "bad-weather animal", survived. And because his chief evolutionary advantage was his aggression, his killer instinct, he gradually became the most dominant species on earth.

This, Ardrey suggests, is why his greatest problem in our modern world is that he will exterminate his own species.

It is a gloomy picture, and it can hardly hold any comfort for antievolutionists who are pleased that we are *not* descended from the ape. But it is not necessarily the last word. Richard Leakey, son of the eminent anthropologist Louis Leakey (whom Ardrey quotes extensively), has argued that all the evidence shows that our primitive ancestors were peaceable creatures and that it was not until he began to create cities – with their overcrowding and other problems – that man became cruel and destructive. And the Finnish paleontologist Björn Kurtén developed his own views in a book entitled – significantly – *Not from the Apes* (1972). This, in summary, is his view:

Our tree-living Ramapithecine ancestors of about fifteen million years ago (in the Miocene era) were furry creatures about the size of a modern-day five-year-old child; but they had forward-looking eyes and human teeth. Kurtén suggests that these highly social creatures developed a "call system" – of warnings and so on – that developed into language. They became capable of "simple thought processes".

With the coming of the droughts – and the savannahs – of the Pliocene era, these creatures came down from the trees – not because they were driven down but because the savannahs offered a richer way of life. The baboons descended from the trees at about the same time. But the baboons remained four-legged herbivores, while the manlike primates became two-legged carnivores. Their upright posture allowed them to see farther into the distance – an advantage for hunters. The need for periods of violent activity – chasing small animals for example – led to the gradual loss of fur.

Since the wandering life was hard on women and small children, the band was inclined to find itself a semipermanent home. The men went hunting while the women remained behind. Family life developed, and two-parent families became the nucleus of the population. Sex played an increasingly important part in their lives, instead of being a "sideshow" (Ardrey's phrase), as it is for animals in the wild. Thinner fur made skin contact more sensuous. Because they walked upright, face-to-face mating gradually replaced sex from the rear. Lips became fuller and female breasts developed. (Kurtén acknowledges that he owes this idea to Desmond Morris's *Naked Ape*.) And at this point, Kurtén agrees that the ability to manipulate weapons caused a development of intelligence. Something very like speech evolved from the "monkey chatter".

Homo erectus came into being about two or three million years ago and coexisted with Dartian man. But while Dartian man had a brain size of about 500 cc, the brain of *Homo erectus* slowly developed until it reached 1,000 cc around 400,000 years ago. There it stopped, and *Homo erectus* gradually faded out.

But about half a million years ago a new species, *Homo sapiens*, came on the scene – no one quite knows how. (One scientist, Allan Wilson, has even suggested that *Homo sapiens* developed from *Homo erectus* in Australia.) What we do know is that his brain developed from *Homo erectus*'s 1,000 cc to modern man's 1,800 cc in such a short period (in evolutionary terms) that scientists speak of "the brain explosion".

What caused this brain explosion? We now know enough about evolution to know that things do not just "happen". Evolution is not "natural"; the shark has remained unchanged for 150 million years. Kurtén has nothing much to suggest, except to point out the obvious – that our evolutionary capacities are drawn out of us by changes in the environment (like the bad weather of the Pleistocene). But as far as we know, there have been no such changes in the past half million years, except a succession of ice ages. It is possible, of course, that these "pressured" man into developing his brain; but it seems more likely that they would favour the development of fur or hair. Ardrey even suggests the possibility that the brain explosion may have been connected with a huge meteor that exploded over the Indian Ocean about seventy thousand years ago (its remains, called *tektites*, can still be found scattered over twenty million square miles) and caused a reversal in the earth's magnetic field. He suggests that if the earth had no magnetic field for a brief intervening period, a rain of cosmic rays may have caused genetic changes in human beings.

Another anthropologist, Otto Kiss Maerth, devoted a book entitled *The Beginning Was the End* (1971) to the theory that human evolution was due to cannibalism – discoveries near Peking in 1929 seemed to show that the ape-men of six hundred thousand years ago ate the brains of their enemies. Maerth suggests that eating brains stimulates both the intelligence and the sexual instinct and that this explains the brain explosion. The objection to this theory is that there is not enough widespread evidence for cannibalism and the eating of brains to account for human evolution.

Ardrey has a more plausible basic hypothesis, which he calls "the hunting hypothesis" – the notion that men had to learn social coopera-tion because they had to learn to hunt together. But Ardrey had originally suggested that Dartian man became a carnivore during the Pleistocene era (in the past million years), when droughts made vegeta-tion scarce. When Louis Leakey discovered evidence at Fort Ternan, in

Kenya, that *Ramapithecus* was a meat eater nearly fifteen million years ago, that view was undermined; yet it only increased Ardrey's conviction that the "hunting hypothesis" explains human evolution. What he failed to explain was why wolves and other animals who hunt in packs have not evolved to the human level.

In fact, this problem has almost certainly been solved by an experimental psychologist named Nicholas Humphrey, who studied the brains of mountain gorillas in Rwanda, in central Africa, and wondered why they had such large brains when their lives are so crudely simple – eating, sleeping, and moving on to new feeding grounds. The answer came as he observed the gorillas closely and noticed their incredible sensitivity to one another's feelings. The most important thing in a gorilla's life is its relation to other gorillas. A gorilla's family life is the equivalent of a university education; it learns to react delicately to the moods, feelings, and reactions of other gorillas. If Humphrey is correct, then the size of the brain has something to do with the complexity of social relations.

The "Humphrey theory" of evolution, then, would run like this: As man became increasingly successful because of his prowess as a hunter, his numbers increased, and social intercourse with other groups became increasingly important. As sensitivity and cooperation became survival factors, the brain flourished.

Yet the "hunting hypothesis" may pave the way to the next step in the argument. If Kurtén is correct in his belief that Dartian man ceased to be a wanderer in the Pliocene era and began to leave the women and children behind while he went hunting, then this would apply even more so to *Homo sapiens* during the great droughts and ice ages of the Pleistocene. Most anthropologists seem to recognize that sex played a basic part in human evolution – from Kurtén and Morris to Maerth, with his brain-eating theory. As Ardrey points out, sex is a sideshow in the world of nature. Wild animals only become interested in it when the female experiences her periodic cycle. But at some point in his evolution, human sexual desire became independent of that cycle, and man began to have sex at all times *except* when the female was menstruating. It seems logical to explain this in terms of the hunting hypothesis. If a hunter had been away from home for weeks, then he would expect to make love to his mate when he returned, whether she was "in heat" or not. Some females would naturally object to this; but they would have fewer offspring than the females who had no such objection – or swallowed their dislike – and eventually, the objectors would die out.

What no one seems to have recognized so far is the importance of sex as an "internal" factor in evolution. When an animal has nothing else to do, it lies down and yawns. When a man has nothing else to do, his thoughts turn as often as not to sex. If there is a pretty girl in the vicinity, he may begin to brood on seduction – even if he happens to have a wife already. If he is too shy or otherwise inhibited, then he may simply daydream about sex. From being a "sideshow", sex has become one of the central interests of human existence.

Now if we imagine Stone Age hunters in a period of scarcity, we can see that they may have had to have spent longer and longer periods away from the women and children of the tribe; a hunting expedition might have lasted a month or longer. Back at home, women were now permanently receptive and were consequently beginning to develop the sexual characteristics males found exciting – larger breasts, full lips, rounded buttocks. When the males came back from a long expedition, some skinny adolescent girls had suddenly begun to change into desirable women. The presence of these unattached females must have introduced an element of competition and excitement. Young men now had good reason for wanting to become successful hunters and fighters – it gave them the pick of the girls.

We note another interesting thing about human beings: that from babyhood onward they have a tendency to idealize possible mates. Little boys fall in love with the prettiest girl in the class and daydream of being cowboys who rescue her from a band of marauding Indians. We do not know, of course, whether dogs and cats experience these emotions, but it seems unlikely. As far as we can see, it seems to have been sex that taught human beings to use the imagination.

This means that, to a large extent, sex provides us with goals and objectives, even when there are no other stimuli. It is an "internal" factor in evolution, a psychological drive that operates most of the time. It could be the factor that explains why man became an "evolutionary animal", an animal who went on striving even when he had a full belly.

Kurtén seems to skirt these ideas when he remarks: "Another semi-solution [to the problem of evolution] was the idea of an inner force of evolution, the *élan vital*, which would automatically carry us forward to new heights of nobility and spirituality. Unfortunately there is no evidence whatever for the existence of such a force". But sex is precisely such a force, as Goethe recognized when he wrote: "The eternal feminine draws us upwards and on".

In the previous paragraph Kurtén had dismissed another possibility: that by improving themselves, human beings produce better offspring. This is known as "the inheritance of acquired characteristics" and is a theory of evolution that was suggested by Darwin's predecessor, Lamarck. The simplest illustration of the difference between the two theories is the problem of how the giraffe came to have a long neck. According to Darwin, food shortages due to drought caused the original short-necked giraffes to become extinct. But the giraffes who, *by chance*, happened to have longer necks, were able to reach the leaves on higher branches and so survived. And eventually, all giraffes had long necks. Lamarck's view was that when food became scarce, giraffes had to make strenuous efforts to reach higher branches, and these efforts gradually lengthened their necks.

The discovery of the genes (by Mendel) made it look as if Darwin was right and Lamarck wrong. For genetics seemed to prove that, even if a giraffe could stretch its neck by effort, it could not transmit this long neck to its children, whose genes would ensure that they had short necks.

In the twentieth century some biologists wondered whether perhaps genes do not mutate at random but in some way that is useful to the organism. But this theory was disproved by the study of bacteria, which showed that genes always mutate at random. At least, healthy and well-nourished bacteria mutate at random, And that is as one would expect. Why should they want to change if they are comfortable and well fed?

But in the late 1980s Dr John Cairns of Harvard decided to study starving bacteria and concluded that some of them *could* deliberately mutate to utilize a new food source. His results have been confirmed by Professor Barry Hall at the University of Rochester, New York. When he deliberately starved his bacteria of an amino acid essential to their survival, some of them mutated so they could manufacture the missing acid, until whole colonies of the mutated bacteria came into existence. It seems, then, that Lamarck was probably right after all. As, incidentally, was Samuel Butler, who objected to Darwin on precisely these grounds (see chapter 23).

But even on a more down-to-earth level, the rigidly Darwinian view is questionable. We all know that efforts made by parents *can* be passed on to their children – that, for example, parents who have educated themselves can pass on their love of learning to their children. The truth is – as Kurtén recognizes – that the brain has a huge *dormant capacity*, which can be awakened by the right stimuli. Man had developed a "modern size" brain long before he had books and music and philosophy to put in it.

Kurtén also recognizes this when he says that our ancestors may have come down from the trees not because there was no longer enough food in the forests but because they were excited by the *possibilities* of the wide savannahs. Again, he is recognizing an evolutionary force, a craving for adventure, for a fuller and richer mode of existence. *Not from the Apes* is devoted to the thesis that man's uniqueness may date back as far as thirty-five million years, when our lineage split off from that of our cousins the apes. In the beginning, that split may have been due to natural selection and survival of the fittest. But in the past half million years or so – perhaps far longer than that – the evolutionary urge seems to have acquired its own momentum, so that even a convinced Darwinian like Sir Julian Huxley (grandson of T. H. Huxley) can state that man has finally become "the managing director of evolution".

We can see, then, that the whole Missing Link controversy was based on simple misunderstanding. Darwin appeared to be saying that man is merely a more intelligent ape and that his intelligence developed by chance. That clearly implies that individual effort counts for nothing. We struggle because we *have* to struggle; that is part of the rat race. But our "higher aspirations" are so much nonsense. We are mere apes.

Human evolution proves the contrary. Man has become an evolutionary animal, an animal who *expects* to change. Striving has become his second nature – a striving based upon his intense romanticism, the same romanticism that made the Greeks romanticize Helen of Troy, that made the troubadours romanticize their chosen "lady", that made Malory romanticize Queen Guinevere and Isolde. And there is every reason to expect our evolution to continue. The dormant capacity that changed Dartian man into modern man lies inside our heads. The brain developed through social intercourse and cooperation, but its excess size meant *dormant capacity*. In other words, *Homo sapiens* developed a modern brain but had very little use for it.

Brain physiologists tell us that, in spite of science, philosophy, art, and technology, modern man still only uses one-fifth of his brain capacity. When he learns to use the other four-fifths, there is every reason to believe that he will be as different from modern man as you and I are from our australopithecine ancestors.

36

Where is the Mona Lisa?

The answer to the above question may seem self-evident: in the Louvre. But the matter is not quite as straightforward as it looks.

The Mona Lisa is better known on the continent of Europe as "La Gioconda", or the smiling woman – the word means the same as the old English "jocund". It was painted, as everyone knows, by the great Italian artist Leonardo, who was born in the little town of Vinci, near Florence, in 1452. Mona Lisa (Mona is short for Madonna) was a young married woman who was about twenty-four when Leonardo met her. She was the wife of a man twenty years her senior, the wealthy Francesco del Giocondo, and when Leonardo started to paint her around 1500 she had just lost a child. Leonardo's biographer Vasari says that her husband had to hire jesters and musicians to make her smile during the early sittings.

For some reason Leonardo became obsessed with her, and went on painting her for several years, always dissatisfied with his work. This has given rise to stories that he was in love with her, and even that she became his mistress; but this seems unlikely. Leonardo was homosexual, and took a poor view of sex, writing with Swiftian disgust: "The act of coitus and the members that serve it are so hideous that, if it were not for the beauty of faces . . . the human species would lose its humanity". Yet there was something about Madonna Lisa that made him strive to capture her expression for at least six years – possibly more. His biographer Antonia Vallentin says she fascinated him more than any other woman he met in his life. He gave the unfinished portrait to Mona Lisa's husband when he left Florence in 1505, but still continued to work on it at intervals when he returned.

In his *Lives of the Painters*, Giorgio Vasari says that Leonardo worked at the Mona Lisa for four years and left it unfinished. "This work is now in the possession of Francis, king of France, at Fontainebleau . . ." And this, we assume, is the famous portrait now in the Louvre. Yet this raises a puzzling question. Leonardo gave the portrait to the man who had commissioned it, Mona Lisa's husband, in 1505, and a mere forty or so years later, when Vasari was writing, it is in the possession of Francis I of France. Surely the Giacondo family would not part with a masterpiece so easily? Besides, the Louvre picture is quite obviously finished . . .

There is another interesting clue. In 1584 a historian of art, Giovanni Paolo Lomazzo, published a book on painting, sculpture and architecture, in which he refers to "the Gioconda *and* the Mona Lisa", as if they were two seperate paintings. The book is dedicated to Don Carlos Emanuele, the Grand Duke of Savoy, who was a great admirer of Leonardo – so it hardly seems likely that this was a slip of the pen . . .

Two Giocondas? Then where is the other one? And, more important, *who* is this second Gioconda?

The answer to the first question is, oddly enough: in the Louvre. The world-famous painting, which has been reproduced more often than any other painting in history, is almost certainly not the Mona Lisa that we have been talking about.

Then where *is* the painting of the woman who so obsessed Leonardo that he could not finish her portrait? There is evidence to show that this original Mona Lisa was brought from Italy in the mid-eighteenth century, and went into the stately home of a nobleman in Somerset. Just before the First World War it was discovered by the art connoisseur Hugh Blaker in Bath, and he picked it up for a few guineas, and took it to his studio in Isleworth. Hence it became known as the Isleworth Mona Lisa. It was bigger than the Louvre painting, and – more important – was unfinished; the background has only been lightly touched in. Blaker was much impressed by it. The girl was younger and prettier than the Louvre Mona Lisa. And Blaker felt that this new Mona Lisa corresponded much more closely to Vasari's description than the Louvre painting. Vasari rhapsodized about its delicate realism:

> The eyes had that lustre and watery sheen which is always seen in real life, and around them were those touches of red and the lashes which cannot be represented without the greatest subtlety . . . The nose with its beautiful nostrils, rosy and tender, seemed to be alive. The opening of the mouth, united by the red of the lips to the flesh tones of the face, seemed not to be coloured, but to be living flesh.

Sir Kenneth Clark, quoting this passage in his book on Leonardo, asks: "Who would recognise the submarine goddess of the Louvre"? To which Blaker would have replied: "Ah, precisely". But the description *does* fit the Isleworth Mona Lisa.

There is another point that seems to establish beyond all doubt that Blaker's picture is Leonardo's Mona Lisa. The painter Raphael saw it in Leonardo's studio about 1504, and later made a sketch of it. This sketch shows two Grecian columns on either side – columns that can be found in the Isleworth Mona Lisa, but not in the Louvre painting.

Blaker believes that the Isleworth Mona Lisa is a far more beautiful work, and many art experts have agreed with him. It is true that the Louvre painting has many admirers; Walter Pater wrote a celebrated "purple passage" about it in *The Renaissance* beginning "She is older than the rocks among which she sits; like the vampire, she has been dead many times. . .", and W. B. Yeats thought this so beautiful that he divided it into lines of free verse and printed it as a poem in his *Oxford Book of Modern Verse*. On the other hand, the connoisseur Bernard Berenson wrote about it: "What I really saw in the figure of Mona Lisa was the estranging image of woman beyond the reach of my sympathy or the ken of my interest . . . watchful, sly, secure, with a smile of anticipated satisfaction and a pervading air of hostile superiority . . ." He felt the beauty of the Louvre Mona Lisa had been sacrificed to technique. No one could say this of the far more fresh and lively Isleworth Mona Lisa.

But if the lady in the Louvre is not Leonardo's Lisa del Giocondo, then who is she? Here the most important clue is to be found in a document by Antonio Beatis, secretary to the Cardinal of Aragon. When Leonardo went to the court of Francis I in 1517 he was visited by the cardinal, and the secretary noted down the conversation. The cardinal was shown works by Leonardo, including St John, the Madonna with St Anne, and "the portrait of a certain Florentine lady, painted from life at the instance of the late Magnifico Giuliano de Medici . . ."

In her biography of Leonardo, Antonia Vallentin speculates that this work *was* the Mona Lisa, and asks: "Did Giuliano [de Medici] love Mona Lisa in her girlhood . . . did he think with longing of her now she was married to Messer del Giocondo, and had he commissioned Leonardo to paint her portrait"? But this delightful romantic bubble is shattered by a mere consideration of dates. Giuliano de Medici, brother of Lorenzo the Magnificent, master of Florence, was murdered in Florence cathedral in 1478. The plotters – mostly rival bankers – hoped to kill Lorenzo too, but Lorenzo was too quick for them. All this happened in the year before Mona Lisa was born.

Then who *was* the lady that Leonardo painted at the orders of Giuliano de Medici? Almost certainly the answer is Costanza d'Avalos, Giuliano's mistress, a lady of such pleasant disposition that she was known as "the smiling one" – la Gioconda . . .

And so it would seem that the painting in the Louvre has been labelled "the Mona Lisa" by a simple misunderstanding. Its subject is obviously a woman in her thirties not, like Mona Lisa del Giocondo, in her twenties. Leonardo took it with him to France, and it went into the collection of Francis I, and eventually into the Louvre. The unfinished Mona Lisa stayed in Italy, was brought to England, and was purchased by Hugh Blaker in 1914. In 1962 it was purchased for some vast but undisclosed sum – undoubtedly amounting to millions – by a Swiss syndicate headed by the art-collector Dr Henry F. Pulitzer, and Pulitzer has since written a short book, *Where is the Mona Lisa?*, setting out the claims of his own painting to be that of Madonna Lisa del Giocondo. Pulitzer's contention is simple. There are two Giocondas – for Madonna Lisa had a perfect right to call herself by her husband's name, with a feminine ending. But there is only one Mona Lisa. And that is not in the Louvre but in London.

37

"The Most Mysterious Manuscript in the World"

The Voynich Manuscript

It was in 1912 that an American dealer in rare books, Wilfred Voynich, heard of a mysterious work that had been discovered in an old chest in the Jesuit school of Mondragone, in Frascati, Italy, and succeeded in buying it for an undisclosed sum. It was an octavo volume, six by nine inches, with 204 pages; it had originally another 28 pages, but these are lost. It is written in cipher, which at first glance looks like ordinary medieval writing. And the pages are covered with strange little drawings of female nudes, astronomical diagrams, and all kinds of strange plants in many colours.

There was a letter accompanying the manuscript, dated 19 August 1666, and written by Joannes Marcus Marci, the rector of Prague University. It was addressed to the famous Jesuit scholar Athanasius Kircher – remembered today mainly for some interesting experiments in animal hypnosis – and stated that the book had been bought for 600 ducats by the Holy Roman Emperor Rudolf II of Prague. Kircher was an expert on cryptography, having published a book on the subject in 1663, in which he claimed to have solved the riddle of hieroglyphics. This in itself may be taken to indicate that Kircher was inclined to indulge in wishful thinking, since we know that it would be another century and a half before Champollion succeeded in reading hieroglyphics. Kircher had apparently already attempted to decipher a few pages of the book, sent to him by its previous owner, who had devoted his whole life to trying to decode it. Now he sent him the whole manuscript.

We do not know how the manuscript came to be in Prague, but the likeliest possibility is that it was taken there from England by the famous Elizabethan "magician" Dr John Dee, who went there in 1584; one writer speculates that Dee may have obtained it from the Duke of Northumberland, who had pillaged monasteries at the behest of Henry VIII. The English writer Sir Thomas Browne said later that Dee's son Arthur had spoken about "a book containing nothing but hieroglyphics" which he had studied in Prague. Marci believed the mysterious book to be by the thirteenth-century monk and scientist Roger Bacon.

The Voynich manuscript (as it came to be known) is a baffling mystery because it *looks* so straightforward; with its drawings of plants it looks like an ordinary medieval "herbal", a book describing how to extract healing drugs from plants. One would expect astronomical or astrological diagrams in a herbal, because the plants were often supposed to be gathered by the full moon, or when the stars or planets were in a certain position.

Kircher obviously had no success with the manuscript; he finally deposited it in the Jesuit College in Rome, whence it came into the hands of the Jesuits of Frascati.

Voynich was fairly certain that the manuscript would not remain a mystery once modern scholars had a chance to study it. So he distributed photostats to anyone who was interested. The first problem, of course, was to determine what language it was in – Latin, Middle English, perhaps even Langue d'Oc. This should have been an easy task, since the plants were labelled, albeit in some sort of code. But most of the plants proved to be imaginary. Certain constellations could be recognized among the astronomical diagrams but again, it proved impossible to translate their names out of code. Cryptanalysts tried the familiar method of looking for the most frequent symbols and equating them with the most commonly used letters of the alphabet; they had no difficulty recognizing 29 individual letters or symbols, but every attempt to translate these into a known language was a failure. What made it so infuriating was that the writing didn't *look* like a code; it looked as if someone had sat down and written it as fluently as his mother tongue. Many scholars, cryptanalysts, linguists, astronomers, experts on Bacon, offered to help; the Vatican Library offered to throw open its archives to the researchers. Still the manuscript refused to yield up its secret – or even one of its secrets.

Then in 1921 a professor of philosophy from the University of Pennsylvania, William Romaine Newbold, announced that he had solved the code; he explained his discovery before a meeting of the American Philosophical Society in Philadelphia. What he had done, he explained, was to start by translating the symbols into Roman letters, reducing them in the process from 29 to 17. Using the Latin *conmuto* (or *commuto*: to change) as a key word, he then went on to produce no less than four more versions of the text, the last of which was (according to Newbold) a straightforward Latin text mixed up into anagrams. These merely had to be unscrambled and the result was a scientific treatise which revealed that Roger Bacon was one of the greatest intellects of all time.

This had, of course, always been suspected. It was Bacon who had inspired Columbus to seek out America by a passage in his *Opus Majus* in which he suggested that the Indies could be reached by sailing westward from Spain. In the days of alchemy and a dogmatic and muddled science derived from Aristotle, Bacon advocated learning from nature by experiment and observation, and was thrown into prison for his pains. In rejecting the authority of Aristotle he was also by implication rejecting the authority of the Church. In his *City of God*, St Augustine had warned Christians to shun science and intellectual inquiry as a danger to salvation. Roger Bacon, like his Elizabethan namesake Francis, could see that such an attitude was tantamount to intellectual suicide. Yet when all this is said, it has to be admitted that Bacon was very much a man of his time, and that the *Opus Majus* is full of statements that a modern scientist would regard as gross errors and superstitions.

But if Newbold was correct, Bacon was one of the greatest scientists before Newton. He had made a microscope and examined biological cells and spermatozoa – these were the tadpole-drawings in the margins – and had made a telescope long before Galileo; he had even recognized the Andromeda nebula as a spiral galaxy. Newbold translated a caption to what he claimed to be a sketch of the nebula: "In a concave mirror I saw a star in the form of a snail . . . between the navel of Pegasus, the girdle of Andromeda and the head of Cassiopeia". (It is known that Bacon understood how to use a concave mirror as a burning-glass.) Newbold declared that he had no idea of what he would find by looking in the region indicated, and was surprised to find that the "snail" was the Andromeda nebula.

But in *The Codebreakers* cipher expert David Kahn has pointed out one of the basic flaws in Newbold's system. Newbold's method depended on "doubling up" the letters of a word, so that, for example, "oritur" became or-ri-it-tu-ur, and this text was solved with the aid of the key word "conmuto" and the addition of a q. But how would this process be carried out in reverse – in other words, when Bacon was turning his original text into a cipher? Kahn says: "Many one-way ciphers have been devised; it is possible to put messages into cipher, but not to get them back out. Newbold's seemed to be the only example extant of the reverse situation".

Newbold died in 1926, only sixty years old; two years later his friend Roland G. Kent published the results of Newbold's labours in *The Cipher of Roger Bacon*. It was widely accepted – for example, by the eminent cultural historian Étienne Gilson.

But one scholar who had been studying Newbold's system was far from convinced. He was Dr John M. Manly, a philologist who headed the department of English at Chicago University, and who had become assistant to the great Herbert Osborne Yardley – described as the greatest codebreaker in history – when US Military Intelligence set up a cryptanalysis department in 1917. Manly had produced the definitive edition of Chaucer in eight volumes, comparing more than eighty versions of the medieval manuscript of the *Canterbury Tales*. One of his most remarkable feats was the deciphering of a letter found in the baggage of a German spy named Lothar Witzke, who was captured in Nogales, Mexico, in 1918. In three days of non-stop application Manly had solved the twelve-step official transposition cipher, with multiple horizontal shiftings of three and four letter groups finally laid out in a vertical transcription. In a military court he was able to read aloud a message from the German minister in Mexico beginning: "The bearer of this is a subject of the empire who travels as a Russian under the name of Pablo Waberski. He is a German secret agent . . ." It was the spy's death warrant (although President Wilson commuted it to life imprisonment).

Now Manly studied Newbold's *Cipher of Roger Bacon*, and concluded that in spite of his undoubted integrity, Newbold had been deceiving himself. The weak point of the cipher was the anagramming process. Most sentences can be anagrammed into a dozen other sentences, a method by which admirers of Francis Bacon have had no difficulty proving that he wrote the plays of Shakespeare (see chapter 51). With a sentence involving more than a hundred letters, there is simply no way of guaranteeing that some particular rearrangement provides the only solution – David Kahn points out that the words "Hail Mary, full of grace, the Lord is with thee" can be anagrammed in thousands of different ways.

Newbold had also made certain "shorthand signs" a basic part of his system of interpretation. When Manly looked at these through a powerful magnifying glass he found out that they were not "shorthand" at all, only places where the ink had peeled off the vellum. By the time he had pointed out dozens of cases in which Newbold had allowed his interpretation to be influenced by his own twentieth-century assumptions, Manly had totally demolished Newbold's claim to have solved "the cipher of Roger Bacon".

Since that time, 1931, there have been many attempts to decipher the Voynich manuscript. In 1933 a cancer specialist, Dr Leonell C. Strong, published his own fragments of translation, and proved to his own satisfaction that the work was a herbal by an English scholar, Anthony Ascham; he even published a recipe for a contraceptive which apparently works. But Strong failed to explain the method by which he arrived at his translations, so they have never achieved wide acceptance.

William F. Friedman, who organized a whole group of specialists to work on the problem in the last year of the Second World War, was frustrated by the end of the war and the disbandment of his group. But Friedman pointed out that the Voynich manuscript differs from other codes in one basic respect. The inventor of a code attempts to frustrate would-be cryptanalysts by trying to remove repetitions that would give him away (for example, a repeated group of three letters would almost certainly be "and" or "the"). The Voynich manuscript actually has far more repetitions than an ordinary text. This led Friedman to hypothesize that the text is in some artificial language which, because of a need for simplicity, would inevitably have more repetitions than a highly complex "natural" language. But this presupposes that Roger Bacon (or whoever wrote the manuscript) was so anxious to conceal his meaning that he went to far greater lengths than even a code-expert would consider reasonable. And for a thirteenth-century monk, who had little reason to fear code-breakers, this seems unlikely . . .

And this, of course, is the very heart of the mystery. We do not know when the manuscript was written, or by whom, or in what language, but even if we knew the answers to these questions it is difficult to think of any good reason for inventing such a baffling code. The earliest ciphers in the Vatican archive date from 1326 (when Roger Bacon was a boy) and these are merely "coded" names relating to the struggle between Ghibellines and Guelphs. These were respectively supporters of the Holy Roman Emperor and the pope; the Ghibellines are called Egyptians and the Guelphs Children of Israel. (It is easy to guess what side the inventor of the code was on.) The earliest Western "substitution" cipher dates from 1401. The first treatise on codes, the *Polygraphia* of Johannes Trithemius, was not printed until 1518, two years after the death of its author. So it is hard to imagine why Roger Bacon or anyone within a century of his death should have gone to so much trouble to invent a code of such apparent sophistication when something much simpler would have sufficed.

Kahn offers one clue to why the author of a herbal (which is what the Voynich manuscript looks most like) should want to conceal his meaning when he speaks of one of the earliest encipherments, a tiny cuneiform tablet dating from about 1500 BC. "It contains the earliest known formula for the making of glazes for pottery. The scribe, jealously guarding his professional secret, used cuneiform signs . . . in their least common values". The author of the Voynich manuscript may have been a highly skilled professional herbalist who wrote down his secrets for his own use and those of his pupils, and was determined to keep them out of the hands of rivals.

This view would have struck the antiquarian bookseller Hans Kraus as altogether too commonplace. When Ethel Voynich died at the age of ninety-six, in 1960, Kraus purchased the manuscript from her executors and put it up for sale at $160,000; he explained that he thought that it could contain information that might provide new insights into the record of man, and that if it could be deciphered it might be worth a million dollars. No one took it at that price, and Kraus finally gave it to Yale University in 1969, where it now lies, awaiting the inspiration of some master-cryptographer.

38

Joan Norkot

The Case of the Bleeding Corpse

When Sir John Mainard, known as "a gentleman of great note and judgment of the law", died in 1690, there was found among his papers an account of an incredible case in which a woman's corpse accused her murderers. The whole document was printed in *The Gentleman's Magazine* of July 1851, a copy having been taken by a lawyer named Hunt. The events it describes are so extraordinary that the magazine took the precaution of heading it: "Singular Instance of Superstition". Yet Mainard's account makes it clear that the event was witnessed by a crowd of people standing in a graveyard, including two clergymen.

The trial in which the evidence was heard took place at Hereford Assizes in Herefordshire in "the fourth year of the reign of King Charles I" (1629), more than sixty years before Mainard's death. Mainard's account is printed in full in the Reverend Montague Summers's *The Vampire in Europe* (1929). An account written by Valentine Dyall in *Unsolved Mysteries* (1954)* is also based on the court records, which it admits are "tantalizingly scanty". The account has an irritating lack of dates, and even of names, but the general outline is clear enough.

There had been, it seems, some trouble between Arthur Norkot and his wife, Joan, one suggestion being that he suspected her of infidelity. It may have been simply overcrowding that caused their disagreements, for Joan lived in a two-room cottage with her husband and baby, as well as with her mother-in-law, Mary Norkot, and her sister and brother-in-law, Agnes and John Okeman.

One morning Joan was found dead in her bed, with her throat cut; the baby was lying – unharmed – beside her. A bloodstained knife was sticking in the bare floorboards.

* Researched by Larry Forrester and Peter Robinson.

Her husband had been away from home that night, according to the relatives. He had gone to visit friends near Tewkesbury. The others swore that it was impossible that Joan Norkot could have been murdered, for anyone entering the cottage would have had to pass through the room in which they slept before entering her bedroom.

At the inquest that followed, it was admitted that there had been "a great deal of trouble" between husband and wife and that Joan had been in "a sour temper with some despondency" before she went to bed. But when the knife was tried in the small hole in the floor that its point had made, it was observed that its handle pointed toward the door and that it was some feet from the bed. If Joan had thrown the knife down after cutting her throat, surely the handle would have been pointing toward the *bed*? In spite of this, a verdict of *felo-de-se* (suicide) was returned, and Joan was duly buried, presumably in unhallowed ground.

It may have been the knife evidence that caused unpleasant rumors to circulate (Mainard merely says "observations of divers circumstances"). The coroner was asked to reopen the case and agreed to a reinvestigation. The body was exhumed, and it was found that the neck was broken. Clearly, the woman could not have broken her own neck. It was noted, moreover, that there was more blood on the floor of the room than on the bed, which seemed odd if Joan had cut her throat in bed. Moreover, Arthur Norkot's alibi collapsed when his friends in Tewkesbury declared that they had not seen him for three years. Altogether, the evidence against the accused was so strong that the prosecution decided not to mention the strangest and most incredible piece of evidence at their trial. But for some reason, the jury did not think it was conclusive, and the four were acquitted. The judge, a man named Harvey, was incredulous and "let fall his opinion that it were better an appeal were brought than so foul a murder should escape unpunished".

This could only be done in the name of Joan Norkot's baby. Accordingly, the four were retried in front of Justice Harvey. And it was at this retrial that a nameless clergyman – the minister of the parish – presented the evidence that the corpse had accused her murderers. The incredulous judge asked if anyone else had seen it, and the old man replied, "I believe the whole company saw it".

What had happened, it seemed, was this: Thirty days after she was buried, the body of Joan Norkot was taken from the grave and the coffin placed beside it, almost certainly on trestles. It must have been an unpleasant sight, since the severed jugular vein would have drained her of most of her blood. Then, in accordance with an ancient superstition, each of the accused was asked to touch the body. According to the superstition, if a corpse is touched by its murderer, the wounds will bleed afresh. Mrs Okeman fell to her knees and prayed to God to grant proof of their innocence. Then, like the others, she was asked to touch the corpse.

The clergyman deposed the following:

> The appellers did touch the dead body, whereupon the brow of the dead, which was all a livid or carrion colour . . . began to have a dew or gentle sweat, which reached down in drops upon the face, and the brow turned and changed to a lively and fresh colour, and the dead opened one of her eyes and shut it again, and this opening the eye was done several times. She likewise thrust out the ring- or marriage finger three times and pulled it in again, and the finger dropt blood from it on to the grass.

It was at this point that the judge expressed his doubts, and the clergyman then turned to his brother, the minister of the next parish, who had also been present. The brother repeated the evidence: that the brow had begun to perspire, that its colour had changed from livid (i.e., a bruised colour) to fresh and normal, that the eye had opened, and that the finger had three times made a pointing motion. (This seems to have been taken to imply that only three of the four accused were guilty.)

What followed was a repetition of the main evidence that had already been presented at the first trial. The body of Joan Norkot lay "in a composed manner" in the bed, the bedclothes undisturbed and her baby beside her. This in itself was evidence enough to convict someone of murder, for it was obviously impossible that she could cut her throat elsewhere in the room – the floor was heavily bloodstained – then lie down and carefully cover herself up. Moreover, the broken neck seemed to indicate that considerable force had been used against her. It is just about possible for a person to break her own neck but not to cut her throat afterwards. It is equally impossible to cut the throat first and then break the neck.

What had happened, quite clearly; was that the husband and wife had quarreled violently and that he had ended with his hands around her throat. She had fallen and struck her head against something, breaking her neck. Now in a panic – for the death was almost certainly accidental – Arthur Norkot conferred with his mother and sister about what could be done, with his brother-in-law, John Okeman, an unwilling participant. To hide the bruises on Joan's throat and her broken neck, the solution seemed to be to cut her throat. But they were in such a panic that they did this on the floor of the room instead of in the bed. Then Joan Norkot was arranged in her bed and the baby – who had probably slept through it all – placed beside her. Someone left a bloodstained fingerprint and thumbprint on her hand. (Chief Justice Hyde, who heard the case, seems to have been so inexperienced in such matters that he had to ask how they could distinguish the prints of the left hand from those of the right.) And as they were leaving the room, someone tossed the bloodstained knife – which probably lay near the door – back into the room, so it stuck in the floor a few feet from the bed. Then Arthur Norkot hastily washed off his bloodstains and took his leave, instructing his mother to "find" the body the next morning and explain that her son was away in Tewkesbury.

It is clear that the attempt to make the murder look like suicide was so bungled that a moderately intelligent investigator could have seen through it right away. But in 1629 scientific crime investigation was unknown. It would be almost another two centuries before Britain even had a police force. If someone was suspected of a crime, the standard method of "investigation" was to torture him until he either confessed or died. No one, it seemed, felt that the evidence against the Norkot family was sufficiently strong for an accusation.

This brings us to the most difficult question of all. Did the corpse really "revive" and accuse the criminals? Any reader who has studied chapter 42 in this volume may concede that the evidence for the "survival" of the human personality is at least plausible. It would even seem that spirits can, under certain circumstances, "possess" the living and cause unexplained movements of material objects ("poltergeist" effects). And in one extraordinary case, the spirit of a murder victim seems to have returned to accuse her killer (see chapter 5). It seems just as conceivable that Joan Norkot was momentarily able to "repossess" her old body in order to accuse her attackers. But it must be immediately admitted that there are no other known examples in the history of paranormal research.

In his *Unsolved Mysteries*, Valentine Dyall suggests a commonsense solution: that the two doctors who presided over the exhumation decided to shock the suspects into a public confession. A tiny pouch of some dark red fluid was stuck to her left hand and a fine thread attached to its stopper. The thread was passed through the wedding ring. Another thread was tied to one of the eyelashes. Then both threads were attached to the coffin handles. When the "touching test" was suggested, each doctor (standing on either side of the coffin) pulled on a thread. The eyelid twitched, the ring-finger jerked, and the "blood" was released so that it ran down the side of the corpse and out of a crack in the bottom of the badly made coffin. The bleeding wound "proved" that Joan had been murdered by someone who had just touched her. The evidence states that someone put his finger into the blood and testified that it was real; but this, Dyall suggests, would obviously have been one of the doctors themselves.

It might be just possible, although one would think that in broad daylight the threads would surely have been visible. And what about the evidence of both clergymen that the face lost its "dead" colour and seemed to come to life? Pure imagination? That is also possible – except that they claimed that this was the *first* thing that happened, before the eye opened or the finger twitched. The imagination theory would be more acceptable if the face had "come to life" *after* the corpse "winked".

Whatever the explanation, the evidence of the two clergymen convinced the court. Arthur Norkot, together with his mother and sister, was sentenced to death. For reasons that Sir John Mainard (who was Sergeant Mainard when he took part in the trial) does not explain, the jury decided to acquit Norkot's brother-in-law, John Okeman. When sentenced, all three repeated, "I did not do it". In fact, Agnes Okeman was reprieved when she was discovered to be pregnant. Mary and John Norkot were hanged. Mainard concludes: "I inquired if they confessed anything at execution, but they did not, as I was told".

39

The *Oera Linda Book*

The Forgotten History
of a Lost Continent

In 1876 there appeared in London a bewildering work entitled the *Oera Linda Book* and subtitled *From a Manuscript of the Thirteenth Century*. It was published by Trubner and Co., one of the most respectable names in publishing, so there could be no suggestion that it was a hoax. And the fact that the original text in Frisian (the language of Friesland, a part of northern Holland) was published opposite the English translation offered scholars the opportunity to check for themselves. Yet if the claims of the *Oera Linda Book* were true, then the history of the ancient world had to be completely rewritten. It suggested that in the third millennium BC, at about the time the Great Pyramid and the original Stonehenge were built, there was a great island continent in northern Europe that was inhabited by a highly civilized race. In 2193 BC this island was destroyed, like the legendary Atlantis, by some immense catastrophe. But enough of its inhabitants escaped to carry their civilization elsewhere – including ancient Egypt and Crete. In fact, the *Oera Linda Book* suggested that the legendary King Minos of Crete (creator of the Labyrinth) was a Frisian and that the same ancient civilization gave democracy to Athens.

All this seemed so extraordinary and so confusing that the first reaction of Dutch and German scholars was to suggest that the book was a forgery. Yet they seem to have agreed that it was not a modern forgery and that it was probably a century to a century and a half old. But that would date it roughly to the 1730s. And it is hard to imagine why anyone would have *wanted* to forge such a document in the 1730s. A century later, in the Romantic era, there would have been some point in creating this mysterious narrative with its marvelous hints of a golden age in the remote past. But it is virtually impossible to imagine why, in that rather dull era of Frederick the Great and the Prince of Orange-Nassau (dull, at any rate, from the literary point of view), anyone should have bothered. It is true that a famous forgery of "ancient" Gaelic poetry – the works of "Ossian", actually written by James MacPherson – became immensely popular in England and on the Continent in the 1760s; but if the *Oera Linda Book* was inspired by MacPherson's Ossian, why did the forger put it in a drawer and forget about it until 1848, when it finally saw the light of day?

According to its Introduction, written in 1871, the *Oera Linda Book* had been preserved in the Linden (or Linda) family from "time immemorial" and was written in a peculiar script that looked a little like Greek. It began with a letter from one "Liko oera Linda", dated AD 803, in which he begged his son to preserve the book "with body and soul", since it contained the history of their peoples. The manuscript was inherited by a certain C. Over de Linden – a modernized version of Oera Linda – in 1848, and a learned professor named Verwijs asked if he could look at it. He immediately recognized its language as ancient Fries, a form of Dutch. The manuscript examined by Verwijs had been copied in 1256 on paper manufactured from cotton and written in a black ink that did not contain iron (which eventually turns brown).

According to the Introduction (by Dr J. O. Ottema), the *Oera Linda Book* records the history of the people of a large island called Atland, which was roughly on the same latitude as the British Isles, in what is now the North Sea (in other words, off the coast of modern Holland). Dr Ottema seems to think that Atland is Plato's Atlantis,* which most commentators have placed somewhere in the mid-Atlantic. But since Plato says only that it was "beyond the Pillars of Hercules" (what is now Gibraltar), Ottema could be correct.

According to the *Oera Linda Book*, Atland had an excellent climate and an abundance of food. And since its rulers were wise and deeply religious, it was a peaceful and contented land. Its legendary founder was a half-mythical woman named Frya – obviously a version of the Nordic *Freya*, the moon goddess, whose name means "a lady". (In the same way, *frey* means "a lord".) Its people worshiped one God, under the (to us) unpronounceable name of Wr-alda. Frya was one of three sisters, the other two being named Lyda and Finda. Lyda was dark-skinned and became the founder of the black races; Finda was yellow-skinned and became the founder of the yellow races. Frya was white.

* See "Atlantis" chapter 2.

All of this is obviously legend. But the *Oera Linda Book* then goes on to describe historical events.

In the year 2193 BC, a great catastrophe of some sort struck Atland, and it was overwhelmed by the sea. Logic suggests that the same catastrophe must have struck the British Isles, since they were so close; but if Atland was as low and flat as Holland, we can understand why it was submerged. (The Dogger Bank, where Atland would have been situated, is the shallowest area of the North Sea.)

According to Plato, Atlantis had been destroyed in a great catastrophe more than nine thousand years earlier. But one modern authority, Professor A. G. Galanopoulos, has argued that all the figures associated with Atlantis (which were recorded by Egyptian priests) were about ten times too great – for example, Plato says that the moat around the royal city was ten thousand stades (more than a thousand miles) long, which would make the royal city about three hundred times larger than Greater London or Los Angeles. If we divide nine thousand years by ten, we get nine hundred. The Egyptian priests told the Athenian lawgiver Solon about Atlantis around 600 BC, which would make the date for the destruction of Atlantis about 1500 BC (nine hundred years earlier). This is roughly the date of the explosion of the volcano of Santorini (north of Crete) that devastated most of the Mediterranean, and Galanopoulos argues that the island of Santorini was Atlantis. The only problem is that Plato placed Atlantis beyond the Pillars of Hercules – in which case, Atland is certainly a contender.

Another reason for the relative neglect of the *Oera Linda Book* is that its narrative seems so unfamiliar and its names are so strange; in this respect it resembles the *Book of Mormon* or that extraordinary work entitled *Oahspe*, which was "dictated" to an American medium named J. B. Newbrough at roughly the same time the *Oera Linda Book* was published. But these two documents claim some kind of "divine" origin, while the *Oera Linda Book* purports to be a historical document.

Nevertheless, the people mentioned in it are not pure invention. A later book speaks at length about a warrior named Friso, an officer of Alexander the Great (born 356 BC), who is described in other Nordic chronicles. (The *Oera Linda Book* also speaks at length of Alexander the Great.) These chronicles state that Friso came from India. The *Oera Linda Book* says that Friso was descended from a Frisian colony that settled in the Punjab about 1550 BC; moreover, the Greek geographer Strabo mentions this strange "Indian" tribe, referring to them by the name *Germania*. The *Oera Linda Book* even mentions Ulysses and recounts how he went in search of a sacred lamp – a priestess had foretold that if he could find it, he would become king of all Italy. After an unsuccessful attempt to buy the lamp from its priestess-custodian, the "Earth Mother" (using treasures looted from Troy), he sailed to a place named Walhallagara (which sounds oddly like Valhalla) and had a love affair with a priestess named Kalip (obviously Calypso), with whom he stayed for several years "to the scandal of all who knew it". From Kalip he obtained a sacred lamp of the kind he wanted, but it did him no good, for he was shipwrecked and had to be picked up, naked and destitute, by another ship.

This fragment of Greek history, tossed into the *Oera Linda Book* is interesting for two reasons. It dates this adventure of Ulysses about 1188, which is about fifty years later than modern archaeology would date the fall of Troy (see chapter 23). But the *Oera Linda Book* could be correct. And it states that the nymph Calypso was actually a *burgtmaagd* (a word meaning "borough maid" – literally, a virgin priestess in charge of vestal virgins). This is consistent with the central claim of the *Oera Linda Book*: that after the "deluge", the Frisians sailed the globe and became the founders of Mediterranean civilization, as well as settling in India. It is obvious why scholars have ignored the book. To take it seriously would mean virtually rewriting ancient history. If, for example, we accept that Calypso's island, Walhallagara, was the island of Walcheren, in the North Sea (as the commentary on the *Oera Linda Book* claims it was), then Ulysses sailed right out of the Mediterranean. It is certainly simpler to accept Homer's version of the story.

After nearly a century of neglect, the *Oera Linda Book* was rediscovered by an English scholar named Robert Scrutton. In his fascinating book *The Other Atlantis*, Scrutton tells how, in 1967, he and his wife – a "sensitive" with strong psychometric powers[*] – were walking over Dartmoor when she experienced a terrifying vision of a flood: great green waves higher than the hills pouring across the land.

Eight years later he found legends of a great deluge in ancient poetry known as the Welsh Triads (which also speak of King Arthur). The Triads explain that long before the Kmry (the Welsh) came to Britain, there was a great flood that depopulated the entire island. One ship survived, and those who sailed in it settled in the "Summer Land" peninsula (which Scrutton identifies as the Crimea – still called Krym – in the Black Sea). These peoples decided to seek other lands, because their peninsula was subject to flooding. One portion went to Italy and

[*] See "Psychometry – Telescope into the Past" chapter 43

the other across Germany and France and into Britain. (In fact, this account does not contradict the little we know about the mysterious people called the Celts, whose origin is unknown.) So the Kmry came back to Britain – probably around 600 BC – and brought their Druidic religion, which involved human sacrifice.

Scrutton went on to uncover many other legends concerning a great catastrophe in ancient Welsh poetry and in the Icelandic Eddas (where it was known as Ragnarok). It is worth mentioning that Ignatius Donnelly, whose book *Atlantis: The Antediluvian World** caused a sensation in 1882, went on to write another classic, *Ragnarok: The Age of Fire and Ice* in the following year; in this volume he attempted to study catastrophe legends of the northern hemisphere and created a remarkable theory of continental drift that later proved to be totally accurate.

Scrutton's research led him to rediscover the *Oera Linda Book* and to become absorbed in its strange yet credible account of ancient history. The first question he asked himself was: what was the precise nature of the catastrophe that destroyed Atland and depopulated Britain? In *The Other Atlantis* (1977) he suggests that it was a giant meteor or asteroid that struck the earth somewhere in the region of the North Pole; the force of the explosion had the effect of tilting the earth's axis into a more upright position, so lands that had formerly had long, hot summers now developed arctic conditions. The Greeks have their legends of the Hyperboreans, a people who live in idyllic conditions in the far north, and Scrutton identifies these with the Atlanders.

This projectile, Scrutton suggests, produced the crater known as the Arctic Ocean – which, he claims, would look like one of the enormous craters of the moon if its water was drained away. Many stones and rocks that modern scientists believe were moved by glaciers were actually, Scrutton suggests, hurled by the explosion. But this part of his theory is open to a simple objection. The opening section of the *Oera Linda Book* says that during the whole summer before the flood "the sun had been hid behind the clouds, as if unwilling to look upon the earth". There was perpetual calm, and "a damp mist hung like a wet sail over the houses and marshes". Then, "in the midst of this stillness, the earth began to tremble as if she was dying. The mountains opened to vomit forth fire and flames".

That seems clearly to be a description of a volcanic catastrophe of the kind that is supposed to have destroyed Atlantis, not a tidal wave caused

* See "Atlantis".

by a meteor. Does this mean that the meteor theory must be abandoned? Not necessarily. A meteor that struck in the region of the North Pole would certainly have produced a tidal wave, but if the polar cap itself was covered with ice, it may not have been great enough to cause a tidal wave that would submerge Britain and Atland. But the volcanic activity that would almost certainly follow such an impact *could* produce a mighty tidal wave, like the one caused by the explosion of Santorini (and later of Krakatoa).

Scrutton also mentions a description in the Finnish epic the *Kalevala* of a time when the sun vanished from the sky and the world became frozen and barren, and quotes a modern introduction that places this at a period when the Magyars (Hungarians) and the Finns were still united – at least three thousand years ago.

Scrutton believes that the "maps of the ancient sea kings" described by Professor Charles Hapgood (and discussed in chapter 49) confirm his view of the catastrophe that destroyed Atland. Once again, there is an objection. Core samples taken in Queen Maud Land (in the Antarctic) show that the last time the South Pole was unfrozen was around 4000 BC So the great maritime civilization that Hapgood believes was responsible for the "ancient maps" must have flourished before then.

This, of course, does not rule out a catastrophe some two thousand years later – perhaps the civilization of Atland lasted for two thousand years, like that of the Egyptians. But if Hapgood is correct, and his great maritime civilization existed more than six thousand years ago and then was either forgotten or destroyed in a great catastrophe, it certainly becomes difficult to reconcile the two theories.

There is, however, one way of reconciling them that is no bolder – or more absurd – than the theories themselves. Hapgood believed that the ancient maps were evidence of a *worldwide* maritime civilization that existed long before Alexander the Great. Let us, then, posit the existence of such a civilization that began sometime after the last great ice age – say, around 10,000 BC. Six thousand years later this civilization is highly developed in the Antarctic and in Atland. In other parts of the world – like the Middle East – it is less highly developed, although there are already cities, and the plow has been developed. For unknown reasons – no one knows what causes ice ages – the cold returns, and the Antarctic civilization freezes up, so its peoples are forced to go elsewhere – notably to Egypt. The Atland civilization, being in more temperate latitudes, is not affected. Then, in 2192 BC, comes the "great catastrophe" that tilted the earth's axis. Now, like the inhabitants of the South Pole, the Atlanders are also forced to move – and of course they move south, to regions that have not been affected by the great catastrophe – like India and the Mediterranean. If this scenario is correct, then both Hapgood and Scrutton could be right.

One thing seems clear: that the ancient maps prove the existence of a great maritime civilization that flourished before Alexander the Great. Like the maps, the *Oera Linda Book* also points to the existence of such a civilization. Even if the *Oera Linda Book* proved to be a forgery, the evidence of the maps would be unaffected. But at the present time, there is no evidence that it is a forgery. In this case, it deserves to be reprinted in a modern edition and carefully studied by historians – as well as read by the general public for its fascinating tales of murder and battle. If it proves to be genuine, the *Oera Linda Book* could revolutionize our view of world history.

40

The "People of the Secret"

Early in 1883 a book called *Esoteric Buddhism* caused an immediate sensation, and quickly went into a second edition. It was by a slender, balding little man called Alfred Percy Sinnett, editor of India's most influential newspaper the *Pioneer*. What caused the excitement was Sinnett's claim, on the very first page, that he had obtained his information from "hidden masters", men who lived in the high mountains of Tibet and who were virtually immortal. Coming from the editor of a newspaper that was regarded as the mouthpiece of the British government in India, this could not be dismissed as "occultist" lunacy. Such a man deserved serious attention when he declared:

> For reasons that will appear as the present explanations proceed, the very considerable block of hitherto secret teaching this volume contains, has been conveyed to me, not only without conditions of the usual kind, but to the express end that I might convey it in my turn to the world at large.

Many people took Sinnett very seriously indeed. The poet W.B. Yeats read the book and handed it to his friend Charles Johnston, who was so impressed that he rushed off to London for permission to set up a Dublin branch of the Theosophical Society, the publisher of Sinnett's book.

It was almost three years later that the general public learned how Sinnett had obtained his "hitherto secret teaching", and the sceptics felt confirmed in their cynicism. In October 1880 Sinnett and his wife had played host to that remarkable lady Madame Blavatsky, who told him that most of her knowledge had been obtained from her "secret Masters" who lived in the Himalayas. She convinced Sinnett of her genuineness by a series of minor miracles. On a picnic, when an unexpected guest had turned up, she ordered another guest to dig in the hillside with a table knife; he unearthed a cup and saucer of the same pattern as the rest of the china. When a woman remarked casually that she wished she could find a lost brooch Madame Blavatsky told the other guests to go and search in the garden; the missing brooch was found in a flower-bed wrapped in paper. And when Sinnett expressed his desire to correspond directly with the "Masters" Madame Blavatsky promised to do what she could, and a few days later Sinnett found lying in his desk the first of what were to become known as "the Mahatma letters". It was from this series of letters that Sinnett obtained his knowledge of "esoteric Buddhism".

Unfortunately, this information about the Mahatma letters was revealed in a report on Theosophy published by the Society for Psychical Research towards the end of 1885, and the rest of the report was damning. It was the result of an investigation by a young man named Richard Hodgson, who had talked to Madame Blavatsky's housekeepers and learned that most of the "miracles" were fraudulent; their most convincing demonstration was to cause a letter – addressed to Hodgson and referring to the conversation they had only just had – to fall out of the air above his head. Hodgson's report had the effect of totally destroying Madame Blavatsky's credibility, and demolishing the myth of the "hidden Masters" in Tibet.

Having said all this, it is necessary to admit that there are still a number of things to be said in Madame Blavatsky's favour. The evidence of many observers shows that she was undoubtedly a genuine "spirit medium". Constance Wachtmeister, a countess who became Madame Blavatsky's factotum in 1884, found it at first a little unnerving. She was sharing a room (divided by a screen) with Madame Blavatsky, and as soon as Madame was asleep the raps would begin, continuing at intervals of ten minutes until about 6 a.m. A lamp was burning by Madame Blavatsky's bed; on one of the first nights the countess was kept awake and slipped behind the screen to extinguish it. She had only just got back into bed when the lamp was relit. Madame Blavatsky was obviously asleep, and in any case the countess would have heard the scrape of a match or tinder box. Three times she extinguished it; three times it promptly relit itself. The raps also continued. The third time she put it out, she saw a disembodied brown hand turning up the wick. She woke Madame Blavatsky, who looked pale and shaken, and explained that she had been "with the Masters" and that it was dangerous to awaken her suddenly.

Charles Johnston describes how he sat watching HPB (as her admirers called her), tapping her fingers idly on a table-top. Then she raised her hand a foot or so above the table and continued the tapping movement; the sounds continued to come from the table. Then she turned towards Johnston, and began to send the "astral taps" on to the back of his hand. "I could both feel and hear them. It was something like taking sparks from the prime conductor of an electric machine; or, better still, perhaps, it was like spurting quicksilver through your fingers".

It is of course possible that all this was fraudulent; but it seems unlikely. If we can accept the hypothesis that there *are* genuine mediums that is, mediums who either possess, or are possessed by, certain "magical" powers then it seems fairly certain that Madame Blavatsky was such a person. And if we can accept that there are genuine mediums, then the next question is whether their powers are the result of some mysterious activity of the unconscious mind, or whether they involve some external force – some emanation of the "collective unconscious", or even "spirits". Most students of the paranormal end up by conceding (however reluctantly) that there *does* seem to be some external force, although understandably many of them find it impossible to concede the existence of spirits.

The psychiatrist Wilson Van Dusen, who studied hundreds of patients suffering from hallucinations in the Mendocino State Hospital, reached the remarkable conclusion that the nature of the hallucinations had been accurately described by the eighteenth-century mystic Emanuel Swedenborg. They seemed to fall into two types, which he calls "higher order" and "lower order". Lower-order hallucinations seemed to be stupid and repetitive; they "are similar to drunken bums at a bar who like to tease and torment just for the fun of it". But higher-order hallucinations seemed "more likely to be symbolic, religious, supportive, genuinely instructive". A gas-fitter experienced a higher-order hallucination of a beautiful woman who showed him thousands of symbols. Van Dusen was able to hold a dialogue with this "woman", with the help of the patient, and after the conversation the patient asked for just one clue to what they had been talking about.

If we can accept this much, then we can also see that Madame Blavatsky's "secret masters" may not have been her own invention. She told Constance Wachtmeister that the raps that resounded from above her bed were a "psychic telegraph" that linked her to the Masters, who watched over her body while she slept. If we are willing to concede that the Masters may have been what Swedenborg calls "angels", or what Van Dusen calls higher-order hallucinations, then it suddenly ceases to be self-evident that HPB was an old fraud. We have at least to consider the hypothesis that *something* was going on which is slightly more complicated.

Madame Blavatsky was not the inventor of the idea of secret masters; the notion is part of an ancient "occult" tradition. The composer Cyril Scott, who was also an "occultist", writes in his *Outline of Modern Occultism* (1935) of the basic tenets of "Occult science":

> Firstly, the occultist holds that Man is in process of evolving from comparative imperfection to much higher states of physical and spiritual evolution. Secondly, that the evolutionary process in all its phases is directed by a Great Hierarchy of Intelligences who have themselves reached these higher states.

Now, many modern thinkers would agree that man is involved in an evolutionary process that involves his mind as well as his body, and many would insist that the process is not entirely a matter of Darwinian mechanisms (see, for example, the contributors to Arthur Koestler's *Beyond Reductionism*). But it is clearly a very long step from this kind of evolutionism to the belief that the evolutionary process is being directed by "higher intelligences".

Such a step was, in fact, taken (on purely scientific grounds) by the cybernetician David Foster, in his book *The Intelligent Universe*. Foster's basic assertion is simply that, to the eye of the cyberneticist, evolution seems to suggest some intelligent intervention. Cybernetics is basically the science of making machines behave as if they are intelligent – as does, for example, a modern washing machine, which performs a number of complex processes, heating water up to a certain temperature, washing the clothes for a certain period, rinsing them, spin-drying, etc. But these processes are "programmed" into the machine, and can be selected by merely turning a dial, or inserting a kind of plastic biscuit – each of whose edges contains a different programme – into a slot. An acorn could be regarded as a device containing the programme for an oak-tree. But to the eye of a cybernetician the acorn, like the plastic biscuit, suggests some form of programming. Could an acorn be programmed solely by Darwinian natural selection? Foster points out that one basic rule about computer-programming is that the intelligence that does the programming must be of a higher, more complex, order than the programme itself. Similarly, in order to drive a car or use an electric typewriter my mind must work faster than the machine; if the machine goes faster than my mind, the result will be disaster or confusion. In cybernetics, blue light could be a programme for red light, but not vice versa on the same principle that Dickens can create Mr Pickwick, but a Mr Pickwick could not create a Dickens. And Foster argues that the energies involved in programming DNA would need to be higher than any form of energy found on earth. He argues that the process would require energies of the same order as cosmic rays. Such an argument obviously implies that the complexity of life on earth can only be accounted for by some intelligence "out there".

We may reject this argument, pointing out that "instinct" may create a complexity that looks like superintelligence. Mathematical prodigies, who can work out problems of bewildering complexity within seconds, are often of otherwise low intelligence. There is no evolutionary necessity for the human brain to work out such problems; so why *has* the brain developed such a power? The physiologist would reply: as a kind of by-product, just as a simple calculating device like an abacus could be used to multiply numbers far beyond the grasp of the human imagination. But those who believe that evolution is basically purposive use such examples as mathematical prodigies to argue that the evolution of man's higher faculties cannot be explained in purely Darwinian terms.

Since Madame Blavatsky (who died in 1891) there have been many "occultists" (I use the word in its broadest sense, as meaning those who are interested in the paranormal) who have believed that they were in contact with higher intelligences. Alice Bailey became an active member of the Theosophical Society after the death of Madame Blavatsky, and was convinced she was in touch with Sinnett's "Mahatma" (it means "great soul") Koot Hoomi. In 1919, disgusted by the power struggles within the society, she founded her own group, and produced a large number of books dictated by an entity called "the Tibetan".

The Rev. Stainton Moses, an early member of the Society for Psychical Research, used "automatic writing" to produce large quantities of a script that was published after his death under the title *Spirit Teachings*. Although Moses published extracts from these in *Light*, he was too embarrassed to admit that some of the "spirits" who dictated them claimed to be Plato, Aristotle and half a dozen Old Testament prophets. Yet there was strong evidence that these scripts were not simply the product of his own unconscious mind. On one occasion Moses asked the "spirit" if it would go to the bookcase, select the last book but one on the second shelf, and read out the last paragraph on page 94. The spirit did this correctly. Moses was still not convinced, so the spirit selected its own book. It dictated a passage about Pope, then told Moses precisely where to find it; when Moses took the book off the shelf, it opened at the right page. The spirit dictated these passages while the books remained closed on the shelf.

In 1963 two Americans, Jane Roberts and her husband Rob, began experimenting with an ouija board, inspired to some extent by "Patience Worth" (see chapter 62). Various personalities identified themselves and gave messages; then after a while a character who identified himself as "Seth" began to come through:

> It was immediately apparent that the board's messages had suddenly increased in scope and quality. We found ourselves dealing with a personality who was of superior intelligence, a personality with a distinctive humor, one who always displayed outstanding psychological insight and knowledge that was certainly beyond our own conscious abilities.

"Seth" went on to dictate a number of books, with titles like *The Seth Material* and *Seth Speaks,* which achieved tremendous popularity. They certainly demonstrate that Seth, whether an aspect of Jane Roberts's unconscious mind or a genuine "spirit", was of a high level of intelligence. Yet when Jane Roberts produced a book that purported to be the after-death journal of the philosopher William James, it was difficult to take it seriously. James's works are noted for their vigour and clarity of style; Jane Roberts's "communicator" writes like an undergraduate:

> Yet, what a rambunctious nationalistic romp, and it was matched with almost missionary fervour by the psychologists, out to root from man's soul all of those inconsistencies and passions that were buried there; and to leash these as well for the splendid pursuits of progress, industry and the physical manipulation of nature for man's use.

There is a clumsiness here that is quite unlike James's swift-moving, colloquial prose. "And to leash these as well . . ." is simply not William James; he would simply have said "And to harness these . . ."

Yet Seth himself often says things of immense and profound importance – for example, his emphasis (in *The Nature of Personal Reality*) on the importance of the conscious mind and conscious decision.

> I quite realise that many of my statements will contradict the beliefs of those of you who accept the idea that the conscious mind

is relatively powerless, and that the answers to problems lie hidden beneath – i.e., in the "unconscious". Obviously the conscious mind is a phenomenon, not a thing. It is ever-changing. It can be concentrated or turned by the ego in literally endless directions. It can view outward reality or turn inward, observing its own contents . . . It is far more flexible than you give it credit for.

Comments like these are so opposed to our familiar dogmas about the unconscious and the "solar plexus" that they make an impact of startling freshness. This is not the usual diffuse verbiage of "inspirational" writing, but the communication of a vision into the powers of the mind. If Seth is an aspect of Jane Roberts, then she is a philosopher of considerable insight.

The experience of the Londoner Tony Neate is typical of the "psychic" who finds himself "in communication" with Van Dusen's "higher order hallucinations". In 1950, at the age of twenty, he began as a skeptic playing with a primitive form of ouija board, a glass on a polished table-top; the glass flew off the table with such violence that it knocked a man over backward. He began to practise psychometry – receiving "pictures" from objects that are held in the hand – and found that his visions of the history of such objects were often accurate. One day when he was practising psychometry he went into a trance, and "spirits" spoke through him. A "spirit" who claimed to be Freud quoted a German book giving the exact page; Tony Neate was able to track down the book in the London Library and found the quotation accurate. A spirit who claimed to be the singer Melba told of a concert she had given in Brussels; again, the statement was found to be accurate.

Then, during the Christmas of 1955, Tony Neate found himself tuned in to a character who called himself Helio-Arcanophus (H-A for short), who claimed to be an inhabitant of Atlantis – the name means high priest of the sun. Tony Neate and his associates founded a society called the Atlanteans, and they moved into a farm complex in West Malvern. The writer Annie Wilson spent some time there, and her book about her experiences, *Where There's Love*, makes it clear that, like Seth, "H-A" has many important and some original things to say. Reading these utterances, it is natural for the skeptic to assume that they originate in the unconscious mind of Tony Neate. But if that is the case, then how can we explain the Freud quotation and the information obtained from "Melba"? And if we are willing to admit that this information was obtained "paranormally" or that *any* information can be obtained paranormally, as in the case of the Glastonbury scripts (see *Time in Disarray*) then it is obviously possible that the same applies to the utterances of Seth and Helio-Arcanophus.

Not all "occult teachings" claim to originate with disembodied entities; others are accompanied by the claim that they have been preserved down the ages by secret societies or brotherhoods. George Gurdjieff, one of the most original thinkers of the twentieth century, spent much of his youth in search of a certain "Sarmoung Brotherhood", and claimed to have received his basic teachings from a monastic brotherhood in the northern Himalayas. The essence of Gurdjieff's teaching consists in the notion that ordinary consciousness is a form of "sleep", that nearly all human activities are entirely "mechanical", and that if man wishes to cease to be mechanical he has to make a tremendous effort of will. But books like *In Search of the Miraculous* (by Gurdjieff's leading follower P.D. Ouspensky) make it clear that behind Gurdjieff's "psychological" teachings lay a highly complex cosmological system, which has no obvious relevance to the psychological teachings, and which it seems unlikely that Gurdjieff invented himself.

This cosmology is further elabourated in the four-volume work of another leading Gurdjieff follower, J.G. Bennett, *The Dramatic Universe*, which is founded on the assertion that "there is a class of cosmic essences called Demiurges that is responsible for maintaining the universal order", and that these Demiurgic Intelligences "work upon time scales far exceeding the span of a human life". Bennett calls the universe "dramatic" to underline his sense of the importance of free will; because the universe is not dead and predetermined, the final outcome is uncertain. "The key to the whole scheme is will-time or Hyparxis. This is the region in which the will is free to make decisions that introduce something new and *uncaused* into the world process". The demiurges have far greater power than man to introduce something new and uncaused into the world process; but they are not infallible. Although their main task is "to guide the evolution of the world from its first lifeless beginning", they have "guided the process by experiment and trial, sometimes making mistakes and retracing their steps, sometimes making great leaps forward, as when life came out of the ocean and land creatures began". Bennett adds that Gurdjieff calls the demiurges "angels", "but this had so many meanings that it is best avoided".

The existence of a secret tradition of hidden teachings is hinted at in Idries Shah's book *The Sufis*, and it was in a review of this book in the *London Evening News* that its literary editor, Edward Campbell, wrote:

For many centuries there has been a strange legend in the East. It suggests that in some hidden centre, perhaps in the Highlands of Central Asia, there exists a colony of men possessing exceptional powers. This centre acts, in some respects at least, as the secret government of the world.

Some aspects of this legend came to the West during the Crusades; the idea was renewed in Rosicrucian guise in 1614; it was restated with variations last century by Mme Blavatsky and the French diplomat Jacoliot; was suggested again by the English author Talbot Mundy, and most recently by the Mongolian traveller Ossendowski in 1918.

In the mysterious Shangri-la of this legend, certain men, evolved beyond the ordinary human situation, act as the regents of powers beyond this planet.

Through lower echelons – who mingle unsuspected in ordinary walks of life, both East and West – they act at critical stages of history, contriving results necessary to keep the whole evolution of the earth in step with events in the solar system.

And in his book *The People of the Secret* (1983), Campbell (under the punning pseudonym Ernest Scott) goes on to suggest that "in the first quarter of the 20th century, Western science had not only reached a critical stage but an impasse and that, simultaneously, material possibly capable of resolving that situation appeared unobtrusively from the East". He goes on to suggest that "this interpretation derives from a source superior to, and qualitatively different from, ordinary intellect", and that "similar 'intervention' occurs at critical points in human history and has done so in all cultures and all ages in a form appropriate to the moment". Campbell refers to the sources of this influence as "the Tradition", and suggests that between 1920 and 1950 part of the intention appears to have been to "reveal publicly *the mechanism of the Tradition's own operation*". And he mentions that two men who were in contact with "the Tradition" were J.G. Bennett and Rodney Collin, both followers of Gurdjieff.

Campbell goes on to suggest a close analogy between the human organism and a civilized culture.

A sperm cell originates a new individual. Suppose a conscious man originates a new culture. Suppose that within life there are a few men, unsuspected and hidden, who are able to process conscious energy and are therefore in touch with the pattern of conscious energy outside life. (In J.G. Bennett's terminology this would correspond to the Demiurgic level.) Such conscious men would be to a human culture as a sperm cell is to tissue cells in the human body.

Campbell then sketches out the "cultural systems" outlined by Rodney Collin in his book *The Theory of Celestial Influence* (Chapter XVI): Aurignacian man, Magdalenian man, Middle and Far Eastern Man (Egypt, Sumer, Ancient India), Graeco-Roman Man, Early Christian Man, Mediaeval Christian Man, Renaissance Man, Modern Man. In this scheme Egypt gave birth to the world of the Greeks, and the Greeks transmitted the "energy of fertilization" to Rome via the philosophy of the Stoics and Epicureans. "Again a period of dazzling achievement seemingly from nowhere". Early Christianity sprang out of Rome, but by the eighth century had fossilized into the corrupt church of the mediaeval papacy. The next culture, according to Campbell, is the medieval church, which originated in Cluny, whose Gothic cathedral "encapsulated all the Gothic cathedrals to come". "In each of these there was a suggestion of a whole unseen cosmology; each an encyclopedia in stone containing, for those who could read . . . a summary of the Plan and Purpose of evolution". Campbell clearly agrees with the author of *The Mystery of the Cathedrals* (see chapter 17) that Gothic cathedrals were alchemical textbooks. The medieval masons were exponents of "the Tradition". Campbell also notes that this was also the period of "esoteric building in Islam", and mentions the joint mission from Cluny and Chartres to Saracen Spain, which returned with knowledge of logarithms, algebra and alchemy.

This was the preparation for the next major stage: the Renaissance. And Renaissance culture finally gave way to the modern epoch around the mid-nineteenth century – Campbell mentions 1859, the year of *The Origin of Species*. Our modern age, Campbell suggests, reached the peak of its development about 1935 with road and air transport and radio and cinema – and indeed, we can see that these developments transformed the mental outlook of the human race just as the invention of printing did in the Renaissance. The modern epoch may well continue for another six or seven hundred years; but the new epoch that will replace it will struggle into being long before our own period comes to an end.

Campbell's starting point, then, is the "Demiurgic intelligences" of J.G. Bennett. He assumes that these are a reality, and that their activities can be seen in human history. From the point of view of this "Hidden Directorate", early Christianity took the wrong turning. He sees the mission of Jesus as an event of universal significance, an attempt to introduce certain energies into the evolutionary process – the energies of a selfless love. Campbell suggests that the Early Fathers "rejected the wisdom component within which lay the techniques of developing consciousness". They reasoned that nothing is necessary for spiritual evolution except the Christ. The "heretic" Arius felt instinctively that this was a mistake. His heresy consisted of the assertion that the Son was *not* the equal of the Father – a dim recognition that Jesus had been "sent" into history at a particular time for a particular purpose. When the Council of Nicaea rejected this view in AD 325, they turned their back on the "Demiurgic Tradition". "Yet", says Campbell,

> Demiurgic responsibility for evolution remained. The Demiurges were still obligated to achieve evolutionary gains, in harmony with growth beyond the earth. Their agents, the Hidden Directorate on earth, were still required to contrive the social environment which would provide the necessary opportunities. The mandate of both is to raise the level of consciousness of mankind in general and of suitable individuals exceptionally. Mankind in the West had subconsciously decided that this was no longer necessary.

The coming of Mohammed once again allowed the Demiurges a foothold. A "school" for the oral transmission of his ideas formed around him. "This inner group of 90 took an oath of fidelity and are said to have adopted the name Sufi". (A moment later, Campbell confuses the issue by stating that this is not to say that Sufism derives from Mohammedanism, and that the Sufic tradition actually goes back through Plato, Hippocrates, Pythagoras and Hermes Trismegistos. But the main thrust of his argument is clear.) In due course the Arabs invaded Spain, and planted the seeds that would become the Renaissance.

Campbell's chapter on "Rome, Christianity and Islam" contains a clear example of what he means by Demiurgic intervention in human history. The monasteries of western Europe, which preserved learning during the Dark Ages, were too remote and inaccessible to serve as real cultural centres. But St Patrick's conversion of Ireland – beginning in AD 432 – caused "the rebirth of Celtic culture by a 'shock' from Christianity". Ireland became a centre of learning – so much so that in 550 a ship had to be chartered to carry scholars from Gaul to Cork. Celtic Christianity valued pagan literature. St Columba and his pupil Columbanus directed the missionary flow back to Europe, and Columbanus founded more than a hundred monasteries. Rome finally brought the Celtic Church to heel in 664 at the Synod of Whitby, but the impulse could not be destroyed. Two Celtic monks were established as dispensers of wisdom at the court of Charlemagne. Campbell makes the fascinating suggestion that the Celtic Church obtained some of its wisdom through "psychokinetic techniques". Psychokinesis is the term invented by students of parapsychology for "mind over matter", and Campbell suggests elsewhere in the book that this is the basic secret of alchemy; it is not quite clear how he believes the Celtic Church used these techniques.

In the ninth century, says Campbell, schools of initiates began to flourish in Córdoba and Toledo, and their efforts were to have far-reaching influences, which can still be traced in the world today. The doctor Al Razi and the scholar Avicenna, both Persians, were only two of an immense number of scholars who "provided the raw material for the coming injection of intellect into Europe". Among these intellectual impulses were the schools of thought that would later become known as Freemasonry and Illuminism, "impulses which at their seventh harmonic were to encompass the French Revolution".

The next five chapter of *The People of the Secret* are an interpretation of European history from the "interventionist" point of view. They consider the Kabbalah, the Tarot and alchemy as vehicles of "the Tradition", and study the historical significance of Catharism, the rise of the Troubadors, and the legends of King Arthur. Again and again, Campbell traces the original seed of these movements back to their Sufic origins.

In the chapter on Gurdjieff, Campbell comments:

Since the early 1950s, a great deal of hitherto unknown material has become available, and in the nature of things this cannot have happened by accident. If it has leaked, it is because those in charge of it have decided to "leak" it.

Separately, the various hints amount to little. Taken together, they suggest for the first time the nature of the organisation, long suspected but never identified, which is concerned with injecting developmental possibilities into the historical process at certain critical points.

On the basis of internal evidence, it may be legitimate to suggest that this organisation is the expression of one of the Centres inferred by J.G. Bennett as directing the evolution of the whole human race. In *The Dramatic Universe*, the Centres of Transformation are the four hypothetical regions where, 35,000 to 40,000 years ago, the human mind was endowed with creativity and man became *Homo sapiens sapiens*. Twelve thousand years ago, these Centres withdrew for some 80 generations to prepare for the debut of modern man. The suggestion is that one of these, immediately responsible for the West, has decided to come, partially at least, into the open in the second half of the 20th century. It may be that the intellectual development of the West is now at such a stage that the parent can only guide the offspring further by taking it into its confidence.

Campbell mentions that attempts by Gurdjieff's pupils to make contact with the monasteries or other teaching centres where Gurdjieff gained his "occult" knowledge were all unsuccessful.

In the 1930s it is believed that Ouspensky made contact with the Mevlevi (Order of Dervishes) and asked them to send someone to England. This they declined to do, but indicated that they were prepared to receive a representative from him. One of Ouspensky's senior pupils was ready to leave for the East in 1939 when War broke out and the project was abandoned.

But in 1961 a journalist seeking material for an article on Sufi practices "was unaccountably introduced to every facility for getting material . . . This journalist, Omar Burke, found himself allowed to visit a secret Dervish community whose location has been identified as Kunji Zagh ("Raven's Corner') in Baluchistan". Burke then wrote up his findings in an article in *Blackwood's Magazine* in December 1961. It was seen by a member of a London Gurdjieff group who realized that one trail to Gurdjieff's source was being openly revealed in a magazine. But when the London group made contact with the "source" they were told that it would be pointless to come to Baluchistan because the current focus of activity was in England.

Campbell argues that Gurdjieff's "source" was the Sufic tradition. What is implied, presumably, by the comment about the "current focus" in London is that this is to be found in the group run by Idries Shah, author of the book *The Sufis*. Bennett had in fact handed over his own teaching centre at Coombe Springs to Shah. In his autobiography *Witness* Bennett describes how in 1962 he was told by an old friend about Idries Shah, who had come to England from Afghanistan to seek out followers of Gurdjieff and "complete their teaching". At a meeting with Shah his first impressions were unfavourable.

He was restless, smoked incessantly, talked too much, and seemed too intent on making a good impression. Halfway through the evening our attitude completely changed. We recognised that he was not only an unusually gifted man, but that he had the indefinable something that marks the man who has seriously worked upon himself.

Shah, he says, did not claim to be a teacher, but he claimed to have been sent by his own teacher, and that "he had the support of the 'Guardians of the Tradition'". He goes on to quote a document Shah gave him, "Declaration of the People of the Tradition", which stated that a "secret, special, superior form of knowledge" really exists, and could be transmitted

to the people to whom this material is addressed . . . This knowledge is concentrated, administered and presided over by three forms of individual . . . They have been called an "Invisible Hierarchy" because normally they are not in communication or contact with ordinary human beings: certainly not in two-way communication with them.

Bennett then goes on to tell how he was persuaded by Shah to hand over Coombe Springs, with no strings attached, and a note of bitterness creeps in when he describes how Shah sold the house for £100,000 only a year later. Yet it remains clear that in spite of a certain personal animosity towards Shah, Bennett still does not discount the possibility that he is precisely what he says he is.

In any case, Campbell's thesis does not stand or fall by whether the reader is willing to accept Idries Shah as a representative of "the secret people". It was Bennett himself who invented the phrase "the Hidden Directorate" in *The Dramatic Universe*. Campbell summarizes the thesis of his book:

The script for the long human story was written by intelligences much greater than man's own . . . Responsibility for this process on Earth lies with an Intelligence which has been called The Hidden Directorate. This may correspond to the level symbolised in occult legend as an Individual (*eg* "The Regent" or "The Ancient of Days", etc). It is to be equated either with the Demi-Urgic level or with the level immediately below.

Side by side with action on humanity-in-the-mass, the Executive and its subordinates are concerned with local attempts to raise the conscious level of individual men exceptionally.

Such specially selected ordinary individuals may aspire to qualify for participation in the work of the Executive. The process by which they may so qualify is the Magnum Opus – the "Great Work". This is equivalent to a vertical ascent to a higher level as opposed to a gradual rise with the evolutionary tide.

In 1857 an American schoolmistress and authoress, Delia Bacon, produced her controversial work *Philosophy of the Plays of Shakespeare Unfolded* (see chapter 51) in which she suggested that "Shakespeare" was actually a group of Elizabethan scholars, probably led by Francis Bacon, whose aim was to express new ideas that would otherwise have led to torture and imprisonment. The book was received with derision, and Delia Bacon went insane and died soon after. Campbell expresses the same theory at two points in *The People of the Secret*, and skeptics will undoubtedly feel that his whole thesis deserves the same reception as Delia Bacon's. The commonsense objection is that men who represented turning-points in human history – Mohammed, Cosimo de' Medici, Darwin, Einstein – were obviously not members of some "Hidden Directorate". And if no "hidden directorate" is needed to explain their existence or their impact on history, then why bother to entertain such an unnecessary hypothesis?

On the other hand, cultural historians have often observed how certain ideas seem to be "in the air" at certain times, and the Germans coined a word to express this phenomenon, the *Zeitgeist*. Every major discovery and invention seems to have been made by at least two people at the same time (evolution, photography, relativity, sound-recording, television). The biologist Rupert Sheldrake has even produced a theory ("morphic resonance") arguing that once *any* difficult process has been achieved, from crystallization of a new substance to the creation of a new idea, it "spreads" like a wave on the surface of a pond, facilitating the process wherever it occurs. Again, Jung's idea of synchronicity (see chapter 54) suggests some connection between the mind and the world of physical matter which finds no support in the western philosophy of science. Such ideas indicate a movement away from the "dead" universe of nineteenth-century science and towards the "intelligent universe" posited by Dr David Foster. It could be argued that a "hidden directorate", responsible for evolution, is only a logical extension of this idea.

Campbell mentions Yeats's book *A Vision* as an example of a work inspired by "the Tradition". This work is a "system" of human types, expressed in terms of the phases of the moon, and was produced by Yeats's wife Georgie through automatic writing. Yeats's "communicators" also sketched out their own vision of history, which has much in common with that advanced in *People of the Secret*. But when Yeats offered to "spend what remained of life explaining and piecing together" this complex system, he received the reply: "No, we have come to give you metaphors for poetry". Even if the "Hidden Directorate" is accepted only on this level, it remains a fascinating and fruitful hypothesis.

41

Poltergeists

The poltergeist or "noisy ghost" is one of the most baffling phenomena in the whole realm of the paranormal. There are thousands of people who do not believe in ghosts, but who will reluctantly admit that the evidence for the poltergeist is too strong to ignore. The favourite theory of such skeptics is that the poltergeist is some unexplained freak of the human mind.

If the poltergeist is a "ghost" or spirit, as its name implies, then its chief characteristic is as a spirit of mischief. Poltergeists cause objects to fly through the air, doors to open and close, pools of water to appear from nowhere. And they are by no means a rarity; at this very moment some case of poltergeist activity is probably going on within a dozen miles of the reader of this book. (I know of a case that is going on within a dozen miles of me as I write this.)

One of the earliest known cases was recorded in a chronicle called the *Annales Fuldenses* and dates back to AD 858. It took place in a farmhouse at Bingen, on the Rhine; the chronicle describes an "evil spirit" that threw stones, and made the walls shake as if men were striking them with hammers. Stone-throwing is one of the most typical of poltergeist activities. The poltergeist also caused fires – another of their favourite activities (although, for some reason, they seldom do serious damage) – in this case burning the farmer's crops soon after they were gathered in. It also developed a voice – a much rarer feature in poltergeist cases – and denounced the man for various sins, including fornication and adultery. Priests sent by the Bishop of Mainz apparently failed to exorcise it; in fact, it is virtually impossible to get rid of a poltergeist by exorcism ceremonies.

It was only after the formation of the Society for Psychical Research in 1882 that the poltergeist was carefully studied. Then it was observed that in the majority of cases there were adolescent children present in the houses where such occurrences took place; it seemed a reasonable assumption that the children were somehow the "cause" of the outbreak. And in the age of Freud the most widely held theory was that the poltergeist is some kind of "unconscious" manifestation of adolescent sexual energies; but no one has so far offered a theory as to exactly how this can occur.

In England one of the most spectacular cases is also one of the earliest to be thoroughly recorded: the so-called "phantom drummer of Tedworth". It took place in the home of a magistrate called John Mompesson in March 1661. The whole household was kept awake all night by loud drumming noises. The magistrate had been responsible for the arrest of a vagrant named William Drury, who attracted attention in the street by beating a drum. Mompesson had the drum confiscated, in spite of Drury's appeals. Drury escaped from custody – he was being held for possessing forged papers – without his drum. It was after this that the disturbances in Mompesson's household began, and continued for two years. The "spirit" also slammed doors, made panting noises like a dog, and scratching noises like huge rats, as well as purring noises like a cat. It also developed a voice and shouted, "A witch, a witch"! It emptied ashes and chamberpots into the children's beds, and caused various objects to fly through the air. In 1663 Drury, who was in prison for stealing a pig, admitted to a visitor that he was somehow responsible for the disturbances, and said they would continue until Mompesson gave him satisfaction for taking away his drum. But the phenomena finally seem to have faded away.

A famous poltergeist haunting took place in the home of the Rev. Samuel Wesley – grandfather of the founder of Methodism – at his rectory at Epworth in Lincolnshire. "Old Jeffrey", as the family came to call it, kept the family awake on the night of 1 December 1716 with appalling groans, and – a few nights later – with loud knocking noises. It also produced sounds of footsteps walking along the corridors and in empty rooms. The "focus" of the disturbances seemed to be nineteen-year-old Hetty Wesley, who was usually asleep when the disturbances began, and who trembled in her sleep. As usual, the disturbances gradually faded away.

The famous case of the "Cock Lane" ghost ended with an innocent man going to prison for two years. The "focus" of the disturbances was ten-year-old Elizabeth Parsons, daughter of a clerk called Richard Parsons. The Parsons family had two lodgers: a retired innkeeper named William Kent and his common-law wife Fanny Lynes, whose sister Elizabeth had been Kent's previous wife. (This was why they could not marry, the law preventing a man from marrying his deceased wife's sister.) One night when Kent was away Fanny Lynes asked the ten-year-old girl to sleep with her to keep her company; they were kept awake by scratching and rapping noises from behind the wainscot. Soon after this Fanny Lynes died of smallpox, and Kent moved elsewhere. The strange rappings continued, and a clergyman named Moore tried to communicate with the "spirit", using a code of one rap for yes, two for no. By this means the "spirit" identified itself as Fanny Lynes, and accused her ex-"husband" of poisoning her with arsenic.

Parsons was unfortunately unaware that poltergeists tell lies more often than not. And he was not displeased to hear that Kent was a murderer, for he was nursing a grudge against him. Kent had lent him money which he had failed to repay, and was now suing him. So Parsons overlooked the fact that the knockings began before the death of Fanny Lynes, and made no attempt to keep the revelations secret.

In due course, Kent heard that he was being accused of murder by a "spirit", and came to the house in Cock Lane, to hear for himself. When the raps accused him of murder he shouted angrily, "Thou art a lying spirit".

The "ghost" became famous. But when a committee – including Dr Johnson – came to investigate, it preferred to remain silent, convincing Johnson that it was a fraud. Then Kent decided to prosecute for libel. The burden of proof lay on Elizabeth's father who was for legal purposes the accuser. There was another test, and Elizabeth was told that if the ghost did not manifest itself this time, her mother and father would be thrown into prison; naturally, she made sure something happened. But servants peering through a crack saw that she was making the raps with a wooden board. She was denounced as a fake. At the trial Parsons was sentenced to two years in prison, as well as to stand three times in the pillory. His wife received a year; a woman who had often "communicated" with the spirit received six months. Even the parson was fined £588 – a huge sum for those days. But when Parsons was standing in the pillory the crowd was distinctly sympathetic and took up a collection for him – an unusual gesture in that age of cruelty, when crowds enjoyed pelting the malefactor in the pillory, sometimes even killing him. Regrettably, we know nothing of what happened to any of the protagonists after the trial. But it is very clear that the unfortunate Parsons family suffered a great injustice. Many witnesses testified earlier that it would have been impossible for Elizabeth to have faked the rapping noises.

One of America's most famous cases occurred on the farm of a

Tennessee farmer named John Bell; the case of the "Bell witch" is also unusual – in fact, virtually unique – in that the poltergeist ended by causing the death of its victim, Bell himself. Bell had nine children, one of whom, Betsy, was a girl of twelve; she was almost certainly the "focus". The disturbances began in 1817 with scratching noises from the walls, and occasional knocks. Then invisible hands pulled bed-clothes off the beds, and there were choking noises that seemed to come from a human throat. Then stones were thrown and furniture moved. The "spirit" frequently slapped Betsy, and her cheek would redden after the sounds of the blow; it also pulled her hair. After about a year the poltergeist developed a voice – a strange asthmatic croak. (Poltergeist voices seldom sound like human voices – it is as if the "entity" is having to master an unfamiliar medium). It made remarks like "I can't stand the smell of a nigger". After its manifestations Betsy was usually exhausted – she was obviously the source of its energy.

Then John Bell began to be attacked; his jaw became stiff and his tongue swelled. The poltergeist, which had now developed a normal voice, identified itself as an Indian, then as a witch called Old Kate Batts. (It used several voices.) It also declared that it would torment John Bell until he died, which it then proceeded to do. It pulled off his shoes, hit him in the face, and caused him to have violent physical convulsions. All this continued until one day in 1820 he was found in a deep stupor. The "witch" claimed that she had given "old Jack" a dose of a medicine that would kill him. And when Bell did in fact die the witch filled the house with shrieks of triumph. Then the disturbances abated. One day in 1821, as the family was eating supper, there was a loud noise in the chimney, and an object like a cannonball rolled out from the fireplace and turned into smoke. The witch's voice cried: "I am going and will be gone for seven years". But she stayed away for good.

One expert on poltergeists, Nandor Fodor, has suggested that the explanation of the Bell witch lies in an incestuous attack made on Betsy by her father, and that the poltergeist is a "personality fragment" that has somehow broken free of the rest of the personality. There is no real evidence for either of these claims.

Another famous American case took place in the home of the Rev. Eliakim Phelps in 1850. This poltergeist began by scattering furniture around and making curious dummies out of stuffed clothes. They were extremely lifelike and were constructed in a few minutes. Then the poltergeist entered the stone-throwing stage (most disturbances seem to go through a number of definite phases), breaking seventy-one window-panes. Paper burst into flames and all kinds of objects were smashed. The twelve-year-old boy, Harry, was snatched up into the air, and on one occasion tied to a tree. His elder sister Anna, sixteen, was pinched and slapped. But when mother and children went off to Pennsylvania for the winter the disturbances ceased.

It was in fact a series of poltergeist disturbances that started the extraordinary nineteenth-century craze known as Spiritualism, which began with typical knocking noises in the home of the Fox family in Hydesville, New York State, in 1848; two daughters – Margaret, fifteen, and Kate, twelve – were obviously the "focuses". A neighbour who questioned the "spirit" (with the usual code one knock for yes, two for no) was told that it was a peddler who had been murdered in the house. (Many years later, human bones and a peddler's box were found buried in the cellar.) The notoriety of the case caused many other Americans to take up "spiritualism", sitting around a table in the dark with clasped hands, and asking for spirits to "manifest" themselves. The Hydesville "spirit" finally delivered a message announcing a new era in spirit communication. And in fact spiritualism swept across the United States, then across Europe.

In the early 1850s a French educator named Léon-Denizard-Hyppolyte Rivail became interested in the new spiritualist craze; when two daughters of a friend proved to be proficient in "automatic writing" Rivail asked the "spirits" all kinds of questions, and received unusually constructive and serious answers. In due course these were published in *The Spirits' Book*, which Rivail published under the pseudonym of Allan Kardec. It became for a while a kind of Bible of Spiritualism, although there was later a split within the movement, many influential Spiritualists rejecting Kardec's belief in reincarnation.

In Paris in 1860 there had been a series of violent disturbances in a house in the Rue des Noyers – the usual window-smashing and furniture-throwing. Rivail requested to speak to the "spirit" responsible, and an entity that claimed to be a long-dead rag and bone man declared that it had used the "electrical energy" of a servant girl in the house to cause the disturbances. The girl, it said, was quite unaware of this – in fact, she was the most terrified of them all. He had been doing these things merely to amuse himself.

"Kardec" was convinced that poltergeists are "earth-bound spirits" – that is, dead people who for various reasons have been unable to advance beyond the purely material plane.

One of the most remarkable American cases of the nineteenth century was recorded in a book called *The Great Amherst Mystery* by Walter

Hubbell, a stage magician who moved into the house of the Teed family in Amherst, Nova Scotia, in 1869 to investigate a poltergeist that concentrated its attention on an eighteen-year-old girl named Esther Cox. The disturbances had begun in the previous year, when Esther's boy-friend, Bob MacNeal, had tried to order her into the woods at gunpoint, presumably to rape her; when interrupted he fled and never returned. Soon after this Esther and her sister Jane were kept awake by mouse-like rustling noises, and a cardboard box leapt into the air. Two nights later, Esther's body seemed to swell like a balloon, but returned to normal after a sound like a thunder-clap. Bedclothes were thrown around the room. Esther's pillow inflated like a balloon. In front of many witnesses, writing appeared on the wall saying, "Esther, you are mine to kill". Esther often complained of an "electric feeling" running through her body. When the poltergeist got into its stride small fires broke out, objects flew around the room, furniture moved, and Esther turned into a kind of human magnet, to which knives and other metal objects stuck firmly. Hubbell succeeded in communicating with the "spirits", who were able to prove their authenticity by telling him the number inside his watch and the date of coins in his pockets. When a barn burned down Esther was accused of arson and sentenced to four months in prison. When she came out again the manifestations stopped.

The Society for Psychical Research was founded in 1882 to investigate "psychical phenomena" scientifically. One of its most influential members, Frank Podmore, author of a valuable two-volume history of Spiritualism, was firmly convinced the poltergeists were usually fakes, caused by stone-throwing children, although he *was* willing to admit that a well-known case at Durweston, on Viscount Portman's estate, was probably genuine. Podmore later had a lengthy correspondence with Andrew Lang, who found Podmore's skepticism too wholesale; Lang is generally conceded to have won this controversy.

In 1990 the famous criminologist Cesare Lombroso investigated a case of poltergeist haunting in a wine shop in Turin. As Lombroso stood in the wine cellar bottles gently rose from the shelves and exploded on the floor. At first Lombroso suspected that the proprietor's wife was the cause of the disturbances, but they continued while she was away. Lombroso's suspicions then focused on a thirteen-year-old waiter. When this boy was dismissed the haunting stopped.

So it was fairly clear to the early investigators that poltergeist phenomena were connected, more often than not, with some particular person, usually an adolescent. (The word poltergeist was seldom used in the early days of psychical research, although it *had* been used to describe various cases by Mrs Catherine Crowe in her best-seller *The Night Side of Nature* in 1848.) But it was not until the late 1940s that the "unconscious mind" theory became popular. Nandor Fodor put forward his theory that poltergeists are "personality fragments" in *The Journal of Clinical Psychopathology* in 1945. Frank Harvey's play *The Poltergeist* had a successful West End run in 1946; it was based on a case that had taken place at Pitmilly House, Boarshill, near Fife, in which £50 worth of fire damage had been caused – Harvey transferred it to a Dartmoor vicarage. His play popularized the "unconscious mind" theory, which had first been put forward about 1930 by Dr Alfred Winterstein, in discussing the case of the Austrian medium Frieda Weisl; the latter's husband described how, when they were first married, ornaments would fly off the mantelpiece when she had an orgasm. The Countess Zoe Wassilko-Serecki had reached similar conclusions when she examined a young Rumanian girl named Eleanore Zugun, who was continually slapped and punched by a poltergeist – bite-marks that appeared on her were often damp with saliva. By the end of the 1940s the "unconscious mind" theory was generally accepted by those psychical investigators who were willing to believe that the poltergeist was not a fraud. This theory was summarized by BBC investigator Brian Branston in his book *Beyond Belief* (1976):

I believe that, on the evidence, we may claim as a working hypothesis that poltergeist phenomena are produced unconsciously by an individual whose psyche is disturbed, that the disturbed psyche reacts on the oldest part of the brain, the brain stem, which by means unknown to science produced the commonly recognisable poltergeist phenomena. And these phenomena are the overt cry for help: as the poem says . . . "I was not . . . waving but drowning".

Yet Branston's own theory has been contradicted by a case he has cited earlier in the chapter on poltergeists – one that took place at Northfleet in Kent. Branston records that "spooks so upset the various tenants that the house finally became empty. Previous tenants named Maxted had young children, and the usual poltergeist phenomena had taken place – mouse-like scratching noises, then the bedclothes pulled off the bed, ornaments disappearing and reappearing, and so on. When Mrs Maxted saw the ghost of a six-year-old girl they decided to move out. The next tenants had no children; they heard strange noises in the bedrooms, and smelt an unpleasant, rotting smell, but it was only after a year that they woke up to find one end of the bed rising up into the air, while beside the bed stood a pinkish-orange phantom, partly transparent, of a woman with no head. They also moved out. But even when the house was empty the next door tenants were able to hear thumping noises, and were alarmed when their own bed began to vibrate. So here, it seems, is a case where the "poltergeist" remained in the house throughout two tenancies, and stayed on when the house was empty.

A similar case was investigated by the present writer.* It took place in the Yorkshire town of Pontefract, in the home of the Pritchard family. Furniture moved, ornaments flew around, green foam gushed out of the taps, the house was shaken by thunderous crashes. A "ghost" – apparently a monk dressed in black – was also seen. But the "haunting" began when the eldest son, Phillip, reached the age of fifteen, and lasted a few days. When his younger sister Diane was fourteen the disturbances began again, and were this time more violent. (Diane had been away on holiday during the first outbreak.) Practically every breakable object in the house was smashed, Diane was thrown repeatedly out of bed and attacked by moving furniture, and a crucifix flew off the wall and stuck to her back, making a red mark. Then, as before, the manifestations faded. Diane herself was aware that the entity was somehow using her energy, and also felt intuitively that it meant her no real harm.

Cases like these suggest that the poltergeist is not a manifestation of the unconscious mind of an unhappy teenager but – as Kardec stated – an actual entity or "spirit", which remains associated with some place, but which can only manifest itself through the surplus energy of a human being – not necessarily a teenager.

This was the conclusion reached by Guy Lyon Playfair, a paranormal-investigator who went to Rio de Janeiro in the early 1960s. Brazil, unlike England and France, remained faithful to Allan Kardec's version of spiritualism, and his two works, *The Spirits' Book* and *The Medium's Book*, became the basic scriptures of Brazil's most influential religion, "spiritism". He investigated a poltergeist for the Brazilian Institute for Psycho-biophysical Research, and began to accept the Brazilian belief that poltergeists are spirits, and that they can be controlled by witch doctors, who may send them to haunt someone they dislike. One young girl named Maria was continually attacked by a poltergeist which tried to suffocate her and set her clothes on fire. A medium relayed a message

* *Poltergeist, A Study in Destructive Haunting*, by Colin Wilson, 1981, Chapter 4.

saying that Maria had been a witch in a previous existence, through whom many people had suffered, and now she was paying for it. Maria committed suicide with poison at thirteen. Playfair's books. *The Flying Cow* and *The Indefinite Boundary* present highly convincing evidence that most poltergeist disturbances are due to "spirits".

In 1977 Playfair and his fellow SPR member Maurice Grosse went to investigate a poltergeist at Enfield in north London. The case is described in detail in a classic book *This House is Haunted*. There were four children in the Harper family, aged respectively thirteen, eleven, ten and seven; it was a one-parent family, and there was considerable psychological tension. The disturbances began with vibrating beds and moving furniture. Playfair tried holding a chair in position with wire; the wire was snapped. A medium who came to the house said that there were several entities, and that eleven-year-old Janet was the "focus". Playfair and Grosse finally established communication with the entity by means of a code of raps; it stated that it had been a previous tenant of the house thirty years ago and was now dead. It began to write messages in pencil. Eventually it developed a strange, harsh voice, identifying itself as Joe Watson. On another occasion the entity called itself Bill Haylock, and claimed that it had come from a nearby graveyard in Durant's Park. One of its standard replies to questions (such as "Do you know you are dead"?) was "Fuck off". Bill Haylock was later identified as a local resident, now deceased. Finally, in 1978, a Dutch clairvoyant, Dono Gmelig-Meyling, spent some time in the house, and somehow put an end to the "haunting". He reported going on an "astral trip", and meeting a 24-year-old girl who was somehow involved in the case. Maurice Grosse's daughter Janet, who was the right age, had been killed in a motor-cycle crash in 1976. Playfair speculates that it was Janet who drew her father's attention to the case, putting it into the head of a neighbour to ring the *Daily Mirror*, and into the head of a *Daily Mirror* journalist to contact the Society for Psychical Research. (Kardec insisted that our minds are far more influenced by "spirits" than we realize.) But the energy required by the poltergeist or poltergeists was undoubtedly supplied by the children, primarily by Janet Harper. (Playfair commented at one stage that half the contents of the local graveyard seemed to be haunting the house.)

The view that poltergeists are "spirits" who make use of some form of human energy remains highly unfashionable among psychical investigators, who prefer the more "scientific" theory of Fodor. Yet the case of the phantom drummer of Tedworth seems to support Playfair's view that poltergeist phenomena can be caused by "witchcraft"; and witches have traditionally claimed to perform their "magic" through the use of spirits. One thing is certain: that Podmore's view that poltergeists are usually due to deliberate fraud is untenable in the face of the evidence. Skeptics point out that most "psychical phenomena" are intermittent, and that they are so much the exception that they may safely be ignored. But there have been literally thousands of cases of poltergeist phenomena, and they continue to occur with a regularity that makes them easy to record and investigate. No one who considers the phenomenon open-mindedly can fail to be convinced that the poltergeist is a reality that defies "purely scientific" explanation.

42

Possession by the Dead

Myth or Reality?

In 1924 the National Psychological Institute in Los Angeles published a book with the arresting title *Thirty Years Among the Dead*, by Carl A. Wickland. It was not, as one might have supposed, the memoirs of a mortuary attendant but an account by a respectable doctor of medicine of his psychological research into Spiritualism. Inevitably, it aroused a great deal of scorn among the medical fraternity, one fortunate result being that first editions are still fairly easy to find in the "occult" sections of secondhand bookshops. Yet this is hardly fair to a work that proves, on closer examination, to be a sober and factual account of Dr Wickland's theory that a great deal of mental illness is caused by "spirit possession".

Wickland, born in Leiden (Sweden) in 1861, had emigrated to Chicago, where he earned his medical degree; he became a member of the National Association for the Advancement of Science and a medical adviser to the Los Angeles branch of the National Psychological Institute. It seems likely that he decided to burn his boats and publish his book because at age sixty-three he was on the verge of retirement anyway, and ridicule would make no difference.

Ridicule was inevitable. Twelve years before Wickland had been born, in 1849, the movement called Spiritualism had been launched in the Corinthian Hall in Rochester, New York, and within a few years, the new "religion" had swept across the Christian world.

It had all started two years earlier in the small town of Hydesville, where strange banging and rapping noises had kept the Fox family awake all night. Mrs Fox asked the unseen knocker whether it was a spirit, and if so, to make two raps; she was answered by two thunderous bangs. Later "communications" in a code of raps seemed to establish that the knocker was the ghost of a peddler who had been murdered by a previous tenant and buried in the basement. (The previous tenant denied it indignantly, but more than half a century later, human bones were unearthed in the basement, behind a make-shift wall.) The raps and bangs turned into typical poltergeist phenomena, which followed the two teenage sisters, Kate and Margaretta, even when they were separated. In the Fox home, bloodcurdling groaning noises and sounds like a body being dragged across the floor made James Fox's hair turn white. Eventually, a "spirit" spelled out a message to the effect that "this truth" must be proclaimed to the world, which led to the launch of the Spiritualist movement in November 1849.

Suddenly, hundreds of "mediums" discovered that they could communicate with spirits; some "physical mediums" could even cause them to "materialize". Scientists were furious and denounced the movement as a revival of medieval superstition; even the foundation of the Society for Psychical Research in London in 1882 – by serious-minded scientists, philosophers, and statesmen – failed to provide Spiritualism with an air of respectability.

So even as late as 1924 Wickland was inviting ridicule with a title like *Thirty Years Among the Dead*. Yet the book's opening chapters soon make it clear that his interest sprang from medical curiosity and was that of a medical man rather than a "believer".

It all began, he explained, with a patient whom he calls Mrs Bl –, who began to practice automatic writing and who soon began to have fits of derangement in which she used vile language and claimed she was an actress; she had to be committed to an asylum. Another woman, "an artist and lady of refinement", became convinced that she was a damned soul and knelt in the mud to pray at the top of her voice. Yet another woman, who owned a millinery shop, posed in her window in her nightclothes, declaring that she was Napoleon, and had to be removed by the police.

At this time (in the mid-1890s) it was generally believed that mental illness could be explained in purely physical terms; many a head physician in a mental home was appointed because he had a working knowledge of brain anatomy. Freud himself was an early convert to this theory (known as *organicism*), his professor, Dr Theodore Meynert, being one of its chief advocates. (Meynert later turned his back on Freud when the latter returned from Paris espousing a new "psychological" explanation of neurosis based on the idea of the unconscious mind.) In America, the favourite theory of mental illness was that it was due to poisons in the system resulting from such causes as infected tonsils or decayed teeth. But Wickland was intrigued by the case of a youth named Frank James who, after a fall from a motorcycle at the age of ten, changed from an affectionate, obedient boy to a juvenile delinquent who spent many terms in reformatories and jails. Declared hopelessly insane, James succeeded in escaping from the criminal asylum and during his recapture was hit on the head with a club. On awakening, he had once again reverted to his earlier personality – gentle and good-natured.

This convinced Wickland of the inadequacy of the "toxemia" theory. And while he was still a medical student, his marriage to a woman who proved to be an excellent "medium" soon provided him with evidence of an alternative theory. One day Wickland was dissecting a leg in medical school, and on his return home, was alarmed when his wife, Anna, seemed to be about to faint. He placed his hand on her shoulder and was startled when she drew herself up and said threateningly, "What do you mean by cutting me"? After a few questions it became clear that he was speaking to the spirit of the owner of the leg he had been dissecting. Wickland guided Anna to a chair, and the spirit objected that he had no right to touch "him". When Wickland replied that he was touching his wife, it retorted, "What are you talking about? I am no woman – I'm a man". Eventually, Wickland reasoned the spirit into recognizing that it was dead and that dissecting its old body would do it no harm. When it asked for a chew of tobacco or a pipe, Wickland had to explain that his wife was a nonsmoker. (The next day he observed that the teeth of the corpse were heavily stained with tobacco.) More detailed explanation finally convinced the man that he was dead, and he left.

This showed Wickland that a "ghost" may believe that it is still alive, particularly if death came unexpectedly. He also encountered a case that seemed to demonstrate that spirits did not need to manifest themselves through a "medium". When he was alone one day, dissecting a female corpse, he thought he heard a distant voice shout, "Don't murder me"! A newspaper on the floor made a rustling noise, as if it was being crushed. Some days later, at a séance, a spirit who gave her name as Minnie Morgan claimed that it was she who had shouted "Don't murder me"! and crushed the newspaper. Minnie also had to be convinced that she was no longer alive.

At séances, entities who spoke through his wife later explained to Wickland that such "homeless spirits" – those who are unaware that they are dead – are attracted by the warmth of the "human aura" – a kind of energy sphere that is supposed to surround the human body – and, under certain circumstances, may attach themselves to the owner of the sphere as a kind of mental parasite. In effect, such spirits are in a state of sleep, in which dreams and reality are confused, and, as in sleep, the dreamer is unaware that he is dreaming.

In one case – of a female musician who had suffered a nervous breakdown – the woman spoke in a "wild gibberish" of English and Spanish (a language of which she was ignorant). Eventually, Wickland succeeded in learning that she was possessed by three spirits: a girl named Mary, and two rival lovers. One had murdered Mary, then the two men had killed each other in a fight; the three spirits were unaware that they were dead and had found themselves able to "possess" the musician, who was psychically weakened. (Wickland's experience was that people who are insane or on the verge of a nervous breakdown are vulnerable to these psychic parasites.) Before the woman was finally cured, another spirit – that of a little girl who had been killed in the San Francisco earthquake – was "removed" from her (by a mild shock treatment involving static electricity generated by a Wimshurst machine, which Wickland found highly effective in "dislodging" these uninvited visitors).

Wickland's book contains so many cases in its 460-odd pages that it is impossible to summarize. But one typical case will illustrate why he was so convinced that he was dealing with real spirits and not with some strange form of hysteria on the part of his wife. In 1904, at a seance in Chicago, Mrs Wickland began to clutch her throat and cry out, "Take the rope away. I am in the dark"! When the "spirit" had been soothed into speaking normally, she declared that she was a sixteen-year-old girl named Minnie Harmening, who had committed suicide by hanging herself in a Chicago suburb called Palatine (Wickland misheard it as Palestine). She had, she said, encountered the spirit of a big man with a black beard in the barn, and he had "hypnotized" her and made her hang herself.

Wickland and his wife were on a visit to Chicago at that time and had not heard of what had become known as the Harmening suicide, which had taken place six weeks earlier. The girl's suicide had baffled her family because it had been without apparent cause (although, Wickland adds, "the girl had always been peculiar", implying that she was mentally deficient). Moreover, there were some suspicious circumstances – the clothes around the neck had been torn, and there were scratches on her throat. The suicide had taken place – as the girl had said – in Palatine, Cook County, Illinois.

The spirit appeared again at the next séance and in reply to questions, explained that as soon as she had kicked the box away, she "came to her senses" and clawed at her clothes, tearing them as she tried to loosen the rope.

Wickland cites many such cases in which he was able to corroborate the evidence of "spirits". But what is obviously of chief interest in this case is that the girl claimed to have been "hypnotized" (she may simply mean strongly influenced) by a black-bearded spirit and induced to kill herself. That is to say, she had, in effect, been "possessed" by the black-bearded spirit.

Unfortunately, Wickland was not generally concerned with the kind of corroboration he provides in this case, with the result that his book is seldom mentioned by modern scientific investigators of the paranormal. (Wickland's own excuse is that the spirits were usually in such a state of confusion that they could not give precise names and dates.) What he might have done is illustrated by his friend F. Lee Howard, a congregational minister, who attended a session in which the Wicklands were attempting to treat the daughter of one of Howard's friends. Howard questioned a "possessing spirit", which declared itself to be that of a suicide victim, and he obtained the name and date. A check with the coroner's records confirmed that such a person had committed suicide on the given date. In another case, a reader of Wickland's book wrote to say that the details given by one of the spirits convinced him that it was his father's cousin.

Another objection raised by modern researchers is that Wickland is often naïve and that he is inclined to mistake mental illness for "spirit possession". For example, the case of Frank James, the boy who became a juvenile delinquent after a fall from a motorcycle, would nowadays be explained in terms of the science of "split-brain physiology". This is based upon the recognition that when the *corpus callosum*, the knot of nerves joining the two cerebral hemispheres of the brain, is severed – as it is sometimes to cure epilepsy – the patient turns into two different people, each of whom resides in a separate hemisphere of the brain. (See also chapter 25.) The normal "everyday self", the person one thinks of as "me", lives in the left hemisphere and is basically a logical and practical person, the one who copes with daily chores. The person who lives in the right is a stranger and seems to be altogether more intuitive and instinctive; he seems more concerned with what goes on inside us. You could say that the left-brain self is objective, the right brain subjective; one is, in effect, a scientist and the other an artist. Most of us are unaware of this "other" (right-brain) self, even though we are connected to it by the *corpus callosum*. In split-brain patients, the "other self" can be studied by directing stimuli to the left eye (actually, the left visual field) or the left side of the body; for some odd reason, the left side of the body is connected to the right brain, and vice versa.

In a well-known case of the 1870s, a French youth named Louis Vivé was bitten by a viper and became paralyzed in both legs for three years; during this time he was quiet and well behaved. One day he had a "hysterico-epileptic" attack, followed by a fifteen-hour sleep; when he woke up, the well-behaved youth had given way to a violent, aggressive, and dishonest delinquent. But, unlike Frank James, Vivé's two personalities continued to alternate. This new "criminal" self had a speech defect and was paralyzed down the right side of his body. After receiving a conviction for theft, Vivé was sent to an asylum at Rochefort, where two doctors became interested in his case. At this time there was considerable interest in the influence of magnets and of various metals on physical ailments like paralysis, and the doctors tried stroking his right side with steel. It had the effect of transferring the paralysis to the left side and restoring the patient to his previous quiet and well-behaved personality. All his memories of the "criminal" period vanished, and he could recall only his "own" earlier self – although his "other self" could be brought back by hypnosis.

Here it seems clear that the "criminal" Vivé was a condition associated with his right brain – hence the speech disorder. (Speech is controlled by the left side of the brain). Another well-known case of "dual personality", that of Clara Fowler (described by Dr Morton Prince in his book *Dissociation of a Personality* – Prince calls her Christine Beauchamp) seems to illustrate the same point. An old friend of Clara's father made a sexual advance that so upset her that she began to suffer from depression and nervous exhaustion. When Prince placed her under hypnosis, another personality emerged, a mischievous child who called herself Sally. From then on, Sally would frequently "take over" the body and play practical jokes, such as going for a long walk in the countryside, then vacating the body and leaving Clara to walk home. Typically, Sally had a bad stutter, suggesting that, like Vivé's alter ego, she was associated with the right brain. (It has been noted that left-handed people who have been forced to learn to write with the right hand often develop a stutter.)

But while it is tempting to explain Wickland's cases in terms of "multiple-personality disorder" and split-brain physiology, it proves in practise to be an impossible enterprise; we can see that, in the case of the Minnie Harmening suicide, no amount of split-brain physiology can explain how Mrs Wickland was able to describe a case of which she had no knowledge.

In fact, Wickland's findings had been anticipated by half a century. In 1855 a French educator named Léon Denizard Hyppolyte Rivail was introduced to a *somnambule* – a person who "channeled" trance communications when hypnotized – named Celina Bequet, through whom the spirit of the famous hypnotist Franz Mesmer was alleged to speak. Accepting without question that he was in touch with the spirits of the dead – a reasonable assumption under the circumstances – Rivail asked hundreds of questions about life after death and published the result in an influential work entitled *The Spirits' Book*. (He used the pseudonym Allan Kardec, suggested to him by "spirits".)

According to *The Spirits' Book*, man consists of body, "aura", intelligent soul, and spiritual soul. The aim of human life, according to the spirits, is evolution, and this comes about through reincarnation – rebirth into new bodies. People who die suddenly, or are unprepared for death by reason of wasted lives, are often unaware that they are dead and become homeless, wanderers on the earth, attracted by human beings of like mind, and sharing their lives and experiences. They are able, to some extent, to influence these like-minded people and to make them do their will through suggestion. Some "low spirits" are activated by malice; others are merely mischievous and can use energy drawn from human beings to cause physical disturbances – these are known as *poltergeists*. When Kardec asked, "Do spirits influence our thoughts and actions"? the answer was, "Their influence upon [human beings] is greater than you suppose, for it is very often they who direct both". Asked about possession, the "spirit" explained that a spirit cannot actually take over another person's body, since that belongs to its owner; but a spirit can assimilate itself to a person who has the same defects and qualities as himself and may dominate such a person. In short, such spirits could be described as "mind parasites".

According to Wickland, one of the most famous murders of the early twentieth century was due to "spirit influence". On the night of 25 June 1906, a wealthy young rake named Harry Thaw sat beside his wife on the roof of Madison Square Garden, watching a new revue. Before her marriage, Mrs Thaw had been Evelyn Nesbit, a beautiful model and showgirl, whom Thaw had persuaded to accompany him to Europe. Thaw was addicted to flogging, and on one occasion, he whipped Evelyn so severely that she was confined to bed for two weeks. When she admitted to him that she had been seduced at the age of fifteen by Stanford White, the architect of Madison Square Garden, Thaw had become almost insane with jealousy. On the night of 25 June, as they were leaving the roof show, Thaw saw White sitting alone at a table, walked up to him, and shot him three times with a pistol.

At Thaw's murder trial, Evelyn gave lurid details of her seduction by the architect (who was more than thirty years her senior), describing how he had taken her virginity after getting her drunk on champagne. ("When I came to I found myself in the bed, naked except for an abbreviated pink undergarment".)* The jury was unable to reach an agreement. At the second trial, Thaw was found not guilty by reason of insanity and confined to an asylum, from which he escaped in 1913; later that year a jury found him to be sane and authorized his release.

Three weeks after the murder, on 15 July 1906, Mrs Wickland fell to the floor during the course of a séance and when moved to a chair, shouted in a brusque voice, "Waiter, bring me a drink"! Asked where she thought she was, she replied, "In Madison Square Roof Garden, of course". Then she began to tremble, explaining that she could see "dead people", and rushed about the room. As soon as this spirit ceased to "possess" Mrs Wickland, another spirit took over, exulting, "I killed the dog"! But this was not Harry Thaw; in reply to questions the spirit said that his name was Johnson and that he had caused Thaw to shoot Stanford White because "he had trifled too long with our daughters". (In fact, White was a famous seducer of chorus girls, keeping a special apartment for that purpose; but then, Thaw shared his taste.) Next, a spirit who claimed to be Thaw's father appeared, begging the people present to "save my boy". (Thaw senior had been dead for some years, and Thaw's mother was overindulgent.) He went on to explain that Thaw had been obsessed by "vengeful spirits" when he killed White and that his son was a "psychic sensitive".

There is nothing in the two books on the case, or in Evelyn Nesbit's book, *The Untold Story*, to suggest that Thaw may have been psychic. But Evelyn's book makes it clear that Thaw was mentally little more than a child. One account states: "Had Thaw been a poor man, he probably would have been in an asylum". At his trial, evidence was presented of insanity in his family – in fact, his elder brother, Horace, had died in an asylum. Evelyn Nesbit's accounts of his violent tantrums – for example, if a waiter dared to try and brush crumbs off the tablecloth he would jerk the cloth away, hurling the dishes to the floor – make it clear that he was mentally disturbed. (The tantrums would vanish with equal suddenness, and Thaw's face would dissolve into a

* See *The Untold Story* by Evelyn Nesbit (1934).

charming and sunny smile.) While this does not support the case for "obsession" by vengeful spirits, it *does* support Wickland's contention that Thaw was the type of person whose mind was open to invasion because he was "not all there".

There *is* one small piece of evidence that suggests that the "spirit" of Thaw's father was what he claimed to be. He begged Wickland to "write to my wife and my attorney, Mr Olcott", and in fact, Judge Olcott *was* Thaw's attorney, a fact that was unknown to the Wicklands.

The classic study of "possession", *Possession, Demoniacal and Other* (1921), is by a Tübingen professor, T. K. Oesterreich. Oesterreich totally discounts the "spirit" explanation, insisting that possession is always a case of hysteria or mental illness. He will not even accept the hypothesis of multiple personality, since he cannot believe that the human personality can "split". One of his most impressive pieces of evidence for the hysteria theory is a lengthy account of the famous case of "Achille", described by the psychiatrist Pierre Janet. Achille, a moderately successful businessman, came from a peasant background and married early. In the winter of 1890, when he was thirty-three, Achille returned from a business trip in a depressed condition, then suddenly went dumb. One day he sent for his wife and child, embraced them despairingly, then went into a cataleptic state for two days. When he awoke he was suffering from delusions; he seemed to think he was in Hell and that demons were burning him and cutting him in pieces. The room, he said, was full of imps, and he was possessed by a devil. After a number of suicide attempts he was sent to the Salpêtrière Hospital in Paris, under the care of the famous physician Charcot. The latter placed Janet in charge of the case.

Janet watched with interest as Achille displayed all the signs of demoniacal possession, as described in the Middle Ages: in a deep voice he cursed God, then in a shrill voice protested that the Devil had forced him to do it.

At first all of Janet's efforts to communicate were a failure; Achille refused to listen to him and resisted all of the doctor's attempts to hypnotize him. Janet saw the solution when he observed that Achille was extremely absentminded – he compared him to someone searching for an umbrella that he holds in his hand. While Achille was raving, Janet quietly inserted a pencil in his hand, then tried ordering him, in a whisper, to make writing movements. The pencil wrote: "I won't". "Who are you"? asked Janet, and the pencil wrote: "The Devil". "I shan't believe you", Janet replied, "unless you can give me proof. Can you make Achille raise his left arm without knowing it"? "Of course", came the answer – and Achille raised his arm. "Why are you doing that"? Janet asked Achille in his normal voice, and Achille looked at his raised arm with astonishment.

The demon went on to demonstrate his powers by making Achille dance, stick out his tongue, and kiss a piece of paper. Finally, Janet asked him if he could put Achille into a deep sleep. Moments later, Achille was in a trance. Now Janet was able to question him about the cause of his illness. He quickly learned that Achille had been unfaithful to his wife while away on his business trip and that deep and intense guilt had caused the depression and other symptoms. Now that he was able to induce hallucinations, Janet made Achille believe that his wife was in the room and had forgiven him for his infidelity. (It is not quite clear from Janet's account whether the wife actually came to the hospital.) After this, Achille's psychological problems soon cleared up.

This is certainly a remarkable case. Yet as a refutation of the "spirit" theory, it is obviously open to one serious objection. According to Wickland, people suffering from nervous traumas or states of intense guilt and misery are more likely to become "obsessed" by spirits than normal healthy persons. Wickland would point out that Achille may have been genuinely "obsessed" by a mischievous spirit and that as soon as Janet had made him feel that he was forgiven, the spirit was "driven out".

In her introduction to Oesterreich's *Possession*, Anita Gregory, an investigator of the paranormal, has some harsh words to say about Wickland and his *Thirty Years Among the Dead*. She points out that there is a basic sameness to all his cases – he always has to convince a spirit that it is dead – and his account of how the spirits of Madame Blavatsky and Mary Baker Eddy expressed contrition for their false doctrines is almost laughable. She also points out that Oesterreich's rationalism is often crude and unconvincing and that he deals with subtleties by ignoring them.

Perhaps the most obvious example of Oesterreich's failure to allow facts to speak for themselves is in his account of one of the most famous of all cases of "possession", that of "the Watseka wonder", a girl named Lurancy Vennum. In July 1877 thirteen-year-old Lurancy, of Watseka, Illinois, had a fit, after which she became prone to trances. In these trances she became a medium, and a number of disagreeable person-alities manifested themselves through her. On 11 February 1878, placed under hypnosis by a local doctor, Lurancy stated that there was a spirit in the room named Mary Roff, and a Mrs Roff who was also present exclaimed, "That's my daughter". Mary had died twelve years earlier, at the age of eighteen. Lurancy then stated that Mary was going to be allowed to take over her body for the next three months.

The next day Lurancy claimed to be Mary Roff. She asked to be taken back to the Roff's home, and on the way there, she recognized their previous home, in which they had lived while she was alive and which was unknown to Lurancy. She also recognized Mary Roff's sister, who was standing at the window. And during the next few weeks, "Mary" showed a precise and detailed knowledge of the Roff household and of Mary's past, recognizing old acquaintances and toys and recalling long-forgotten incidents. On 21 May, the day she had declared she had to leave, she took a tearful farewell of her family, and on the way home, "became" Lurancy again. The case was investigated by Richard Hodgson, one of the most skeptical members of the Society for Psychical Research, who was convinced of its genuineness.

Readers of Hodgson's account of the "Watseka wonder" will find it very hard to find loopholes; Mary provided such detailed proof of her knowledge of her early years, and of the family background – recognizing unhesitatingly anyone Mary had known – that the notion of trickery or delusion becomes untenable; it is perhaps the single most convincing case of "possession" in the history of psychical research. But Oesterreich merely quotes William James's summary of the case (from *The Principles of Psychology*), making no attempt to analyze it and passing on quickly to other matters – in spite of the fact that James himself had spoken of "the plausibility of the spiritualistic interpretation of the phenomenon". And Anita Gregory concludes her introduction by admitting that she is unable to declare that all the people in Oesterreich's book are frauds, dupes, lunatics, and psychopaths, ending with the words: "So I shall conclude . . . that the phenomena described by Oesterreich are very much in need of an explanation".

Oesterreich's *pièce de résistance* is a long account of the famous case of the "devils of Loudun", which, in 1952, was made the subject of a full-length study by Aldous Huxley. In 1633 Urbain Grandier, the parish priest of the small French town of Loudun, was charged with bewitching the nuns in a local convent and causing them to be possessed by demons, so that they screamed blasphemies and obscenities and writhed about on the floor displaying their private parts. Grandier had become notorious for his immoralities – he had impregnated two of his penitents and seduced many others – and had made many enemies. Inquisitors claimed to find "devil's marks" on his body, and in a trial that was a travesty of justice, he was found guilty and sentenced to be burned alive. Even under torture, and later at the stake, Grandier maintained his innocence. His death made no difference, and the nuns continued to be possessed by "demons" for many years.

Oesterreich, like Aldous Huxley, takes the view that all this could be explained simply in terms of hysteria, while another authority, Rossell Hope Robbins, goes even further in his *Encyclopedia of Witchcraft and Demonology* and attributes the manifestations to outright imposture. But a careful reading of Huxley's own book makes either of these explanations seem implausible. It is easy to see how sex-starved nuns could deceive themselves into believing that they were possessed by devils – the Mother Superior of the convent, Sister Jeanne des Anges, admits in her autobiography that she made no real attempt to combat the possession because she enjoyed the sexual stirrings aroused in her by the demons.

But it is far more difficult to understand what then happened to the exorcists themselves. Brother Lactance, who had overseen the torture, became "possessed" and died insane within a month; five years later Brother Tranquille died of exhaustion after months of battling against the "invaders" of his psyche, and was amazed to witness his body writhing on the ground and hear himself uttering blasphemies that he was powerless to prevent. Brother Lucas, another of Grandier's persecutors, met the same fate. The "witch pricker", Dr Mannouri, also died in delirium. Brother Jean-Joseph Surin, a genuinely saintly man, who was called to Loudun to try and exorcise the nuns after Grandier's execution, himself fell victim to the "devils" and became periodically insane for twenty-five years.

It is difficult to believe that ordinary hysteria could produce such results. Surin described in a letter how the "alien spirit" was united to his own, "constituting a second me, as though I had two souls". Considering these facts, the skeptical Anita Gregory admits that "one is probably not justified in assuming that . . . the Loudun pandemonium [was] necessarily nothing but collective delusion". And bearing in mind Kardec's comment that "a spirit does not enter into a body as you enter into a house . . . he assimilates himself to a [person] who has the same defects and the same qualities as himself", the hypothesis that the Loudun "pandemonium" was caused by Wickland's earthbound spirits seems, on the whole, more plausible than the religious-hysteria theory.

It is difficult to draw a clear dividing line between "possession" and poltergeist manifestations. Poltergeists are "noisy ghosts" who cause objects to fly through the air, and scientific observation of dozens of cases has established their reality beyond all doubt. The most widely held current view is that they are a form of 'spontaneous psychokinesis" (mind over matter) caused by the unconscious mind of an emotionally disturbed adolescent, but this theory fails to explain how the unconscious mind can cause heavy objects to fly through the air. (In labouratory experiments, "psychics" have so far failed to move any object larger than a compass needle.) According to Kardec's "informants", poltergeists are earthbound spirits who are, under certain conditions, able to draw energy from the living and make use of negative energies "exuded" by the emotionally disturbed and the sexually frustrated.

In the Amherst case of 1878, poltergeist phenomena began to occur in the home of an unmarried girl named Esther Cox, who lived with her sister and her sister's husband, Daniel Teed. After an attempt at abduction and rape, Esther's boyfriend had hastily left the area, and Esther was deeply upset. A few days later, rustling noises – sounding like a mouse – came from a box under her bed; a few nights after that, following a hysterical fit, Esther's body began to swell like a balloon. There were then two loud bangs, and she ceased swelling and fell asleep. All of this was repeated a few days later; the bedclothes also flew off the bed, and the pillow inflated. As the family stood around the bed, there was a scratching noise above it, and an invisible hand or claw traced on the plaster the words: *Esther, you are mine to kill*. At a later stage of the manifestation, Esther turned into a human magnet – knives stuck to her – and some iron spokes in her lap became too hot to touch. When spontaneous fires broke out, Esther was accused of causing them and sentenced to four months in jail. By the time she was released, the manifestations had ceased.

Ten years later, in 1889, a farm in Quebec province run by a man named George Dagg became the scene of equally bizarre poltergeist manifestations: milk pans overturned, small fires started, windows smashed, and water poured on the floor. In this case, the "focus" (or the person who seemed to be causing it) was a young girl named Dinah McLean, an orphan. The poltergeist often attacked Dinah, making her scream; like Esther Cox, she also seemed to be able to hear it, although no one else could. Later, it began to talk in a gruff voice, uttering violent obscenities and alleging that it was the Devil. But after some dialogue with George Dagg – during which it admitted to causing the fires and throwing stones – it declared its willingness to leave the following Sunday. Crowds of neighbours gathered, and the poltergeist talked freely, seeming to have an intimate knowledge of their lives. (The Fox poltergeist had also been able to supply all kinds of personal information to the neighbours.) It also alleged that it was not the

"Devil" of the previous day but an angel sent by God; but it proceeded to contradict itself and then lost its temper and used foul language. Finally, it declared that it would leave the following morning after taking leave of the village children. The next morning, the children rushed in from the yard to say that they had just seen a beautiful man in white, who had picked up two of them – Mary and Johnny – in his arms and declared that Johnny was a fine little fellow, then put them down and ascended into the sky. After this, the manifestations ceased.

In both these cases, the poltergeist masqueraded as some kind of demonic entity but was clearly nothing of the sort – an observation that seems to suggest that poltergeists, like the devils of Loudun, are probably also "earthbound spirits".

Another investigator who came to believe that "possession" was due to spirits was Max Freedom Long, an American schoolmaster who arrived in Hawaii in 1917, at the age of twenty-seven, and began to make a study of its native "magicians", the kahunas or "keepers of the secret" – the last representatives of the ancient Huna religion. According to Huna belief, Long discovered, man has three "selves": the "low self", the "middle self", and the "high self". The low self is basically emotional and corresponds roughly to Freud's unconscious mind. The middle self is our ordinary, everyday consciousness. The high self might be called the superconscious mind and can foresee the future. After death, the three selves may become separated, and it is the low self that sometimes becomes a poltergeist, and the middle self may become a "ghost". In his book describing these investigations – offputtingly entitled *The Secret Science Behind Miracles* – Long also discusses the phenomenon of multiple personality and expresses the view that this is often due to "possession", either by a low self or a middle self or a combination of the two. He describes the case of a California girl with a secondary personality that took over the body for years at a time. When doctors tried to amalgamate the two under hypnosis, a third personality appeared, who told them that the girl should be left as she was, with two spirits sharing the body. This third personality warned that if they persisted, it would withdraw and leave them with a corpse; Long believed this third person to be the girl's "high self".

Two more eminent American investigators came to accept the possibility of "possession". The philosopher William James was converted from his early skepticism to a belief in "spirits" through the mediumship of Mrs Leonore Piper, whose "control", Phinuit, was able to tell him all kinds of things that he could not possibly have learned by normal means. James was to agree that if a medium could be "possessed" by a spirit, then it was possible that other people might be and that this could explain cases of "demoniacal possession".

James's close friend, Professor James Hyslop, was another skeptic who was "converted" by Mrs Piper. But he had a more practical reason for becoming convinced of the reality of "possession". When Hyslop was president of the American Society for Psychical Research in 1907, he was visited by a goldsmith named Frederick Thompson, who believed that he had become "possessed" by the spirit of a painter named Robert Swain Gifford, whom he had met on a few occasions. After Gifford's death, Thompson had begun to hear Gifford's voice urging him to draw and paint – something he had never done before – and although he had no artistic training, Thompson began to paint in Gifford's style. What convinced Hyslop was that Thompson painted accurate pictures of places that he had never seen but that Gifford *had*. Some of these proved to be identical to Gifford's final sketches – which Thompson had never seen – and when Hyslop visited the New England swamps and coastal regions, he recognized them as the subject of these sketches.

Hyslop consulted a neurologist, Dr Titus Bull, about Thompson. And Bull himself went on to conclude that many cases of mental illness really involved "possession". In one case, the patient, who had suffered a head injury, claimed that he had been "taken over" by the spirit of a painter named Josef Selleny, who had been a friend of the Emperor Maximilian and who was "forcing" him to paint. (Wickland, as we know, believed that such accidents as head injuries could provide opportunity for alien "entities" to invade.)

Lengthy research by Bull's assistant, Helen Lambert, finally uncovered the existence of a real Josef Selleny (the encyclopedias mistakenly spelled his first name *Joseph*, but the patient spelled it correctly), who had, indeed, been a friend of the Emperor Maximilian. A medium who worked with Dr Bull was able to reveal that the patient was being possessed by several "entities", one of whom seized possession of her body and grabbed Bull by the throat.

Eventually, the various entities were dislodged or persuaded to go away. Mrs Lambert's account, later published in her book *A General Survey of Psychic Phenomena*, sounds remarkably like many cases described by Carl Wickland. The few available cases make it clear that Bull's name deserves a distinguished place in the annals of psychical research; unfortunately, most of his records have been lost.

Clearly, views like those of William James and Titus Bull will find no acceptance with the majority of doctors and scientists. Yet in recent years, belief in "possession" as a cause of some mental illness has received support from two eminent psychiatrists, Adam Crabtree and Ralph Allison. In his book *Multiple Man* (1986), Crabtree asserts that he has come to accept, merely as a convenient working hypothesis, the notion that certain multiple personalities are "possessed" by spirits, inviting us to believe that he is waiting for someone to suggest an alternative psychological theory that will cover all the facts. But the cases he describes make it virtually impossible to imagine such a hypothesis.

Crabtree's first experience with "possession" involved a young patient named Sarah Worthington, who was in a condition of suicidal depression. In a semitrance state, Sarah spoke in a completely different voice, which sounded like that of an older woman used to exercising authority. This "voice" identified herself as Sarah's grandmother and explained that she wanted to "help Sarah". It began to emerge that the grandmother also had a problem: many years earlier, she had left her seven-year-old son alone in the house, then rushed back when she heard that the neighbourhood was on fire. Her son had, in fact, been removed to a safe place by neighbours, but she had spent a traumatic hour searching for him. Later, her indifference to her daughter, Sarah's mother (she greatly preferred her son), had created psychological problems, which had been inherited by Sarah. Now the grandmother believed that she was trying to help Sarah, who had always felt rejected; in fact, her presence was troubling the girl, who was intuitively aware that she had been "invaded". The case sounds oddly similar to many described by Carl Wickland. But in this case, it was unnecessary to persuade the "spirit" to go away; when Sarah realized that the obscure inner presence she felt was her grandmother, she came to accept it, and all her suicidal impulses vanished.

In another case, a girl named Susan was convinced that she was "possessed" by her dead father, who had been killed in a car crash. He had always been sexually obsessed with her, creeping into her bedroom when she was asleep to fondle her genitals; her unconscious knowledge of what was going on made her contemptuous of him. But the close rapport between them meant that when he died, he had found refuge in his daughter's body, unaware that he was dead. When Crabtree was able to persuade him to leave her, her problems vanished.

But from the point of view of "demoniacal possession", perhaps the most interesting case in Crabtree's book is that of a history professor whom he calls Art. About to be married for the second time, Art was experiencing strange feelings of reluctance, as if "under great pressure from some inner force that he could not control". A censorious inner voice would criticize anyone whom he liked. Art's own theory was that some negative aspect of his personality had unconsciously assimilated the critical attitudes of his mother, Veronica, who was now living in Detroit. When Crabtree placed Art in a light trance, he was able to open a dialogue with the "mother", and she told him, "Art is mine and his life is mine . . . I have to make sure Art knows how kooky all these friends of his are".

Art's description of his mother revealed that she was sexually obsessed with her son. Until he was in his late teens, she would call him into her bed when her husband had left for work and arouse him into a state of sexual excitement that she refused to satisfy. Oddly enough, the Veronica who "possessed" Art was also aware of herself as "Veronica who lived in Detroit", and she described the life of her alter ego as drab and dull. Crabtree suggested that life might become more interesting if she spent more time with "Veronica in Detroit", and the entity agreed to try it. When Art's mother had an operation to remove a cancerous growth, the entity realized that it had been robbing her of vitality by concentrating on Art and began spending less time with Art. The real Veronica's life now underwent a remarkable transformation, and she began seeing more of people and enjoying herself. Art, surprisingly enough, found he missed the censorious inner voice and recognized how much he had encouraged it, using it as an excuse for not making his own decisions. As he faced this fact, his problems vanished.

Here we may assume either that Art himself was suffering from delusions – a reasonable enough hypothesis, under the circumstances – or that, in some odd way, his mother *was* somehow "possessing" him from a distance, in spite of the fact that she was still alive. This, admittedly, sounds farfetched – until we take into account the mother's transformation after her operation. And if Art's mother *was* somehow "in two places at once", the implications are very strange indeed.

Can one person "possess" another? In Frederic Myers's classic *Phantasms of the Living*, there is an interesting account of a girl who was convinced that a man she scarcely knew was taking control of her dreams and trying to force her into sexual slavery (see chapter 60). If this is possible, and if disembodied "spirits" exist, then it would seem to follow that, under certain circumstances, "possession" by a spirit is a possibility.

Although Crabtree claims to treat the notion of "possession" merely as a working hypothesis, it can be seen that his work lends support to the views expressed by Wickland. This is even more so in the case of the

California psychiatrist Ralph Allison, whose *Minds in Many Pieces* (1980) is a major work in the field of multiple personality disorder (usually shortened to MPD). Allison had been practicing for almost a decade when he encountered his first case of MPD – a woman named Janette who had tried to kill her husband and children. A colleague advised Allison that he thought Janette was a case of MPD, and when Allison induced her to relax deeply and asked if he could speak to the "other person", a woman with a harsh, grating voice emerged and identified herself as Lydia. At one point, Janette had been raped in the hospital by several orderlies; now, as Lydia mentioned her interest in "drinking, dancing, fucking", and placed herself in a provocative position, Allison began to suspect that the orderlies may not have been entirely to blame. Eventually, a third personality named Karen emerged – a balanced, sensible woman – and with her help, Allison was able to cure Janette. (He came to call such personalities "the inner self-helper".)

In this case, the basic hypothesis of multiple personality covered the facts; that a traumatic childhood had caused the "prime personality" to withdraw from the problems of life, like an ostrich burying its head in the sand. But Allison's next patient, a girl named Carrie, forced him to take the "possession" hypothesis seriously. Carrie was another "multiple" with a history of childhood traumas, including a gang rape. Even without hypnosis, an alter ego named Wanda emerged and talked to Allison. But it seemed clear that Wanda was not responsible for the suicidal impulses Carrie was experiencing. When told that a "psychic" claimed that Carrie was possessed by the spirit of a drug addict who had died of an overdose in New York in 1968, Allison decided to "give the concept of spirit possession a try". Under deep hypnosis, Carrie agreed that the drug addict was influencing her life, and Allison's makeshift "exorcism" – performed with a swinging crystal ball on a chain – apparently succeeded. Unfortunately, it failed to dislodge two other personalities, and Carrie eventually committed suicide.

Yet Allison continued to reject the notion of "spirit possession" until he encountered a girl named Elise, who revealed several personalities under hypnosis. Most of these were able to describe their history – what traumas had caused them to be "born". But one of them claimed to be a man named Dennis, who explained that he had entered Elise's body when she was experimenting with black magic as a teenager and that he enjoyed remaining there because he enjoyed having sex with another of Elise's personalities, a girl named Shannon. The sex was not, as might be supposed, a bodiless intercourse between two "spirits"; when

Shannon took over Elise's body and had sex with a man, Dennis would enter the man's body. And although Elise and Shannon shared the same body, Dennis was not interested in having sex with Elise, only with Shannon. Eventually, with the help of another "inner self-helper", Elise was cured. It was this case that finally convinced Allison that multiple personality may sometimes be a case of spirit possession.

Another case confirmed this. In curing a girl named Sophia (by "integrating" her various personalities), Allison discovered that two personalities remained "left over". Under hypnosis, Sophia was regressed to birth and described how the doctor who had been her mother's lover had suffocated two triplets at birth but had been interrupted before he could dispose of the third – Sophia. The other two children had then moved into Sophia's body. Armed with this knowledge, Allison was able to rid Sophia of her two sisters and cure her.

Allison concluded that there were many possible causes of multiple personality, such as compulsive neurosis and violent traumas. But he also listed "possession" by another living person – as in the case of "Art" and his mother – possession by a dead person – as in Dr Bull's case of the painter Gifford – and possession by a "nonhuman spirit". By this he was referring to what would once have been called "demoniacal possession". In a paper on multiple personality, the parapsychologist Stanley Krippner reveals that an increasing number of psychiatrists accept the "spirit hypothesis".

What, then, is to be made of this bewildering mass of evidence about "possession", which most doctors would dismiss as childish fantasy? Belief in possession depends, clearly, on the prior assumption that "spirits" actually exist and that what happens at séances, for example, is genuine "possession" by the dead. This is doubted by many eminent parapsychologists and even by some mediums themselves; they prefer to believe that all that is involved in such cases is telepathy and some form of extrasensory perception (ESP). But, as we have seen, William James himself was finally convinced by Mrs Piper. So was Richard Hodgson, who had her shadowed by private detectives to see how she acquired her information – and who learned nothing whatever. But he was staggered when Mrs Piper told him about a girl named Jessie, to whom he had been engaged in Australia and who had subsequently died; Mrs Piper's "control", Phinuit, was able to report to Hodgson a conversation with Jessie about which no one else knew.

Hyslop himself was inclined to believe that that mediumship was a matter of "super ESP" until he was finally convinced by William James – many years after James's death. Hyslop received a letter from an Irish medium, telling him that a spirit who called himself William James (and of whom the medium had never heard) had asked him to contact Hyslop and remind him of the "red pajamas". James had once agreed with Hyslop that whichever of them died first should try to communicate with the other. At first, the message about red pajamas meant nothing to Hyslop. Then he suddenly remembered. When he and James had visited Paris as young men, their luggage had failed to arrive, and Hyslop had been forced to go out and buy some pajamas. All he had been able to find at short notice was a bright red pair, and James had teased him for days about his poor taste in pajamas. It was this message that finally convinced Hyslop of the survival of the dead.

If, like Hyslop, we can accept the notion of "survival", and if, like Kardec, we can accept that spirits can, under certain conditions, share the human brain, then it is hard to see why we should not also accept that they can influence people's actions – that is, "possess" them. It is important to note that "spiritualists" are in general agreement that such "possession" is rare, since it is impossible for a spirit actually to dislodge the incumbent, or even to share the body, unless there is a close affinity between "possessor" and "possessed".

The Loudun case seems to provide support for this view. Kardec states that poltergeists can only manifest themselves by stealing human energy, particularly sexual energy. Sister Jeanne's autobiography makes it clear that her own sexual frustrations alone could have provided a host of "entities" with the necessary energy. And by the time a dozen or so nuns were writhing on the floor and making suggestions that caused even hardened roués to blush, the convent must have been awash with sexual energy. Most cases of possession in nunneries seem to involve the same feverish sexuality. Two decades before the Loudun case, fourteen-year-old Madeleine de Demandolx de la Palud was seduced by Brother Louis Gaufridi, twenty years her senior; the liaison was broken up and she was sent to a nunnery at Aix-en-Provence. Two years later Madeleine began to see devils and smashed a crucifix. Her hysteria soon spread to the other nuns; Madeleine accused Gaufridi not only of seducing her but of introducing her to various diabolic practices. Gaufridi was asked to try and exorcise the demons, and when he failed, was put in prison.

At his trial, Madeleine declared that her allegations were all imaginings, after which she began to move her hips back and forth in a lascivious manner. The judge chose to disbelieve her; Gaufridi was tortured until he "confessed", then was burned at the stake.

It is important to realize that fornication among the clergy was a commonplace occurrence in the seventeenth century and that seduction of nuns by their confessors was far from rare. In 1625 a French orphan named Madeleine Bavent was seduced by a Franciscan priest, appropriately named Bonnetemps. In the following year she entered a convent run by Brother Pierre David, who secretly belonged to the Illuminati – a sect that believed that the Holy Spirit could do no harm and that therefore, sex was perfectly acceptable among priests. David apparently insisted that Madeleine should strip to the waist as he administered communion; other nuns, she later claimed, strolled around naked. She claimed that she and David never engaged in actual intercourse – only mutual masturbation – and that when David died in 1628, his successor, Brother Mathurin Picard, continued to caress her genitals during confession.

It was after Picard's death in 1642 (when Madeleine was thirty-five) that the nuns began to manifest the usual signs of possession: writhing on the ground, contorting their bodies, and making howling noises like animals, as they alleged they were being ravished by demons. Fourteen of the fifty-two nuns exhibited these symptoms, and all put the blame on Madeleine.

Madeleine then told the full story of David, Picard, and the latter's assistant, Brother Boulle. She claimed that Picard and Boulle had indulged in various "magical" acts involving communion wafers and menstrual blood and eventually in "sabbats", in which a Black Mass was recited. The priests had draped their erections with consecrated wafers with a hole cut in the middle and "thus arrayed gave themselves to the women present" – Madeleine being favoured five or six times.

Madeleine was accused of being a witch and was discharged from the order; Picard's corpse was dug up, excommunicated, and tossed onto a refuse heap. This led the priest's brother to create a scandal, and the result was a trial that ended with Boulle being tortured and burned alive, together with another priest named Duval. Madeleine, confined in a convent and brutally treated, made several suicide attempts and finally died at the age of forty. The nuns were all dispersed to other convents.

Madeleine's descriptions of sabbats and Black Masses sound like pure invention. But half a century later the notorious *chambre ardente* ("lighted chamber") affair revealed that many priests did, in fact, take part in such practices. When Louis XIV was informed by his chief of police that many women were asking for absolution for murdering their husbands, he ordered an investigation. It revealed that an international poisoning ring, organized by men of influence, existed. A number of fortune-tellers provided their clients with poisons and love philters, while priests performed Black Masses involving the sacrifice of babies and magical ceremonies in which they copulated with women on altars. These facts duly emerged in secret sessions of the "lighted chamber", and were recorded in detail. (The king later ordered all records to be destroyed, but the official transcript was overlooked.) One hundred and four of the accused were sentenced, thirty-six of them to death, while two of the fortune-tellers were burned alive. It is difficult for us to understand why the Church was involved in this wave of demonology – the likeliest explanation is that seventeenth-century rationalism was undermining its authority and that the protest against this authority took the form of licentiousness and black magic. Whatever the explanation, the *chambre ardente* transcripts leave no doubt that it really happened.

One interesting question remains: whether, as Ralph Allison believes, there is such a thing as possession by "nonhuman" entities – i.e., whether some form of "demoniacal possession" is a reality. Of all these cases involving "possession", the Loudun affair remains the most puzzling. Even if we can accept Wickland's belief that human beings can be influenced by "earthbound spirits", it is difficult to understand how five of the exorcists became victims of the demonic possession and four actually died of it. None of the patients described by Wickland, Crabtree, or Allison was driven to this extreme.

One possible clue is provided by a curious little book that appeared in Cape Town, South Africa, in 1972. It is entitled *Who Are the Dead?*, and the author is listed as Helen Quartermaine – which is not, apparently, her real name.

The author's view, briefly, is that in addition to the physical body, all human beings possess a "personality body" – also known as the psyche – which is made of a finer matter than the physical body. This personality body permeates the physical body – the author uses the image of a ball of wool soaked in water to illustrate how the personality body "imbues" the physical body. The points of contact between the two bodies, she says, are the seven endocrine glands, also known as the seven chakras of Hinduism.

So far, Helen Quartermaine is simply echoing the "occult tradition", in which the personality body is sometimes called the astral body. (Occult tradition also recognizes the human "aura", or etheric body, which might be regarded as its "life field" – the equivalent of a magnet's magnetic field.) But she goes on to make some far more startling assertions. Our problem, she says, is to keep these three "bodies" in alignment. In most people the two "higher bodies" tend to jut out of the right side. This lopsidedness means that the left side is unprotected and can easily be "invaded" by other disembodied personalities. When people get angry or upset, she explains, the personality receives a shock and is displaced sideways. And it may remain this way for a long time. Life force drains away into the physical body, and the result is serious depletion. She goes on to say: "Considering the endless list of trifling incidences which can cause a person to be malpositioned within his three bodies . . . it follows that *all* of us play host to our dead, by leaving the door of our physical bodies open to admit them. Worse follows, however, for we must also leave ourselves open to their mental, physical and emotional sicknesses".

She goes on to describe how the dead may attach themselves to those they love. Thus far she is in basic agreement with Wickland. But she then states: "Sometimes, of course, the motivating force is quite the opposite, and hate becomes the destroying power. There are many well-known cases of revenge striking from beyond the grave".

Ms Quartermaine next cites the case of Barbara Graham, executed in the gas chamber at San Quentin in June 1953 for her part in the murder of an elderly widow, Mabel Monahan, in the course of robbery. By 1953 Barbara, then thirty, had become a gangster's moll as well as an alcoholic and drug addict. On 9 March she agreed to help the gang enter Mrs Monahan's house in Burbank, California, by knocking on the door and asking to use the phone to contact a garage. Her four accomplices, Jack Santo, Baxter Shorter, Emmett Perkins, and John L. True, rushed into the house behind her and tied up the sixty-three-year-old widow while they searched the house for the fortune she was supposed to be guarding for the owner of a gambling casino. What actually happened is uncertain; the body of the woman, strangled with a strip of bedsheet, was found three days later by the gardener; her head, wrapped in a pillowcase, had been battered by a heavy blunt instrument.

The case was puzzling, since the victim's purse contained $500, and $10,000 worth of jewelry was untouched. But after questioning various underworld figures, the police called on Baxter Shorter, who – under a promise of complete immunity – told them that Santo, Perkins, True, and Barbara Graham had been involved. (A man named William Upshaw had also agreed to take part but had backed out.) Barbara, he said, had rung the doorbell, and when the old lady opened the door, True and Perkins had rushed in. When Shorter finally went in to see what was taking them so long, he saw Barbara pistol-whipping Mrs Monahan. Santo had tied the pillowcase around her head and Perkins had strangled her. A search of the house failed to reveal the gambler's hoard, and they left empty-handed.

Shorter's story was accepted and he was released. But he was soon kidnapped by Perkins – who was still free – and murdered. Later, Perkins, Santo, and Barbara Graham were arrested in a motel. Barbara denied that she was present in the Monahan home; whether or not this was true, it is certain that many people in court did not believe that she had done the beating, as True alleged. But the main evidence against her was that she had attempted to bribe a fellow prisoner – in fact, a police officer – to provide her with an alibi for $2,500. She had also told the policeman that Shorter had been "well taken care of".

Barbara Graham was tried, together with Santo and Perkins (her lover). Mainly on True's evidence, she was found guilty. She died in the gas chamber on the same day as Santo and Perkins (who had been sentenced to death for a second time for the murder of a whole family committed during the course of robbery).

Helen Quartermaine states:

[Barbara Graham] swore she was innocent, but when the verdict found her guilty she pledged herself to see that all the men concerned with her conviction would also, like herself, die prematurely. This list included the three men who were said to be her accomplices.

The first to die after her execution was the one who had turned prosecution witness and whose evidence damned her; he was involved in the collision of two boats on the Mississippi and killed outright. The other two men were retried at a later date and found guilty; they were also executed. This was only the beginning. The District Attorney in charge of her prosecution died very suddenly and unexpectedly from cancer. The fear grew when the warden of San Quentin prison . . . was struck dead by heart failure. Next came the abrupt death, again from cancer, of the Superior Court Judge who sentenced her. In February 1958, the man who informed the police against Mrs Graham was crushed to death on a journey by cars piling up. Another informer on the lady's catalogue of revenge has since disappeared, and police have strong reason to suspect he may have been murdered.

This account has several minor inaccuracies. Santo and Perkins died the same day, not "at a later date". John True died in January, not February, 1958, when a Dutch freighter rammed a small craft in a fog. William Upshaw was not the man who informed the police on Barbara Graham – but he certainly died when he drove into a road obstruction in California. The "other informer" – Shorter – had died long before Barbara Graham.

Helen Quartermaine is convinced that these deaths were actually caused by Barbara Graham's "personality body", out for revenge. Wickland, as we have seen, believed that such influence is possible and that Harry Thaw killed Stanford White under the influence of an entity – or entities – seeking revenge. Helen Quartermaine argues that the kind of lapse of attention that caused William Upshaw to drive his car into an obstruction, or that caused the Dutch freighter in the fog to run down the boat carrying divers (including John True), could easily be induced by a "vengeful spirit".

John True and William Upshaw were responsible for the death sentence that sent Barbara Graham to the gas chamber. The Loudun inquisitors were responsible for the torture of Urbain Grandier and for his agonizing death at the stake. Helen Quartermaine would undoubtedly regard the possession of the Loudun inquisitors as the revenge of Urbain Grandier on his tormentors.

Whether plausible or not, the suggestion may be regarded as a disturbing footnote to Wickland's *Thirty Years Among the Dead*.

43

Psychometry

"Telescope into the Past"

In the winter of 1921 members of the Metapsychic Institute in Paris met together to test a clairvoyant. Someone produced a letter and asked someone to pass it to her; before it could reach her it was grabbed by a novelist called Pascal Forthunny, who said scathingly: "It can't be difficult to invent something that applies to anybody". He then closed his eyes and pronounced solemnly: "Ah yes, I see a crime, a murder . . ." When he had finished the man who had brought the letter said: "That was written by Henri Landru". Landru was the "Bluebeard" who was then on trial for the murders of eleven women. The sceptic Forthunny had discovered that he possessed the curious ability known as psychometry – the ability to "sense" the history of an object by holding it in the hand.

According to the man who invented the word – an American doctor named Joseph Rodes Buchanan – it is an ability we all possess, although most of us have unconsciously suppressed it. Buchanan – who was a professor of medicine in Kentucky – came to suspect the existence of such a faculty in 1841, when he met a bishop named Leonidas Polk, who claimed that he could always detect brass when he touched it – even in the dark – because it produced a peculiar taste in his mouth. Buchanan was interested in the science known as phrenology – the notion that the "bumps" on our skulls reveal our characters – and he was interested to discover that Polk seemed to have a highly developed "bump" of sensibility. So he decided to perform a scientific test on students who had a similar bump. Various metals were wrapped in paper, and Buchanan was delighted to discover that many of his students could detect brass, iron, lead and so on by merely pressing their fingertips against the paper. They could also distinguish substances like salt, sugar, pepper and vinegar.

Buchanan concluded that the answer lay in some "nerve aura" in the fingertips, which can detect different metals exactly as we could distinguish them by touching them with the tip of the tongue. This appeared to be confirmed by his observation that it seemed to work better when the hands are damp with perspiration – for after all, a damp skin is more "sensitive" than a dry skin. But this explanation began to seem inadequate when he discovered that one of his best "sensitives" – a man named Charles Inman – could sense the contents of sealed letters, and the character of the writers. Buchanan's explanation was that the "nerve aura" of the writer had left some kind of trace on the letter, and Inman was able to pick up this trace through his own nerve aura. In other words, Inman's "sensitivity" was abnormally developed, in much the same way as a bloodhound's sense of smell. But that theory also broke down when he discovered that Inman displayed the same insight when presented with photographs – daguerreotypes – in sealed envelopes. Even the argument that the photograph had been in contact with the "sitter", and had therefore picked up something of his "nerve aura", ceased to be convincing when Buchanan discovered that newspaper photographs worked as well as daguerreotypes.

The professor of geology at Boston University, William Denton, read Buchanan's original paper on psychometry – the word means "soul measurement" – and decided to try it himself. His sister Anne was "highly impressible", and she proved to be an even better psychometrist than Inman; she was not only able to describe the character of letter-writers; she was even able to describe their physical appearance and surroundings.

This led Denton to ask himself whether, if a writer's image and surroundings could be "impressed" on a letter, "why could not rocks receive impressions of surrounding objects, some of which they have been in the immediate neighbourhood of for years". So in 1853 Denton began testing his "sensitives" with geological and archaeological specimens, "and was delighted to find that without possessing any previous knowledge of the specimen, or even seeing it, the history of its time passed before the gaze of the seer like a grand panoramic view". When he handed his sister a piece of volcanic lava from Hawaii, she was shaken to see "an ocean of fire pouring over a precipice and boiling as it pours". Significantly, she also saw the sea with ships on it, and Denton knew that the lava had been ejected during an eruption in 1840, when the American navy had been in Hawaii. A fragment of bone found in a piece of limestone evoked a picture of a prehistoric beach with dinosaurs. A fragment of Indian pottery brought a vision of Red Indians. A meteorite fragment brought visions of empty space, with the stars looking abnormally large and bright. A fragment of rock from Niagara brought a vision of a boiling torrent hurling up spray (which she thought was steam). A piece of stalactite brought an image of pieces of rock hanging down like icicles. To make doubly sure that his sensitives were not somehow picking up unconscious hints or recognizing the specimens, Denton wrapped them in thick paper. He also discovered that when he tried the same specimen a second time – perhaps a month later – it produced the same result, although the picture was never identical.

In one of his most interesting experiments he showed his wife a fragment of Roman tile which came from a villa that had belonged to the orator Cicero. She described a Roman villa and lines of soldiers; she also saw the owner of the villa, a genial, fleshy man with an air of command. Denton was disappointed; Cicero had been tall and thin. But by the time Denton came to write the second volume of *The Soul of Things* he had discovered that the villa had also belonged to the dictator Sulla, and that Sulla *did* fit his wife's description.

Another impressive "hit" was the "vision" induced by a piece of volcanic rock from Pompeii. Mrs Denton had no idea what it was, and was not allowed to see it; but she had a vivid impression of the eruption of Vesuvius and the crowds fleeing from Pompeii. Denton's son Sherman had an even more detailed vision of ancient Pompeii, complete with many archaeological details – such as an image of a boat with a "swan's neck" – which proved to be historically accurate.

Denton was immensely excited; he believed that he and Buchanan had discovered a so far unknown human faculty, a kind of "telescope into the past" that would enable us to relive great scenes of history. In effect, everything that had ever happened to the world was preserved on a kind of "newsreel" (although this was not, of course, an image that occurred to Denton) and could be replayed at will.

But while the evidence for the psychometric faculty is undoubtedly beyond dispute, Denton was not aware of how far it can be deceptive. The third volume of *The Soul of Things*, published in 1888, contains "visions" of various planets that we now know to be preposterous. Venus has giant trees like toadstools and animals that sound as if they were invented by Hieronymus Bosch; Mars has a summery temperature (in fact it would be freezing) and is peopled with four-fingered men with blue eyes and yellow hair; Jupiter also has blue-eyed blondes with plaits down to their waists and the ability to float like balloons. Denton's son Sherman (who was responsible for most of these extraordinary descriptions) had clearly developed the faculty that Jung calls "active imagination", and was unable to distinguish it from his genuine psychometric abilities.

What impresses the modern reader about Denton's *Soul of Things* and Buchanan's *Manual of Psychometry* (optimistically sub-titled The Dawn of a New Civilization) is their thoroughly scientific approach. This also impressed their contemporaries at first. Unfortunately, the period when they were conducting their experiments was also the period when the new craze known as Spiritualism was spreading across America and Europe. It had started with curious poltergeist manifestations in the home of the Fox family in New York state (see chapter 41) in the late 1840s. By 1860 it was a world-wide phenomenon. Scientists were appalled, and most of them dismissed it as sheer delusion. Anything that seemed remotely connected with the "supernatural" became the object of the same skepticism, and the researches of Buchanan and Denton never attracted the attention they deserved. Denton died in 1883, Buchanan in 1900, both in relative obscurity.

The next major experiments in psychometry were made by Dr Gustav Pagenstecher, a German who moved to Mexico City in the 1880s, and who regarded himself as a hard-headed materialist. Some time after the First World War, Pagenstecher was treating the insomnia of a patient called Maria Reyes de Zierold by hypnosis. One day, as she lay in a hypnotic trance, she told him that her daughter was listening at the door. Pagenstecher opened the door and found the daughter there. He began testing Maria for paranormal abilities and discovered that while under hypnosis she could share his own sensations; if he put sugar or salt on his tongue she could taste it; if he held a lighted match near his fingers she felt the heat of the flame. Then he began testing her for psychometric abilities. Like Denton's subjects, she could describe where some specimen came from. Holding a sea-shell, she described an underwater scene; holding a piece of meteorite, she described hurtling through space and down through the earth's atmosphere. ("I am horrified! My God"!) Dr Walter Franklin Prince, who tested her on behalf of the American Society for Psychical Research, handed her what he thought was a "sea bean" which he had found on the beach. She described a tropical forest. Professional botanists confirmed that the "bean" was a nut from a tree that grew in the tropical forest, and that was often carried down to the sea by the rivers.

Another eminent experimenter of the 1920s was Dr Eugene Osty, director of the Metapsychical Institute at which the novelist Pascal Fortunny correctly identified the letter from the mass murderer Landru. In his classic work *Supernormal Faculties in Man*, Osty described many experiments in psychometry with various "sensitives". In 1921 he was handed a photograph of a sealed glass capsule containing some liquid; it had been found near the great temple at Baalbek. One of his best psychics, a Mme Moral, held the photograph in her hand – it was so blurred it could have been of anything – and said immediately that it reminded her of "a place with dead people", and of one old man in particular. She "saw" a vast place, like an enormous church, then went on to describe the man, who was obviously a high priest. The capsule in the photograph contained the blood of a man who had been sacrificed in some distant land, and had been placed in the priest's grave as a memento.

At the time Osty himself had no idea what the photograph represented, and was surprised when the engineer who had found it was able to confirm that it had been discovered in a rich tomb in the Bekaa valley.

This story raises again the central problem about psychometry. Buchanan's original hypothesis – that it was simply a matter of "nerve aura", so the psychometrist could be regarded as a kind of human bloodhound – ceases to be plausible if the information can be picked up from a photograph, which could not be expected to retain any kind of "scent". Even Denton's assumption that every object somehow "photographs" its surroundings seems dubious. In that case a piece of Roman pavement could only have "photographed" a limited area, and Mrs Denton's view of Roman legionaries would have been simply of hairy legs towering up above her.

The likeliest hypothesis is that the faculty involved is what is traditionally known as "clairvoyance", a peculiar ability to "know" what is going on in some other place or at some other time. But Bishop Polk's ability to distinguish brass in the dark is obviously not clairvoyance. Here, as in so many other areas of the "paranormal", it is practically impossible to draw neat dividing lines.

Many modern psychometrists – like Gerard Croiset, Peter Hurkos and Suzanne Padfield – have been able use their faculty to help the police solve crimes: Suzanne Padfield was even able to help the Moscow police catch a child-murderer without leaving her home in Dorset. But it is significant that Croiset disliked being called a psychometrist or clairvoyant, and preferred the more ambiguous word "paragnost" – meaning simply the ability to "know" what lies beyond the normal limits of the senses.

44

Rennes-le-Château

The Treasure of Béranger Saunière

The mystery of Rennes-le-Château is the riddle of a poor priest who discovered a secret that made him a millionaire and which profoundly shocked the priest to whom he confided it on his deathbed.

In June 1885 a new curé came to the little village of Rennes-le-Château, on the French side of the Pyrenees; he was 33-year-old Béranger Saunière, and he was returning to the area in which he had been brought up. His early account books survive, and they show that he was very poor – the income on which he supported himself and his housekeeper was the equivalent of six pounds sterling a year.

It was six years later that Saunière decided to restore the church altar, a stone slab cemented into the wall and supported at the other end by two square Visigothic pillars. One of these proved to be hollow, and inside it Saunière found four parchments in wooden tubes. Two were genealogies of local families; the other two were texts from the New Testament, but written without the usual spaces between the letters. It seemed fairly obvious that these were in some sort of code – in fact, the code of the shorter text was straightforward. Saunière only had to write down the letters that were raised above the others, and he had a message that read: "A Dagobert II roi et à Sion est ce trésor et il est la mort": to Dagobert II, king, and to Sion belongs this treasure, and he is there dead. (The final phrase "et il est la mort" could also be translated "and it is death" – meaning, perhaps, "it is death to interfere with it".) So these secret messages were about a treasure. Dagobert was a seventh-century French king of the Merovingian dynasty. The author of these parchments was almost certainly a predecessor of Saunière, a priest named Antoine Bigou, who had been the curé of Rennes-le-Château at the time of the French Revolution.

Saunière took the parchments to the Bishop of Carcassonne, Monseigneur Félix-Arsène Billard, and the bishop was sufficiently intrigued to send Saunière to Paris to consult with various scholars and experts in cryptography. Among these were the Abbé Bieil, director of St Sulpice. Bieil's nephew was a brilliant young man named Emile Hoffet, who was a student of linguistics. Although Hoffet was training for the priest-hood, he was in touch with many "occultists" who flourished in Paris in the 1890s, an era which had seen a revival of interest in ritual magic; Hoffet introduced Saunière to a circle of distinguished artists, which included the poet Mallarmé, the dramatist Maeterlinck and the com-poser Claude Debussy. It was probably Debussy who introduced Saunière to the famous soprano Emma Calvé, and the relationship that developed between them may have been more than friendship – Sau-nière was a man who loved women and food.

Before he left Paris, Saunière visited the Louvre and purchased reproductions of three paintings, including Nicolas Poussin's *Les Ber-gers d'Arcadie* – the Shepherds of Arcady – which shows three shep-herds standing by a tomb on which are carved the words "Et in Arcadia Ego" – usually translated as "I [Death] am also in Arcadia".

When Saunière returned to Rennes-le-Château three weeks later he was hot on the trail of the "treasure". He brought in three young men to raise the stone slab set in the floor in front of the altar, and discovered that its underside was carved with a picture of mounted knights; it dated from about the time of King Dagobert. When his helpers dug farther down they discovered two skeletons, and – according to one of them who survived into the 1960s – a pot of "worthless medallions". Saunière then sent them away, locked the church doors, and spent the evening there alone.

Now Saunière, accompanied by his housekeeper – a young peasant girl named Marie Denarnaud – began to spend his days wandering around the district with a sack on his back, returning each evening with stones which he used to construct a grotto in his garden. Whether this was the only purpose of his explorations is not known. He also com-mitted a rather curious piece of vandalism on a grave in the churchyard. It belonged to Marie, Marquise de Blanchefort, whose headstone had been designed by the same Abbé Bigou who had concealed the parch-ments in the column. Saunière obliterated the inscriptions on the stone that covered the grave, and removed the headstone completely. How-ever, he was unaware that both inscriptions had already been recorded in a little book by a local antiquary. The inscription on the gravestone is shown opposite:

The vertical inscriptions on either side of the gravestone are easy to read: a mixture of Greek and Latin letters carries the inscription *Et in*

Arcadio Ego – linking it with the Poussin painting. The central inscription: "Reddis Regis Cellis Arcis" may be read: "At royal Reddis, in the cave of the fortress". "Reddis" is one of the ancient names for Rennes-le-Château, which was also known to the Romans as Aereda.

The inscription on the headstone has many odd features. In the first line, the *i* of *ci* (*ci gît* means "here lies") has been carved as a capital T. The M of Marie has been left at the end of the first line. The "e" of "noble" is in the lower case. The word following "negre" should read "Dables" not "Darles", so should have an R, not a B. Altogether there are eight of these anomalies in the inscription, making up two sets of four, one in capital letters and one in lower case. The capitals are TMRO, while the lower case are three e's and a p. Only one word can be formed of the capitals: MORT – death. Only one word can be formed of the lower-case letters: *epée* – sword. In fact these two words proved to be the "keyword" to decipher the longer of the two parchments found in the pillar . . .

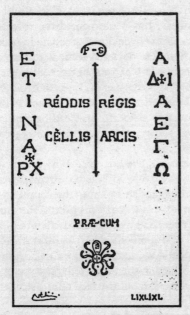

CT GIT NOBLe M

ARIE DE NEGRe

DARLES DAME

DHAUPOUL De

BLANCHEFORT

AGEE DE SOIX

ANTE SEpT ANS

DECEDEE LE

XVII JANVIER

MDCOLXXXI

REQUIESCAT IN

PACE

(P.S.) PRAE-CUM

Whether Saunière deciphered it alone, or whether his obliging friends at St Sulpice unknowingly handed him the vital clues, may never be known. All that *is* known is that shortly after this Saunière began spending money at a remarkable rate. He contacted a Paris bank, who sent a representative to Rennes-le-Château solely to attend to Saunière's business. Then he built a public road to replace the dirt track that had run to the village, and also had a water supply piped in. He built a pleasant villa with a garden that had fountains and shady walks. To house his library he built a gothic tower perched on the edge of the mountainside. He began to collect rare china, antiques and precious fabrics. He began to entertain distinguished visitors, like Emma Calvé and the Secretary of State for Culture. One of his visitors was recognized as the Archduke Johann von Habsburg, cousin of Franz- Josef, Emperor of Austria. His guests were given the very best of food and wine (and it may be significant that Saunière eventually died of cirrhosis of the liver).

Understandably, Saunière's superiors were curious about his wealth and wanted to know where it came from. Saunière told them coolly that he was not at liberty to divulge the source of his wealth – some of it came from rich penitents who had sworn him to secrecy. He had also been paid well for saying masses for the souls of the dead. The old bishop decided to mind his own business, but a new one later revealed a pertinacious curiosity, and when Saunière declined to satisfy it, ordered his transfer to another parish. Saunière declined to be transferred. A new priest was appointed to Rennes-le-Château, but the villagers still continued to treat Saunière as their spiritual pastor. Eventually, in 1917, Saunière suffered a stroke, and died at the age of sixty-four. A priest from a neighbouring parish who was called to his deathbed emerged looking pale and shaken, and a local account, doubtless exaggerated, says that he "never smiled again".

His housekeeper, Marie Denarnaud, lived on until 1953 in considerable affluence. When after the Second World War the French government issued new currency, and demanded to know the source of any large sums (the aim being to trap tax-evaders and profiteers) she burned piles of ten-franc notes in the garden, and lived for the remainder of her life on the proceeds of the sale of Saunière's villa. She was evidently determined not to betray Saunière's secret. Just before her death she confided to the purchaser of the villa that she would tell him a secret that would make him both rich and powerful; but she died after a stroke that left her speechless.

The obvious solution to the mystery is that Saunière discovered the treasure mentioned in the parchment, and somehow turned it into modern currency. In which case the mystery is simply what clues he found in the parchment, and how he followed them up to discover the concealed hoard.

Henry Lincoln, a modern investigator, became fascinated by the problem after reading a book called *Le Trésor Maudit* [*The Accursed Treasure*], by Gérard de Sède, in 1969. He made many visits to Rennes-le-Château, and eventually made a programme for BBC television called "The Lost Treasure of Jerusalem . . .?" Lincoln went to Paris to see Gérard de Sède, and before the programme was made de Sède had presented him with the solution of the "long cipher" from the Visigothic column. De Sède claimed that this had been broken with the help of French army experts who had used a computer. Lincoln suspected that this was untrue, and British Intelligence confirmed his suspicion that the code could not have been broken by computer.

The code was unbelievably complex – so complex that Lincoln does not even attempt to explain it in the book he later wrote on the mystery. Cracking it involved a technique known to cipher experts as the Vigenère process, which involves writing out the alphabet twenty-six times in a square, with the first line beginning with A, the second with B, the third with C, and so on. Then the key word Mort Epée is placed over the whole message in this case, of the longer of the two parchments and the letters are transformed by a simple process using the Vigenère table. But the new text is still meaningless. The next step is to move each letter one letter farther down the alphabet. It is still meaningless. The next step is to use a new key word on the jumble. This new key word is the entire text of the headstone beginning "Ci gît noble Maria" etc, and to take from the gravestone the two lots of letters "P.S" and "Prae cum" (Latin for "before" and "with"). This new "keyword" is applied backward to the text, ending with "P.S." and "Prae cum". Then all the letters are moved two spaces down the alphabet. Next, the text is divided into two groups of 64, and these are laid out on two chessboards, and the knight makes a series of knight's moves on the chessboards. Then the letter contained in each square of this series is written down. And now at last the message emerges – although it still looks quite absurd. The message runs: BERGERE PAS DE TENTATION QUE POUSSIN TENIERS GARDENT LE CLEF PAX DCLXXXI PAR LA CROIX ET CE CHEVAL DE DIEU J´ACHEVE CE DAEMON DE GARDIEN A MIDI POMMES BLEUES. This may be translated: SHEPHERDESS WITHOUT TEMPTATION TO WHICH POUSSIN AND TENIERS HOLD THE KEY PEACE 681 WITH THE CROSS AND THIS HORSE OF GOD I REACH THIS DAEMON GUARDIAN AT MIDDAY BLUE APPLES.

This message, we must presume, led Saunière to the treasure. Which raises the interesting question: *how* did he succeed in deciphering the message? True, he had the all-important "key words" from the grave of Marie de Blanchefort. But even if he also knew about the Vigenère table and the knight's moves, that would still make the decipherment an unbelievably complex task for an ordinary parish priest without training in cryptography. Leaving aside for the moment the actual meaning of the message, who handed Saunière the thread that guided him through this complex labyrinth?

Lincoln concluded, logically, that there must be someone who had already known some of the basic answers to the mystery or, more likely, some group or organization. This, presumably, was the organization from which his own informant, Gérard de Sède, had received his own information. This guess seemed to be supported by the number of books and pamphlets about Saunière and Rennes-le-Château that had appeared since 1956. Many of these were under obvious pseudonyms like "Anthony the Hermit". They proved to be available in the Bibliothèque Nationale, although some of them were curiously difficult to get hold of and one of them was constantly engaged for three months. And it was in the Bibliothèque Nationale that Lincoln found one of his most vital clues: a number of miscellaneous items gathered together in stiff covers under the title *Dossiers secrets*. And one of these documents spoke about a secret order called the Priory of Sion. We may recall that the shorter of the two documents Saunière found in the pillar ended with the letters P.S., while the longer document – the one containing the "shepherdess" message – is signed with the letters NO-IS which back to front reads "Sion". According to this document, the Grand Masters of this secret order included the alchemist Nicolas Flamel (who is reputed to have made gold), Leonardo da Vinci, Isaac Newton, Victor Hugo – and Claude Debussy. Saunière had met Debussy in Paris. This then could explain where he had received the key to the code.

And what exactly was the Priory of Sion? It was, according to the *Secret Dossiers*, the inner hierarchy of the order of "warrior monks" called the Knights Templars. In the year AD 1118, after the first Crusade had opened the Holy Land to Christian pilgrims, a knight called Hugues de Payens conceived the apparently absurd idea of policing the dangerous roads of the Holy Land with a small band of knights. They were successful beyond all expectation, and were granted a wing of Solomon's temple on Mount Sion in Jerusalem as their headquarters. As grateful pilgrims left them legacies they became immensely wealthy – they were also virtually the bankers of the Holy Land. Their downfall came two centuries later when the French king Philip the Fair (Philippe le Bel) had them all arrested in one sudden swoop – it was 13 October 1307 – and accused them of all kinds of horrible blasphemies and indecencies. Dozens of them were tortured and executed, and in

1312 the order was dissolved. Philip had gained his chief objective – to lay his hands on their wealth – but he was unsuccessful in his attempt to seize the treasures of one of their major strongholds, Bezu, which is near Rennes-le-Château . . .

Mount Sion is just outside Jerusalem, and Jerusalem is often referred to as Sion in the scriptures. According to the *Secret Dossiers*, the Order of Sion (as it was at first called) was the secret society that originally created the Templars, and it was unaffected by the latter's downfall in 1307. And what was the purpose of the Priory? It was apparently to restore the Merovingians – the dynasty founded by King Clovis at the beginning of the sixth century AD – to the throne of France. Later Merovingian kings were distinctly feeble – in fact, they became known as "the feeble kings" (*rois fainéants*) – and left most of the work to their major-domos (or Mayors of the Palace). In AD 679 one of these major-domos organized the murder of King Dagobert II – a lance was driven through his eye while he was asleep – and in due course the major-domos became kings: they were known as the Carolingians.

According to the *Secret Dossiers*, Dagobert's son Sigisbert fled south to Languedoc, and inherited the title duke of Razés and count of Rhedae from his uncle. Rhedae is another old name for Rennes-le-Château (which was then a large town), and Razés is the name of the county (or comté) in which Rennes is situated. And three centuries later, another descendant of Dagobert, Godfrey de Bouillon, led the First Crusade and freed Jerusalem from the Moslems.

It seems rather a strange ambition – to restore to the throne of France a dynasty known as "the feeble kings". Why should anyone bother? It seems as irrelevant and absurd as wanting to restore the Tudors or Stuarts to the English throne. And what connection could there be between this curious aspiration and the "treasure" that made Saunière a rich man? As Lincoln pursued his researches, he found himself drawn into an increasingly bewildering labyrinth of mystery and rumour.

To begin with, Gérard de Sède told him, while he was preparing the original television programme, that the tomb shown in Poussin's painting had now been discovered. It was at a place called Arques, a few miles east of Rennes-le-Château. The tomb is close to the Château of Arques, and is in fact an exact duplicate of the tomb in Poussin's painting. One can even see Rennes-le-Château in the background of the painting. The first vertical line of the tombstone inscription on Marie de Blanchefort's grave reads "Et in Arc". The central inscription reads "At royal Reddis in the caves of the fortress". An odd-looking circle surrounds the letters P.S. which starts *before* the P and curls back so that it ends before the S. The letter before P is O. The letter before S is R. O and R together spell "or", the French for gold. The message seems to be saying that the gold is at Royal Reddis in the caves of the fortress. Why royal Reddis? Because it is associated with the Merovingian line of kings . . .

So we can being to see why the coded message on the parchment said that Poussin held the key; it was presumably to this painting it was referring. But the message also mentioned the painter Teniers, a Flemish artist who was a contemporary of Poussin. What part does he play in the mystery? Lincoln discovered that there is a copy of Poussin's *Shepherds of Arcady* at Shugborough Hall, in Staffordshire – a bas relief which is a reversed mirror image of the painting. But also at Shugborough Hall there is a painting of St Anthony by Teniers. The temptation of St Anthony was one of Teniers's favourite subjects. But this one is different – it simply shows St Anthony in meditation: no temptation. And in the background there is a shepherdess. "Shepherdess, no temptation, that Poussin and Teniers hold the key . . ." Shugborough Hall is the seat of the earls of Lichfield, and Lincoln discovered that it had been a hotbed of masonic activity in the seventeenth century. In 1715 one of the earls helped his cousin when he escaped from Newgate prison. The cousin was called Charles Radclyffe, and he is listed in the *Secret Dossiers* as one of the Grand Masters of the Priory of Sion. The offence for which Radclyffe was imprisoned was, significantly, aiding the Old Pretender in his attempt on the throne of England. Radclyffe became the secretary of the Young Pretender in France – and presumably Grand Master of the Priory of Sion – and was executed after Culloden in 1746. So there could be good reasons why more clues to the Rennes-le-Château mystery are to be found at Shugborough Hall. Unfortunately, Lincoln found himself unable to decipher these clues.

What precisely *is* the treasure of Rennes-le-Château? The obvious guess is that it is the treasure of the Templars of Bezu, which Philippe le Bel failed to lay his hands on. And this could well be correct. But there is another clue that is contained in the longer of the two coded parchments. In the middle of the message there are twelve letters raised above the others; these have to be discarded before the decoding process begins. But in addition there are eight small letters that occur at random throughout the text, and these spell the words Rex Mundi, King of the World. This links the message with a religious sect called the Cathars, which might be regarded as an early form of Protestantism. The Cathars or "Pure Ones" held a belief that was derived from a much older sect called the Manichees: that everything to do with the world of matter is evil, and everything to do with the world of spirit is good. They believed that this world was not created by God but by a "demiurge" or demon, who is the King of this world. Although they accepted salvation through Christ, they did not believe that he was crucified on the cross. This sect of early puritans became so powerful in the Languedoc – where Rennes-le-Château is situated – that the pope called a crusade against them, and in 1209 a huge army invaded Languedoc and murdered thousands of people. The last stand of the Languedoc Cathars occurred in 1244; the Cathars took refuge in the citadel of Montségur, situated on a mountain-top. After a ten-month siege they surrendered, and were offered lenient terms by the besiegers – all who renounced their faith could go free. Heretics who refused to surrender would be burned alive. They were given two weeks to think about it; at the end of that time two hundred heretics were dragged down the mountain (about two hundred family members were spared) and burnt on a huge pyre. But during those two weeks four men escaped from the citadel carrying the "treasure" of the Cathars – two months earlier another two Cathars had escaped with more "treasure". These were not caught.

So Saunière's treasure may have been that of the Cathars of Mont-ségur. But surely this cannot have been very substantial – after all, six men scrambling down a steep mountain-side cannot carry much gold and silver. It is, of course, conceivable that they were carrying some other form of treasure – the holy objects of the Cathars. But if that is so, what were these holy objects?

For completeness we should mention yet another treasure associated with the area: the treasure of the Visigoths (or Western Goths), the German "barbarians" who played an important part in the downfall of Rome. In Dagobert's time Rennes-le-Château was a Visigoth bastion, and Dagobert was married to a Visigoth princess. In their triumphant march across Europe the Visigoths accumulated vast treasures, which seem to have included some of the treasures from the Temple at Jerusalem, removed after the Roman emperor Titus took Jerusalem in AD 69. Much of this treasure was never recovered.

But for Henry Lincoln the Priory of Sion materials in the *Secret Dossiers* were leading to another and far stranger line of enquiry. After his first television programme on Rennes-le-Château (he went on to make three) he received a curious letter from an Anglican priest which claimed that the treasure did not involve gold or precious stones. It consisted of "incontrovertible proof" that the Crucifixion was a fraud, and that Jesus was still alive as late as AD 45. (The date of the crucifixion is usually assumed to be about AD 33.) Lincoln went to see the priest, who declined to go into detail. But he admitted that his information came from an Anglican scholar named Canon Alfred Leslie Lilley. Lilley had maintained contacts with Catholic scholars based at St Sulpice, and had been acquainted with Emile Hoffet, the trainee priest who had introduced Saunière to Debussy and others.

And it gradually became clear that this was in fact the "great secret" of the Priory of Sion. The real founder of the Merovingian dynasty was not the legendary King Merovech (or Merovée), but Jesus himself, and *this* was why the descendants of the Merovingians felt that they had a right to the throne of France. In the course of his investigations Lincoln had encountered repeated mentions of the Holy Grail or "Sangreal". One legend asserted that it was in the possession of the Templars, another that it was the "treasure" carried down Montségur by the four Cathars. But "sang real" also means "royal blood". The Grail was supposed to be the cup from which Jesus drank at the last supper, and Glastonbury legends assert that it was taken there by Joseph of Arimathea. In two of the Gospels, Jesus is described as being a descendant of King David, and therefore of royal blood; the notice "The King of the Jews" displayed above the cross is generally assumed to be sarcasm, but it may have referred to a claim actually made by the close followers of Jesus.

It was in a book, *The Holy Blood and the Holy Grail* (1982), co-authored by Michael Baigent and Richard Lee, that Lincoln finally revealed this astonishing theory. It is difficult to discover from the book how far this is his own deduction from the evidence, and how far he received the information from sources like Gérard de Sède, or from M. Pierre Plantard de Saint-Clair, who claims to be a lineal descendant of Dagobert II, and the chief Merovingian pretender to the throne of modern France. But the theory itself is straightforward enough. It is that Jesus did not die on the cross – that the sponge that was proffered to him contained a drug. Lincoln points out that Jesus seems to have taken only a few hours to die, while most people took days, even weeks. His death forestalled the breaking of his legs – an act of mercy that prevented a crucified man from supporting himself on his nailed feet, and ensured his swift suffocation as his weight dragged on his arms. The sponge was offered in the nick of time. The theory also involves the assumption that Jesus was married, and that his wife was probably Mary Magdalene, who may have been identical with Mary the sister of Martha and of Lazarus. According to the theory, Jesus left Palestine and came to Languedoc, although he may have ended his life at the siege of Masada in AD 74. The hillside tomb depicted by Poussin could well be the actual tomb of Jesus.

Whether or not there is historical evidence for this theory, there is certainly evidence that this is the belief held by the Priory of Sion and by Saunière himself. He built himself a tower to house his library and called it the Magdala tower (Magdala being the name of the village from which Magdalene came). He called his house the Villa Bethania, after Bethany, the home of the other Mary, and the place from which two of the disciples fetch the ass on which Jesus rides into Jerusalem. Lincoln suggests that the man who provided the ass was Lazarus, and that it was all part of a carefully laid plan which would involve the false crucifixion.

There is a curious and baffling piece of evidence concerning Nicolas Poussin. In 1656 Nicolas Fouquet, Louis XIV's Minister of Finance, dispatched his younger brother Louis to Rome on a mission that involved a visit to Poussin. On 17 April Louis wrote Nicolas a letter commenting that Poussin had displayed "overwhelming joy" on receiving the letter Fouquet had sent him. It then goes on:

> He and I have planned certain things of which in a little while I shall be able to inform you fully; things which will give you, through M. Poussin, advantages which kings would have great difficulty in obtaining from him, and which, according to what he says, no one in the world will ever retrieve in centuries to come; and, furthermore, it would be achieved without much expense and could even turn to profit, and they are matters so difficult to enquire into that nothing on earth at the present time could bring a greater fortune nor perhaps ever its equal . . .

The comment about "advantages which kings would have great difficulty in obtaining (or drawing) from him" is fairly clearly a reference to Louis XIV. It looks as if Fouquet is involved in some interesting plot behind Louis's back. Five years later Fouquet was arrested on vague charges of misappropriation of funds, and finally sentenced to life imprisonment. (One theory suggests that he was the Man in the Iron Mask.) Louis XIV went to great trouble to obtain the painting of the *Shepherds of Arcady* – which is also engraved on Poussin's tomb – yet instead of placing it on display, kept it in his private apartments.

Let us then see if we can begin to piece together the basic outline of this incredibly complicated story. It begins with Jesus, who is alleged to have arranged his own crucifixion and subsequent "resurrection", presumably with the aim of "creating faith" and establishing Christianity. Whether or not this is true, we are invited to believe that the Merovingian dynasty believed that it was descended directly from Jesus.

When Dagobert was murdered the Church endorsed the regicide; Pepin the Short, first of the Carolingians, repaid the pope by taking an army to Italy, inflicting defeats on the pope's enemies the Lombards, and handing over the captured territory, which became the basis of the Papal States. So the Merovingians came to regard themselves as the enemies of the Church of Rome. A secret society called the Priory of Sion was formed, with the object of placing the Merovingians back on the throne of France. It held some important sacred object – possibly the Grail, possibly some "incontrovertible proof" of the descent of the Merovingians from Jesus. Its secret password was probably the phrase "Et in Arcadia Ego". In the twelfth century the Knights Templars became the military arm of this secret society – which means, presumably, that they shared the secret about the crucifixion – a secret, we must bear in mind, that could have undermined the foundations of the Catholic Church, which was founded upon the notion of the Vicarious Atonement. No crucifixion, no atonement, no Church . . .

The oddest aspect of the destruction of the Templars was the accusations of blasphemy and worship of demons. But if the Templars *did* possess this knowledge, then they *were* dangerous, both to the Church and to the State (*i.e.*, to the kings of France). There is also much historical evidence of a close alliance between the Templars and the Cathars. The Cathars gave large amounts of land to the Templars, and Bertrand de Blanchefort, fourth Grand Master of the Templars, came of a Cathar family. Bertrand's descendants fought besides the Cathars of Languedoc against the invaders who were sent by the pope to stamp out Catharism.

By the sixteenth century the Merovingians were represented by the house of Lorraine (which became Habsburg-Lorraine – so the Habsburgs were also Merovingians). They tried hard to depose the ruling house of Valois, but although they finally succeeded in bringing about their extinction, they had exhausted themselves in the process and had no eligible candidate to put forward. When Louis XIII died there was another determined attempt by the conspirators to prevent Louis XIV coming to the throne; but this again failed. (Readers who wish to study this historical aspect in more detail are recommended to read Lincoln's fascinating book.)

The story of Fouquet's downfall seems to suggest that he was hoping to use the secret of the Priory of Sion to overthrow the king. It is not clear how Poussin was associated with the mystery, but he was presumably a member of the Priory, and was asked to encode its major secret – probably that of the "incontrovertible evidence", or of the Grail – in his picture *The Shepherds of Arcady*. Lincoln argues that the painting embodies some secret geometry involving a pentagram which would enable the "treasure" to be located. King Louis's interest in the painting suggests that he hoped to find the treasure first.

During the early years of Louis's reign the Grand Master of the Priory was, according to the *Secret Dossiers*, a German minister named Johann Valentin Andreae; and this introduces an interesting new complication. Andreae is believed to have been the author of a curious work called *The Fama Fraternitas of the Worthy Order of the Rosy Cross*, published in 1614. This claimed that an ascetic called Christian Rosenkreuz, who lived to be 106, had spent his whole life in a search for occult wisdom, and had founded an order called the Brotherhood of the Rosy Cross, or Rosicrucians. He lay buried in a secret tomb for 120 years, surrounded by lighted candles, before a brother found the tomb. Now, anyone who wished to become party to this secret wisdom only had to make their interest known and they would be contacted . . . Many people published pamphlets announcing their desire to be initiated but (as far as is known) none of them was ever contacted. Two more Rosicrucian works were published, and scholarship has established that the author of the third of these, *The Chemical Wedding of Christian Rosenkreuz*, was Andreae. Rosicrucianism exerted a powerful influence on the minds of scholars and occultists in the seventeenth, eighteenth and nineteenth centuries. Now, according to Lincoln's sources, Andreae is revealed as a Grand Master of the Priory (twenty years after publication of the *Fama*), and we are apparently to assume that the Priory of Sion became closely identified with the Rosicrucians, and later with the various Masonic lodges.

Lincoln writes:

It was in the eighteenth century, however, that the Merovingian bloodline probably came closest to the realisation of its objectives. By virtue of its intermarriage with the Habsburgs, the house of Lorraine had actually acquired the throne of Austria, the Holy Roman Empire. When Marie Antoinette, daughter of François de Lorraine, became queen of France, the throne of France, too, was only a generation or so away. Had not the French Revolution intervened, the house of Habsburg-Lorraine might well, by the early 1800s, have been on its way to establishing dominion all over Europe.

With the Revolution, these hopes evaporated. And for some reason the Abbé Antoine Bigou, the priest of Rennes-le-Château and confessor of the Blanchefort family (of which, we may recall, one member had been a Master of the Templars) felt that both he and the secret of Rennes-le-Château were in danger. Why is not clear – the sans-culottes could hardly kill every priest in France. Possibly he thought they had been betrayed or were likely to be. At all events, he went to the trouble of writing the two coded parchments and concealing them, together with the two genealogical tables, in the Visigothic pillar. We do not know what the two tables contained – perhaps the line of descent from Jesus down to the living members of the Priory of Sion. (According to Lincoln's informant, M. Plantard, the Merovingian Pretender, they are now in a London bank vault.) Then Bigou fled to Spain, where he soon died.

So the scene was set for Saunière's appearance nearly a century later, and for his discovery of the parchments. What happened then? Saunière went to Paris, and contacted the very person – Emile Hoffet – who was able to put him in touch with the modern Priory of Sion. The Priory may well have lost touch with the secrets of Rennes-le-Château, if Bigou had hidden the "treasure", and so would have been delighted to see him. We must assume that Saunière accepted the "incontrovertible proof" that Jesus had not died on the cross but had founded a royal dynasty, and became a member of the Priory. He then returned to Rennes-le-Château, and used the knowledge he had gained – presumably from Debussy – to find the "treasure". Those excursions in the area, when he claimed to have been collecting stones for a grotto, must have been part of the treasure-hunt. He found his "treasure", and became a rich man. But we know that much of his money came from the Habsburg family – at one point he was accused of being an Austrian spy because he was being paid by the Habsburgs – but that some of it was paid to him by the Abbé Henri Boudet, curé of nearby Rennes-les-Bains. Boudet also passed on money to the Bishop of Carcassonne. It would seem, then, that Boudet too was a member of the Priory of Sion.

When Saunière died, after enjoying his new-found wealth for less than a quarter of a century, he shocked the priest who administered the final rites by admitting that he was not, in the strict sense of the word, a Christian. He had dropped hints to the same effect in the restorations in his church: the devil inside the door (Rex Mundi) – Asmodeus, the legendary guardian of Solomon's treasure – and many baffling touches in the tableau of the crucifixion, such as a money bag at the foot of the cross. Over the door he had inscribed the words TERRIBILIS EST LOCUS ISTE: this place is terrible. The words are from the dedicatory mass sung for new churches, and "terrible" here means "awe-inspiring"; but it still seems odd that Saunière should have chosen them for the motto of his church, seen immediately before the visitor encounters its "demon guardian".

Lincoln seems to feel that the solution to the mystery of Saunière's wealth is that it came from the Priory of Sion. But this is disputed by other writers. Brian Innes, who conducted a four-part investigation of the mystery in a magazine called *The Unexplained* in 1980, points out that quantities of gold have been found in the area. In 1645 a shepherd boy called Ignace Paris was executed for theft; he was in possession of gold coins, and claimed that he had found these after falling down a ravine and finding his way into a cave full of treasure. Innes says that more recently a slab of gold weighing nearly 45 lb has been found near Rennes-le-Château, made from fused Arab (or Crusader) coins, and that in 1928 the remains of a large gold statue were found in a hut on the edge of a stream that flows below the village.

In their book *The Holy Grail Revealed: The Real Secret of Rennes-le-Château*, Patricia and Lionel Fanthorpe also argue strongly that Saunière found real treasure, not merely some ancient secret. Yet they are also inclined to agree with Lincoln that there was also some "object" referred to as the Grail which could confer power on those who owned it: they compare it to the Ring of Power in Tolkien's *Lord of the Rings*, and even suggest in one place, that it might be of "extra-terrestrial origin", linking Rennes-le-Château with the "ancient astronaut" theories of Erich von Däniken.

None of the theories can provide a complete solution to the mystery of Rennes-le-Château, but on the whole Lincoln comes closest to it. For the twentieth-century reader, the notion that Jesus survived the crucifixion and founded a dynasty is not particularly "terrible". Yet we can see that for Nicolas Poussin and Louis Fouquet this notion would have seemed hair-raising, a kind of spiritual dynamite, sufficient to undermine sixteen centuries of Christianity and the authority of the pope. Even for Saunière, living at the end of the skeptical nineteenth century, it must have seemed quite startling.

Is it likely that we shall ever get to the bottom of the mystery? It is well within the realms of possibility. Presumably the Priory of Sion knows precisely what Saunière found near Rennes-le-Château in the hillside tomb or the old fortress, and its increasing tendency to "go public" may mean that we shall sooner or later be told the whole story. But even if that does not happen, the solution could still lie in the message on the second parchment – in solving the puzzle contained in Poussin and Teniers, in working out the meaning of "Peace 681" (which could refer to the year 1799, since Templar Freemasons dated the calender from the year 1118), the horse of God, the demon of the guardian at noon, and the blue apples. But whoever discovers the secret can be reasonably certain of one thing: that the treasure itself will be missing.

Postscript to Rennes-le-Château

Publication of *The Holy Blood and the Holy Grail* in 1982 created a sensation. Suddenly, the little village of Rennes-le-Chateau became famous, and busloads of tourists arrived every summer – some of them guided by Henry Lincoln himself.

Lincoln came to feel that an important part of the mystery of Rennes-le-Chateau lay in the landscape itself.

Looking at the code discovered in the parchment, Lincoln noted the phrase: "Poussin holds the key . . ." and, as we have seen, the actual tomb shown in Poussin's painting was discovered in the area of Rennes-le-Chateau at nearby Arques. And in fact, the tomb, although it had no Latin inscription, was otherwise identical, even to the stone on which the shepherd in the painting is resting his foot.

Lincoln had not only noticed that there was a hidden pentagram in one of the parchments, but that there was something odd about the geometry of Poussin's painting. He showed it to Professor Christopher Cornford, of the Royal College of Art, and Cornford not only agreed with him that there was a pentagram hidden in the painting, but that the structure was based on the Golden Section, a geometrical division much used in ancient times. (This is also known by the Greek letter phi, and is basically a way of dividing a line in such a ratio that the smaller part is to the greater as the greater is to the whole line – and in numerical terms equals 1.618.) What makes the Golden Section so important is that nature, for some odd reason, is using it all the time, from spiral seashells to spiral nebulae. It is present in the petal arrangements around the heads of flowers, and in the human body. And for some reason, when used in the divisions of a painting, it produces an oddly pleasing effect.

Now the pentagram is one of the most ancient magical symbols. And the reason is almost certainly that it was associated with the planet Venus.

If we imagine the earth as the centre of the solar system (as the ancients believed it was) it becomes obvious that there will be moments when every planet will be "eclipsed" by the sun, when the sun comes between the planet and the earth. Mercury, for example, is "eclipsed" three times, and if we draw lines between these three points in the heavens, they form an irregular triangle. Mars is "eclipsed" four times, and the figure is an irregular rectangle. In fact, all the planets make irregular figures – except Venus. And this makes a regular pentagram or pentacle.

Now in writing a book called *From Atlantis to the Sphinx* I had concluded that astronomy is far, far older than we might imagine. There is even evidence that it dates back more than a hundred thousand years, to Neanderthal Man. And in their book *Hamlet's Mill* George Santillana and Hertha von Dechend have demonstrated very clearly that the precession of the equinoxes – that apparent slow backward movement of the constellations, due to a slight wobble on the earth's axis, which takes almost twenty-six thousand years to complete its cycle – was known to every major civilization of the ancient world. This admittedly sounds absurd, since it would seem to involve many centuries of close observation of the heavens. But Santillana and Dechend leave little doubt that it was so.

The implication is that the pentagram symbolizing Venus has been sacred for many thousands of years.

Now Lincoln also discovered the pentagram in the geometry of Rennes-le-Chateau.

When he looked at an ordnance survey map of Rennes-le-Chateau region, one thing was immediately obvious: that three of its key sites – Rennes, the Templar Chateau of Bezu, and the Blanchefort chateau – formed three points of a triangle. And all were on hilltops.

When Lincoln drew the triangle on his map, and proceeded to measure its lines, he received a surprise. It was a precise isosceles triangle, that is, with two sides exactly equal. With Bezu at the appex of the triangle, the lines from Bezu to Blanchefort, and from Bezu to Rennes-le-Chateau, were equal.

This could not be an accident. At some remote point in time, someone had observed that the three hilltops made a precise triangle, and in due course they had been chosen as part of a secret pattern.

Now Lincoln found himself wondering if, by any remote chance, there were two more hilltops which would form the rest of the pentagram. Of course, he felt that would be asking too much . . .

Yet when he studied the map, he was staggered to find that there were indeed two such hilltops, in precisely the right places. The eastern one was called La Soulane, and the western one Serre de Lauzet. And when the five hilltops were joined up on the map, they formed an exact pentacle.

This was obviously an amazing natural freak. But there was one more surprise to come. When Lincoln looked for the centre of the map, he found that it was marked by another hill, called La Pique.

Admittedly, although the summit of La Pique looked on the map like the dead centre, it was actually two hundred and fifty yards to the south east of centre. But that was to be expected. After all, this was not a man-made landscape. It was incredible enough that La Pique fell at the centre of the pentacle.

So this was the basic secret of Rennes-le-Chateau: that it was part of a sacred landscape. Perhaps this is why Rennes-le-Chateau was chosen by the Merovingian King Dagobert as his home (and explains why his son Sigisbert fled there after his father's murder). The royal blood of the Merovingians was associated with a *magic* landscape.

The implication is that the goddess to whom the Rennes-le-Chateau "Temple" was originally dedicated was Venus, and explains why Mary Magdalen – who was identified with Venus in the Middle Ages – figures so largely in the area.

In other words, the whole area of Rennes-le-Chateau was regarded as sacred because of its geometry. At the centre of its landscape lay a natural pentagram.

That being so, it seems inevitable that in the Christian era, churches would be built so as to conform to this geometrical pattern. And in fact, an enthusiast named David Wood studied the map of the area, and quickly discovered that a precise circle could be drawn through five churches, including Rennes-le-Chateau, connected by a pentacular geometry. His book *Genisis* contains some remarkable insights into the geometry of the area, which Lincoln (who introduces the book) acknowledges to be remarkable. However, Lincoln – probably in common with most readers of the book – is unable to agree with Wood's explanation of the mystery, which involves a super-race who came from Syrius 200,000 years ago, and became the gods of Ancient Egypt. Such speculations, while fascinating, are obviously unproven and unprovable.

But one interesting discovery made by David Wood – and accepted by Lincoln – is that the geometry of the Rennes-le-Chateau area is, incredibly, measured in English miles, not in kilometres. Lincoln argues effectively that the kilometre (which is supposed to be one ten millionth of the distance from the North Pole to the Equator) is a slipshod and meaningless measurement, and that the world would be better off to return to miles.

Equally controversial are the speculations contained in a book called *The Tomb of God* (1996) by Richard Andrews and Paul Schellenberger, whose geometrical constructions leave them to locate the tomb of Jesus at the foot of a mountain near Rennes-le-Chateau, and who are convinced that Saunière was murdered. But a BBC television programme about the book seemed to demonstrate that the BBC's attitude to Rennes-le-Chateau had changed since Lincoln's three programmes, and that they had become hard line skeptics.

What was certainly most absurd was the programme's attempt to demonstrate that the Priory of Sion story, and the whole Rennes-le-Château affair, was a hoax that has now been exploded. For even if it could be demonstrated that Pierre Plantard, who claims to be a Merovingian descendant of Dagobert, was an imposter, the mystery of Saunière and his fortune would remain as baffling as ever.

Then where did that wealth come from? The answer is almost certainly: not from any hidden treasure but from the Priory of Sion – that is, from modern descendants of the Merovingians, particularly the house of Hapsburg in Austria. Andrews and Schellenberger (whose book is excellently researched, even if its conclusions seem dubious) produce evidence that Henri Boudet, the priest of nearby Rennes-les-Bains, was Saunière's paymaster, and that he passed on sums like three and a half million gold francs to Saunière's housekeeper Marie Denardaud, and seven and a half million to Bishop Bellard, who appointed Saunière to Rennes-le-Château. It seems clear that there were many other people in the secret.

As to Pierre Plantard, who seems to have given Lincoln the basic information that enabled him to solve the mystery of the parchments, the case against him has been laid out by Lynn Picknett and Clive Prince in a book called *The Templar Revelation*. Plantard came to prominence in occupied Paris in 1942 as the Grand Master of a quasi-Masonic order called The Order of Alpha-Galates, which was "markedly uncritical" of the Nazis. In fact, the Nazis seemed to approve of it. But then, they would; part of Himmler's job was to establish that the Germans had a noble origin in the remote days of the Norse sagas, and to create a modern mystical order with its roots in the Aryan past. Pierre Plantard, whom Picknett and Prince describe as "a one-time draftsman for a stove-fitting firm, who allegedly had difficulty paying the rent from

time to time", then changed his name to Pierre Plantard de Saint-Clair
and later played an important part in bringing about the return to power
of General de Gaulle in 1958. From 1956, the Priory of Sion had been
depositing "enigmatic documents" in the Bibliotheque Nationale. The
implication was that these documents had been concocted as part of the
"hoax". In fact, Lincoln's books *The Holy Place* and *Key to the Sacred
Pattern* make it clear that there is no reason whatever for believing that
the Priory of Sion is some kind of hoax or that Pierre Plantard is not
exactly what he says he is.

On the other hand, it is necessary to admit that the BBC may have
been justified in its negative attitude towards *The Tomb of God* by
Andrews and Schellenberger. As already noted, their theory suggests
that Jesus is buried at the foot of a mountain near Rennes-le-Chateau.
They find all kinds of geometrical figures in Saunière's parchments,
then use these as a map to locate the "tomb of God". They add the word
"sum" (am) to *"et in Arcadia ego"* to make an anagram that reads "I
touch the tomb of God, Jesus" They suggest that the "blue apples"
referred to in Saunière's parchment are grapes, and that they symbolize
the body of Jesus. The puzzling phrase "horse of God" they seem to
think refers to a railway engine, and an important part in their argument
is played by a railway line that was built in the 1870s. Finally they
suggest that Saunière and his two fellow priests were murdered, for
reasons they fail to make clear.

Another theory cited by Picknett and Prince holds that the tomb of
Jesus is situated under the public toilet in Rennes-le-Chateau.

Henry Lincoln's most powerful argument concerns the actual mea-
surements of the earth. He mentions a remarkable book called *Historical
Metrology* (1953) by a master engineer named A.E. Berriman, an
incredibly erudite volume covering ancient Egypt, Babylon, Sumer,
China, India, Persia and many other cultures, which begins with the
question: "Was the earth measured in remote antiquity"?, and sets out
to demonstrate that indeed it was. It argues that ancient weights and
measures were derived from measuring the earth – which, of course,
means that ancient people had already measured the earth.

The book must have struck Berriman's contemporaries as hopelessly
eccentric. He says that one measure was a fraction of the earth's
circumference, that a measure of land area (the acre) was based on a
decimal fraction of the square of the earth's radius, and that certain
weights were based on the density of water and of gold. It sounds almost
as if Berriman is positing the existence of some ancient civilization
which vanished without a trace, except for these ancient measures.

In the last analysis, one of the most interesting things Lincoln has done, with his thirty-year investigation of Rennes-le-Chateau, is to demonstrate the existence of some ancient science of earth measurement. Since medieval times, this science seems to have been in the custody of the Church, and we must naturally suspect the involvement of the Templars. But Lincoln is inclined to believe that it may be far older even than that – dating back to the age of the megaliths.

Berriman seems to be making the same point in *Historical Metrology*. His argument, as noted above, is that prehistoric measurement was geodetic in origin – that is, was derived from the size of the earth.

One of his most powerful arguments occurs at the beginning of his first chapter.

He points out that although the Greeks did not know the size of the earth, the earth's polar circumference happens to be precisely 216,000 Greek stade, or stadia. The Greek stade is 600 Greek feet, and the Greek foot is .15 longer than the British foot.

If we want to find out how many Greek stade there are to one degree of the earth's circumference, we divide 216,000 by the 360 degrees in a circle. And the answer, significantly turns out to be 600 – the same as the number of feet in the stade.

If we then divide by 60 – to get the number of stade in one minute of the circumference – we get 10 stade.

And if we go further, and divide again by 60, to find the number of Greek feet in one second of the earth's circumference, we see that it is precisely 100.

This simply cannot be chance. Distances do not normally work out in neat round figures. It is obvious (a) that the Greeks took their stade from someone else, and (b) that someone else knew the exact size of the earth.

Berriman is full of these puzzling facts – for example, that the area of the great bath of Mohenjo Daro, in the Indus Valley, is a hundred square yards.

As to this "English connection", Lincoln has an amusing but fascinating speculation. Early in his investigation into Rennes-le-Chateau, he went to the Bibliotheque Nationale with Gerard de Sede, and de Sede suggested he should request a book called *Le Vraie Langue Celtique* (*The True Celtic Tongue*) by the Abbe Henri Boudet, who was, as we have noted, priest of nearby Rennes-les-Bains, and a close friend of Saunière.

Lincoln was able to obtain Boudet's book, and found it baffling as well as funny. Boudet seemed to think that the original language of mankind before the Tower of Babel was English, or rather Celtic. This part of the book Lincoln describes as "linguistic tomfoolery". And since Boudet was known to be an intelligent man, Lincoln suspects he had his tongue in his cheek. But the volume then turns into something far more interesting. Boudet goes on to discuss the complex megalithic structures of the area. The subtitle of the book is "The Cromlech of Rennes-les-Bains" – a cromlech is a megalith made up of large flat stones resting on two upright stones, rather like a huge dining table.

It looks as if Boudet's job was simply to hint at the mystery of the whole area, and imply that it dates back to megalithic times. But Lincoln is also inclined to suspect that his intention is to tell his reader that one major key to the secret of the area lies in English – perhaps in English measures, such as the English mile. And is Boudet also hinting that the original measures of mankind are English – such as the mile?

Let me try to summarize the conclusions of this postscript.

The Rennes-le-Chateau area appears to be an enormous sacred site centred on a natural pentacle. Lincoln believes it has been sacred for at least a thousand years, for the "temple" – consisting of churches, castles and villages – must have been designed at least a thousand years ago.

But the pentacular structure of the mountains of the area can only be seen from the air or from a good map. And we know that there were no good maps a thousand years ago, except portolans, the maps sailors used to navigate from port to port. And we will see in the section on the "Maps of the Ancient Sea Kings" that Professor Charles Hapgood believed that some of the portolans may date back to the age when there was no ice covering Antarctica – at least 5.000 BC, and perhaps earlier.

A.E. Berriman's conclusions about the Greek stade point in the same direction. If the ancient Greeks – before Eratosthenes, about 200 BC – did not know the size of the earth, then how is it possible that the Greek stade should be a very precise measure of the earth's polar circumference? *Someone* knew the size of the earth. That "someone" may have been the ancient Egyptians, or perhaps even the Sumerians, whose civilization dates from around 4,000 BC. But then, neither the Egyptians nor the Sumerians had any means of measuring the size of the earth so precisely. Was the earth, in fact, measured by some much earlier civilization, dating back long before the Egyptians or the Sumerians? In our book *The Atlantis Blueprint*, Rand Flem-Ath and I have argued that Antartica was Atlantis and that a great civilization existed in Atlantis – as Plato suggests – as long ago as 10,500 BC.

But even if a "worldwide maritime civilization" existed at that time, as Hapgood suggests, it would still have been virtually impossible to measure the earth's polar circumference except by the rather inaccurate geometrical means used by Eratosthenes. (See Chapter on the Ancient Sea Kings.)

Erik van Daniken would undoubtedly argue that the earth was measured from spacecraft in ancient times. Rand Flem-Ath and I (CW) are both inclined to suspect that the real answer lies in the notion that civilization may be tens of thousands of years older than anyone suspects.

If that is so, then the mystery of Rennes-le-Chateau may stretch back much further than the Templars or the Merovingians and have its origin in some remote period of prehistory.

45

Did Robin Hood Really Exist?

Next to King Arthur, Robin Hood is the most famous of British heroes, and he shares with King Arthur the indignity of having his existence doubted by modern scholarship. The folklorist Lord Raglan concluded that he was really a Celtic god, while in *The God of the Witches* Margaret Murray argues that his name means *Robin of the Hood*, and that he was probably the devil (or horned god) in ancient witchcraft festivals. Yet there is also convincing evidence that Robin was a real person, and that – as the ballads declare – he plundered the king's deer in Sherwood Forest and had a long-standing feud with the Sheriff of Nottingham.

The first literary reference to Robin Hood occurs in William Langland's *Piers Plowman*, dating from around 1377. Langland makes a priest remark that he could not say his paternoster without making mistakes, but "I know rhymes of Robyn Hood and Randolf Earl of Chester". So there were already ballads of Robin Hood by that date. In 1510 Wynkyn de Worde, one of the earliest printers, brought out *A Lytell Geste of Robyn Hood*, which did for Robin Hood what Malory had done for King Arthur in the middle of the previous century. And by the time he appears in Sir Walter Scott's *Ivanhoe* (1847) Robin had become the boon-companion and ally of Richard the Lion Heart, the heroic outlaw of the woods. All that was needed then was for some folklorist to notice how often Robin Hood's name is associated with folk festivals, like the Hobby Horse ceremony which takes place on May Day in Padstow, Cornwall,* to suggest that Robin Hood was really Robin Wood, and that his name is derived from the Norse god Woden . . . In fact he appears as Robin Wood in T.H.White's *Sword in the Stone*, in which he becomes a contemporary of King Arthur, who (if he ever existed) was said to have died about AD 540.

---

* Actually 8 May, but the date has become displaced over the centuries.

Those who assume there is no smoke without fire are inclined to believe that Robin Hood was a real outlaw who at some time lived in Sherwood Forest, and who became so popular during his own lifetime that, like Billy the Kid, he soon became the subject of tales and ballads. Yet it seems unlikely that he was around as early as Richard the Lion Heart (1157–99), or he would surely have been mentioned in manuscripts before *Piers Plowman* two centuries later. In his *Chronicle of Scotland*, written about 1420, Andrew Wyntoun refers to Robin Hood and Little John for the year 1283, which sounds altogether more likely – about a century before *Piers Plowman*.

And where precisely did he operate? One important clue is that there is a small fishing town called Robin Hood's Bay in Yorkshire, not far from Whitby, and that up on the nearby moors there are two tumuli (or barrows) called Robin Hood's Butts. Another is that in medieval England the forest of Barnsdale in Yorkshire joined Sherwood Forest in Nottinghamshire. A sixteenth-century life of Robin Hood among the Sloane Manuscripts says he was born in Locksley, in Yorkshire, about 1160. *The Chronicle of Scotland* associates Robin with "Barnysale" presumably Barnsdale. So the evidence suggests that he was a Yorkshireman.

Later legends declare that he was "Sir Robin of Locksley", or even the Earl of Huntingdon. But it is clear from the earlier ballads that he was a yeoman – a farmer who owns his own land – and that this is partly why he became such a hero: not because he was a nobleman, but because he was a representative of the people. (A small tenant farmer would be only one stage above a landless peasant.)

One of the most important clues to Robin's identity emerged in the mid-nineteenth century, when the Historic Documents Commission was cataloguing thousands of documents which represented eight centuries of British history. It was in 1852 that the antiquary Joseph Hunter claimed that he had stumbled upon a man who sounded as if he might be the original Robin Hood. His name in fact was Robert, and he was the son of Adam Hood, a forester in the service of the Earl de Warenne. (Robin was simply a diminutive of Robert – not, in those days, a name in its own right.) He was born about 1280, and on 25 January 1316 Robert Hood and his wife Matilda paid two shillings for permission to take a piece of the earl's waste ground in "Bickhill" (or Bitch-hill) in Wakefield. It was merely the size of a kitchen garden – thirty feet long by sixteen feet wide. The rent for this was sixpence a year. The Manor Court Roll for 1357 shows a house "formerly the property of Robert Hode" on the site – so by that time Robert Hood was presumably dead.

Now, 1316 was midway through the reign of Edward the Second, the foppish, homosexual king who was finally murdered – by having a red-hot spit inserted into his entrails – in September 1327. After his coronation (in 1307) he dismissed his father's ministers and judges and made his lover, Piers Gaveston, Earl of Cornwall – to the fury of his barons. It was the most powerful of these, Thomas, Earl of Lancaster, who forced Edward to accept the rule of twenty-eight barons (called Ordainers), and who finally executed Piers Gaveston in 1312. Edward's lack of attention to affairs of state allowed the Scots – against whom his father Edward I had fought so successfully – to throw off their English masters. Edward II was defeated at Bannockburn in 1314, two years before Robin Hood hired the piece of waste ground and set up home with his wife Matilda. So it is understandable that when the Earl of Warenne was ordered by the king to raise a troop to fight the Scots Robert Hood failed to oblige, and the records show that he was accordingly fined. But when a second muster was raised in 1317 Hood's name was not listed among those fined – which led J.W.Walker, a modern historian, to conclude that this time Robin Hood joined the army. Five years later it was the Earl of Lancaster who raised the army, to fight against the king. Again, Hood's name is not among those fined, so it again seems that he answered the summons. Lancaster's army was defeated at Boroughbridge, and Lancaster was captured and beheaded. The quarrel had been about Edward's new favourites, the Despensers, father and son, whom he had been forced to banish; now he was able to recall them.

Many of Lancaster's supporters were declared outlaws, and Walker discovered a document that stated that a "building of five rooms" on Bichhill, Wakefield, was among the property confiscated. Walker believes that this was Robert Hood's home, and that the outlaw now took refuge in the nearby forest of Barnsdale, where he soon became a highly successful robber.

Now, it must be understood that if Robert Hood *was* the legendary Robin, and he took refuge in the forest, living off the deer population, he was risking horrible penalties. When William the Conqueror brought the Normans to England he declared that the forests – which covered a third of the land – were his own property; any peasant who killed deer risked being literally flayed alive. Under William the Saxons suffered as much as countries occupied by the Nazis in the Second World War. Two and a half centuries later the Normans regarded themselves as Englishmen, and the French language had ceased to be used in England, but the laws were still harsh. The "forest laws" had been mitigated, so a man could no longer have his hands or his lips sliced off for poaching a deer; but the penalty was still a heavy fine, a year's imprisonment, and sureties for his future good behaviour. If he could not find guarantors he had to "abjure the realm" – quit the kingdom for ever.

The battle of Boroughbridge was fought on 16 March 1322, near the Ure river in Yorkshire; dismounted men-at-arms and archers drove back the cavalry, then another royalist army moved up behind the rebels and forced them to surrender. Lancaster was captured and tried; evidence revealed that he had been contemplating an alliance with the king's old enemy Robert the Bruce. Lancaster – the king's cousin – was beheaded. And Robin Hood, deprived of his home, became an outlaw in the king's forest.

But if Walker is correct in identifying Robert Hood of Wakefield as Robin Hood, he was not an outlaw for long. In the spring of the following year the king made a progress through the north of England, reaching York on 1 May. From 16 May to 21 May he stayed at Rothwell, between Wakefield and Leeds, and spent three days hunting at Plumpton Park in Knaresborough Forest. And the *Lytell Geste* makes this visit a part of the story of Robin Hood, describing how the king "came to Plumpton Park/And failed [missed] many of his deer". Where the king was accustomed to seeing herds of deer, now he could find only one deer "that bore any good horn". Which made the king swear by the Trinity "I wish I could lay my hands on Robin Hood":

> I wolde I had Robyn Hode
> With eyen I myght hym se.

So, according to this ballad, one of the foresters suggested that the king should disguise himself as an abbot, riding through the greenwood with a band of monks. The ruse was successful; Robin and his men stopped the "abbot", but recognized him as the king. And the king thereupon found Robin so likable that he invited him to join the royal household as a *vadlet*, a gentleman of the royal bedchamber. The king continued on his travels until February 1324, when he returned to Westminster. The royal household accounts for April record payment of the past month's wages to Robyn Hod and twenty-eight others. The first record of a payment to Robyn Hod is in the previous June. The ballad tells us that after being a servant of the king for somewhat over a year Robin asked the king's permission to return to Barnsdale. And the household accounts for November 1324 record that Robyn Hod, formerly one of the "porteurs" (gentlemen of the bedchamber) had been given five shillings "because he is no longer able to work". The ballad says that Robin asked the king's leave to return to Barnsdale, and was given permission to stay for seven days. But he never returned; instead he regrouped his merry men, and lived on in the greenwood for another twenty-two years. If this is based on fact, then he died about 1346, in his mid-sixties.

The king's fortunes took a downward turn after Robin's departure. He had recalled the banished Despensers, and the younger of the two had become his "favourite" – to the disgust of his queen, who had already had to contend with Piers Gaveston. She was a Frenchwoman, daughter of Philip the Fair. Now she began to take a romantic interest in an unpleasant and ambitious young baron called Roger de Mortimer, who had been thrown into the Tower for his opposition to the Despensers. Queen Isabella became his mistress, and it was probably she who plotted Mortimer's escape. He fled to Paris, and was joined there by Isabella, who was on a mission for the king. They landed at Orwell, in Suffolk, with an army of almost three thousand. When the king heard the news he fled, and was captured, and imprisoned in Berkeley Castle. He was forced to abdicate, and his son (aged fifteen) was crowned Edward III. On the night of 21 September 1327 horrible screams rang through the castle. The next morning it was announced that the king had died "of natural causes". There were no marks on the body, but it is said that his features were still contorted with agony. A chronicle of some thirty years later states that three assassins entered his cell when he was asleep, and held down the upper half of his body with a table. Then a horn was inserted into the anal orifice, and a red-hot iron bar was used to burn out the king's insides.

Mortimer and Isabella ruled England as regents for four years; then the young king asserted himself, had Mortimer seized in Nottingham Castle, and had him executed as a traitor at Tyburn. The loss of her lover almost drove the queen mad. But she was restored to favour, and lived on for another twenty-eight years.

It is of course conceivable that the Robin Hood who lived in Edward's reign had no connection with the legendary outlaw of Sherwood Forest; one reference book (*Who's Who In History*) says that he was alive in 1230, in the reign of Henry III, on the grounds that records show that the Sheriff of Yorkshire sold his possessions in that year (for 32s 6d) when he became an outlaw; but the same reference book admits that the Robyn Hode of Wakefield is also a good contender. There is something to be said for this earlier dating, for it would give more time for the legend of Robin Hood to spread throughout England. But there is also a great deal to be said for Robin Hood of Wakefield. If he became an outlaw in 1322, as a result of the Lancaster rebellion, then he spent only one year in Sherwood Forest before the king pardoned him. The story of his pardon by the homosexual king certainly rings true – as does his appointment as a gentleman of the bedchamber. It is natural to speculate that he may have found that his duties in the bedchamber involved more than he had bargained for, although at this time the king's favourite was the younger Hugh le Despenser (executed by Mortimer and Isabella in 1326). So he returned to the greenwood, and became a hero of legend. We do not know whether he became the arch-enemy of the Sheriff of Nottingham, but the sheriff – who would be the equivalent of a modern Chief Constable – would have been responsible for law and order in Nottinghamshire and south Yorkshire, and would certainly have resented a band of outlaws who lived off the king's deer. One chronicle states that Robin also had a retreat in what became known as Robin Hood's Bay, and ships in which he could escape to sea. (He is also said to have operated as far afield as Cumberland.) If a concerted attempt had been made to flush him out, it would probably have succeeded. But most of the peasants and tenant farmers would have been on Robin's side. There had been a time when the forests of England were common land, and half-starved peasantry must have felt it was highly unreasonable that thousands of square miles of forest should be reserved for the king's hunting, when the king could not make use of a fraction of that area.

But there could be another reason that Robin was allowed to operate without too much opposition. When he was at court he must surely have met the fourteen-year-old boy who would become Edward III, and Edward would be of exactly the right age to look with admiration on a famous outlaw. This is only speculation, but it could undoubtedly explain why Robin was allowed to become the legendary bane of authority in the last decades of his life.

Authority has its own ways of striking back. According to the Sloane Manuscript, Robin fell ill, and went to his cousin, the Prioress of Kirklees, to be bled – the standard procedure for treating any illness in those days. She decided to avenge the many churchmen he had robbed, and allowed him to bleed to death. Another account says that she betrayed him at the request of her lover, Sir Roger de Doncaster. Still another source states that the man responsible for Robin's death was a monk who was called in to attend him, and who decided that the outlaw would be better dead. He was buried in the grounds of the nunnery, within a bowshot of its walls. Grafton's Chronicle (1562) says he was buried under an inscribed stone, and a century later another chronicle reported that his tomb, with a plain cross on a flat stone, could be seen in the cemetery; in 1665 Dr Nathaniel Johnstone made a drawing of it; Gough's *Sepulchral Monuments* also has an engraving of the tombstone. In the early nineteenth century navvies building a railway broke up the stone – it is said they believed its chips to be a cure for toothache. So the last trace of the real existence of Robin Hood disappeared. But by that time the grave of the prioress had been discovered among the ruins of the nunnery, and it bore some resemblance to the tomb of Robin Hood. It also mentioned her name – Elizabeth Stainton.

The real significance of Robin Hood is that he lived in a century when the peasants were beginning to feel an increasing resentment about their condition – a resentment that expressed itself in the revolutionary doctrines of John Ball, and which exploded in the Peasants' Revolt of 1381, only a short time after Robin is first mentioned in print by Langland. The Peasants' Revolt is generally considered to mark the end of the Middle Ages; but it is in the ballads of Robin Hood that we can see that the state of mind known as the Middle Ages is coming to an end.

46

The Mystery Death
of Mary Rogers

The mysterious death of the "cigar girl" Mary Rogers, which caused a sensation in New York in the summer of 1841, would hardly cause a raised eyebrow in the same city today. That the mystery has never been forgotten is largely the work of Edgar Allan Poe, who transformed it into a classic detective story. Half a century after the death of the cigar girl, information came to light that suggested that Poe's "guess" had been at least partly correct – and that led one writer to suggest that Poe himself may have committed the murder.

Mary Cecilia Rogers was born in New York in 1820; her mother, who became a widow when the child was five, supported herself by running a boarding-house in Nassau Street. Mary grew up into a tall, very beautiful young woman with jet-black hair. This led a cigar-store owner named John Anderson, whose shop was on Broadway, to offer her a job as a salesgirl. In 1840 this was regarded as an imaginative piece of business enterprise, for New York was even more "Victorian" than London, and young unmarried girls did not exhibit themselves behind shop counters, particularly in shops frequented exclusively by young men. Mary's mother objected to the idea, but her daughter's enthusiasm finally won her over. She drew many new customers to the shop, although – as Thomas Duke is careful to note in his *Celebrated Criminal Cases of America* (1910) – "the girl's conduct was apparently a model of modest decorum, and while she was lavish in her smiles, she did not hesitate to repel all undue advances".

She had been working in the store about ten months when one day in January 1841 she failed to appear. Her mother had no idea where she was, and according to Duke, "Mr Anderson was unable to account for her absence". The police searched for her and the newspapers reported her disappearance. Six days later she reappeared, looking tired and rather ill, and explained that she had been visiting relatives in the country. Her mother and her employer apparently corroborated the story. But when a rumour began to circulate that she had been seen during her absence with a tall, handsome naval officer Mary abruptly gave up her job – only a few days after returning – and was no longer seen on Broadway. A month later she announced her engagement to one of her mother's boarders, a clerk called Daniel Payne.

Five months later, on Sunday 25 July 1841, Mary knocked on her fiancé's door at 10 a.m. and announced that she was going to see her aunt in Bleecker Street; Payne said that he would call for her that evening. Payne also spent the day away from home, but when a violent thunderstorm came on towards evening he decided not to call for Mary, but to let her stay the night with her aunt. Mrs Rogers apparently approved. But when Mary failed to return home the following day she began to worry. When Payne returned from work and learned that Mary was still away, he rushed to see the aunt in Bleecker Street – a Mrs Downing – and was even more alarmed when she told him that she had not seen Mary in the past forty-eight hours.

It was two days later on Wednesday morning that three men in a sailing-boat saw a body in the water off Castle Point, Hoboken. It was Mary, and according to the *New York Tribune* "it was obvious that she had been horribly outraged and murdered". She was fully clothed, although her clothes were torn, and the petticoat was missing. A piece of lace from the bottom of the dress was embedded so deeply in the throat that it had almost disappeared. An autopsy performed almost immediately led to the conclusion that she had been "brutally violated". Oddly enough, Daniel Payne did not go to view the corpse, although he had earlier searched for her all over New York, including Hoboken. But after being interrogated by the police, Payne was released.

A week passed without any fresh clues, and a large reward was offered. Then the coroner received a letter from some anonymous man – who said he had not come forward before from "motives of perhaps criminal prudence" – and who claimed to have seen Mary Rogers on the Sunday afternoon of her disappearance. She had, the writer said, stepped out of a boat with six rough-looking characters, and gone with them into the woods, laughing merrily and apparently under no kind of constraint. Soon afterwards a boat with three well-dressed men had come ashore, and one of these accosted two men walking on the beach and asked if they had seen a young woman and six men recently. They said that they had, and that she had appeared to go with them willingly. At this the trio turned their boat and headed back for New York.

In fact, the two men came forward and corroborated this story. But although they both knew Mary Rogers by sight, neither of them could swear that the girl they had seen was definitely Mary.

The next important piece of information came from a stagecoach-driver named Adams, who said he had seen Mary arrive on the Hoboken ferry with a well-dressed man of dark complexion, and that they had gone to a roadhouse called "Nick Mullen's". This tavern was kept by a Mrs Loss, who told the police that the couple had "taken refreshment" there, then gone off into the woods. Some time later she had heard a scream from the woods; but since the place "was a resort of questionable characters" she had thought no more of it.

Two months after the murder, on 25 September, children playing in the woods found the missing petticoat in a thicket; they also found a white silk scarf, a parasol and a handkerchief marked "M.R." Daniel Payne was to commit suicide in this spot soon after.

A gambler named Joseph Morse, who lived in Nassau Street, was arrested and apparently charged with the murder; there was evidence that he had been seen with Mary Rogers on the evening she disappeared. The following day, he had fled from New York. But Morse was released when he was able to prove that he had been at Staten Island with another young lady on the Sunday afternoon. One odd story in the *Tribune* declared that Morse believed that the young lady *was* Mary Rogers, and that when he heard of the disappearance he assumed she had committed suicide because of the way he had treated her – he had tried to seduce her in his room. He was relieved to learn that the girl with whom he had spent the afternoon was still alive.

In the following year, 1842, Poe's "Mystery of Marie Roget" was published in three parts in *Snowden's Ladies' Companion*. But for anyone looking for a solution of the Mary Rogers mystery, it should be treated with extreme caution. Poe argues that Mary Rogers was not murdered by a gang but by a single individual. His original view seems to have been that the motive was rape; later he heard the rumour that Mary had died as a result of an abortion, and made a few hasty alterations in his story to accommodate this notion. He argues that the signs of a struggle in the woods, and the battered state of her face, indicate that she was killed by an individual – a gang would have been able to overpower her easily. He also speaks of a strip from the girl's skirt that had been wound around the waist to afford a kind of handle for carrying the body; but the evidence of two witnesses who dragged the body out of the water makes no mention of this "handle". In spite of this, there can be no doubt that Poe's objections to the gang theory carry a great deal of weight.

In an issue of a magazine called *The Unexplained* (No. 152) Grahame Fuller and Ian Knight suggest that Poe himself may have been the killer of Mary Rogers. A witness thought he had seen her with a tall, well-dressed man of swarthy complexion on the afternoon she died; the authors point out that Poe had an olive complexion and was always well dressed. But Poe was only five feet eight inches tall – hardly a "tall man". They also argue that Poe may have killed Mary Rogers in a fit of "alcoholic insanity". In 1841 Poe's wife Virginia was dying of tuberculosis and he was under considerable stress; he wrote later: "I became insane, with long intervals of horrible sanity. During these fits of unconsciousness I drank, God only knows how often or how much". Yet none of Poe's biographers have ever suggested that he was a violent person – on the contrary, most emphasize his gentleness and courtesy. There have been plenty of alcoholic men of genius, a few of whom – like Ben Jonson or Caravaggio – have killed men in duels or quarrels; but there is not a single example of one who has ever committed a murder. Besides, no witness suggested that the man who was seen with Mary Rogers was blind drunk. On the whole, the notion of Poe as a demonic killer, writing "The Mystery of Marie Roget" to boast about his crime, must be relegated to the realm of fantasy.

What was not known to Poe in 1842 is that Mary's employer, John Anderson, had been questioned by the police as a suspect; like all the others, he was released. But fifty years later – in December 1891 – new evidence was to emerge. By that time Anderson had been dead ten years; he became a millionaire, and died in Paris. Apparently he had told friends that he had experienced "many unhappy days and nights in regard to her" (Mary Rogers), and had been in touch with her spirit. His heirs contested his estate, and in 1891 his daughter tried to break her father's will on the grounds that when he signed it he was mentally incompetent. The case was settled out of court, and the records destroyed. But a lawyer named Samuel Copp Worthen, who had been closely associated with Anderson's daughter Laura Appleton, knew that his firm had kept a copy of the testimony in the Supreme Court of New York in 1891, and he made it his business to read it. He finally described what he had learned in the periodical *American Literature* in 1948. It revealed that Anderson had been questioned by the police about the death of Mary Rogers, and that this had preyed on his mind, so that he later declined to stand as a candidate for mayor of New York, in case someone revealed his secret.

The most significant part of the testimony was the assertion that Anderson had admitted to paying for an abortion for Mary Rogers and had got "in some trouble over it". But he had insisted that he had not "had anything, directly, himself, to do with her problems".

This would obviously explain Mary's week-long disappearance from the cigar store, and the fact that she looked tired and ill when she returned. It probably also explains why she decided to leave the store a week later – not because of gossip about the naval officer, but because she needed more time to convalesce.

Worthen's theory is that in the six months after leaving the cigar store Mary again got herself pregnant, and once more appealed to Anderson for help. When she left home that Sunday morning she intended to go to Hoboken for an abortion. (In fact, there was a story that Mrs Loss, the tavern-owner, had admitted on her deathbed that Mary Rogers had died during an abortion; there is no hard evidence for this confession, but it is known that the District Attorney was inclined to the abortion theory of Mary's death.) She died during the abortion, and her body was dumped in the river to protect the abortionist – the dark-skinned man with whom she was seen on the ferry – and Mrs Loss's family.

How does this theory fit the known facts? The answer is: very well indeed, particularly if we make the natural assumption that the father of the second unborn child was Daniel Payne – for it seems unlikely that Mary agreed to marry him, then continued her affair with her former lover. (Nothing is known about this former lover, but Anderson is obviously a suspect.) We must assume, then, that Payne knew perfectly well that Mary was on her way to Hoboken to have an illegal operation. We may also probably assume that the pregnancy was still in its early stages, and that Mary anticipated very little trouble – after all, she had recovered from the earlier abortion in a week, though it still left her feeling ill. Mary's mother was probably also in the secret. Duke comments: "It was generally believed at the time that the murdered girl's mother knew more about her daughter's mysterious admirer than she chose to tell".

What of the evidence about the gang? It is possible, of course, that a young girl was actually seen entering the woods with a gang of men, and that this was nothing to do with Mary Rogers. But it far more probable that the anonymous letter claiming that Mary had entered the woods with six ruffians was sent by Mrs Loss or one of her friends – it came from Hoboken. Then all she had to do was to persuade two of her relatives or friends to claim that they were the men on the beach, and that they had seen Mary enter the woods and seen the boat with three men that landed shortly afterwards . . . The result would be a perfect red herring, directing the attention of the police away from her own abortion parlour.

What of the petticoat found later in the woods? This, significantly enough, was found by Mrs Loss's children. We may assume that the petticoat, the umbrella and the handkerchief were left behind in Mrs Loss's roadhouse when Mary's body was dragged to the water in the middle of the night, and were later planted in the woods, in a place where the bushes were broken, to suggest evidence of a struggle.

And what of the evidence that Mary had been raped? This, apparently, was the coroner's report; we do not know whether she was examined by a doctor or if so what the doctor concluded. What we *do* know is that Mary's body was already decomposing, and that because of the hot July weather it was buried within a few hours of being taken out of the water; so any inquest would have been performed in haste. In 1841 the science of legal medicine was in its infancy, and it is doubtful whether anyone took a vaginal swab and examined it under a microscope for spermatozoa. What was probably taken for evidence of rape was actually evidence of an abortion that had gone wrong.

Duke reports that Daniel Payne committed suicide "at the same spot in the woods where his sweetheart was probably slain". Other writers on the case have questioned this (notably Charles E. Pearce in *Unsolved Murder Mysteries*, 1924). But Payne's suicide would certainly be consistent with the theory that he was the father of the unborn child.

It is a disappointing – if obvious – solution to one of the great "murder mysteries", that Mary Rogers died in the course of an abortion. Why is it not more generally known? Partly because Poe himself obscured the truth. In the 1850 edition of Poe's works published in the year after his death "Marie Roget" appeared with a footnote that stated:

> It may not be improper to record . . . that the confessions of *two* persons (one of them the Madame Dulac of the narrative [Mrs Loss]) made at different periods long subsequent to the publication confessed, in full, not only the general conclusion but absolutely *all* the chief hypothetical details by which the conclusion was attained.

But this is obviously impossible. Mrs Loss only seems to have confessed that Mary had died in the course of an abortion in her tavern. Poe's theory was that she was murdered by a man "in a passion" who then dragged her body to the seashore. The likely truth seems to be that she died of an air embolism, and that the abortionist, with the aid of Mrs Loss, made the death look like murder by tying a strip of cloth round her throat; the two of them then probably carried it to the water. Poe's "Marie Roget", far from being an amazingly accurate reconstruction of the murder, is simply a bad guess. Poe may not have been a murderer, but he was undoubtedly a liar.

47

"Saint-Germain the Deathless"

He is still regarded by many "occultists" as one of the most exciting and mysterious figures in the history of magic; some even believe that he is still alive. But everyone who has written about him has ended by wondering whether the secrets of "Saint-Germain the deathless" are a matter of mystery or merely of mystification. Since the enormous dossier on him collected at the orders of Napoleon III was destroyed by fire during the Commune, the question must remain unanswered. "Thus", says one historian, "once again an 'accident' upheld the ancient law which decrees that the life of an adept must always be surrounded by mystery".

When the Comte de Saint-Germain (he admitted the name was false) first appeared in France about 1756 he looked about fifty years old. He was a brilliant conversationalist, spoke many languages, possessed a knowledge of medicine, and was a first-rate experimental chemist. He was a small man, who dressed in black velvet with a white satin cravat (a sign of self-restraint in those days of magnificent male wardrobes), and whose manners were meticulously correct. He was obviously wealthy – he wore many diamonds and he had numerous servants. These seem to have been extremely well trained. When a sceptic said to one of them: "Your master is a liar" the man replied: "I know that better than you. He tells everyone that he is four thousand years old. But I have been in his service only a hundred years, and when I came the count told me that he was three thousand years old. Whether he has added nine hundred years by error, or whether he is lying, I do not know". Another servant – his valet – was asked about some point of ancient history and replied: "Perhaps the count forgets that I have been in his service only five hundred years".

It sounds as if he was an accomplished leg-puller, or perhaps merely a charlatan; but if so, it is not clear what he hoped to gain. He seems to have been wealthy; he was an accomplished violinist, a skilful painter, and had a wide knowledge of music and painting – apparently he could identify most paintings at a glance. In *Historical Mysteries*, Andrew Lang suggests that he was the son of the ex-queen of Spain, Marie de Neuberg, who lived in Bayonne after the death of her husband Charles II. Marie's lover was the finance minister, Count Andanero, and Lang thinks it possible that Saint-Germain was his son.

Before going to France, Saint-Germain had been in Vienna. He had met the Marshal de Belle-Isle, who had contracted some illness while campaigning in Germany; Saint-Germain cured him, and the marshal brought him back with him to Paris. Soon after, he cured a lady of the court of mushroom poisoning, and became a friend of Madame de Pompadour, mistress of Louis XV. The ladies of the court found him intriguing. Countess von Gergy, whose husband had been ambassador to Venice around 1710, thought she recollected his name, and asked him if his father had been there; Saint-Germain replied – typically – that he himself had been there at the time. "Impossible" said the countess; the man she had known had been at least forty-five at the time. Saint-Germain smiled mysteriously. "I am very old". He then added various details about Venice, which convinced the countess that he knew what he was talking about. "You must be a devil"! exclaimed the countess, at which Saint-Germain began to tremble as if he had cramp and hurriedly left the room.

A decade earlier, Saint-Germain had been in London, and in 1745 was arrested as a spy of the Young Pretender, who was just marching on Derby. Horace Walpole noted in a letter:

> . . . the other day they seized an odd man who goes by the name of Count Saint-Germain. He has been here these two years and will not tell who he is, or whence . . . He sings, plays on the violin wonderfully, composes, is mad, and not very sensible. He is called an Italian, a Spaniard, a Pole; a somebody that married a great fortune in Mexico, and ran away with her jewels to Constantinople; a priest, a fiddler, a vast nobleman. The Prince of Wales has had unsatisfied curiosity about him, but in vain . . .

No one knows where he was between 1745 and 1755. But by the late 1750s he was the talk of Paris. Madame du Hausset, a *femme de chambre* of Madame de Pompadour, wrote:

> A man who was as amazing as a witch came often . . . This was the Count de Saint-Germain, who wished to make people believe that

he lived for several centuries. One day Madame said to him, while at her toilet, "What sort of man was Francis I . . ."? "A good sort of fellow", said Saint-Germain, "too fiery – I could have given him a useful piece of advice but he would not have listened". He then described, in very general terms, the beauty of Mary Stuart and La Reine Margot. "You seem to have seen them all . . ." "Sometimes", said Saint-Germain, "I amuse myself, not by making people believe, but by letting them believe that I have lived from time immemorial". Then Madame de Pompadour asked him about Madame de Gergy, who thought she had known Saint-Germain in Venice fifty years ago. "It may be so", said Saint-Germain, "But I admit that even more possibly the respected lady is in her dotage".

It seems clear from this that Saint-Germain treated the tales of his great age as a joke, and made no real attempt to impose them on Madame de Pompadour. The king's foreign minister, the Duc de Choiseul, further confused the issue by hiring an impostor to impersonate Saint-Germain in the salons of Paris, and to discredit him by making absurd claims – such as claiming to have been a close friend of Saint Anne, mother of the Virgin Mary, and making remarks like "I always knew Christ would come to a bad end".

So what do we actually know of the life of Saint-Germain? An autograph letter of 1735 proves that he was in The Hague in November of that year, but does not tell us why. Saint-Germain would then be about twenty-five years old. We know he was in England from 1743 to about 1745, and was arrested as a spy. The story given in Mrs Cooper-Oakley's book on him is that someone who was jealous of him (because of a rivalry about a lady) planted a treasonable letter in his pocket, then had him arrested; he was able to prove his innocence.

By 1755 he was wealthy and was living in Vienna, where he was taken up by the Marshal de Belle-Isle and brought to Paris, where – as already noted – his conversation and his wide culture soon made him a favourite of the salons. He claimed to live off some food or elixir which he made himself, and would sit through dinners without eating. In fact his greatest interest seems to have been chemistry, and he had apparently discovered some process for dyeing silk and leather. He told the king that he could remove flaws from diamonds, and went off with a stone worth six thousand francs. A month later he returned the stone flawless, and a jeweller valued it at ten thousand francs. In all probability Saint-Germain simply substituted another stone, and gained the king's gratitude at the low price of four thousand francs. The result was that the king set up a labouratory at the Trianon, and installed Saint-Germain in apartments at the castle of Chambord, to work on his dyeing processes – the king hoped these would eventually bring large sums to the royal treasury, which badly needed replenishing. He became so much a familiar of Louis that the Duc de Choiseul wrote indignantly: "It is strange that the King is so often allowed to be almost alone with this man, though when he goes out he is surrounded by guards. . . ." He also referred to Saint-Germain as "the son of a Portuguese Jew".

In 1760 the king apparently sent Saint-Germain on a diplomatic mission to Holland – although this was kept secret from his ministers; Saint-Germain's mission was to investigate overtures of peace with England – the king was hoping to persuade England to abandon her ally Prussia. Saint-Germain found himself staying in the same hotel as that other amusing adventurer Casanova, who was trying to negotiate a loan for France. They already knew one another, and Casanova was convinced that Saint-Germain was a charlatan. He says of him in his Memoirs:

> This extraordinary man, intended by nature to be the king of impostors and quacks, would say in an easy and assured manner that he was three hundred years old, that he knew the secrets of universal medicine, that he possessed a mastery over nature, that he could melt diamonds. . . . Notwithstanding his boastings, his bare-faced lies and his manifold eccentricities, I cannot say I thought him offensive.

Nevertheless, Casanova seized the opportunity to destroy Saint-Germain's credit by producing a bogus "cabalistic" oracle warning against him. Meanwhile the Duc de Choiseul had got wind of the plot – he was against making peace – and sent orders for Saint-Germain to be arrested and conveyed to the Bastille. But the Dutch Ambassador decided to drop a word in Saint-Germain's ear, and he took the next boat to London. Louis was too embarrassed to admit that he and Belle-Isle had been behind Saint-Germain's mission.

Saint-Germain's enemies had succeeded in bringing about his downfall – although there can be no doubt that his own tactlessness and naivety also played their part; he buttonholed the most unsuitable people and told them about his mission. In England he met the German ambassador, and may have hoped to go and join Frederick the Great in

Saxony; the ambassador wrote in haste to the Prussian secretary of state begging him to do his best to hinder Saint-Germain's journey, on the grounds that he was dangerously impetuous, and might fascinate the king and persuade him to undertake "many disastrous measures". He seems to have had no doubt of Saint-Germain's power to fascinate. Saint-Germain was apparently obliged to return secretly to Holland, where he purchased an estate, calling himself Count Surmount – he seems to have been short of cash, for he paid only part of the purchase price. The French ambassador described him as "completely discredited". But he had found himself a new patron – or dupe – in Cobenzl, minister in the Austrian Netherlands, who wanted to exploit Saint-Germain's chemical processes in factories at Tournai. Cobenzl told Kaunitz, the Austrian chancellor, of all kinds of "miracles", such as turning base metals into gold, dyeing silks and other materials all kinds of glorious colours, and tanning skins to produce marvellously soft leather. Cobenzl seemed positively infatuated with Saint-Germain, although he added: "The only thing I can reproach him with is frequent boasting about his talents and origins." And although Cobenzl later came to take a dim view of the "genius's" character, he never doubted the tremendous commercial value of his processes. The factories in Tournai were set up, and Saint-Germain managed to pocket a hundred thousand gulden for secrets he had promised to give gratis. Even so, he vanished without parting with all the promised secrets. But the factories in Tournai apparently did well – from which we may infer that Saint-Germain's "processes" were genuine enough.

Saint-Germain's movements during the next decade are unknown, but he himself claimed to have been twice to India, and to have been involved in the Russo-Turkish war in the Mediterranean (1768–74). He certainly went to St Petersburg and became a friend of Count Alexei Orlov, commander of the Russian expedition to the Archipelago. His favourite beverage, tea made from sennapods (a mild laxative), became known as Russian tea and was supplied in bulk to the Russian navy. For reasons that are not clear, he was raised to the rank of a Russian general. In 1774 he was living at Schwabach, in Anspach, and found himself a new patron, Charles Alexander, margrave of Brandenburg. The margrave was duly impressed when he went with Saint-Germain to meet Orlov and saw the latter embrace him with great warmth. Soon Saint-Germain was the margrave's guest in his castle at Triersdorf, living quietly and continuing his experiments. He was now calling himself Count Tzarogy. But one day his desire to impress and astonish led him to tell his host that he was really Prince Rakoczy of Transylvania. But when the margrave visited Italy in the following year, and began to tell stories about his astonishing guest, he learned that the last three sons of the royal house of Transylvania were dead, and that his guest sounded like the notorious trickster Saint-Germain, who was really the son of a tax-collector of San Germano. Gemmingen, the Anspach minister who was sent to confront Saint-Germain, reported that "Prince Rakoczy" did not deny that he called himself Saint-Germain. He had had occasion to use many aliases to avoid his enemies; but he had never disgraced any of the names he bore. This on the whole was true, and the margrave had to admit that his guest had always behaved quietly and modestly, and never tried to part him from large sums of money. All the same, he was disillusioned, and declined to see Saint-Germain again. So in 1776, in his mid-sixties, Saint-Germain once again took to the road. He visited Leipzig, Dresden, Berlin and Hamburg, then went to Berlin hoping to see Frederick the Great; but the king had no wish to make the acquaintance of a discredited adventurer.

Finally, Saint-Germain found another patron, Prince Charles of Hesse-Cassel, who was cool and uninterested to begin with, but gradually succumbed to Saint-Germain's charm and enthusiasm. Prince Charles was not disposed to doubt any of Saint-Germain's stories, including that he was Prince Rakoczy, that he had been brought up in the household of the last of the Medici, and that he was now eighty-eight years old. He set Saint-Germain up in a factory in Eckenforde, in Schleswig-Holstein, and there the adventurer lived out his last years quietly, suffering periodically from depression and rheumatism, and dying in February 1784, to the grief of Prince Charles, who described him as "one of the greatest sages who ever lived".

No sooner was Saint-Germain dead than rumours that he was still alive began to circulate. A journal published in the following year said he was expected to return soon. Madame de Genlis was convinced she had seen him in Vienna in 1821. In 1836 a volume of *Souvenirs* by the Countess d'Adhémar, who claimed to be familiar with the court at Versailles in the last days of the monarchy, claimed that she had seen Saint-Germain as late as 1793, and that he had warned her about the death of Marie Antoinette. He told her she would see him five times more, "and do not wish for a sixth", and she claims that she saw him five times between then and 1820. But G.B. Volz, who conducted an investigation of the life of Saint-Germain in the 1920s, asserts that the countess never existed and that the *Souvenirs* are a forgery. In 1845 Franz Graffer declares in his *Memoirs* that he had seen Saint-Germain, and that he had announced that he would appear in the Himalayas towards the turn of the century – a claim that in due course led Madame Blavatsky to include him among her "Secret Masters" in Tibet, and to quote him with respect in *The Secret Doctrine*. But again, the *Memoirs* of Franz Graffer are thought to be a forgery. On the other hand, Madame Blavatsky went to the trouble of visiting the then Countess d'Adhémar in 1885, and Mrs Cooper-Oakley, whose book on Saint-Germain appeared in 1912, discovered that there were still documents about him in the possession of the d'Adhémar family. As late as January 1972, a young man called Richard Chanfray appeared on French television claiming to be Saint-Germain, and apparently transformed lead into gold, using only a camping stove.

When all the claims and counter-claims have been taken into account, what can we say of the "man of mystery"? First – regretfully – that he cannot be taken seriously as a mage or a secret Master. Whether the Prussian ambassador in Dresden is correct when he says "inordinate vanity is the mainspring of his mechanism", there can be no doubt that Saint-Germain *was* a vain man who talked too much – too many contemporaries make this comment for it to be untrue. But a man may be vain and talkative, and still possess genius (Bernard Shaw being the example who immediately springs to mind). It is also perfectly clear that Saint-Germain was a genuine enthusiast, with an extraordinary range of talents. He himself never claimed to be a "mage", or a student of occultism. In fact, he insisted that he was a materialist whose chief desire was to benefit humanity. Diderot and D'Alembert would no doubt have found him an ideal contributor to their *Encyclopedia*.

The real mystery about Saint-Germain is that he was a man of genius, and at the same time a charlatan. He had what we would now call a strongly developed sense of publicity, a desire to intrigue and fascinate. And this in itself argues that he was not what he claimed to be. He was undoubtedly *not* the last surviving member of the Transylvanian royal family – precise details are known about its last three surviving members. But this desire to pose as a king in exile suggests that Saint-Germain was born in fairly humble circumstances, and that he spent a great deal of his childhood and youth daydreaming about fame and glory. The annals of charlatanism are full of Walter Mittys and Billy Liars, but it is difficult to recollect a swindler who was really born in a palace or a stately home. We may probably assume, then, that Saint-Germain was not the bastard son of the Queen of Spain. But it seems equally clear that he managed to acquire himself a good education, and that chemistry was the love of his life. In different circumstances he might have become a Lavoisier or Robert Boyle or Michael Faraday.

His natural brilliance made him contemptuous of the intelligence of his fellow-men, and when he claimed to be three hundred years old, or dropped hints about his acquaintance with Francis I, he probably told himself that he was poking fun at human stupidity.

The only real mystery is where he acquired the money to pose as a prince. Since he seems to have been an honest man (if we except the little affair of the Tournai factory), the answer, presumably, is that he was able to turn his chemical researches to commercial use. It is a disappointing conclusion that the Man of Mystery, the Secret Master, was merely a brilliant industrial chemist. But it is the only theory that corresponds to the facts as we know them.

48

The Miracles of Saint-Médard

The strange events that took place in the little Paris churchyard of Saint-Médard between 1727 and 1732 sound so incredible, so preposterous, that the modern reader is tempted to dismiss them as pure invention. This would be a mistake, for an impressive mass of documents, including accounts by doctors, magistrates and other respectable public figures, attests to their genuineness. The miracles undoubtedly took place. But no doctor, philosopher or scientist has even begun to explain them.

They began with the burial of François de Pâris, the Deacon of Paris, in May 1727. François was only thirty-seven years old, yet he was revered as a holy man, with powers of healing. He was a follower of Bishop Cornelius Jansen, who taught that men can be saved only by divine grace, not by their own efforts. The Deacon had no doubt whatever that his own healing powers came from God.

Great crowds followed his coffin, many weeping. It was laid in a tomb behind the high altar of Saint-Médard. Then the congregation filed past, laying their flowers on the corpse. A father supported his son, a cripple, as he leaned over the coffin. Suddenly, the child went into convulsions; he seemed to be having a fit. Several people helped to drag him, writhing, to a quiet corner of the church. Suddenly the convulsions stopped. The boy opened his eyes, looking around in bewilderment, and then slowly stood up. A look of incredulous joy crossed his face; then to the astonishment of the spectators he began to dance up and down, singing and laughing. His father found it impossible to believe, for the boy was using his withered right leg, which had virtually no muscles. Later it was claimed that the leg had become as strong and normal as the other.

The news spread. Within hours cripples, lepers, hunchbacks and blind men were rushing to the church. At first few "respectable" people believed the stories of miraculous cures – the majority of the Deacon's followers were poor people. The rich preferred to leave their spiritual affairs in the hands of the Jesuits, who were more cultivated and worldly. But it soon became clear that ignorance and credulity could not be used as a blanket explanation for all the stories of marvels. Deformed limbs, it was said, were being straightened; hideous growths and cancers were disappearing without trace; horrible sores and wounds were healing instantly.

The Jesuits declared that the miracles were either a fraud or the work of the Devil; the result was that most of the better-off people in Paris flatly refused to believe that anything unusual was taking place in the churchyard of Saint-Médard. But a few men of intellect were drawn by curiosity, and they invariably returned from the churchyard profoundly shaken. Sometimes they recorded their testimony in print: some, such as one Philippe Hecquet, attempted to explain the events by natural causes. Others, such as the Benedictine Bernard Louis de la Taste, attacked the people who performed the miracles on theological grounds, but were unable to expose any deception or error by them, or any error on the part of the witnesses. The accumulation of written testimony was such that David Hume, one of the greatest of philosophers, wrote in *An enquiry concerning human understanding* (1758):

> There surely never was a greater number of miracles ascribed to one person . . . But what is more extraordinary; many of the miracles were immediately proved upon the spot, before judges of unquestioned integrity, attested by witnesses of credit and distinction, in a learned age. . . . Where shall we find such a number of circumstances, agreeing to the corroboration of one fact?

One of those who investigated the happenings was a lawyer named Louis Adrien de Paige. When he told his friend, the magistrate Louis-Basile Carré de Montgéron, what he had seen the magistrate assured him patronizingly that he had been taken in by conjuring tricks – the kind of "miracles" performed by tricksters at fairgrounds. But he finally agreed to go with Paige to the churchyard, if only for the pleasure of pointing out how the lawyer had been deceived. They went there on the morning of 7 September 1731. And de Montgéron left the churchyard a changed man – he even endured prison rather than deny what he had seen that day.

The first thing the magistrate saw when he entered the churchyard was a number of women writhing on the ground, twisting themselves into the most startling shapes, sometimes bending backward until the backs of their heads touched their heels. These ladies were all wearing a long cloth undergarment that fastened around the ankles. M.Paige explained that this was now obligatory for all women who wished to avail themselves of the Deacon's miraculous powers. In the early days, when women had stood on their heads or bent their bodies convulsively, prurient young men had begun to frequent the churchyard to view the spectacle.

However, there was no lack of male devotees of the deceased Abbé to assist in the activities of the churchyard. Montgéron was shocked to see that some of the women and girls were being sadistically beaten – at least, that is what at first appeared to be going on. Men were striking them with heavy pieces of wood and iron. Other women lay on the ground, apparently crushed under immensely heavy weights. One girl was naked to the waist: a man was gripping her nipples with a pair of iron tongs and twisting them violently. Paige explained that none of these women felt any pain; on the contrary, many begged for more blows. And an incredible number of them were cured of deformities or diseases by this violent treatment.

In another part of the churchyard, they saw an attractive pink-cheeked girl of about nineteen, who was sitting at a trestle table and eating. That seemed normal enough until Montgéron looked more closely at the food on the plate, and realized from its appearance as well as from the smell that reached him that it was human excrement. In between mouthfuls of this sickening fare she drank a yellow liquid, which Paige explained was urine. The girl had come to the churchyard to be cured of what we would now call a neurosis: she had to wash her hands hundreds of times a day, and was so fastidious about her food that she would taste nothing that had been touched by another human hand. The Deacon had indeed cured her. Within days she was eating excrement and drinking urine, and did so with every sign of enjoyment. Such cases might not be remarkable in asylums; but what was more extra-ordinary – indeed, preposterous – was that after one of these meals she opened her mouth as if to be sick, and milk came pouring out. Monsieur Paige had collected a cupful; it was apparently perfectly ordinary cow's milk.

After staggering away from the eater of excrement, Montgéron had to endure a worse ordeal. In another part of the churchyard a number of women had volunteered to cleanse suppurating wounds and boils by sucking them clean. Trying hard to prevent himself vomiting, Montgéron watched as someone unwound a dirty bandage from the leg of a small girl; the smell was horrible. The leg was a festering mass of sores, some so deep that the bone was visible. The woman who had volunteered to clean it was one of the *convulsionnaires* – she had been miraculously cured and converted by her bodily contortions, and God had now chosen her to demonstrate how easily human beings' disgust can be overcome. Yet even she blenched as she saw and smelt the gangrened leg. She cast her eyes up to heaven, prayed silently for a moment, then bent her head and began to lap, swallowing the septic matter. When she moved her face farther down the child's leg Montgéron could see that the wound was now clean. Paige assured him that the girl would almost certainly be cured when the treatment was complete.

What Montgéron saw next finally shattered his resistance and convinced him that he was witnessing something of profound significance. A sixteen-year-old girl named Gabrielle Moler had arrived, and the interest she excited made Montgéron aware that, even among this crowd of miraculous freaks, she was a celebrity. She removed her cloak and lay on the ground, her skirt modestly round her ankles. Four men, each holding a pointed iron bar, stood over her. When the girl smiled at them they lunged down at her, driving their rods into her stomach. Montgéron had to be restrained from interfering as the rods went through the girl's dress and into her stomach. He looked for signs of blood staining her dress. But none came, and the girl looked calm and serene. Next the bars were jammed under her chin, forcing her head back. It seemed inevitable that they would penetrate through to her mouth; yet when the points were removed the flesh was unbroken. The men took up sharp-edged shovels, placed them against a breast, and then pushed with all their might; the girl went on smiling gently. The breast, trapped between shovels, should have been cut off, but it seemed impervious to the assault. Then the cutting edge of a shovel was placed against her throat, and the man wielding it did his best to cut off her head; he did not seem to be able even to dent her neck.

Dazed, Montgéron watched as the girl was beaten with a great iron truncheon shaped like a pestle. A stone weighing half a hundredweight (25 kilograms) was raised above her body and dropped repeatedly from a height of several feet. Finally, Montgéron watched her kneel in front of a blazing fire, and plunge her head into it. He could feel the heat from where he stood; yet her hair and eyebrows were not even singed. When she picked up a blazing chunk of coal and proceeded to eat it Montgéron could stand no more and left.

But he went back repeatedly, until he had enough materials for the first volume of an amazing book. He presented it to the king, Louis XV, who was so shocked and indignant that he had Montgéron thrown into prison. Yet Montgéron felt he had to "bear witness", and was to publish two more volumes following his release, full of precise scientific testimony concerning the miracles.

In the year following Montgéron's imprisonment, 1732, the Paris authorities decided that the scandal was becoming unbearable and closed down the churchyard. But the *convulsionnaires* had discovered that they could perform their miracles anywhere, and they continued for many years. A hardened skeptic, the scientist La Condamine, was as startled as Montgéron when, in 1759, he watched a girl named Sister Françoise being crucified on a wooden cross, nailed by the hands and feet over a period of several hours, and stabbed in the side with a spear. He noticed that all this obviously hurt the girl, and her wounds bled when the nails were removed; but she seemed none the worse for an ordeal that would have killed most people.

So what can we say of the miracles from the standpoint of the twentieth century? Some writers believe it was a kind of self-hypnosis. But while this could explain the excrement-eater and the woman who sucked festering wounds, it is less plausible in explaining Gabrielle Moler's feats of endurance. These remind us rather of descriptions of ceremonies of dervishes and fakirs: for example, J.G.Bennett in his autobiography *Witness* describes watching a dervish ritual in which a razor-sharp sword was placed across the belly of a naked man, and two heavy men jumped up and down on it – all without even marking the flesh. What seems to be at work here is some power of "mind over matter", deeper than mere hypnosis, which is not yet understood but obviously merits serious attention.

It would be absurd to stop looking for scientific explanations of the miracles of Saint-Médard. But let us not in the meantime deceive ourselves by accepting superficial "skeptical" explanations.

49

The Sea Kings of 6000 BC

The Maps That
Contradict the History Books

In 1966 Charles Hapgood, a professor of the history of science, caused something of a scandal when he published a book entitled *Maps of the Ancient Sea Kings*. For what Professor Hapgood was arguing, with a logic that was difficult to fault, was that civilization may be far, far older than historians now recognize: that as long as twelve thousand years ago, when man was still a wandering hunter, ancient seafarers may have been sailing across the Atlantic. These conclusions were not the outcome of wild speculation, they were the logical result of the study of old maps that had been available for centuries.

The story began in 1956, when a cartographer named M. I. Walters, at the U.S. Navy Hydrographic Office, found himself looking at a copy of a strange map that had been presented to the Office by a Turkish naval officer. It was obviously very old – in fact, it was dated 919 in the Muslim calendar, which is AD 1513 by Christian reckoning. It was basically a map of the Atlantic Ocean, showing a small part of North Africa, from what is now Morocco to the Ivory Coast, and all of South America. These were in their correct longitudes, a remarkable – in fact, almost unbelievable – achievement for those days, when most maps were laughably crude. (One of the most famous medieval maps shows Italy joined to Spain; another shows the British Isles shaped like a teapot.) It was also, for 1513, an astonishingly accurate map of South America. And what was even more surprising was that it apparently showed Antarctica, which was not discovered until 1818. Oddly enough, it also showed the mid-Atlantic ridge, which seems an unbelievable piece of knowledge for any period before the invention of sonar depth soundings – unless, of course, it had been observed while it was still above water.

The original mapmaker had been a Turkish pirate named Piri Re'is (Re'is means "admiral"), who had been beheaded in 1554. He had been the nephew of a famous pirate, Kemal Re'is, and had held a high post, equivalent to the governorship of Egypt. Piri Re'is had made the interesting statement that he had based his map on twenty old maps, one of them made by Christopher Columbus and others from the great library of Alexandria, destroyed by invading Arabs in AD 640.

In fact, the Piri Re'is map had been known since 1929, when it had been discovered in the Topkapi Palace museum in Istanbul, and there was already a copy in the Library of Congress. But thus far, no one had paid much attention to it. Walters decided to try and remedy that and showed the map to his friend, Captain Arlington H. Mallery, a navigator who was devoting his retirement to studying old maps. Mallery was allowed to borrow the map, and when he brought it back, he had some startling – indeed, incredible – comments. Mallery agreed that the land shown to the south was Antarctica; what was more, the map had apparently been made before the Antarctic continent was covered with ice. But that seemed absurd. The coast of Antarctica had certainly been covered with ice in the time of Alexander the Great; the last time men could have seen it without ice was many thousands of years ago, long before the earliest known maritime civilizations. And that could only mean one of two things: either that ships had sailed the seas at a time when, according to historians, our ancestors were living in caves, or – what sounded equally outrageous – that there had once been a flourishing civilization on Antarctica itself, whose men made maps that were copied down through the ages, up to the time of Alexander the Great.

These suggestions caused considerable controversy, which came to Hapgood's attention. He was interested because it sounded as if the Piri Re'is map might support some of the conclusions he had drawn about the movements of the earth's crust – and would publish in a book entitled *Earth's Shifting Crust* in 1958. Hapgood's starting point had been the puzzle of the great ice ages, which are still unexplained by science. Hapgood's own suggestion was that, for some unknown reason, the amount of sunlight varies from age to age. Ice caps form unevenly at the poles, and this lack of balance affects the rotation of the earth – just as an off-balance wheel begins to vibrate as it spins. This, Hapgood suggested, causes masses of ice to dislodge, as well as the tectonic plates to which they are stuck. And the movement of these plates causes a catastrophic shake-up of the earth's crust. Hapgood estimated that the last such catastrophic movement took place between ten and fifteen thousand years ago. Before that, he suggested, Antarctica was 2,500 miles closer to the equator than it is today and had a temperate climate. Albert Einstein wrote an introduction to the book, in which he declared that Hapgood's theories deserved careful attention.

When Hapgood learned of Mallery's views on the Piri Re'is map, he decided that, instead of arguing about whether it was genuine, it would be more sensible to subject it to careful, detailed study. He therefore assembled a group of students at Keene State College in New Hampshire and set them the task of studying a number of ancient maps, including that of Piri Re'is.

Hapgood's first surprise was that the maps known as *portolans* – those used by seafarers in the Middle Ages (the word means "from port to port") – had been known to scholars for centuries and that no one had paid much attention to them, even though some showed, for example, that Cuba had been known before Columbus "discovered" it in 1492. His next surprise was that these portolans were often as accurate as modern maps. It seemed odd that land-based mapmakers should have been content with crudities when their marine counterparts were so sophisticated.

Hapgood also noted that A. E. Nordenskiold, a leading scholar whose study of early maps had appeared in 1889, believed that the portolans of the fifteenth and sixteenth centuries were based on far older maps that dated back centuries before Christ. One of Nordenskiold's main reasons for this belief was that the great geographer and astronomer Ptolemy, who was active in Alexandria around AD 150, made maps that were less accurate than these medieval portolans, even though he had the greatest library in the world at his disposal. Was it likely that ordinary medieval seamen, working by rule of thumb, could surpass Ptolemy unless they had some ancient maps to guide them?

The arguments Hapgood uses to support this thesis, based on the research of his students, are too long and too technical to describe at length here. But one thing that was obvious was that although Piri had combined the twenty maps he admitted using to the best of his ability, he had often allowed them to overlap – or fail to overlap. He had shown the Amazon river twice but had left out a nine-hundred-mile stretch of the coastline. The problem was to try to understand how these errors had come about.

One error could be pinned down to the Greek astronomer Eratosthenes, the first man to calculate the size of the earth with accuracy. He knew that on June 21 the sun at midday was reflected in a certain well in Syene, on the Nile, and that towers did not cast a shadow. But in Alexandria, they did. He had only to measure the length of the shadow of a tower in Alexandria at midday on June 21 to calculate the angle of the sun's rays. This proved to be 7 degrees. Since he knew the distance from Syene to Alexandria, he could easily work out how many miles were required for 360 degrees. Due to a miscalculation of distance, Eratosthenes increased the circumference of the earth by about $4\frac{1}{2}$ degrees; but it was an amazingly accurate calculation for 240 BC. Hapgood discovered that if he allowed for this $4\frac{1}{2}$ degree error, Piri's map became even more accurate. This was an additional piece of evidence that Piri's map was based on ancient Greek models.

Another problem is the obvious one known to all geographers – that the earth is a sphere, and a map that is flat is bound to distort it. Today mapmakers use a "projection" based on division into latitude and longitude. But the old mapmakers, it seemed, used a simpler method. They chose a centre, drew a circle around it, then subdivided this into sixteen segments, much like dividing a cake into sixteen slices. Along the outer edge of every "slice" they drew various squares – a complicated method, but one that worked well enough. The original centre of the Piri Re'is map was actually off the map, but calculation indicated that it had to be in Egypt. At first, Alexandria seemed the obvious place. But more careful calculation showed that the place had to be further north. When it turned out to be Syene, Hapgood knew he was on the right track.

But this in itself, Hapgood realized, had some interesting implications. When the geographers of Alexandria made their maps – which included Eratosthenes's $4\frac{1}{2}$ degree error – it is unlikely that they sailed off to visit the various places they were mapping. They presumably used older maps. And those older maps must have been incredibly accurate – without the $4\frac{1}{2}$ degree error. This suggests that the older mapmakers possessed a more accurate and advanced mapmaking science than the Greeks.

In fact, there is one interesting piece of evidence that this is so. Toward the end of the second century BC the Greek grammarian Agatharchides of Cnidus, who was a tutor to one of the Ptolemy kings of Egypt, was told that, according to ancient tradition, one side of the base of the Great Pyramid – built around 2500 BC – was precisely one-eighth of a minute of a degree in length – that is, it was that part of the earth's circumference. (A minute is a sixtieth of a degree.) The pyramid's base is just over 230 meters. If 230 is multiplied by 8, then by 60, then by 360, the result is just under foty thousand kilometers, or just under twenty-five thousand miles – a remarkably accurate estimate of the length of the equator. Now it is possible, of course, that whoever designed the pyramid chose the length of its base at random and that some later geographer, after Eratosthenes, worked out that it was an eighth of a minute. But our knowledge of the ancient Egyptians, and the importance they attached to sacred geometry, suggests that they knew exactly what they were doing – and that they knew the circumference of the earth in 2500 BC.

When Napoléon invaded Egypt in 1798, one of the learned men he took along with him, Edmé François Jomard, studied the Great Pyramid carefully and made some important discoveries: The four sides of the pyramid point to the four points of the compass – north, south, east, and west – with incredible accuracy. The pyramid is ten miles from Cairo, which is at the base of the Nile Delta – so called because it is a triangle of streams running into the sea – and if diagonals are drawn from the pyramid, they neatly enclose the delta. Moreover, a line drawn from exactly halfway along the north face slices the delta into two exact halves. All of these facts indicate that the ancient Egyptians had some extremely precise method of measuring long distances and did not do it by rough guesswork.

The French meter is supposed to be precisely one ten-millionth of the distance from equator to pole. Jomard's study of the pyramid convinced him that the Egyptians had also used a measure based on the earth's size – in this case, 1 divided by 216,000.

All of this is staggering. How could a fairly primitive agricultural civilization know the size of the earth? What is equally hard to understand is why this knowledge had to be rediscovered by Eratosthenes more than two thousand years later – until we recall that until Columbus sailed to America, there was a general belief that the earth is flat. Knowledge can be lost very easily.

Hapgood made another interesting discovery from his study of the Piri Re'is map: that the original maps from which it was drawn must have used a slightly different length for the degree of latitude than the degree of longitude. Why? Well, presumably because if you are trying to project the surface of a sphere onto a flat sheet of paper, the lines of longitude get shorter as they draw toward the poles, while the lines of latitude (since they run parallel across the globe) are less affected. The first European to use this projection method was Gerardus Mercator, in 1569. It looked as if the ancient mapmakers had already used the same method.

Hapgood concluded that the "evident knowledge of longitude implies a people unknown to us, a nation of seafarers, with instruments for finding longitude undreamed of by the Greeks."

What was equally impressive was Hapgood's confirmation of Mallery's conclusion that the coast of Queen Maud Land, on the Antarctic continent, had been drawn without the ice sheets. In 1949 an expedition mounted by Norway, Britain, and Sweden was able to establish the outline of the land under the ice by various sophisticated techniques for taking depth soundings through the ice caps. This indicated that Piri Re'is probably based his map on some original map of the Antarctic before the Ice Age – which, as we recall, Hapgood had placed (in *Earth's Shifting Crust*) between ten and fifteen thousand years ago.

The Piri Re'is map was not the only one examined by Hapgood and his students. Hapgood asked the Library of Congress to allow him to look at all the old maps of the period and was startled to find hundreds of them laid out for his inspection. It was a 1531 map by one Oronteus Finaeus that filled him with a conviction that he had made a discovery equal in importance to the Piri Re'is map. It showed the South Pole – which was amazing enough for a date nearly three centuries before its official discovery. What was positively staggering was that it was a map of the whole polar cap, as if drawn from the air, showing a remarkable resemblance to the pole as we know it today. And again, all the evidence suggested that it had been made in the days before the pole was covered with ice – it, too, showed the coast of Queen Maud Land and mountain ranges now under the ice, as well as rivers flowing into the sea. Certain mistakes on the map reappeared in all other contemporary maps, suggesting that all of them had been based on some old map, possibly dating back to Alexander the Great. But the 1949 core samples left no doubt that the Antarctic was covered with ice at the time of Alexander the Great (356–23 BC). So the original maps must have been much older.

How much older? The core samples showed that the last warm period in the Antarctic ended six thousand years ago, or around 4000 BC, so the "Antarctic civilization" posited by Hapgood must have flourished before this. Now this, in itself, is not particularly astonishing. Man was fishing ten thousand years ago and began to farm soon after that. Jericho, the oldest market town so far discovered, was fortified between eight and ten thousand years ago, and its inhabitants used polished limestone dishes because they had not yet learned to bake pottery. On the other hand, writing was not invented until about 3500 BC, in Sumeria. Domestication of camels and donkeys was to cause an expansion in trade about five hundred years later. So the Oronteus Finaeus map suggested that some kind of writing – because it is hard to conceive of a map without "labels" – must have existed nearly three thousand years earlier. Besides, mapmaking is a sophisticated science requiring, among other things, some knowledge of geometry – and the earliest knowledge of geometry seems to date from Babylon about 1500 BC, nearly five thousand years later than the "Antarctic civilization."

A Turkish Hadji Ahmed map of 1550 (fourteen years before the birth of Shakespeare) shows the world from a northern "projection," as if hovering over the North Pole. Again, the accuracy is incredible. But what may be its most interesting feature is that Alaska and Siberia *seem* to be joined. Since this projection shows a heart-shaped globe, with Alaska on one side of the "dimple" and Siberia on the other, this could merely indicate that the map-maker did not have enough space to show the Bering Strait which divides the continents. If this is not so, the consequences are staggering: we know that a land bridge *did* exist in the remote past, but it may have been as long as 12,000 years ago.

Other early portolans were equally remarkable for their accuracy. The "Dulcert Portolano" of 1339, for example, shows that the cartographer had precise knowledge of an area from Galway to the Don Basin in Russia. Others showed the Aegean dotted with islands that do not now exist – they were presumably drowned by melting ice; an accurately drawn map of southern Great Britain, but without Scotland and with indications of glaciers; and a Sweden still partially glaciated.

Perhaps the most interesting piece of evidence uncovered by Hapgood is a map of China that he found in Needham's *Science and Civilisation in China*, dating from AD 1137 and carved in stone. Hapgood's studies of Piri Re'is and other European portolans had made him familiar with the "longitude error" mentioned above; now he was astonished to find it on this map of China. If he was correct, then the Chinese had also known the "original" maps on which Piri Re'is's map was based.

And this, of course, suggested the staggering idea that some worldwide seafaring civilization had existed before Alexander the Great and that it had disappeared while the civilization of Mesopotamia was still primitive and illiterate. This is the suggestion that Hapgood – shunning all academic caution – outlines in his book's last chapter, "A Civilisation That Vanished." He points out that we had to wait for the eighteenth century to develop an accurate method of measuring longitude and the circumference of the earth, and until the nineteenth for the exploration of the Arctic and Antarctic. According to Hapgood: "The maps indicate that some ancient people did all these things." And this civilization disappeared, either in some catastrophe or over a long period of time, and was simply forgotten. If it existed in Antarctica – and possibly the

Arctic – then its disappearance is easily explained by the return of the ice cap about six thousand years ago.

And what does all this mean? Hapgood was content simply to postulate a maritime civilization that sailed the seven seas when, according to historians, the only seafarers were fishermen who hugged the coasts of the Mediterranean. But others were anxious to dot the is and cross the ts. They saw his "advanced civilization of the Ice Age" as a proof of the real existence of Atlantis, supposedly destroyed in some great prehistoric catastrophe, while others seized upon it as proof that the earth had been visited by "spacemen" at some remote epoch in the past. The "ancient astronaut" theory (see chapter 14) was popularized in books like *The Morning of the Magicians* (1960) by Louis Pauwels and Jacques Bergier, and *Chariots of the Gods?* (1957) by Erich von Däniken. All these speculations – popularized in the 1968 film *2001: A Space Odyssey* – had the same effect on the scientists of the 1960s that the Spiritualist explosion of the 1860s had on their nineteenth-century predecessors. Serious inquiry was underminded by "guilt by association." Hapgood ceased to be taken seriously, even by a minority of his fellow academics.

In 1979 a revised edition of *Maps of the Ancient Sea Kings: Evidence of Advanced Civilisation in the Ice Age* made reviewers aware that Hapgood did not deserve to be tarred with the same brush as von Däniken. It is perfectly conceivable that some of his arguments may prove to be false and that the mistakes of unskilled mapmakers may explain the extra islands in the Aegean, the missing upper half of England, the mid-Atlantic ridge, and even the land bridge across the Bering Strait. But his main argument remains unaffected. Portolans of the Middle Ages show Antarctica long before it was explored, and the skill with which they are drawn suggests that they are based on far older maps. Perhaps the resemblance between the Chinese map of 1137 and the portolans is coincidence, and there was no "worldwide maritime civilization." But at the very least, there must have been some fairly sophisticated civilization long before the so-called birth of civilization in Mesopotamia or China – perhaps buried beneath Antarctic ice.

Hapgood is inclined to undermine his own case with specious arguments. For example, he points out that in *Gulliver's Travels* (1726), Swift gives a strangely accurate description of the two moons of Mars, which were not discovered for another century and a half. Hapgood suggests that Swift was relying on "some ancient source," when the true explanation is probably the curious serendipity that can be found so often in the history of art and literature. (I point out in my book

Starseekers that in *Eureka*, Poe anticipated the Big Bang theory of the origin of the universe, as well as the discovery that atoms can be broken down into positive and negative particles.) In other words, we are dealing with something closer to Jung's "synchronicity."

To be fair to von Däniken and *The Morning of the Magicians*, it must also be admitted that Hapgood's carefully argued analysis of the portolans *does* offer some support for the "ancient astronaut" theory. The Oronteus Finaeus map *does* look as if it has been based on an aerial view. So does the 1550 Hadji Ahmed map of the world seen from above the North Pole. Moreover, it is still difficult to see how the lines and the vast drawings on the desert floor at Nazca could have been drawn by people who were unable to look down on them from the air – although primitive balloons would have been as effective as spacecraft for that purpose.

But the theories that have appealed to Hapgood's findings for support (including those based on the *Oera Linda Book*, discussed in chapter 39) cannot be regarded as evidence either for or against his findings. All that is quite certain is that Hapgood's evidence for an ancient maritime civilization that preceded any of those we know is virtually incontrovertible.

50

Sea Monsters

Unknown Giants of the Deep

On 10 October 1848, the *Times* of London carried the following report: "When the *Daedalus*, frigate, Captain M'Quhae, which arrived on the 4th inst., was on her passage from the East Indies between the Cape of Good Hope and St. Helena, her captain, and most of her officers and crew, at four o'clock one afternoon, saw a sea serpent".

The report brought a flood of angry letters from naval men who felt that the *Times* was failing in its duty to the public by printing such rubbish. Understandably, the public took a different view, and newspapers all over the country seized upon the story. A conference was hastily called at the Admiralty, which concluded that an immediate investigation was required.

The first step was to contact Captain Peter M'Quhae, to find out whether there any substance to the story. To the embarrassment of Admiral Sir W. Gage, who was in charge of the investigation, M'Quhae replied that despite certain glaring inaccuracies, the *Times* story was essentially correct: he had indeed seen a sea monster. He had noted the event in the ship's log and had planned to report the incident through normal channels.

His story was as follows: At five o'clock on 6 August 1848, while the *Daedalus* was between the Cape of Good Hope and St. Helena, one of the midshipmen reported a strange creature swimming slowly toward them off the starboard bow. Most of the crew were at supper, and there were only seven men on deck, including the captain, the watch officer, and the ship's navigator. All of them witnessed what M'Quhae described as "an enormous serpent" – judged to be about 100 feet long – as it swam in a straight line past the frigate, apparently oblivious to its existence. The captain judged it to be travelling at around twelve to fifteen miles an hour and described how it had remained within the range of their spyglasses for nearly twenty minutes. Although the afternoon was showery and dull, M'Quhae stated that it was still bright enough to see the creature clearly and that it swam close enough that "had it been a man of my acquaintance I should have easily recognized his features with the naked eye".

He described the large, distinctly snakelike head projecting just above the waves on a neck about fifteen inches thick, followed by sixty feet or so of serpentine back, which crested above the surface of the water. The colour was uniformly dark brown, apart from the throat, which was a yellowish white. To M'Quhae it seemed to slip through the water effortlessly, without the aid of fins or the undulatory swimming typical of snakes and eels. This odd fact may be explained by a mane of hair or seaweed that ran along its back and that may have obscured its means of propulsion. At no point did the creature open its mouth to reveal "large jagged teeth" (as the *Times* had reported). The witnesses had all agreed that it appeared neither frightened nor threatening but rather that it was traveling forward "on some determined purpose". M'Quhae had made a sketch of the creature which, at the admiral's request, he converted into a larger drawing to accompany his statement.

To the credit of the Admiralty, it quickly made the controversial report publicly available. On 13 October the *Times* printed the report in full, and fifteen days later the *Illustrated London News* printed several pictures of the "*Daedalus* sea serpent" based on M'Quhae's drawing. The "purposeful" sea monster became a subject of sometimes heated national debate.

The other six witnesses named by M'Quhae backed his version of events, but it was clear from the outset that there was some difference of opinion on details. The magazine *Zoologist* published an extract from the journal of the watch officer, Lieutenant Edgar Drummond, covering the day of the sighting. Drummond had judged the head to be about ten feet long – rather large for a sixteen-inch neck to support. He estimated the visible part of the body at about twenty feet long, and although he mentioned that the captain claimed to see another twenty feet of tail just beneath the surface, this still came short of M'Quhae's estimate of sixty feet of wave-cresting body. Drummond also disagreed about what his captain referred to as a "mane" on the creature's back, preferring to describe it as some sort of dorsal fin.

Few skeptics were rude enough to accuse the witnesses of being downright liars, but many hinted that this was their view. One wrote to the *Times* asking why M'Quhae did not order his men to put about and give chase to the creature. Another, perhaps with tongue in cheek, demanded why he had not fired a broadside at it.

A more useful contribution to the discussion was a letter in the *Literary Gazette* that pointed out that the description of the *Daedalus* monster was remarkably like that of a sea serpent described by the Danish Bishop Pontoppidan in his influential zoological study, *A Natural History of Norway* (1753). It continued: "One might fancy the gallant Captain had read the old Dane, and was copying him, when he tells of the dark brown colour and white about the throat, and the neck clothed as if by a horse's mane or a bunch of sea-weed, the exact words of the historian". Through all this M'Quhae maintained a dignified silence. It took the intervention of one of Europe's leading men of science to persuade him to comment.

Sir Richard Owen, curator of the Hunterian Museum, an anatomist, naturalist, and paleontologist of immense reputation, came forward to lead the crusade of *Daedalus* sea-serpent debunkers. Owen was considered by many people to be the greatest living authority on zoology. Pugnaciously conservative, he would later become Darwin's most bitter and most venomous opponent.

Owen began by sending the *Times* a copy of a lengthy letter he had written to a friend who had inquired whether the *Daedalus* sea serpent might not be a survival of the Saurian age – one of the most popular theories that had emerged during the controversy. Owen dismissed M'Quhae's suggestion that the creature was a giant sea snake, implying that the captain should leave scientific deductions to the experts. After a careful consideration of M'Quhae's statement, Owen came to the conclusion that the creature was almost certainly a mammal of some sort, and – since his analysis was based on the preconceived idea that the sighting was of some species already known to science – he went on to suggest one that might fit the bill: the *Phoca proboscidea* or sea elephant. (The level of Owen's expertise on sea serpents may be judged from his remark that alligators are often encountered by vessels at sea; in fact, alligators are relatively weak swimmers and cannot even live in turbulent stretches of river.)

The sea elephant is, in fact, an enormous seal (it may grow to twenty feet in length) that is native to the seas around Antarctica. Owen's suggestion was that one of these creatures might have been swept north on an iceberg, from which it would swim periodically to eat fish. When the ice melted, it would have been forced to swim until its strength gave out. Perhaps, he wrote, it was dying when the *Daedalus* encountered it, thus explaining its lack of interest in them. In his opinion, what M'Quhae had mistaken as a forty-foot stretch of semisubmerged reptilian body was, in fact, the turbulence its horizontal tail made as it swam along in a straight line. The "mane" that the captain noted was, Owen pointed out, typical of bull sea elephants – also known as Anderson's sea lions. He then went on to deny the existence of all sea serpents on the grounds that science had found no evidence of them and concluded with the assertion: "A larger body of evidence from eye-witnesses might be got together in proof of ghosts than of sea-serpents".

In a letter to the *Times* M'Quhae replied, a little testily, that the creature seen that day had not been a sea elephant, which he would have quickly recognized, or for that matter a seal of any kind. As an experienced sailor he was quite capable of telling the difference between water turbulence and the passage of a large, solid body. He also insisted that he had not heard of the account of a sea serpent given by Bishop Pontoppidan until it had been mentioned by the *Literary Gazette* correspondent and that therefore it could not have influenced him to embroider the account of what he had seen.

Finally, he ended by stating categorically that there had been no hysterical excitement among the witnesses and that he himself was certain that no kind of optical illusion could have misled them about the details given in the report. His statement, he concluded, would stand as it was "until some more fortunate opportunity shall occur of making a closer acquaintance with the 'great unknown' – in the present instance assuredly no ghost". The letter was his final word on the controversy, and its general tone was one of a man sick to death of the whole subject.

Ten years after the *Daedalus* sighting, a Captain Frederic Smith wrote to the *Times* describing how his lookout on the *Pekin* had sighted what they took to be a sea serpent with a "huge head and neck, covered with a long shaggy-looking kind of mane", but that had proved to be a twenty-foot length of seaweed. The letter ended by concluding that the *Daedalus* serpent was almost certainly a piece of seaweed as well. This drew a reply from an officer of the *Daedalus* in which he stated that the "serpent" was "beyond all question a living animal, moving rapidly through the water". He went on to describe how they had observed it at close quarters for some time. Again, the circumstantial details of the report are impressive.

At least the British Admiralty indicated their belated support for M'Quhae's story by placing his report in their official records, the first such claimed sighting to be dignified in this way.

In fact, there had been dozens of sightings of sea serpents before 1848 – Bernard Huevelmans's book *In the Wake of the Sea Serpents* (1968) lists about 150 between 1639 and 1848. The 1639 sighting is second-hand, but there are dozens of other reports that are as circumstantial as

M'Quhae's. For example, Captain George Little, of the frigate *Boston*, described how, in May 1740, he was lying in Broad Bay, off Maine, when "I discovered a large Serpent or monster coming down the Bay, on the surface of the water". A cutter full of armed men went off to take a closer look, but "when within a hundred feet . . . the serpent dove. He was not less than from 45 to 50 feet in length; the largest diameter of his body, I should judge, 15 inches; his head nearly the size of a man, which he carried four or five feet above the water. He wore every appearance of a common black snake".

Huevelmans quotes 587 sightings between 1639 and 1966. One of the 1966 sightings was made by two Englishmen, John Ridgeway and Chay Blyth. Ridgeway wrote in *A Fighting Chance*:

> I was shocked to full wakefulness by a swishing noise to starboard. I looked out into the water and suddenly saw the writhing, twisting shape of a great creature. It was outlined by the phosphorescence in the sea as if a string of neon lights were hanging from it. It was an enormous size, some thirty-five feet or more long, and it came towards me quite fast. . . . It headed straight at me and disappeared right beneath me. . . . I was frozen with terror at this apparition.

And Huevelmans concludes his chapter – and his sightings – with a report by two vacationers near Skegness in eastern England, who saw "something like the Loch Ness monster" a hundred yards out to sea: "It had a head like a serpent and six or seven pointed humps trailing behind".

Huevelmans goes on to quote Sir Arthur Conan Doyle as saying that if one okapi had been shot in Africa, its existence might be doubted. If ten men shoot an okapi, the evidence would be strong. If fifty men shoot one, "it would become convincing". So 587 sightings – even if some are dismissed as fraud or genuine mistakes – undoubtedly deserve to be classified as convincing. Huevelmans then analyses the sightings and classifies them into seven basic types: the "super-otter", with a flat head and long, otterlike body; the many-humped serpent, with its row of regular humps; the many-finned serpent, with pointed projections along both sides; the merhorse, a creature with a mane; the long-necked serpent, with a long, slender neck like a prehistoric diplodocus; and the "super-eels", which resemble giant snakes. He toys with a classification called the "Father-of-all-the-turtles" – looking, as one might suppose, like a giant turtle – but finally dismisses it as suspect and doubtful. The first five he believes to be mammals, while the super-eel – on the evidence of body fragments – seems to be a fish.

Bishop Pontoppidan, whom we have already encountered, was not the first to describe the sea serpent. As early as 1539 a Swedish bishop named Olaf Mansson (Latinized as Olaus Magnus) published in Venice a map of the north that clearly showed two sea serpents. And in a *History of the Goths, Swedes, and Vandals*, published in 1555, he describes a "serpent 200 feet long and 20 feet thick" that lives in the sea caves off Bergen. This story, accompanied by terrifying pictures of serpents devouring ships, was cited by many subsequent encyclope-dists. Two hundred years later Bishop Pontoppidan devoted a chapter of his *Natural History of Norway* to various monsters, including the sea serpent, the kraken, and the mermaid. In the case of the sea serpent he took the trouble to obtain a firsthand account by one Captain Lorenz von Ferry, who ordered a boat to pursue the creature, and was able to describe in some detail the horselike head with a white mane and black eyes, and the many coils or folds – he thought there were seven or eight, with about a fathom (six feet) between each fold.

The main interest of Pontoppidan's comments at this juncture is that his book aroused considerable skepticism in Britain when it was trans-lated in 1765 and that a Captain (later Admiral) Charles Douglas, who tried to find out what he could about such monsters, took a distinctly skeptical view of the evidence of some witnesses. Oddly enough, he recorded that while many Norwegians believed in the existence of "Stoor worms" (sea worms), they were inclined to dismiss the kraken, a giant octopus, as a myth. And it continued to be dismissed as a myth until its existence was finally accepted by science in the 1970s. The legends of the kraken – a vast octopoid monster that sometimes attacked swimmers, ships, and even coastal villages – can be traced back as far as the ancient Roman scholar Pliny, who described a "polyp" with thirty-foot-long arms that climbed ashore to steal fish being salted at Carteia in Spain and that was killed only after a violent encounter. Yet it should be noted that just about every seagoing culture in the world has had its equivalent of the kraken myth.

By comparison, Bishop Pontoppidan's kraken seemed relatively harmless. He notes that local fishermen had discovered that there was a certain place off the coast of Norway where the recorded depth of eighty to one hundred fathoms would at times diminish to twenty or thirty fathoms, and that during these times the sea around would become turbid and muddy and the fishing in the area spectacularly abundant. This, they believed, was due to the kraken, a vast tentacled beast a mile and a half in circumference, which swam up from the seabed and attracted the fish by venting its excrement. The monster posed no danger to men provided they removed their boats from the area before it came to the surface. This kraken seemed to be curiously passive – it looked like a group of surfacing islands interconnected by a weedlike substance and surrounded by waving "horns", some "as high and as large as the masts of middle-siz'd vessels". After eating its fill of the fish "beached" on its immense bulk, it would sink to the bottom again.

By the end of the eighteenth century science had dismissed such creatures as mythical. But the large number of nineteenth-century sightings of sea serpents off the coast of America began to erode the skepticism, while huge sucker marks found on sperm whales, and fragments of enormous tentacles found in their stomachs, made it clear that the giant squid was no myth either.

In November 1861 crewmen on the French gunboat *Alecton* saw a giant squid near Tenerife and tried to harpoon it. The creature was clearly dying, since they were able to slip a noose around it; but it broke in two as they tried to heave it aboard. The squid was about twenty-four feet long, and the mouth measured eighteen inches across. The *Alecton* arrived at Tenerife with enough of the monster to leave no possible doubt of its existence, and an account of it was read before the French Academy of Sciences on 30, December 1861. Yet a zoologist named Arthur Mangin still expressed disbelief and wanted to know why the creature had not simply dove below the surface. It was more likely, he thought, that everybody concerned in the report was a liar.

But in the 1870s so many giant squids expired on the beaches of Newfoundland and Labrador that it became impossible to doubt their existence. And in 1896 an enormous though mutilated corpse was washed up on the beach in St. Augustine, Florida, and photographed and examined by Dr DeWitt Webb. It took four horses, six men, and a block and tackle to move the six- or seven- ton bulk farther up the beach. The experts decided that it was a dead whale. But seventy-five years later, scientific examination of the few pieces that had been preserved demonstrated that it was a giant octopus (not a squid) that must have been about 200 feet across – big enough that its bulk would have occupied most of Picadilly Circus or Times Square.

Fortunately, actual encounters with such monsters have been rare. But some of the most vivid accounts date from the Second World War. On 25, March 1941 in a remote part of the South Atlantic, the Allied vessel *Britannia* was attacked by a German raider flying the Japanese flag. The Germans fired on the vessel until she was ablaze, then gave the crew five minutes to abandon ship before they sank her. Because the *Britannia* had an insufficient number of lifeboats, many of the crew found themselves clinging to fragile rubber rafts in the open ocean, hundreds of miles from land and well off the normal shipping lanes. One of these was overloaded with twelve exhausted men, among whom were Lieutenants Rolandson and Davidson of the Royal Navy and Lieutenant R. E. Grimani Cox of the Indian Army, who survived to give an account of their experiences.

They had no food or water and no shelter from the sun. To avoid swamping the raft they had to take turns hanging precariously from its sides, where they had no defense against the attacks of Portuguese men-of-war, which Cox later described as "stinging like a million bees". By the second day some of the men had become delirious; on the third the sharks started to close in. For three days the wounded and thirst-maddened survivors were picked off one by one. Then, to the sailors' joy, the circling sharks suddenly disappeared.

One of the survivors gazed into the ocean depths and saw, to his horror, a huge shape surfacing beneath them. An enormous tentacled creature surfaced beside them and flailed its "arms" over the raft. It grabbed an Indian sailor, "hugging him like a bear", and dragged him into the sea. Satisfied with its prey it moved off but later renewed its attack. Lieutenant Cox's arm was badly mauled by a grasping tentacle, but this time the sailors managed to fight it off. Several days later Cox, Rolandson, and Davidson, the only survivors of the original twelve, were rescued by a Spanish ship.

When, in 1943, Cox was examined by the British biologist, Dr John L. Cloudsley-Thompson, the latter observed a number of circular scars on Cox's arm showing that disks of skin and flesh, each measuring about one and a quarter inches in diameter, had at some time been savagely gouged out of it. In Cloudsley-Thompson's opinion the injuries closely resembled those made by the serrated suckers of a squid; and from their size he deduced that the squid in question would have had to have been approximately twenty-three feet long. Richard Owen and his fellow skeptics would have regarded this as a monster of unprecedented proportions, but the only surprise for Cloudsley-Thompson was that a giant squid so "small" could abduct a full-grown man.

Another account of a giant squid also dates from the war years. J. D. Starkey describes how he would lower a cluster of electric bulbs over the side of an Admiralty trawler to attract fish, which could then be easily caught. One night in the Indian Ocean he found himself gazing at a "green unwinking eye". Shining a powerful torch into the water, Starkey saw tentacles two feet thick. He walked the length of the ship, studying the monster, with its parrotlike beak, and realized that it had to be more than 175 feet long. The squid remained there for about fifteen minutes; then "as its valve opened fully . . . without any visible effort it zoomed into the night".

The major problem, as far as science is concerned, is that it seems virtually impossible to study sea monsters in their natural habitat. Like the notorious Loch Ness monster, they seem oddly shy. One student of "lake monsters", the late Ted Holiday, even came to believe that some of them must be regarded as paranormal phenomena – a conclusion he reached because of his observation that some of the lakes in which monsters have been observed are too small to support a large creature. Holiday's encounters with the Loch Ness monster also developed in him a conviction that it seemed to have a sixth sense about when it could show itself without danger of being photographed.

Another "monster watcher" – Tony "Doc" Shiels – reached a similar conclusion. In 1975 and 1976 there were many sightings of a sea monster off Falmouth, in Cornwall; it was christened "Morgawr", meaning "Cornish giant". Shiels succeeded in taking an excellent photograph of Morgawr, which had the same "plesiosaur-like" shape as the Loch Ness monster – a long neck and a bulky body with "humps" on the back. Shiels subsequently went to Loch Ness and immediately succeeded in snapping two photographs of the monster. But his book *Monstrum*, subtitled *A Wisard's Tale*, makes it clear that he believes that his own monster-sightings have involved some kind of encounter with the world of the paranormal.

This need not imply that creatures like Morgawr and "Nessie" are ghosts, as Holiday was at one point inclined to believe. It may merely imply that they possess highly developed telepathic powers that have enabled them, thus far, to avoid the monster-hunters with considerable success. Which in turn may imply that those who wish to study them must also possess such powers.

The mystery of the underwater monsters is still far from solved. But at least there is now enough evidence to make it clear that Olaus Magnus and Bishop Pontoppidan deserve an apology.

51

Who Was Shakespeare?

Early in 1616, a respectable middle-class gentleman of Stratford-upon-Avon decided it was time to make his will; a few months later in April he died, apparently after a drinking bout with two old friends from London, the playwrights Ben Jonson and Michael Drayton. And then, for a considerable time, he was more or less forgotten. Within seven years of his death, a monument was erected to him in the parish church. In 1656 the antiquary Sir William Dugdale, who was interested in coats of arms, reproduced an inaccurate sketch of it in his *Antiquities of Warwickshire*. It showed a gentleman with a drooping moustache, whose hands rested on a woolsack – a symbol of trade. Few people in Stratford seemed to be aware that this mournful-looking tradesman was a famous actor-playwright who had performed before Queen Elizabeth.

More than a century later, in the 1770s, a clergyman named James Wilmot retired to his native Warwickshire, and devoted his declining years to the study of his two favourite writers, Francis Bacon and William Shakespeare. Since the village of which he was now the rector – Barton-on-the-Heath – was only half a dozen miles from Stratford, he began making inquiries to find out if any stories and traditions of the great actor-playwright now survived in his native town. Apparently no one knew of any. But from the study of Shakespeare's plays, Wilmot had concluded that he must have been a man of wide learning, and must therefore have possessed a considerable library. Over the course of many years he made diligent inquiries in the area, investigating small private libraries for fifty miles around. He found nothing whatever – not a single volume that might have belonged to Shakespeare. And finally he was struck by an astonishing conviction: that the man called Shakespeare was not the author of the plays attributed to him. The man who possessed all the qualifications for writing them was his other favourite author, Francis Bacon.

Wilmot was apparently so overwhelmed by this realization – for by this time, Shakespeare was becoming recognized as one of the greatest of English playwrights – that he decided to keep his strange convictions to himself. But almost thirty years later, when he was eighty, some of his caution had evaporated. And when he was visited by an Ipswich Quaker in 1803 Wilmot finally revealed his embarrassing secret. The Quaker, James Cowell, was researching Shakespeare's life because he had agreed to read a paper about him to his local philosophical society, and no standard biography had yet been published. Cowell was shaken, but more than half convinced. Two years later he read his paper on Shakespeare, and told his astonished fellow-townsmen about the re-markable old vicar and his alarming theories. The Ipswich philosophers were apparently "thrown into confusion". Perhaps Wilmot heard about their reaction; at all events, he left instructions in his will that all his Shakespeare papers should be burnt, and this was duly carried out. And Cowell's lecture lay undiscovered until more than a century later, when an eminent Shakespearian scholar described Wilmot in *The Times Literary Supplement* as "The first Baconian".* Professor Allardyce Nicoll did not intend it as a compliment, for he regarded the proponents of the Baconian theory of Shakespeare's authorship as cranks.

And why should anyone reach such an apparently eccentric conclu-sion? Why should the gentleman of Stratford-upon-Avon not be the author of *Hamlet* and *Lear*, just as most people assumed he was? In fact the notion is not quite as absurd as it sounds. The most baffling thing about Shakespeare is the lack of actual connection between the "gentle-man of Stratford" and the author of the plays. Shakespeare went to London in his twenties; within a few years he was a successful actor and playwright, and by the time he reached his mid-thirties (in 1601) he was one of the most popular writers of the time. The author of *Coriolanus* and *The Tempest* must have known he possessed genius – he says as much in sonnet 55, beginning:

> Not marble, nor the gilded monuments
> Of princes, shall outlive this powerful rime.

And when he returned to Stratford in his mid-forties he had become a wealthy man through the use of his talents. Is it conceivable that he did not even bother to take a single printed copy of any of his works with him – there were many extant – and that he even left behind in London

* 25 February 1932.

the library he must have accumulated over the years? Of course, he may have done so – but in that case, what happened to them? Why are they not mentioned in his will?

Shakespeare scholars reply that in Elizabethan times acting was not regarded as a particularly respectable profession – hardly more so than pimping – and that Shakespeare may have preferred to keep it to himself. This is true. But writers, then as now, were regarded as a cut above most other professions, and Shakespeare was also the author of the sonnets, *The Rape of Lucrece* and *Venus and Adonis*. The sonnets appeared in 1609, two years before he retired to Stratford – surely he would have taken a few copies with him to distribute to his friends and family? Surely he would have made sure that copies of his works went to his beloved daughter Susanna to whom he left most of his estate in the will, and to her husband, the distinguished physician Dr John Hall, who was later to refuse a knighthood from Charles I? Again, the scholars reply that he may well have done so, and that Shakespeare's books simply vanished over the next fifty years or so – by which time admirers were beginning to show an interest in the playwright. It could be true, but it sounds somehow unlikely.

The Rev. Wilmot had another reason for doubting that the gentleman of Stratford wrote the plays. They seem to reveal a man of wide learning and experience: a knowledge of medicine, law, botany and foreign countries, as well as of court life. Where would a butcher's son from Stratford have the opportunity of gaining such knowledge? Francis Bacon, on the other hand – philosopher, essayist and Lord Chancellor – was known as one of the most erudite men of his time. . . .

For Wilmot one of the main problems was that Shakespeare's reputation had increased so much since his death that it was difficult to sort out the truth from the later legends. Until 1660 – when the theatres opened again after the Puritan interregnum – he remained half forgotten (although his collected plays had appeared in 1623). There was a Shakespeare revival during the Restoration, but his plays were "adapted" and almost totally rewritten. John Aubrey's *Brief Lives* (1682) has an extremely "brief" life of Shakespeare – a mere two pages – in which he says that Shakespeare was a butcher's son, and that he would make dramatic speeches when he had to kill a calf. By that time the Stratford vicar John Ward had noted in his diaries (1661–3) the legend about Shakespeare dying after a drinking bout with Jonson and Drayton. By 1670 Shakespeare's reputation with the playgoing public was as high as it had been in 1600, and unscrupulous booksellers were getting rid of all kinds of old plays by declaring they were by Shakespeare. The "Shakespeare boom" was largely the work of Sir William Davenant, who was reputed to be Shakespeare's godson – perhaps his son – and who devoted much of his life to reviving the reputation of his idol. The first *Life* of Shakespeare appeared in 1709, as the introduction to Nicholas Rowe's six-volume edition of Shakespeare; Rowe obtained much of his information from the actor Thomas Betterton, another worshipper of the bard, who had made a pilgrimage to Stratford to collect stories and traditions in about 1708. It was Rowe who first printed the story about how Shakespeare fled from Stratford after being caught poaching the deer of Sir Thomas Lucy. From then on the legends multiplied: stories of carousing in Warwickshire villages – notably "drunken Bidford" – of rhymes about fellow-townsmen, of holding horses' heads outside the theatre when he first came to London, of his love affairs, his appearances before Queen Elizabeth and King James, and dozens more. In 1769 Shakespeare was now regarded with such reverence that the burghers of Stratford decided to hold bicentenary celebrations, and asked the famous actor David Garrick to take charge of the Jubilee. (They were, in fact, five years too late – Shakespeare was born in 1564 – but no one seemed to mind this.) Shakespeare had already become a source of income to the tradesmen of Stratford. Rain spoiled the celebrations, and Garrick lost a small fortune; nevertheless, the Jubilee may be said to have established the "Shakespeare Industry" as Stratford's chief source of income.

But in the same year, 1769, Herbert Lawrence, a friend of Garrick's, published an amusing allegory called *The Life and Adventures of Common Sense* which describes how a plausible rogue and habitual thief named Shakespeare stole some of the attributes of Wisdom, Genius and Humour and used them to write plays. It was not meant to be a serious accusation, but it seemed to demonstrate a mildly satirical attitude to the Shakespeare Industry. Soon after this the Rev. James Wilmot moved to Barton-on-the-Heath and began those researches that led him to conclude that Shakespeare's real name was Francis Bacon. But when the Quaker James Cowell imparted these conclusions to the Ipswich Philosophical Society in 1803 he swore them to silence about the name of their author, and they seem to have kept their word.

The absurd episode of the Ireland forgeries demonstrates the extent to which "Bardolatry" (as Shaw was to call it) had gained a foothold by the 1790s. Samuel Ireland, a prosperous author of travel books, worshipped Shakespeare, and allowed various tradesmen of Stratford to sell him a large number of Shakespeare relics, including a goblet carved from the mulberry tree planted in Shakespeare's garden and the chair on which Shakespeare sat in his courting days. Ireland's youngest son William craved his father's affection, and began forging small Shakespeare items, such as a mortgage deed. His father's greed led him finally to forge whole Shakespeare plays which for a while fooled many experts. The bubble finally burst in 1796, when Ireland's play *Vortigern* was presented at Drury Lane; at the line: "And when this solemn mockery is ended" the audience burst into boos and jeers. When William finally confessed to the forgeries his father flatly refused to believe him, remaining convinced that such "works of genius" were beyond the powers of his untalented son. In the previous century there had been a far more sensible and balanced attitude – Samuel Pepys thought *Twelfth Night* "but a silly play" and *A Midsummer Night's Dream* "the most insipid, ridiculous play that I ever saw in my life". By the mid-nineteenth century, Shakespeare was regarded as a godlike genius whose feeblest lines were regarded as beyond criticism. Matthew Arnold expressed this attitude of mindless worship in a sonnet that began:

> Others abide our question. Thou art free.
> We ask and ask: Thou smilest and art still,
> Out-topping knowledge. For the loftiest hill
> That to the stars uncrowns his majesty . . . etc.

It was probably this kind of uncritical veneration that lay at the root of the various heresies that began to spring up in the mid-nineteenth century. In 1848 the American consul at Vera Cruz, Joseph C. Hart, wrote a book on *The Romance of Yachting* in which he paused to reflect: "Ah, Shakespeare – Immortal Bard – who were you"? And in the next thirty-five pages, Hart digresses from yachting to suggest the theory that the Stratford actor was merely a hack who inserted bawdy lines into plays that had been written by starving poets. In 1857 William Henry Smith published *Bacon and Shakespeare* in which he pointed out that nothing we know about Shakespeare indicates that he could be the author of the plays, while Bacon had all the necessary qualifications.

He had already been anticipated by a brilliant and attractive American lady, Delia Bacon, who had started life as a schoolteacher, then become an author and lecturer. Her special subjects were history and literature, and her study of Shakespeare convinced her – for the reasons we have already discussed – that the retired actor of Stratford was an unlikely author for the plays. She became convinced that the evidence for Bacon's authorship lay in England, probably in the tomb itself. She gained the support of that eminent Bostonian Ralph Waldo Emerson, and of a New York banker who admired Bacon, Charles Butler. She sailed for England in the spring of 1853, armed with an introduction to Carlyle from Emerson. Carlyle took to her at once and gave her support; so did Nathaniel Hawthorne, who was American consul in Liverpool. She spent three years living in lodgings and writing her book to prove that Bacon was Shakespeare. The publishers Chapman and Hall sent her a rejection note declining to have any part in "an attack on one of the most sacred beliefs of the nation and indeed of all nations" – a phrase that expresses the almost religious bigotry that had become typical of the British attitude to Shakespeare. In 1856 she moved to Stratford and charmed the clerk of the church into allowing her to spend some time locked alone in the church; but at the last minute her nerve failed her – or perhaps she was merely demoralized at the thought of trying to rip up the floor of the church and dig down seventeen feet, the reputed depth of the grave.

In 1857, Delia Bacon finally brought out her *Philosophy of the Plays of Shakespeare Unfolded*. (Hawthorne, with whom she had quarrelled, paid for it.) But it proved to be a confused and confusing book – it is not even clear whether her "suspect" is Bacon, Raleigh, Spenser, Sidney or the Earl of Oxford. Her main thesis was obviously absurd – that a group of enlightened scholars concocted the plays, using the Stratford actor as a "front", in order to express convictions that might otherwise have led to imprisonment and torture. Reviewers were understandably scathing. After so many years of effort, Delia was shattered, and her mind gave way soon after. A nephew found her in a lunatic asylum, and took her back to New England, where she died at the age of forty-eight.

Delia Bacon's success was greater than she lived to realize; she had raised the question of Shakespeare's authorship, and now many others took it up, including Emerson, Whitman, Oliver Wendell Holmes and Henry James senior. In England the prime minister, Lord Palmerston, read William Henry Smith's book and became a Baconian.

In 1867 there came to light one of the most interesting and convincing pieces of evidence connecting Bacon and Shakespeare. A librarian commissioned by the Duke of Northumberland to examine manuscripts in Northumberland House came upon a folio volume consisting of twenty-two sheets folded double. It seemed clear that it had belonged to Francis Bacon – at least, it contained mostly copies of works written by him. Nine pieces remained in the folder, and there were probably more. The cover, headed "Mr ffrauncis Bacon", also has the word "Nevill" written twice at the top. Just below this are the words "Ne vele velis", the family motto of Bacon's nephew Sir Henry Nevill. The script

contains two different sets of handwriting, probably those of ama-
nuenses – presumably Bacon's. The cover contains a list which seems
to be a table of contents – since it mentions a number of pieces which are
actually in the folder, such as four essays by Bacon, "Philipp against
monsieur" – a letter from Sir Philip Sidney dissuading the Queen from
marrying the Duke of Anjou, "Speeches for Lord Essex at the tylt" –
speeches by Bacon written for the Earl of Essex, and "Loycester's
Common Wealth" – an incomplete copy of Leicester's Commonwealth.
But the cover also lists items that were no longer in the folio, including
Nashe's banned play *The Isle of Dogs*, and "Richard the Second" and
"Richard the Third". And immediately above these Shakespeare titles:
"By Mr ffrauncis William Shakespeare".

In fact this evidence is less powerful than it looks at first. "Richard
the Second", while not actually banned, was something of a "sensitive"
play, and Shakespeare had been obliged to omit some lines from the first
quarto edition of 1597 (which is also the likeliest date for the Northumberland manuscript). When Essex rebelled in 1601 he paid for a
special performance of *Richard II*, hoping that a play about a king who
was deposed might inspire Londoners to join his insurrection. (It was
unsuccessful, and he was executed.) The "sensitive" lines about deposi-
tion were restored in an edition after Queen Elizabeth's death. *Richard
III* was about the same sensitive subject, and may also have been
regarded as dubious. As a Privy Councillor of the queen, and her legal
adviser, it was Bacon's job to study "sensitive" works – he had also read
a work by Dr Hayward on Richard II which had "much incensed Queen
Elizabeth"; Dr Hayward was committed to the Tower for treason, but
Bacon told the queen the book was harmless.

So we may assume that the Northumberland folder originally contained several "banned" works on which Bacon had been asked to give
an opinion. A closer look at the cover shows that the name "Mr ffrauncis
Bacon" and "Mr ffrauncis" has been doodled several times perhaps by
Bacon himself; Shakespeare's name has also been doodled repeatedly.
But a close examination of the manuscript shows that it is quite untrue
to claim that someone has doodled "Mr ffrauncis William Shakespeare". "ffrauncis" and "William Shakespeare" are on different levels,
and the surname Bacon is written directly below "Mr ffrauncis" (with
the phrase "your sovereign" written upside down between them).
"William Shakespeare" is written directly above the titles of his two
plays and obviously refers to them.

So, regretfully, the Northumberland MS must be abandoned as a
proof that there was a closer connection between Bacon and Shake-

speare than is generally supposed; all it proves is that Bacon had read *Richard II* and *Richard III* in the course of his duties as the queen's adviser.

Thirty-one years after Delia Bacon's book there appeared the most influential of all the works of the "Shakespeare heretics", Ignatius Donnelly's *The Great Cryptogram, Francis Bacon's Cipher in the So-called Shakespeare Plays.* Donnelly was an American congressman, famous for *Atlantis: the Antediluvian World*, which is still regarded as a sourcebook by those who believe in the existence of Plato's sunken continent. But in the vast two-volume work on Bacon he tried to prove that Bacon had hidden ciphers about himself in the plays of Shakespeare, to prove his own authorship. (Bacon was in reality fascinated by ciphers.) After years of studying the plays and trying out every possible key to the cipher he finally began to perceive such obscure messages as: "Seas ill said that More low or Shak'st spur never writ a word of them", meaning, according to Donnelly: "Cecil said that Marlowe or Shakespeare never writ a word of them." The book inspired thousands of cranks to seek for "ciphers" in Shakespeare and other famous authors, and provoked a few wits and satirists to demonstrate that almost any sentence can be rearranged to produce astonishing messages – Ronald Knox wrote a delightful essay proving by this method that Queen Victoria was the real author of *In Memoriam*, describing herself, for example, as "Alf's pen-poet".

Another Baconian who was convinced that Bacon concealed his identity under various ciphers and anagrams was Dr Orville W. Owen of Detroit, who finally extracted a long message in blank verse from the plays, and found that it ordered him to cut up all the works of Bacon and Shakespeare into separate pages and stick them around the outside of a wheel. Owen used two wheels, and a thousand-foot strip of canvas that passed around them, with the pages stuck on to it. By incredibly complex reasoning, he extracted more codes from this dismembered text, and used it to extract the information that Bacon was really the son of Queen Elizabeth and her lover the Earl of Leicester; *Hamlet* was written as a personal attack on his mother, who retaliated by sending Bacon to exile in France. . . . The cipher also revealed that the Queen had finally been strangled by her chief minister Robert Cecil. The deciphered material also informed Owen that Bacon had concealed vital manuscripts proving his authorship in various boxes hidden near a castle at the confluence of the rivers Severn and Wye. Owen and a band of faithful followers spent fifteen years searching the countryside in the region of Chepstow (where there is a ruined castle). They dug dozens of holes and tunnels around the castle, and even under the river Wye, but eventually had to admit defeat. Another party hired boatmen to take them up and down the river, looking for hidden flights of steps that might lead to secret chambers. To the armchair student of human eccentricity, it all sounds marvellously funny; but the people who wasted their fortunes and their lives on this wild-goose chase must have felt that it was closer to tragedy.

In fact, anyone who takes the trouble to read a biography of Francis Bacon will see why it is impossible that he could have written Shakespeare's plays. Their characters are utterly different. The author of *A Midsummer Night's Dream* and *Twelfth Night* is obviously a kindly and good-natured human being; it is easy to understand why his friends referred to him as "gentle Shakespeare". No one would have called Bacon gentle. He was a man of immense intelligence who was permanently dissatisfied with himself and with his lot in life. He was driven by the most superficial kind of ambition: "political power is what I want, power over men and affairs". He was a calculating, rather heartless man who believed that successful men should learn how to "work" their friends by discovering their weaknesses. His father died before he had time to make provision for him in his will, and Bacon found himself practically penniless at the age of nineteen. His uncle Lord Burghley (William Cecil) was Lord Treasurer, and could easily have procured his nephew advancement; but he preferred to help his son Robert. Bacon became a lawyer. Then he decided to pay court to the Queen's favourite, the accomplished and dashing Earl of Essex; with charm and flattery he had soon gained the earl's friendship. Essex frequently gave him money – Bacon was a spendthrift – and tried hard to persuade the Queen to grant him various offices. When she passed over Bacon in favour of another candidate for Master of the Rolls, Essex soothed his protégé's disappointment by presenting him with a large estate. In 1596 Essex captured Cadiz, and became one of the most popular men in England. But – to Bacon's alarm – he began to overreach himself. After an unsuccessful expedition against the Irish, Essex was politically ruined. He tried to foment a rebellion, and was arrested and put on trial. Everyone recognized that he was guilty of hot temper rather than a desire to overthrow the Queen, and it seemed likely that his punishment would not be heavy. At this point Bacon betrayed his friend; he delivered a brilliant speech in which he accused Essex of treason, and declared that, "as a friend", he knew Essex meant to seize the throne. Essex was sentenced to death and executed.

It is impossible to exonerate Bacon. He did it to gain favour with the

Queen and further his own career; in return for sending Essex to his death he received twelve hundred pounds. But not the advancement he hoped for. Elizabeth distrusted him.

When Elizabeth died Bacon set out to flatter James I, and succeeded. He was knighted, and became Attorney-General in 1613. Five years later he finally reached the climax of his ambition, was ennobled and became Lord Chancellor. Three years later he was impeached for accepting bribes; he admitted his guilt and was banned from office and fined £40,000. He devoted the last five years of his life to writing.

Bacon is a baffling character, a strange mixture of greatness and pettiness. He was the most intelligent man of his time, and in some ways one of the nastiest. It would be difficult to conceive a character more totally unlike Shakespeare's. The dramatist had genius; yet in a sense was not particularly intelligent. He wrote as naturally as a bird sings. The pessimism in which he frequently indulges is the pessimism of a child who has just lost a favourite toy, not the gloomy cynicism of the brilliant intellectual who despises his own craving for success. It is as impossible that Bacon could have written Shakespeare as that Schopenhauer could have written *Alice in Wonderland*.

Bacon was only the first of many candidates. In 1891 an archivist named James Greenstreet wrote a series of articles in *The Genealogist* suggesting that Shakespeare was the Earl of Derby, William Stanley. In 1599 a Jesuit spy had told a correspondent on the continent that the earl was not available to take part in a plot against the Queen because he was "busy in penning comedies for the common players". Greenstreet died soon after publishing the articles, but the theory was revived fifteen years later by an American, Robert Frazer, in a book called *The Silent Shakespeare*. A later exponent of the theory, Professor Abel Lefranc, wrote four large volumes whose purpose was to prove that Shakespeare was thoroughly familiar with France and the French. He also pointed out that the plot of *Measure for Measure* was based on a real-life story from Paris in which there was a distinct similarity between the names of the characters and Shakespeare's inventions.

The dramatist Christopher Marlowe was another candidate, advanced in 1895 in a novel called *It Was Marlowe* by a San Francisco attorney, William G. Ziegler. It was not taken seriously, but the theory was revived in 1955 by an American scholar, Calvin Hoffman, in *The Murder of the Man Who Was Shakespeare*. Marlowe became famous with his first play, *Tamburlaine*, in 1587, when he was only twenty-three, and he probably collabourated with Shakespeare on Henry VI. In 1593 he was murdered in a quarrel about how much he owed towards a bill in a tavern; his murderer was acquitted. At the time of his murder Marlowe was in serious trouble; his fellow-playwright Thomas Kyd had been charged with atheism, and alleged that the papers found in his room actually belonged to Marlowe. Kyd was tortured but released, and seems to have died not long after. Marlowe had a powerful protector, Sir Thomas Walsingham, the cousin of the queen's spy-master Sir Francis Walsingham. At the time of his death he was due to stand trial, and might well have been executed. Hoffman's theory is that Marlowe was spirited away to Europe, and that another man was killed in his place and buried in his grave. And Marlowe went on to write the plays of Shakespeare. Hoffman's chief argument is that an analytical method invented by Dr Thomas Corwin Meadenhall – it involves noting the average length (in letters) of an author's words – demonstrated that Bacon could not have written Shakespeare, but that Marlowe *could*.

But once again a reading of the works of the two men reveals that they were quite different in character. One of the most basic differences was that Marlowe was homosexual, and Shakespeare was clearly not. The Shakespeare scholar Dr A.L. Rowse has pointed out that one major difference between the work of Marlowe and that of Shakespeare is that Shakespeare is fond of bawdy jokes and sexual *double entendres*, while Marlowe's work shows the prudery that is often characteristic of homosexuals – the distaste for crude smut. This observation leaves Calvin Hoffman's case with very little support.

Around 1914 an elementary schoolmaster named John Thomas Looney (an unfortunate name, but pronounced Loney) became convinced that the Stratford actor could not have written the plays, and began a systematic search for an Elizabethan who possessed the right qualifications. He deduced the character of the author from his work, then made a list of the basic requirements of such a person: he ended with a list of seventeen. By 1920 he had decided that only one man fitted the picture: Edward de Vere, the seventeenth Earl of Oxford. His book *Shakespeare Identified* is generally agreed to be as absorbing as a detective story, but his "unfortunate name" prevented it being taken seriously by the general public. (Other writers on the Shakespeare problem included S.E. Silliman, who supported Marlowe's case, and George Battey, who believed Shakespeare was Daniel Defoe.) But although his book was soon forgotten, the theory was taken up by another American scholar, Charlton Ogburn, whose huge tome *The Mysterious William Shakespeare* (1984) is, in spite of its size, immensely readable. But although Ogburn argues convincingly that Oxford was a fine lyric poet who might well have written "Hark, hark the lark" and

"Full fathom five", he has an almost impossible task convincing the reader that late plays like *A Winter's Tale, Lear* and *The Tempest* were written before 1604, the year Oxford died. Looney overcame that problem by suggesting that these plays were written by other people – Raleigh being the author of *The Tempest* and Fletcher of *Henry VIII*; Ogburn argues vigorously that they were all written much earlier than supposed; but his arguments will leave most people as unconvinced as Looney's did.

One of the minor problems of Shakespeare scholarship is the identity of the lady called Anne Whateley, to whom, according to an entry in the Bishop of Worcester's register, Shakespeare was due to be married in November 1582; a licence was issued to William Shakespeare just before his marriage to Anne Hathaway. "Whateley" could have been a slip of the pen on the part of the clerk, but surely he would not have written "of Temple Grafton" when he should have written "Shottery"? Says Sir Sidney Lee: "He was doubtless another of the numerous William Shakespeare's who abounded in the diocese of Worcester". This view is disputed by William Ross, a Scottish architect, who became convinced that Anne was the true author of Shakespeare's plays. In *The Story of Anne Whateley and William Shaxpere* (1939), Ross tells a touching story of how in 1581 the seventeen-year-old Shakespeare, employed in his father's business, called at a nunnery in Temple Grafton, near Stratford, and became acquainted with a nun called Anne Whateley, who fell in love with him. She began to write sonnets to him, the first of which began "From fairest creatures we desire increase". But after she had given him thirty-two sonnets, the youth confessed that he was having a love affair with an older woman, Anne Hathaway, and in sonnet 33 she becomes the "basest cloud" that hides the face of the sun. When Anne Hathaway became pregnant Shakespeare experienced revulsion, and persuaded Anne Whateley to marry him; but the Hathaway family stepped in and took legal steps to force "Shaxpere" to marry Anne Hathaway. Anne is of course the "dark Lady", for whom Anne Whateley began to experience a tormented, ambivalent kind of love. In fact, according to Ross, Anne Whateley eventually wrote about Shakespeare's desertion – to London – from Anne Hathaway's point of view, the result being *A Lover's Complaint*, a triumph of identification of one woman with another.

But how did a girl who had spent most of her life in a nunnery become such an excellent craftsman? The answer, according to Ross, is that she was also the collabourator of one of the major poets of the age, Edmund Spenser. Spenser met Anne Whateley about 1576, when Shakespeare was only twelve, and fell in love with her. Spenser's first major poem, *The Shephearde's Calender*, appeared three years later, and, according to Ross, "the surmise that she collabourated in it is not an improbable one". And she then went on to write Spenser's most celebrated work, *The Faerie Queene*. A few years later she also dashed off Marlowe's *Hero and Leander*. In fact, "a perusal of the plays attributed to Marlowe makes it quite evident that their real author was Anne Whateley. These plays . . . were preliminary efforts, written when she was acquiring proficiency in the technique of the theatre. Her full achievement as a creative artist was reserved for Shakespeare alone." The question of whether she was also responsible for the bawdy passages is not explored, but we may probably assume that these vulgar touches were added by the Stratford actor.

The reader of *Anne Whateley and William Shaxpere* may experience a sudden suspicion that the author is pulling his leg, and that the book is intended as a satire on the whole anti-Shakespeare industry. This would be unfounded. William Ross presented the present writer with a copy in 1963, when he was seventy-three, and it was perfectly clear from his accompanying letter that he was totally sincere, and that since publishing the book in 1939 he had been working assiduously on his theory and accumulating more evidence. And it was also clear that nothing would convince him that the different styles of *The Faerie Queene*, *Hero and Leander* and *King Lear* indicate the presence of three different authors.

This seems to be the major problem with most of the anti-Shakespearians. They examine the problem through a magnifying glass, and cannot see the wood for the trees. And most of them are so lacking in any faculty of literary criticism that they cannot tell a good poem from a bad one. Most of them can be highly convincing for a few pages at a time, but the whole argument is always less than the sum of its parts. Neither Bacon nor Derby nor Oxford nor Marlowe nor even Anne Whateley finally emerge as a more convincing candidate than the Stratford actor.

But what of the Stratford actor? It seems, to put it mildly, unlikely that a man whose father was illiterate and whose children were illiterate, and who could not even be bothered to keep copies of his own books in the house, should have written *Hamlet* and *Othello*. We may reject all the other candidates as absurd; but at the end of the day we still find ourselves facing the same problems that made the Rev. James Wilmot conclude that, whoever wrote the plays and sonnets, it was not William Shakespeare.

52

The Skull of Doom

The Strange Tale of the Crystal Skull

For the past twenty years the weirdest gem in the world has belonged to a lady who keeps it on a velvet cloth on a sideboard in her house. It is a fearsome skull, weighing 11 pounds 7 ounces (5.19 kilograms), carved of pure quartz crystal, and its owner believes it comes from a lost civilization. Its eyes are prisms and it is said, the future appears in them. It has been called the "skull of doom".

That passage from Arthur C. Clarke's television series "Mysterious World" may serve as an introduction to one of the most interesting mysteries of the twentieth century. The skull belonged to an explorer and adventurer named Albert ("Mike") Mitchell-Hedges, born in 1882. On his death in 1959 it passed into the possession of his ward, Anna Mitchell-Hedges, born in 1910, who claimed to have discovered it in a "lost city" in South America – the Mayan city of Lubaantun, in British Honduras. According to her own account: "I did see the skull first – or I saw something shining and called my father – it was his expedition, and we all helped to carefully move the stones. [Lubaantun means 'place of fallen stones'.] I was let pick it up because I had seen it first". It was found, apparently, underneath the altar in the ruins of a Mayan temple. The date she gives – 1924 – conflicts with an earlier account in which she is said to have discovered it on her seventeenth birthday, which would have been three years later. What she found was the upper part of the skull; the jaw, she says, was found three months later under rubble twenty-five feet away.

Mitchell-Hedges, according to Anna, felt that the skull belonged to the local Indians, descendants of the ancient Mayas, and he gave it to them. But when he prepared to leave for England in the rainy season of

1927, the grateful Indians returned it to him as a present for his kindness to them.

The ancient Mayas are themselves something of a mystery. Their earliest history seems to date back to 1500 BC, but their great "classic" period extends roughly from AD 700 to 900. During this period they developed a high level of civilization, with writing, sophisticated mathematics, a calendar, and impressive sculptures. Then, with startling suddenness, Mayan civilization collapsed – no one knows why. Disease and earthquakes have been suggested, yet there is no evidence for either. Neither is there evidence of violence. It seems that the Mayas simply abandoned their cities and melted away into remote places. And their great civilization reverted to a far more primitive level. Their partially deciphered writings offer no clue to the mystery.

Mitchell-Hedges believed that there was a connection between the Mayas and the legendary continent of Atlantis, which is said to have vanished beneath the waves of the Atlantic Ocean in prehistoric times. Another explorer, Colonel Percy Fawcett, believed that he had evidence that survivors from Atlantis had reached South America and that the evidence lay in Brazil. Fawcett vanished without a trace on an expedition to Brazil in 1924. Mitchell-Hedges believed that the survivors had come ashore farther north, in the Yucatán Peninsula of Central America, and one of the objects of his expedition to Honduras was to look for proof of this theory. He never found it, but he *did* find clues to the lost treasures of Sir Henry Morgan, a pirate who had captured Panama (with considerable brutality) in the seventeenth century.

What, in fact, do we know about the "skull of doom"? Remarkably little. It is made from a single block of rock crystal, or clear quartz. Mitchell-Hedges declared that it was probably 3,600 years old, but that would take it back a thousand years before the earliest date suggested for the Mayas. He also suggested that it must have taken 150 years to create, by the grinding and polishing of rock with sand. In *Chariots of the Gods*? Erich von Däniken has (predictably) taken an even bolder line, explaining (mistakenly) that "nowhere on the skull is there a clue showing that a tool known to us was used!" and suggesting that it was created by the "Ancient Astronauts" who (according to von Däniken) built the Great Pyramid. A modern crystal expert, Frank Dorland, has said that he could make a similar skull in three years, but that would be with the aid of modern technology.

Inevitably, the experts are divided on the subject of the skull's origin. Most seem to agree that it was probably carved in Mexico, from rock crystal found in Mexico or Calaveras County, California, and that it could have been manufactured in the past five hundred years. But if that date is correct, then it runs counter to the claim of Mitchell-Hedges that it was found in a Mayan temple that had been abandoned for a thousand years. The Aztecs – the likeliest manufacturers of the skull – founded their capital, Tenochtitlan, around AD 1325.

Regrettably, this is also the view of practically everybody who has looked into the matter. Mike Mitchell-Hedges was undoubtedly a very remarkable man, and Anna's total devotion to him is understandable. When he met her in Toronto in 1917, she was a seven-year-old orphan by the name of Anna Le Guillon and was in the charge of some men who intended to put her into an orphanage. Mitchell-Hedges was touched by her plight and adopted her, a decision, as she later said, that neither of them had reason to regret.

But for all his kindness and erratic brilliance as an explorer, Mitchell-Hedges was not another Captain Scott or Colonel Fawcett; his character was altogether closer to that of the swashbuckling Sir Henry Morgan. He was a man with a keen sense of humor, and he enjoyed telling – and even printing – tongue in cheek tall stories. His life of adventure was inspired by his childhood reading of Rider Haggard stories and Arthur Conan Doyle's *Lost World*, and his own books – with titles like *Land of Wonder and Fear* and *Battles with Giant Fish* – reflect the character of a man who was, in some respects, an overgrown schoolboy. He was not so much a liar as an Elizabethan adventurer born out of his time.

It has been suggested that Mitchell-Hedges brought the crystal skull from London to Lubaantun and "planted" it under the altar for his adopted daughter to find on her seventeenth (or fourteenth) birthday, something of which he would have been perfectly capable.

Yet his autobiography, *Danger My Ally* (1954), suggests that all was not as straightforward as Anna's account suggests. You would expect a man who had made such an important find to describe it in some detail; instead, he dismisses it in a few lines, explaining; "How the skull came into my possession I have reason for not revealing". But why not, if Anna's story about its discovery is accurate? After all, it would reflect credit on his adopted daughter. He also describes at length far less important artifacts he found in Lubaantun. Stranger still, he has removed *all* reference to the skull from the American edition of the book. There can be only one reason for this: he does not want to be caught in a lie but is still not willing to tell the truth.

Anna Mitchell-Hedges stuck firmly to the Lubaantun story. *Daily Express* journalist Donald Seaman has described how he heard it directly from her own lips. In 1962 Seaman, who was writing a book about espionage, came upon a photograph of the recently convicted spy Gordon Lonsdale that showed him posing with two middle-aged women. Careful research revealed that one of the women was Anna Mitchell-Hedges. Curious to know what she was doing with a spy, Seaman contacted her at her home in Reading and went to see her, accompanied by photographer Robert Girling.

Anna Mitchell-Hedges proved to be a stout, formidable-looking woman in her fifties, and when they arrived she was still attired in her dressing gown. The story behind the photograph proved to be innocent enough; it had been taken at a historic castle, where she and her friend had fallen into conversation with the man who later proved to be at the centre of the Portland spy case; a passing commercial photographer had snapped them, extracted payment from Anna Mitchell-Hedges, and later forwarded the photograph to her. She hadn't seen Lonsdale since that time.

Perhaps feeling guilty that she had brought them to Reading on a wild goose chase, she asked them if they would like to see the "skull of doom". Neither had ever heard of it, but they politely said yes. She asked them to follow her and led them to the master bedroom, where she groped around under the bed. Seaman, who was expecting to see an object the size of an egg, was surprised when she brought out something that might have been a large cabbage, wrapped in newspapers. They accompanied her back to the sitting room, where she unwrapped it on the table.

Both Seaman and Girling stared with amazement at the magnificent and bizarre object that lay on the table. The life-size human skull seemed to be made of polished diamond – in the dim light it had a greenish hue, as if lit from the inside or from underneath. Its lower jaw moved like that of a human jaw, adding a gruesome touch of realism. They agreed later that neither had seen anything at once so beautiful and so oddly disquieting. This, Anna Mitchell-Hedges told them, was the "skull of doom", found in a Mayan temple in 1927. It had received its nickname from the local natives, who were convinced that it had magical powers and should be treated with the respect due to a supernatural being. It had become the focus of a number of legends about people who encountered misfortune after showing it insufficient respect.

She went on to tell them that in 1927 her father had been looking for the treasure buried by the pirate Henry Morgan in 1671. They had learned that in the area of the Mayan city of Lubaantun, in British Honduras, natives had names like Hawkins and Morgan. Her father was also convinced that the remains of the lost civilization of Atlantis were in the same area. But the skull was the only ancient artifact he had found.

Now that her father was dead (he died in 1959), Anna wanted to return to Honduras to look for the treasure, and in order to raise the money, she was willing to sell the skull, as well as a drinking mug that had been presented to King Charles II by Nell Gwyn (and that had been authenticated by scholars).

"How much is the skull worth?" asked Seaman.

"Probably about a quarter of a million".

"My God! Aren't you afraid to keep it in the house?"

"I think I could deal with any burglars". Anna Mitchell-Hedges opened her dressing gown, and revealed a Colt 45 revolver strapped to her waist.

There was some talk about the possibility of the *Daily Express* helping to finance the expedition to Lubaantun and allowing Seaman to go along to report on it. To his great regret, the proposal was turned down by the editor. But Donald Seaman has never forgotten that menacingly beautiful object that seemed to glow with its own light.

But, as we have seen, the Lubaantun story remains dubious. Norman Hammond, an archaeologist who also excavated Lubaantun, failed to mention the crystal skull in his book on Lubaantun, and he explained to Joe Nickell, a skeptical investigator (who figures in the introduction to this book) that this was because the crystal skull had nothing to do with the site. "Rock crystal is not found naturally in the Maya area" he writes and goes on to mention that the nearest places where it has been found are Oaxaca, in southern Mexico, and the Valley of Mexico, where some other small crystal skulls – of Aztec manufacture – have been found. He adds that as far as the documentary evidence shows, Anna Mitchell-Hedges was never in Lubaantun. This seems to be verified by others on the expedition. (Hammond is also on record as saying, "I have always thought that it is most likely a *memento mori* [something designed to remind us that we must all die] of sixteenth- to eighteenth-century origin. While a Renaissance origin is not improbable, given the sheer size of the rock crystal block involved, manufacture in Quing-dynasty China for a European client cannot be ruled out".)

When we learn that Mitchell-Hedges himself was caught in a lie – his assertion that he served with the Mexican revolutionary Pancho Villa and fought at the Battle of Laredo – and that he lost a libel suit against the *Daily Express*, which claimed in 1928 that he had staged a fake robbery for the sake of publicity, it begins to look as if the whole crystal skull story must be dismissed as pure invention. In fact, the first reference to the skull occurs in a journal entitled "Man – A Monthly Record of Anthropological Science" in 1936, in which two experts compare the skull with another in the British Museum and refer to the former as "the Burney skull".

The Burney referred to is Sydney Burney, an art dealer, and Sotheby's records show that he put the skull up for auction in late 1943; but since no one bid more than £340 for it, Burney decided to keep it. It was then, apparently, sold to Mitchell-Hedges in 1944 for £400.

When Nickell asked Anna Mitchell-Hedges about this story, he was told that Mitchell-Hedges had left the skull with Burney as security for a loan to finance an expedition and that Burney had no right to offer it for sale. But there is not a scrap of evidence to prove that the skull was in the possession of Mitchell-Hedges before 1944. Moreover, a letter from Sydney Burney, dated 21 March 1933 to someone at the American Museum of Natural History declares that before he (Burney) became its owner, the skull had been in the possession of the collector from whom Burney bought it, and before that, in the collection of an Englishman.

So it would seem almost certain that Mitchell-Hedges invented his story of finding the skull in a Mayan temple and that his daughter has continued to support this false version out of an understandable sense of gratitude and loyalty to her adopted father. Presumably this also applies to Mitchell-Hedges's claim that the skull had been used to "will someone to death" (Anna Mitchell-Hedges explained that this should be regarded as an expression of his sense of humor) and to various other claims about the skull's supernatural powers – like the newspaper report of a cameraman who fled in terror from the darkroom when his enlarging bulb exploded as he was trying to enlarge a photograph of the skull.

It all sounds rather disappointing – particularly when we learn that traces of "mechanical grinding" have been found on the teeth. The consensus seems to be that the "mystery" surrounding the "skull of doom" is a hoax.

Yet such a view would be premature. To begin with, the other – and far less "perfect" – crystal skull, which is in possession of the British Museum (and sits at the top of the stairs in the Museum of Man, near Piccadilly Circus in London), is generally accepted as genuine, and it also shows traces of mechanical grinding. The Mexican Indians used a grinding wheel driven by a string stretched across a bow. It seems relatively certain that both skulls originated in Mexico. The Museum of Man skull was bought at Tiffany's, the New York jeweler, in 1898 and cost £120.

In 1963 Anna Mitchell-Hedges allowed the aforementioned scholar and crystal expert, Frank Dorland, to borrow the skull and take it to California for tests; he studied it for seven years. One of his most important conclusions was that the skull could well be as old as twelve thousand years, although more recent work has undoubtedly been done on it. Dorland sent the skull to the labouratory of the Hewlett-Packard Electronics company, which manufactures crystal oscillators. They suggested that the skull had taken a very long time to manufacture – perhaps three hundred years (twice as long as Mitchell-Hedges's estimate.) If this is correct, then it seems probably – almost certain – that it was a religious object, created on the orders of priests and kept in a temple. In that case, its purpose would be connected with divination. It would be kept on an altar – probably covered up (like the crystal balls of clairvoyants) – and exposed for certain ceremonies, probably lit from underneath.

Dorland also reported that he was told by friends of Mitchell-Hedges that the skull was brought back from the Holy Land by the Knights Templars during the Crusades and that it was kept in their Inner Sanctum in London until it finally found its way on to the antiques market.

This is in many ways more plausible than the Mayan temple story. The Templars, founded in 1118 by Hugh de Payens of Champagne, was a religious order whose members swore to devote their lives to the defense of the Holy Land and its Christian pilgrims. Their success was extraordinary and their wealth became legendary. This led to their downfall, for their money was coveted by King Philip IV of France, who organized a mass arrest of Templars on 13 October 1307. They were accused of black magic, of blasphemy, of renouncing Christ, and of sexual perversions. One of the major accusations was that they worshiped the demon Baphomet in the form of a stuffed head *or a human skull* and that the cords they wore around their robes were hallowed by being wrapped around this skull.

Some of the lesser accusations against the Templars are acknowledged to be true by scholars, among them the belief that they practiced ritual magic. Hundreds of Templars were executed; yet the king never succeeded in laying his hands on their fabled "treasures". Nothing seems less likely than that the "skull" worshiped by the Templars was an ordinary human skull, and the Mitchell-Hedges skull would certainly be a perfect candidate for the mysterious talisman.

And what of its "mystical" properties? Anna Mitchell-Hedges declared that Adrian Conan Doyle, son of Arthur, was unable to bear the skull and disliked even being in the same room with it. She said he could tell when it was around, even when it was not visible. Such assertions as these are usually dismissed as typical attempts at legend building. But Frank Dorland himself concluded, after seven years of contact with the skull, that it had mystical properties. He described hearing sounds of "high-pitched silver bells, very quiet but very noticeable" and sounds like an "a capella choir". And staring into the skull, he saw images of "other skulls, high mountains, fingers and faces". He stated that the first night he kept the skull in his house, he heard the sound of prowling jungle cats.

This, of course, could be pure autosuggestion. But what happened after a visit from "satanist" Anton LaVey could not be dismissed in this way. LaVey called on Dorland with the editor of an Oakland newspaper; he claimed that the skull was created by Satan and was thus the property of his church. (LaVey has a keen sense of humor as well as of publicity.) LaVey ended by playing at some length on Dorland's organ, so that when he left, it was too late to return the skull to the safe deposit box where it was kept. That night, once again, there were many strange sounds that kept Dorland and his wife awake. But when they got up to investigate, they found nothing. The next morning they found that many of their belongings had been displaced, and a crystal rod used as a telephone dialer had leapt thirty-five feet to the front door.

Dorland's theory is not that the skull itself possesses a "spirit" (or poltergeist) but that it had absorbed something from LaVey's presence – that perhaps La Vey's "vibes" and those of the skull conflicted, producing physical effects. This theory is not as farfetched as it sounds. Clairvoyants use crystals because they claim they can absorb living energies; they keep them covered with black velvet because these energies escape when exposed to daylight. Since the time of the oldest known magical beliefs, crystals have been held in special esteem because of their powers.

Oddly enough, there is now some kind of scientific backing for this notion. For a decade or more the biologist Rupert Sheldrake has been arguing that learning among human beings and animals is "transmitted" by a process that he calls *morphic resonance*. The most famous story illustrating this process is of the monkeys on Kojima Island, off the coast of Japan, that learned to wash their potatoes in the sea because the salt improved the taste; subsequently, asserts zoologist Lyall Watson (in *Lifetide*), monkeys on other islands, with no connection with the original group, began doing the same thing. Morphic resonance might thus be regarded as a kind of telepathy, and Sheldrake believes that it plays an active part in evolution.

The strange thing is that this phenomenon applies not only to living creatures but to crystals as well. Some new chemicals are extremely difficult to crystallize in the labouratory. But once they have been crystallized anywhere in the world, the process suddenly becomes faster in all labouratories. At first it was suspected that this was because scientists were carrying traces of the crystal in their hair or clothes when they visited other labouratories; but this theory had to be discounted. It seems that crystals, like living creatures, can "learn" by morphic resonance. So the notion that they can absorb living energies and radiate them again is less outlandish than it seems.

It seems probable that we shall never know the truth about the "skull of doom", but its resemblance to the British Museum skull suggests that it was probably of Aztec manufacture. What we know of the Aztecs – and their religion of human sacrifice – suggests that it was created as some kind of religious object, possibly used for scrying (short for *descrying*) – that is, for purposes of divination, as a modern clairvoyant uses a crystal ball. But for whatever purpose it was created, most of those who have seen it seem to agree that it is one of the most beautiful man-made objects in the world.

53

Spontaneous Human Combustion

On the evening of Sunday 1 July 1951 Mrs Mary Reeser, aged seventy-seven, seemed slightly depressed as she sat in her overstuffed armchair and smoked a cigarette. At about 9 pm her landlady, Mrs Pansy Carpenter, called in to say goodnight. Mrs Reeser showed no disposition to go to bed yet; it was a hot evening in St Petersburg, Florida.

At five the next morning, Mrs Carpenter awoke to a smell of smoke; assuming it was a water pump that had been overheating, she went to the garage and turned it off. She was awakened again at eight by a telegraph boy with a telegram for Mrs Reeser; Mrs Carpenter signed for it and took it up to Mrs Reeser's room. To her surprise, the doorknob was hot. She shouted for help, and two decorators working across the street came in. One of them placed a cloth over the doorknob and turned it; a blast of hot air met him as the door opened. Yet the place seemed empty, and at first they could see no sign of fire. Then they noticed a blackened circle on the carpet where the armchair had stood. Only a few springs now remained. In the midst of them there was a human skull, "charred to the size of a baseball", and a fragment of liver attached to a backbone. There was also a foot encased in a satin slipper; it had been burnt down to the ankle.

Mrs Reeser was a victim of a baffling phenomenon called spontaneous human combustion; there are hundreds of recorded cases. Yet in their standard textbook *Forensic Medicine*, Drs S. A. Smith and F. S. Fiddes assert flatly: "Spontaneous combustion of the human body cannot occur, and no good purpose can be served by discussing it". This is a typical example of the kind of wishful thinking in which scientists are prone to indulge when they confront a fact that falls outside the range of their experience. In the same way the great chemist Lavoisier denied the possibility of meteorites.

The example of Mrs Reeser is worth citing because it is mentioned by

Professor John Taylor in his book *Science and the Supernatural*, a book whose chief purpose is to debunk the whole idea of the "paranormal", which, according to Professor Taylor, tends to "crumble to nothing" as it is scientifically appraised. Yet he then proceeds to admit that there are instances that seem "reasonably well validated", and proceeds to cite the case of Mrs Reeser.

Twenty-nine years later, in October 1980, a case of spontaneous combustion was observed at close quarters when a naval airwoman named Jeanna Winchester was driving with a friend, Leslie Scott, along Seaboard Avenue in Jacksonville, Florida. Suddenly, Jeanna Winchester burst into yellow flames, and screamed, "Get me out of here". Her companion tried to beat out the flames with her hands, and the car ran into a telegraph pole. When Jeanna Winchester was examined it was found that 20 per cent of her body was covered with burns. But Jeanna Winchester survived.

Michael Harrison's book on spontaneous combustion, *Fire From Heaven* (1976), cites dozens of cases; they make it clear that the chief mystery of spontaneous combustion is that it seldom spreads beyond the person concerned. On Whit Monday 1725, in Rheims, Nicole Millet, the wife of the landlord of the Lion d'Or, was found burnt to death in an *unburnt* armchair, and her husband was accused of her murder. But a young surgeon, Claude-Nicholas Le Cat, succeeded in persuading the court that spontaneous human combustion *does* occur, and Millet was acquitted – the verdict was that his wife had died "by a visitation of God". The case inspired a Frenchman called Jonas Dupont to gather together all the evidence he could find for spontaneous combustion, which he published in a book *De Incendiis Corporis Humani Spontaneis*, printed in Leyden in 1763.

Another famous case of this period was that of Countess Cornelia di Bandi, of Cesena, aged sixty-two, who was found on the floor of her bedroom by her maid. Her stockinged legs were untouched, and between them lay her head, half burnt. The rest of the body was reduced to ashes, and the air was full of floating soot. The bed was undamaged and the sheets had been thrown back, as if she had got out – perhaps to open a window – and then been quickly consumed as she stood upright, so the head had fallen between the legs. Unlike the wife of innkeeper Millet, the countess had not been a heavy drinker. (One of the most popular theories of spontaneous combustion at this period was that it was due to large quantities of alcohol in the body.)

Two nineteenth-century novelists used spontaneous combustion to dispose of unwanted characters. Captain Marryat borrowed details from a *Times* report of 1832 to describe the death of the mother of his hero Jacob Faithful (in the novel of the same name), who is reduced to "a sort of unctuous pitchy cinder" in her bed. Twenty years later, in 1852, Dickens put an end to his drunken rag-and-bone dealer Krook in *Bleak House* by means of spontaneous combustion – Krook is charred to a cinder that looks like a burnt log. G.H. Lewes, George Eliot's lover, took issue with Dickens and declared that spontaneous combustion was impossible, so in his preface to *Bleak House* Dickens contradicts Lewes and cites thirty examples from press reports. Yet at the end of his article on Krook in *The Dickens Encyclopedia* (1924), Arthur L. Hayward states dogmatically: "The possibility of spontaneous combustion in human beings has been finally disproved". He fails to explain what experiments have "finally disproved" it.

Harrison's book, which gathers together the result of many studies, leaves no possible doubt of the reality of spontaneous combustion. But what causes it? At present it must be confessed that the phenomenon baffles medical knowledge. But Harrison offers some interesting clues. He speaks of the researches of an American doctor, Mayne R. Coe junior, who was interested in the subject of telekinesis – mind over matter. Coe was able to move aluminium strips pivoted on the points of needles by moving his hand over them – this was obviously due to some natural physical "magnetism". He began various yoga exercises in an attempt to develop his bioelectricity; sitting one day in an easy-chair, he felt a powerful current passing downward from his head throughout his body; he thought it was of high voltage but low amperage. He suspended a cardboard box from the ceiling on a length of string, and found that he could cause it to move from a distance – when the room was dry, from as much as eight feet. He then charged his body with 35,000 volts DC, using an electric current, and found that he could move the box in exactly the same way. This seemed to prove that he was in fact generating a high voltage current with his mental exercises. He also went up in an aeroplane to an altitude of 21,000 feet, where the air was extremely dry, and produced electric sparks after he had charged his body to 35,000 volts. Coe theorized that this could explain the phenomenon of levitation – when the yogi's body floats off the ground – with the positively charged human body repelling the negatively charged earth.

Harrison also cites cases of human "batteries" and magnets people (usually children) who have developed a powerful electric charge. In 1877 Caroline Clare of London, Ontario, turned into a human magnet, who attracted metal objects and could give a powerful electric shock to as many as twenty people holding hands. She was suffering from adolescent depressions at the time. Frank McKinistry of Joplin, Missouri, developed a magnetic force which caused his feet to stick to the earth. In 1895 fourteen-year-old Jennie Morgan of Sedalia, Missouri, generated a charge sufficient to knock a grown man on his back, and when she touched a pump handle sparks flew from her fingertips. It is also worth noting that many teenagers who became the focus of "poltergeist effects" (see chapter 41) developed magnetic or electrical properties; in 1846 a French girl named Angélique Cottin became a kind of human electric battery; objects that touched her flew off violently, and a heavy oak loom began to dance when she came near it. On the other hand, Esther Cox, the "focus" of the disturbances at Great Amherst in Nova Scotia, developed a magnetism that made cutlery fly to her and stick fast. It seems that there must be two kinds of charges, positive and negative.

According to Dr Coe, each human muscle cell is a battery, and a cubic inch could develop 400,000 volts. (The inventor Nicola Tesla used to demonstrate that the human body can take immense electrical charges – enough to light up neon tubes – provided the amperage is kept very low.)

But this seems unlikely to explain spontaneous combustion: the whole point of Tesla's experiments was that he did *not* burst into flame. It is high amperage that can cause "burn-ups". (If two 12-volt car batteries are connected by thin wire, the wire will melt; even thick wire becomes hot.) And this could begin to explain why the surroundings of victims of spontaneous combustion are undamaged; they are non-conductors.

Victims of spontaneous combustion tend to be the old and the young. On 27 August 1938, the 22-year-old Phyllis Newcombe was dancing vigorously in Chelmsford, Essex, when her body glowed with a blue light which turned into flames; she died within minutes. In October of the same year a girl called Maybelle Andrews was dancing in a Soho nightclub with her boy-friend, Billy Clifford, when flames erupted from her back, chest and shoulders. Her boy-friend, who was badly burned trying to put her out, said that there were no flames in the room – the flames seemed to come from the girl herself. She died on the way to hospital. In such cases it seems just conceivable that the activity of dancing built up some kind of static electricity. Michael Harrison even points out that "ritual dancing" is used by primitive tribes to build up emotional tension in religious ceremonies, and suggests that this is what has happened here.

Michael Harrison also points out some curious geographical links. On 13 March 1966 three men were "spontaneously combusted" at the same time. John Greeley, helmsman of the SS Ulrich, was burnt to a cinder some miles west of Land's End; George Turner, a lorry-driver, was found burnt at the wheel of his lorry at Upton-by-Chester – the lorry overturned in a ditch; in Nijmegen, Holland, eighteen-year-old Willem ten Bruik died at the wheel of his car. As usual in such cases, the surroundings of all three were undamaged. Harrison points out that the three men were at the points of an equilateral triangle whose sides were 340 miles long. Is it conceivable that the earth itself discharged energy in a triangular pattern?

Another investigator, Larry Arnold, put forward his own theory in the magazine *Frontiers of Science* (January 1982): that so-called "ley lines" – lines of "earth force" may be involved. The man who "discovered" ley lines, Alfred Watkins, noted how frequently places called "Brent" occur on them (brent being an old English form of "burnt"). Other "ley-hunters" have suggested that megalithic stone circles are placed at crucial points on ley lines – often at crossing-points of several leys. It is again interesting to note how many stone circles are associated with the idea of dancing – for example, the Merry Maidens in Cornwall; Stonehenge itself was known as "the Giants' Dance". It has been suggested that ritual dances occurred at these sites, so that the dancers would somehow interact with the earth energy (or "telluric force").

Larry Arnold drew a dozen or so major leys on a map of England, then set out to find if they were associated with mystery fires. He claims that one 400-mile-long "fire-leyne" (as he calls them) passed through five towns where ten mysterious blazes had concurred. He also notes several cases of spontaneous combustion occurring on this "leyne". He cites four cases which occurred on it between 1852 and 1908.

Harrison believes that spontaneous combustion is basically a "mental freak", where the mind somehow influences the body to build up immense charges. The answer could lie in either of the two theories, or in a combination of the two.

54

Synchronicity
or "Mere Coincidence"?

The *Sunday Times* journalist Godfrey Smith was thinking of writing something about the "saga of lost manuscripts" – Carlyle's manuscript of *The French Revolution,* burnt by a careless maid, T.E. Lawrence's *Seven Pillars of Wisdom,* left in a taxi, Hemingway's suitcase full of early manuscripts, stolen from a train – and decided to call on the literary agent Hilary Rubinstein, a treasure-house of similar stories. But before he could introduce the subject into the conversation a girl sitting with them – the wife of the novelist Nicholas Mosley – mentioned that her husband was upset because he had just had the first 150 pages of his new novel stolen from his car. Smith remarked in his *Sunday Times* column: "We are back in what J. W. Dunne called serial time, and Arthur Koestler called synchronicity, and some of us still call coincidence . . ."

It was Jung in fact who coined the word "synchronicity" for meaningful coincidence. But Arthur Koestler was equally intrigued by the subject, and discussed it in a book called *The Roots of Coincidence* in 1972. In the following year he wrote an article about coincidence in *The Sunday Times* and appealed to readers for examples. Many of these were utilized in his book *The Challenge of Chance* (1973), co-authored by Sir Alister Hardy and Robert Harvie. He begins with a section called "The Library Angel", describing coincidences involved with books. In 1972 Koestler had been asked to write about the chess championship between Boris Spassky and Bobbie Fischer, so he went to the London Library to look up books on chess and books on Iceland. He decided to start with chess and the first book that caught his eye was entitled *Chess in Iceland* by Williard Fiske.

He then tells of how Dame Rebecca West was trying to check up on an episode related by one of the accused in one of the Nuremberg war-crimes trials, and how she discovered to her annoyance that the trials are published in the form of abstracts under arbitrary headings and are therefore useless to a researcher. After an hour of fruitless searching she approached a librarian and said: "I can't find it . . .", and casually took a volume off the shelf and opened it. It opened at the page she had been searching for.

This anecdote is particularly interesting because it involved an apparently "random" action, a casual reaching out without logical purpose. The word "synchronicity" was coined by Jung in connection with the *I Ching*, the Chinese *Book of Changes*, which the Chinese consult as an "oracle". The method of "consulting" the *I Ching* consists of throwing down three coins at random half a dozen times and noting whether there are more heads or tails. Two or three tails gives a line with a break in the middle, thus three heads gives an unbroken line. The six lines, placed on top of one another, form a "hexagram":

The above hexagram is number 58, "The Joyous – Lake", with a "Judgement:": "The Joyous, Success – Perseverance is favourable". But from the logical point of view it is obviously impossible to explain how throwing down coins at random can provide an answer – even if the question has been very clearly and precisely formulated in the mind before the coins are thrown.

The experience of Rebecca West can provide a glimmering of an answer. She was looking for a particular passage. We may assume that some unconscious faculty of "extra-sensory perception" guided her to the right place before she began to speak to the librarian, and then guided her hand as she casually reached out. But could it also cause the book to open in the right place? This would seem to require something more than "ESP", something for which Horace Walpole coined the word "serendipity", "the faculty of making happy and unexpected discoveries by chance". And what of the "chance" that caused the librarian to be standing in the right place at that moment? We have here such a complex situation that it is difficult to conceive of some purely "passive" faculty – a kind of intuition – capable of accounting for it. Unless we wish to fall back on "coincidence", we have to think in terms of some faculty capable to some extent of "engineering" a situation as well as merely taking advantage of it. And the use of the *I Ching* also seems to presuppose the use of such a faculty in causing the coins to fall in a certain order.

For most of his life Jung was unwilling even to conceive of such a possibility – at least publicly. (He was, in fact, using the *I Ching* as an oracle from the early 1920s.)

In 1944, when he was sixty-eight years old, Jung slipped on an icy road and broke his ankle; this led to a severe heart attack. While hovering between life and death, Jung experienced curious visions, in one of which he was hovering above the earth, out in space, then saw a kind of Hindu temple inside a meteor. "Night after night I floated in a state of purest bliss". He was convinced that if he recovered his doctor would have to die – and in fact the doctor died as Jung started to recover. The result of these strange experiences was that Jung ceased to be concerned about whether his contemporaries regarded him as a mystic rather than a scientist, and he ceased to make a secret of his lifelong interest in "the occult". In 1949 he wrote his influential introduction to Richard Wilhelm's edition of the *I Ching*, in which he speaks about the "acausal connecting principle" called synchronicity; in the following year he wrote his paper *On Synchronicity*, later expanded into a book. Unfortunately, Jung's fundamental premise in both these seminal works is basically nonsensical. Western science, he says, is based on the principle of causality, but modern physics is shaking this principle to its foundations; we now know that natural laws are merely statistical truths, and that therefore we must allow for exceptions. This is, of course, untrue. The philosopher Hume had argued that causality is not a basic law of the universe; a pan of water usually boils when we put it on a fire, but it *might* freeze. Kant later used this argument to demonstrate that the stuff of the universe is basically "mental". We can now see that these arguments were fallacious. It is true that a pan of water might freeze when placed on a fire, if the atmospheric pressure were suddenly increased a thousandfold. But this would not be a defiance of the law of causality, merely a change in some of the basic conditions of the experiment. And by the same argument, we can see that modern physics has not demonstrated that the laws of nature are "statistical", and that once in a billion times they might be "broken". A law of nature cannot be broken except for some very good "legal" reason.

So Jung's talk about an "acausal connecting principle" may be dismissed as verbal mystification, designed to throw dust in the eyes of scientists who would otherwise accuse him of becoming superstitious in his old age. The example Jung gives of synchronicity makes this clear. He tells how, on 1 April 1949, they had fish for lunch, and someone mentioned the custom of making an "April fish" (i.e., April fool) of someone. In the afternoon a patient showed him pictures of fish which she had painted. In the evening he was shown a piece of embroidery with fish-like monsters on it. The next morning another patient told him of a dream of a fish. At this time Jung was studying the fish symbol in history, and before this string of coincidences began had made a note of a Latin quotation about fish. It is, says Jung, very natural to feel that this is a case of "meaningful coincidence" – i.e., that there is an "acausal connection". But if the coincidence is "meaningful", then there must be a causal connection – even if (as Jung is implying) it is not one that would be recognized by science. Jung is in fact suggesting that there is some hidden connection between the mind and nature.

Jung was not the first to consider this possibility. The Austrian biologist Paul Kammerer – who committed suicide after being accused of faking some of his experiments – was fascinated by odd coincidences, and wrote a book, *The Law of Series*, about it. The book contains a hundred samples of coincidence. For example, in 1915 his wife was reading about a character called Mrs Rohan in a novel; on the tram soon after she saw a man who resembled her friend Prince Rohan; that evening Prince Rohan dropped in to see them. In the tram she had heard someone ask the man who looked like Rohan whether he knew the village of Weissenbach on Lake Attersee; when she got off the tram she walked into a delicatessen shop, and the assistant asked her if she knew Weissenbach on Lake Attersee . . .

Kammerer's theory was that events *do* happen in "clusters", which are natural but not "causal". He thought of it as some unknown mathematical law – a "law of seriality". In short, "absurd" coincidences *are* a law of nature. He spent his days carefully noting all kinds of things – the age, sex and dress of people walking past him in a park or sitting on a tram – and observed the typical "clustering".

Jung offers one of the most amusing examples of "clustering" in his book on synchronicity – it was originally told by the scientist Camille Flammarion in his book *The Unknown*. The poet Emile Deschamps was given a piece of plum pudding by a certain M. Fortgibu when he was at boarding-school – the dish was then almost unknown in France, but Fortgibu had just returned from England. Ten years later Deschamps saw plum pudding in the window of a Paris restaurant and went in to ask if he could have some. He was told that unfortunately the pudding had been ordered by someone else – M. Fortgibu, who was sitting there, and who offered to share it. Years later he attended a party at which there was to be plum pudding, and he told the story about M. Fortgibu. As they sat eating plum pudding the door opened and a servant announced "Monsieur Fortgibu". In walked Fortgibu, who had been invited to another apartment in the same building, and had mistaken the door.

This seems to be a good example of Kammerer's seriality; if there is any "meaning" in the coincidence, it is not apparent. But another example given by Flammarion is a different matter. When he was writing a book a gust of wind carried the pages out of the window; at the same moment it began to rain. He decided there would be no point in going to get them. A few days later the chapter arrived from his printer. It seemed the porter of the printing office had walked past, seen the pages on the ground, and assumed he had dropped them himself; so he gathered them together, sorted them, and delivered them to the printer. What was the subject of the chapter? The wind . . .

So it would seem there are two types of coincidence: serial "clusterings", which are purely "mechanical", and synchronicities, which might seem to imply that the mind itself has been able to influence the laws of nature – as when Rebecca West snatched the book at random off the shelf.

Koestler gives an even stranger example of synchronicity. The writer Pearl Binder was planning a satirical novel in association with two collabourators. They invented a situation in which camps for the homeless had been set up in Hyde Park. They decided to have a refugee Viennese professor, a broken-down old man with a Hungarian-sounding name – such as Horvath-Nadoly. Two days later they read in the newspaper that a homeless foreign old man had been found wandering alone at night in Hyde Park, and had given his name as Horvath-Nadoly. Here all three collabourators had contributed to the impossible coincidence. So if it is to be regarded as "meaningful" rather than an example of "serial clustering", then it has to be supposed that all three participated in some odd form of telepathy and/or precognition; i.e., that called upon to "invent" a situation at random, their unconscious minds preferred to cheat by supplying them with details about a real person – just as, asked to invent a name on the spur of the moment, we shall probably choose a name we have just seen or heard . . .

This "unconscious" explanation – preferred by Jung – can explain dozens of curious coincidences involving literature. In 1898 a novelist named Morgan Robertson wrote a book about a ship called the *Titan*, "the safest vessel in the world", which hit an iceberg on her maiden voyage across the Atlantic; fourteen years later his story came to life in the tragic maiden voyage of the *Titanic*. Moreover, the editor W. T. Stead had written a story about a ship that sank, and concluded: "This is exactly what might take place, and what will take place, if liners are sent to sea short of boats". Like the liner in Morgan Robertson's novel, the *Titanic* did *not* have enough boats. And W. T. Stead was one of those who drowned.

In 1885 a playwright named Arthur Law wrote a play about a man called Robert Golding, the sole survivor of the shipwreck of a vessel called the *Caroline*. A few days after it was staged, Law read an account of the sinking of a ship called the *Caroline*; the sole survivor was called Robert Golding.

In 1972 a wrter named James Rusk published a pornographic novel called *Black Abductor* under a pseudonym; its plot was so similar to the true story of the kidnapping of heiress Patty Hearst in 1974 by the "Symbionese Liberation Army" – even to the name of the victim, Patricia – that the FBI later interrogated Rusk to find if he had been involved in the kidnapping plot. He had not; it was again "pure coincidence".

In the month preceding the Allied invasion of Normandy – D-Day – the *Daily Telegraph* crossword puzzle gave most of the codewords for the operation: Utah, Mulberry, Neptune and Overlord (the last being the name of the whole operation). MI5 was called to investigate, but found that the compiler of the crosswords was a schoolmaster named Dawe who had no idea of how the words had come into his head.

To explain "synchronistic" events, Jung was inclined to refer to a phrase of the French psychologist Pierre Janet, *abaissement du niveau mental*, "lowering of the mental threshold", by which Janet meant a certain lowering of the vital forces – such as we experience when we are tired or discouraged and which is the precondition for neurosis. Jung believed that when the mental threshold is lowered "the tone of the unconscious is heightened, thereby creating a gradient for the unconscious to flow towards the conscious". The conscious then comes under the influence of what Jung calls the "archetypes" or "primordial images". These images belong to the "collective unconscious", and might be – for example – of a "great mother", a hero-god, a devil-figure, or an image of incarnate wisdom. Jung thought that when the archetype is activated odd coincidences are likely to happen.

Jung worked out his idea of synchronicity with the aid of the physicist Wolfgang Pauli. Pauli himself seemed to have some odd power of causing coincidences. Whenever he touched some piece of experimental apparatus it tended to break. One day in Göttingen a complicated apparatus for studying atomic events collapsed without warning, and Professor J. Franck is said to have remarked: "Pauli must be around somewhere". He wrote to Pauli, and received a reply saying that at the time of the accident his train had been standing in the station at Göttingen, on its way to Copenhagen. Pauli, understandably, was intrigued by Jung's ideas about synchronicity, and Jung's book on the subject was published together with a paper by Pauli on archetypal ideas in the work of Kepler – Kepler had apparently stumbled on the idea of archetypes three centuries earlier, although he meant something closer to Plato's "ideas". Pauli had created a hypothesis called "the exclusion principle", which says that only one electron at a time can occupy any "planetary orbit" inside an atom. He gave no physical reason for this notion; it simply seemed to him to have a pleasing mathematical symmetry, rather like Avogadro's hypothesis that equal volumes of gases will have equal numbers of molecules. In his own essay on Kepler in *The Encyclopedia of Philosophy*, Koestler tried to show that Kepler had arrived at his correct results about the solar system through completely nonsensical ideas about the Blessed Trinity and other such notions, the implication being that creative minds have some instinct or intuition that *shows* them scientific truths, on some principle of symmetry or beauty, rather than through logical reasoning. And this in itself implies that there is some strange basic affinity between mind and nature, and that mind is not some accidental product that has no "right" to be in the universe. It was this intuition that drew Jung and Pauli together.

More to the point is a passage in the writing of the medieval "magician" Albertus Magnus:

A certain power to alter things indwells in the human soul and subordinates the other things to her, particularly when she is swept into a great excess of love or hate or the like. When therefore the soul of man falls into a great excess of any passion, it can be proved by experiment that the [excess] binds things together [magically] and alters them in the way it wants. Whoever would learn the secret of doing and undoing these things must know that everyone can influence everything magically if he falls into a great excess.

That is to say, a psychological state can somehow affect the physical world. But Albertus's "great excess" is clearly the opposite of Jung's "lowering of the mental threshold". One is a lowering of vitality, the other an intensification of it.

Some of the concepts of "split-brain physiology" – a science developed after Jung's death in 1961 – may be able to throw a useful light on these problems. The brain is divided into two hemispheres, rather like a walnut. Brain physiology has established that the left cerebral hemisphere is concerned with our conscious objectives – language, logic, calculation – while the right deals with intuition, pattern-recognition and insight. The remarkable discovery made by Roger Sperry was that when the bridge of nerves – called the corpus callosum – which connects the two halves is severed to prevent epilepsy the patient turns into two people. One split-brain patient tried to hit his wife with one hand while the other held it back. The person I call "me" lives in the left hemisphere; the person who lives in the other half – the "intuitive self" – is a stranger. When a female patient was shown an indecent picture with her right brain, she blushed; asked why she was blushing, she replied: "I don't know".

The right-brain "stranger" is an artist; the left-brain "me" is a scientist. There is some interesting evidence that it is this right-brain "stranger" who is involved in so-called "extra-sensory perception" – telepathy, dowsing, "second sight" – and that his main problem is somehow to communicate the things he knows to the logical self, which is too preoccupied in its own practical purposes to pay attention to the "still, small voice" of the "other self".

The "stranger" can at times "take over". When the English boxer Freddie Mills fought Gus Lesnevitch in 1946 he was knocked down in the second round and concussed. He remembered nothing more until he heard the referee announcing the tenth round. But in the intervening seven rounds he had boxed brilliantly against the much heavier Lesnevitch, and was ahead on points. As soon as he "recovered" consciousness he began to lose. His "other self" had taken over when he was knocked down in the second round. Here is an example where a "lowering of the mental threshold" produced positive results.

If, then, we credit the "other person" with some kind of "extra-sensory perception", it would be possible to explain such phenomena as the activities of "the library angel" – for example, how Rebecca West located the trial she was looking for by reaching out casually. It knows where the trial is located, but it cannot communicate its knowledge to the left brain, which is obsessively searching through the catalogues. Then a librarian approaches, and it sees its chance as he stops near the book. She is prompted to go and complain to the librarian – a relatively easy task, since she is seething with exasperation – and then the "other self" reaches out for the book and, with that intuitive skill that we see in great sportsmen, opens it at the right place . . . (It would be interesting to know if Rebecca West reached out with her left hand – for the left side of the body is controlled by the right brain, and vice versa.)

And how does the ESP hypothesis apply to another story told by Rebecca West and quoted by Koestler? Again she was in the London Library, and had asked an assistant for Gounod's Memoirs. As she was waiting she was approached by an American who had recognized her, and who wanted to know if it was true that she possessed some lithographs by the artist Delpeche. She said she did, and they were still talking when the assistant returned with the book. She opened it casually, and found herself looking at a passage in which Gounod describes how kind Delpeche had been to his mother.

Now here, we can see, the chain of coincidences had been set in motion – by her request for the book – before the stranger came and asked her about Delpeche; so we cannot accuse her "other self" of engineering the whole situation. What we *can* suppose is that the "other self" was somehow aware that the Gounod Memoirs contained a reference to the artist they were speaking about at that very moment, and drew her attention to it by causing her to open the book in the right place . . .

Why? One possible answer is self-evident. Modern man has become a "split-brainer"; for the most part, he lives in the left brain. This means that he is only aware of *half* his identity. Whenever he is reminded of that other half – for example, when music or poetry produce a sudden "warm glow", or when some smell reminds him vividly of childhood – he experiences the strange sense of wild elation that G.K. Chesterton called "absurd good news". The more he feels "trapped" in his left-brain self by fatigue, discouragement, foreboding – the more he actually cuts himself off from that deep inner sense of purpose and well-being. If he had some instant method of re-establishing contact with this inner power – Abraham Maslow called such contacts "peak experiences" – his life would be transformed. It must be irritating for that "other self" to see the left-brain self plunging itself into states of gloom and boredom that are completely unnecessary, and so wasting its life – *both* their lives. So, as a fruitful hypothesis, we might regard "synchronicities" – like the one involving Gounod's Memoirs – as attempts by the "other self" to remind the left-brain personality of its existence, and to rescue it from its sense of "contingency" – the feeling that Proust describes, of feeling "mediocre, accidental, mortal".

There is, unfortunately, another type of synchronicity that cannot be explained on the ESP hypothesis and this is the very type that Jung originally set out to explain. ESP cannot explain how the *I Ching* could produce a "meaningful" answer to a question (if, of course, it actually does so). Common sense tells us that the throwing down of coins can only produce a chance result, *unless* the coins are somehow "interfered with" as they fall. The Chinese believe that the *I Ching* is some kind of living entity – presumably a supernatural one – and we may assume that this entity answers the question by causing the coins to fall in a certain way. The Western psychologist, rejecting the supernatural explanation, can only fall back on the notion that the unconscious mind – the "other self" – can somehow influence the fall of the coins by some form of psychokinesis, "mind over matter". And while this may be more or less satisfactory in explaining how the *I Ching* works, it still fails to explain, for example, the fish synchronicities that Jung found so intriguing: the Latin inscription about a fish, the mention of "April fish", the patient who had painted fish, the embroidery with fish-like monsters, the other patient with the dream of a fish. Psychokinesis can hardly explain this series of coincidences.

This is true also of a type of "cluster" coincidence described by Koestler. A doctor wrote to him commenting that if a patient with some rare and unusual complaint turns up at a surgery, he could be fairly certain that a similar case would turn up later during the same surgery, and that if a patient with a certain name – say, Donnell – should ring him, then another patient called Donnell would be almost certain to turn up at the surgery. Another letter mentioned similar "clusters" of various types: a dentist noting how often he had "runs" of patients with the same kind of extraction problem, an eye specialist noting how often he had runs of patients with the same eye problem, even a typewriter-repairer noticing how often he had runs of the same make of machine for repair, or runs of different machines with the identical problem.

Obviously there can be no "explanation" for such oddities unless a mathematician discovers some completely new law of seriality. But again, we can note that such coincidences tend to produce in us much the same effect as more personal experiences of "serendipity" – a sense that perhaps the universe *is* less meaningless and inscrutable than we assume. And this – as every reader of Jung's book will agree – is what Jung felt about synchronicity. In fact, a hostile critic might object that Jung – who was the son of a parson – is trying to introduce God by the back door. All his attempts to argue in favour of a "scientific" principle of synchronicity are unconvincing because the words "acausal connecting principle" involve a contradiction in terms – unless, that is, he is willing to admit that it is "pure chance", in which case he has undermined his own argument. A coincidence is either "meaningful" or it is not; and if it is meaningful, then it is not a coincidence.

In the last analysis, accepting or rejecting "synchronicity" is a matter of individual temperament. I personally am inclined to accept it because my own experience of "coincidences" inclines me to the belief that they *are* often "meaningful". On the morning when I was about to begin the article on Joan of Arc in the present book, I noticed in my library a bound series of the *International History Magazine*, and decided to spend half an hour looking through it in case it contained material for this book. I opened the first volume at random, and found myself looking at an article on Joan of Arc, whose editorial introduction raised the question of whether she survived her "execution". In fact, the article proved to be useless: the author made no mention of the controversy about the Dame des Armoires. Does this not in itself suggest that the coincidence was "non-meaningful"? Not necessarily. I have cited elsewhere (see chapter 57) Jacques Vallee's interesting theory about synchronicity. When he was researching a cult that used the name of the prophet Melchizedek he spent a great deal of time looking up every reference to Melchizedek he could find. In Los Angeles he asked a woman taxi-driver for a receipt: it was signed M. Melchizedek. A check with the Los Angeles telephone directory revealed that there was only one Melchizedek in the whole area.

Vallee points out that there are two ways in which a librarian can store information. One is to place it in alphabetical order on shelves. But computer scientists have discovered that there is a simpler and quicker method. They prefer to store information as it arrives – the equivalent of a librarian putting books on the shelves side by side as they come into the library – and having a keyword or algorithm that will retrieve it. (In a library, the equivalent might be as follows: as each new book comes into the library, some kind of "beeping" mechanism is attached to its spine; each beeper is adjusted to respond to a certain number code, like a telephone. When the librarian requires a certain book, he dials the number on his pocket beeper, and then goes straight to the book that is beeping.)

Vallee suggests that "the world might be organised more like a randomised data base than a sequential library". It was as if he had stuck on the universal notice-board a note saying; "Wanted, Melchidezeks", and some earnest librarian had said: "How about this one?" "No, that's no good – that's just a taxi driver . . ."

This picture, like Jung's, suggests that there *is* some mutual interaction between the mind and the universe, and that the key to "retrieving information" is to be in the right state of mind: a state of deep interest or excitement: Albertus Magnus's "excess of passion".

Another personal example. I was led to write the present article partly by the "Joan of Arc coincidence", partly by another coincidence that happened a day or two later. I had received in the post a copy of the biography of the American novelist Ayn Rand by Barbara Branden. I was reading this in bed the next day when the post arrived. This included a paperback novel sent to me by an American reader, with a letter enclosed. The letter began: "In Barbara Branden's recent biography of Ayn Rand you are mentioned in a footnote . . ."

Half an hour later, about to go to my study, I noticed a newspaper clipping that my wife had left for me outside the door. I asked her "What's this?", and she said: "It's an article that mentions Hemingway – I thought it might interest you." In fact it was the article about coincidence and lost manuscripts by Godfrey Smith, quoted at the beginning of the present article.

As it happened, I decided not to write the coincidence article immediately; I had planned first of all to write a piece about the disappearance of Mary Rogers. I took Poe's short stories from my bookshelf and opened it at "The Mystery of Marie Roget". The opening paragraph reads: "There are few persons, even among the calmest thinkers, who have not occasionally been startled into a vague yet thrilling half-credence in the supernatural, by *coincidences* of so seemingly marvellous a character that, as mere coincidences, the intellect has been unable to receive them." It confirmed my decision to write this article.

As if to underline this point, a further coincidence occurred after I had written the preceding sentence, which happened to be at the end of a day's work. About to leave my study, I noticed among an untidy pile of books a title I had no recollection of seeing before: *You Are Sentenced to Life* by W.D. Chesney, published by a private press in California; it was a book about life after death. I had obviously bought it a long time ago and had never – as far as I know – even glanced into it. I decided it was time to remedy this. Later in the afternoon, I spent an hour glancing through it, reading a section here and there; then, just before closing it, I decided to glance at the very end. The top of the last page was headed: ORDER OF MELCHIZEDEK, and was a reprint of a letter from Grace Hooper Pettipher, "Instructor within the Order of Melchizedek", requesting a copy of another book published by the same press. I doubt whether, in two thousand or so books in my study, there is another reference to Melchizedek; but I had to stumble upon this one after writing about Melchizedek in an article about synchronicity.

It is my own experience that coincidences like this seem to happen when I am in "good form" – when I am feeling alert, cheerful and optimistic, and not when I am feeling tired, bored or gloomy. This leads me to formulate my own hypothesis about synchronicity as follows. As a writer, I am at my best when I feel alert and purposeful; at these times I feel a sense of "hidden meanings" lurking behind the apparently impassive face of everyday reality. But this is not true only for writers; it applies to all human beings. We are *all* at our best when the imagination is awake, and we can sense the presence of that "other self", the intuitive part of us. When we are tired or discouraged we feel "stranded" in left-brain consciousness. We feel, as William James says, that "our fires are damped, our draughts are checked". We can be jarred out of this state by a sudden crisis, or any pleasant stimulus, but more often than not these fail to present themselves. It must be irritating for "the other self" to find its partner so dull and sluggish, allowing valuable time and opportunity to leak away by default. A "synchronicity" can snap us into a sudden state of alertness and awareness. And if the "other self" can, by the use of its peculiar powers, bring about a synchronicity, then there is still time to prevent us from wasting yet another day of our brief lives.

The Melchizedek coincidence seems to me of another kind, designed to confirm that we are on "the right track". When in the late 1960s I first turned my attention to the field of the paranormal, and began writing a book called *The Occult*, such coincidences became common-place. I have described in that book how I needed a reference from some alchemical text. I knew that the book containing the reference was in one of the books facing my desk; but it was towards the end of the day, and I was feeling tired and lazy. Besides, I had forgotten where to find the reference, and my heart sank at the prospect of a fruitless search through half a dozen volumes . . . Conscience finally triumphed and I heaved myself to my feet, crossed the room, and took a book off the shelf. As I did so the next book fell off the shelf; it landed on the floor, open, at the passage I was looking for. And I felt that curious flash of gratitude and delight that we always experience in these moments, as if some invisible guardian angel has politely tendered his help.

Now, a book falling off a shelf and opening at the right page is obviously closer to the procedure of the *I Ching* than, for example, Mrs Kammerer's chain of coincidences about Prince Rohan and Lake Attersee, or Flammarion's story about M. Fortgibu. Yet it seems equally obvious that, in a basic sense, there is a family resemblance between them. The problem arises if we attempt some kind of classification. When Rebecca West reached out and found the right book, this sounds like ESP. But a book falling off a shelf at the right page obviously involves some extra element besides ESP – something closer to psychokinesis. But neither ESP nor psychokinesis can begin to explain Mrs Kammerer's chain of coincidences; and in the case of M. Fortgibu and the plum pudding, it becomes absurd. We seem to be dealing with the mysterious entity that Charles Fort called "the cosmic joker", and any respectable parapsychologist is bound to draw back in horror at the very idea.

But even if synchronicity declines to fit into any of our scientific theories, this is no reason to refuse to believe in its existence. Science still has no idea of how or why the universe began, of the nature of time, or of what lies beyond the outermost limit of the stars. In fact, science continues to use terms like space, time and motion *as if* they were comprehensible to the human intellect; no one accuses Cantor of being an occultist or mystic because he devised a mathematics of infinity. Science continues to grow and develop in spite of its uneasy metaphysical foundations.

From the purely practical point of view, the chief problem of human existence is individual lack of purpose. In those curious moments of relaxation or sudden happiness that we all experience at intervals, we can *see* that it is stupid to lose purpose and direction, and that if only we could learn to summon this insight *at will*, this fatal tendency to forgetfulness could be permanently eradicated, and life would be transformed. It is obvious in such moments that if we could train ourselves to behave *as if* there were hidden meanings lurking behind the blank face of the present, the problem would be solved. If "synchronicities" can produce that sense of meaning and purpose, then it is obviously sensible for us to behave *as if* they were meaningful coincidences, and to ignore the question of their scientific validity.

55

Time in Disarray

Time Slips and Precognitions

The late Ivan T. Sanderson, the eminent naturalist and scientist, once had a curious experience of Paris. But it was the Paris not of today, but of five centuries ago; and, to make the story still more paradoxical, it happened in Haiti.

Before beginning his account (in *More "Things"*), Sanderson is careful to note that he has never taken any interest in "the occult" – not because he actively disbelieves in it, but because "I have only one life to lead . . . and I've been far too busy trying to catch up with the more pragmatic facts of it".

Sanderson and his wife were living in a small village named Pont Beudet in Haiti; together with his assistant Frederick G. Allsop, he was engaged in a biological survey. One beautiful evening the three of them decided to drive to Lake Azuey in their ancient Rolls-Royce. Taking a short cut down an old dirt road, they drove into a squashy mass of mud, and went in up to their axles. They got out and began to walk. They walked through most of the night until they were exhausted. They encountered a car with an American doctor on his way to a case, but he had no room for three of them; he promised to try and pick them up on his way back. They plodded on in the moonlight. Then:

> . . . suddenly, on looking up from the dusty ground I perceived absolutely clearly in the now brilliant moonlight, *and casting shadows appropriate to their positions*, three-storied houses of various shapes and sizes lining both sides of the road. These houses hung out over the road, which certainly appeared to be muddy with patches of large cobblestones. The houses were of (I would say) about the Elizabethan period of England, but for some reason I *knew* they were in Paris! They had pent roofs, some with dormer windows, gabled timbered porticos, and small windows

with tiny leaded panes. Here and there, there were dull reddish lights burning behind them, as if from candles. There were iron-frame lanterns hanging from timbers jutting from some houses and they were all swaying together as if in a wind, but there was not the faintest movement of air about us. I could go on and on describing this scene as it was so vivid: in fact, I could *draw* it. But that is not the main point.

I was marvelling at this, and looking about me, when my wife came to a dead stop and gave a gasp. I ran smack into her. Then she went speechless for a time while I begged to know what was wrong. Finally she took my hand and, pointing, described to me *exactly what I was seeing*. At which point, *I* became speechless.

Finally pulling myself together, I blurted out something like "What do you think's happened?" but my wife's reply startled me even more. I remember it only too well: she said, "How did we get to *Paris* five hundred years ago?"

We stood marvelling at what we apparently *both* now saw, picking out individual items, pointing, questioning each other as to details, and so forth. Curiously, we found ourselves swaying back and forth, and began to feel very weak, so I called out to Fred, whose white shirt was fast disappearing ahead.

I don't remember what happened then but we tried to run towards him and, feeling dizzy, sat down on what we were *convinced* was a tall, rough curbstone. Fred came running back asking what was wrong but at first we did not know what to say. He was the "keeper" of the cigarettes, of which we had about half a dozen left, and he sat down beside us and gave us each one. By the time the flame from his lighter had cleared from my eyes, so had fifteenth-century Paris, and there was nothing before me but the endless and damned thorn bushes and cactus and bare earth. My wife also "came back" after looking into the flame. Fred had seen nothing, and was completely mystified by our subsequent babble, but he was not sceptical and insisted that we just sit and wait for the truck . . .

When eventually they arrived back home they were surprised to find that their servant woman had a hot meal waiting for them, and a large bowl of hot water, in which she insisted on washing Mrs Sanderson's feet; the head man had prepared hot baths for Sanderson and Fred Allsop. They would not explain how they knew that Sanderson and his companions would be back at dawn. But one of the young men in the village later said to Sanderson: "You saw things, didn't you? You don't believe it, but you could *always* see things if you wanted to."

Sanderson had obviously experienced a kind of "time slip" into the past, and there are dozens – perhaps hundreds – of other recorded examples, the most famous undoubtedly being that of the two English ladies, Eleanor Jourdain and Charlotte Moberly, who in August 1901, walking in the gardens at Versailles, found themselves back in Versailles in 1789, just before the downfall of Louis XVI. Ten years later, their book describing their experience caused a sensation because it was so obvious that the two ladies – principals of an Oxford college – were of unquestioned integrity. Professor C.E.M. Joad, speaking about their "adventure", used the phrase "the undoubted queerness of time". But he made no attempt to explain the mechanism of "time slips".

In my book *Mysteries* I record an equally remarkable example, taken directly from the person concerned, Mrs Jane O'Neill of Cambridge. In 1973 she was the first person to arrive at the scene of a serious accident, and helped injured passengers out of the wrecked bus. Later she began to suffer from insomnia, and the doctor told her this was due to shock. On holiday with a friend in Norfolk, she began experiencing "visions" – sudden vivid pictures that lasted just a few seconds. After one of these she told her friend, "I have just seen you in the galleys", and the friend replied: "That's not surprising. My ancestors were Huguenots and were punished by being sent to the galleys."

But the most remarkable event took place on a visit to Fotheringay church. She stood for some time in front of the picture of the Crucifixion behind the altar. Later, when she commented on it back in the hotel room, her friend asked: "What picture?" A year later, when they revisited the church, the inside seemed quite different from the first visit, and there was no picture behind the altar. She wrote to Joan Forman, an expert on "time slips", and through her contacted an antiquarian who was able to tell her that what she had seen had been the church as it *had* been before it had been pulled down in 1553.

Both Sanderson and Jane O'Neill were convinced that what they were looking at was real, not a hallucination, although the Sandersons felt dizzy when they tried to run. One of Jane O'Neill's "visions" was of two figures walking beside a lake, "and I knew, though I don't know why, that one of them was Margaret Roper", the daughter of Sir Thomas More. Sanderson and his wife "knew" that they were looking at fifteenth-century Paris. So it seems clear that the vision was not some simple objective hallucination, like a mirage in the desert, but was due to some extent to their own minds. Sanderson and his wife presumably shared it because of some telepathic rapport of the kind that often develops between married couples. But this fails to explain why they saw Paris in Haiti. (Haiti was, of course, French, but not until the eighteenth century.)

In the mid-nineteenth century a theory of "time slips" was developed by two American professors, Joseph Rodes Buchanan and William Denton. Through his experiments with his students,* Buchanan came to believe that human beings possess a faculty for "reading" the history of objects; he called this "psychometry" (see chapter 43). Denton tested his own students with all kinds of geological specimens, and found that the "sensitive" ones among them saw "mental pictures" that were closely related to the object they were holding (and which Denton wrapped in thick brown paper, so they could have no idea of what it was). A piece of lava brought "visions" of an exploding volcano; a fragment of meteor conjured up visions of outer space; a piece of dinosaur tooth brought visions of primeval forests. Denton was convinced that all human beings possess this faculty, which he described as "a telescope into the past".

But while the "time slips" described by Sanderson and Jane O'Neill obviously have much in common with "psychometric" visions, they were unquestionably far more than mental pictures or impressions. Yet this is not to say that they were not mental pictures. After her experience of the accident, Jane O'Neill kept on "seeing" the injuries of the passengers; such visions are known as "eidetic imagery". The scientist Nicola Tesla possessed it to such an extent that he could construct a dynamo in his mind and actually watch it running. After experimenting all day with images of the sun, Isaac Newton found that he could produce a visual hallucination of the sun by simply imagining it. Like the strange abilities of calculating prodigies (see chapter 26), this seems to be a faculty that all human beings possess, but that most of us never learn how to use. We may speculate that Jane O'Neill's traumatic experience activated this dormant faculty, and that it somehow continued to operate spasmodically in the succeeding months. If the image of the sixteenth-century church was some kind of "eidetic image" floating in front of her eyes, there is no reason why she should have recognized it as a hallucination unless she tried to touch the picture above the altar; most of us accept the evidence of our senses without question. The same argument probably applies to the experience of Miss Moberly and Miss Jourdain at Versailles. They *saw* men and

* Described in my book *The Psychic Detectives*.

women dressed in the style of Louis XVI (and assumed it was a rehearsal for a costume drama) but naturally, they did not try to touch them, or even to speak to them. (Being English, they would have required an introduction!)

Another "time slip" collected by Joan Forman offers us a further clue. Mrs Turrell-Clarke, of Wisley-cum-Pyrford in Surrey, was cycling along the modern road there on her way to evensong when the road suddenly became a field path, and *she seemed to be walking along it*. She was wearing a nun's robes, and she saw a man dressed in the peasant dress of the thirteenth century, who stood aside to allow her to pass. A month later, sitting in the village church, she suddenly saw the church change to its original state, with earth floor, stone altar, lancet windows, and brown-habited monks intoning the same plainsong chant that was at present being sung by the choir in the "modern" church. At this moment Mrs Turrell-Clarke felt she was at the back of the church, watching the proceedings. So it seems clear that what happened was that her viewpoint changed, and she found herself *looking through someone else's eyes* – the eyes of a lady walking along the road and the eyes of a woman standing at the back of the church. When Jane O'Neill found herself looking at Sir Thomas More's daughter walking by a lake she wondered whether there might be some "family" connection, since her own unmarried name was Moore. She may even have suspected that she had somehow slipped back into a previous incarnation. Again, it seems clear that she was seeing the scene through someone else's eyes – which explains how she knew that she was looking at Margaret Roper. And since the Sandersons knew they were looking at fifteenth-century Paris, we may assume that they were also looking through "someone else's eyes".

The late T.C. Lethbridge, a retired Cambridge don who devoted the last years of his life to studying the paranormal, came to the interesting conclusion that "ghosts" are in fact a kind of "tape recording": that powerful emotions can "imprint" themselves on some sort of magnetic field, and that these "recordings" can be "picked up" by a person who is sensitive to them – for example, by a good dowser. (Dowsing involves sensitivity to the electromagnetic field of water.) Lethbridge himself, for example, experienced a strange feeling of foreboding and depression in a spot where the body of a suicide was concealed in a hollow tree. Joan Forman has also expressed her conviction that time slips "have some connection with the human electromagnetic field". She herself was standing in the courtyard of Haddon Hall in Derbyshire when she saw a group of four children playing on the steps and yelling with laughter.

When she took a step forward the group vanished, but she later recognized one of the girls in an ancestral painting that hung on the walls. She also cites the experience of a Norwich teacher, Mrs Anne May, who was leaning against a monolith at the Clava Cairns, near Inverness, when she "saw" a group of men in shaggy tunics and cross-gartered trousers, dragging one of the monoliths over the turf; when a group of tourists walked into the glade the figures vanished; apparently Mrs May had caught a glimpse of the original bronze-age builders of the monolithic circle. Joan Forman believes that the contact with the monolith was the "trigger factor" that caused Mrs May to see her vision, and that in her own case it was the spot she was standing on.

Most students of the paranormal would admit another possibility: the notion that what is being "contacted" is the mind of someone who lived in the distant past. In 1907 the architect Frederick Bligh Bond was appointed by the Church of England to take charge of the excavations at Glastonbury Abbey. What his employers did not know was that Bond was interested in spiritualism. Together with a friend named Bartlett, Bond attempted "automatic writing", the aim being to learn where to start digging in the abbey grounds. When they asked about Glastonbury the pencil – which they were both holding – wrote: "All knowledge is eternal and is available to mental sympathy". And soon a communicator who signed himself Gulielmus Monachus – William the Monk – began giving extremely detailed instructions on where to excavate, and as a result Bond unearthed two chapels, each of precisely the dimensions given by William the Monk. Another "communicator", Johannes, made the following interesting remark:

> Why cling I to that which is not? It is I, and it is not I, butt parte of me which dwelleth in the past and is bound to that whych my carnal self loved and called "home" these many years. Yet I, Johannes, amm of many partes, and ye better parte doeth other things . . . only that part which remembereth clingeth like memory to what it seeth yet.

Bond's downfall came when he wrote a book describing how he had obtained the information that had made his excavations so successful; the Church of England dismissed him. But the book, *Gate of Remembrance*, remains an astonishing proof that a twentieth-century mind *can* apparently attain some kind of direct access to the past. "All knowledge is eternal and is available to mental sympathy". And the comments of Johannes seem to imply that a "parte of me which dwelleth in the past

. . . clingeth like memory to what it seeth yet". It seems, therefore, remotely possible that some "time slips" may involve contact with a mind "which dwelleth in the past".

Many writers describing time slips mention an odd sense of "crossing a threshold". When Miss Jourdain returned alone to Versailles a few months after her "adventure" with Miss Moberly she suddenly felt "as if I had crossed a line and was in a circle of influence", and saw oddly dressed labourers in bright tunics. A girl named Louisa Hand told Joan Forman how, when she was a child, she had entered her grandmother's cottage, and been puzzled to find herself in a place with older furniture. Thinking she had entered the wrong place, she went out to check, then went back in; still the room was different. But when she went in a third time things had returned to normal. She also mentioned the sensation of "crossing a threshold", and of a feeling of silence associated with it.

It would seem, then, that the "psychometric" theory of Buchanan and Denton could account for the time-slip phenomenon. But this is far from the truth. It is also possible to "slip" the other way, into the future. Joan Forman cites the case of a teacher from Holt, Norfolk, who while involved in a "traffic contretemps" in the town noticed that a launderette that had been under construction was now finished and in use. He told his wife, who went there the next day with a bag of soiled laundry, and found that the place was still half-finished. The teacher had seen the shop as it *would* be in six weeks' time.

Most of the cases of "future visions" cited in *The Mask of Time* are involved with dreams. In 1927 J.W. Dunne's book *An Experiment With Time*, with its study of "precognitive dreams", caused a sensation. Dunne described a number of occasions on which he had dreamt of events that he would read about later in the newspapers. T.C. Lethbridge later had much the same experience; he carefully observed his dreams, and noticed how often he dreamt of some trivial event of the next day; for example, he woke up dreaming of the face of a man he did not know; the face seemed to be enclosed in a kind of frame, and the man was making movements with his hands in the area of his chin, as if soaping his face prior to shaving. The next day, driving along a country road, he saw the face of the man of his dream; he was behind the windscreen of an oncoming car – the "frame" – and his hands were moving on the steering wheel, which was directly under his chin. Joan Forman cites many similar cases. All tend to have the same "trivial" quality, as if the glimpse of the future is some kind of freak accident. One schoolteacher, lying in bed with a high temperature, had an odd hallucination involving hedgehogs walking round the bedroom floor, and building a high nest with sticks and straw. Three months later he was packing ceramic figures made by his pottery class to take them to the kiln; he packed them in a kind of layered nest, with straw between the layers. Several ceramic hedgehogs were on the floor around his feet. Suddenly he recognized his hallucination. Just before he began the packing operation, he experienced a feeling of "a peculiar mechanical inevitability".

An Oxford scientist, Michael Shallis, has written a book on the nature of time,* in the course of which he mentions two of his own odd experiences of "prevision". As a twelve-year-old boy he went into the house one day and called out to ask his mother what they were having for dinner. As he did so he experienced a feeling of *déja vu*, and knew that his mother would reply that they were having salad for dinner which she did.

This kind of "prevision" is fairly common. Joan Forman quotes a letter she received from a man who often knew with absolute certainty that a cricketer would be bowled out before the ball left the bowler's hand; he comments that this often annoyed the batsman, who felt that he had somehow caused it. One explanation for such an ability might be some kind of unconscious "computer" that swiftly assessed the whole situation – the stance of the batsman, the skill of the bowler – and "saw" that the loss of the wicket was inevitable. But another experience cited by Shallis suggests that the problem is rather more complex than this.

A few years ago I was teaching a student physics in an upstairs lecture room. I had reached the part of the tutorial where we were discussing radioactive half lives and I was again swamped with the deja-vu feeling. I knew I was going to suggest that I needed to show him some examples from a certain book in my office and then go and collect it. I resisted saying this to him, but the feeling it had all happened before was strong. I was determined to break the pattern of the event. I turned to my student and asked him if we had done this work before, believing that he might be sharing the experience. He looked puzzled and replied no. I struggled to avoid continuing the experience. I resolved not to go and fetch the book. Having made that resolution I turned again to the student and said: "I think I had better show you some examples of these. I will just pop down to my room and get a book". My awareness of the experience itself did not make it go away, even when I tried not to repeat its pre-set pattern.

* *On Time*, 1982.

There is an alarming implication in the words "repeat its pre-set pattern". *Is* it possible that we do what we "have" to do, whether we want to or not, and that our sense of free will is a delusion? Shallis goes on to say:

> There is an element of precognition itself in the experience, because the situation is so "familiar" that one knows what will happen next. It is different from precognition, however, in that it is familiar; one is in a sense reliving a part of one's life, not predicting or sensing a remote event.

J.W. Dunne's explanation for such experiences involves what he calls "serial time". Basically, he is suggesting that there are several "times". When we say "time flows", it means we are measuring it *against* something. That something must be another kind of time, "time number two". And this in turn could be measured against "time number three". We also have several "selves". Self number one is stuck in time number one; but we have another self which is not the physical body, which can rise above self number one and foresee the future.

In his book *Man and Time*, J.B. Priestley tells a story that seems to illustrate the difference between the two selves. A young mother dreamed that on a camping holiday she left her young son by the river while she went off to get the soap, and that when she came back he was drowned. On a camping holiday some time later she was about to go off and get the soap when she suddenly recognized the scene of her dream; so she tucked the baby under her arm before she went off to the tent . . .

The implication here is important. We *do* possess a degree of free will, but it is hard to exercise in the material world of "time number one". It is like swimming against the current. Our human problem is not to remain stuck in "time number one", the material world, with its repetitious futility, but to learn to spend as much time as possible in the mental world, the world of "time number two".

Priestley argues that Dunne is making things unnecessarily complicated in arguing for an infinite number of selves; according to Priestley, there are only three. Self number one is simply involved in living; it might say, for example: "I feel depressed." Self number two says: "I know self number one is depressed." Self three says: "I know self two knows self one is depressed. But then, self one is a self-indulgent idiot." Self one experiences; self two is conscious of experience; self three passes judgment on the experience. Priestley gives an example; in a plane accident, self one was hurled out of his seat; self two knew there was about to be an accident. Self three thought: "Now I shall know what it's like to be fried alive." It "does not really care; it is as if it goes along with the other two just for the ride."

This is perhaps one of the most interesting and important observations to arise from these speculations about the nature of time; the experience of what seems to be a "higher self". In his important book *A Drug-Taker's Notes*, R.H. Ward describes his experience under dental gas:

> . . . I passed, after the first few inhalations of the gas, directly into a state of consciousness already far more complete than the fullest degree of ordinary waking consciousness, and that I then passed progressively upwards . . . into finer and finer degrees of heightened awareness. But although one must write of it in terms of time, time had no place in the experience. In one sense it lasted far longer than the short period between inhaling the gas and "coming round", lasted indeed for an eternity, and in another sense it took no time at all.

Ward's observation here emphasizes that the nature of time is essentially *mental*. It might almost be said that the sense of time is produced by the stress between the physical world and the "higher self", and that when this stress vanishes there is a sense of timelessness. The stress vanishes as a result of a withdrawal *inward*, as if towards another level of reality inside us, an inner world with its own reality. Ward says that when he later tried to recall the essence of his experience he found himself repeating "Within and within and within . . ." like a recurring decimal.

He also quotes from the experience of a friend he calls A, who was on his way back from the station when he experienced mild indigestion. The thought occurred to him

> It belongs only to my body and is real only to the physical not-self. There is no need for the self to feel it . . . Even as I thought this the pain disappeared; that is, it was in some way left behind . . . the sensation of "rising up within" began . . . First there is the indescribable sensation in the spine, as of *something mounting up*, a sensation which is partly pleasure and partly pleasure and partly awe . . . This is accompanied by an extraordinary feeling of *bodily*

lightness, of well-being and effortlessness . . . Everything was becoming "more", everything was *going up to another level*.

Here it sounds as if A's "self number three" had decided to actively intervene, and the result was a sense of leaving the pain behind.

If there is any general conclusion to be drawn from these experiences of the "undoubted queerness of time", it is this: that we are somehow mistaken in our natural and very understandable assumption that the physical world is the basic and perhaps the only reality. Experiences of "time slips" and of precognition suggests that when the mind can slip into another "gear" it escapes its normal enslavement to time, and achieves a state of serene detachment "above" time.

The puzzling thing about such a notion is its implication that time is somehow unreal, or at least less real than we take it to be. Common sense and science are in agreement that the future cannot be predicted with any precision because it has not yet happened. Every "cause" in the world of the present moment could have many different effects. When a gas is heated its molecules begin to move faster, and an increasing number of collisions will occur. Each of these collisions causes the molecules to change course, and so leads to a different set of collisions. So it would be virtually impossible to determine which molecules will be colliding with others in ten minutes' time; everything depends upon chance. In the same way, the five billion or so people in the world at the present moment will interact in unpredictable ways, and will determine what is happening in a week from now. In the case of the gas molecules, a sufficiently complex computer could in theory predict what will be happening a week from now; but no computer could make similar predictions about people.

Experiences of time slips and of precognition contradict this assertion. They clearly imply that in some sense the future *is* to some extent predetermined, as if it had already happened. This is, in fact, precisely what the materialist would assert. Free will is an illusion; therefore human beings obey mechanical laws. Yet apparently this cannot be entirely true, or Priestley's mother would not have been able to prevent her baby from drowning. In fact, the very existence of precognition means that the future cannot be entirely determined, for to know the future in advance is to be able, to some extent, to alter it. Even though Michael Shallis obeyed his compulsion to go to look for the book, he had nevertheless made an effort not to do so – thereby revealing that he was not completely "determined". (And, presumably, he would have been able to overcome the compulsion if he had felt strongly enough about it

– for example, if his sense of *déja-vu* had warned him that he would meet with a serious accident on his way to his office.)

It is a disconcerting thought: that life is somehow basically "scripted". But what seems to be more important is the recognition that, with the right kind of effort, we can depart from the "script". Priestley takes issue with Professor Gilbert Ryle's view – in *The Concept of Mind* – that man is merely a living body, not a body controlled by a self or soul. Ryle calls this view "the ghost in the machine". Experiences of "time in disarray" seems to support Priestley and contradict Ryle: in fact, to confirm the view that we have at least three "selves" as distinct from the physical body, and that the third of these selves corresponds roughly to what Kant (and Husserl) meant by the "transcendental ego", or "the self that presides over consciousness".

56

The Great Tunguska Explosion

On 30 June 1908 the inhabitants of Nizhne-Karelinsk, a small village in central Siberia, saw a bluish-white streak of fire cut vertically across the sky to the north-west. What began as a bright point of light lengthened over a period of ten minutes until it seemed to split the sky in two. When it reached the ground it shattered to form a monstrous cloud of black smoke. Seconds later there was a terrific roaring detonation that made the buildings tremble. Assuming that the Day of Judgment had arrived, many of the villagers fell on their knees. The reaction was not entirely absurd; in fact, they had witnessed the greatest natural disaster in the earth's recorded history. If the object that caused what is now known as "the Great Siberian Explosion" had arrived a few hours earlier or later it might have landed in more heavily populated regions, and caused millions of deaths.

As it later turned out, the village of Nizhne-Karelinsk had been over 200 miles away from the "impact point", and yet the explosion had been enough to shake debris from their roofs. A Trans-Siberian express train stopped because the driver was convinced that it was derailed; and seismographs in the town of Irkutsk indicated a crash of earthquake proportions. Both the train and the town were over 800 miles from the explosion.

Whatever it was that struck the Tunguska region of the Siberian forestland had exploded with a force never before imagined. Its shock-wave travelled around the globe twice before it died out, and its general effect on the weather in the northern hemisphere was far-reaching. During the rest of June it was quite possible to read the small print in the London *Times* at midnight. There were photographs of Stockholm taken at one o'clock in the morning by natural light, and a photograph of the Russian town of Navrochat taken at midnight looks like a bright summer afternoon.

For some months the world was treated to spectacular dawns and sunsets, as impressive as those that had been seen after the great Krakatoa eruption in 1883. From this, as well as the various reports of unusual cloud formations over following months, it is fair to guess that the event had thrown a good deal of dust into the atmosphere, as happens with violent volcanic eruptions and, notably, atomic explosions.

Perhaps the strangest aspect of the Great Siberian Explosion was that no one paid much attention to it. Reports of the falling object were published in Siberian newspapers but did not spread any further. Meteorologists speculated about the strange weather, but no one came close to guessing its real cause.

It was not until the Great War had been fought, and the Russian Revolution had overthrown the tsarist regime that the extraordinary events of that June day finally reached the general public. In 1921, as part of Lenin's general plan to place the USSR at the forefront of world science, the Soviet Academy of Sciences commissioned Leonid Kulik to investigate meteorite falls on Soviet territory. It was Kulik who stumbled upon the few brief reports in ten-year-old Siberian newspapers that finally led him to suspect that something extraordinary had happened in central Siberia in the summer of 1908.

Leonid found the reports confusing and contradictory. None of them seemed to agree quite where the object had exploded. Some even claimed that the "meteor" had later been found. But when his researchers began to collect eyewitness reports of the event Kulik became convinced that whatever had exploded in the Tunguska forest was certainly not a normal meteorite.

These reports described how the ground had opened up to release a great pillar of fire and smoke which burned brighter than the sun. Distant huts were blown down and reindeer herds scattered. A man ploughing in an open field felt his shirt burning on his back, and others described being badly sunburnt on one side of the face but not the other. Many people claimed to have been made temporarily deaf by the noise, or to have suffered long-term effects of shock. Yet, almost unbelievably, not a single person had been killed or seriously injured. Whatever it was that produced the explosion had landed in one of the few places on earth where its catastrophic effect was minimized. A few hours later, and it could have obliterated St Petersburg, London or New York. Even if it had landed in the sea, tidal waves might have destroyed whole coastal regions. That day the human race had escaped the greatest disaster in its history, and had not even been aware of it.

Finally Kulik discovered that a local meteorologist had made an estimate of the point of impact, and in 1927 he was given the necessary backing by the Academy of Sciences to find the point where the "great meteorite" had fallen.

The great Siberian forest is one of the least accessible places on earth. Even today it remains largely unexplored, and there are whole areas that have only ever been surveyed from the air. What settlements there are can be found along the banks of its mighty rivers, some of them miles in width. The winters are ferociously cold, and in the summer the ground becomes boggy, and the air is filled with the hum of mosquitoes. Kulik was faced with an almost impossible task: to travel by horse and raft with no idea of exactly where to look or what to look for.

In March 1927 he set off accompanied by two local guides who had witnessed the event, and after many setbacks arrived on the banks of the Mekirta river in April. The Mekirta is the closest river to the impact point, and in 1927 formed a boundary between untouched forest and almost total devastation.

On that first day Kulik stood on a low hill and surveyed the destruction caused by the Tunguska explosion. For as far as he could see to the north – perhaps a dozen miles – there was not one full-grown tree left standing. Every one had been flattened by the blast, and they lay like a slaughtered regiment, all pointing towards him. Yet it was obvious that what he was looking at was only a fraction of the devastation, since all the trees were facing in the same direction as far as the horizon. The blast must have been far greater than even the wildest reports had suggested.

Kulik wanted to explore the devastation; his two guides were terrified, and refused to go on. So Kulik was forced to return with them, and it was not until June that he managed to return with two new companions.

The expedition followed the line of broken trees for several days until they came to a natural amphitheatre in the hills, and pitched camp there. They spent the next few days surveying the surrounding area, and Kulik reached the conclusion that "the cauldron" as he called it, was the centre of the blast. All around, the fallen trees faced away from it, and yet, incredibly, some trees actually remained standing although stripped and charred, at the very centre of the explosion.

The full extent of the desolation was now apparent; from the river to its central point was a distance of thirty-seven miles. So the blast had flattened more than four thousand square miles of forest.

Still working on the supposition that the explosion had been caused by a large meteorite, Kulik began searching the area for its remains. He thought he had achieved his object when he discovered a number of pits filled with water – he naturally assumed that they had been made by fragments of the exploding meteorite. Yet when the holes were drained they were found to be empty. One even had a tree-stump at the bottom, proving it had not been made by a blast.

Kulik was to make four expeditions to the area of the explosion, and until his death he remained convinced that it had been caused by an unusually large meteorite. Yet he never found the iron or rock fragments that would provide him with the evidence he needed. In fact, he never succeeded in proving that anything had even struck the ground. There was evidence of two blast waves – the original explosion and the ballistic wave – and even of brief flash fire; but there was no crater.

The new evidence only deepened the riddle. An aerial survey in 1938 showed that only 770 square miles of forest had been flattened, and that at the very point where the crater should have been the original trees were still standing. That suggested the vagaries of an exploding bomb, rather than that of the impact of a giant meteor – like the one that made the 600-foot-deep crater at Winslow, Arizona.

Even the way that the object fell to earth was disputed. Over seven hundred eyewitnesses claimed that it changed course as it fell, saying that it was originally moving towards Lake Baikal before it swerved. Falling heavenly bodies have never been known to do this, nor is it possible to explain how it could have happened in terms of physical dynamics.

Another curious puzzle about the explosion was its effect on the trees and insect life in the blast area. Trees that had survived the explosion had either stopped growing, or were shooting up at a greatly accelerated rate. Later studies revealed new species of ants and other insects which are peculiar to the Tunguska blast region.

It was not until some years after Kulik's death in a German prisoner-of-war camp that scientists began to see similarities between the Tunguska event and another even more catastrophic explosion: the destruction of Hiroshima and Nagasaki with thermonuclear devices.

Our knowledge of the atom bomb enables us to clear up many of the mysteries that baffled Kulik. The reason there was no crater was that the explosion had taken place above the ground, as with an atomic bomb. The standing trees at the central point of the explosion confirmed this; at both Nagasaki and Hiroshima, buildings directly beneath the blast remained standing, because the blast spread sideways. Genetic mutations in the flora and fauna around the Japanese cities are like those witnessed in Siberia, while blisters found on dogs and reindeer in the Tunguska area can now be recognized as radiation burns.

Atomic explosions produce disturbances in the earth's magnetic field, and even today the area around the Tunguska explosion has been described as "magnetic chaos". It seems clear that an electro-magnetic "hurricane" of incredible strength has ruptured the earth's magnetic field in this area.

Eye-witness accounts of the cloud produced by the explosion again support the view that it was some kind of atomic device; it had the typical shape of the atomic "mushroom cloud". Unfortunately, the one conclusive piece of evidence for the "atom bomb" theory is lacking: by the time the area's radiation levels were tested, more than fifty years later, they were normal.

Later investigators also learned that Kulik had been mistaken in his theory about the water-filled holes; they were not caused by meteorite fragments but by winter ice forcing its way to the surface through expansion, then melting in summer. Kulik's immense labours to drain the holes had been a waste of time.

Unfortunately, none of the new evidence that has been uncovered by Russian – and even American – expeditions has thrown any light on the cause of the explosion. UFO enthusiasts favour the theory that the object was an alien space craft, powered by atomic motors, which went out of control as it struck the earth's atmosphere. It has even been suggested that such a space craft might have headed towards Lake Baikal because it was in need of fresh water to cool its nuclear reactors; before it could reach its objective the reactors superheated and exploded.

The scientific establishment is naturally inclined to discount this theory as pure fantasy. But some of its own hypotheses seem equally fantastic. A.A. Jackson and M.P. Ryan of the University of Texas have suggested that the explosion was caused by a miniature black hole – a kind of whirlpool in space caused by the total collapse of the particles inside the atom. They calculated that their black hole would have passed straight through the earth and come out on the other side, and the Russians were sufficiently impressed by the theory to research local newspapers in Iceland and Newfoundland for June 1980; but there was no sign of the Tunguska-like catastrophe that should have occurred if Jackson and Ryan were correct.

Other American scientists suggested that the explosion was caused by antimatter, a hypothetical type of matter whose particles contain the opposite electric charge to those of normal matter. In contact with normal matter, anti-matter would explode and simply disappear. Only atomic radiation would be left behind. But there is even less evidence to support this theory than there is for the black-hole explanation.

Slightly more plausible – but still highly improbable – is the theory of the English scientist Frank Whipple that the earth had been struck by a comet. Astronomers still have no idea where comets originate, or how they are formed. The two chief objections to the comet theory are that it would be unlikely to produce a "nuclear" explosion, and that it would have been observed by astronomers long before it reached the earth. Supporters of the comet theory have pointed out that a comet coming in from the direction of the sun might be very hard to detect, and that the explosion of a comet might produce an effect similar to that of solar flares, which produce radio-activity. But none of the 120 observatories questioned by the Russians have any record of a comet on the trajectory of the Tunguska object.

More recently, it has been pointed out that the Tunguska event took place on 30 June and that on that same day each year the earth's orbit crosses that of a meteor stream called Beta Taurids, producing a "meteor shower". If one of these meteors had been exceptionally large, it could have survived burning up in the earth's atmosphere, and as its super-heated exterior reacted against its frozen interior, it would have shattered like molten glass suddenly plunged into freezing water. If this theory is correct, then it seems that Kulik was right after all. But that only reminds us that Kulik was unable to find the slightest shred of evidence for his theory. Eight decades after it took place, it seems increasingly unlikely that the mystery of the Tunguska explosion will ever be solved.

Postscript to The Great Tunguska Explosion

Since this article was written, new research has suggested that the "Tunguska object" was almost certainly a small comet or meteor, and not, as some have suggested, an exploding space craft, or even a miniature black hole. A comet seems less likely than a meteor, since comets travel relatively slowly, and would surely have been seen approaching the earth. Professor Alexis Zolotov (the leader of the 1959 expedition to Tunguska) calculated that, whatever the object was, it was about 130 feet in diameter, and exploded about three miles above the ground with a force of 40 megatons, 2,000 times greater than the atomic bomb at Hiroshima.

57

Unidentified Flying Objects

"Flying Saucers" have undoubtedly been *the* great mystery of the era that followed the Second World War, and theories to explain them have ranged from the belief that they are superior beings from another planet (or another dimension) to the suggestion that they are some kind of supernatural occurrence, allied to ghosts. Among intellectuals the most popular theory is that of Jung, who suggested that UFOs (unidentified flying objects) are "projections" of the unconscious mind, which is a polite, scientific way of saying that they have no more objective reality than the pink elephants of a dipsomaniac. But most of these Jungians choose to ignore – or are unaware of – Jung's later retraction of this view; he told his niece not long before his death that he had come to accept that UFOs *are* real objects.

The story of modern sightings began on 24 June 1947 when a businessman named Kenneth Arnold was flying his private plane near Mount Rainier in Washington State; against the background of the mountain, he saw nine shining discs travelling very fast – he estimated their speed at a thousand miles an hour, far beyond the speed of which any aircraft was capable at that time. Arnold said they were flying in formation, like geese, and that they wove in and out of the mountain peaks; he later compared their flight to a "saucer skipped across the water". So UFOs came to be referred to as "flying saucers".

Arnold's story was widely reported in the American Press, for he had a good reputation and was taken seriously – he had been out searching for the wreckage of a lost plane at the time he made the sighting, and obviously had no reason to invent such a story. Four days later, two pilots and two intelligence officers saw a bright light performing "impossible manoeuvres" over Maxwell Air Force Base in Montgomery, Alabama, and in Nevada on the same day another pilot saw a formation of "unidentified flying objects". As these and other sightings were reported the Press began to give prominence to stories of flying saucers, and by the end of that year there had been hundreds of sightings – a number that soon grew into thousands.

In January of the following year, 1948, an "unidentified object" was spotted in the sky above Godman Air Force Base in Kentucky. Three F-51 Mustangs were diverted from a training exercise to investigate, and one of these, flown by Captain Thomas Mantell, had soon outdistanced the other two. The radio tower received a call: "I see something above and ahead of me – I'm still climbing." "What is it?" "It looks metallic and is tremendous in size". Then he announced: "It's above me and I'm gaining on it. I'm going to twenty thousand feet". But these were the last words Mantell spoke. Later that day the remains of his plane were found ninety miles away from the base.

The story was a sensation – "airman destroyed by flying saucer". The Air Force announced that what Mantell had mistaken for a flying saucer was actually the planet Venus – a story that seemed, to put it mildly, unlikely. But then, the Air Force had shown the same confidence ten days after Arnold's original sighting when it had announced that Arnold had been "hallucinating".

It was obvious that the newspaper publicity was causing a certain amount of hysteria, and that many people thought they had seen flying saucers when they had only seen weather balloons or aircraft tail-lights. But was it conceivable that thousands of people – in fact, millions – could all be mistaken? For by 1966, a Gallup Poll revealed that five million Americans had seen flying saucers. And some of these sightings were at close quarters. A few days after Arnold's original sighting, the SS *Llandovery Castle* sailed from Mombasa *en route* to Cape Town. At about eleven one evening a Mrs A.M. King, of Nairobi, was on deck with another woman when they saw what appeared to be a bright star approaching the ship. Then a searchlight switched on, illuminating the sea about fifty yards from the ship. They saw an object made of steel and "shaped like a cigar cut at the rear end". It was about four times as big as the ship, and was travelling in the same direction; soon it vanished at a great speed, flames issuing from the "flattened" end.

Yet in spite of an increasing number of reports of this type, and thousands of "sky sightings", the Air Force continued to insist that UFO sightings were hoaxes, mistakes or downright lies. An official investigation, known as "Project Sign", began in September 1947, and later became known as "Project Blue Book". One of its advisers was the astronomer J. Allen Hynek, who began as a skeptic, but was soon convinced by the obvious truthfulness of witnesses that UFOs were a reality. But the Air Force remained adamantly skeptical. By the mid-1960s the belief that it was involved in a cover-up became so persistent that in 1965 the Air Force itself ordered that a new scientific panel should be set up; Edward U. Condon, a well-known physicist, was appointed head of this panel, and it was sponsored by the University of Colorado. But when the panel issued its report in 1969 it was obvious that the scientists of the University of Colorado had reached the same conclusion as the Air Force investigators – one newspaper headline summarized the findings of the 965-page report in the headline: "Flying Saucers Do Not Exist – Official".

One basic problem was that many of the sightings were too preposterous to be taken seriously; the whole field of investigation had become a happy hunting-ground for cranks. In a book called *Flying Saucers Have Landed* a Polish-American named George Adamski claimed that in 1952 he and a number of other saucer enthusiasts drove into the California desert – their route dictated by Adamski's "hunches" – and saw a huge cigar-shaped object in the sky. With a camera, Adamski wandered off alone, and saw a flying saucer land half a mile away. He hurried to the spot, and found a flying saucer, and a small man with shoulder-length blond hair, who identified himself in sign language as an inhabitant of the planet Venus. Then he flew off in his space craft. His friends had witnessed the encounter from a distance, and later signed notarized statements to this effect. In a second book, *Inside the Space Ships*, Adamski told how he had been taken for a trip in a flying saucer – called a "scout ship" – with his Venusian acquaintance, plus a man from Mars and a man from Saturn. On this occasion they flew into space and went on board the mother ship. On another occasion Adamski was taken to the moon, where he saw rich vegetation, including trees, and four-legged furry animals. He was also shown live pictures of Venus on a television screen, and saw that it had cities, mountains, rivers and lakes. Adamski died in 1965, four years before the moon landings, but three years after a space probe – Mariner II – had swept past Venus and revealed that it has an atmosphere of sulphuric acid gas, and that the surface is too hot to support life. But such small setbacks left Adamski unmoved – he was always able to claim that a mere space probe was less reliable than real Venusians – and he spent the final years of his life happily lecturing to audience of UFO enthusiasts all over the world.

Adamski's friend Dr George Hunt Williamson, who had been one of the witnesses of Adamski's original "contact", achieved a similar celebrity. In a book called *The Saucers Speak*, he told of how he had originally made contact with the inhabitants of flying saucers by means of automatic writing, and how later, a radio operator (whom he calls Mr R.) was able to establish direct contact. The "space men" were from the planet Mars, which they called Masar, and they explained that the earth was in grave danger of destroying itself. "Good and evil forces are working now. Organization is important for the salvation of your world." These space intelligences had been observing the earth for seventy-five thousand years, and were now prepared to save the world by revealing all kinds of astonishing secrets about Life, God and the Creator's place in the Divine Scheme. In a book called *Secret Places of the Lion* Williamson revealed some of these secrets – he claimed he had found them in a great library in a lost city high in the mountains of Peru, where a Master teacher, a survivor of the Elders, still lives and works. (This Master is thousands of years old – he lived on earth in the days when giants still roamed the planet.) This library (the author thanks one of the monks for translating its ancient records) reveals that the Star People came to earth eighteen million years ago (long before man appeared), and ever since then have been helping man to evolve. Their records are held in tombs and secret chambers, and one of their space-ships is at present hidden in the base of the Great Pyramid, which was built 24,000 years ago (and not a mere 4,500, as Egyptologists believe). These Star People were continually reincarnated as the great leaders and prophets of mankind, so Tiyi, the wife of the pharaoh Amenhotep III, later became the Queen of Sheba, Nefertiti, Queen Guinevere (wife of King Arthur) and Joan of Arc, while the Egyptian crown prince Seti became Isaiah, Aristotle, the apostle John and Leonardo da Vinci. *The Secret Places of the Lion* is a history of earth according to the ancient records, and is admittedly excellent value as historical entertainment. But the reader could be forgiven for thinking that Williamson decided that if Adamski could get away with it, then so could he . . .

In 1960 there appeared in France an extraordinary book called *Morning of the Magicians*, by Louis Pauwels and Jacques Bergier; it became an instant best-seller, and was translated into many languages. It discussed various "mysteries" – alchemy, astrology, black magic, mysterious ancient artifacts and the Great Pyramid – but its main argument is that much "lost knowledge" was brought to our planet by visitors from outer space. It discusses, for example, the so-called Piri Reis maps, dating to the sixteenth century, which show Antarctica (although it was not discovered until three centuries later), and also show a land bridge between Siberia and Alaska – a bridge that vanished thousands of years ago, giving way to the Bering Strait – and argues that such maps prove that the earth must have been surveyed from the air more than two thousand years ago. It is also full of inaccuracies – for example, describing Piri Reis (who was a Turkish pirate who was beheaded in 1554) as an American naval officer of the nineteenth century. But it caused widespread excitement, and seemed to justify the increasing number of "ufologists" who believed that the "saucers" had been appearing for centuries, and that they are even described in the Bible (as the fiery chariots of the prophet Ezekiel, for example).

But it was in 1967 that the "ancient astronaut theory" finally reached a worldwide audience, in the form of a book called *Memories of the Future*, translated into English as *Chariots of the Gods?* (One newspaper serialized it under the headline "Was God an Astronaut?") Its author, Erich von Däniken, borrowed liberally – and without acknowledgement – from predecessors like Williamson, Bergier and Pauwels, but presented his own "evidence" with a certain individual panache. His argument consists basically of the assertion that various ancient monuments – the Great Pyramid (naturally), the Easter Island statues, the Mexican pyramids, the megaliths of Carnac and Stonehenge – must have been erected with the aid of space men, because their technology would have been beyond the skills of the builders to whom they are attributed. It is full of misinformation – for example, he manages to multiply the weight of the Great Pyramid by five, and cites "legends" from the *Epic of Gilgamesh* which are simply not to be found in that work. Most of his major arguments proved to be faulty. He insists that the Easter Island statues were too big to be erected by natives; but the explorer Thor Heyerdahl persuaded modern Easter Islanders to carve and erect a similar statute in a few weeks. He asserts that the pyramids had to be built by ancient astronauts because the Egyptians had no rope – but pyramid texts show the use of rope. What Däniken claimed to be a picture of a man taking off in a space ship on the Palenque funerary tablet in Guatemala was shown by scholars to be a typical Mayan religious inscription, full of their basic symbols – birds, serpents and so on. He cites the mysterious Nazca lines on the plains of Peru as examples of structures that could only be understood when seen from the air, and suggests that they were giant runways for space craft – he even has a photograph of an aircraft "parking bay". But the lines are drawn on the pebbly surface of the desert, and would be instantly blown away if an aircraft tried to land on them. The "parking bay" turned out to be a detail from the leg of a bird – its knee – and was hardly large enough to park a bicycle. Däniken insisted that this was a mistake made by an editor; but he has allowed it to stand in subsequent editions of his book.

The mistake about the desert surface seems typical of Däniken's cavalier attitude to facts. Another can be found in *Gold of the Gods*, where Däniken offers a photograph of a skeleton carved out of stone, and wants to know how ancient sculptors knew about skeletons in the days before x-rays – overlooking the fact that every graveyard was full of them. It is also in *Gold of the Gods* that Däniken claims to have been taken into an underground city where he examined a secret library with books made of metal leaves. His companion, he said, was an explorer named Juan Moricz. When Moricz flatly denied the whole story Däniken hastened to concede that he had invented the underground library, but insisted that in Germany authors of popular non-fiction works are permitted to use certain "effects" – that is, to tell lies – provided they are merely incidental and do not touch the facts . . . And in spite of these embarrassments, Däniken continued to publish more books, each one of which, he claimed, helped to establish his astronaut theory beyond all possible doubt.

Understandably, then, the increasing flood of books by "ufologists" aroused most serious investigators to fury or derision.

Yet there were notable exceptions. J. Allen Hynek, as we have already observed, was part of Project Blue Book, and the evidence he studied finally convinced him that, no matter how many cranks, simpletons and downright liars managed to obscure the facts, these facts unequivocally indicated the real existence of flying saucers, and even of "space men". It was Hynek who coined the phrase "close encounters of the third kind" meaning encounters with grounded saucers and "humanoids" and he begins his chapter on such encounters (in *The UFO Experience, A Scientific Enquiry*): "We come now to the most bizarre and seemingly incredible aspect of the entire UFOs phenomenon. To be frank, I would gladly omit this part if I could without offense to scientific integrity . . ." And he goes on to consider a number of cases which, although they sound preposterous, were too well-authenticated to be dismissed. One typical case will suffice.

On 11 August 1955 a flying saucer was seen to land in farming country near Kelly-Hopkinsville, Kentucky. An hour later members of the Sutton family were alerted by the barking of the dog to the presence of an intruder near their farmhouse, and saw "a small 'glowing' man with extremely large eyes, his arms extended over his head". The two Sutton men fired at him with a rifle and shotgun, and there was a sound "as if I'd shot into a bucket", and the "space man" turned and hurried off. When another visitor appeared at the window the rifle was again fired and they ran outside to see if the creature had been hit. As one of them stopped under a low portion of the roof a claw-like hand reached down from it and touched his hair. More shots were fired at the creature on the roof, and although it was hit directly it floated down to the ground and hurried away. For the next three hours the eleven occupants of the house remained behind bolted doors, frequently seeing the "space men" at the windows. Finally, they all bolted out of the house, piled into two cars, and drove to the nearest police station. Police could find no signs of the spacemen, but as soon as they were gone the creatures reappeared. The next day a police artist got witnesses to describe what they had seen; the pictures that emerged was of tiny creatures with round heads and saucer-like eyes, and arms twice as long as their legs.

The family was subjected to a great deal of harassment as a result of their story; but serious investigators who questioned them had no doubt whatever that they were telling the truth.

Perhaps the most famous case of a "close encounter of the third kind" was that of Barney and Betty Hill. In September 1961 they were returning through New Hampshire from a holiday in Canada when they saw a flying saucer apparently in the process of landing. Two hours later they found themselves thirty-five miles from this spot, with no recollection of what had happened in the meantime. Eventually they consulted an expert in amnesia, Dr Benjamin Simon, who placed them under hypnosis; the Hills then described – independently – what had happened. They had been taken aboard the "saucer" by a number of uniformed men who looked more or less human (Barney said they reminded him of red-haired, round-faced Irishmen), subjected to a number of medical tests or experiments – skin and nail shavings were taken, and Betty Hill had a needle inserted into her navel – then they were hypnotized and told to forget everything that had happened. Allen Hynek himself was later present when Barney Hill was placed under hypnosis, and was allowed to question him. He ended by being convinced of the genuineness of the experience.

What has been called the "ultimate in contact stories" happened to Antonio Villas-Boas, a 23-year-old Brazilian farmer. On 15 October 1957, Villas-Boas claims that he was ploughing his fields when an egg-shaped UFO descended in front of his tractor. He tried to run away, but was grabbed by "humanoids" in tight grey overalls and helmets, and carried into the saucer. The space men communicated with sounds like yelps or barks. Villas-Boas was stripped naked and washed, then a blood sample was taken. After this a beautiful naked woman – about 4 foot 6 inches tall – came into the room. She soon induced Villas-Boas to make love to her, although he says that she had an off-putting way of grunting at intervals that made him feel he was having intercourse with an animal.

Villas-Boas's story would be an obvious candidate for the "hoax" category but for one thing. Dr Olavo T. Fontes examined him soon after the "encounter", and found that Villas-Boas had been subjected to a very high dose of radiation. And at the point on his chin where he claimed the needle had been inserted for the blood sample the doctor found two small marks. Villas-Boas's story is documented with convincing details in *The Humanoids*, edited by Charles Bowen.

Like Hynek, the journalist John Keel was also mildly skeptical about flying saucers until he tried the unusual expedient of studying the subject instead of passing a priori judgements. In 1952 he prepared a radio documentary on things seen in the sky, and came to believe that – even then – there had been too many sightings of flying saucers to dismiss them as mistakes or lies. In 1953, in Egypt, he saw his first UFO, a metallic disc with a revolving rim, hovering over the Aswan dam in daylight. Yet even so, it was not until 1966 that he decided to undertake a careful study of the subject, and subscribed to a press-cutting bureau. What then staggered him was the sheer number of the sightings – he often received 150 clippings in a day. (In those days press clippings were only a few pence each; twenty years later, at about a pound each, the experiment would be beyond the resources of most journalists.) Moreover, it soon became clear that even these were only a small percentage of the total, and that thousands of sightings were going unrecorded. (This is in fact the chief disadvantage of an article like this one; it cannot even begin to convey the sheer volume of the sightings. Any skeptic should try the experience of reading, say, a hundred cases, one after the other, to realize that the "delusion" theory fails to hold water.) What also fascinated Keel was that so many witnesses who had seen UFOs from their cars had later seen them over their homes; this suggested that the "space men" were not merely alien scientists or explorers, engaged in routine surveying work.

In the following year, 1967, Keel was driving along the Long Island Expressway when he saw a sphere of light in the sky, pursuing a course parallel to his own. When he reached Huntington he found that cars were parked along the roads, and dozens of people were staring at four lights that were bobbing and weaving in the sky; the light that had followed Keel joined the other four. Keel was in fact on his way to interview a scientist, Phillip Burckhardt, who had seen a UFO hovering above some trees close to his home on the previous evening, and had examined it through binoculars; he had seen that it was a silvery disc illuminated by rectangular lights that blinked on and off. The nearby Suffolk Air Force Base seemed to know nothing about it.

Like Hynek, Keel was impressed by the witnesses he interviewed; most were ordinary people who had no obvious reason for inventing a story about UFOs. His study of the actual literature convinced him that it was 98 per cent nonsense; but most individual witnesses were obviously telling the truth. Keel had soon accumulated enough cases to fill a 2000-page typescript; this had to be severely truncated before it was published under the title *UFOs: Operation Trojan Horse.*

As his investigation progressed, Keel became increasingly convinced that UFOs had been around for thousands of years, and that many biblical accounts of fiery chariots or fireballs are probably descriptions of them. In 1883 a Mexican astronomer named Jose Bonilla photographed 143 circular objects that moved across the solar disc. In 1878 a Texas farmer named John Martin saw a large circular object flying overhead, and actually used the word "saucer" in a newspaper interview about it. In 1897 people all over American began sighting huge airships – cigar-shaped craft. (This was before the man-made airship had been invented.) Dozens of other early "UFO" sightings have been chronicled in newspaper reports or pamphlets; Chapter 26 of Charles Fort's *Book of the Damned* – written thirty years before the UFO craze – is devoted to strange objects and lights seen in the sky. One of the most convincing sightings was made by the Russian painter Nicholas Roerich (who designed Stravinsky's *Rite of Spring* ballet); in his book *Altai Himalaya* (1930) he describes how, making his way from Mongolia to India in 1926, he – and the whole party – observed a big shiny disc moving swiftly across the sky. Like so many modern UFOs, this one suddenly changed direction above their camp. (In many UFO reports, the object seems to defy the laws of momentum by turning at right angles at great speed.) It vanished over the mountain peaks.

Keel was also interested by the parallels between reports of "space men" and descriptions by people who claim to have had supernatural experiences. The "angel" that instructed Joseph Smith – founder of the Mormons – to go and dig for engraved gold tablets sounds very like the kind of space visitor described by Adamski and so many others. During the First World War three children playing in meadows near Fatima, Portugal, saw a shining globe of light, and a woman's voice spoke from it. (Only two of the three heard it, although all saw it, suggesting that it was in their minds rather than in the objective world.) Crowds began to visit the spot every month where the "Lady of the Rosary" (as she called herself) appeared to the three children – only the children were able to see and hear her. But on 13 October 1917, when the Lady had announced that she would provide a miracle to convince the world, the rainclouds parted, and a huge silver disc descended towards the crowd of seventy thousand people. It whirled and bobbed – exactly like the UFOs Keel had seen – and changed colour through the whole spectrum; all watched it for ten minutes before it vanished into the clouds again. Many other people in the area saw it from their homes. The heat from the "object" dried the wet clothes of the crowd. Keel cites this and other "miracles" (such as one that occurred in Heede, Germany), and argues that they sound curiously similar to later UFO accounts.

There also seemed to be a more sinister aspect to the UFO affair; witnesses began to report that "government officials" had called on them and warned them to be silent; these men were usually dressed in black, although sometimes they wore military uniforms. No government department had – apparently – ever heard of them. Albert K. Bender of Bridgeport, Connecticut, suddenly closed down his International Flying Saucer Bureau in 1953, and declared that three dark-skinned men with glowing eyes had pressured him into abandoning his researches. Most UFO enthusiasts blamed the government; but when Bender published his full account ten years later it was obvious that something much stranger was involved; the three men materialized and dematerialized in his apartment, and on one occasion had transported him to a UFO base in Antarctica. Jacques Vallee, another scientist who had become interested in the UFO phenomenon, noted the similarity between this story and medieval legends about fairies and "elementals".

When Keel began to investigate sightings in West Virginia of a huge winged man who seemed to be able to keep up with fast-moving cars, he himself began to encounter vaguely hostile entities. A photographer took his picture in an empty street, then ran away. Just after arranging to meet another UFO expert, Gray Barker, a friend revealed that she had been told about the meeting two days ago before Keel had even thought of it. "Contactees" would ring him up and explain that they were with someone who wished to speak to him; then he would have conversations with men who spoke in strange voices. (He sometimes got the feeling he was speaking to someone in a trance.) Keel would be instructed to write letters to addresses which upon investigation proved to be non-existent; yet he would receive prompt replies, written in block letters. On one occasion, he stayed at a motel chosen at random, and found a message waiting for him at the desk. He says (in *The Mothman Prophecies*): "Someone somewhere was just trying to prove that they knew every move I was making, listened to all my phone calls, and could even control my mail. And they were succeeding". The entities also made many predictions of the assassination of Martin Luther King, of a planned attack on Robert Kennedy, of an attempt to stab the pope; but they frequently seemed to get the dates wrong. Keel concluded that "our little planet seems to be experiencing the interpenetration of forces or entities from some other space-time continuum".

The British expert on UFOs, Brinsley Le Poer Trench (the Earl of Clancarty), reached a similar kind of conclusion on the basis of his investigations. He expresses them (in *Operation Earth*) as follows:

> . . . there exist at least two diametrically opposed forces of entities interested in us. Firstly, those that are the real Sky People who have been around since time immemorial. Secondly, those that live in an area indigenous to this planet, though some of us believe they also live in the interior of the earth. There is obviously a "War in the Heavens" between these two factions. However, it is not considered that battles are going on in the sense that humans usually envisage them. It is more of a mental affray for the domination of the minds of mankind.

Jacques Vallee, one of the most serious and intelligent writers on the subject, finally came to a similar conclusion. In earlier books like *Anatomy of a Phenomenon* and *Challenge to Science: The UFO Enigma*, he studied case reports with unusual thoroughness (and many statistical tables). In *Passport to Magonia* (1970) he pointed out that the picture we can form of the world of the UFO occupants is more like the mediaeval concept of Magonia, a land above the clouds, than some inhabited planet. By 1977 he had come to the strange conclusion that UFOs are basically "psychic" in nature, a view he expressed in a book called *The Invisible College*. The invisible college is a group of scientists who are engaged in the study of UFO phenomena, and who decline to be intimidated by conservative scientific attitudes. Vallee, himself a computer expert, reached the conclusion that UFO phenomena are a "control system" – that is, that they are designed to produce a certain specific effect on the human mind. He explains in *Messengers of Deception* (1979): that after a year researching the similarity between UFO phenomena and psychic phenomena "I could no longer regard the 'flying saucers' as simply some sort of spacecraft or machine, no matter how exotic its propulsion". He went back to his computers, and concluded: "The most clear result was that the phenomenon behaved like a conditioning process. The logic of conditioning uses absurdity and confusion to achieve its goal while hiding its mechanism. I began to see a similar structure in the UFO stories".

Absurdity and confusion are certainly one of the most puzzling and irritating aspects of the UFO stories. Vallee devotes a chapter of *The Invisible College* to studying the case of Uri Geller. Geller, the Israeli psychic and "metal-bender", was "discovered" by the scientist Andrija Puharich. Geller's powers aroused such worldwide interest that it seemed inevitable that the first full-length book about him would become a bestseller. In fact Puharich's *Uri: A Journal of the Mystery of Uri Geller* (1974) came close to destroying Puharich's reputation as a serious investigator. It seems to be full of baffling confusions and preposterous and inexplicable happenings. Yet it also provides some vital clues to the mystery of "space intelligences". In 1952, long before he met Geller, Puharich was studying with a Hindu psychic named Dr Vinod when Vinod went into a trance and began to speak with an English voice; this trance-entity announced itself as a member of "the Nine", superhuman intelligences who had been studying the human race for thousands of years, and whose purpose is to aid human evolution. Three years later, travelling in Mexico, Puharich met an American doctor who also passed on lengthy messages from "space intelligences" – the odd thing being that they were a continuation of the messages that had come through Dr Vinod. When Puharich met Geller in 1971 the "Nine" again entered the story; while Geller was in a trance a voice spoke out of the air above his head explaining that Geller had been programmed by "space intelligences" from the age of three – the aim being to prevent the human race from plunging itself into catastrophe. Puharich goes on to describe UFO sightings, and an endless series of baffling events, with objects appearing and disappearing and recorded tapes being mysteriously "wiped". Puharich assured the present writer (CW) that he had left out some of the more startling items because they would be simply beyond belief.

After Puharich's break with Geller, the "Nine" continued to manifest themselves through mediums. The story is told in *Prelude to a Landing on Planet Earth* by Stuart Holroyd, and it is even more confusing than Puharich's book. The "Nine" finally sent Puharich and his companions on a kind of wild-goose chase around the Middle East and other remote places; the main purpose was apparently to pray for peace, and the "intelligences" assured them that they had averted appalling international catastrophes.

In fact, the mention of mediums may provide a key to the mystery.

Modern spiritualism began in the mid-nineteenth century, when "spirits" began to express themselves through the mediumship of two teenage girls named Fox; soon thousands of "mediums" were causing mysterious rapping noises (one knock for yes, two for no), making trumpets and other musical instruments float through the air and apparently play themselves, and producing spirit voices – and even spirit forms – by going into a trance. No one who has studied the phenomena in depth can believe that they were all fraudulent. Moreover, the theory that they were somehow produced by the unconscious minds of the participants must also be reluctantly dismissed, since in many cases "spirits" were able to use different "mediums" in order to reveal fragments of the same message – fragments which interlocked like a jigsaw puzzle.

But what soon becomes equally clear to any student of the subject is that the "spirits" cannot be taken at their own valuation. As often as not, they told lies. Emanuel Swedenborg, the eighteenth-century visionary, warned that there are basically two varieties of spirit, a "higher order" and a "lower order". A psychiatrist, Wilson Van Dusen, who studied hundreds of cases of hallucinations at the Mendocino State Hospital in California, noted that "the patients felt as if they had contact with another world or order of beings. Most thought these other persons were living. All objected to the term 'hallucination'". And he noted that the hallucinations seemed to fall into Swedenborg's two categories: "helpful" spirits (about one-fifth of all cases), and distinctly unhelpful spirits whose aim seemed to be to cause the patients misery, irritation and anguish.

It is, of course, a major step for any normal, rational person to accept the real existence of disembodied spirits, or "discarnates". Yet anyone who is willing to study the evidence patiently and open-mindedly will undoubtedly arrive at that conclusion. In fact, anyone who has ever tried automatic writing or the ouija board or "table turning" has probably reached the conclusion that there are "intelligences" that are capable of manifesting through human beings. But the question of the precise nature of these entities is altogether more baffling. It seems clear that some can be taken seriously, others not. Many seem to behave like the traditional demons of the Middle Ages, telling whatever lie happens to enter their heads on the spur of the moment. Some of these "intelligences" – known as poltergeists – can even manifest their presence by causing objects to fly around the room, or causing mysterious bangs and crashes. One interesting characteristic of the poltergeist is that it can cause an object travelling at high speed to change direction quite abruptly, in defiance of the Newtonian laws of motion. This also seems to be one of the characteristics of the flying saucer.

Jacques Vallee was intrigued by the number of cases in which UFOs behaved in a manner that contradicted the notion that they were simply the artifacts of some superior civilization; some have dissolved into thin air; some have vanished into the earth; some have expanded like balloons, then disappeared. Some "spacemen" seem to have the power of reading thoughts and of predicting events which will occur in the future. Many of them like Puharich's "Nine" insist that their purpose is to prepare the human race for some astonishing event, like a landing of UFOs on earth; but the landing never seems to occur.

Yet it may be simplistic to believe that UFOs are simply an up-dated version of medieval demons or nineteenth-century "spirit communicators". Vallee's belief is that the phenomenon is "heuristic" that is, is designed to teach us something. Modern science and philosophy have accustomed us to materialistic theories of the universe, to the notion that living creatures are a billion-to-one accident, and that the human reality is simply the reality of our bodies and brains. In *Flying Saucers, A Modern Myth of Things Seen in the Skies*, Jung suggested that UFOs may be modern man's response to his craving for religious meanings, and Vallee seems to accept at least the basic implication of this theory. Like Jung, he also seems to believe that coincidences may be more than they seem. In *Messengers of Deception*, he describes his interest in a modern religious cult called the Order of Melchizedek, which believes that its basic doctrines have been received through extra-terrestrial intelligences. Then, as noted in chapter 54, he began collecting all he could find about the biblical prophet Melchizedek. In February 1976 he asked a female taxi-driver in Los Angeles for a receipt; when he looked at the receipt it was signed "M. Melchizedek". He looked up Melchizedek in the Los Angeles phone directory; there was only one . . .

This leads Vallee to an interesting speculation about the underlying reality of the world. He points out that we are confined to our space-time continuum, and all our concepts of knowledge are based on space and time. So in a library our "information retrieval system" is based on alphabetical order. But modern computer scientists have developed another method; they "sprinkle the records throughout storage as they arrive, and . . . construct an algorithm for retrieval based on some type of keyword . . ." He concluded: "The Melchizedek incident . . . suggested to me that the world may be organized more like a randomized data base than a sequential library". In a computer "library", the student enters a request for "microwave" or "headache" and finds twenty articles that he never even suspected had existed. Vallee had entered a request for Melchizedek, and some psychic computer had asked: "How about this one?"

In *The Flying Saucer Vision* (1967), the English writer John Michell also takes his starting-point from Jung. Michell accepts Jung's view that the UFO phenomenon is somehow connected with the "religious vacuum" in the soul of modern man. He associates UFOs with ancient legends about gods who descend in airships, and his conclusions are not dissimilar to those of von Däniken, although rather more convincingly argued. But Michell also has an original contribution to make to "ufology". In his researches he had stumbled upon Alfred Watkins's book *The Old Straight Track* (1925), in which Watkins argues that the countryside is intersected with ancient straight trackways which were prehistoric trade routes, and that these tracks connect "sacred sites" such as churches, stone circles, barrows and tumuli. Watkins called these "ley lines". Michell argues that the ley lines are identical with lines that the Chinese call "dragon paths" or *lung mei*. The Chinese science of *feng shui*, or geomancy, is basically a religious system concerned with the harmony between man and nature; it regards the earth as a living body. *Lung mei* are lines of force on the earth's surface, and one of the aims of *feng shui* is to preserve and concentrate this force, and prevent it from leaking away. Michell was mistaken to state that *lung mei* are straight lines, like Watkins' leys – in fact, the Chinese regard straight lines with suspicion; the essential quality of *lung meis* is that they are crooked. But Michell takes an important step beyond Watkins in regarding ley lines as lines of some earth force; he believes that ancient man selected spots in which there was a high concentration of this force as their sacred sites. Points where two or more ley lines cross have a special significance. Michell also points out that many sightings of flying saucers occur on ley lines, and particularly on their points of intersection – for example, Warminster, in Wiltshire, where a truly extraordinary number of sightings have been made. In a book called *The Undiscovered Country*, Stephen Jenkins, another serious investigator of such matters, points out how often crossing-points of ley lines are associated with all kinds of "supernatural" occurrences, from ghosts and poltergeists to strange visions of phantom armies. Once again we seem to have an interesting link between UFOs and the "supernatural".

Two more investigators deserve a mention in this context: T.C. Lethbridge and F.W. Holiday. Lethbridge was a retired Cambridge don who became fascinated by dowsing, and the power of the pendulum to detect various substances under the earth. (I have spoken of him at length in my book *Mysteries*.) Towards the end of his life (he died in 1971), Lethbridge became interested in flying saucers, and in a book called *Legend of the Sons of God* (1972) suggested that UFOs may be associated with ancient standing stones – in fact, that such stones may have been set up in the remote past as "beacons" for ancient space craft. Lethbridge knew nothing of ley lines, but his own investigations led him to conclusions that are remarkably similar to Michell's.

F.W. Holiday was a naturalist and a fishing journalist who became fascinated by the mystery of the Loch Ness monster (*qv*) and wrote a book suggesting that it was a giant slug, or "worm" (using this word in its medieval sense of "dragon"). But after years of study of the phenomenon he found the Loch Ness monster and other lake monsters as elusive as ufologists have found flying saucers. He became increasingly convinced that both flying saucers and lake monsters belong to what he called "the phantom menagerie" (see chapter 19 on The Grey Man of Ben MacDhui). This view was expressed in his book *The Dragon and the Disc*, and in his posthumous work *The Goblin Universe*. Like Vallee, Holiday finally became convinced that the answer to the UFO enigma lies in "the psychic solution". It must be acknowledged that there is a great deal of evidence that points in this direction. On the other hand, it would be premature to discount the possibility that they may be spacecraft from another planet or galaxy; this is a matter on which it would be foolish not to keep an open mind.

58

Vampires: Do They Exist?

The problem of the vampire can be stated simply. Any rational person will agree that the notion that vampires actually exist *has* to be pure superstition. Blood-drinking supernatural beings do not and cannot exist. There has to be some simpler, more sensible, explanation. The objection to this view is that a number of early accounts of vampires have such an air of sobriety and authority that it is difficult to dismiss them as pure fantasy. Here, for example, is an eighteenth-century report known as *Visum et Repertum* ("Seen and Discovered"), signed by no fewer than five Austrian officers, three of them doctors:

After it had been reported in the village of Medvegia [near Belgrade] that so-called vampires had killed some people by sucking their blood, I was, by high decree of a local Honorable Supreme Command, sent there to investigate the matter thoroughly, along with officers detailed for that purpose and two subordinate medical officers, and therefore carried out and heard the present enquiry in the company of the Captain of the Stallath company of haiduks [Balkan mercenaries and outlaws opposed to Turkish rule], Hadnack Gorschiz, the standard-bearer and the oldest haiduk of the village. [They reported], unanimously, as follows. About five years ago, a local haiduk called Arnod Paole broke his neck in a fall from a hay wagon. This man had, during his lifetime, often described how, near Gossova in Turkish Serbia, he had been troubled by a vampire, wherefore he had eaten from the earth of the vampire's grave and had smeared himself with the vampire's blood, in order to be free of the vexation he had suffered. In twenty or thirty days after his death, some people complained that they were being bothered by this same Arnod Paole; and in fact, four people were killed by him. In order to end this evil, they dug up Arnod Paole forty days after his death – this on the advice of their Hadnack, who had been present at such events before; and they found that he was quite complete and undecayed, and that fresh blood had flowed from his eyes, nose, mouth, and ears; that the shirt, the covering, and the coffin were completely bloody; that the old nails on his hands and feet, along with the skin, had fallen off, and that new ones had grown. And since they saw from this that he was a true vampire, they drove a stake through his heart – according to their custom – whereupon he gave an audible groan and bled copiously. Thereupon they burned the body to ashes the same day and threw these into the grave. These same people also say that all those who have been tormented and killed by vampires must themselves become vampires. Therefore they disinterred the above mentioned four people in the same way. Then they also add that this same Arnod Paole attacked not only people but cattle, and sucked out their blood. And since some people ate the flesh of such cattle, it would appear that [this is the reason that] some vampires are again present here, inasmuch as in a period of three months, seventeen young and old people died, among them some who, with no previous illness, died in two or at most three days. In addition, the haiduk Jovitsa reports that his stepdaughter, by name Stanacka, lay down to sleep fifteen days ago, fresh and healthy, but that at midnight she started up out of her sleep with a terrible cry, fearful and trembling, and complained that she had been throttled by the son of a haiduk by the name of Milloe [who had died nine weeks earlier], whereupon she had experienced a great pain in the chest, and become worse hour by hour, until finally she died on the third day. At this, we went the same afternoon to the graveyard, along with the aforementioned oldest haiduks of the village, in order to cause the suspicious graves to be opened, and to examine the bodies in them. Whereby, after all of them had been [exhumed and] dissected, the following was found:

1. A woman by the name of Stana, twenty years old, who had died in childbirth two months ago, after a three-day illness, and who had herself said before her death that she had painted herself with the blood of a vampire – wherefore both she and the child, which had died soon after birth and through careless burial had been half

eaten by dogs – must also become vampires. She was quite complete and undecayed. After the opening of the body there was found in the *cavitate pectoris* a quantity of fresh extravascular blood. The vessels of the *arteriae*, like the *ventriculis cordis*, were not, as is usual, filled with coagulated blood; and the whole viscera – that is, the lung, liver, stomach, spleen, and intestines – were quite fresh, as they would be in a healthy person. The uterus was, however, quite enlarged and very inflamed externally, for the placenta and lochia had remained in place, wherefore the same was in complete putrefaction. The skin on her hands and feet, along with the old nails, fell away on their own, but on the other hand completely new nails were evident, along with a fresh and vivid skin.

2. There was a woman by the name of Militsa, sixty years old, who had died after a three-month sickness and had been buried ninety or so days earlier. In the chest much liquid blood was found, and the other viscera were – like those mentioned above – in good condition. During her dissection, all the haiduks who were standing around marveled greatly at her plumpness and perfect body, uniformly stating that they had known the woman well from her youth and that she had throughout her life been very lean and dried up; they emphasized that she had come to such surprising plumpness in the grave. They also said that it was she who had started the vampires this time, because she had been eating of the flesh of those sheep who had been killed by previous vampires.

3. There was an eight-day-old child which had lain in the grave for ninety days and which was also in a condition of vampirism.

4. The son of a haiduk, sixteen years old, named Milloe, was dug up, having lain in the earth for nine weeks, after he had died from a three-day illness, and was found to be like the other vampires. [This is obviously the vampire who had attacked the stepdaughter of the haiduk Jovitsa.]

5. Joachim, also the son of a haiduk, seventeen years old, had died after a three-day illness. He had been buried eight weeks and four days and, on being dissected, was found in similar condition.

6. A woman by the name of Ruscha who had died after a ten-day illness and been buried six weeks earlier, in whom there was much fresh blood, not only in the chest but also in *in fundo ventriculi*. The same showed itself in her child, which was eighteen days old and had died five weeks earlier.

7. No less did a girl of ten years of age, who had died two months previously, find herself in the above-mentioned condition, quite complete and undecayed, and had much fresh blood in her chest.

8. They caused the wife of the Hadnack to be dug up, along with her child. She had died seven weeks earlier, her child – who was eight weeks old – twenty-one days previously, and it was found that mother and child were completely decomposed, although earth and grave were like those of the vampires lying nearby.

9. A servant of the local corporal of the haiduks, by the name of Rhade, twenty-three years old, died after a three-month illness, and after being buried five weeks, was found completely decomposed.

10. The wife of the local standard-bearer, along with her child, were also completely decomposed.

11. With Stanche, a haiduk, sixty years old, who had died six weeks previously, I noticed a profuse liquid blood, like the others, in the chest and stomach. The entire body was in the above-mentioned condition of vampirism.

12. Milloe, a haiduk, twenty-five years old, who had lain for six weeks in the earth, was also found in a condition of vampirism.

13. Stanoicka [earlier called Stanacka], the wife of a haiduk, twenty-three years old, died after a three-day illness and had been buried eighteen days earlier. In the dissection I found that her countenance was quite red and of a vivid colour, and as was mentioned above, she had been throttled at midnight, by Milloe, the son of a haiduk, and there was also to be seen, on the right side under the ear, a bloodshot blue mark [i.e., a bruise] the length of a finger [demonstrating that she had been throttled]. As she was being taken out of the grave, a quantity of fresh blood flowed from her nose. With the dissection I found – as so often mentioned already – a regular fragrant fresh bleeding, not only in the chest cavity but also in the heart ventricle. All the viscera were found in a completely good and healthy condition. The skin of the entire body, along with the nails on the hands and feet, were as though completely fresh.

After the examination had taken place, the heads of the vampires were out off by the local gypsies and then burned along with the bodies, after which the ashes were thrown into the river Morava. The decomposed bodies, however, were laid back in their own graves. Which I attest along with those assistant medical officers provided for me. *Actum ut supra*:

L.S. [signed] Johannes Fluchinger, Regimental Medical Officer of the Foot Regiment of the Honorable B. Furstenbusch.

L.S. J.H. Siegel, Medical Officer of the Honorable Morall Regiment.

L.S. Johann Friedrich Baumgarten, Medical Officer of the Foot Regiment of the Honorable B. Furstenbusch.

The undersigned attest herewith that all which the Regiment Medical Officer of the Honorable Furstenbusch had observed in the matter of vampires – along with both medical officers who signed with him – is in every way truthful and has been undertaken, observed, and examined in our own presence. In confirmation thereof is our signature in our own hand, of our own making, Belgrade, 26 January 1732.

L.S. Buttener, Lieutenant Colonel of the Honorable Alexandrian Regiment.

L.S. J.H. von Lindenfels, Officer of the Honorable Alexandrian Regiment.

As we study this strange account (which is admittedly difficult to do without skipping), there is an obvious temptation to dismiss it as a farrago of peasant superstition. Yet this is no secondhand tale of absurd horrors; the three doctors were officers in the army of Charles VI, Emperor of Austria – that newly emerging power that was succeeding the Holy Roman Empire. They were thoroughly familiar with corpses, having been serving in the army that had fought the Turks since 1714 and that defeated them four years later.

A brief sketch of the historical background may clarify the emergence of vampires in the first half of the eighteenth century. For more than four centuries the Turks had dominated eastern Europe, marching in and out of Transylvania, Walachia, and Hungary and even conquering Constantinople in 1453. Don John of Austria defeated them at the great sea battle of Lepanto (1571), but it was their failure to capture Vienna after a siege in 1683 that caused the breakup of the Ottoman Empire. During the earlier stages of this war between Europe and Turkey, the man whose name has become synonymous with vampirism – Dracula, or Vlad the Impaler – struck blow after blow against the Turks, until they killed and beheaded him in 1477.

Vlad Tepes (the Impaler), king of Walachia (1456–62, 1476–77), was, as his nickname implies, a man of sadistic temperament whose greatest pleasure was to impale his enemies (which meant anyone against whom he had a grudge) on pointed stakes; the stake – driven into the ground –

was inserted into the anus (or, in the case of women, the vagina), and the victim was allowed to impale himself slowly under his own weight. (Vlad often had the point blunted to make the agony last longer.) In his own time he was known as Dracula, which means "son of a dragon" or "son of the Devil". It is estimated that Dracula had about one hundred thousand people impaled during the course of his lifetime. When he conquered Brasov, in Transylvania, he had all its inhabitants impaled on poles, then gave a feast among the corpses. When one nobleman held his nose at the stench, Vlad sent for a particularly long pole and had him impaled. When he was a prisoner in Hungary, Vlad was kept supplied with birds, rats, and toads, which he impaled on small stakes. A brave and fearless warrior, he was finally killed in battle – or possibly assassinated by his own soldiers – and his head sent to Constantinople. Four hundred and twenty years later, in 1897, he was immortalized by Bram Stoker as the sinister Count Dracula, no longer a sadistic maniac but a drinker of blood.

By the time of the outbreak of vampirism in Medvegia in the early 1730s, Vlad's hereditary enemies, the Turks, had been driven out of Serbia, and the Austrians were now in Belgrade – which had originally fallen to the troops of Suleiman the Magnificent in 1521. The Austrians soon became aware of a strange superstition among the peasantry; they dug up corpses and beheaded them, alleging that they were *vampires*, or *upirs*.

Tales of the "living dead" had been current since the days of ancient Greece. The Greeks called the creature a *lamia* or *empusa* and seemed to identify it with a witch. Lamias were not blood drinkers but cannibals. The biographer Philostratus tells a story of the philosopher (and magician) Apollonius of Tyana, who instantly recognized the fiancée of his disciple Menippus as a lamia, and with a few magical words caused the whole wedding feast to disappear into thin air. The girl then admitted that it was her intention to make a meal of Menippus. (Keats sentimentalizes the story in his poem *Lamia*; unable to believe any evil of a pretty girl, he makes her a lovelorn snake and Apollonius the cold, rational philosopher who destroys their happiness.)

Tales of the "undead" – known as *vrykolakas* – persisted in Greece down through the centuries, and on January 1, 1701, a French botanist named Pitton de Tornefort visited the island of Mykonos and was present at a gruesome scene of dissection. An unnamed peasant, of sullen and quarrelsome disposition, was murdered in the fields by persons unknown. Two days after his burial, his ghost was reported to be wandering around at night, overturning furniture and "playing a thousand roguish tricks". Ten days after his burial, a mass was said to "drive out the demon" that was believed to be in the corpse, after which the body was disinterred and the local butcher given the task of tearing out the heart. His knowledge of anatomy seemed to be defective, and he tore open the stomach and rummaged around in the intestines, causing such a vile stench that incense had to be burned. In the smoke-filled church, people began shouting "vrykolakas" and alleging that some of the smoke poured out of the corpse itself. Even after the heart had been burned at the seashore, the ghost continued to cause havoc until the villagers finally burned the corpse on a pyre.

De Tornefort took a highly superior attitude about all this, convinced that it was simply mass hysteria: "I have never viewed anything so pitiable as the state of this island. Everyone's head was turned; the wisest people were stricken like the others". Although the year was only 1701, de Tornefort's attitude was that of a typical French rationalist of the eighteenth century.

Twenty years later, after the Turks were driven out of eastern Europe, western Europe was astonished by these gruesome tales of disinterments – of which the one quoted above is so typical. And now it was no longer possible to take an attitude of amused superiority, since many of the accounts were firsthand. An account of what happened when a man named Peter Plogojowitz was exhumed dates from 1725, seven years before the story of the vampires of Medvegia. It is recounted by another official:

After a subject by the name of Peter Plogojowitz had died, ten weeks past – he lived in the village of Kisilova, in the Rahm district [of Serbia] – and had been buried according to the Raetzian custom, it was revealed that in this same village of Kisilova, within a week, nine people, both young and old, died also, after suffering a twenty-four-hour illness. And they said publicly, while they were yet alive, but on their deathbed, that the above-mentioned Peter Plogojowitz, who had died ten weeks earlier, had come to them in their sleep, laid himself on them, and throttled them, so that they would have to give up the ghost. The other subjects were very distressed and strengthened even more in such beliefs by the fact that the dead Peter Plogojowitz's wife, after saying that her husband had come to her and demanded his opanki, or shoes, had left the village of Kisilova and gone to another. And since with such people (which they call vampires) various signs are to be seen – that is, the body undecomposed, the skin, hair, beard, and nails growing – the subjects resolved unanimously to open the grave of Peter Plogojowitz and see whether any such above-mentioned signs were to be found on him. To this end they came here to me, and, telling of these events, asked me and the local pope, or parish priest, to be present at the viewing. And although I at first disapproved, telling them that first the praiseworthy administration should be dutifully and humbly informed, and its exalted opinion about this should be heard, they did not want to accommodate themselves to this at all but rather gave this short answer: I could do what I wanted, but if I did not accord them the viewing and the legal recognition to deal with the body according to their custom, they would have to leave house and home, because by the time a gracious resolution was received from Belgrade, perhaps the entire village – and this was supposed to have happened once before when it was under the Turks – could be destroyed by such an evil spirit, and they did not want to wait for this.

Since I could not hold such people from the resolution they had made, either with good words or threats, I went to the village of Kisilova, taking along the Gradisk pope, and viewed the body of Peter Plogojowitz, just exhumed, finding it, in accordance with thorough truthfulness, that first of all I did not detect the slightest odor that is otherwise characteristic of the dead, and the body – except for the nose, which was somehow sunken – was completely fresh. The hair and the beard – even the nails, of which the old ones had fallen away – had grown on him; the old skin, which was somewhat whitish, had peeled away, and a new fresh one had emerged under it. The face, hands, and feet, and the whole body, were so constituted, that they could not have been more complete in his lifetime. Not without astonishment, I saw some fresh blood in his mouth, which according to the common observation, he had sucked from the people killed by him. In short, all the indications were present (as remarked above) as such people are supposed to have. After both the pope and I had seen this spectacle, while the people grew more outraged than distressed, all the subjects, with great speed, sharpened a stake – in order to pierce the corpse of the deceased with it – and put this at his heart, whereupon, as he was pierced, not only did much blood, completely fresh, flow also through his ears and mouth, but still other wild signs (which I pass by out of high respect) took place. [He means that the corpse had an erection.] Finally, according to their usual practice, they burned the aforementioned body, *in hoc casu*, to ashes, of which I (now) inform the most laudable administration, and at the same time would like to request, obediently and humbly, that if a mistake was made in this matter, such as is to be attributed not to me but to the rabble, who were beside themselves with fear.

Imperial Provisor, Gradisk District

Here again we have a respectable official vouching for the fact that the corpse looked remarkably fresh and had fresh blood in the mouth.

Let us consider these accounts in more detail. To begin with, it seems clear that the vampire is not a physical body that clambers out of its grave – as in *Dracula* – but some sort of ghost or spectral "projection". In the long account of the Medvegia vampires signed by Dr. Fluchinger et al., we find that the vampire lies down beside its victim and throttles her; a mark on the girl's throat seems to indicate that this is what happened. There is nothing here of the Draculalike vampire who sinks his pointed fangs into the victim's flesh. What the villagers allege is that the body has been *taken over* by a demonic entity, which attacks the living and somehow drains their vitality. The corpse that is the home of the demonic entity then flourishes in the grave and even continues to grow new skin and nails. The detail of blood in the chest seems a little puzzling, until, we look again at the account and see that the blood is found in the breast cavity (*cavitate pectoris*) of the woman named Stana, while the lungs are mentioned separately later in the same sentence; in other words, when the breast was opened up, exposing the heart, fresh blood was found. There is no reason, in this particular instance, to suppose that this is the blood of the victim; it is presumably the vampire's own.

The many skeptics who have written on the subject of vampires usually produce the same rationalizations. These are typified by the long article on vampirism in Rossell Hope Robbins's *Encyclopedia of Witchcraft and Demonology* (1959). He points out that there must have been many premature burials and that when the grave of such an unfortunate was opened, the corpse would be found in a contorted position that suggested that it had come to life. He also points out that "the existence of maniacs who crave for blood" could have given rise to the legend of the vampire. The sudden deaths of a large number of people in a space of weeks is explained by plague or other unknown forms of illness. Paul Barber, in *Vampires, Burial and Death* (from which the above translations have been quoted), takes much the same line, although he admits that the premature burial theory fails to explain the Medvegia "outbreak". But he goes on to point out that different bodies decay at different rates and that therefore, there is nothing surprising in the description of a two-month-old body that remains as fresh as when it was buried.

All this is plausible enough. But if we read straight through the accounts by Fluchinger and the Gradisk provisor (a steward to a religious house), we see that these rationalizations simply fail to provide an adequate explanation of what has taken place. It is true that the account of Arnod Paole, the soldier who became a vampire, is second-hand, having occurred five years before the officers went to investigate the new outbreak of vampirism. We may therefore doubt whether he gave an "audible groan" as they drove a stake through his heart, and all the other details of the hearsay account. But even if we suppose that some plague was really responsible for the deaths of the seventeen villagers, it is hard to explain why eleven of the corpses were undecayed, while only four corpses were decomposed in the manner one might expect.

In fact, the real problem with all these debunkers of the vampire theory is that they do their debunking piecemeal; that is, they concentrate on some small point that they feel they can disprove and then behave as if they have produced a total explanation that makes any further discussion unnecessary. Those people who – like myself – find their theories inadequate might well agree that vampires *cannot* really exist. But they simply cannot agree that the skeptics have proved their point and produced a convincing explanation for the many highly detailed stories.

Paul Barber also cites an interesting case known as the Shoemaker of Breslau. He takes his version from an 1868 collection of Prussian folklore by J. Grasse, but there is an earlier version of the same story in Henry More's *Antidote Against Atheism* (1653). This describes how, on September 21, 1591, a well-to-do shoemaker of Breslau, in Silesia – one account gives his name as Weinrichius – cut his throat with a knife and soon after died from the wound. Since suicide was regarded as a mortal sin, his wife tried to conceal it and announced that her husband had died of a stroke. An old woman was taken into the secret, and she washed the body and bound up the throat so skillfully that the wound was invisible. A priest who came to comfort the widow was taken to view the corpse and noticed nothing suspicious. The shoemaker was buried on the following day, September 22, 1591.

Perhaps because of this unseemly haste, and the refusal of the wife to allow neighbours to view the body, a rumor sprang up that the shoemaker had committed suicide. After this, his ghost began to be seen in the town. Soon it was climbing into bed with people and squeezing them so hard that it left the marks of its fingers on their flesh. This finally became such a nuisance that in the year following the burial, on April 18, 1592, the council ordered the grave to be opened. The body was complete and undamaged by decay but "blown up like a drum." The skin had peeled away from the feet, and another had grown, "much purer and stronger than the first." He had a "mole like a rose" on his big toe – which was interpreted as a witch's mark – and there was no smell of decay, except in the shroud itself. Even the wound in the throat was undecayed. The corpse was laid under a gallows, but the ghost continued to appear. By May 7 it had grown "much fuller of flesh." Finally, the council ordered that the corpse should be beheaded and dismembered. When the body was opened up, the heart was found to be "as good as that of a freshly slaughtered calf." Finally, the body was burned on a huge bonfire of wood and pitch and the ashes thrown into the river. After this, the ghost ceased to appear.

Barber agrees that "much in this story is implausible" but points out that so many details – notably the description of the body – are so precise as to leave no doubt "that we are dealing with real events."

But what are these "real events"? Before we comment further, let us consider another well-known case from the same year, 1592 (which is, of course, more than a century earlier than the famous vampire outbreak we have been discussing). This case has also been discussed by both More and Grasse and concerns an alderman of Pentsch (or Pentach) in Silesia named Johannes Cuntze (whose name More Latinizes to Cuntius). On his way to dinner with the mayor, Cuntze tried to examine a loose shoe of a mettlesome horse and received a kick, presumably on the head. The blow apparently unsettled his reason; he complained that he was a great sinner and that his body was burning. He also refused to see a priest. This gave rise to all kinds of rumors about him, including that he had made a pact with the Devil.

As Cuntze was dying, with his son beside the bed, the casement opened and a black cat jumped into the room and leapt onto Cuntze's face, scratching him badly; he died soon after. At his funeral on February 8, 1592, "a great tempest arose"; it continued to rage as he was buried beside the altar of the local church.

Before he was buried, there were stories that his ghost had appeared and attempted to rape a woman. After the burial the ghost began to behave like a mischievous hobgoblin, throwing things about, opening doors, and causing banging noises so that "the whole house shaked again." On the morning after these events animal footprints or hoof marks were found outside in the snow. His widow had the maid sleeping in her bed; the ghost of Cuntze appeared and demanded to be allowed to take his proper place beside his wife. And the parson of the parish (who is mentioned as the chronicler of these events) dreamed that Cuntze was "squeezing" him and woke up feeling utterly exhausted. The spirit was also able to cause a nauseating stench to fill the room.

The conclusion is much as in the story of the shoemaker of Breslau. Cuntze was finally disinterred on July 20, six months after his burial, and was found to be undecayed, and when a vein in the leg was opened, the blood that ran out was "as fresh as the living." After having been transported to the bonfire with some difficulty – his body had apparently become as heavy as a stone – he was dismembered (the blood was, again, found to be quite fresh) and burned to ashes.

In fact, there are even earlier accounts of the walking dead. The French expert on vampires, Jean Marigny, remarks:

Well before the eighteenth century, the epoch when the word "vampire" first appeared, people believed in Europe that the dead were able to rise from their graves to suck the blood of the living. The oldest chronicles in Latin mention manifestations of this type, and their authors, instead of employing the word "vampire" (which did not yet exist) utilized a term just as explicit, the word *sanguisugae* (Latin for "leech," or "bloodsucker"). The oldest of these chronicles date from the twelfth and thirteenth centuries and, contrary to what one might expect, are not set in remote parts of Europe, but in England and Scotland.*

Marigny goes on to cite four cases described by the twelfth-century chronicler, William of Newburgh, author of *Historia rerum Anglicarum*. These are too long to cite here (although they can be found in full in Montague Summers's *The Vampire in Europe*). The first, "of the extraordinary happenings when a dead man wandered abroad out of his grave," describes a case in Buckinghamshire, recounted to the chronicler by the local archdeacon. It describes how a man returned from the grave the night after his burial and attacked his wife. When this happened again the following night, the wife asked various neighbours to

---

* "La Tradition Legendaire du Vampire en Europe" in *Les Cahiers du G.E.R.F.* (Groupe d'Etudes et de Recherche sur la Fantastique, Grenoble University of Languages and Letters, 1987).

spend the night with her, and their shouts drove the ghost away. Then, like Cuntze and Weinrichius, the ghost began to create a general disturbance in town, attacking animals and alarming people. That he *was* a ghost, and not a physical body, is proved by the comment that some people could see him while others could not (although they "perceptibly felt his horrible presence"). The archdeacon consulted the bishop, Hugh of Lincoln, whose learned advisers suggested that the body should be dug up and burned to ashes. Hugh of Lincoln felt this would be "undesirable" and instead wrote out a charter of absolution. When the tomb was opened, the body proved to be "uncorrupt," just as on the day it was buried. The absolution was placed on his chest and the grave closed again; after that, the ghost ceased to wander abroad.

William of Newburgh's other account sounds slightly more like the traditional vampire in that the ghost – of a wealthy man who had died at Berwick on Tweed – had an odor of decomposition that affected the air and caused plague. The body was exhumed (it is not recorded whether it was undecayed) and burned.

The third story concerns a priest, chaplain of a lady of rank, at Melrose Abbey, whose life had been far from blameless; after death, his ghost haunted the cloister and appeared in the bed-chamber of the lady of rank. The body was exhumed and burned.

In the fourth story, a dissolute lord of Alnwick Castle, in Northumberland, spied on his wife's adultery by lying on top of the "roof" that covered her four-poster bed. The sight of his wife and her lover "clipping at clicket" so incensed him that he fell down and injured himself, dying a few days later without absolution. He also returned as a ghost to haunt the district, his stench causing a plague that killed many people. When the corpse was exhumed, it proved to be "gorged and swollen with a frightful corpulence"; when attacked with a spade, there gushed out such a stream of blood "that they realized that this leech had battened on the blood of many poor folk." The body was cremated and the haunting ceased.

These stories have the touches of absurdity that might be expected from an ecclesiastical chronicler of that period; yet their similarity to the other chronicles cited suggests that they have some common basis. The same applies to another work, *De nugis curialum* by Walter Map (1193), also cited at length by Summers.

All these cases took place long before western Europe heard tales of vampires from former Turkish dominions, and, except in the case of the "leech" of Alnwick, there is no suggestion of blood drinking. But in most ways, the revenants behave very much like Peter Plogojowitz and the vampires of Medvegia. They haunt the living, climb into bed with people when they are asleep, and then throttle them, leaving them drained of energy. And when the bodies are disinterred, they are found to be undecayed. It seems very clear that there is no basic difference between the vampires of 1732 and the revenants of 1592. And when we look more closely into the accounts of the vampires, we discover that they are energy suckers rather than blood suckers. Peter Plogojowitz has fresh blood in his mouth, but it is merely a matter of hearsay that he sucked the blood of his victims – the account mentions only throttling. Otherwise, these earlier revenants behave very much like the paranormal phenomena known as poltergeists – they throw things and create disturbances.

One of the earliest accounts of poltergeist activity can be found in a document known as *Sigebert's Chronicle*, by one Sigebert of Gembloux (Belgium), which dates from the ninth century. One passage runs as follows:

> There appeared this year [858] in the diocese of Mentz [near Bingen, on the Rhine] a spirit which revealed himself at first by throwing stones, and beating against the walls of houses as if with a great mallet. He then proceeded to speak and reveal secrets, and discovered the authors of several thefts and other matters likely to breed disturbances in the neighbourhood. At last he vented his malice upon one particular person, whom he was industrious in persecuting and making odious to all the neighbours by representing him as the cause of God's anger against the whole village. The spirit never forsook the poor man but tormented him without intermission, burnt all the corn in the barns, and set every place on fire where he came. The priests attempted to frighten him away be exorcisms, prayers, and holy water, but the spectre answered them with a volley of stones which wounded several of them. When the priests were gone he was heard to bemoan himself and say that he was forced to take refuge in the cowl of one of the priests, who had injured the daughter of a man of consequence in the village. He continued in this manner to infest the village for three years together, and never gave up until he had set every house on fire.

The account in another document, the *Annales Fuldenses*, from which Sigebert of Gembloux condensed this account, mentions that the man the spirit tormented was a farmer and that the spirit accused him of adultery and of seducing the daughter of his overseer.

Now at this point, oddly enough, we leave the realm of superstition – if the vampire is indeed superstition – and enter that of actuality. For the poltergeist is undoubtedly one of the best-authenticated of all psychical phenomena; there are hundreds, perhaps thousands, of accounts on record. Poltergeists specialize in mischief and seem to be the juvenile delinquents of the psychic world. They drive people to distraction with their pranks, causing objects to fly through the air (and sometimes change course abruptly in midflight) and often making a racket that can be heard for miles. Allowing for the exaggerations of the medieval chronicler, the above case from Sigebert has the ring of authenticity. It is true that speaking poltergeists are unusual; nevertheless, there *are* a number of cases on record (see chapter 41).

Generally speaking, poltergeists do no harm; Giraldus Cambrensis remarks of a Pembrokeshire poltergeist of A.D. 1191 that it seemed to intend "to deride rather than to do bodily injury." Again, however, there are a few exceptions. The psychical investigator Guy Lyon Playfair mentions a Brazilian case in which the poltergeist drove a girl to suicide by tormenting her. And the poltergeist known as the "Bell witch," whose malign activities continued from 1817 to 1821 in Robertson County, Tennessee, fixed its attentions on one particular man, farmer John Bell, and – like Sigebert's poltergeist – "tormented him without intermission," beating him black and blue and finally poisoning him.

What exactly is a poltergeist? Writers like Sigebert and Giraldus Cambrensis took the understandable view that it was a spirit. Modern psychical research is inclined to find such a view embarrassing. Frank Podmore, one of the founders of the Society for Psychical Research, concluded in 1890 that they are mischievous children throwing stones. But conscientious investigators soon realized that such a view was untenable. In the mid-twentieth century they finally came to terms with the poltergeist by deciding that it was an example of "recurrent spontaneous psychokinesis" (RSPK) or "mind over matter". A few gifted psychics are able to move small objects, such as pins, compass needles, or scraps of paper, by concentrating on them. No one has yet succeeded in doing anything more spectacular with "mind force" – even some thing as modest as throwing a stone.

On the other hand, it was soon noticed by investigators that nearly all poltergeist occurrences seemed to centre around an emotionally disturbed adolescent or one on the point of puberty. If these individuals were somehow causing the poltergeist effects, then they must be doing so unconsciously. One of the strongest advocates of this theory was the

Freudian psychiatrist Nandor Fodor, who was also a distinguished psychical investigator. Fodor argued that the Freudian unconscious is to blame for the "spontaneous psychokinesis" and that the energies involved are the powerful sexual energies of puberty. Neither Fodor nor any other adherent of the theory could explain how the unconscious mind could cause heavy objects to fly through the air and even cause them to penetrate solid walls. But the theory had a satisfyingly scientific ring and was soon generally accepted.

In the early 1970s, however, one investigator came to have strong doubts about this theory. He was Guy Lyon Playfair, a Cambridge graduate who had gone to teach English in Rio de Janeiro. He became interested in the paranormal after a personal experience of "psychic surgery" and joined the Brazilian Institute for Psycho Biophysical Research (IBPP). In Brazil, a large proportion of the population are adherents of a religion known as Spiritism, based on the writings of the Frenchman Allan Kardec, which accepts communication with the dead and the active role of spirits in human existence. After engaging in a number of poltergeist investigations, Playfair was less inclined to dismiss Spiritism as nonsense – in fact, he concluded that Kardec is correct in asserting that poltergeists are spirits. His investigations into the Brazilian form of voodoo, known as *umbanda*, also convinced him that it actually works and that *umbanda* practitioners often perform their "magic" by means of spirits. The experiences that led him to these conclusions are described in his book *The Flying Cow*.

In a book entitled *Poltergeist*, I have described how my own investigations led me to conclude that Playfair was correct (see also chapter 41) and how the "spontaneous psychokinesis" theory simply fails to cover all the facts. After being a convinced adherent of this theory, I found myself forced by the evidence to accept the embarrassing view that poltergeists are spirits. Since that time I have met many psychical researchers – particularly in America – who are at least willing to entertain that possibility.

The same (as we shall see elsewhere in this volume) applies to the closely related field of "possession", the notion that human beings may be possessed by "unclean spirits". The standard view is stated in Aldous Huxley's well-known study, *The Devils of Loudun*, in which it is taken for granted that the nuns who writhed on the ground and uttered appalling blasphemies were in the grip of sexual hysteria. Here, even more than in the case of the poltergeist, it seems natural to assume that we are dealing with psychological illness – and no doubt in many cases this is so. Yet a number of American psychiatrists – among them

Morton Prince, Ralph Allison, and Adam Crabtree – have produced studies of "multiple personality" in which they admit that it is difficult to explain certain cases except in terms of possession by the spirit of a deceased person. (See chapter 42.)

Another piece of interesting evidence for this view of possession can be found in Professor Ian Stevenson's study, *Twenty Cases Suggestive of Reincarnation*. He describes the case of a Hindu boy named Jasbir Lal Jat, who apparently died at the age of three in 1954. Before he could be buried, he revived – but with a new personality completely unlike the old one. This new Jasbir claimed to be a man named Sobha Ram, who had died in the village of Vehedi after a fall from a cart. He claimed to be of Brahmim caste and made difficulties about his food. The family dismissed his claims as childish imagination. But when Jasbir was six, a Brahmin woman from Vehedi came to the village, and Jasbir insisted that she was his aunt. She was, in fact, the aunt of a man named Sobha Ram who had died of a fall from a cart at precisely the same time Jasbir had revived. Taken to Vehedi, Jasbir showed an intimate knowledge of the place and of Sobha Ram's relatives, convincing his own father and mother that he was telling the truth. The conclusion must be that *if* Jasbir was Sobha Ram, then the "spirit" of the latter took possession of the vacant body at the moment Jasbir "died".

In his classic work, *Human Personality and Its Survival of Bodily Death*, Frederic Myers, one of the founding members of the Society for Psychical Research, devotes a chapter to "Trance, Possession and Ecstacy". He begins by acknowledging that when spiritualist "mediums" go into a trance, they are "taken over" by spirits and that this constitutes the phenomenon that was once called "possession". He adds that in some cases, the spirit messages may be deceptive and that "they suggest – nor can we absolutely disprove the suggestion – a type of intelligence inferior to humans, animal-like, and perhaps parasitic". This is as far as he is willing to go in conceding that possession may occasionally be nonbenevolent. But he goes on to cite many cases of what he calls "psychic invasion" – that is, cases in which someone has seen the "spirit" of another person, often someone who has died at exactly that moment. In other cases, the person who "appears" is still alive. A Mrs T., living in Adelaide, recounts how, lying in bed but still wide awake, she saw a former lover standing in the bedroom, as well as another man, whom she felt to be a cousin who had "been the means of leading him astray". The former lover, who looked very pale, told her that his father had just died and that he had inherited his property. Because her husband was skeptical about this vision, she wrote it down.

Some weeks later she heard that her lover's father had died at exactly the time of the vision and had left him his property.

Another case, cited in *Phantasms of the Living* (which Myers co-authored), has a slightly more sinister touch. A nineteen-year-old girl described how she had begun having dreams of a man with a mole on the side of his mouth, and how these filled her with repugnance. The dreams always began with a feeling of some kind of "influence" coming over her. (In spite of her reticence, it is clear that these dreams were of a sexual nature and that the man was forcing her to participate in sex acts.) Two years later, at a party in Liverpool, she felt the same "influence" and turned around to find herself looking into the face of the man with the mole. She was introduced to him, and he insisted that they had met before, which she denied. But when he reminded her of a Birmingham music festival, she suddenly remembered that she had experienced the same unpleasant sense of "influence" there and had then fainted. After this the man began to pursue her and even began talking about the dreams. She felt instinctively that if she admitted to these, she would be in his power; therefore, she pretended not to understand. Eventually, she left Liverpool and ceased to see him.

Here it seems clear that the man had recognized her as the kind of person over whom he was able to exercise some psychic "influence" and had somehow invaded her dreams. If we can once concede the possibility of such "invasion", as well as the possibility of "spirits", then the notion of vampires suddenly seems less absurd.

In a remarkable book entitled *Hungry Ghosts*, the British journalist Joe Fisher has described his own strange experience of "spirits". Fisher had written a book about reincarnation, in the course of which he had become convinced of its reality. One day, after being interviewed on the radio in Toronto (where he lives), he received a phone call from a woman who explained that she had accidentally become a mouthpiece of "discarnate entities". She was being hypnotized in an attempt to cure her of leukemia, and various "spirit guides" had begun speaking through her mouth. (Myers points out that a "spirit" can only enter a body when the usual "tenant" is absent, a point to note when considering that early accounts of vampires involve attack *during sleep*.)

The first time Fisher went to the woman's house, a "spirit" named Russell spoke through her mouth with a reassuring Yorkshire accent and told him that he had a female "guide", a Greek girl named Filipa, who had been his mistress in a previous existence three centuries earlier. This struck Fisher as plausible, since he had always felt some affinity with Greece. He began attending the seances regularly and devoting some time every morning to relaxing and trying to contact Filipa. Eventually he succeeded; buzzing noises in his ears would be succeeded by a feeling of bliss and communication. Filipa was a sensual little creature who liked to be hugged, and Fisher implies that, in some sense, they became lovers. It broke up his current love affair; his live-in girlfriend felt she was no match for a ghost.

Other people at the séances were told about their "guides" or guardian angels. One guide was an ex-RAF pilot named Ernest Scott, another an amusing cockney named Harry Maddox. Fisher's disillusionment began when, on a trip back to England, he decided to try and verify Ernest Scott's war stories – having no doubt whatever that they would prove genuine. The airfield was certainly genuine; so was the squadron Ernest claimed to have belonged to; the descriptions of wartime raids were accurate; so were the descriptions of the squadron's moves from airfield to airfield. But there had been no Ernest Scott in the squadron, and a long search in the Public Record Office failed to turn up his name. Fisher went back to Canada in a bitter mood and accused Ernest of lying. Ernest strenuously denied it. Anyway, he said, he was due to reincarnate in another body, so had to leave. The "guide" Russell later told Fisher that Ernest had been reborn in England and gave the name of the parents and date of birth. Oddly enough, when Fisher checked on this it proved to be accurate. He even contacted the parents, who were intrigued but decided they had no wish to get more deeply involved.

With Russell's approval, Fisher tried to track down the farm in Yorkshire where Russell claimed he had lived in the nineteenth century. Here again, many of the facts Russell had given about the Harrogate area proved to be accurate; but again, the crucial facts were simply wrong. It seemed that Russell was also a liar. And so, upon investigation, was the lovable World War I veteran Harry Maddox. His accounts of World War I battles were accurate; but Harry did not exist.

Finally, Fisher took his search to Greece. In spite of his disillusion with the other guides, he had no doubt whatever that Filipa was genuine. She possessed, he states early in the book, "more love, compassion and perspicacity than I had ever known". The problem was that all his attempts to locate Theros – a village near the Turkish border – in atlases or gazetteers had failed. Yet that could be because it had been destroyed by the Turks in the past three centuries. But a town called Alexandroupoli, which Filipa had mentioned, still existed. After a long and frustrating search for the remains of Theros, Fisher went to Alexandroupoli, a city that he assumed had been founded by Alexander the Great. But a brochure there disillusioned him. Alexandroupoli was a mere two centuries old; it had not even existed at the time when he and Filipa were supposed to have been lovers. Like the others, Filipa was a liar and a deceiver.

In a chapter entitled "Siren Call of the Hungry Ghosts", Fisher tries to analyze what has happened to him. The answer seems simple. He had been involved with what Kardec called "earthbound spirits", spirits who either do not realize they are dead or have such a craving to remain on earth that they remain attached to it:

> These earthbound spirits or, in Tibetan Buddhist phraseology, *pretas* or "hungry ghosts", are individuals whose minds, at the point of physical death, have been incapable of disentangling from desire. Thus enslaved, the personality becomes trapped on the lower planes even as it retains, for a while, its memory and individuality. Hence the term "lost soul", a residual entity that is no more than an astral corpse-in-waiting. It has condemned itself to perish; it has chosen a "second death".

Fisher also quotes Lieutenant Colonel Arthur E. Powell's book entitled *The Astral Body*:

> Such spooks are conscienceless, devoid of good impulses, tending towards disintegration, and consequently can work for evil only, whether we regard them as prolonging their vitality by vampirising at séances, or polluting the medium and sitters with astral connections of an altogether undesirable kind.

And Fisher cites the modern American expert on out-of-the-body journeys, Robert Monroe:

> Monroe tells of encountering a zone next to the Earth plane populated by the "dead", who couldn't or wouldn't realize they were no longer physical beings . . . The beings he perceived "kept trying to be physical, to do and be what they had been, to continue being physical one way or another. Bewildered, some spent all of their activity in attempting to communicate with friends and loved ones still in bodies or with anyone else who might come along".

Kardec had insisted that most human beings can be unconsciously influenced by spirits, since they can wander freely in and out of our bodies and minds. And a psychical investigator named Carl Wickland, whose *Thirty Years Among the Dead* is a classic of Spiritualism (see chapter 42), declared that "these earthbound spirits are the supposed 'devils' of all ages; devils of human origin. . . . The influence of these discarnate entities is the cause of many of the inexplicable and obscure events of earth life and of a large part of the world's misery". Wickland states that these entities are attracted to the magnetic light emanating from mortals; they attach themselves to these auras, finding an avenue of expression through influencing, obsessing, or possessing their victims.

Such spirits can easily be contacted by means of an Ouija board, a smooth tabletop with letters arranged in a semicircle; the "sitters" place their fingers on an upturned glass, which moves of its own accord from letter to letter, spelling out words. Anyone who has ever tried it will have noticed that the "spirits" seldom tell the truth. G. K. Chesterton devotes several pages of his *Autobiography* to experiments with an Ouija board, and while he concedes that the force that moves the glass is, in some sense, "supernatural", he nevertheless concludes: "The only thing I will say with complete confidence about that mystic and invisible power is that it tells lies".

This is interesting, because Chesterton became a Roman Catholic convert, and the Catholic church has always been strongly opposed to "Spiritualism". This is not because the Church rejects life after death, but because it is deeply suspicious of the kind of entities that "come through" at séances, taking the view that spirits have no reason to hang around the "earth plane", any more than adults want to hang around their old childhood schools. Unlike H. G. Wells, Julian Huxley, or other modern rationalists, Chesterton did not reject "spirit communication" as a fraud or delusion; but, like Joe Fisher, he was unable to accept the "spirits" at face value.

If we can at once concede the possibility of "psychic invasion", as well as the possibility of "spirits", then the notion of vampires suddenly seems less absurd. In *The Magus of Strovolos*, an American academic, Kyriacos C. Markides, has described his friendship with a modern Cypriot mystic and "magus", Spyros Sathi, known as Daskalos, who lives in Nicosia. Daskalos, like Myers and Fisher, takes the actual reality of spirits for granted, but he also speaks without embarrassment of possession and vampirism.

Some of Markides's stories of Daskalos are so extraordinary that most readers will suspect him of extreme gullibility. Yet Daskalos's teachings, as quoted by Markides, make it clear that he deserves to be classified with such twentieth-century teachers as Steiner and Gurd-jieff. And Markides offers many examples that seem to leave no doubt whatsoever of the genuineness of Daskalos's psychic powers. He was able to describe Markides's house in America in remarkable detail, although he had no way of learning such details. On another occasion, when Markides and a friend were searching for Daskalos, Markides remarked jokingly that perhaps he was visiting a mistress; when they found him and asked where he had been, Daskalos snapped, "Visiting a mistress", then went on to say that he had overheard all their "silly conversation". It becomes clear that Daskalos takes "possession" for granted, and Markides tells a number of stories, in some of which he was personally involved.

There are, Daskalos claims, three kinds of possession: by ill-disposed human spirits; by demonic entities; and by elementals (the latter being human thoughts and desires that have taken on a life of their own). He goes on to describe a case of spirit possession of the first type. Daskalos was approached by the parents of a girl who claimed that she was being haunted by the spirit of her dead fiancé. Although they had lived together, she had refused to allow him to possess her until they were married. He died of tuberculosis, haunted by unfulfilled cravings. "Each night before she would go to bed he would semi-hypnotise her and induce her to keep the window of her room open. He would then enter inside a bat and would come to her. The bat would wedge itself on her neck and draw blood and etheric [energy]". The local priest told Daskalos how to deal with the situation. He must wait in the next room, and when he heard the bat entering, should go in and quickly shut the window; then, since the bat would attack him, he must stun it with a broom. Then he must wrap the bat in a towel and burn it in a brazier [stove]. Daskalos did this, and as the bat burned, the girl screamed and groaned. Then she calmed down and asked, "Why were you trying to burn me?" The "haunting" ceased thereafter.

Daskalos told another story that has elements of vampirism. On a journey in southern Greece he had encountered another girl who was being haunted by a former lover, a shepherd who had been in love with her and had died in a motor accident. Five years later, when looking for some goats, the girl saw the shepherd – whose name was Loizo – and he followed her, finally making her feel so sleepy that she felt obliged to sit down. He then "hypnotized" her and caused her to experience intense sexual pleasure. When she reported the incident, she was medically examined and found to be a virgin. But three days later the shepherd came to her bed and made love to her. Medical examination revealed that she was no longer a virgin. Daskalos noticed two reddish spots on her neck. The girl told him: "He kisses me there, but his kisses are strange. They are like sucking, and I like them".

The doctor who examined the girl believed that she had torn the hymen with her own fingers; Daskalos seems to accept this but believes that Loizo made her do this.

Daskalos claimed that two days later, he saw the shepherd coming into the house and greeted him. Loizo explained that he had wanted the girl for many years and had never had sexual relations with a woman – only with animals like donkeys and goats. Now that he was possessing her, he had no intention of letting her go. He refused to believe it when Daskalos told him he was dead. Daskalos warned him that if he persisted in possessing the girl, he would remain "in a narcotised state like a vampire". His arguments finally convinced the shepherd, who agreed to go away.

These two cases, taken in conjunction with the others we have considered, offer some interesting clues about the nature of the vampire. According to Daskalos, the "earthbound spirit" of the dead fiancé was able to enter an ordinary bat and then to suck her blood. This was an expression of his sexual desire, his desire to possess her. There have been many cases of so-called Vampirism in the history of sex crimes. In the early 1870s an Italian youth named Vincent Verzeni murdered three women and attempted to strangle several more. Verzeni was possessed by a powerful desire to throttle women (and even birds and animals). After throttling a fourteen-year-old girl named Johanna Motta, he disemboweled her and drank her blood. Verzeni admitted that it gave him keen pleasure to sniff women's clothing, and "it satisfied me to seize women by the neck and suck their blood". So it is easy to imagine that the earthbound fiancé mentioned by Daskalos should enjoy drinking the girl's blood. But we can also see that his desire to "possess" her was also satisfied in another way – by somehow *taking control of her imagination*.

Again, in the case of Loizo, we can see that the shepherd had entered the girl's body and taken possession of her mind so that he could cause her to tear her own hymen with her fingers. This implies – as we would expect – that the lovemaking was not on the physical level, since Loizo possessed no body. (Joe Fisher seems to hint at something similar when he describes his relationship with Filipa.)

All of this has interesting implications. The act of lovemaking seems to involve a paradox, since it is an attempt at the mingling of two bodies, an attempt that is doomed to failure by their separateness. In the *Symposium*, Plato expresses the paradox in an amusing myth. Human beings were originally spherical beings who possessed the character-istics of both sexes. Because their sheer vitality made them a challenge to the gods, Zeus decided that they had to be enfeebled. So he sliced them all down the centre, "as you and I might slice an apple", and turned their faces back to front. And now the separated parts spent their lives in a desperate search for their other half, and they ceased to constitute a challenge to the gods.

It is plain that, in its crudest form, the male sexual urge is basically a desire for "possession" and that the act of physical penetration is an act of aggression. (Most writers on Dracula, for example, have noted that it is basically a rape fantasy.) As a man holds a woman in his arms, he experiences a desire to absorb her, to blend with her, and the actual penetration is only a token union. So we might say that a "vampire" like Loizo is able to achieve what every lover dreams about: a possession that involves total interpenetration, union of minds.

The notion of vampirism that begins to emerge from all this is simple and (provided one can accept the notion of "earthbound spirits") plausible. Daskalos told Markides that those who commit suicide may become trapped in the "etheric of the gross material world", unable to move to the higher psychic planes. A person who commits suicide dies in "a state of despair and confusion" and "may vibrate too close to the material world, which will not allow him to find rest". He becomes a "hungry ghost", wandering in and out of the minds of human beings like a man wandering through a deserted city. In all probability, he is unaware that he is dead. (The wife of Peter Plogojowitz declared that he came to her asking for his shoes; since shoes would obviously be of no use to a ghost, we must conclude that he was unaware that his feet had "dematerialized".) Under normal circumstances, the spirit would be incapable of influencing his involuntary host or of making his presence felt; only if the host happens to vibrate with the same desires, to be "on the same wavelength", can true "possession" occur.

It also seems clear that some human beings have a greater ability than others to sense the presence of these entities; we call such people "psychic". They may be totally unaware that they are psychic unless some chance event happens to reveal it. In a book entitled *The Para-normal*, the psychologist Stan Gooch has described how, at the age of twenty-six, he attended a séance in Coventry with a friend and sponta-neously fell into a trance condition. When he awoke, he learned that several "spirits" had spoken through him.

It was during this period, Gooch reveals in a later book entitled *Creatures from Inner Space*, that he had his first experience of a "psychic invasion". He was lying in bed one Saturday morning with his eyes closed when he felt a movement on the pillow beside his head, as if someone had gently pressed a hand against it. The movement continued for some time; but when he opened his eyes, he was alone.

Twenty years later, lying half awake in the early morning, he became aware that someone else was in bed with him. He felt that it was a composite of various girls he had known: "On this first occasion my conscious interest in the situation got the better of me, and the succubus [female demon] gradually faded away. On subsequent occasions, however, the presence of the entity was maintained, until finally we actually made love". He notes that "from some points of view the sex is actually more satisfying than that with a real woman, because in the paranormal encounter archetypal elements are both involved and invoked".

Oddly enough, Gooch does not believe that his succubus was real; he thinks such entities are creations of the human mind. He cites cases of hypnotized subjects who have been able to see and touch hallucinations suggested by the hypnotist, and a book entitled *The Story of Ruth*, by Dr Morton Schatzman, which describes how a girl whose father had tried to rape her as a child began to hallucinate her father and believe that he was in the room with her. He seems to believe that his succubus was a similar hallucination. Yet this view seems to be contradicted by other cases he cites in the book.

The first of these concerns a policeman, Martin Pryer, who had always been "psychic". At one point he decided to try practicing the control of hypnagogic imagery – the imagery we experience on the verge of sleep – and soon began having alarming experiences. On one occasion, a strange entity began to cling to his back like a limpet and held on until he staggered across the room and switched on the light. On another occasion, he thought that a former girlfriend was outside the window, and when he asked what she was doing, she replied, "You sent for me". Then a female entity seemed to seize him from behind, clinging to his back; he sensed that it wanted him to make love to her "in a crude and violent manner". After some minutes it faded away.

Gooch goes on to describe the experiences of an actress friend named Sandy, who was also "psychic". One night, she woke up and felt that the spotlight in the corner of her ceiling had changed into an eye that was watching her. Then she felt an entity – she felt it was male – lying on top of her and trying to make love to her. "One part of her was quite willing for the lovemaking to proceed, but another part of her knew that she wanted it to stop." The entity became heavier, and another force seemed to be dragging her down through the mattress. She made an effort to imagine that she was pulling herself up through the mattress, and the pressure suddenly vanished. But when she went into the bathroom, she discovered that her mouth was rimmed with dark streaks, and when she opened it, it proved to be full of dried blood. There was no sign of a nosebleed or any other injury that could account for the blood.

Guy Playfair has described a similar case in *The Flying Cow*. A girl named Marcia, who had a master's degree in psychology, was on the beach at São Paolo when she picked up a plaster image of the sea goddess Yemanja, which had obviously been thrown into the sea as an offering. Against the advice of her aunt, she took it home. After this, she experienced a series of disasters. She began to feel exhausted and lose weight. Her pressure cooker blew up, burning her hands and face, and her oven exploded. She began to experience suicidal impulses. Then one night, an "entity" entered her bed, and she felt a penis entering her. It happened on several subsequent occasions. In desperation, she went to consult an *umbanda* specialist, who urged her to return the statue to the beach. As soon as she did this, the run of bad luck – and the psychic rapes – ceased.

Such cases make it difficult to accept Gooch's view that these entities are a kind of hypnotic hallucination. It seems obvious that he arrived at that conclusion because his "succubus" seemed to be a blend of previous girlfriends. But according to the "earth-bound spirit" hypothesis, we would assume that the entity simply put these ideas into his mind – that is, into his imagination. He writes: "In short, this entity, though possessing physical and even psychological attributes familiar to me, was none the less essentially its own independent self." And he agrees that the "archetypal elements" were, to some extent, "invoked" – that is, that he himself was conjuring them up. Sandy was able to free herself from the "psychic invasion" by *imagining* that she was pulling herself back up through the mattress, indicating that the entity was controlling her imagination, not her body.

We also note that these "psychic invasions" occurred when all three subjects – Gooch, Martin Pryer, and Sandy – were either asleep or hovering between sleep and waking, and therefore in a trance condition akin to mediumship.

The evidence, then, all seems to suggest that the vampire, like the poltergeist, is an "earthbound spirit," a "hungry ghost" that draws vitality from human beings. Daskalos's remark to Loizo, that "he would remain in a narcotised state like a vampire," indicates that such spirits become, in effect, drug addicts who are unable to progress to a higher level while in the grip of their addiction.

One of the few contemporary "vampirologists" is a graduate of the State University of New York named Stephen Kaplan. In his book *Vampires Are . . .* (1984) he describes how he became interested in the subject. In the course of his studies in anthropology, he noticed that "many of the customs and rituals of the primitive cultures we were studying showed striking similarities to vampire myths and legends." This led him to suppose that there might be some basis of truth in vampire legends, and in 1971 he founded the Vampire Research Center on Long Island. As a result of interviews on the radio, he received many calls, most of which were hoaxes. The first real "vampires" he encountered were a couple who liked to taste blood. (In fact, blood is an emetic, so it would be impossible to drink it in quantity.) The woman used to whip her companion until he bled, then lick the cuts. They had formed a small group that would indulge in these practices. Another woman Kaplan interviewed obtained blood by trading sexual favours.

Without exception, the people Kaplan interviewed were "sexually disturbed". (In *The Sexual Anomalies and Perversions* by Dr Magnus Hirschfeld, there is a section devoted to vampirism, in which it becomes clear that it is related to necrophilia; Hirschfeld describes, for example, a gravedigger named Victor Ardisson who drank animal blood and performed various perverted acts on female corpses whom he disinterred.) But Kaplan suggests that genuine vampirism is "the draining of physical energy from one individual to another, often via the blood". He speaks of "psychic vampires", people who seem to drain our physical energies. He comments that the process seems to be the reverse of "psychic healing", whereby the healer is able to transfer energy to the patient.

In an article on sexual occultism in the magazine *The Unexplained*, the occult historian Francis King describes the process by which a "magician" can cause sexual arousal in a selected victim:

The would-be lover sits as near as possible to his intended victim. He gauges her breathing by the rise and fall of her breast, and, once he has established the exact rhythm, begins to breathe in precise unison with her. The sorcerer continues this for a period of between three and five minutes, and then contracts the muscles of his anus from five to ten seconds. This, supposedly, establishes an "astral link" between the two people involved, by bringing into action the man's *muladhara chakra*, the centre of psychic activity that, according to some occultists, controls the libido. It is situated, they claim, in a part of the "subtle body" roughly corresponding to the area between the anus and the genitals. The magician then gradually increases his rate of breathing until it reaches the rate characteristic of the height of sexual activity. The "astral link" ensures that the emotions normally associated with this rapid breathing are communicated to the woman, and she immediately experiences sexual arousal. The magician then begins a conversation.

He goes on to theorize that vampirism is a way of draining "psychosexual energy" from the victim.

What is being suggested is that a man can establish a telepathic link between himself and a woman he desires and use it to influence her desires. In *God Is My Adventure*, Rom Landau tells a story of the philosopher and mystic George Gurdjieff, which seems to indicate that he was also able to do this. One man told Landau of an occasion when he was lunching with an attractive female novelist:

Gurdjieff caught her eye, and we saw distinctly that he began to inhale and to exhale in a peculiar way. I am too old a hand at such tricks not to have known that Gurdjieff was employing one of the methods he must have learned in the East. A few moments later, I noticed that my friend was turning pale; she seemed to be on the verge of fainting. And yet she is anything but highly strung. I was very much surprised to see her in that strange condition, but she recovered after a few moments. I asked her what the matter was, "That man is uncanny", she whispered. "Something awful happened", she continued. "I ought to be ashamed . . . I looked at your "friend" a moment ago, and he caught my eye. He looked at me in such a peculiar way that within a second or so I suddenly felt as though I had been struck right through my sexual centre. It was beastly!"

It seems likely that the "man with the mole" described in *Phantasms of the Living* possessed the same curious ability and that this explained why the girl had fainted at the Birmingham music festival; it also seems clear that, having established the "psychic link", he was able to invade her dreams in the manner of a "vampire".

Let us, then, attempt an outline of a theory of vampirism that is in accordance with the various accounts that have been quoted. The story of Arnod Paole, like so many others, makes it clear that he was not a willing vampire; the *Visum et Repertum* states that he had been "troubled by a vampire" in Turkey and had eaten earth from the grave to free himself of the affliction. This was not successful, and the earthbound spirit returned after death to vampirize people in Medvegia. If we assume that vampirism is an experience akin to sexual satisfaction, then the implication is that Paole's unquiet spirit became a vampire, much as many sexually abused children grow up to become child abusers. But this view suggests that sex itself may be regarded as a form of benevolent vampirism; the act of lovemaking, which has to rest content with an interpenetration of bodies, is an attempt at mutual absorption. In that case, the actions of sex criminals must be seen as a form of nonbenevolent vampirism. (The sex murderer Ted Bundy told police interrogators: "Sometimes I feel like a vampire".) If we can accept this view, then it is not difficult to accept that some "earthbound spirits" or "hungry ghosts" also attempt to maintain their link with the world by a form of psychic vampirism.

Only one question remains: if vampirism is a draining of psychic energy, why do so many accounts mention the drinking of blood? Stephen Kaplan suggests that genuine vampirism is "the draining of physical energy from one individual to another, often via the blood". The *Visum et Repertum* mentions that fresh blood was flowing from Paole's eyes, nose, mouth, and ears. Gooch's friend Sandy found that her mouth was full of dried blood after the "psychic attack", although she had no injury that might account for it.

But why should a "vampire" leave its own blood behind? Is it possible that the blood *was* Sandy's own and that the "incubus" (male demon) had the power to draw it from her, like a leech, without breaking the skin? This notion opens up an entirely new realm of speculation about vampires – a realm which, for lack of further evidence, we must at present leave unexplored.

59

Velikovsky's Comet

When the bulky manuscript of *Worlds in Collision* landed on the desk of a New York editor in 1947 its tattered state left no doubt that it had been rejected many times. All the same, the editor was impressed. According to the author, Immanuel Velikovsky, the earth had been almost destroyed about three and a half thousand years ago by a near-collision with a comet; in the earthquakes and volcanic eruptions that followed, cities were wiped out and whole countries laid waste. It was a fascinating and erudite book, and its author – who was apparently a respectable psychiatrist – had the ability to write a clear and vigorous prose.

The editor cautiously recommended it. His superiors were worried; Macmillans was a reputable publisher with a large textbook list; they could not afford to be accused of encouraging the lunatic fringe. So they compromised, and offered Velikovsky a small advance and a contract that gave them the option to publish, but no guarantee that they would do so. A year later they finally decided to go ahead, and *Worlds in Collision* made its belated appearance on 3 April 1950. Within days it had climbed to the top of the best-seller list. When it appeared in England the following September its reputation had preceded it, so that it sold out its first impression even before publication. But by that time Macmillans' doubts had been justified; the denunciations of the book were so violent that they were forced into retreat, and *Worlds in Collision* had to be passed on to another publisher. By then Velikovsky had become one of the most famous and most vilified men in America.

Who was this controversial psychiatrist who also seemed to be an expert on astronomy, geology and world history? Immanuel Velikovsky was a Russian Jew, born in Vitebsk in June 1895 who had studied mathematics in Moscow. He went on to study medicine, qualifying in 1921, then studied psychiatry in Vienna with Freud's pupil Stekel. In 1924 he moved to Palestine to practise, and became increasingly interested in Biblical archaeology. The turning-point in his career was a reading of Freud's *Moses and Monotheism* (1937). In this book Freud proposes that Moses was not a Jew but an Egyptian, and that he was a follower of the monotheistic religion of the Pharaoh Akhnaton (see chapter 11), the king who replaced the host of Egyptian gods with one single sun god. Freud proposed that Moses fled from Egypt after the death of Akhnaton (probably murdered) and imposed his religion on the Jews.

The obvious historical objection to this theory is that Moses is supposed to have lived about a century after the death of Akhnaton; but Freud contested this view, and moved fearlessly into the arena of historical research. Dazzled by his boldness, Velikovsky decided to do the same. His researches into Egyptian, Greek and Near Eastern history soon convinced him that much of the accepted dating is hopelessly wrong. But they led him to an even more unorthodox conclusion: that the pharaoh Akhnaton was none other than the legendary Oedipus of Greek myth, and that the story arose out of the fact that Akhnaton had murdered his father and married his mother.

Velikovsky went on to construct a theory beside which even Freud's heterodox views seemed conservative; that the various events that accompanied the plagues of Egypt – the crossing of the Red Sea, the destruction of the Egyptian armies by floods, the manna that fell from heaven – were the outcome of some great cosmic upheaval. And at this point Velikovsky came across exactly what he was looking for: a papyrus written by an Egyptian sage called Ipuwer, which contained an account of events that sounded strangely like the Bible story in Exodus.

In 1939 Velikovsky moved to the United States, and continued his researches in its libraries. What precisely *was* the "great catastrophe"? The Austrian Hanns Hoerbiger had put forward the theory that the earth has had several moons (see chapter 2), and that the collapse of one of these moons on the earth caused the great floods and upheavals recorded in the Bible and in other ancient documents. But Velikovsky came to reject the Hoerbiger theory. There was a far more exciting clue. Before the second millennium BC – and even later – the planet Venus was not grouped by ancient astronomers with the other planets. That might have been because it was so close to the sun that they mistook it for a star – in fact, it is called the morning star. But what if it was because Venus was not in its present position at that time? Velikovsky found tantalizing references in old documents to something that sounded like a near-collision of a comet with the earth. In legends from Greece to Mexico he found suggestions that this catastrophe was somehow linked with Venus. Only one thing puzzled him deeply: that other legends seemed to link the catastrophe with Zeus, the father of the gods, also known as Jupiter. He finally reconciled these stories by reaching the astonishing conclusion that Venus was "born out of Jupiter – forced out by a gigantic explosion. Venus began as a comet, and passed so close to Mars that it was dragged out of its orbit; then it came close to earth, causing the Biblical catastrophes; then it finally settled down near the sun as the planet Venus.

It sounds like pure lunacy; but Velikovsky argued it with formidable erudition. And, unlike the usual crank, he spent a great deal of time searching for scientific evidence. He needed, for example, a spectroscopic analysis of the atmospheres of Mars and Venus, and he decided to approach the eminent astronomer Harlow Shapley. Shapley had himself become a figure of controversy in 1919 when he announced his conclusion that our solar system is not – as had previously been believed – at the centre of the Milky Way, but somewhere much closer to its edge; perhaps it was the blow to human self-esteem that caused the opposition. At all events, Velikovsky seems to have reasoned that Shapley might be sympathetic to his own heterodox ideas. Shapley was polite, but said he was too busy to read *Worlds in Collision*; he asked a colleague, a sociologist named Horace Kallen, if he would read it first. Kallen did so, and was excited; he told Shapley that it seemed a serious and worthwhile book, and that even if it should prove to be nonsense, it was still a bold and fascinating thesis. The Macmillan editor agreed, and Velikovsky got his contract.

Three months before its publication, in January 1950, a preview of *Worlds in Collision* appeared in *Harper's* magazine, and aroused widespread interest. Shapley's reaction was curious. He wrote Macmillans a letter saying that he had heard that they had decided *not* to publish the book after all, and that he was greatly relieved; he had discussed it with various scientists, and they were all astonished that Macmillan should venture into "the Black Arts".

Macmillans replied defensively that the book was not supposed to be hard science, but was a controversial theory that scholars ought to know about. Shapley replied tartly that Velikovsky was "complete nonsense", and that when he had introduced himself to Shapley in a New York hotel Shapley had looked around to see if he had his keeper with him. The book, he said, was "quite possibly intellectually fraudulent", a legpull designed to make money, and if Macmillans insisted on publishing it, then they had better drop Shapley from their list.

Macmillans ignored this attempt at blackmail, and published the book in April. No doubt they were astonished to find that they had a best-seller on their hands. America has a vast audience of "fundamentalists" – people who believe that every word of the Bible is literally true, and are delighted to read anything that seems to offer scientific support for this view. (The same audience made Werner Keller's *The Bible as History* a best-seller in 1956.) Now they rushed to buy this book that seemed to prove that the parting of the Red Sea and the destruction of the walls of Jericho had really taken place. So did thousands of ordinary intelligent readers who simply enjoyed an adventure in speculative thought.

Scientists did not share this open-mindedness. One exception was Gordon Atwater, chairman of the astronomy department at New York's Museum of Natural History; he published a review urging that scientists ought to be willing to consider the book without prejudice; the review resulted in his dismissal. James Putnam, the editor who accepted *Worlds in Collision*, was dismissed from Macmillan. Professors deluged Macmillan with letters threatening to boycott their textbooks unless *Worlds in Collision* was withdrawn. Macmillans failed to show the same courage that had led them to ignore similar veiled threats from Shapley; they passed on Velikovsky to the Doubleday corporation, who had no textbook department to worry about, and who were probably unable to believe their luck in being handed such a profitable piece of intellectual merchandise. Fred Whipple, Shapley's successor at Harvard, wrote to Doubleday[*] telling them that if they persisted in publishing Velikovsky, he wanted them to take his own book *Earth, Moon and Planets* off their list. (Twenty years later, he denied in print ever writing such a letter.)

Velikovsky himself was rather bewildered by the sheer violence of the reactions; it had taken him thirty years to develop his theory, and he had expected controversy; but this amounted to persecution. He was willing to admit that he could be wrong about the nature of the catastrophe; but the historical records showed that *something* had taken place. Why couldn't they admit that, and *then* criticize his theory, instead of treating him as a madman? The only thing to do was to go on collecting more evidence.

And more evidence was produced in intimidating quantities during the remaining twenty-nine years of Velikovsky's life; he died on 17 November 1979, at the age of eighty-four. In 1955 came *Earth in Upheaval*, in many ways his best book, presenting the scientific evidence for great catastrophes. But again it outraged scientists – this time

---

[*] In fact, to the Doubleday subsidiary, Blakiston: see *Velikovsky Reconsidered*, p. 25.

biologists – by suggesting that there are serious inadequacies in Darwin's theory of "gradual evolution", and arguing that a better explanation would be the effect of radiation due to "catastrophes" on the genes. Then came four books in a series that Velikovsky chose to call *Ages in Chaos*, whose main thesis is that historians of the ancient world have made a basic mistake in their dating, and that a period of about six or seven centuries needs to be dropped from the chronological record. In Velikovsky's dating, Queen Hatshepsut, generally assumed to have lived about 1500 BC, becomes a contemporary of Solomon more than four centuries later (in fact, Velikovsky identifies her with the Queen of Sheba), while the pharaoh Rameses II – assumed to live around 1250 BC – becomes a contemporary of Nebuchadnezzar more than six centuries later. The great invasion of barbarians known as the Sea Peoples, usually dated about 1200 BC, is placed by Velikovsky in the middle of the fourth century BC, about the time of the death of Plato. The arguments contained in *Ages in Chaos* (1953), *Oedipus and Akhnaton* (1960), *Peoples of the Sea* (1977) and *Rameses II and his Time* (1978) are of interest to historians rather than to scientists, but, like the earlier works, are totally absorbing to read. Two other projected volumes, *The Dark Age in Greece* and *The Assyrian Conquest*, have not so far been published. But a third volume of the *Worlds in Collision* series, *Mankind in Amnesia*, appeared posthumously in 1982. It expands a short section in *Worlds in Collision* arguing that catastrophic events produce a kind of collective amnesia. It is his most Freudian book, but it reveals that he never lost that curious ability to produce a state of intellectual excitement in the reader, even when his arguments seem most outrageous.

How far does Velikovsky deserve to be taken seriously? Should he be regarded as another Freud, or merely as another Erich von Däniken? It must be admitted that the basic thesis of *Worlds in Collision* sounds preposterous: that various Biblical events, like the parting of the Red Sea and the fall of the walls of Jericho, can be explained in terms of an astronomical catastrophe. But it is possible to entertain doubts about this aspect of Velikovsky's thesis without dismissing the most important part of his theory: that Venus may be far younger than the rest of the solar system. Moreover, whether or not Velikovsky is correct about the origin of Venus, there can be no doubt whatever that many of his controversial insights have been confirmed. Astronomers object that Jupiter was not likely to be the source of a "comet" because it is too cold and inactive. However, a standard textbook of astronomy – Skilling and Richardson (1947) states "From the fact that Jupiter is 5.2 times as far from the source of heat as is the earth, it can be seen that it should receive only $1/5.2^2$, or $1/27$ as much heat as does the earth. The temperature that a planet should have as the result of this much heat is very low – in the neighbourhood of $-140°C$". But space probes have since revealed that the surface temperature on Jupiter is around $-150°C$, and that its surface is extremely turbulent, with immense explosions. The same textbook of astronomy states that the temperature on the surface of Venus "may be as high as boiling water". Velikovsky argued that it should be much higher, since Venus is so "young" in astronomical terms. Mariner 2 revealed that the temperature on the surface of Venus is about $900°C$. It also revealed the curious fact that Venus rotates backward as compared to all the other planets, an oddity that seems incomprehensible if it was formed at the same time and evolved through the same process.

Russian space probes also revealed that Venus has violent electrical storms. Velikovsky had argued that the planets have powerful magnetic fields, and that therefore a close brush between the earth and a "comet" would produce quite definite effects. The discovery of the Van Allen belts around the earth supported Velikovsky's view. There also seem to be close links between the rotation of Venus and Earth – Venus turns the same face to earth at each inferior conjunction, which could have come about through an interlocking of their magnetic fields. In the 1950s Velikovsky's assertion about electromagnetic fields in space was treated with contempt – in *Fads and Fallacies in the Name of Science*, Martin Gardner remarked dismissively that Velikovsky had invented forces capable of doing whatever he wanted them to do. His electromagnetic theory also led Velikovsky to predict that Jupiter would be found to emit radio waves, and that the sun would have an extremely powerful magnetic field. One critic (D. Menzel) retorted that Velikovsky's model of the sun would require an impossible charge of 10^{19} volts. Since then, Jupiter *has* been found to emit radio waves, while the sun's electrical potential has been calculated at about 10^{19} volts. It could be said that many of Velikovsky's theories are now an accepted part of astrophysics except, of course, that no one acknowledges that Velikovsky was the first one to formulate them.

Another matter on which Velikovsky seems to have been proved correct is the question of the reversal of the earth's magnetic poles. When molten volcanic rocks cool, or when clay or brick is baked, the magnetic minerals in it are magnetized in the direction of the earth's magnetic field. At the turn of the century Giuseppe Folgerhaiter examined Etruscan vases, looking for minor magnetic variations, and was astonished to find that there seemed to have been a complete reversal of the magnetic field around the eighth century BC. Scientists explained his findings by declaring that the pots must have been fired upside down. But in 1906 Bernard Brunhes found the same complete reversal in certain volcanic rocks. Further research revealed that there had been at least nine such reversals in the past 3.6 million years. No one could make any plausible suggestion as to why this had happened. Velikovsky's suggestion was that it was due to the close approach of other celestial bodies and that the earth's brush with Venus should have produced such a reversal. His critics replied that there have been no reversals in the past half-million years or so. But since then two more have been discovered – one 28,000 years ago, the other about 12500 BC, and one of Velikovsky's bitterest opponents Harold Urey, has come to admit that the "celestial body" theory is the likeliest explanation of pole-reversal. Yet so far the crucial piece of evidence – volcanic rock revealing a reversal about 1450 BC – has not been forthcoming.

Those who regard Velikovsky as an innovator comparable to Freud should also be prepared to admit that he had many of Freud's faults – particularly a tendency to jump to bold and unorthodox conclusions, and then to stick by them with a certain rigid dogmatism. Yet it must also be admitted that whether or not his Venus theory proves to be ultimately correct, his "guesses" have often been amazingly accurate. Like Kepler, who came to all the right conclusions about the solar system for all the wrong reasons (including the belief that it is somehow modelled on the Holy Trinity), Velikovsky seems to possess the intuitive genius of all great innovators. Even one of his most dismissive critics, Carl Sagan, admits: "I find the concatenation of legends which Velikovsky has accumulated stunning . . . If twenty per cent of the legendary concordances . . . are real, there is something important to be explained".

60

Vortices

The Bridge Between
the Natural and the Supernatural?

In 1839 a gray-bearded professor read a paper entitled "An Essay on the Figure of the Earth" to the Royal Society in Edinburgh; it exhibited a high order of mathematical ability, and its author had been awarded a gold medal by Edinburgh University. But the professor who read it was not, in fact, its author; the actual author was a boy of fifteen named William Thomson, and he was not allowed to read his own work because it might have embarrassed the learned audience to be lectured by a fresh-faced teenager. In due course, William Thomson went on to become one of the most celebrated scientists of his day, the discoverer of the Second Law of Thermodynamics (the recognition that the universe is "running down"), of "absolute zero", and of the moving coil galvanometer. He was also instrumental in laying the first trans-atlantic cable and in bringing Bell's telephone to Britain. At the age of sixty-eight he was made Lord Kelvin, and the absolute scale of temperature still bears his name.

Yet if Kelvin had been asked what he considered his most important achievement, he would undoubtedly have replied: the vortex (or whirl-pool) theory of atoms – a theory that has now been totally forgotten. In fact, most of his contemporaries would have agreed; the 1875 edition of the *Encyclopaedia Britannica* carries a two-page entry on his vortex theory of atoms, written by the eminent mathematical physicist James Clerk Maxwell. The idea had come to Kelvin in 1867, in a flash of inspiration, and only a few weeks later, he delivered a paper on his theory to the same Royal Society in Edinburgh that had listened to his first paper twenty-eight years earlier.

Kelvin had been a child prodigy; the son of James Thomson, a Belfast professor of mathematics, he had started attending his father's lectures at the age of eight and had entered the University of Glasgow (to which his father had moved) at the age of eleven. A trip to Europe at the age of sixteen had introduced him to Fourier's book on the mathematical theory of heat; from then on, he was determined to become a physicist – or, as they called it in those days, a "natural philosopher".

The dazzling idea that struck him in 1867 seems to have developed from his observation of smoke rings. A simple way to create these is to introduce smoke into a box that has a round hole in one of its sides. If you give the opposite side of the box a vigorous slap (particularly if that side is made of some soft material like toweling), a smoke ring will shoot out of the hole. But if you try to stop the smoke ring with your hand, it will not dissolve like a bubble, as you might expect. It will simply bounce off your hand like a rubber ball. If you make two smoke rings collide head on, they vibrate from the impact like two charging bulls meeting head on, then bounce away from each other. In short, they behave like solid objects.

In 1803 an English chemist named John Dalton had suggested that matter is finally made up of tiny hard balls called "atoms", which are indivisible. He had borrowed the idea from the Greek philosopher Democritus but had backed it up with highly convincing evidence. Dalton's theory had led to a number of important breakthroughs in physics and chemistry, such as the recognition of how atoms fuse together to form molecules – so that two atoms of hydrogen, for example, combine with one of oxygen to form water.

That still left many problems. For example, *why* are atoms of hydrogen and oxygen quite different? You would think that if the universe were made up of primordial particles, all those particles would be the same.

Kelvin went on to explain that "vortices" of energy can form different substances because there can obviously be many different types of vortices – different sizes, speeds, and so on. Within ten years or so most physicists accepted Kelvin's view that atoms are vortices; it simply seemed to make sense. In 1882 a brilliant twenty-six-year-old Cambridge scientist, J. J. Thomson (no relation to William Thomson), won a prize for a paper on the motion of vortex rings. Yet fifteen years later, Thomson's discovery of the electron apparently made Kelvin's vortex theory obsolete. Kelvin himself intensely disliked the "new physics" that arose from the study of the disintegration of radioactive particles and declined to believe that atoms could fall apart.

The discovery of the electron led to quantum physics, to the theory of relativity, and, eventually, to the "discovery" of subelectronic particles like quarks – all of which seemed to make the vortex theory doubly irrelevant.

In 1968 a twenty-year-old science student at Kelvin's old university, Belfast, went to see his professor of zoology, Dr G. Owen. The student's name was David Ash, and he was thinking of transferring from physics and zoology to medicine. He expected some resistance and was startled when his professor showed him to a chair and then strode about the room delivering a diatribe on the way young men believe everything their elders tell them. All they cared about, he complained, was getting a degree and a good job. Learning for the sheer joy of learning had vanished.

When Ash left the professor's study, he was fired with sudden determination. He would stop thinking about a career and devote himself to *real* learning – to inventing theories and exploring ideas for the sheer joy of it. Fortunately, his father, Dr Michael Ash, was the author of some highly unorthodox theories of medicine and raised no serious objection. After a period as a science teacher, Ash became a consultant on nutrition and alternative medicine and devoted all his spare time to developing his own unorthodox theories of the nature of matter, based on an idea that he called "primordial spin" – or vortices. He had come across the idea in a physics textbook printed in America in 1904 that championed Kelvin's "outmoded" idea. In due course, Ash joined forces with a young science graduate, Peter Hewitt, to argue these ideas in a book entitled *Science of the Gods* – which, in spite of its catchpenny title, is a serious attempt to create a theory of the nature of matter that can transcend the serious limitations of contemporary science.

One of the most irritating of these limitations must be obvious to any reader of this book: that science seems incapable of dealing with certain fundamental mysteries of human existence. You and I have no idea of where we were a hundred years ago and where we shall be a hundred years hence. It is a real question, and it is as important as anything we could ask; yet science regards it as a pseudoquestion. Neither can modern science deal with such mysteries as precognition – glimpses of the future – second sight – glimpses of things that are happening elsewhere – or out-of-the-body experiences. If it humbly admitted that these are at present beyond its range, there would be no problem. But it insists that these problems do not exist, that they are simply a sign of human gullibility and self-deception. Yet anyone who has taken a serious look at these problems knows this to be escapist nonsense.

In the 1870s a group of British scientists and philosophers decided to form a society that would study claims about ghosts and life after death; in 1882 it was launched under the title The Society for Psychical Research. Most of its members – scientists like J. J. Thomson, literary men like Tennyson and Mark Twain, and statesmen like Gladstone – were skeptics but were willing to admit that there *was* something here that needed explaining. Lewis Carroll wrote: "That trickery will *not* do as a complete explanation of all the phenomena . . . I am more than convinced". He thought that perhaps spirits could be explained as some unknown natural force "allied to electricity". By the 1890s the Society had made important investigations of ghosts, out-of-the-body experiences, and telepathy and had proved beyond all doubt that – as Carroll suspected – they could not be explained as trickery. But at that point they got stuck. All their hopes of turning the "paranormal" into a science melted away like ghosts at cockcrow. And, more than a century later, the position is still unchanged. As far as science is concerned, the paranormal does not exist – or is, at best, a kind of crank fringe activity.

That is why David Ash and Peter Hewitt are asking one of the most important and relevant of all scientific questions: can some new approach provide science and the paranormal with a common foundation?

In the third chapter of their book, they raise the question of "the key to the supernatural". Energy, they say, is the prime reality. But is our physical universe the *only* reality? If matter and light are two forms of energy (as Einstein showed), is it not possible that there are other forms of energy, so-called nonmaterial forms? To anyone interested in the paranormal, the answer is obviously yes. The entity known as the poltergeist has been proved to have the ability to make solid objects pass through walls (so that, for example, in one case a picture fell out of its frame without either breaking the glass or the sealed cardboard at the back of the frame). Neither matter nor light can pass through solid walls; ergo, some other form of energy must exist.

If, as Kelvin believed, matter is made up of "vortices" or whirlpools, what are these whirlpools *in*? Ash replies that the very question is based on a misconception. Before Einstein, scientists believed that light was a vibration in the "ether" – an unknown fluid that pervades all space. Two physicists named Michelson and Morley showed that the "ether" does not exist. Light seems to be "pure movement", not a movement *in* something. A simple illustration might clarify this idea. Suppose I toss a book across the room – as I am always tossing books from my worktable onto the camp bed that serves as a halfway house to the bookshelf, while the book is in motion, it remains in every way the same book; a tiny Martian scientist sitting on it would detect no difference whatever. Yet its motion is undoubtedly real. You must regard its motion as a kind of invisible additive. Now try to imagine this invisible additive on its own. It is impossible, of course; but that does not prove that it cannot exist. When you look at the night sky you cannot imagine space going on forever; yet common sense tells you it does, even beyond the edge of the universe. Ash is suggesting that, just as energy is more "fundamental" than matter, so "pure movement" is more fundamental than energy.

So why should energy be restricted to the speed of light? Ash writes: "If movement could have a faster speed, it would give rise to a completely different type of energy". This he calls super-energy. (In fact, physicists have suggested in recent years the possibility of a particle called the *tachyon*, which is faster than light.)

According to Ash: "Objects of super-energy would share the same *form* as things in our world, but their *substance* would be entirely different". They would actually coexist with our physical world but would be, under normal circumstances, undetectable. And this, Ash suggests, could be the explanation of ghosts, poltergeists, "miracles" (like those of the Hindu guru Sai Baba, who can "materialize" objects out of thin air), precognition, and all other so-called paranormal phenomena.

The skeptic will ask: does Ash's suggestion bring us any closer to understanding the paranormal? In a sense, yes, it does. Most scientific theories begin as an attempt to explain some puzzling phenomenon, such as thunder and lightning. The super-energy theory can certainly help to explain a wide variety of "paranormal" phenomena.

Let us begin with an extremely simple one: dowsing. A "diviner" can hold a forked twig in his hands and detect underground water. This can be explained in purely electrical terms. Moving water produces a weak electric field, and men – and animals – seem to have an inbuilt sensitivity to this field – obviously part of our survival mechanism.

A Cambridge don named T. C. ("Tom") Lethbridge, who was also an archaeologist, often used his own dowsing abilities to detect buried objects. He also discovered that a pendulum – a weight on a piece of string – worked just as well as a dowsing rod – the pendulum would swing in a circle over things he was looking for. He then made another discovery that sounds absurd but that all dowsers will verify: that he could "ask the pendulum questions" and that it would reply in the negative or affirmative by swinging back and forth or in a circle. The theory advanced by scientists – like Sir William Barrett – is that the unconscious mind knows the answer and causes the muscles to make the pendulum move in a circle or a "swing".

During his Cambridge days, Lethbridge used the pendulum to explore a giant Celtic figure cut in a hillside but now buried beneath the turf.* And after his retirement to an old house in Devon, he continued his investigations into the "power of the pendulum". Instead of a short pendulum, he tried a pendulum made of a long piece of string, which he was able to shorten or lengthen by winding it round a stick. His first experiment was to place a silver dish on the floor and then to hold the pendulum over it and carefully unwind the string. When it reached 22 inches, it went into a circular swing. He tried it over copper; this went into a circular swing at 30½ inches. He now tried the 30½ -inch pendulum in his garden and soon unearthed a small copper tube with it.

So far, Lethbridge was merely "proving" that different metals caused the pendulum to respond at different lengths. He next proved to his satisfaction that all substances have their characteristic "rate" (length of the pendulum swing): oak (11 inches), mercury (12½), grass (16), lead (22 – the same as silver), potatoes (39). Many substances, of course, "share" a rate with others, but Lethbridge found that the weight "circled" a distinct number of times for each – for example, sixteen times for lead and twenty-two for silver.

Now certain that he was on to something of scientific importance, he became more ambitious. One of the strangest and most absurd phenomena connected with the pendulum is "map dowsing". It sounds preposterous, but a good dowser can locate water by swinging his pendulum over a map. At this point we have to leave "scientific" explanations behind, and fall back on ESP (extrasensory perception) or on the powers of the unconscious mind. Lethbridge reasoned that if the pendulum is equally at home with an abstraction like a map, it should be at home with abstractions in general – love, anger, evolution, death. It ought, for example, to have a different rate for male and female. He and his wife, Mina, tried throwing stones against a wall; then he tested them with the pendulum. Those Mina had thrown reacted at 29 inches, those Lethbridge had thrown at 22. These, it seemed, were the "rates" for male and female.

Other stones – sling stones from an Iron Age fort – showed a reaction at 40 inches. Could it be that the stones had been thrown in the course of battle, and 40 was the rate for anger? Lethbridge set his pendulum at 40 inches and thought of something that annoyed him; it immediately began to swing in a circle.

* These excavations – and Lethbridge's subsequent career – are described at length in my book *Mysteries* (1978).

So Lethbridge had established, at least to his own satisfaction, that emotions and ideas, as well as substances, caused the pendulum to react at a definite rate. The rate for death was 40, and this was also the rate for black, cold, anger, deceit, and sleep – obviously connected ideas. When he drew a circle divided into 40 compartments, and placed each quality or object in its appropriate compartment, he found that "opposite" qualities occurred where you would expect to find them: safety at 9, danger at 29, pleasant smells at 7, unpleasant smells at 27, and so on.

In a moment of idleness, he tried placing the substances at their appropriate distance from the centre – sulphur at 7 inches along line 7, chlorine 9 inches along line 9, and so on – then joined up the dots with a line – which was, of course, a spiral. Spirals (vortices) seem to play an important part in most primitive religions; they are found carved on rocks all over the world. The vortex obviously embodies some important primitive idea. And now, looking at his own spiral, it struck Lethbridge that a spiral can go on indefinitely. Why should the "dowsing spiral" stop at 40?

So Lethbridge proceeded to experiment with the pendulum extended beyond 40 inches. And he discovered that every substance now reacted at its "normal" rate, *plus* 40; sulphur at $43\frac{1}{2}$, silver at 62, and so on. There was one small difference. If he held a $43\frac{1}{2}$-inch pendulum over a heap of sulphur, it reacted most strongly *slightly to one side* of the heap; the same applied to everything else he tested. It was as if, in this realm beyond 40, energies were slightly diffracted, like a stone at the bottom of a fish tank that appears slightly to one side of its proper position.

When the pendulum was extended beyond 80, all the same effects occurred again, including the "diffraction effect". And when it was extended beyond 120, it was the same all over again.

Lethbridge's deduction from these observations may sound totally arbitrary, although in his books he makes it sound reasonable enough: that since 40 is the "rate" for death, then the pendulum beyond 40 is reacting to a level of reality "beyond death" and to yet another level at 80, another at 120, and so on, possibly ad infinitum. (He found it impossible to test a pendulum at more than 120 inches because it was too long.)

One of the oddities that Lethbridge observed is that in "our" world – below 40 – there is no "rate" for time; this is presumably because we are *in* it, and so time appears "stationary", as a stream would to a boat drifting along it. At the second level – beyond 40 – time "registers" at 60 inches but – oddly enough – seems to have no forward motion. (I do not profess to understand what he meant.) Then, in the world beyond 80, time disappears again.

Lethbridge concluded that many "worlds" coexist on different "vibration rates". We cannot see the world "beyond 40" because it moves too fast for us, so to speak, just as you cannot read the name of a station if the train goes through it too fast. But some people – "psychics" – are better at reading fast-moving words, so to speak, and keep catching glimpses of the next level of reality.

Lethbridge is of interest in this context because he did not begin as an occultist but as an archaeologist trained in scientific method. The notion of "other realities" forced itself upon him little by little, as a result of experiences that he found hard to explain. He always declined to go further than the facts would allow, but the facts often forced him to go further than he wanted. Personal experience convinced him, for example, of the reality of ghosts, poltergeists, and what he called "ghouls" – unpleasant sensations associated with certain places where tragedies have occurred. Yet he preferred to believe that these could be explained in terms of "tape recording" – "imprints" of human emotions on some kind of electrical field.

Lethbridge died in 1971, but he would undoubtedly have approved of David Ash's vortex theory and of the notion that paranormal events can be explained in terms of super-energy (or, as he would have said, higher vibrational rates). He would probably have added that each level of reality has its own level of super-energy and that there is no obvious limit to the number of levels.

This notion of levels is fundamental to occultism. Madame Blavatsky taught that there are seven levels of reality, the first three of a descending order and the last three of an ascending order. Earth is situated at the bottom, at level four, the "heaviest" and densest of all levels. Yet the sheer density of matter means that human beings are capable of greater achievement than on any other level – just as a sculptor can create more permanent works of art out of marble than out of clay.

Another thinker who attempted to bridge the gap between science and the paranormal was Arthur Young, inventor of the Bell helicopter.* In books such as *The Reflexive Universe*, Young also speculated that there are "seven levels of existence", which include (in order) subatomic particles, atoms, molecules, plants, animals, humans, and what might be called "true humans", or human beings who have moved to the next evolutionary stage. This seventh level is also that of light.

* For a fuller account of Arthur Young, see my book *Mysteries* (1978), pages 608–10.

To most scientists, such speculations will sound suspiciously "mystical". Yet the most interesting scientific development of the second half of the twentieth century has been the recognition by scientists themselves that some of the implications of relativity physics and quantum theory *are* "mystical". Consider the strange paradox of the "photon that interferes with itself" (for the sake of brevity I will quote my own book, *Beyond the Occult*):

> If I shine a beam of light through a pinhole it will form a circle of light on a screen (or photographic plate). If two pinholes are opened up side by side, the result – as you might expect – is two overlapping circles of light. But on the overlapping portions there are a number of dark lines. These are due to the "interference" of the two beams – the same effect you would get if two fast streams of traffic shot out on to the same roundabout. Now suppose the beam is dimmed so only one photon at a time can pass through either of the holes. When the image finally builds up on the photographic plate you would expect the interference bands to disappear. Instead, they are there as usual. But how can one photon at a time interfere with itself? And how does a photon flying through one hole "know" that the other hole is open? Could it possess telepathy, as Einstein jokingly suggested? . . . Perhaps the photon splits and goes through both holes? But a photon detector reveals that this is not so: only one photon at a time goes through one hole at a time. Yet, oddly enough, as soon as we begin to "watch" the photons, they cease to interfere, and the dark bands vanish. The likeliest explanation is that the photon is behaving like a wave when it is unobserved, and so goes through both holes, and interferes. The moment we try to watch it, it turns into a hard ball.

In 1957 a Princeton physicist named Hugh Everett III suggested an apparently preposterous idea to explain this apparent paradox. The "wave" we call a quantum is not a real wave. We impose reality on it because our minds work that way. It is a "wave of possibilities". (Heisenberg's famous "uncertainty principle" – that you cannot know both the speed and the position of a photon – and the amusing paradox of Schrödinger's cat – that a cat in a box can be neither dead nor alive, but in an "intermediate" state – are examples of the same notion.) If the two "holes" can somehow interfere with each other, even though there is only one photon, then the two alternative paths of the electron must exist side by side, so to speak. But where? Everett suggested that one of them exists in a parallel "alternative universe". In these parallel universes (or perhaps they are just different ways of seeing the same universe), a tossed coin could come down heads in one and tails in the other. A wave is actually two particles in two different worlds – or rather, many different worlds, for every "alternative" splits into two more, and so on.

Anyone who finds this idea absurd should study *Parallel Universes* (1988) by the physicist Fred Alan Wolf, in which the implications of the theory are developed in all their Alice-in-Wonderland complexity. The physicist Sir Fred Hoyle has suggested that the paradoxes of quantum physics can be explained only if we assume that *future* possibilities can somehow influence the present and that therefore, in some very real sense, the future has already taken place – a possibility that is already familiar to all students of precognition – those sudden flashes of foreknowledge of the future.

Clearly, the need to find a deeper foundation that can embrace science and the "paranormal" is one of the most vital notions that has emerged during the twentieth century. Yet obviously, even this way of expressing it perpetuates the misunderstanding, since it speaks of science and the paranormal as if they were separate entities, rather than part of the same whole. The philosopher Edmund Husserl was struggling toward the same insight in his last book, *The Crisis in the European Sciences*, when he pointed out that the Greeks had *divided* reality into the world of the physically real and the world of ideas. Galileo then taught scientists how to handle this physical world in terms of mathematics, and suddenly science was confined to the world of physical reality. And since scientists declined to admit any other reality, science became oddly lopsided. (This is what Alfred North Whitehead meant when he accused science of "bifurcating" nature, dividing reality into the "solid" realm of physics and the – comparatively unimportant – realm of lived experience, which includes art, religion, and philosophy.) Husserl argued that we have to take a stand against "scientific reality" and rethink science until it can comfortably include the full range of our human reality. Husserl, of course, was not remotely interested in the paranormal, and his work is doubly important because it shows how a philosopher (who began his career with a book on mathematics) can reach the same philosophical conclusions closely related to those of Lethbridge or David Ash from the other end, so to speak.

In *Science of the Gods*, Ash and Hewitt have made a brave attempt to show how the vortex theory can explain many kinds of "psychic phenomena" in scientific terms, from ghosts and miracles to reincarnation and UFOs. It is an exciting and imaginative program that – inevitably – falls short of its objective. But at least it makes us aware that when Kelvin had his flash of "vision" in 1867 and developed it into the vortex theory of atoms, he may have laid the foundation for a new and more comprehensive science of reality.

61

Who Was Harry Whitecliffe?

According to a book published in France in 1978, one of England's most extraordinary mass murderers committed suicide in a Berlin gaol in the middle of the jazz era. His name was Harry Whitecliffe, and he murdered at least forty women. Then why is his name not more widely known – at least to students of crime? Because when he was arrested he was masquerading under the name Lovach Blume, and his suicide concealed his true identity from the authorities.

The full story can be found in a volume called *Nouvelles Histoires Magiques – New Tales of Magic* – by Louis Pauwels and Guy Breton, published by Editions J'ai Lu. In spite of the title – which sounds like fiction – it is in fact a series of studies in the paranormal and bizarre; there are chapters on Nostradamus, Rasputin and Eusapia Palladino, and accounts of such well-known mysteries as the devil's footprints in Devon (see my chapter 12).

According to the chapter "The Two Faces of Harry Whitecliffe", there appeared in London in the early twenties a collection of essays so promising that it sold out in a few days; it consisted of a series of marvellous pastiches of Oscar Wilde. But its author, Harry Whitecliffe, apparently preferred to shun publicity; he remained obstinately hidden. Would-be interviewers returned empty-handed. Then, just as people were beginning to suggest that Whitecliffe was a pseudonym for some well-known writer – Bernard Shaw, perhaps, or the young T.S. Eliot – Whitecliffe finally consented to appear. He was a handsome young man of twenty-three, likeable, eccentric and fond of sport. He was also generous; he was said to have ended one convivial evening by casually giving a pretty female beggar five hundred pounds. He professed to adore flowers, but only provided their stems were not more than twenty centimetres long. He was the kind of person the English love, and was soon a celebrity.

Meanwhile he continued to write: essays, poetry and plays. One of his comedies, *Similia*, had four hundred consecutive performances in London before touring England. It made him a fortune, which he quickly scattered among his friends. By the beginning of 1923 he was one of the "kings of London society".

Then, in September of that year, he vanished. He sold all his possessions, and gave his publisher carte blanche to handle his work. But before the end of the year he reappeared in Dresden. The theatre there presented *Similia* with enormous success, the author himself translating it from English into German. It went on to appear in many theatres along the Rhine. He founded a press for publishing modern poetry, and works on modern painting – Dorian Verlag – whose editions are now worth a fortune.

But he was still something of a man of mystery. Every morning he galloped along the banks of the river Elbe until nine o'clock; at ten he went to his office, eating lunch there. At six in the evening, he went to art exhibitions or literary salons, and met friends. At nine, he returned home and no one knew what he did for the rest of the evening. And no one liked to ask him.

One reason for this regular life was that he was in love – the girl was called Wally von Hammerstein, daughter of aristocratic parents, who were favourably impressed with the young writer. Their engagement was to be announced on 4 October 1924.

But on the previous day Whitecliffe disappeared again. He failed to arrive at his office, and vanished from his flat. The frantic Wally searched Dresden, without success. The police were alerted – discreetly – and pursued diligent inquiries. Their theory was that he had committed suicide. Wally believed he had either met with an accident or been the victim of a crime – he often carried large sums of money. As the weeks dragged by her desperation turned to misery; she talked about entering a convent.

Then she received a letter. It had been found in the cell of a condemned man who had committed suicide in Berlin – he had succeeded in opening his veins with the buckle of his belt. The inscription on the envelope said: "I beg you, monsieur le procureur of the Reich, to forward this letter to its destination without opening it." It was signed: Lovach Blume.

Blume was apparently one of the most horrible of murderers, worse than Jack the Ripper or Peter Kürten, the Düsseldorf sadist. He had admitted to the court that tried him: "Every ten days I have to kill. I am driven by an irresistible urge, so that until I have killed, I suffer atrociously. But as I disembowel my victims I feel an indescribable pleasure." Asked about his past, he declared: "I am a corpse. Why bother about the past of a corpse"?

Blume's victims were prostitutes and homeless girls picked up on the Berlin streets. He would take them to a hotel, and kill them as soon as they were undressed. Then, with a knife like a Malaysian "kriss", with an ivory handle, he would perform horrible mutilations, so awful that even doctors found the sight unbearable. These murders continued over a period of six months, during which the slum quarters of Berlin lived in fear.

Blume was finally arrested by accident, in September 1924. The police thought he was engaged in drug trafficking, and knocked on the door of a hotel room minutes after Blume had entered with a prostitute. Blume had just committed his thirty-first murder in Berlin; he was standing naked by the window, and the woman's body lay at his feet.

He made no resistance, and admitted freely to his crimes – he could only recall twenty-seven. He declared that he had no fear of death – particularly the way executions were performed in Germany (by decapitation), which he greatly preferred to the English custom of hanging.

This was the man who had committed suicide in his prison cell, and who addressed a long letter to his fiancée, Wally von Hammerstein. He told her that he was certain the devil existed, because he had met him. He was, he explained, a kind of Jekyll and Hyde, an intelligent, talented man who suddenly became cruel and bloodthirsty. He thought of himself as being like victims of demoniacal possession. He had left London after committing nine murders, when he suspected that Scotland Yard was on his trail. His love for Wally was genuine, he told her, and had caused him to "die a little". He had hoped once that she might be able to save him from his demons, but it had proved a vain hope.

Wally fainted as she read the letter. And in 1925 she entered a nunnery and took the name Marie de Douleurs. There she prays for the salvation of a tortured soul . . .

This is the story, as told by Louis Pauwels – a writer who became famous for his collabouration with Jacques Bergier on a book called *The Morning of the Magicians*. Critics pointed out that that book was full of factual errors, and a number of these can also be found in his article on Whitecliffe. For example, if the date of Blume's arrest is correct – 25 September 1924 – then it took place before Whitecliffe vanished from Dresden, on 3 October 1924 . . . But this, presumably, is a slip of the pen.

But who was Harry Whitecliffe? According to Pauwels, he told the Berlin court that his father was German, his mother Danish, and that he was brought up in Australia by an uncle who was a butcher. His uncle lived in Sydney. But in a "conversation" between Pauwels and his fellow-author at the end of one chapter, Pauwels states that Whitecliffe was the son of a great English family. But apart from the three magistrates who opened the suicide letter – ignoring Blume's last wishes – only Wally and her parents knew Whitecliffe's true identity. The judges are dead, so are Wally's parents. Wally is a 75-year-old nun who until now has never told anyone of this drama of her youth. We are left to assume that she has now told the story to Pauwels.

This extraordinary tale aroused the curiosity of a well-known French authoress, Françoise d'Eaubonne, who felt that Whitecliffe deserved a book to himself. But her letters to the two authors – Pauwels and Breton – went unanswered. She therefore contacted the British Society of Theatre Research, and so entered into a correspondence with the theatre historian John Kennedy Melling. Melling had never heard of Whitecliffe, or of a play called *Similia*. He decided to begin his researches by contacting Scotland Yard, to ask whether they have any record of an unknown sex killer of the early 1920s. Their reply was negative; there was no series of Ripper-type murders of prostitutes in the early 1920s. He next applied to J.H.H. Gaute, the possessor of the largest crime library in the British Isles; Gaute could also find no trace of such a series of sex crimes in the 1920s. Theatrical reference books contained no mention of Harry Whitecliffe, or of his successful comedy *Similia*. It began to look – as incredible as it sounds – as if Pauwels had simply invented the whole story.

Thelma Holland, Oscar Wilde's daughter-in-law, could find no trace of a volume of parodies of Wilde among the comprehensive collection of her late husband, Vyvyan Holland. But she had a suggestion to make – to address inquiries to the Mitchell Library in Sydney. As an Australian, she felt it was probably Melling's best chance of tracking down Harry Whitecliffe.

Incredibly, this long shot brought positive results: not about Harry Whitecliffe, but about a German murderer called Blume – not Lovach, but Wilhelm Blume. The *Argus* newspaper for 8 August 1922 contained a story headed "Cultured Murderer", and sub-titled: "Literary Man's Series of Crimes". It was datelined Berlin, 7 August.

Wilhelm Blume, a man of wide culture and considerable literary gifts, whose translations of English plays have been produced in

Dresden with great success, has confessed to a series of cold-blooded murders, one of which was perpetrated at the Hotel Adlon, the best known Berlin hotel.

The most significant item in the newspaper report is that Blume had founded a publishing house called Dorian Press (Verlag) in Dresden. This is obviously the same Blume who – according to Pauwels – committed suicide in Berlin.

But Wilhelm Blume was not a sex killer. His victims had been postmen, and the motive had been robbery. In Germany postal orders were paid to consignees in their own homes, so postmen often carried fairly large sums of money. Blume had sent himself postal orders, then killed the postmen and robbed them – the exact number is not stated in the *Argus* article. The first time he did this he was interrupted by his landlady while he was strangling the postman with a noose; and he cut her throat. Then he moved on to Dresden, where in due course he attempted to rob another postman. Armed with two revolvers, he waited for the postman in the porch of a house. But the tenant of the house arrived so promptly that he had to flee, shooting one of the policemen. Then his revolvers both misfired, and he was caught. Apparently he attempted to commit suicide in prison, but failed. He confessed – as the *Argus* states – to several murders, and was presumably executed later in 1922 (although the *Argus* carries no further record).

It seems plain, then, that the question "Who was Harry Whitecliffe"? should be reworded "Who was Wilhelm Blume"? For Blume and Whitecliffe were obviously the same person.

From the information we possess, we can make a tentative reconstruction of the story of Blume-Whitecliffe. He sounds like a typical example of a certain type of killer who is also a confidence man – other examples are Landru, Petiot, the "acid bath murderer" Haigh, and the sex killer Neville Heath. It is an essential part of such a man's personality that he is a fantasist, and that he likes to pose as a success, and to talk casually about past triumphs. (Neville Heath called himself "Group Captain Rupert Brooke".) They usually start off as petty swindlers, then gradually become more ambitious, and graduate to murder. This is what Blume seems to have done. In the chaos of postwar Berlin he made a quick fortune by murdering and robbing postmen. Perhaps his last coup made him a fortune beyond his expectations, or perhaps the Berlin postal authorities were now on the alert for the killer. Blume decided it was time to make an attempt to live a respectable life, and to put his literary fantasies into operation. He moved to Dresden, called himself

Harry Whitecliffe and set up Dorian Verlag. He became a successful translator of English plays, and may have helped to finance their production in Dresden and in theatres along the Rhine. Since he was posing as an upper-class Englishman, and must have occasionally run into other Englishmen in Dresden, we may assume that his English was perfect, and that his story of being brought up in Australia was probably true. Since he also spoke perfect German, it is also a fair assumption that he was, as he told the court, the son of a German father and a Danish mother.

He fell in love with an upper-class girl, and told her a romantic story that is typical of the inveterate daydreamer: that he was the son of a "great English family", that he had become an overnight literary success in London as a result of his pastiches of Oscar Wilde, but had at first preferred to shun the limelight (this is the true Walter Mitty touch) until increasing success made this impossible. His wealth is the result of a successful play, *Similia*. (The similarity of the title to *Salome* is obvious, and we may infer that Blume was an ardent admirer of Wilde.) But in order to avoid too much publicity – after all, victims of previous swindles might expose him – he lives the quiet, regular life of a crook in hiding.

And just as all seems to be going so well – just as success, respectability, a happy marriage, seem so close – he once again runs out of money. There is only one solution: a brief return to a life of crime. One or two robberies of postmen can replenish his bank account and secure his future . . . But this time it goes disastrously wrong. Harry Whitecliffe is exposed as the swindler and murderer Wilhelm Blume. He makes no attempt to deny it, and confesses to his previous murders; his world has now collapsed in ruins. He is sent back to Berlin, where the murders were committed, and he attempts suicide in his cell. Soon after, he dies by the guillotine. And in Dresden the true story of Wilhelm Blume is soon embroidered into a horrifying tale of a Jekyll-and-Hyde mass murderer, whose early career in London is confused with Jack the Ripper . . .

Do any records of Wilhelm Blume still exist? It seems doubtful – the fire-bombing of Dresden destroyed most of the civic records, and the people who knew him more than sixty years ago must now all be dead. Yet Pauwels has obviously come across some garbled and wildly inaccurate account of Blume's career as Harry Whitecliffe. It would be interesting to know where he obtained his information; but neither Françoise d'Eaubonne nor John Kennedy Melling have been successful in persuading him to answer letters.

62

Patience Worth

Or the Ghost Who Wrote Novels

On an August day in 1912 two women sat in a house in St Louis, Missouri, and played with an ouija board. They were Emily Grant Hutchings and Pearl Curran, and both were married to successful businessmen – their husbands were in fact playing cards in the next room. It was Mrs Hutchings who was interested in trying to "contact the spirits"; her friend Pearl Curran thought it was all a waste of time. And on that first August afternoon she proved to be right. The pointer of the ouija board spelt out a few recognizable words, but it was mostly nonsense.

But in spite of her friend's boredom, Emily Hutchings insisted on trying again. They tried repeatedly over the next ten months. And finally, on 22 June 1913, the board spelled out the word PAT several times, then went on to write:

> Oh, why let sorrow steel thy heart?
> Thy bosom is but its foster-mother,
> The world its cradle and the loving home its grave.

This was not only intelligible, but intelligent – although a careful reading is required before it can be seen to make sense.

That same afternoon the board went on to utter a number of similar sentiments, most of which sound like the utterances of a sentimental lady novelist of the Victorian period:

"Rest, weary heart. Let only sunshine light the shrine within. A single ray shall filter through and warm thy frozen soul".

There were several more aphoristic sentences of the same nature.

The next time the ladies met was on 2 July 1913, and once again the ouija board began spelling out words with bewildering speed. "Dust rests beneath, and webs lie caught among the briars. A single jewel gleams as a mirrored vision of rising Venus in a mountain lake . . ." And after more poetic sentiments of the same kind, it declared: "All those who so lately graced your board are here, and as the moon looks down, think ye of them and their abode as a spirit song, as spirit friends, and close communion held twixt thee and them. Tis but a journey, dost not see"? And when the ladies asked for some elucidation the board replied: "Tis all so clear behind the veil . . ." And when they asked its name it answered: "Should one so near be confined to a name? The sun shines alike on the briar and the rose . . ." But at the next session, six days later, it finally condescended to reveal its identity. "Many moons ago I lived. Again I come – Patience Worth my name". But she seemed reluctant to disclose more details. "About me you would know much. Yesterday is dead". And she was inclined to express herself in aphorisms; at a later séance, when they asked her to hurry up, she replied: "Beat the hound and lose the hare." She had a sharp tongue and a ready wit, although the old-fashioned language often made it difficult to understand. She seems to have taken a dislike to a Mrs Pollard, Pearl Curran's mother, who was present at some of the sessions, and when asked by Emily Hutchings what she thought of Mrs Pollard, replied: "The men should stock her". Did she mean that Mrs Pollard should be put in the stocks? asked Mrs Hutchings. "Aye, and leave a place for two" snapped Patience.

But shortly before Christmas Patience displayed an interesting ability to predict the future. Mrs Hutchings asked her what Pearl Curran intended to give her for Christmas; Patience replied: "Fifteen pieces, and one cracked". In fact Mrs Curran had ordered a set of kitchen jars for her friend, and when they were delivered the next day one of the fifteen proved to be cracked. Asked what Emily Hutchings intended to give Pearl Curran for Christmas, Patience answered: "Table store, cross-stitched". Again this was accurate – she had bought some cross-stitched table linen. Asked by Mrs Pollard for an inscription for a present to her daughter, Patience replied: "A burning desire never to be snuffed; a waxing faith, ever to burn". It was remarkably appropriate: Mrs Pollard had bought her daughter a candle and snuffer.

Eventually Patience offered a little more information about herself. She was a Quaker girl, born either in 1649 or 1694 (the board dictated 1649, then changed its mind and added 94) and had been born in Dorset. She had worked hard – apparently on a farm – until her family emigrated to America, and had shortly thereafter been killed by Indians. She was certainly a talkative lady – even the incomplete records of the sessions with her, cited in *The Case of Patience Worth* by Walter

Franklin Prince, are exhausting to read. And she was inclined to dictate lengthy "poems" which lack rhyme and show an uncertainty about metre. Her best-known utterance runs as follows:

> Ah God, I have drunk unto the dregs,
> And flung the cup at Thee!
> The dust of crumbled righteousness
> Hath dried and soaked unto itself
> E'en the drop I spilled to Bacchus,
> Whilst Thou, all-patient,
> Sendest purple vintage for a later harvest.

This has most of the characteristics of Patience's literary utterances. On first reading, it seems meaningless; on a second or third reading, it yields up its meaning. But the reader may be left in some doubt as to whether it was worth saying in the first place.

In 1915 Patience became something of a celebrity when Caspar Yost, the editor of the Sunday supplement of the *St Louis Globe-Democrat*, wrote a series of articles about her, although he was careful not to identify the two ladies who had "discovered" her. The articles caused a sensation, and Yost went on to write a book. Another St Louis journalist, William Marion Reedy, editor of *Reedy's Mirror* – and one of the best literary critics of his time also attended some of the séances, and to his own astonishment was much impressed by Patience. Yost and Reedy were responsible for making the name of Patience Worth known all over America.

By now Patience had embarked upon more ambitious literary composition. First came *Red Wing*, a six-act medieval play. Next there was a 60,000 word medieval novel, *Telka*. And here it must be admitted at once that Patience is a disappointing writer. If the works were literary masterpieces, or even highly competent hack-work, they would deserve to be kept permanently in print. In fact, they are so long-winded as to be almost unreadable. "Historical" novels like *Telka* and *The Sorry Tale* (set in the time of Jesus) are written in an "archaic" style that demands close attention and offers no adequate reward. This is from *The Sorry Tale*: "And his beard hung low upon his breast, and he spoke unto the Rome's men: 'The peace of Jehovah be upon you' And they spat upon his fruits and made loud words, saying: 'Behold, Jerusalem hath been beset of locusts and desert fleas . . .'" It reads like second-rate Biblical pastiches. A 'modern' novel, *Hope Trueblood*, begins: "The glass had slipped thrice, and the sands stood midway through, and still the bird hopped within its wicker. I think the glass had slipped through a score of years, rightfully set at each turning, and the bird had sung through some of these and mourned through others. The hearth's arch yawned sleepily . . ." And after half a page of this the reader is also yawning sleepily.

Certainly Patience seems to have known little of the virtue of brevity. When a psychic named Arthur Delroy addressed a meeting in St Louis he remarked that the ouija board was of no more value than a doorknob, and that Patience's language was not archaic English but the kind of language learned at Sunday school. (He added unkindly that he would not be surprised to learn that Mrs Curran had spent a great deal of time at Sunday school.) When this was reported to Patience, she replied: "Tis fools that smite the lute and set it awhir o'folly song, when sage's hand do be at loth to touch." To this Delroy replied, in Patience's own style: "Nay, thou puttest me among the nobles. I be not the wise man from the East who wouldst prithee never be the last word, but wouldsy patiently wait, yea, t'll'st the millionth Patient utterance . . ." Her reply, if she made one, is not recorded.

In November 1915 Mr and Mrs Curran decided to go to the east coast, where Patience was widely known, and to take the ouija board. Asked if she was willing to accompany them, Patience replied in her usual long-winded style: "E'en as doth the breath o' thee to hug, so shall I, to follow thee. Think ye I'd build me a cup and leave it dry"? And when Patience was interviewed by the eminent psychologist Morton Prince in Boston he also found her wordiness rather trying. Asked if she objected to the investigation, she replied at inordinate length, beginning: "Ye be at seek o' a measure o' smoke's put . . ." He repeated the question, and Patience explained lucidly: "Ye turn up a stone, ayea, and aneath there be a toad, aye, and he blinketh him at the light . . ." And when Prince in desperation repeated the question a third time, she explained: "Here be a one who hath 'o a ball o' twine and be not a satisfied with the ball, but doth to awish that I do awind it out. List thee, brother, at thy poke aneath the stone! Tis well and alike unto me." And hours of interrogation brought forth a great many more of these labyrinthine obscurities. Patience seems incapable of using one word where ten will do, bringing to mind Lincoln's remark: "He can compress the most words into the smallest ideas of any man I ever met." It was impossible to get her to answer even the simplest question with a direct reply. When Prince asked her how old she was when she came to America, she replied: "A goodly dame", and when he repeated the question, advised him to look at a parable she had written about an ass.

Patience herself ended the interview – the last – with an abrupt "Good night."

Prince's feeling was that they had been basically a waste of time. Whether or not Patience was genuine, she was certainly evasive. Mrs Curran flatly refused Prince's suggestion that she should be hypnotized, and the Currans gave to the newspapers an account of the interviews that struck Prince as inaccurate, leading to some bad-tempered exchanges.

After this unsatisfactory encounter, the Currans went on to New York, where Patience met her future publisher Henry Holt, and rambled on in her usual infuriatingly prolix manner. But Holt was impressed, and in the following February – 1916 – brought out Caspar Yost's book *Patience Worth – A Psychic Mystery*, which met, on the whole, with an excellent reception. Critics described Patience as a "powerful, unique but impalpable personality" and her work as "entertaining, humourous and beautiful". But a dissenting note was sounded by Professor James Hyslop, of the American Society for Psychical Research, who deplored the total lack of scientifically convincing evidence, and dismissed Patience as a "fraud and a delusion".

In June 1917 Henry Holt published the vast pseudo-Biblical epic *The Sorry Tale*, more than a quarter of a million words long. Again, many papers were ecstatic; the *Boston Transcript* wrote: "If, however, on account of its psychic claims, one approaches the story with unbelief or scoffing, one is instantly rebuffed by its quality", while *The Nation* said that it "deserved to be weighed as a piece of creative fiction". The modern reader will find these claims incomprehensible; the writing is atrocious, and often illiterate. "Sheep, storm-lost, bleated, where, out upon the hills, they lost them". "The temples stood whited and the market place shewed emptied." "And the Rome's men bared their blades and the air rocked with cries of mock prayers from Rome's lips." If Patience had been an ambitious shop girl the novel would have been dismissed as a bad joke.

On the other hand, the book seemed to indicate a knowledge of ancient Rome that Mrs Curran insisted she had never possessed. The distinguished psychical investigator G.N.M. Tyrrell, writing thirty years later, said: "There is not here the greatness of genius, but . . . there is a fount of inspiration which might have provided the material for a work of genius had it been expressed through the conscious mind of, say, a Coleridge instead of . . . Mrs Curran", and he went on to quote Caspar Yost's view that the book revealed an intimate knowledge of the Rome of Augustus and Tiberius, and also of the topography of Jerusalem and the Holy Land. But then, of course, Yost was a somewhat biased witness, having been one of the original "discoverers" of Patience Worth.

One of the most bizarre episodes in the entire story began in August 1916, while *The Sorry Tale* was still being dictated. In her usual circumlocutory way, Patience announced that her works would bring in a great deal of money ("a-time a later the purse shall fatten"), but that this money "be not for him who hath". The Currans were told "ye shall seek a one, a wee bit, one who hath not", and added "Aye, this be close, close." And soon it became clear that what Patience meant – she seems to have been incapable of saying anything in plain words – was that the Currans, who were childless, should adopt a baby, and that this baby would be in some sense Patience's own daughter. By "the merest accident", a pregnant widow was located – her husband had been killed in a mill accident – and she agreed to relinquish her unborn child to the Currans. Patience seemed quite certain it would be a daughter. And one evening, as she was dictating *The Sorry Tale*, Patience broke off abruptly with the comment "This be 'nuff' ". An hour later the Currans heard that the baby had been born. It was indeed a girl, and had red hair and brown eyes – a description Patience had formerly given of herself. On Patience's instructions the child was called Patience Worth Wee Curran.

In that same year – 1916 – Emily Hutchings called upon the eminent literary critic William Marion Reedy, and showed him the first ten thousand words of a novel about Missouri politics and journalism. In recent years Emily had dropped out of the limelight, for it had become clear that her presence was not essential for Patience to manifest herself. Reedy was impressed by the novel, and congratulated her. A week later he probably felt like eating his words when Emily called again, and confessed that the novel had been "dictated" by the spirit of Mark Twain – then proceeded to produce several pages with the help of the ouija board. The novel was accepted, and published under the title of *Jap Herron*, and was well received – although it was generally agreed that its quality was much inferior to the works Mark Twain had produced while he was alive. An effort by Mark Twain's publishers to suppress the novel was unsuccessful.

During this period Patience's fame continued to grow. The Victorian novel *Hope Trueblood* met with an enthusiastic reception from many respectable journals, although the reading public found that even Patience's "modern" style was too wordy. In England the book was issued without any indication of its "psychic" origin, and received mixed reviews; but at least most of the critics seemed to assume that it was the first novel of an English writer. The Currans also launched *Patience Worth's Magazine*, to make Patience's poems and lesser writings accessible to her admirers; it was edited by Caspar Yost, and ran to ten issues.

But by 1918 there were signs that Patience's vogue was coming to an end. In *The Atlantic Monthly* that August a writer named Agnes Repplier poured scorn on this latest fad for books written by spirits, and expressed dismay at the thought that Patience, being dead, might be on the literary scene for ever. Of Patience's books, Miss Repplier said tartly that "they were as silly as they were dull". In retrospect, it seems surprising that no other reputable critic had already made this assessment.

The blast of ridicule was in effect the end of Patience Worth's period of literary celebrity; Agnes Repplier had stated that the emperor was naked, and now everybody realized that it had been obvious all along. A new book by Caspar Yost on Patience's religion and philosophy was turned down by Henry Holt; so was a volume of Patience's poems. Pearl Curran (who had always strenuously denied that she had any writing talent) herself wrote a short story about a Chicago salesgirl – who, significantly, is "taken over" by a secondary personality – and it was accepted by the *Saturday Evening Post*; but Pearl's most recent biographer, Irving Litvag, admits (in *Singer in the Shadows*) that the story "never rises above the level of bad soap opera".

When William Marion Reedy died in 1920 Patience lost one of her most influential defenders. And another sign of Patience's sinking reputation was a hostile article by a critic called Mary Austin in the *Unpartizan Review*; what made it worse was that the magazine was published by Henry Holt.

John Curran's health began to fail, and he died in June 1922, after fourteen months of illness. Pearl, who was now thirty-nine years old, was pregnant with their first child; a girl was born six months later. Pearl had four people to support – herself, her mother, Patience Wee and her new daughter – on a dwindling income. Far from making them a fortune, Patience's literary works had cost them money; the novels had sold poorly, and the magazine was an expensive production. Pearl was forced to accept an offer to give several lectures in Chicago; she was reluctant to do this because she had always insisted that her position as Patience's mouthpiece brought her no profit; but there was no alternative. The death of her mother was another blow. But at this point a New York admirer, Herman Behr, came to the rescue; he not only made her an allowance of $400 a month but also paid for the publication of Patience's poems, which appeared under the title *Light From Beyond*. But it failed to revive the interest of the American reading public in the Patience Worth phenomenon. In the age of James Joyce and Ernest Hemingway and John Dos Passos, the rambling productions of Patience Worth seemed irrelevant.

Litvag comments: "The next three years were lonely, rather despairing ones for Pearl Curran. No longer a celebrity, largely ignored by the public . . . periodically in ill health, she was often depressed and morose". In 1923 she allowed Patience Wee to go to California. In 1926 she married a retired doctor, Henry Rogers, many years her senior; but the marriage was unsuccessful, and ended in divorce. In 1930 Pearl moved to California, where in Los Angeles she once again acquired some degree of celebrity among a group of devoted admirers. In 1931 she married again – this time to a man to whom she had been briefly engaged when she was nineteen; she and her husband – Robert Wyman – moved to Culver City, and Patience began to dictate a new literary work, a play about Shakespeare. At séances she continued to be as garrulous and evasive as ever – the simplest question could be guaranteed to provide a five-minute answer. In 1934 Patience Wee who was eighteen married, and Patience provided a lengthy blessing, signed "Thy Mither".

Then in November 1937 Pearl, who was fifty-four, suddenly announced to her old friend Dotsie Smith that "Patience has just shown me the end of the road, and you will have to carry on as best you can". She seemed to be in excellent health. But on Thanksgiving Day she caught a cold; on 3 December 1937 she died of pneumonia in a Los Angeles hospital. That was in effect the end of the Patience Worth phenomenon. Patience Wee, who by the age of twenty-seven had been twice married, died equally suddenly in 1943, after a mild heart ailment had been diagnosed; inevitably, there were those who felt that Patience had finally claimed her "daughter".

The last chapter of Irving Litvag's book on Patience is entitled "Who was Patience Worth"?, but he admits almost immediately that he has no idea. Writers on the case tend to be equally divided between the two obvious theories: that Patience was a "secondary personality" of Pearl Curran, and that she was more or less what she claimed to be, a "spirit". Both Morton Prince and Walter Franklin Prince (they were unrelated) had produced classic studies of cases of multiple personality; Morton Prince's "Sally Beauchamp" case (described in *The Dissociation of a Personality*) has achieved the status of a classic; Walter Franklin

Prince's "Doris Fischer" case deserves to be equally well known, but never achieved circulation beyond the pages of the *American Journal for Psychical Research* (1923) and *Contributions to Psychology* But anyone who reads the Patience Worth case after studying Sally Beauchamp and Doris Fischer is bound to feel that they have very little in common. Most "multiple personalities" have a history of childhood abuse and misery; Pearl Curran seems to have had a normal childhood, and to have been a perfectly ordinary, unremarkable person until the coming of Patience Worth. Although it *is* conceivable that Pearl Curran was a case of dual personality, the clinical evidence for it is not particularly convincing.

For those who are willing to accept the possibility of life after death, the most convincing explanation is certainly that Patience was a "spirit". But that does not necessarily mean that she was really what she claimed to be. Anyone who has studied "spirit communication" soon recognizes that "spirits" are very seldom what they claim to be; G.K. Chesterton put in more bluntly and said that they are liars. If Patience *was* a seventeenth-century Quaker who was killed by Red Indians, it is difficult to understand why she was so evasive and why she failed to answer straightforward questions that might have enabled the Currans to prove that such a person really existed. Litvag's book leaves one with the conviction that if Patience was a spirit, then it was probably the spirit of a frustrated would-be writer with a strong tendency to mythomania.

63

Zombies

The Evidence for the Walking Dead

Ever since 1932, when Bela Lugosi starred in *White Zombie*, the zombie legend has been a Hollywood standby, challenging the vampire, the walking mummy, and the Frankenstein monster in popularity. No one who has seen a film like *King of the Zombies* can ever forget the shot of a zombie marching on like a robot while someone fires bullet after bullet into its chest.

Zombies, according to Alfred Metraux's book, *Voodoo* (1959), are "people whose decease has been duly recorded and whose burial has been witnessed, but who are found a few years later . . . in a state verging on idiocy". In Port-au-Prince, Haiti, says Metraux, "there are few, even among the educated, who do not give some credence to these macabre stories". Understandably, such tales have met with skepticism outside Haiti.

One of the first Western observers to record an actual incident of zombiism was the black ethnographer Zora Neale Hurston, who had trained in America under the great Franz Boas. In October 1936 a naked woman was found wandering in Haiti's Artibonite Valley; her name was Felicia Felix-Mentor, and she had died at the age of twenty-nine and been buried. Zora Hurston went to visit her in the hospital at Gonaïves and described her as having "a blank face with dead eyes" and eyelids "white as if they had been burned with acid".

According to Zora Hurston, people were "zombified" if they betrayed the secrets of the Haitian secret societies. No one believed her, and Metraux writes patronizingly of "Zora Houston [*sic*], who is very superstitious". Nevertheless, Metraux tells a story involving two members of "high society". After his car broke down, one of them was invited to the home of a little white bearded man, a *houngan* or vodoun (voodoo) priest. Piqued by his guest's skepticism about a *wanga* (magical charm), the old man asked him if he had known a certain M.

Celestin – who had, in fact, been one of the visitor's closest friends. Summoned by a whip crack, a man shambled into the room, and to his horror the visitor recognized his old friend Celestin, who had died six months earlier. When the zombie reached out for the visitor's glass – obviously thirsty – the *houngan* stopped him from handing it over, saying that nothing could be more dangerous than to give or take something from the hand of a dead man. The *houngan* told his visitor that Celestin had died from a spell and that the magician who had killed him had sold him for twelve dollars.

Other stories recounted by Metraux make it clear that he considers zombies to be people who have literally died and then been raised from the dead. Understandably, he rejects this as superstition. In fact, as we shall see, Zora Hurston was correct and Metraux was wrong.

Haiti, in the West Indies, was discovered by Columbus in 1492, but it was not until two centuries later that it became a base for pirates and buccaneers. French colonists developed Haiti's rich sugar trade, using black slaves kidnapped from Africa. The Spanish ceded Haiti (or Saint-Domingue, as it was called) to the French in 1697.

The slaves were treated with unbelievable cruelty – for example, hung from trees with nails driven through the ears or smeared with molasses and left to be eaten alive by ants. Another horrifying practice involved filling a slave's anus with gunpowder and setting it alight, an act the Frenchmen often referred to as "blasting black's ass". In spite of the risks, slaves ran away whenever they could and hid in the mountains, until, eventually, certain mountainous regions became "no-go areas" for whites. In the 1740s a slave named Macandal, who had lost his arm in a sugar press, escaped to the mountains and taught the runaway Maroons (as the slaves were known) to use poison against their oppressors. Mass poisoning of cattle was followed by mass poisoning of the colonists. Macandal was eventually betrayed and sentenced to be burned alive (although, according to legend, he used his magical powers to escape). But from then on, the secret societies spread revolt among the black slaves. After the great revolts of the 1790s, French authority virtually collapsed, and although it was savagely restored under Napoléon, he was never able to conquer the interior of the island. A series of black emperors ruled until 1859, but the island has alternated between a state of virtual anarchy and harsh authoritarian rule ever since, both of which have nurtured the secret societies.

Zora Hurston asserted that "zombification" was effected by means of a "quick-acting poison". It was not until the early 1980s, however, that a young American anthropologist, Wade Davies, heard rumours that zombification was, in fact, a process involving certain known poisons, chief among which was that of the puffer fish – a delicacy dear to the Japanese, although it has to be prepared with extreme care. (More on this follows.)

Summoned to meet a New York psychiatrist named Nathan Kline, Davies was told of two recent cases that seemed to demonstrate beyond all doubt that zombification was not a myth. In 1962 a Haitian peasant in his forties, Clairvius Narcisse, was admitted to the Albert Schweitzer Hospital in the Artibonite Valley, suffering from fever; he died two days later and was buried the next day. Eighteen years later, in 1980, a man walked up to Narcisse's sister Angelina and identified himself as her brother, Clairvius. He asserted that he had been "zombified" by order of his brother, with whom he had been disputing about land. He had been removed from his grave and taken to work with other zombies. After two years, their master was killed and he escaped to wander the country for the next sixteen years. It was not until he heard of his brother's death that he dared to make himself known.

Narcisse's identity was confirmed, and the BBC made a short film about the case. In the same year, a group of "zombies" was found wandering in the north of the country – where Narcisse had been forced to work, confirming Narcisse's story of the escape.

In 1976 a thirty-year-old woman named Francina Illeus, known as "*Ti Femme*", was pronounced dead. Three years later she was found alive by her mother and recognized by a scar on her temple; her coffin was found to be full of rocks. She believed that she was poisoned on the orders of a jealous husband.

In 1980 another woman, Natagette Joseph, aged sixty, was recognized as she wandered near her home village; she had "died" in 1964.

When Davies went to Haiti to investigate, his attention focused on *Datura stramonium*, known in America as jimsonweed and in Haiti as zombie's cucumber. He went to see Max Beauvoir, an expert on vodoun. He interviewed Clairvius Narcisse and confirmed his story. He also discovered that Narcisse was not simply the victim of a vengeful brother; he had been something of a Casanova and had left illegitimate children – whom he declined to support – all over the place. Davies later concluded that "zombification" is not simply a matter of malice. The secret societies had a sinister reputation, but it seemed that they were less black than they were painted and often acted as protectors of the oppressed. Zombification, it seemed, was often a punishment for flagrant wrongdoing.

Davies's research led him to a highly poisonous toad, the *Bufo marinus*, and to two varieties of puffer fish, so called because they inflate themselves with water when threatened. Both are full of deadly neurotoxin called *tetrodotoxin*, a fatal dose of which would just cover the head of a pin. Captain Cook had suffered severely after eating the cooked liver and roe of a puffer fish. The Japanese throw away all the poisonous parts of the fish and eat the flesh raw – as *sashimi* – but the deadly liver is also eaten after being cleaned and boiled.

But it was clear to Davies that the poison of the puffer fish is not the sole secret of "zombification". In his extraordinary book *The Serpent and the Rainbow* (1985), he describes his search for samples of zombie poison. His aim was to obtain samples and take them back to be tested in the laboratory. But although he met a number of *houngans* and witnessed some remarkable ceremonies – in a number of which he saw people "possessed" by spirits (so that one woman was able to place a lighted cigarette on her tongue without being burned) – his quest came to a premature end when one of his major backers died and another suffered a debilitating stroke. But his book leaves very little doubt that the secret of "zombification" is a poison that can produce all the signs of death. When the body is dug up, an antidote is administered (Davies was able to study some antidotes and concluded that the "magical" powers of the priest seem to be as important as the ingredients themselves), and then the victim is often stupefied by further drugs that reduce the subject to a level of virtual idiocy.

A 1984 BBC programme introduced by John Tusa confirmed that "zombification" results from a poison that affects certain brain centres, reducing consciousness to a dream level.

Wade Davies was left in no doubt about the reality of "zombification". But his investigation into the vodoun religion also seems to have convinced him that not all the phenomena of vodoun can be explained in such naturalistic terms.

Index